# SCENE DESIGN AND STAGE LIGHTING

# SCENE DESIGN AND STAGE LIGHTING

### SEVENTH EDITION

## W. OREN PARKER
CARNEGIE-MELLON UNIVERSITY

## R. CRAIG WOLF
SAN DIEGO STATE UNIVERSITY

HARCOURT BRACE COLLEGE PUBLISHERS

Fort Worth   Philadelphia   San Diego   New York   Orlando   Austin   San Antonio
Toronto   Montreal   London   Sydney   Tokyo

| | |
|---|---|
| Senior Vice President, Editorial | Ted Buchholz |
| Publisher | Christopher P. Klein |
| Acquisitions Editor | Barbara J. C. Rosenberg |
| Developmental Editor | Cathlynn Richard |
| Senior Project Editor | Charles J. Dierker |
| Senior Production Manager | Kathleen Ferguson |
| Art Director | Vicki Whistler |

Scale model on cover, and sketches for part openers, from
*The Miser,* designed by Ralph Funicello.

ISBN: 0-15-501620-2

Library of Congress Catalog Card Number: 95-77200

In memoriam

Lee Watson
Ned Bowman
Gary Gaiser

# PREFACE

The seventh edition of *Scene Design and Stage Lighting* reflects changes in the theatre from Broadway to a more diversified professional theatre that is expanding both westward and north into Canada. The work of educational and regional theatres, particularly those located near our borders, reflects the exciting influence of multiculturalism. Recent emphasis has been less on original plays (although there are signs of a resurgence of new plays and musicals) and more toward adaptation or revival of old favorites.

Fortunately for designers in the theatre, the accent is on production. Scene design continues to move away from box-set realism, and designers are expected to be more diversified and mobile than in the past. Lighting design, reflecting new technology in instrumentation and control, has become more precise and selective. Today's lighting styles are showing the influence of a current trend toward harshness. And sound is enjoying an ever-increasing role in theatre design. Technological advances in this area are occurring so rapidly that keeping abreast requires full-time attention.

As theatre has become more technical with respect to both lighting and production, the need for greater professionalism and teamwork between designers has increased. Parts I and II of this book have been revised to include this new direction and the changes in technical production. The single sound chapter of the sixth edition has been expanded into two: the first devoted solely to design and the second to equipment. The lighting chapters have been extensively rewritten to reflect current practice and technology. A new section has been added on nontheatrical opportunities in lighting design.

This edition, like preceding ones, would not have been possible without the valuable assistance of former students and professional colleagues. We would like to thank the following reviewers:

Sandy Black, Ryerson Polytechnical Institute; M. Barret Cleveland, Colorado State University; Linda Essig, University of Wisconsin–Madison; Lynne Porter, University of North Texas; Gerald B. Stephens, University of Florida–Tampa; Michael Tomko, Santa Monica College; and Dr. A. F. C. Wehlberg, University of Florida–Gainesville.

We also wish to acknowledge the artistic contributions of Samuel Ball, Albert Filoni, Ralph Funicello, Chris Parry, Jeff Ladman, Cameron Porteous, David Segal, and Susan Tzu, as well as the special assistance of Kevin Abbott,

Peter Davidson, Georg Schieber, William Teague, and Charles Weeks. Special thanks are due to Richard Block for all of his hard work on the edition, to Peter Nordyke for his invaluable collaboration on the sound chapters, and to Mary Neuru for reading the manuscript from a student's point of view. Additional special thanks are extended to the Yale Theatre Collection and to the Shaw Festival, Canada.

Finally, as always, a debt of gratitude is due to our patient and ever-supportive colleagues, Teschie and Barbara. This seventh edition is dedicated to you.

# CONTENTS

# PART III    STAGE LIGHTING AND SOUND    323

# SCENE DESIGN AND
# STAGE LIGHTING

# PART I

# THE DESIGN CONCEPT

# INTRODUCTION

Although design in the theatre may branch off into various areas of specialization, it primarily materializes in three basic forms: first, as an environmental background, or *scenery*; then as *costumes* for the actor within that setting; and finally, unifying all, as *stage lighting*.

The paths leading to a career designing in the theatre are numerous and varied. They may come from within the theatre itself or from the outside world. An actor or director gifted with a visual sense of theatre can contribute to design just as surely as can the trained visual artist who, equipped with the practical ability to draw and paint, possesses a strong desire to be in the theatre. A student from the latter background standing at the threshold of training for a career in design for the theatre may puzzle over what the future holds. The sudden but transitory flush of excitement involving one's first experiences in the theatre shouldn't obscure the need for a long-range artistic commitment to hard work. Anyone interested in achieving creative and personal fulfillment as a scene, costume, or lighting designer must first thoroughly understand the complexity of theatre as an art form.

Theatre today is undergoing significant change. During this century its literary form, its physical form, and in some cases its theatrical form (that is, the basic idea of theatre itself) have undergone changes. The influence of television has been pervasive—more and more scripts are written as a series of short scenes set in numerous locales. The popularity of thrust stages has increased, inviting the audience to be more directly involved both physically and emotionally. The trends toward more conceptual art and spectacle, along with influences from Eastern Europe, have redefined our very notion of what constitutes "theatre," and have challenged our ideas of its form, expanding the possibilities of involving, manipulating, and affecting an audience through various types of performance. The availability and affordability of computer technology have opened the door to more complex movement and control. All these changes in some measure affect designers and their position in the theatre.

## THEATRICAL FORM

Theatrical form in its simplest description is the communication of ideas between two groups: performers and audience. The assembly of audience and performer, or *performance,* is the presentation of ideas by the performers to the audience. These ideas may range from the very ancient to the most topical, from the profound to the absurd, and at the same time be either sentimentally obvious or intellectually obscure. The performance can exist in a number of styles and descriptions and in a variety of physical forms. Theatrical styles will be discussed in detail later; it is more important in an introduction to elaborate on the description of types of theatrical forms and the variety of physical forms, or theatre structures, that make up our some-times controversial, frequently exciting, but always interesting contemporary theatre.

There are several types of theatrical venues that involve the designer. The most obvious are the *literary form,* or drama; the *musical form,* including opera and book musicals; and, for want of a better name, the *audiovisual form,* which is nonverbal communication that places emphasis on sound and sight and not on the spoken word (for example, ballet and modern dance). Other possible outlets that have become more common in recent years include industrials (theatre that is performed to promote a product or company); parties for company executives, salespersons, and/or managers; rock concerts and videos; theme parks; and performance art.

Of these forms, the literary form, or drama, has so dominated theatre historically that the word *drama* has become synonymous with *theatre.* The significance of drama to the designer is evidenced by the fact that the major portion of a designer's training for the theatre is spent in learning to interpret and expand the ideas of the playwright.

In recent years the dominance of the literary form has been challenged by musical theatre. Characterized for so long by either lighthearted musical comedies or the heavier fare of "grand opera," the new musical theatre has tried to unite these extremes. At the same time, opera has been undergoing a resurgence that in part reflects the influence of the intricate staging of musicals and the philosophy of modern scenography. Opera scenery of the past was for the most part a background of theatrical realism and painted atmosphere. In contrast, modern stage design's interpretive form, color, and light relate much more closely to the emotion of the music and the theme of the libretto. Today's staging brings visual unity and nonverbal support to an already powerful theatrical form (Figure 1–1).

Challenging all of these theatrical forms is the recent penchant for *spectacle,* exemplified by such productions as *Sunset Boulevard,* The Who's *Tommy,*

## Figure 1–1
### Theatrical Forms

(a) Dance. Movement and music are the means of communicating in this modern dance performance of *Window Dressers* presented by Malashock Dance & Company at the Old Globe Theatre. Choreographed by John Malashock, Lighting by Ashley York Kennedy, Costumes by Deborah Dryden, Set Design by Ralph Funicello. Photo courtesy of Ralph Funicello.

(b) Drama. Theatrics at their most dramatic in *Hamlet* at the Old Globe Theatre, San Diego, 1990. Director—Jack O'Brien, Set Design—Ralph Funicello, Lighting—Peter Maradudin, Costumes—Lewis Brown. Photo courtesy of Ralph Funicello.

(c) *Lohengrin* at Le Grand Théâtre de Genève, June 1994, Geneva, Switzerland. Director—Robert Carsen, Set and Costume Design—Paul Steinberg, Lighting Design—Dominique Bruguière. Photograph © George Mott.

and *Phantom of the Opera.* Spectacular lighting, sound, and engineering technology, made possible by computer control and computer-generated design, bring to the stage a powerful and innovative production style. The audience, dazzled by pyrotechnics and special effects, is left breathless with a memorable experience that will forever influence their attitude toward "live theatre." As well, technology from the fields of film and science is being combined with theatre technology more and more. Several decades ago, the use of film and live actors so innovatively employed in *Laterna Magika* (from what once was Czechoslovakia) changed our notion of theatre and what can be done physically on stage. Within the past five years there have been experiments with holograms on stage. And what is virtual reality if not theatre?

## PHYSICAL FORM

The various types of theatrical form often determine in a general way their physical form. For example, the size of a theatre for most musical productions, with their presentational style and spectacular scale, is the opposite of the needs of much drama, which tends to be more intimate in nature. Both have clung in the past to the traditional proscenium theatre arrangement, with the audience facing the stage. The physical shape of new theatres, however, has undergone a variety of changes, discussed in detail in Chapter 2. Like the innovations in theatrical form, many new theatres contain either variations of the conventional proscenium shape (Figure 1–2) or are completely different in form, while a few try to combine both by converting at will from a conventional form to an unconventional one.

**Figure 1–2**
**Proscenium Theatre**

The Princess of Wales Theatre in Toronto is a showcase of all that is best in contemporary design. Built to accommodate the spectacular opening of *Miss Saigon*, the theatre combines the architectural work of Peter Smith, interior design of Yabu Pushelberg, artistic talent of Frank Stella, and is a marriage of the finest ideas in theatre design from this century and the last. Photo courtesy Mirvish Productions.

## Figure 1–3
### Thrust Stages

(a) Tyrone Guthrie Theatre, Minneapolis. Photo courtesy of the Guthrie Theatre.
(b) Mark Taper Forum, Los Angeles, 1985. *Measure for Measure*, Director—Robert Egan, Set Design—Ralph Funicello, Lighting—Martin Aronstein, Costumes—Robert Blackman. Photo courtesy of Ralph Funicello.
(c) Stratford Festival Theatre, Stratford, Ontario. Photo courtesy the Stratford Festival.

Designed primarily for drama and possibly intimate musicals, many recent theatres have taken on the new-old forms of the thrust and arena stages (Figures 1–3 and 1–4). Prompted by the desire to bring the audience closer to the actor, these variations either partially or completely surround the acting area with seats. These shapes give the theatre back to the actor and the

**Figure 1–4**
**Arena Theatres**

(a) The Arena Stage in Washington D.C., a classic example of theatre-in-the-round. Photo courtesy Capitol Photo Service, Inc. (b) *Fiddler on the Roof* as presented on Casa Manāna's arena stage in Fort Worth, Texas. Photo courtesy of Casa Manāna.

**Figure 1—5**
Open Staging

*All's Well That Ends Well* was designed for the Colorado Shakespeare Festival open stage production by Steven L. Gilliam Photo courtesy of Steven L. Gilliam.

playwright. This trend toward thrust and arena presents many different challenges to the designer. The staging emphasizes the costumes and the properties, while often minimizing the background. The desire for spectacle, however, often demands a great deal of scenery in these venues.

In an effort to find a form midway between thrust and proscenium staging, different uses of the proscenium form have evolved. In one such case, the picture-frame feeling is reduced by extending the apron of the stage (Figure 1—5) and doing away with the traditional act curtain. The result gives the illusion of a thrust into the audience and at the same time provides a stage that scenically can function like the proscenium.

The "black box" (Figure 1—6) is a name given to a flexible space within which a variety of audience—performer arrangements can be created. This popular theatre form often employs an ingenious stage space as well as the potential for clever staging. The challenge to the designer is to be functionally simple and at the same time theatrically expressive. The black box as a theatre form is comparable to the arena, thrust, and proscenium theatres.

It is no longer rare for a theatre to be created in a wide range of non-theatre structures (Figure 1—7). The audience—performer arrangement has been altered to fit into an old garage, a deserted warehouse, a gymnasium, a ballroom, an out-of-use church, and many other unexpected locations. The often unusual relationship between the seating arrangement and performance area is part of the theatrical experience and can function as an element of the production. Unconventional arrangements free the audience and the performer from any preconceived notion of what will be seen or what can be done. In *Tony and Tina's Wedding,* the audience serve as wedding guests. In at

**Figure 1–6**
**Black Box Theatre**

A unique example of a black box, The Walt Disney Modular Theatre at California Institute for the Arts has movable floor units and wall panels which allow for multiple set configurations. The theatre was designed by Jules Fisher in collaboration with Herb Blau. Photography by Steven A. Gunther and photo courtesy CalArts.

**Figure 1–7**
**Nontheatre Forms**

(a) Outdoor production of *The Music Man* at St. Louis MUNY. Set design by Steven L. Gilliam. Photo courtesy of David Burnside.
(b) The Hip Pocket Theatre in Fort Worth, Texas is built around a tree. Photo courtesy Hip Pocket Theatre.
(c) The Round House, on the outskirts of London, provides theatre in an old railroad roundhouse.

least one production of *Tamara*, the action of several scenes takes place simultaneously, with the audience choosing what path to follow for the evening—either remaining in one room or following one particular character.

## SCENE DESIGN

Theatrical form, of which scene design is a vital part, combines many related arts into the very intricate, sometimes frustrating, but always fascinating art of the theatre. In drama, or literary theatre, for instance, the written words of the playwright are transformed for the audience by the director and fellow artists into an audible and visible expression of the author's ideas. The scene design gives visual substance to the performance.

### THE TOTAL VISUAL EFFECT

Scene design in the modern theatre is concerned with the total visual effect of a dramatic production. In any production this is the sum of all the elements that depend on being seen to make their impression on the audience. The scenic background is perhaps the largest visual element that supports the spoken word of the dramatic form. The design of a setting, however, is not confined to creating the color and shape of framed pieces of scenery alone. It also includes the selection and style of the furniture and set-dressing, as well as careful consideration of the actors' costumes to blend or contrast with the background and, because a dramatic production is not a static form, to allow easy and appropriate movement of the actors. As well, in discussion with the lighting designer, the set designer considers the quality of the lights that reveal the scene.

The visual requirements of a script may be as simple as those of Thornton Wilder's play *Our Town*, which all but eliminates physical elements of scenery, or as complicated as those of Jerome Kern's *Showboat*, which requires vast quantities of spectacular background. In either case the visual elements have to be designed by someone.

### QUALITIES OF DESIGNERS

Beginning designers are expected to know so many things at once that they may be puzzled where to begin. They will soon find that if they wish to design for the stage they must quickly develop three qualities that are directly related to the specific demands of modern theatre. Anyone who aspires to be a designer will need the vision and imagination of the creative artist, the ingenuity and skills of the stage artisan, and above all the knowledge and sense of theatre of the actor, director, and playwright.

To function as creative artists in the theatre, designers must be talented and articulate in line, color, and form. They must be able to bring meaning and visual significance to a stage picture through imaginative and creative qualities developed by training in the nonverbal techniques of design, drawing, and painting.

As stage artisans, designers must be able, through the use of unique materials and theatrical techniques, to bring substance to their ideas with skill and dispatch and within the structural limitations of their medium. To create a design that can be wholly realized, they must know the structure of scenery, the limitations of materials, the methods of moving scenery, and must have at least a general understanding of lighting.

As a collaborating artist, the scene designer makes an important visual contribution to the dramatic form. Through the study of dramatic structure and perception of the playwright's goals, the designer is better able to find the author's image and bring its visual interpretation onto the stage. Awareness of the necessary movements of the actors and directing techniques helps the designer create a proper environment to support the action of the play. This is the designer's theatrical quality. A strong sense of theatre is needed in order to bring a theatrical flair to designs while still keeping them in proportion to the dramatic import of the play.

## DESIGN COLLABORATION

Within the realm of the total visual effect are several areas of design concentration. In this age of specialization, productions are rarely designed by one designer. Usually, the design of a production is divided between a scene designer, a costume designer, and a lighting designer. The three designers (often four if there is a sound designer) work as a team in collaboration with the director. Each area of design is directly influenced by the others, creating the total visual effect of any theatrical production. This visual effect is determined by a response to the script and the overall approach to the production as decided on by the artistic team. Each of the designers cannot with integrity design without a concern for the rest of the artistic team. If the actors will be wearing delicate fabrics, heavy textures probably are best avoided. If the costumes will be big due to padding or some other understructure, as is typical of several periods, the set must be large enough to accommodate. Is it possible for the lighting designer to light an actor in any area of the set? Does the setting allow for the lighting to achieve the mood of the play? Constant communication among the designers and with the director is critical throughout the production process.

It is important for the design team to consider how the director will use the space—physically and visually—for the production. Although the final action and positioning of the actors is the prerogative of the director, the arrangement of the space has a direct bearing. Part of the job of the scene designer is to allow the director to create theatrical stage pictures by arranging the actors within the setting in a manner appropriate to the script. The floor plan of a setting influences the ease or effectiveness of the actors' movements. The restrictions of a poor floor plan are usually more obvious than the virtues of a successful one.

Light brings atmosphere and focus to a production as well as a flexible means of modifying color and modeling scenic forms. The lighting reveals or hides what is necessary in the most subtle or the most blatant manner. It is innately theatrical. A good lighting designer will illuminate the actors and the set in such a way that members of the audience sense the mood and the tone of the moment often without being aware of how they are being manipulated. The scene designer must be aware of the design potential of light in modern theatre and embody the appropriate theatrical sense of light in the design of the set.

Costume design is an essential part of the total visual effect, and although it most directly concerns the actor, it complements the scene design. The costume gives meaning to the individual character and at the same time places each character in proper relationship to the total visual effect.

Each of the three designers must work to bring all of their contributions together to form one whole. If they have helped to create the world of the play in a given production, they have done their job well. Although an audience may leave the theatre with a lasting impression of the scenery, the lighting, or the costumes, they come to the theatre to see and hear an actor interpret a role.

There are times when one person is working on two or more of the areas of design. Although historically it was once most common to find the same person designing sets and lights, today any combination is possible. In some situations one designer will be responsible for all three areas of design. (It is possible for sound to be included here, but it is a rare occurrence.) Although it might seem that this would be easier, the lack of input from other designers can prove difficult and even less satisfying. In addition, designing in one area at a time is time-consuming. The responsibility for more than one area can prove to be cumbersome without additional artistic help.

Whether the attributes of the artist and the artisan are found in one person or separate individuals, the ultimate goal of scene design is the same. Designing for the stage means working within specific time limitations and a predetermined stage space—be it thrust, arena, or proscenium. At the same time, the designer must strive to satisfy the visual requirement of each production . . . ballet, opera, or drama.

# SCENE DESIGN AND THE THEATRE

# 2

Materials and techniques that are the bases of scene design must have a direct influence on the final design form. These materials and techniques create a medium through which design is transmitted. Each medium requires a specific handling, which gives it an individual effect. A painting, for example, may be done in an oil, watercolor, or fresco medium. Scene design, however, does not stand alone; it is a part of the overall dramatic form. A scene designer may draw sketches or make models, but final designs do not reach a full state of expression until they are on stage with actors in a theatre. As a result the scene designer is concerned not only with the media of canvas, paint, and wood—and more and more, the computer—but also with theatrical materials or material that can be adapted to theatrical uses and techniques. If new or old materials and techniques are to be used intelligently, the designer must have an awareness of the theatre as a medium of expression.

## THE THEATRICAL MEDIUM

The basic communicative qualities of scene design are the same as in any other visual art—color, line, and form have the potential to create emotional response on the stage just as they do in a poster or display design. Any differences in the design form are traceable to special materials and stage techniques associated with the functions of scene design. In order to understand, at least in general terms, the extent and limitations of the materials and techniques of this medium, the beginning designer must develop an awareness of the theatre as an organization, a show, a machine.

### THEATRE AS AN ORGANIZATION

The preparation of any production requires the close cooperation of many specialists. The theatrical medium brings together the writer, actor, director, designers, and audience. Certain elements are critical to ensure the success of a play, regardless of the level of theatre. The producing organization must always be efficient in (1) selecting a play; (2) selecting and rehearsing the actors; (3) designing the scenery, lighting, costumes, and sound; (4) building and painting the sets, building the costumes, and lighting the production; and (5) promoting an audience. Professional theatre, as well as some college, university, and community theatres, must also consider (1) procuring financial backing and establishing the budget, and (2) selecting a theatre. Lack of cooperation or understanding, complicated by faulty planning in any phase of the organization, can weaken the production as a whole (Figure 2–1).

As in any other well-functioning organization, there must be a guiding force or chief interpretive artist for the playwright. This could be the director, producer, department chair, or another leader, depending on the particular situation. It is the director's basic overall approach to the production, however, that brings a unifying control to the visual elements, acting style, and literary interpretation. The designers' contribution to the production is, of course, a vital part of the visual statement. Designers are, nevertheless, a part

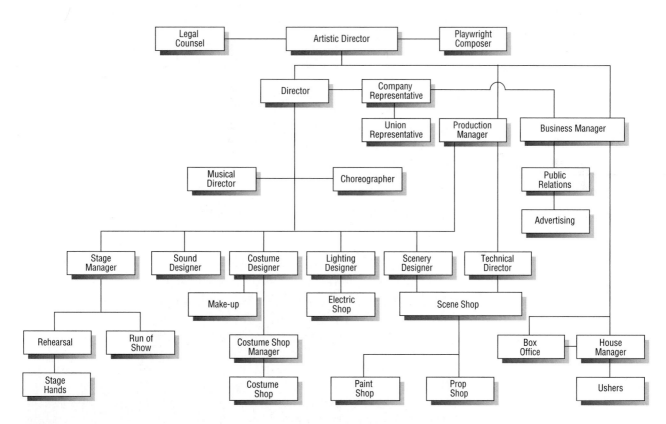

**Figure 2–1**
**A Producing Theatre's Organizational Chart**

An average theatre organization. Personnel would vary with size of organization or type of productions.

of the organization and its collaborative effort, which may mean subordinating personal triumph many times for the good of the whole. Great moments of unified achievement in the theatre are usually experienced when the goal of the production is placed above individual gain.

In addition to being aware of their general relationship to the overall production plans, designers need to know the specific organization of their own area of theatre—design, technical production, and lighting. A thorough knowledge of backstage and scenery-shop organization often leads to a more efficient production as well as a more faithful reproduction of design ideas. Because of its specialized nature, the personnel organization of designing and technical production is discussed in detail in Chapter 10.

## THEATRE AS A SHOW

The designer's awareness of the theatre as a show emphasizes the temporal quality of scenery, the dramatic qualities of the visual elements, and above all the sense of joining with an audience to give a performance.

As a performing art the theatre has a feeling of immediacy and audience relationship that does not exist as completely in other art forms. It is true that a painting has an audience, or viewers, too, but the painting remains a painting even without viewers. A theatrical performance without an audience, however, is little more than a rehearsal. The audience and its participation are vital parts of the theatrical medium. Consequently, the theatre's almost total dependence on an audience gives it a temporal quality that becomes an intrinsic part of the medium.

The direct influence of this temporal quality brings about a specific attitude toward scene design and the structure of scenery, for although scenery may look solid for the most part, it must be lightweight and portable to move easily from scene to scene or from audience to audience. And finally, when the production reaches its last curtain, the usefulness of the scenery ends. It is doomed to storage, rebuilding, or destruction.

The performance aspect of the theatre has a direct bearing on the attitude of designers. There is a tendency to think that the actors are the only performers, which is not the case. *All* the artists and workers in the theatre are performers. A performance is the collaborative effort of all performers. Its success is dependent on the teamwork of its members. Any sense of achievement lies in the reaction of the audience to a good performance. They are more often than not responding to an overall experience rather than to an individual performance. Visual artists working in the theatre are not their own bosses; they are collaborators in a joint venture.

The dramatic qualities of scenery are, of course, mainly achieved through the versatility of the designer's use of the visual art form. A dramatic quality more specifically related to the theatre is the use of proportion or scale. The theatre, more than other art forms, is an overstatement of life. Even a realistic play is drawn a little sharper and greater than real life. Any idea, no matter how significant, will make little impression on an audience if it is merely stated.

The size and distance of the audience in relation to the performance have an influence on the scale of any overstatement in scenery. If, for example, the theatre is large and the audience is at a great distance from the performance, the scenery has to take on an increased scale just to be in proportion to the size of the auditorium and stage. But whether it is a musical spectacle at a great outdoor arena or a drama of intimate proportions in a vest-pocket theatre, the theatrical medium has the capacity of offering a broad spectrum of electrifying moments.

## THEATRE AS A MACHINE

Although the technology of the theatre is in other hands, the designer should be aware of the tools backstage. Most scenery-moving techniques occur on the stage of the proscenium theatre where the emphasis, more often than not, is on production. The effortless movement of scenery, either in view of the audience or hidden by a curtain, is part of its theatrical magic.

Scenery and properties are, of course, moved in the thrust and arena stages, as well as the in the black box theatres. The movement can be mechanized, but more often is either a part of the action of the performance or is moved in view of the audience as an accepted feature of the theatre form.

There are a number of typical scenery-moving machines that the designer should know. A flying system is particular to the proscenium theatre, although makeshift versions can be used in a thrust or arena theatre. Tracked wagons for lateral or diagonal movement and a turntable or revolving stage are also commonly used. Elevators can be part of a design. Some stages are equipped with a built-in revolving stage or elevator system. All of these sytems might have an influence on the production scheme.

The computer has added efficiency to the control of backstage movement as well as greater safety, and is rapidly becoming a common tool for designers. Most lighting systems are now run by computer—and although still prohibitively expensive for some theatres, the computer will certainly become a built-in feature of stage equipment of the future. It is already becoming more commonly used as a design tool. For a more thorough discussion of scenery-moving techniques, please see Chapter 10.

## THE PHYSICAL STAGE AND ITS AUDITORIUM

The most important step for beginning designers is to learn their new medium by becoming acquainted with the physical stage. They need to know the actual shape and physical makeup of the performance area, for each defines the space in which they must work.

## PROSCENIUM THEATRE

In the contemporary theatre the stage has various forms based on the relationship of the audience to the stage area. The most common form is the proscenium type of theatre, where the audience is arranged on one side of a raised stage area. The enclosed stage is open to the audience through the proscenium opening. Early proscenium openings were surrounded by a decorative frame to separate the audience from the play in an artificial and often unrelated manner. The proscenium wall of the modern stage is merely a masking to hide stage machinery, lights, and scenery storage from view.

**Figure 2—2**
**The Proscenium Opening**

Three drawings to illustrate some of the design options of the proscenium opening.
(a) Altering the proportions of the proscenium to fit the scale of the design by lowering the teaser (horizontal frame) and narrowing the tormentor (vertical right and left frames).
(b) The setting is held free of the proscenium opening, thereby establishing a surrounding environment that may be in harmony or contrast to the scenic forms.
(c) A totally different effect is achieved by thrusting a portion of the setting through the proscenium opening.

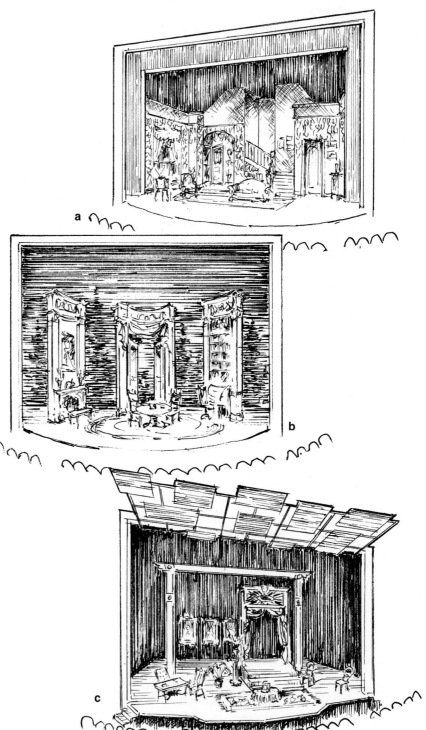

**The Proscenium Opening**     The modern proscenium theatre attempts to minimize the frame of the opening separating the audience from the stage (Figure 2–2). It is less of a demarcation than the old picture-frame prosceniums. The relationship of the design space to the proscenium opening is an early decision for the designer. Does the setting relate or attach to the frame of the opening; hold free in an open staging manner; or, does it pierce the opening to begin on the apron? Each has a different visual impact and staging capabilities. To close-in the opening reduces the scale of the production but provides more backstage space for the storage of scenery. To hold free expands the design space into open staging. And piercing the opening reaches toward the audience as if to break through the plane of the opening.

The proscenium opening can be reduced in proportion by lowering the inner overhead masking known as the *teaser*, and by closing-in the side masking, the *tormentor*.

a

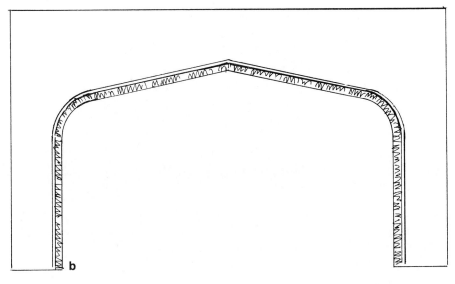

b

**Figure 2–3**
Show Portal

Sometimes called a *false proscenium,* the show portal is located upstage of the fixed proscenium and has two basic functions:
(a) The show portal may be decorative to set the tone or style of the production; or,
(b) it can be a simple frame to bring unity to a variety of scenes.

**Show Portal**     Rather than close-in the proscenium opening, the designer may choose to use a *show portal* (Figure 2–3). Sometimes called a *false proscenium*, the show portal is usually hung upstage of the tormentor and teaser. It is designed to make a visual statement and set the tone of the show. The reverse is also a feature of the show portal. It may be very simple and neutral in tone and shape to provide a unifying feature.

## SIGHTLINES

After learning the size and shape of the stage area, the designer is interested in the sightlines of the auditorium to determine how much of the stage is in view. The proscenium theatre has a characteristic sightline problem that varies only slightly with the different patterns of seating arrangement. If the flare of the seating arrangement is very wide, for example, people sitting on the extreme right side of the auditorium see very little of the left side of the stage and vice versa. Similarly, persons sitting in a very steep second balcony see very little of the back wall of the setting. If the auditorium floor is flat without a gradient, or if the stage floor is unusually high, the audience does not see the stage floor and sees very little even of the actors' legs as they walk upstage.

The designer must know these extreme sightline conditions in order to plan a setting that brings the most important areas into the view of all the audience. It is not necessary to find the sightline of every seat in the house but only of the extreme or critical locations.

The extreme vertical sightlines are difficult to locate, for they are found on a sectional view of the auditorium and stage that frequently is not available to the designer. The extreme vertical sightlines are drawn from the front row upward and from the last row in the balcony downward. On occasion, when a large balcony overhangs a considerable portion of the orchestra, it is necessary to consider a vertical sightline from the last row of orchestra seats (Figure 2–4a).

The extreme horizontal sightlines are drawn from the seats farthest to the right and left in the audience. The horizontal sightlines are located on the plan of the stage and auditorium (Figure 2–4b).

From the pattern of extreme sightlines, the designer can see how much of the stage is in view to each member of the audience. In Figure 2–4b, for example, the horizontal sightline (4) shows the designer how far onstage a person sitting in this seat can see and how much of the stage-right wall cannot be seen. In this manner, the designer consults the sightlines of an auditorium in order to efficiently plan the use of stage areas for staging the action of the play.

## STAGING FOR THE PROSCENIUM THEATRE

The designer uses the sightlines of a theatre in two different ways: first, when studying the staging of the play, to develop the design form; and then later, for technical reasons, to check the masking of the nearly completed setting.

When planning the staging, in collaboration with the director, the designer maps out the arrangement of properties, levels, and general floor plan

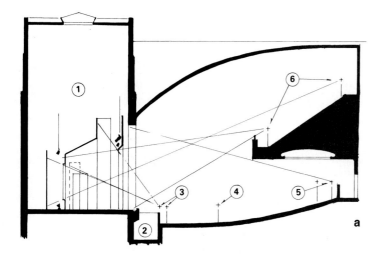

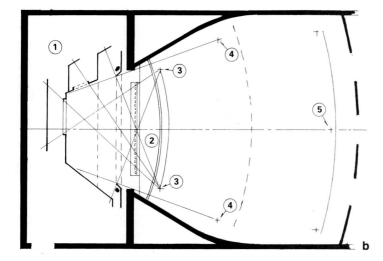

**Figure 2—4**
Sightlines

(a) Sectional view.
(b) Plan of auditorium and stage.
In each view
  (1) is the stage area,
  (2) orchestra pit,
  (3) front row end seats,
  (4) widest part of the auditorium, which determines the splay of the seating arrangement,
  (5) back row of the orchestra,
  (6) balcony seats.

to facilitate the easy flow of the play's actions. Because the designer is thinking like a director at this point, the staging is more than a traffic pattern for the actors. It allows the director to create appropriate stage pictures, bringing into focus each scene or moment in the play with the proper degree of relative importance to the other moments. Because actors and audience face each other, directions can become confusing. On the stage, all directions are related to the actors' right or left as they face the audience. *Stage left* is to the actors' left and the reverse holds for *stage right*. Because stage floors in the past used to slope toward the footlights, *downstage* is towards the audience and *upstage* is away. *Offstage* refers to the right and left areas out of view, while *backstage* is the entire area behind the proscenium. (The same directions apply to the thrust stage. In an arena space, however, this system does not work. Rather, the stage directions are commonly given in terms of the hands of a clock, the position of "12" being an arbitrary choice.)

The designer, through composition of the visual elements, can alter the basic value of any stage area. Due to their position on the bare stage, certain areas are stonger than others. The very nature of the proscenium theatre makes an actor standing downstage nearer the audience more important than an actor in an upstage position. The relative importance of the various positions on a bare stage is shown in Figure 2–5a by first dividing the stage into six equal parts and then numbering the areas in the order of their importance.

Such devices as raking or angling the side walls of a set to force the action in the weak upstage left and right areas toward the center, placing furniture to bring important scenes into good sightlines, and using levels in the upstage areas to increase their importance are just a few examples of staging techniques in scene design.

When the stage is cut, left to right, by a series of portals or large arches, the staging becomes more two-dimensional. It falls into a series of horizontal planes related to the portals, each traditionally referred to by numbers. Beginning at the apron the downstage strip is number one, the next number

## Figure 2–5
### Stage Area

(a) The stage divided for easy identification into basic areas that are numbered in order of relative importance:
    (1) downstage center,
    (2) downstage right;
    (3) downstage left,
    (4) upstage center,
    (5) upstage right,
    (6) upstage left.
(b) A second method of dividing the stage, a series of horizontal planes determined by the location of portals or wings and numbered from downstage to upstage.

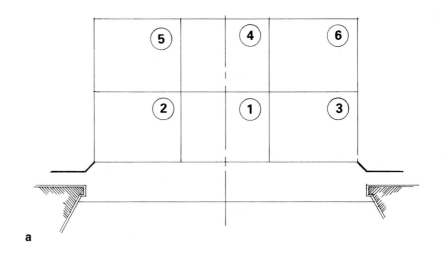

a

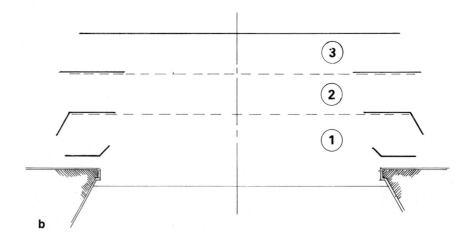

b

two, and so on upstage. The staging can be directed by indicating whether an actor or piece of scenery is to be in "one," "two," or "three," as desired (Figure 2–5b).

## STAGING IN FRONT OF THE PROSCENIUM

Two variations of the proscenium theatre are the *extended apron* and the *thrust stage*. Both are outgrowths of the desire to break through the frame of the proscenium in an effort to reduce the distance between the audience and the actor. Each is a part of the contemporary trend or revolt from the romantic theatricality of the past, which depended on a certain aesthetic distance to complete its illusion. Although the extended apron and thrust stage are not necessarily new forms in the theatre, they are very much a part of present-day staging and represent a space in which today's stage designer must be prepared to work.

**Extended Apron**     Although somewhat alike in shape, the apron and thrust stages differ in the arrangement of their respective audiences. The extended apron plays to a seating arrangement similar to that of the proscenium theatre with only slight differences in sightlines. The greatest change occurs in the vertical sightlines caused by the increased gradient. The necessity to keep an actor in full view and in a position well ahead of the proscenium results in a steeper rate of rise in each successive row of seats.

The extended apron is usually equipped with access openings or doors within each flanking wall ahead of the proscenium opening. The forestage area may be used in conjunction with proscenium staging, allowing elements of the scene to spill out onto the side stages, or in a more formalized manner, with all action originating on the apron.

The most flexible form of apron stage is illustrated in Figure 2–6, which shows how the area ahead of the proscenium opening can be modified by the use of elevators or removable platforms and seats to one of three variations: (a) full extended apron, (b) side stages with orchestra pit, or (c) regular proscenium staging with additional seats.

**Thrust Stage**     The thrust stage, or open stage as it is sometimes called, is as the name suggests a stage thrust out into the audience area. With seats arranged on three sides of the peninsula-shaped acting space, the bulk of the audience is closer to the actors than it would be in conventional seating. Semipermanent elements of scenery or an architectural background make up the fourth side of the theatre (Figure 2–7).

Though in appearance the thrust stage is structurally related to the proscenium theatre, its chronological development stems from the arena theatre. The long-felt need in theatre-in-the-round for greater variety of staging and a stronger axis of visual composition led to a semicircular grouping of seats around the thrust stage. At the same time, the widely diversified sightlines are an obvious improvement over the limited angle of view of the proscenium theatre. Since the upstage portion of the stage is anchored to the structural

### Figure 2–6
### Flexible Apron

A proscenium-form theatre equipped with a flexible apron that when raised or lowered can assume a number of shapes.
(a) The apron raised to stage level, providing an extended apron ahead of the proscenium opening with entrances from the sides and through the apron floor.
(b) The apron lowered to orchestra-pit level for a musical production.
(c) The apron at auditorium level. This arrangement with the extra seats is for a proscenium production.

a

b

part of the theatre, a rather important axis is established in the opposite direction.

The strong visual axis, however, has its shortcomings. The people sitting in the end seats of the right and left sides have a radically different compositional view. This is even more in evidence if the seating arc is greater than a semicircle, in which case the audience in the extreme side seats may find themselves enjoying a vista that approaches a rear view. The ideal configuration seems to be slightly less than semicircular, thereby providing a more equitable distribution of seats without losing the sense of close contact with the actors, which is so much a part of both the thrust stage and arena theatre concept.

The features of an ideal thrust stage that influence design are the extreme conditions of both the horizontal and vertical sightlines as well as the basic aim of this theatre type to simplify the amount of scenery needed to establish the locale. The abnormally wide horizontal sightlines force the use of conventional scenery to the back wall, with properties and levels utilized on the stage to set the scene. The sharp vertical sightlines, owing to the steeper gradient, make the floor treatment an important part of the design.

Both the apron and thrust stages, because of their exposed positions, work most easily with one fixed setting or relatively simple modifications during act changes. Any speedy change of locale is somewhat awkward and depends on the ingenuity of the director to stage it visually or to resort to the uncertainty of a "blackout" change.

The apron and thrust stages potentially provide more flexibility of staging. The three-quarters facing of the thrust stage, plus the presence of actors' entrances from the audience area, as well as the unconventionality of the theatre itself continuously encourage a greater use of style and design detail than is called for in the proscenium theatre. Costumes and properties become the center of the visual composition with most of the environment only suggested or defined with light.

### ARENA THEATRE

Another familiar stage form is the arena type of staging where the audience encircles the stage area. The scale of arena staging can vary from an intimate theatre-in-the-round to an arena the size of Madison Square Garden, with many sizes and variations in between (Figure 2–8).

**Figure 2–7**
**Thrust-Stage Theatre**

With seats on three sides of the stage area, the thrust stage and its background can assume a great variety of forms other than the conventional living-room interior in the illustration. Entrances can be made from the audience tunnels, the sides, through the stage floor, and from the back.

**Figure 2–8**
**Arena Theatre**

The audience surrounds the stage area, which may or may not be raised. Any use of scenic elements is limited to properties and an occasional open set piece.

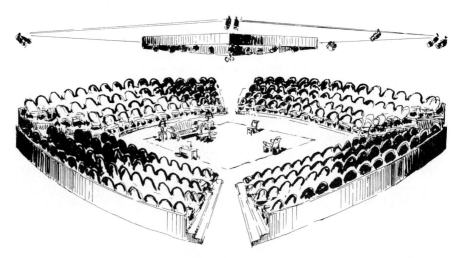

The sightlines of arena staging are drastically different from the proscenium type of theatre and present a different set of challenges and unique opportunities to the designer. It is much more difficult to hide actors, props, or machinery, for example. The visual elements normally have to be confined to small, low units or open pieces that can be seen through.

Design detail becomes more important because of the intimacy of the theatre and the lack of larger elements of scenery in the composition. This type of staging is intentionally simple, depending on a suggestion of scenery to set the scene and stimulate the audience's imagination to fill in the rest.

## FLEXIBLE STAGING

Flexible staging is an outgrowth or expansion of arena staging (Figure 2–9). It is obvious that arena staging has some advantages over proscenium staging, but on the other hand there are many plays that do not lend themselves to arena presentation.

Flexible staging, as a technique, is associated with the black box theatre form, which provides an area for easy changing of the stage–audience arrangement. Within this flexible space the staging can be altered from arena

**Figure 2–9**
Flexible Staging

The seat platforms and stage are movable and thereby able to assume a variety of arrangements. The audience partially surrounds the stage area, which may have a limited amount of scenic background.
(a) L-shaped arrangement.
(b) Proscenium-type.
(c) U-shaped, with the audience on the three sides of the stage.
(d) The audience split to produce a number of acting areas.

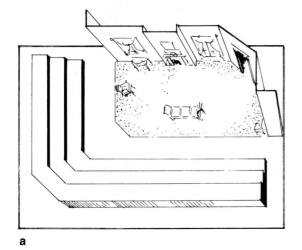

a

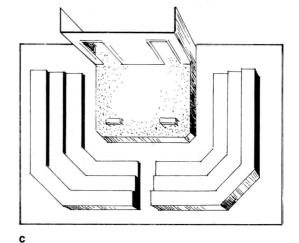

c

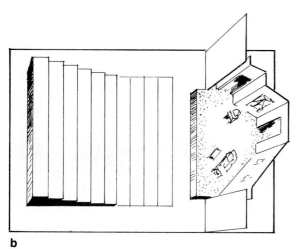

b

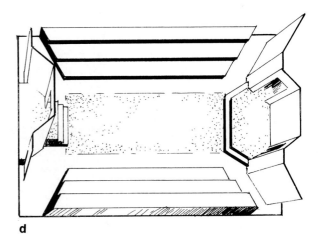

d

staging to three-quarters round, or to proscenium-type staging (Figure 2–10). Ballroom or cabaret staging is a further variation, with the audience on two sides and a small stage or bit of scenery at one end, or both. The sightlines vary, of course, depending on the type of staging. When the seats are arranged for proscenium-type staging there is a decided improvement in the sightlines over the conventional proscenium theatre. The seating is usually

**Figure 2–10**
**The Black Box Theatre**

The cutaway section reveals the basic areas of this flexible theatre. The corridor or passageway surrounding the audience–performance space has adjustable openings to provide entrances and exits for both the audience and actors to fit the specific arrangement.
(a) The encircling cat-walk provides easy access to the tension-wire grid covering the entire theatre space. Flexible lighting positions are available as well as limited flying or hanging of scenic elements. Sheaves or pulleys can be mounted under the cross beams and belaying pins can be inserted into the railing.
(b) Photograph of the tension wire grid. Photo courtesy of George Schieber.

a

b

arranged with a negligible flare, thereby creating good sightlines for the entire house (Figure 2–9b).

Flexible staging offers many exciting design and directing possibilities. Its main drawback is the relatively small audience capacity, which limits its commercial use. A more serious handicap is the loss of time and energy that occurs during the changing of the theatre from one arrangement to another. It is, however, an excellent staging medium for experimentation in new dramatic forms and for establishing greater intimacy between the actors and audience.

## CHECK LIST

Before venturing too far into the designing of a production, the designer should check the stage or performance area for the following:

· Floor plan—showing offstage space and heights
· Flying system—number of lines and spacing
· Traps—sizes and area
· Overhead obstructions—ducts or vents
· Load-in door—size and access to stage
· Sightlines
· Lighting positions and control
· Local fire code—restrictions and tests

# SCENE DESIGN AS A VISUAL ART

# 3

The exciting interplay of line, color, and form in a vibrant stage setting or the subtle refinements of an inconspicuous scenic background do not happen by chance. The proper integration of color and style of costumes and the dramatic presence of light in the stage scene depend on an understanding on the part of all the designers of the principles of design. To create a setting, the scene designer uses, either consciously or intuitively, well-established rules and fundamentals of design common to all the visual arts. The beginning designer should have a knowledge of these fundamentals to aid in the development of final design forms.

## DESIGN AND THE DESIGNER

We think of design as a creation of order that is the work of the artist. Artists bring two things to their work: *emotion* and *intellect*. Both are expressed in the feeling and rationale of a work of art. The emotional aspect of creating is individual and introspective. Its intangibility is sometimes called *talent*. It is hard to quantify and impossible to teach. The intellectual side of design, however, can be measured and defined in terms of *composition*. Within emotion or feeling lie desire, imagination, and a sense of theatre which are so necessary to creativity. Intellect, or the mind, on the other hand, cultivates the practical skills as well as the conceptual and interpretive powers of design. The merging of emotion and intellect is the beginning of the creative process that spawns the design form.

Beginning designers may wonder how this abstract definition of design applies to their special interest in the theatre. It means that during the process of designing, for example, there are two forces at work: a personal vision or feeling for the final design form, and the practical realities that are tempered by thoughtful judgment and taste. Both are regulated by the dictates of the playwright, the concepts of the director, and the limits of the performance space. In other words, emotion and feeling become the *ideal,* thought and intellect the *reality,* the first being the *goal* and the second the *realization.* The greater the skill and ability to realize the ideal, the more successful the designer.

## COMPOSITION AND THE ELEMENTS OF DESIGN

Composition, in general terms, is the composing or organizing of the elements of design in space into a unified *form.* The result may be a single form or the interaction of several forms acting as a whole. The elements of design are the elemental factors that make up the visual form, whether it be a two-dimensional shape or a three-dimensional sculptural object.

The elements of design can also be thought of as forces that, by manipulation, can singly dominate a composition and help give the form *meaning.* The reason for or meaning of any visual form brings to the composition a unity of purpose that is particularly important when designing in the theatre. The meaning attached to the designing of a visual form may be dictated from the outside, or may come from within the artist, often formulated by the simple desire for personal expression.

The major factors that make up a visual form can be listed in the order of their importance to the creative process:

Line

Dimension

Movement

Light

Color

Texture

Of these elements, *line* and *color* are the most forceful; in terms of design, *light* and *movement* are unique to the theatre. All the elements interact, one influencing the other as the composition takes shape. Although none usually stands alone, each has unique features that contribute to the overall effect sought by the designer.

### LINE

Line, as an element of design, *defines* form. It is a most important force in a composition because it is present in many different ways. Line can enclose space as *outline* and create shape (two-dimensional form), or as *contour lines* it can suggest three-dimensional form. Line in a composition can appear as *real line* in many different modes (straight, curved, spiral, and so on), as *linear shapes* that take on a line-like quality, or as *suggested line* simulated by the eye as it follows a sequence of related shapes (Figure 3–1).

**Figure 3—1**
**Real Line and Linear Shapes**

(a) Examples of real line. Straight, curved, subtle and strong reverse curves, serpentine and spiral.
(b) Real line can enclose space and create shape. Some shapes are linear, thereby taking on line characteristics by assuming direction and attitude.
(c) Suggested line. The eye will follow a line suggested by repetition of shapes, parallel lines, concentric circles, gradation of size or color, or a shape that points.

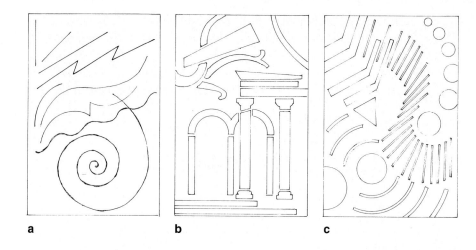

a            b            c

Line is a path of action and therefore cannot help but take on a sense of *direction* and become a part of *movement*. This is particularly true when the form is *linear* in shape (Figure 3–2). It soon becomes apparent that in an arrangement of several linear shapes the lines not only assume a direction but also take on an *attitude* toward each other, be it one of harmony or opposition.

The use of line, suggested line, and shapes with linear characteristics becomes a vital force in any form or arrangement of forms (Figure 3–1c). A composition may use line as a dynamic force with a sense of violent action or as a static force with a feeling of strength and stability.

## DIMENSION

Dimension is the *size* or *mass* of form. As an element of design, dimension is not only concerned with the size of a shape or the mass of a three-dimen-

**Figure 3—2**
**Linear Form in Composition**

The production of *Twelth Night* presented in San Diego's Old Globe Theatre in 1994 exhibits clear use of linear form in its composition.
Director—Laird Williamson;
Lighting—Chris Parry;
Costumes—Andrew Yelusich;
Set Design—Ralph Funicello;
Photo courtesy Ralph Funicello.

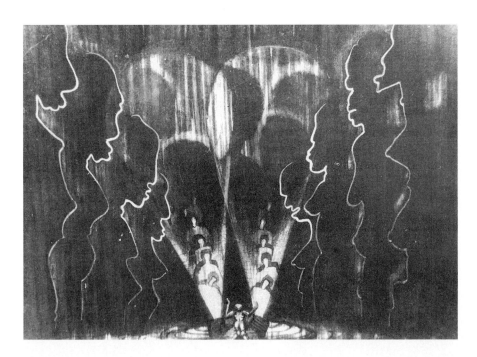

**Figure 3—3**
Dimensional Relationship

The scale of form and proportional relationship to other forms in a composition. Large to small, small to small, and so on. Scene from Eugene O'Neill's *Emperor Jones*. Photo courtesy of the Yale Theatre Collection.

sional form, but also with the relationship of the size of one shape to another—large to small, large to large, and so forth (Figure 3–3). *Real dimension* is always present in a two-dimensional shape, but, of course, becomes *suggested dimension* when a three-dimensional form is represented on a two-dimensional surface.

Dimension, in addition, includes the amount of space between forms in a composition. The size of the interval has a definite effect on the apparent size or mass of the form and its proportional relationship. The prominence or recession of the interval or size of mass is, of course, influenced further by the use of color, light, and texture. The proportional relationship between interval and mass also begins to establish a rhythm or sense of *movement*.

## MOVEMENT

Movement is the *action* of form. It is the kinetic energy of composition. Motion in design is always present, even in a static composition. The pattern of optical signals that touch the retina and then the brain is a continuous flow and hence mobile in character.

The *real movement* of form within a composition is very much a part of stage design (Figure 3–4). The movement of light, of the actors, and on occasion animated elements of scenery is commonplace in the theatre.

*Simulated movement,* as the name indicates, is the implied movement in a static medium such as a drawing, color sketch, or sculpture. The designer or artist may suggest motion in a sketch, for instance, by the blurring of a shape or the indication of shock waves. The costume sketch in Figure 3–5 illustrates simulated movement in the flow of the skirt and the eccentric balance of the figure.

**Figure 3—4**
Real Movement

The movement of actors and lights is the kinetic energy that brings life to a stage composition. Photo courtesy Randy Choura.

The movement of the eye, or *optical motion,* is a type of movement that is present in any fixed arrangement of forms. The use of suggested line (one characteristic of *line*) stimulates optical motion as the eye is led from one shape to the next.

Optical motion begins with an intuitive sense of *orientation* that everyone has or has experienced. It provides the basis for an interpretive feeling of movement frequently so subtle the viewer does not distinguish the effect as a product of optical motion. The tendency of the viewer, for example, to interpret a diagonal line extending from the lower left to upper right corner of a composition as an upward motion is a product of orientation. It is a part of the left-to-right orientation common to us all as well as the fixed association of a top and bottom to all compositions. See Figure 3—6 for further examples.

Movement also involves the fourth dimension—*time.* The interval and size of form relationship (mentioned earlier) cause a kind of movement or rhythm. The interval spacing or *tempo* may be staccato, pulsating, or ponderous in its timing. The vibration of repeated shapes, complementary colors, rapid changes of direction, and high contrasting areas are all visible examples of optical motion.

a

### Figure 3–5
### Simulated Movement

Movement in the costume sketch is suggested in the action of the skirt and the eccentric balance of the figure.
(a) A dancer in Smetana's *Bartered Bride* by Czech designer Karl Svolinsky.
(b) Detail of a relief sculpture entitled ''Passage'' suggests the fluidity of movement though cast in bronze. Sculpture and photograph courtesy of New England artist Harold Tovich.

b

a

c

b

d

### Figure 3–6
### Optical Movement

Within these four simple overall patterns the eye is stimulated into individual paths of movement.
(a) Herringbone or wave motion.
(b) Diaper or diagonal pattern.
(c) Vertical or linear.
(d) Primarily horizontal with a secondary diagonal movement.

(a) and (b) are active patterns, while (c) and (d) are more passive.

Although orientation brings an instinctive sense of movement to a composition, the designer has many means of controlling optical motion. Strong direction can be countered, reversed, or subtly changed by altering the *position* or *attitude* of the forms in relation to each other. The outline of the form itself can establish a direction, as can the other elements of design, such as color and light.

Another interesting phenomenon of movement is its *transferability*. Both real motion and optical motion can be transferred to a static object. A simple figure or shape placed against a busy or pulsating background will appear to dance or vibrate itself. This unwanted optical motion can happen to pictures, for example, if they are hung on a background of vibrant wallpaper. Real motion can also be transferred from a moving background to a fixed object in the foreground. Most everyone, for example, has experienced the sense of motion while sitting in a stationary railroad car or bus when the adjacent vehicle begins to move. The technique of moving the background behind the actor or fixed scene to create the illusion of movement in the scene is frequently used on the stage.

It goes without saying that all movement on the stage has to be carefully controlled and coordinated. Movement catches the eye and can detract from the scene as easily as it can enhance it. Ask any actor who has been "upstaged" by the innocent waving of a handkerchief or scarf by a fellow actor.

**Movement and Composition**     A stage composition is in a constant state of flux. Actors change position and grouping; elements of scenery change location; or, a static arrangement changes by the movement of light with color and a shift of direction. Figure 3–7 illustrates with four drawings how composition can be changed by the movement of light and the positioning of actors.

## LIGHT

Light *reveals* form. Although it has not been traditionally viewed as an element of design, light is a most dominant presence in all areas of stage design. As such, it must be considered a basic influence at the beginning of the creative process and not something to be added later.

Light can be thought of in three different ways: first, as *real light* capable of revealing form; second, as real light having its *own* design form; and last, as *simulated light* as it might appear in a two-dimensional representation of a three-dimensional form.

The design potential of light is inherent in its physical characteristics. The four variants of light are *intensity, color, distribution,* and *movement.* By controlling its brightness, color, and direction, light becomes a strong factor in creating a design form.

*Intensity* is the actual or comparative brightness of light. The actual brightness of the sun, for example, can be contrasted with the comparative brightness of automobile headlights at night. Spotlights in a darkened theatre offer the designer the same comparative brightness under more controlled conditions.

The ability of light to transmit and reveal *color* is one of its most dramatic qualities. The modification of local color of form by colored light is a design technique unique to the theatre. Color modification and the additive mixing

**Figure 3–7**
**Light in Composition**

Use of the distribution, color, and movement of light in this production of *Prometheus Bound*, designed by Donald Oenslager, was unique for its time. Produced at Yale in 1939 and conceived much earlier, it represents the kind of innovative use of light we accept as modern practice. Within the simple "gray gauze box" sitting in space, through which light could penetrate, wash with color, project on its surfaces, or make it disappear before our eyes, we watched the anguishes of Prometheus unfold. Lighting—Stanley McCandless. Costumes—Frank Bevan.

of colored light are two basic concepts of color as a quality of light that have to be understood by all designers in the theatre.

*Distribution* is the energy path of light. The control of the distribution of light gives it *direction* and *texture* as a design feature. The various kinds of distribution begin with the general radiation of direct emanation, through the more specific reshaping of the light rays by reflection and optics, to the parallel rays of the laser beam. The sharp versus soft-edged quality of a light beam, coupled with its degree of brightness, gives *texture* to light. It is easy to see how a knowledge of the distribution of light can affect the design form by the introduction of *highlight, shade,* and *shadow* into composition. Besides the atmospheric quality that light can add to a composition, there is the obvious design character of an exposed light source such as candelabra, chandeliers, or visible lighting instruments.

The fourth variant of light is *movement*—and the scene designer must be aware that stage lighting is in a near-constant state of motion. Movement of light can be described as the visible change of any or all of the other three qualities of light. The subtle change of intensity, for example, can alter the focus or center of interest within the composition, as does the more obvious movement of a *follow spot.* Change of color in a sky or background modifies the atmosphere or mood of a scene. The rapid change of the direction and texture of the distribution of light can have a dramatic or emotional impact on the viewer, such as that experienced during the vibrant movement of light in a rock show.

As mentioned before, real light can also take on its own design form. Patterns of light can be projected over a form as a part of the composition, or the projected image can be the entire composition. Although the use of light as projected scenery can be thought of as a medium in itself, it is, however, still a visual art and therefore draws on the same fundamentals of design for its realization.

The use of *simulated light* is most often present in the designer's sketch, where it represents the effect of light in the composition. Although *line* is used first to represent three dimensions, the added use of simulated light and its shades and shadows is the designer's most effective way of representing three-dimensional form in a sketch or backdrop. However, the most successful use of simulated light in a sketch or painting is based on a firsthand knowledge of what real light can and does do.

**Light and the Scene Designer**     Of all the techniques within the theatrical medium affecting scene design and the structure of scenery, lighting is the most influential. Because lighting technique will be covered in great detail later, it will not be necessary here to do more than point out its general influence on the materials and structure of scenery.

The use and control of lighting is strictly a theatrical technique, born and developed in the theatre. It is an additional element of design that gives the production designers a greater flexibility in composition than occurs in any other visual art form.

Light is visible energy. Among its characteristics is the apparent ability to transmit some of its energy onto whatever surface it falls. The energy of light reveals, brightens, and adds color to an inert object, thereby increasing its vitality. By the same token, it might be argued that color also brings life to a painting, but it is not as animated as, for example, light through a stained glass window or a projected color image on the stage.

Of all the components that make up a stage composition, the two most active and vital are the *actor* and *light*. The power of light to animate form makes it a forceful design statement in a stage composition. For a dynamic example of designing for light, refer again to Figure 3–7.

Aside from its design possibilities, light on the stage has an unavoidable effect on the structure and materials of scenery. The scene designer must consider in advance the relative changes in the intensity of light and the position of the light source, which may determine whether an area of scenery is to be opaque, translucent, or transparent. In the making of transparent or translucent pieces of scenery, the pattern of the framing and the location of the seams have to be carefully considered. Frequently the design is altered slightly to conceal or modify a seam or structural element. Conversely, opaque areas should not be neglected, for a strong backing light may reveal an interesting but unwanted pattern of framing.

Unfortunately the design of the lighting often comes late in the planning of a setting, almost as an afterthought. This sometimes reflects an indifference or unawareness of the theatricality and compositional value of light itself. Lighting is too important a part of the theatrical medium, however, not to be considered in the beginning along with the other theatrical techniques that condition the design and structure of scenery.

## COLOR

Color *modifies* form. As an element of design it is a powerful stimulus that can change the dimension of form, reverse the direction of line, alter the interval between forms, and generate optical motion. Color in the theatre comes from two basic sources: pigment or dye present on the surface of the form, or color transmitted by light.

Color in either light or pigment has three variants: *hue, value,* and *chroma.* A specific color can be thought of in terms of its *hue,* which is the color's wavelength or position in the spectrum; its *value,* signifying the color's black-to-white relationship; and its *chroma,* indicating the color's degree of purity (saturation) or freedom of neutrality.

**Value**    Although value has been defined as a variant of color, it is an important medium of expression itself. Suggested form can be modeled on paper without color in shades and highlights using various black-to-white tones, as illustrated in Figure 3–8.

Value is experienced early in the process of designing scenery. Many preliminary sketches are expressed in black and white with occasional gray tones. For more on color, see Chapter 8.

**Figure 3—8**
Value Sketch

Value sketch of a set for T.S.
Eliot's *Family Reunion*. The
scene is the cavernous manor
house of the family matriarch
where they are gathered for her
funeral. Scene designer—Laurie
Bennett.

## TEXTURE

Texture is the *tactile* aspect of form. As a design feature, it adds interest by embellishing the surface and thereby giving character to the finished form. The composition takes on a temperament partially inspired by the makeup of its texture. Surfaces may vary from the extremes of highly polished to rough/natural in quality (Figure 3–9). A rough-hewn surface or decorative bas-relief, for example, each stimulates different emotional responses. Each illustrates the purpose of texture as a design element.

The reason for using texture in the theatre is to catch, interrupt, and reflect light. The irregular shadows and highlights of a textured surface enrich a design form; thus the dependency of texture on light is a crucial component of design.

Texture in the theatre has two dimensions. First, it may be seen as *real* texture; the various surface treatments just described are examples of real texture. But it may also occur as *simulated* or painted texture. The two-dimensionality of painted texture is used for the same design reasons as real

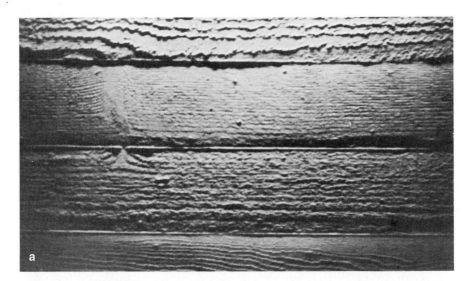

**Figure 3—9**
**Texture and Light**

(a) Rusticated surface emphasized with side lighting.
(b) Decorative bas-relief.
(c) This small but expressive
scene design illustrates the
dominance of texture in a composition. Designer—Vladimir
Suchanek, Bratislava.

## Figure 3–10
### Texture in Costumes

Used to augment character, real texture is an important aspect of costume design.
(a) Texture used to age or distress a costume.
(b) Texture as rich ornamentation.

texture, but the surface is treated with paint to add interest and character (Figure 3–10).

The earliest concept of the word *texture* was associated with weaving. The size and makeup of the warp and weft had a tactile sense that was either smooth or rough to the touch. A tactile image also appeared in the woven pattern and color variation. The same textural trait can be seen in techniques of paint and in surface decoration. The enrichment of a surface using a repeated motif or geometric patterns, such as on wallpaper, is one example of simulated or visual texture, as are mosaic, parquetry, and tiled surfaces. See Figure 3–11.

**Light and Texture**    Real texture is best revealed by directional side-lighting, while painted texture appears more real under a wash of light without a strong sense of direction. A wash of light is shadowless and therefore does not cast telltale shadows (such as wrinkles) in a drop that may expose the simulated texture as a painted surface. Conversely, a wash of light on a textured detail such as a cornice or molding will deny its three-dimensionality and sometimes require the addition of painted shadows and highlights to create the appearance of reality.

**Using Texture to Design for Light**    Since the function of real texture is to divide light into interesting shadows and highlights as a design feature, it is not too difficult to apply the concept of "real texture" to scenic forms as a whole. Although scenic forms are large in scale they, too, should be designed to interact with light.

The successful unity of light and scenic form results most often from the close creative collaboration of the lighting and scene designers. The theat-

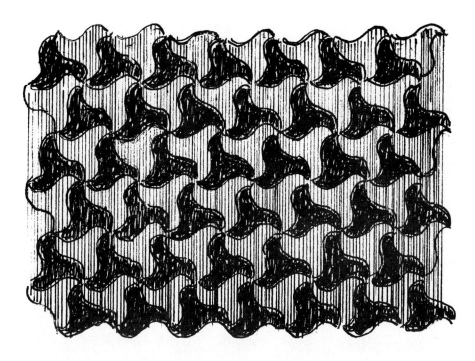

**Figure 3–11**
**Visual Texture**

An overall pattern can visually
simulate texture and enrich the
surface it decorates.

rical value of light to scenic form, first envisioned by Adolphe Appia and Edward Gordon Craig at the beginning of the twentieth century and fully realized later by the inventiveness of Josef Svoboda, is very much a part of present-day scenography. The use of abrupt surface changes, reflective covering, density variations from opaque to transparent, as well as the addition of highly textured areas on scene forms, all contribute to the unity of lighting and scenic form.

Figure 3–12 is an excellent example of designing for light. The illustration shows two moments in the National Theatre of London production of *Richard III* on the open stage of the Olivier Theatre. The open stage, or thrust stage, lends itself very well to the more dramatic use of light and scenic form.

## PRINCIPLES OF COMPOSITION

The elements of design are the raw materials ready to be brought together into some order or purpose. *Composition* is the organization of these elements into a unified form. The principles of composition are the various ways the designer can control and use the design elements to bring a fusion of interest and meaning to the stage. A good composition brings into play two controls: *harmony* and *contrast*. The manipulation of these controls—through variation, pattern, gradation, and so forth—is how the designer creates interest or appeal in a stage setting.

### HARMONY

The simplest act of bringing order to disorder is to sort unrelated objects into groups that have some sequential relationship or continuity. The objects

## Figure 3–12
### Designing for Light

These two atmospheric drawings are facsimiles of the London National Theatre's production of Shakespeare's *Richard III*. Revolving forms and sliding panels cast shadows and slash the stage with shafts of light in a series of dramatic compositions. A striking example of designing for light. Scene Designer—Ralph Koltai. Lighting Designer—David Hersey. Director—Christopher Morahan.

may have in common a similarity of shape, color, or texture. Repetition, then, is a basic control. The repetition of one or more of the elements of design shows the presence of outside control. The repeated use of line or linear forms, for example, can dominate a composition, although other elements of design may be present.

Although repetition is one of the easiest and quickest ways to bring harmonious control to a composition, it suffers the danger of becoming monotonous. The possible monotony of repetition can be relieved with a little contrast or variation.

## CONTRAST

The designer depends on contrast to create form. Form cannot be revealed without contrast, as is evident in the examples of the absence of contrast occasionally seen in nature. The protective coloration of an animal or bird, for instance, reduces contrast to the point of making it invisible against the background. But in the theatre, such lack of contrast—an actress in a red gown sitting on a matching red sofa—would be disastrous. Between the two extremes lie infinite variations.

The most visible examples of harmony and contrast are found in the use of color and value tones. A design with a single color scheme would be harmonious. The further colors are apart in the spectrum, the greater the contrast. The same thing occurs with value coupling. Black and white, for example, are extreme value contrasts. On the other hand, value tones that are close together are more harmonious. Again, refer to Chapter 8 on color.

## VARIATION

When the repetition of one element produces monotony, a variation of one or more of the other elements can add interest to the composition. It is interesting to note that in Donald Oenslager's designs for Aeschylus's *Prometheus Bound* (Figure 3–7), although the design is dominated by the use of light, the manipulation of the direction, distribution, and intensity of light is the major variation brought to a rather simple form. Color of the scenic form in this production was held under strict control. The overall tonality was gray or neutral with moments of color achieved through the use of colored light.

## PATTERN

The injection of variation into composition to relieve repetition establishes a rhythm as the variation recurs. This is the basis of most pattern compositions, which exist in two forms: border and overall patterns. The rhythm of the variation repeat (or *motif*, as it is called) is known in terms of its relative positions. That is to say, the motif may be placed in relative positions of alternation, opposition, or inversion (Figure 3–13).

The motifs may be placed in alternation by alternating their position in relation to a central axis without changing the original direction of the pattern. To place motifs in opposition tends to break the rhythm into a series of static arrangements, creating a feeling of stability. To place the motifs in inversion takes the direction out of the movement, especially if used in an overall pattern. Inversion is frequently used in textile patterns permitting the material to hang either up or down without the motif appearing to be upside down. These arrangements can be combined and compounded into numerous variations of each element of design, thereby adding interest to the border or pattern composition.

An analysis of border designs may seem unrelated to scene design. However, a border or pattern is a type of composition. It has an obvious control that is easy to see and study. The same control appears with a subtler and

**Figure 3–13**
Pattern Composition

(a) Border motifs in repetition,
(b) motifs in opposition,
(c) motifs in inversion, and
(d) motifs in alternation.
*Overall patterns.* The same motif is shown in four variations of the many methods of creating an overall pattern such as wallpaper. Inserts indicate the geometry of the control.
(e) Diaper.
(f) Scale.
(g) Ogee.
(h) Vertical stripes.

a

b

c

d

e

f

g

h

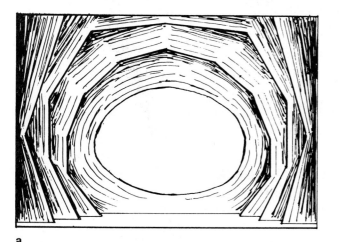

a

b

less restricted handling in the composition of a setting. Besides, pattern composition as found in wallpaper, paneling, and cornice decorations still occupies a large part of the scene designer's time.

## GRADATION

The variation of motifs within a border composition can, as has been shown, establish a rhythm or feeling of movement. The feeling of movement or change is frequently desired in composition of a stage setting where the controls will be less obvious. The sequential controls of a border composition are sometimes too obvious or abrupt. Sharp contrasts can be reduced by the use of the sequence of gradation, which by transitional steps softens contrasting elements and at the same time brings a feeling of movement into the stage picture. The graded wash of a sky-drop, with the dark blue at the top gradually becoming lighter near the bottom, is an example of gradation of the value of a color. The use of gradation may occur in line, shape, or in any of the elements of design. The resulting feeling of movement in the composition is free of the repetitive rhythm of the pattern composition (Figure 3–14).

**Figure 3–14**
The Sequence of Gradation

(a) Gradation of shape from a rectangle to an oval opening.
(b) Gradation of value in the sky and of direction of the steps.

## COMPOSITION AND SPACE

Space is to the scene designer what a block of wood or stone is to the sculptor. The space in and around the stage becomes an area to enclose or leave open, to light or leave dark, to flatten out or to create the illusion of even greater depth.

Although undefined space is limitless in scope, it can be defined in two-dimensional terms. Figure 3–15 graphically illustrates the definition of two- and three-dimensional space and solid form by showing the many options a scene designer has to create a space or a form within a space. If the lines in the drawing that define a space—often referred to as a *space frame*—were considered to be outlining a plane of solid surface, the final arrangement

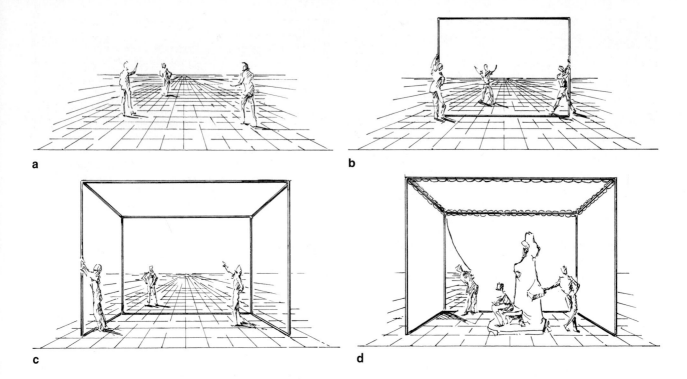

**Figure 3—15**
**Definitions of Space**

(a) Undefined space.
(b) Two-dimensional space frame.
(c) Three-dimensional space frame.
(d) Hollow solid surrounding a sculptural solid.

would be known as a *hollow solid*. The hollow solid is a familiar scenic form associated with proscenium theatre. The *sculptural solid,* designed to be viewed from all sides, is more suitable for the thrust and arena stages. The first, like scenery, defines a space that becomes the design form itself. The second creates a form within a space.

Designing within the limits of two-dimensional space begins with a perception of the relationship of *figure* and *ground*. Ground, often background, is a two-dimensional plane. In the simplest example, it can be likened to a sheet of drawing paper. The figure or shape outline has to be in contrast to the ground to be visible. An example of figure is the enclosure of a portion of the ground by an outline. For greater contrast, the figure may be filled with a flat tone or color.

The spatial feeling of a composition made up of a single figure and ground is flat. As figures or large shapes are overlapped, one figure becomes the ground for the other and composition begins to take on depth. The ground may be simple with a textured or patterned figure, or in reverse, with a complicated ground and simple figures.

The composition of a wing-and-backdrop type of setting is an example of the use of figure and ground in scene design. The flat plane of each wing when contrasted against the adjacent wing gives an illusion of space that belies their two-dimensionality, especially when other signs of space are used.

Up to now the figure has been thought of as an outline, or outline and flat tone. The figure can also represent a solid with not only height and width but also a depth or thickness. The representation of volume in outline or in solid areas is also an indication of space. The outline itself may be varied in

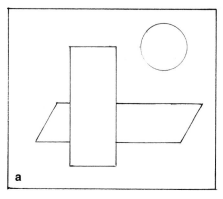

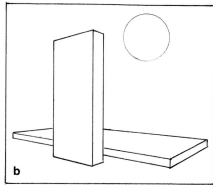

**Figure 3–16**
Sequence of Composition

(a) Flat outline.
(b) Slight perspective or feeling of space.
(c) Dimension and texture.
(d) Light and shadow.

thickness and the ground modeled to accentuate the three-dimensional or plastic qualities.

To heighten the three-dimensional quality of the form is to model it in light and shade as if coming from a definite light source. The direction of the light and the cast shadows help to describe the form and place it in space.

The final exploit of space perception is the illusion of literally breaking through the plane of the drawing paper with the use of perspective. Perspective and the shadows of directional lighting are combined to achieve a total effect, a feeling of space in two-dimensional form (Figure 3–16).

## COMPOSITION AND UNITY

The composition of a stage setting is expected to bring a unity to the overall arrangements of the visual forms. In addition to the unifying effect of harmony expressed in the sequence of repetition and gradation, scene design needs a greater sense of unity to bring strength to stage composition. The compositional unity of a scene design is first dependent on *balance and movement* and then on *proportion and rhythm*. At first glance, balance and movement may seem the same as proportion and rhythm; however, a closer analysis will show that they are related but not the same. Balance and movement are the outward, more obvious expressions of the subtler, more sensitive effects of proportion and rhythm.

Unity suggests balance, a balance of the forces within the composition. These forces are the forces of tension, attraction, attention, and movement that exist between the forms of a stage design. All scenery forms have mass and size (dimension), which means that their proportion must be considered. And lastly, the proportional relationship between forms cannot help but bring rhythm into the composition, whether it is static or dynamic in feeling.

**BALANCE AND MOVEMENT**

Balance is described as the relationship of forces within a composition. But what is the visual expression of a force? The strong visual pull of attraction and attention are forces. The intense colors of a poster attract the eye. The attention value of the poster contains the interest and meaning that stimulate a response in the viewer.

These two forces, attraction and attention, are of significance to scene design. Many times a setting has to make a telling effect in the opening moments of a play and then have sufficient attention value to sustain interest through two hours of performance.

A visual expression of tension also exists between forms. The degree of tension is dependent on the interval or space between forms. The space between the finger of God and Adam as God gives life to man in Michelangelo's fresco in the Sistine Chapel is an example of tension. The spark of life can almost be seen. If the fingers were touching, or moved farther apart, the tension would be absent. Tension as a force is found in the composition of a setting in the spacing of scenery masses, the grouping of furniture, or in the relationship of the actor to the scenery and furniture.

Another example of a force in composition is the force of gravity and the viewer's unconscious reaction to it. Gravity has probably the greatest effect on balance. A viewer reacts to visual signs with an organic sense of balance schooled by a lifetime of living with the pull of gravity. Because of this, an unsupported heavy object may seem to be falling, as does a leaning object, unless its center of gravity holds it in balance. Also, a recognizable shape in an unnatural position may cause a feeling of imbalance. The reverse is also true. To abstract a recognizable shape, the designer sometimes consciously uses unnatural position as pure design in an effort to deny reality.

Depth perception is also crucial in the theatre. It allows a viewer to judge whether objects are in the same plane or are receding in proper order. However, this sense of depth on the part of the theatre audience can be fooled, by altering the signs of space perception through perspective foreshortening, into seeing more distance than is actually on the stage.

Movement as a contributor to unity is concerned with *change* and *time*. The harmonious and progressive change of the sequence of gradation is an example of movement as the eye is led, step by step, through a change of color, form, dimension, or direction.

A well-organized form has a firmly established plan of movement. Some arrangements of form stimulate a greater sense of movement than others. Some cause a different kind of movement, such as a precarious balance of tension. The plan of movement within a composition, in any event, is a closed plan, always staying or returning to the overall form.

In the theatre, as has been noted, the inclusion of time in actual movement is quite apparent. The actors move from area to area; the lights dim and brighten; scenery, on occasion, moves in view of the audience. All these are part of the composition of the dramatic form and involve the element of time. The element of time, however, exists in a fixed composition, too.

There is an interval of time as the eye follows the pattern of movement through a composition. The interval is minute, of course, when compared to the broader movements on stage. The visual change can lead the eye, abruptly or gradually in terms of time, over the movement plan of a composition.

## PROPORTION AND RHYTHM

The second means of obtaining unity in a composition is through the use of proportion and rhythm. Proportional judgment is probably one of the initial signs of talent. A certain amount can be acquired by training and sharpened by analysis, but a sense of proportion is largely intuitive.

Proportion is the ratio of something to something else. On stage it is natural to relate proportion to the human figure, for the actor is a part of the total composition. In the theatre this is referred to as *scale*. The designer is constantly checking the size of a form in ratio to human scale (Figure 3–17). Some productions demand a greater scale or an increased ratio of the size of surrounding forms to the actor.

Proportion can also be linked to the reason or function of a visual form. The proportion of a chair as a visual form, for example, depends on how the chair is to be used. A simple dining-room side chair is small when compared to the scale and grandeur of a canopied throne chair. Stage settings and even entire productions can differ in scale for similar reasons. The proportions of the ballroom scene in *Romeo and Juliet,* for example, are of more significance than the scale of Friar Laurence's cell; similarly, the pageantry of *Henry VIII* demands greater scale as a production than *The Merchant of Venice,* which is of more intimate proportions.

Many forms and arrangements of forms, however, are not associated with human scale. In addition to the concept of proportion as scale, a proportional relationship exists between one form and another and between the space used between forms. Perhaps more important is the proportional relationship of forms to their surrounding space. The rhythm and proportions of a sculptural arrangement of forms set in an unbound space, for example, may seem different from a similar arrangment of shapes framed or confined within a rectangular shape such as a proscenium opening.

Although scene designing, at least in its formative stages, composes within a rectangular or near-rectangular shape, it is also concerned with the freer compositions of the nonproscenium stage. Designing for nonproscenium theatre approaches the use of sculptural techniques to create a desirable proportional relationship between scenic forms in a more or less undefined

**Figure 3–17**
Scale

(a) The feeling of scale in a stage setting is linked to the size of the human figure. In these two examples the design forms are identical in size. Their scale changes in relation to the size of the figure in the composition.
(b) An oversized puppet dominates other characters in a children's show. Puppeteer—Mario Donate, Puerto Rico.

space. Whereas the composition within a proscenium frame is viewed basically from a frontal direction, nonproscenium scenic forms have to be composed satisfactorily for viewers from all directions.

As balance is linked to movement, so proportion is joined with rhythm. The space between forms and the attitude of one shape to another create a rhythm in the composition. Rhythm is a type of movement that recurs at intervals or completes a cycle. The proportional relationship between forms establishes a rhythm, as does the subdivision of single form.

A conscious inner relation and rhythm is present in stage composition in many ways. It may appear in the quiet dignity of a formal arrangement or in the vigorous movement of a dynamic composition. Or it may be expressed in the rhythmic flow of harmonious forms or in a nervous, staccato organization of shapes.

Rhythm as a unifying factor is usually expressed in the lines or linear qualities of a stage composition. The use of actual lines or the feeling of a line caused by the position and direction of one shape to another results in a rhythmic movement that may be as strong or as subdued as the designer desires. Diagonal lines and lines parallel to the diagonals give a greater sense of movement than the use of strong horizontal and vertical lines, which tend to stop movement.

Although the rhythm of straight lines is more bold and forceful than curved lines, curved lines have infinitely greater variety. The rhythm of a curved line may have the grace of flowing lines, the turbulence of reverse curves, the whirl of a spiral, as well as the repetition and order of interlaced geometric curves such as circles and ovals.

Whether the rhythm of a stage composition is dominated by straight or curved lines, it eventually becomes a part of the basic movement plan. Likewise, the proportional relationship of forms, which determines the rhythm, forms a balance, resulting in greater feeling of unity, especially when the rhythm is visibly repetitious.

## COMPOSITION AND INTEREST

In addition to maintaining unity in a stage composition, the designer tries to bring interest and meaning to the setting. Any meaning attached to the scenic forms of the composition is, of course, a part of the designer's interpretation of the scenic requirements of the play that are a result of an attempt to bring visual substance to the playwright's ideas.

A stage setting, however, can fulfill all the scenic requirements of the play and still not be interesting. Just what makes one setting for a play more interesting than another?

A setting is interesting many times because of a unique and daring design interpretation that stimulates an intellectual response on the part of the audience. This is frequently possible when the play is a classic or one familiar to the audience. European scene designers constantly produce exciting and innovative design approaches to well-established classics. In university and community theatres in the United States, where people are going to see a production or interpretation of a well-known play more often than a new play, the emphasis is also often on the design idea or an exciting production scheme.

The designer, unfortunately, cannot take such great liberties with a new play. Here the audience is seeing the play for the first time and will not appreciate too "intellectual" an approach unless it is a part of the production scheme. It is more important first to stimulate the proper emotional response and not allow a self-conscious design to overwhelm the play.

The way in which a designer achieves balance in composition also accounts for one design being more interesting than another. A mechanical balance of the design forms may bring unity to a composition but can still be monotonous and uninteresting. An interesting composition varies or stretches the balance into a more exciting arrangement of forms without losing unity.

### CENTER OF INTEREST

Unless the composition is an overall pattern, it is organized about a center of interest, or *focal point*. This is a point in the composition (not necessarily the center) to which the eye of the viewer is led by either obvious or subtle means. The leadlines that are present in the movement plan of the composition direct the eye to the center of interest. In addition to the focal center there may also be secondary areas of interest as well as intriguing bits of detail within the composition that hold attention yet do not detract from the main point of focus.

A stage setting is usually designed around a strong center of interest with important secondary areas. Although the setting as a background has its own center of interest, the true center of interest in the total visual effect is the actor. As was mentioned earlier, a stage composition is a fluid, ever-changing thing with a different center of interest for each scene.

Fortunately, stage lighting, costume colors, and the movement of actors all help to make any change of emphasis rather simple. By dimming most of the lights and brightening one area, stage lighting can easily bring focus to a specific point on the stage, as can the color of a costume in relation to the setting and to other costumes in the scene. The movement of the actor can also be used to change the center of focus, as is so effectively demonstrated in a ballet or group-dance composition. The mobility of the actor allows the director to use groups of actors as a composition tool in order to direct the interest of the audience to any portion of the stage setting. The contributions of stage lighting, costumes, and groupings of actors toward the complete stage composition all serve to emphasize the importance of the visual side of the theatre as well as to underline the function of scene design as a visual art.

# 4 THE DESIGN IDEA

A design idea is concerned first with the function it will perform. A scenic idea may warrant pure decoration, as for a beauty pageant; the mood-inducing staging of a ballet; or a realistic environment for a cola commercial. In other words, design serves the story line that is unfolding, defining its very own function.

## FUNCTION OF SCENE DESIGN FOR DRAMA

Scene design, like other kinds of creative design, is the creating of a form to fulfill a purpose or function. The function of scene design is obviously linked with the dramatic form it serves. Scene design, in providing a visual support to the dramatic form, is an integral part of the modern theatre. Its function, as a result, is woven into the philosophy of modern theatre practice. The basic concept of present-day theatre, as a playwriting and play-production unity, has brought scenery out of the "pretty background" class into full partnership in the production of a play. The scene designer brings to the production a visual expression of the author's aim. As a result, scene design becomes a fusing of the visual effect and the basic intent of the play into a single dramatic impression.

The function of scene design can be more clearly revealed by looking at the dramatic form of the play itself. The form of the play should enable the designers to understand the relationship of scenery to action and the actors, to dominant mood, to theme, and to the story in general.

### PLACING THE ACTION

If scene design is supposed to bring to the play a visual expression of the author's intent, the designer must first examine the *action* of the play and the kind of people involved in the action. Unless completely abstract, every play (or any other storytelling theatrical form, such as ballet or pantomime) presents a conflict. Out of the conflict, whether of heroic proportions or a simple domestic problem, comes the action of the play. The action of the play is the force that moves it forward and makes it a living, breathing form. Dramatic action is a combination of physical or bodily action, visual movement, dialogue, and characterization. Characterization creates sympathy or repulsion on the part of the audience for the figures caught in the action. The characters either create the conflict or are shaped by the conflict in the ensuing action.

**The Scene of Action**     By incorporating all the elements of the total visual effect, scene design creates in visual terms the scene of the action. At the same time, it is more than just a place—it is an environment for the action. Sometimes the scene or elements of the scene may become a part of the action, which can be seen in the frankly theatrical use of scenery in a farce or musical comedy. The scene, on the other hand, may recede into the background and become a witness to the action, to be more felt than seen.

**Characterization**     Character development or *characterization* bears an important relationship to the environment of the scene. The people in the action react in accordance with, or in opposition to, their surroundings. The influence of the characters on scene design, sometimes subtle, sometimes symbolic, is on occasion more obvious. When the place is an interior, a study of the people living in the house gives the designer many important clues for details. For example, the family of Grandpa Vanderhof and his bizarre friends in Kaufman and Hart's *You Can't Take It with You* certainly contribute a wealth of detail about the kind of house and collection of curios that make up the environment of the play.

**Time and Place**     The action of the play must occur in a specific *time* and *place*, which are usually calculated, by the author, to establish the proper atmospheric surroundings for the action. Place, even though it may be in limbo, makes a visual impression on the audience. A specific time in the historical past can prepare a state of mind in the audience as much as can the absence of a specific time or place.

Although time and place are linked with the overall atmospherics, the connection is sometimes rather loose and may merely suggest a place that carries connotations of the atmosphere inherent in the play. The first act of Anouilh's *Legend of Lovers*, for example, is set in a French provincial railroad station in the early twentieth century (Figure 4–1). A closer examination of the play shows that it is not a literal station but a point where travelers pause as they come and go between this life and the life hereafter. Specific time is thus of very little importance except that it is not contemporary.

**ESTABLISHING THE MOOD**

The second function of scene design is to establish in the visual elements of the surroundings an expression of the dominant atmosphere, or *mood*. Scene design aims to create in this first impression an expression of the mood and

**Figure 4–1**
Legend of Lovers

Courtesy of Yale School of
Drama Theatre Collection.

its relationship to the action and characters. Mood can be described as the quality of a play that, when properly transmitted, creates a state of mind and emotional response in the audience. It can be expressed in such words as *sparkling, warm, gloomy, violent, earthy, mystic,* and so forth. Some more general expressions of mood are *tragedy, comedy, farce,* and the like, that are also used to define a type of play. Figure 4–2 provides two illustrations of how creative set design can be used to establish opposite moods.

A play, it can be argued, is the dramatization of a mood, a theme, and a story. All three elements are always present in a play, but one may be emphasized over the other two. Hence, a play may be primarily a dramatization of mood with theme and story in a secondary position; the plays with mood dominating seem to be at the extreme ends of the emotional scale. A tragedy is usually a mood-dominated play, as is low comedy or farce.

The relationship of mood to action is stressed, for on occasion a visual atmosphere is established in contrast to the apparent mood of a play. Comedy scenes are sometimes played in the ghostly surroundings of a haunted house, or tragedy against the raucous background of a street carnival. The contrasting moods combine into a single dramatic impression. Hence, fun in the haunted house might turn into farce, and murder at the Mardi Gras may become irony.

## Figure 4–2
### Mood

(a) Dramatic use of movement and light intensity in the avalanche scene in Henrik Ibsen's *Brand*. Designer—Richard Hay. Photo courtesy Hank Kranzler.
(b) The opposite mood is seen in the exaggerated architectural detail in the setting of Georges Feadeau's *Cat Among the Pigeons*. Designer—Richard Seger.

Tragedy, of course, frequently begins in a lighter mood that may or may not be expressed in the surroundings. A festive scene may have an air of foreboding that anticipates the approaching tragedy.

### REINFORCING THE THEME

*Theme* is, of course, closely linked with mood as well as with the storytelling part of the dramatic form. The theme of some plays is clearly apparent, especially if the author is using the dramatic form as a pulpit or soapbox to lampoon society or government. Comedy often carries a message to an unsuspecting audience as effectively as does the more direct approach of the serious play with a strong story line.

An example of an expression of theme in scenery is found in Shaw's *Heartbreak House* (Figure 4–3). The living room of Captain Shotover's house is designed like the fantail of an ancient sailing ship. The incongruity of this misplaced bit of architecture is a constant visual symbol of the lack of purpose and aimlessness of the cultured, frank, charming, unconventional people who live in it.

The expression of theme in scenery cannot always be easily achieved. More often the theme is treated with subtlety and in symbols known only to the designer and his muse. The most obvious example of a theme-oriented play is found in the political theatre. Removed from the fictional format of literary theatre, the political theatre is free to move to its objective with dramatic and theatrical directness. The most familiar political theatre, stemming from Germany in the 1930s, is that of Bertolt Brecht and Erwin Piscator.

**Figure 4–3**
Theme

*Heartbreak House* by Bernard Shaw. (a) The traditional design of the bizarre room in the form of an ancient sailing ship. Designer—James Russel. Photo courtesy Morris Shapiro.
(b) Designer Michael Levine chose not to follow Shaw's nautical image. He achieved a disquieting atmosphere by creating an all white room dressed with oversized clutter. A few minutes into the first act, the ceiling begins to rise from a normal level to an absurd, yet droll, height. Shaw Festival Theatre, Canada. Photo courtesy David Cooper.

Their "theatre of alienation" had a sociopolitical orientation that was frankly aimed at the elimination of capitalism as a social and political way of life.

Although impact of the message has lessened as audiences have become more sophisticated and tolerant of shock, the political theatre remains a vital theatrical form exerting a strong influence on modern theatre practice and design. Light projections using mixed media of film and live actors to express theme have become the hallmark of political theatre, as have the conscious efforts to bring real-life objects and true materials to the stage in an attempt to remove scenery (and all of theatre for that matter) from the world of make-believe and playacting. The effect on the young designer is evident in the freedom of present-day stage design from the taboos of illusion and sentimentality that dominated the romantic world of make-believe.

## STAGING THE STORY

*Story* is the connecting thread that holds together the other elements in a complete dramatic form. It is the train of related incidents bringing continuity to the many events in a play. Story is probably more important to the theatre than to other art forms. The expression of an idea in the theatre is dependent on having and holding the audience's attention every moment. The theatre audience, if confused, cannot turn back the pages, like a novel reader, and reread a passage for clarification. An engrossing story can hold an audience spellbound. A good storyteller, of course, uses mood to create the atmosphere for a story. The storyteller can also use the story to make a point, which is apparent in plays with strong themes. Any good play usually has a good story, but a play that is dominated by the dramatization of story is primarily dedicated to telling an interesting tale, whether it be of love, adventure, intrigue—the list is long and varied.

Because the environment of a story-dominated play is usually real, the designing problem becomes one of selection of realistic details and forms that place the action and establish the mood. This, more often than not, has already been accomplished by the author through the choice of realistic location for the scene of the action. A more important contribution of design in the story-dominated play is the staging of the action. *Staging*, or fitting the action on the stage, provides the areas, levels, and properties in such a way as to allow the continuous flow of action so necessary to telling a good story.

The many English and French so-called bedroom farces are story-dominated plays that depend heavily on staging. The skillful juxtaposition of hallways, doors, closets, and the ever-present bedroom—all visible to the audience—is necessary to facilitate the fast pace and split-second timing of the nonsensical action of the story. An unusual example of imaginative farce staging is Alan Ayckburn's *Taking Steps*. The three floors of a house are staged on one level. Light helps to define the change of floor levels as well as the actors when they pantomime going up and down nonexistent stairs. Once the audience catches on to the convention, its imagination separates the different levels of the house. The cleverness of the staging adds humor to the performance and develops an interesting production style.

## DESIGN AND OTHER THEATRICAL FORMS

Theme and mood are present in any theatrical form—ballet, mime, and audiovisual performances, for instance, as well as plays and other literary forms. The high-tech lighting of a rock show imparts a stirring theme through the atmospheric senses of sight and sound. Although classical ballet usually has a story line, its modern counterpart frequently does not. Hence the decorative background of ballet that sets the locale and mood of the dance has given way to the limited use of scenery in the form of stylized properties, and is more expressive of theme than anything else. Mime, both group and solo, is the most absolute of the theatrical forms. Imagination supplies the scenic background and hand props. Although the same thinking is involved, the skill of the performer, rather than the designer, creates the mood of the locale in the minds of the audience. Mime is sometimes incorporated into literary theatre. The pantomimed props and scenery in *Our Town* is an example, as well as the imagined costume in *The Emperor's New Clothes*. In ballet the miming of dialogue by the dancers is a conscious control or theatrical convention that has little to do with the scenic background except that it establishes a performing style.

### DESIGN QUESTIONS

In other words, whatever type of theatrical event a designer may be asked to do, he or she asks more or less the same questions:

1. What is the reason for this event? (commercial, charity function, historical celebration, etc.)
2. What is the atmosphere? (happy, serious, etc.)
3. What is it saying? (How will scenery, costumes, and lights help you say it?)
4. How and where will it be staged? (theatre, stadium, on the street, etc.)
5. What is the style? (entertainment, documentary, pageant, etc.)

## HOW TO BEGIN

At this point, beginning designers should be conscious of the importance of scene design in relation to the play. They should be aware of the influences of the theatrical medium and be familiar with the intricacies of the creative process. But, they may ask, how does one get an idea for a design?

It is impossible to set down universal rules for developing a design idea; there are as many methods as designers. And an individual method is often so subjective and intuitive that it is of little value to another designer as a way of working; each must and usually does develop his or her own method of reaching the inner reservoir of creative ideas. Still, although it is possible to make recommendations and to point to examples of good design, the actual conquest of an idea is the designer's individual struggle.

The design idea, of course, does not exist until the play becomes a production and the written word becomes dialogue and visible action. It is the individual expression of the artistic imagination, theatrical sense, and technical ingenuity of the designer through the visual control of line, color, and form. The design concept is often evident as a visual theme with variations that weave through a complicated setting or series of settings, bringing unity of thought to the whole. Many times the theme is so subtle that only the trained eye of another designer can see and appreciate its presence.

The design idea is aimed at stimulating an intellectual or emotional response in the audience. The control of the design elements may be broad and sensational to arouse primitive emotions, or they may be subtle and refined to stimulate an intellectual response. Good design is the result of logical yet imaginative thinking and intuitive feeling expressed through an idea or central theme.

The ideas for many an inspirational setting have been worked out on the back of an envelope during a coffee break or have been virtually completed before the author has finished the third act. Although this is frequently the pace at which a scene designer is expected to work, it is hardly a practical procedure for an inexperienced designer.

## ANALYSIS OF THE SCRIPT, LIBRETTO, OR SCENARIO

All parts of a production are based on written words of the play. It is logical, then, that the designer begins his conceptual work with the study of the play's script. Ideally, the play is analyzed from a number of separate readings. Each subsequent reading will likely lead to a better understanding of the play.

The designer's first reading of the play is for its *content*. The designer should react as a member of the audience, avoiding any preconceived image of the scenery other than the author's description. In this way a first impression will serve as an overall response that will help answer these questions: What kind of a play is it? What is the action and where is it taking place? What is the dominant mood? Is the play a comedy? Or is it a tongue-in-cheek satire with political overtones? Is it a tragedy of classical proportions or a domestic misunderstanding?

The scene of the action often suggests or sets the *atmosphere* of a play. A deserted house on a stormy night for a mystery or a love scene by candlelight are typical examples. The action, however, is not always in harmony with its surroundings but may be in opposition or contrast to its environment.

The mood of a play or scene often suggests *color* to the designer. Out of the mood of the environment comes the overall tonality of the play, which often can be expressed most forcefully with color or even the absence of color.

The second reading is for the play's *intent*. It is a more careful reading—between the lines and within parentheses. What is the author saying? What is the theme? What is the style? Has the author expressed a point of view through allegorical symbols or in daily-life realism? Has the playwright soared into the realm of epic poetry or dropped into the lusty imagery of sidewalk prose? In the style of the play the designer finds a clue to the degree of reality or unreality of the scenic environment.

From the theme of the play the designer can usually find a visual image that leads to a design concept. And from the style of the play the designer gets an indication of the form of the design. Style and form interact, for style influences form. A realistic style implies realistic forms; a fantasy or dream suggests unreal forms.

It is not unusual for the designer to continue rereading the play throughout the production process.

**The Opera Libretto and the Ballet Scenario**     The *libretto* is the text or dialogue of an opera, which is sung rather than spoken. Like plays, operas vary widely. Some opera libretti are stilted and void of drama, while others are full of action and are highly dramatic. By definition, the music contains most of the excitement and atmosphere, so the only way to comprehend the full dramatic intensity of an opera is to listen to it.

Opera is a "larger than life" performance style—therefore the designer is looking for more than a functional background. He or she is searching for a visual image or metaphor in the music to support the theme of the text.

Because ballet is a stylized performance technique relying on pantomime to tell the story, the scenery is often highly decorative and atmospheric. The *scenario* of a ballet is an outline of the story with an occasional description of the action, all of which is minimal information for the designer. However, many classical ballets are based on familiar stories that can be researched for additional background.

As with opera, the designer for a ballet should listen to the music. Because ballet is dance, the music will convey the mood and tempo of the movement. The choreographer who plans the movement, however, may interpret a familiar story and musical composition in a very individualistic style. There are, for example, many versions of the popular ballet *The Nutcracker*. Hence the designer must not only be familiar with the scenario and the music but must also rely heavily on the choreographer for inspiration. Although these obstacles may seem restrictive, designing for ballet provides an opportunity for imaginative and creative design that does not exist in other theatrical forms.

## DETERMINING THE VISUAL STYLE

*Style* can be defined as the degree of reality expressed in the writing or literary form of the play, which in turn influences the mode of the performance and the visual form of the scenery and costumes. Because style in the theatre is felt, heard, and seen in so many different ways, it is difficult to define in specific terms. Literary, acting, directing, and visual styles, as well as period styles, unite to form a single production style. Style is sometimes visually obvious, but more often it will be unnoticed by the audience unless some element of it is jarring or incorrect in terms of the whole.

**Production Style and Reality**     The overall style of a production is expressed in the degree of reality of the performance. There are many kinds of reality in the theatre: the lifelike copy of nature (*naturalism*), the *fantasy* of dreams, the *make-believe* quality of storytelling, the immediacy of *documentary* or of *improvisational* style, and the performance reality of the *theatrical* style. The two extreme realities in a performance are the lifelike quality of naturalism and the theatrical reality of presentational theatre. It might be seen as the difference between the *actor* and the *performer.*

The theatrical reality of the performer is something that *is* happening at the moment—as opposed to an actor's dramatic re-creation of something that *has* happened, but in such a way as to make the audience believe they are experiencing it for the first time. Each is a different degree of reality to which the audience reacts with contrasting emotions. Although an audience may justly appreciate an actor's convincing performance, the reality is still make-believe. If, for example, a light cue is missed or scenery falls down, the make-believe spell is broken by the unfortunate intrusion of reality. A presentional style, however, might keep technical mishaps and muffed lines in the routine to give the performance an immediate reality.

Occasionally production styles are combined. The docudrama style (documentary and literary styles) is often used to capture the emotion of an actual happening. It has the factual reality of a documentary but is actually a fictional style. The documentary format heightens the reality and holds the audience while the story unfolds.

The docudrama, as a style, is less convincing on the stage than in the more immediate media of radio and television. A classic example of the emotional impact of a docudrama style occurred in 1938. Orson Welles's famous radio adaptation of H. G. Wells's *War of the Worlds* was presented as a newscaster's report of the landing of Martians. The docudrama was so real that many listeners were on the verge of panic.

**Visual Style and Form**     The effect of style on form is more easily seen in visual styles than in the performance styles just discussed, although the two are related. Visual styles can be defined in similar degrees of reality.

The representional style, for example, is lifelike. The design form is represented in a painting or sculpture rendered as near to its natural form and color as the technical skill of the artist allows.

The nonrepresentational style, the opposite reality, is ornamental. Because its goal is sensation, the interplay of sheer form and color becomes important. The designer does not attempt to create a form that bears any resemblance to natural or manmade objects.

Between these two extremes lie as many degrees of realism, symbolism, abstraction, or complete nonobjectivity as designers care to define.

The effect of style on form is more apparent as the degree of reality decreases. The form is distorted into an abstract but recognizable shape. The

**Figure 4—4**
Style and Form

The scenic tree is used to illus-
trate the influence of style on
form.
(Top) Lifelike apple tree for *On
Borrowed Time*.
(Center) Fanciful forest for
*Iolanthe*.
(Bottom) Abstract trees from the
forest scene in *The Visit*.

metamorphosis of a tree form on the stage can be used to illustrate the
influence of style on form. For example, in Figure 4—4 the realistic apple tree
in Osborn's *On Borrowed Time* contrasts with the decorative forest in Gilbert
and Sullivan's *Iolanthe* and with the abstract trees in the forest scene of Dürrenmatt's *The Visit*. The trees in the latter production were reduced to pen-
dants of gauze that were slashed with side-lighting and projected patterns
on the floor.

As a visual art, scenery styles conform to the same degrees of reality as
do production styles. Scenery style, in fact, is the most important visual
element supporting the overall production style (Figure 4—5).

## Figure 4-5
### Visual Styles of Scenery

(a) Realism. Real forms in life-like arrangements for *Killing Mother*. Scene and lighting design—William Teague.

(b) Anti-Illusionary Scenery. *Puntila* by Bertolt Brecht. An example of Brecht's aversion to illusionary or "make-believe" scenery. Real, unconventional textures such as the straw-covered portals, unpainted old boards, and a brass sun are used. The result is of course not realism but stylization which, though denying illusion, is still theatrical. Photo courtesy Nelson.

(c) Surrealism. The unnatural juxtaposition of a large, tilted mirror upstage revealing the entrance-way, and a reverse image of the action on stage attempts to express the irrational subject matter in *Right You Are If You Think You Are* by Luigi Pirandello. Designer—William Matthews. Photo courtesy Feinstein.

(d) Fragmentary Scenery. A view from the wings of a setting for the operatic version of Eugene O'Neill's *Mourning Becomes Electra* at the Metropolitan Opera, New York. The highly stylized interpretation of the stately Classic Revival style is achieved by the imaginative use of textured surfaces and exposed structural members. Designer—Boris Aronson. Photo courtesy Gary Renaud.

(e) Suggested Scenery. Elements of scenery have been manipulated to convey a backstage scene for *Dalliance*, Tom Stoppard's adaptation of Schnitzler's *Liebelei*. Designer—John Conklin. Long Wharf Theatre. Photo © T. Charles Erickson.

(f) Concept Based on Period Theatre. An interesting concept for an opera version of Shakespeare's *Two Gentlemen of Verona*. Designer Henry Haymann developed a Victorian Toy Theatre look inspired by a fifteenth century Serlioian Street Scene. Three River Shakespeare Festival, Pittsburgh. Photo courtesy Jeffery Cepull.

(g) Symbolism. An oversized symbolic image dominates the world of Shakespeare's *Pericles*. Designer—John Conklin. Hartford Stage Company. Photo © T. Charles Erickson.

a

b

c

d

e

**Style and Costumes**     Although both scenery and costume design are visual arts, the respective influence of *style* on *form* is not the same. A costume design is always linked to the *character* and *life style* envisioned by the playwright, as well as the *human form* of the actor. The author created the character in a certain style, be it realistic, allegorical, or symbolic. The actor and the costume interpret the character. Any visible style change in costumes usually starts with the director's concept of the play, which might be a spoof of a period piece or a radical departure in form, such as the changing of a drama into a musical.

The human body can be stylized or dehumanized. Picasso's cubistic costume designs for the Ballet Russe's *Le Parade* is a good example (Figure 4–6). Although realism can itself be a style, any departure from the real is a more obvious example. For an actor to change form by donning a bear costume, for instance, is not really a style change, especially if the bear suit is very realistic. If the bear is suggested by only a headpiece or mask, then a more imaginative style is created.

The British musical *Cats* offers a wonderful example of costume style. The actors and dancers suggest that they are cats with stylized makeup, painted body tights, and movement. Their performance, however, is not to imply that they are humans impersonating cats, but that cats are like humans.

The focus of a theatrical performance is on the actors (character) and their costumes. A costume style is the most impressionable part of the stage composition. Its brilliance, cleverness, or dullness can stimulate or confuse an audience.

**Figure 4–6**
Costume Styles

(a) A facsimile of Pablo Picasso's costume design for the American Manager in the ballet *Parade* staged by Diaghliev's Ballet Russe. Picasso's cubistic style dehumanizes the human form into an assemblage of abstract shapes.
(b) Period style and character. Group costumes in same period style with subtle character differences. The *Cut Purses* in *Cyrano*. Designer—Susan Tsu.

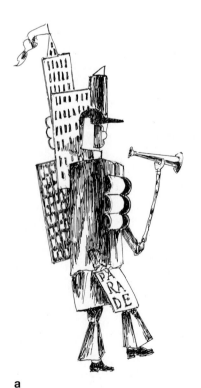

a                    b

a

b

**Figure 4—7**
Style and Light

(a) The abstract use of light, form, and costumes in a production of Harold Pinter's *Old Times*. Lighting design—Craig Wolf.
(b) A very light-conscious design allowing the atmospheric, motivated, and decorative use of light. *Faust* designed by Albert Filoni.

**Style and Light**     It is obvious that lighting and scene designers must be aware of all styles in the theatre, for they are called on to visually support (and occasionally contrast) the acting, literary, and directing styles and create a unified production style. A lighting style can be developed by the manipulation of the *qualities of light*. The varying proportions of *intensity* (brightness), *color*, *distribution*, and *movement* of light contribute to the production style and the degree of reality in the stage picture, as shown in the examples in Figure 4—7.

The reality of light on the stage is easily seen in its degree of conformity (or lack of comformity) to light in nature. We are so used to seeing each other under normal angles, distribution, and colors of the sun that when these angles deviate, or when colors change too much, we consider the light "unreal" or "theatrical." The low angle and rich colors of a sunset are frequently so dramatic that they seem to belong on the stage. For the same reason, light on an actor from a low angle seems unnatural or stylized.

Although much of stage lighting may seem naturalistic, there are types of theatrical productions and performances that are more dependent on a style of color, distribution, and movement of light than on general illumination or visibility. Ballet, for example, is a theatrical extension of life into a highly stylized performance technique. Realistic illumination is less important than the theatrical atmosphere, exotic colors, and arbitrary angles of light that make up this style of production.

The theatrical reality of Brecht, on the other hand, strips away atmosphere and illusion. Lighting instruments are exposed and uncolored to reinforce the feeling that what we are seeing is happening *now*, on the stage, in the reality of the performance.

## DEVELOPING THE DESIGN CONCEPT

A concept is the *idea* or *visual theme* of design. It is the product of creative thinking, visual imagination, and collaboration with the director. The concept provides the *control* and *direction* toward a final design. The clearer and stronger the design concept, the easier every subsequent design decision will be.

Because designing for the theatre is a collaborative effort, the design concept is often the visual interpretation of a literary, musical, or dance form and conforms to the production style of the director or choreographer. A good concept makes a strong design statement, which then becomes a visual style.

**Historical Style and Concept**    Historical styles, both period and national, are significant in their own right. The effect of each period on form is quite clear. The geometric and flamboyant tracery of Gothic, for example, is distinct from the reverse curve of the baroque and the whiplash of art nouveau. The same is true of national styles. There is a difference, for example, in the forms of the rococo in France, Germany, and Austria.

When a historical style is used on the stage, however, it becomes a *concept*, for it is not the period that is being demonstrated but a conceptualization of the historical style. The historical scenes in Miller's *The Crucible*, for example, are conceptual versions of seventeenth-century America. It is not too difficult to see that period style can take on many degrees of reality. A historical period can be authentically reproduced, suggested, or even spoofed.

Historical moments in theatre frequently serve as a framework for a contemporary idea. The Shevelove/Gilbart/Sondheim musical *A Funny Thing Happened on the Way to the Forum*, for example, is a burlesque of Roman comedy with a present-day message. *Girl Friend* is a nostalgic spoof of life and the theatre of the 1920s. The melodramatic revival of such plays as *Under the Gaslights* is an exaggeration of period mannerism as a concept.

**Style and Theatre Forms**    Today's theatre is moving away from naturalism toward a more imaginative use of style. The stage, rather than trying to compete with the photographic realism of the movies and television, has turned to more abstract, stylized, and sometimes expressionistic styles in both writing and staging.

An interesting contrast of styles has developed in the production concepts of the two nonproscenium theatre forms, the thrust and the arena stages (Figure 4–8). Where the emphasis of the proscenium theatre was on *production*, we find the thrust and arena theatres concentrating on *performance*. The lack of scenic elements on the thrust and arena stages calls on the imagination of the audience to complete the scene. Invisible walls and doors, different locales indicated by levels on the floor, hanging fragments overhead, and the color of light are common theatrical conventions on thrust and arena stages.

**Figure 4–8**
**Style and the Theatre Form**

The thrust and arena stages often force the designer into theatrical conventions or stylization inherent in the scale and sightlines of their physical form.
(a) O'Neill's *A Moon for the Misbegotten*. Designed by Anne Mundell for the Pittsburgh Public Theatre. Photo by Ric Evans.
(b) *A Tempest*, freely adapted from Shakespeare's *The Tempest* for a small thrust stage. Designer—Peter Davidson. Photo © Davidson.

They establish an abstract degree of reality the audience is asked to accept. On the other hand, furniture and hand properties are painstakingly real, and the actors' costumes are fully detailed in a contrast of styles. Because the audience is physically closer to the action, it is virtually in the scene and a part of the action. There is a more subjective or intimate alliance of audience and performer when the proscenium wall is removed, although the reality is very much a theatrical reality.

The proscenium theatre, on the other hand, depends on aesthetic distance and a more objective relationship with its audience. There is, however, a great latitude of expression from bare-stage to full-stage productions in a variety of styles, and on occasion, a thrust through the proscenium for closer contact with the audience.

**Acting and Literary Styles**     Dramatic form combines the literary and acting styles. Along with scenery style, they all have an effect on each other and must have some degree of unity in order to create a strong dramatic form.

The literary style reveals through dialogue the degree of reality represented in the play. The style of a play may capture a cross section of life, such as Elmer Rice's *Street Scene*, or it may be as expressionistic as the treatment of Mr. Zero's problems in Rice's *The Adding Machine*.

The epic style of Brecht and his attempts to denude the stage of illusion or any visual make-believe obviously has had its influence on scenery style. By appealing to the intellectual side of the members of his audience, and denying them any escape into sentimentality, Brecht forces them to listen and, perhaps more important, to react. The belief that any reaction, even the shock of unconventionality, is better than having a passive, hypnotized audience is reflected in elements of scenery. Thus, a barren stage, the presence of *real* materials and textures, exposed lighting instruments, and clear unatmospheric lighting create the essence of his scenes.

Paradoxically, this opposition to the fakery of illusionary scenery and the effort to free the theatre of conventionality actually imposes a new system of theatrical hocus-pocus. The result is almost a scenic stylization that the audience responds to in vicarious recognition of its unconventional cleverness.

The acting style of today, for the most part, is believably real when compared to the highly mannered period examples of the seventeenth, eighteenth, and nineteenth centuries. Acting style, however, may vary from naturalism to conform with the style of a specific drama. It takes its cue, as does scenery, from the literary style of the play.

The theatre contains many examples of conflicting literary and acting styles. One illustration is the nineteenth-century conception of opera, in which a stilted literary style was combined with a presentational acting style of singing dialogue—both set against a conflicting background of painted realism. Today, the style of the scenery has been brought closer to the less realistic acting and writing styles to form a more unified and convincing art form.

Scene design, as a visual art, can reinforce and heighten literary and acting styles. Strangely enough, it can on occasion be a contrast to the acting style without breaking the unity of the production. The designer has always felt that stylized scenery does not necessarily call for stylized acting, as was demonstrated so expertly in Jo Mielziner's setting for Miller's *Death of a Salesman*. The reverse, however, is not true. If the acting is stylized, the scenery must be, too. The important thing is that the audience will accept any degree of departure from the real in scenery as long as it is consistent and in good taste.

**Finding a Concept**     The search for a concept cannot help but be influenced by personal taste, background, and experience. An experienced designer falls into the habit of mentally storing ideas and then waiting for the opportunity to use them. By observing people, nature, and unusual happenings, the designer develops an eye to see and record.

Ideas in one art medium can be transposed to another. To work, for example, in the manner of a famous painter—colors from the palette of Cézanne, the light of Rembrandt, or the forms of Picasso—can suggest a compositional control of light and form within a stage production. Similarly, the dramatic colors and the compositional use of light by Turner are another example of elements that are very adaptable to a stage color concept.

In Chapter 3 we mentioned that the strong emphasis of a single element such as line, color, or light in a composition becomes a design control leading to a concept. For example, each act (or scene) could be keyed to a single color, moving us in a specific pattern. If planned carefully, this progression of color and intensity will reinforce the emotional climax.

Movement as an element of design is frequently used in a lighting concept. It can be expressed in the movement of color and the distribution of light in dance, or to interpret the rhythm of music in color and form.

Light can also dominate a composition and become a concept. Patterns of exposed sources, specific distribution, or projected images can become a visual style with light as the central force. Natural light and colors can also be an inspiration. The crushing intensity of the sun, the dampness of a forest, or the fog of a river can be lighting concepts that give the designer a control or way of thinking and creating.

A thematic image can lead to a variety of uses of symbolic form, color, or atmosphere. Symbolism in scenery and light should be extremely subtle, serving basically as a control for the director and the designers; obvious symbolism could cause a negative response on the part of the audience and should be used with caution. Too much symbolism in scenic forms can be so overwhelming that the actor and playwright's words are anticlimactic.

**Working with the Director**     During this formative stage there is only so much a designer can do alone. From the beginning there is a need for close communication with the director, especially if a strong directorial concept is considered in the design. Directorial influence on design can vary from a complete hands-off "solve-it-yourself" attitude to a "this-is-what-I-want" directive. A more equally balanced collaboration is, naturally, ideal. One-sided domination can lead to personality clashes that abort the creative process. The most successful and unified productions are usually the result of mutual respect and openmindedness on the part of both the designer and the director.

The collaboration, of course, begins with talking. Preliminary discussions can lead to agreement about the nature of the play, the dramatic image, and general atmosphere (colors, style, staging, and directorial concept). Talk, however, has its limits. Words have a way of triggering a different image in each individual. At some point the designer must put visual impressions on paper. Only then can the designer and director really begin to communicate.

An understanding and agreement about the production style is probably the most important part of the designer–director collaboration, and probably the most difficult. This can only come about after a thorough exchange of ideas (as well as drawings) among the artistic team (the director and the set, light, and costume designers). It is more than conceivable that only after much discussion, exploration of ideas, and perhaps discovery that the final determination of "production style" will be found.

The theatre, as we have seen, brings together many ideas. During production, the director is the only one with an overall view and therefore must be responsible for coordinating the various styles as the show is being put together. The lack of immediate communication to the designer or designers of directorial changes or style adjustments in other areas of design can lead to conflicts at a time in the production schedule when it is too late to make changes. The best-laid plans can go astray without constant supervision and communication on the part of the director. An experienced designer soon learns to not take anything for granted and makes frequent checks with the director and other areas of design.

## REREADING THE PLAY

After reaching a mutual understanding with the director and fellow designers on theme, production style, and general interpretation of the play, the designer returns to the script for another reading. This reading of the play is for its *technique*. Close attention is paid to the physical requirements of the plot structure and, if there are many scenes, to the changes of locale. The action and staging requirements are examined to determine the number of people in a scene, the types of entrances and exits, references in the dialogue to the scene, bits of action hidden from one actor but visible to the audience, and so on—all leading to the development of the basic idea and scheme of production.

It is also a good idea to reread the play after initial designs are prepared. This is a good chance to rethink the play with your design in mind. Often this rereading will point out specific problems with the design and perhaps suggest better answers to questions about staging or the "look" of the design. Further readings might prove necessary during the course of production.

## PLANNING THE SCHEME OF PRODUCTION

The design solution of a multiscene play, which is known as a *scheme of production*, brings scenery-handling techniques into the design concept. The design idea is developed around a method of handling the numerous changes of scene. The kinds of changes and the methods of handling scenery, such as wagons and turntables, are discussed fully in Chapter 10 and indicate the necessity of designing a large production around at least a basic scheme for moving the scenery.

Although discussed separately, a scheme of production is, of course, closely related to style. Many times the designer, through a scheme of production, establishes certain conventions that the audience is expected to accept and that, consequently, create a scenery style. Conversely, a scenery style may dictate how the scenery is to be handled, thereby becoming a scheme of production.

**Unit Setting**     The movement of scenery may be reduced by the various uses of a unit setting. This form of setting is based on the retention or reuse of certain elements of scenery to simulate a change of scene. This is usually accomplished by repeating either the plan, design shape, or color in the various settings. The design shapes and colors, for example, may be varied in each setting although they are placed in identical floor plans, or the same shape can be moved to a variety of positions.

A unit setting can be used in two different ways, either as a cleverly camouflaged method of reusing scenery unbeknown to the audience, or as an obvious device that becomes a unifying force for the production, as well as a means of simplifying scene changes (Figure 4–9).

**Projected Scenery**     Light projections as scenery are included with many production schemes for handling multiscene shows. The rear projection of a design onto a translucent screen makes the shifting of a scene as simple as the changing of a slide.

Because projected scenery is *light* and not *paint*, it has a strong dramatic quality that tends to dominate the scene. It becomes in a sense an actor rather than scenery. Projected scenery, when used correctly as an integral part of the play, functions best in a nonrealistic or abstract production where the scenery is part of the action and not just background.

Brecht, for example, used the screen as an actor. He frequently projected instructive messages or illustrative images on the screen, more as an instrument of propaganda or idea than as a visual background to set the scene. It is a classroom or documentary technique which, when used in dramatic surroundings, serves to heighten his epic theatre.

In spite of its limitations and dominating characteristics, projected scenery can be used as a highly dramatic and exciting production scheme. Many production designs have been based on projected scenery with successful results (Figures 4–10 and 4–11).

## Figure 4–9
## The Unit Setting

The production for Shaw's *Arms and the Man.* Designer—Eduard Kochergin. Photo © David Cooper, courtesy Shaw Festival, Canada.

**COLOR PLATE 4–8b**
**PAINTER'S ELEVATIONS**
Color layout for one of several wings for *The Nutcracker,* also dye on scrim.

**COLOR PLATE 4–8a**
**PAINTER'S ELEVATIONS**
Color elevation for dye painting on sharkstooth scrim. All architectural features were filled to become opaque on a "cross fade" that dissolves into a snow scene, for the ballet *The Nutcracker*.

a

b

**Color Plate 4–7**
**Computer-Generated Art**
(a) Computer-genrated design using several programs including sketch, perspective, color, texture and light for *The Sea Gull*. Designer–Keven Abbott. (b) Design created on Photoshop program to seve as one of the many projected backgrounds for *Much Ado About Nothing*, Orlando Shakespeare Festival. Designer–Samuel Ball.

a

b

**COLOR PLATE 4–6**

**SKETCH MODEL**

(a) Full-color sketch model of portions of the first act of the operetta *Firefly*. (b) Sketch model of interior setting for *Little Foxes*. Model photos by Margo.

**COLOR PLATE 4–4**
**PRODUCTION MODEL**
A 1/4-inch scale model for a production of *Hamlet* directed by Jack O'Brien. Scenery–Ralph Funicello, lighting–Peter Maradudin, and costumes–Lewis Brown. Produced by The Old Globe Theatre, San Diego, Calif., 1990. Photo courtesy of Ralph Funicello.

**COLOR PLATE 4–5**
**BRITISH MODEL**
Color reproduction of British model (Figure 4–18) for Shaw's *Arms and the Man*. Designer–Eduard Kochergin. Photo © David Cooper, Shaw Festival, Canada.

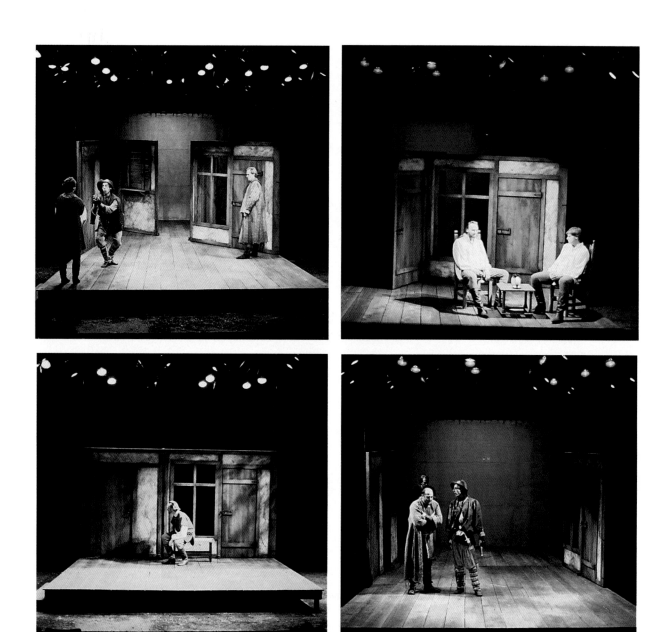

**COLOR PLATE 4–3**
**UNIT SETTING**
Another example of unit setting in *Arden of Haversham*, setting and lighting designed by Tim Saternow for The Empty Space in Seattle, Wash., 1991. *See also* Figure 4–9; photo courtesy Tim Saternow.

**COLOR PLATE 4–2**
**PROJECTIONS ON SCENERY**
Bringing the outside into the interior in an interesting setting for *Berkley Square*. Designer–Cameron Porteous.
Photo © David Cooper, courtesy of Shaw Festival, Canada.

**COLOR PLATE 4–1**
**LIGHT AND REALISM**
Interesting use of light and realism in color reproduction of production shot for Figure 4–14, *The Cherry Orchard*.
Photo courtesy Tim Saternow.

## Figure 4–10
### Projected Scenery

(a) Two of the fifteen variations of *The Turn of the Screw* by Benjamin Britten are set in a gloomy Victorian country house. The eerie mood of the opera lends itself to the effective use of projections. Two basic screens are backed by a third upstage, creating a three-dimensional effect. Designer—Patrick Robertson. Lighting Designer—David Hersey. Courtesy Noel Staunton, English National Opera, London.
(b) Sometimes the screen is as interesting as the projection. This intricate screen is a part of the design for *Faith, Hope, Charity* by Ödön von Horvath. Designer—William Mathews, Photo courtesy Nelson.
(c) A scene from *Faith, Hope, Charity*.

**Figure 4–11**
Projections on Scenery and Dancers.

The Nikolais Dance Theatre production of *The Tent*. Photo courtesy of Bryan Manley.

## PRESENTATION OF THE DESIGN IDEA

The designer's presentation communicates his or her ideas to the other members of the design and production team. The designer might, at varying points in the production process, present color sketches, floor plans, and/or models. The importance placed on each form of presentation can vary with the director (some will only be able to understand models, some like to see sketches, etc.), the particular skills of the designer, and perhaps the type of theatre company or the scale of production. The sketch, for example, might be a collage expressing the atmosphere and visual impact of the setting, while placing more emphasis on a larger scaled model with more detail. On the other hand, a single setting with many changes of scenic elements and lighting might be best presented with a series of photographs. Every production is different and the designer should be prepared to present his or her work in any way or ways that best communicate the design ideas.

### PRELIMINARY STUDIES

The designer's first impressions of a design concept may have been formed as early as the first reading of the play, only to be substantially revised or rejected after a closer study of the script in the second and third readings. A first impression is often correct, but sometimes it is wrong, and the designer may find it difficult to change this early impression. For this reason the beginning designer may be wise during the first reading of a new play to keep an open mind free of preconceptions until all the facts are accumulated. For instance, an idea may first appear to the designer in the form of an interesting

## Figure 4–12
### Scene Designer's Preliminary Sketches

Four of many designer's thumbnail sketches made in counsel with the director while developing a scheme of production for *The Visit*. These sketches are a quick, easy, and descriptive method of communicating in the early stages of planning.

floor plan, to be developed later into a related elevational drawing, or the reverse—as a decorative shape or historical form that must be adjusted to a workable floor plan.

Preliminary studies usually consist of small, freehand, thumbnail sketches and rough floor plans (Figure 4–12). After consultation with the director, the tentative ideas of the designer are ready to be expanded into a more complete form of presentation, assuming a conclusive agreement between the designer and the director. These first sketches are visual ideas that will be developed in detail later. (If the preliminary sketch is used as a step in the teaching of scene design, it is interesting to save these first ideas to compare with the final design form.)

Some designers use a so-called *mood sketch* to study the atmosphere of a scene (Figure 4–13). By working off a dark or black background, such as gray or black velour paper, the scenic forms are easily revealed in an atmospheric light.

## THE SKETCH

Although scene design is essentially a three-dimensional art form, the two-dimensional sketch medium is used to present the design idea. The sketch can be rendered in color and perspective to show atmosphere that would be difficult to accomplish in a model. (Besides, the designer does not always have time to build even a rough model.) Many sketches can be made to show changes in lighting, scenery, and composition of the actors. More importantly, the sketch can be done relatively quickly, so less time and energy (and soul) are invested in a single drawing. It is easier to accept the rejection of a sketched design if the designer remembers that it represents no more than an idea still to be developed.

What is represented on the sketch depends somewhat on the working relationship the designer has with the director (or producer). The first time a designer and director are paired on a project is always the most difficult. It takes time to learn one another's habits and "language." Once everyone on the artistic team has knowledge of each other's working habits, it is easier to determine the kinds of presentations that will prove successful. Because a new designer does not have examples of past work to support his or her ideas, the concept is bought or rejected on the strength of the sketch. In addition, of course, the young designer must be able to back up all ideas with faithful execution.

The sketch should catch a significant moment in the play. The designer usually picks a moment that will best show the setting and still express the dominant mood of the play (see again Figure 4–13). The sketch is an idealized drawing of the total visual effect, which serves as a goal for the execution and guide for the lighting. The colors in the sketch are meant generally to represent a moment of the play with the actors on the set, in costume and under lights, providing the total visual effect. Supplementary sketches are sometimes needed to show what would happen at another dramatic moment, with different lighting and actor grouping.

**Figure 4–13**
**Designer's Sketches**

(a) An atmospheric sketch of the main setting for the ballet version of *Winterset*. The massive scale of Jo Mielziner's original design is transformed into wing and back drop for ballet.
(b) Completed sketch of the barn scene from Dürrenmatt's *The Visit*.
(c) Banquet scene from *The Visit*.

## Figure 4–14
### Sketch, Model, and Set

(Top to bottom) Designer's sketch, designer's model, and completed setting for *The Cherry Orchard*. Design—Tim Saternow and R. Michael Earl.

a

ACT II

b

c

In the purest sense, however, the sketch is only a means of presenting an idea. It is not the final design and therefore should not be displayed or judged as a complete art form. A stage setting is not complete until it is on the stage, lighted, and viewed in the context of the action of the play and the actors' movements. The judgment of the success or failure of a design in the final analysis is based on how it functions under finished performance conditions rather than as a beautiful sketch.

The sketch is *not* meant to be a working drawing. Although it maintains a consistent proportion to show the actor-scenery relationship, it is not necessarily drawn to an accurate scale. It is possible, however, to execute a design from a carefully proportioned sketch if large portions of the set are parallel to the footlights, as in a wing-and-backdrop setting.

If the designer is a member of an established producing group, such as summer stock or television, the sketch may take on a different character. The designer, director, builder, and painter may be so used to working with each other that much will be understood without being set down on paper. The designer's sketch becomes schematic, with marginal notes. It is carried just as far as necessary to convey the idea and is drawn for the designer's professional colleagues. The designer will resort to a full sketch or model only when trying something experimental, which needs careful explanation.

The sketch is always accompanied by a *floor plan.* If the floor plan is drawn to scale and the sketch is in good proportion, the director and others concerned with the production can form an accurate opinion as to how the actual setting will look.

## THE MODEL

Although the sketch has been pictured as the prime means of presenting an idea, it is often preliminary to a model. Most directors today will expect a model, but it depends on the personalities involved. Because of the three-dimensionality of scenery, some designers prefer to work directly in the model form of presentation. The model gives a true indication of the space relationships of scenery and actors and is, therefore, of interest to the director when planning the staging (Figure 4–15).

Within the model, each piece of scenery is constructed to an accurate scale, thus giving the designer a miniature preview of how the setting is going to look. Because the model is three-dimensional, composition and sightlines can be checked from all the extreme angles of view. In addition to being a means of presentation, the model can also be used to check the appropriateness of scale, proportion, or shape. If the model is for the designer's use only, a very rough version can be built, saving time and energy.

The scale of the model varies with the designer. Some like to work at the scale of $\frac{1}{2}$ inch equal to one foot, while others prefer a smaller scale. The $\frac{1}{4}$-inch scale model is a convenient size for fast execution, which sometimes is important. The smaller scale is also convenient because it is easier to make changes and experiment with than a larger scale. Some designers will work in scale as small as $\frac{1}{8}$ inch equals a foot. The advantage to this is that the overall sense of the design can be determined quickly. It is also much easier

**Figure 4–15**
Model and Production Setting

Design for thrust stage *North-shore Fish*. Designer—Peter Davidson, photo © Davidson.

to carry a very small model with you to a design meeting and just as much information can be imparted. It is cheaper—less material is needed—and it is easier to store. What this ultimately means is that the designer can experiment more with the design without investing huge amounts of time or money.

**Constructing The Sketch Model**     Sometimes called a *working model*, the sketch model is made of paper (two-ply bristol board) and is used by the designer to check the three-dimensional qualities of a setting or portions of a set (Figure 4–16). The model is usually uncolored, but if three-ply bristol board is used and the paint is applied before cutting and shaping, the model can be made in full color.

a

b

**Figure 4–16**
Sketch Model

Full color models painted on 3-ply Bristol board.
(a) Scenic forms from the operetta *Firefly*.
(b) Work models. Quick black and white studies made before creating a larger, more accurate model. Model photos by Margo.

If the model is made carefully and to scale, it is of great value to those who will be constructing the scenery. It is a three-dimensional assembled view. The British use a model in this manner—a carefully detailed 1:25 scale model—to present a final design (Figure 4–17). The scale, which is about $\frac{1}{2}$ inch to one foot in the United States, is large enough to provide the stage technicians with the information they need to develop construction drawings. The designer is depending on the skill and craftsmanship of the carpenters and scenic artists to interpret the model into full-scale scenery.

**Figure 4–17**
**British Model**

The British and all English-influenced countries such as Canada use a carefully detailed scaled model in place of designer's and painter's elevations. The carpenter and the painters work directly from the model. The setting is for *You Never Can Tell* designed by Cameron Porteous. Photo © David Cooper, courtesy of Shaw Festival, Canada.

## THE COSTUME SKETCH

The costume designer's ideas are also presented in sketch form (Figure 4–18). Individual costume designs are usually in full color, while group designs might be in black and white with color notes or swatches.

The costume sketch, besides presenting a design to be viewed in correlation with the overall tonality and style of the production, is first and foremost the designer's interpretation of an individual character. For this reason, the actor is also interested in the costume sketch to gather visual reinforcement and insight of his or her character and lifestyle.

Unlike the scene designer's sketch where the colors are usually modified by the lighting of the scene, the costume sketch can indicate colors of the costumes as they will be seen. Therefore, a costume sketch in color, supplemented by fabric swatches and with a few penciled details or an additional view of the design, can become a reference drawing for costume construction.

## TECHNICAL PRESENTATION

Once a design idea has been fully developed and is ready to be translated into full scale reality, the designer has to prepare a series of detailed presentations to the artisan who will be building and painting the setting. These are scaled and dimensioned drawings that provide information as to the profile, size and location of openings and decorative detail of every unit of scenery. The designer and the design staff prepare these drawings in the form of designer's elevations, from which the technical director develops rear elevations and construction drawings. All are discussed in detail in Chapter 5.

**Designer's Elevations**     Design elevations are usually presented at a scale of $\frac{1}{2}$ inch to one foot. An elevation that is a head-on view of a unit of scenery

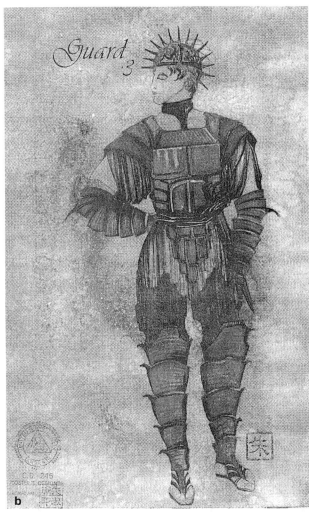

appears in other forms also, such as the cartoon or layout for decorative painting or with color added—a guide for the painters.

**Painter's Elevation**     For the artists who will be painting the scenery, the designer prepares scaled elevations that indicate the colors and painting technique of each unit of scenery. Figure 4–19 shows the technical presentation of a large cut-drop representing the downstage portion of a detailed wooded landscape. The first drawing (Figure 4–19a) is the cartoon, or line drawing indicating the basic layout of the composition. The cartoon is important to the painter, for as can be seen in Figure 4–19b, the outline is lost in the fully painted forest scene. The cut-drop not only has cut out spaces, but is also translucent in the sky areas.

The two drawings (cartoon and painter's elevation) provide the scenic artist with information for the layout, open spaces, translucent and opaque areas, colors, and painting techniques. For a more detailed explanation of methods of layout, proportional enlargement, and scenery painting techniques, please refer to Chapter 9.

**Figure 4–18**
**Costume Design Presentation**

(a) Unusual presentation of group costumes for *The Plough and the Stars*. Designer—Susan Tsu.
(b) An interesting concept for the armor of the guards in Sophocles' *Antigone*. The legging and gauntlet are crustacean forms, while the breast plate has the markings of the turtle. Designer—Susan Tsu.

**Figure 4–19**
Technical Presentation, Painter's Elevations

Elevations for the scenic artists are developed in two categories. (a) First comes the cartoon or line drawing supplying the painters with a layout of the design. It may or may not be gridded with squares for scale reference, as some painters prefer to plan their own grid.
(b) The second elevation provides the painters with the complete design indicating color and painting techniques. Between the two drawings of this cut drop the painters have information pertaining to the layout, open spaces, translucent and opaque areas, colors and painting techniques.

a

b

## COMPUTER-GENERATED DESIGN

The scene designer, with the aid of a computer, can expand a preliminary sketch into a fully developed design. Working on a personal computer with the aid of available software, the designer is able to model a form or group of forms into a three-dimensional composition in very little time. After texture and color or tone have been added, the designer can light the composition to fit the action and atmosphere. In simple terms, the design is developed in the following manner:

1. The basic sketch outline, or *wire frame* of the design form, is modeled into a three-dimensional drawing. To give definition and dimension to the model, its surfaces may need to be textured.

2. A *texture mapping* program allows the designer to choose, from a *library* of textures, the most suitable texture and color or tone for the individual areas throughout the composition. The texture adds shape, direction, and a sense of detail to the design as well as providing each surface a degree of absorption and reflection of light.

3. From an *object library*, the designer chooses furniture or properties to be placed in the setting, along with figures and their dress.

4. The final step, the lighting of the composition, is the most exciting, though time-consuming. Through a *lighting editor* program, the designer can select offstage positions for motivating light sources, front lighting positions for the actors, as well as atmospheric background illumination. Light sources on the stage—such as lamps, torches, or candelabras—are also established. The computer analyzes the distribution of each light source, calculates the amount of reflection off the various textures, and plots the direction of the many overlapping shadows cast by the numerous light sources. The photographic realism of the printout is an excellent presentation of a design idea (Figure 4–20).

Other methods of computer-generated design are more two-dimensional in form. The designer, for example, can create directly on the screen of a personal computer such as the Macintosh®. With aid of the mouse (which moves the pointer) the designer is able to draw directly or select data from a library of software programs. A library of geometric shapes is a useful aid, and another is the texture mapping program mentioned earlier. A printout of this type of design can serve as a presentation drawing for a painter's elevation or as a design for a projection.

The final example of the computer as an aid to design is in the use of the *photo-shop* program along with an extra piece of hardware, a *scanner*. The scanner captures an object or shape on the screen. The object or collection of shapes can then be manipulated by reversing, duplicating, overlapping it, or can be composed with other forms. The final arrangement of forms is similar to a collage of found art, and with original coloring can be as real or abstract as the designer wishes.

The computer is extremely useful as a tool. Although it does not solve any problems, it allows the designer to change, adapt, or rethink work quickly and easily. Computer-aided drawing may take some time to understand. Some programs have a very steep learning curve. It should also be noted that much of the hardware and software required for the computer is still expensive. This will no doubt change in the future, making the computer a much more commonly used tool for designers.

## LIGHTING DESIGN PRESENTATION

Since the lighting designer is a member of the artistic team, he or she should be present at discussions of the play. Certainly the lighting designer will

**Figure 4–20**
**Computer-Generated Design**

Two basic approaches to the use of the computer as design tool.
(a) A design idea is developed in steps beginning with the basic outline, through modeling with a three-dimensional program to the adding of color and texture and finally the lighting of the form or collection of forms. Setting for *Hamlet* designed by Kevin Abbott.
(b) Computer-generated design using PhotoShop for *Much Ado about Nothing*, courtesy Samuel Ball.

provide insights to the production different from the other designers and can be instrumental in developing the production style as well as influencing the floor plan and setting. It is important that the set and lighting designers work hand in hand during the initial stages of the design process.

Obviously the lighting designer has been influenced by the script and has formed some general ideas of atmosphere and color. An early discussion of light colors is important, especially to the costume designer. Swatch books of gel colors are convenient, if imperfect, aids for indicating light colors to others.

At later production meetings, the lighting designer will be able to present visual indications of color, distribution, and atmosphere through the use of *value sketches,* a *storyboard,* or a *lighting score.* A storyboard illustrates with simple tones on the basic forms of the setting, the changes or movement of intensity, direction of light within a scene, or from scene to scene (Figure 4–21). The lighting score indicates with simple symbols a scene-by-scene analysis of the motivational sources, brightness, mood, focus, and direction of key light on

**Figure 4–21**
**Lighting Design Presentation**

The lighting story board, an early presentation before the final light plot, is a variation of the mood sketch showing atmospheric and distribution changes scene by scene. The illustration shows one of many light changes.

the actors. Further and more detailed discussion of the lighting designer's presentation techniques be found in Chapter 20.

As the lighting concept is developed, the lighting designer turns to his or her final presentation: the *light plot.* The plot is a plan or *top view* of the layout of all lighting instruments in the production and a *sectional view* showing the height and direction of each lighting position. Beside each unit is a brief notation of the instrument's number, type, (function or purpose,) color, circuit, and dimmer hookup. A more complete explanation of the light plot is also found in Chapter 20.

## THEATRICAL DESIGN OUTSIDE THE THEATRE

Frequently the designer in the theatre supplements his or her income by designing for related but commercially oriented uses of theatrical techniques. Figure 4–22 shows one example. Such spheres as *trade shows,* (such as auto or fashion shows), *in-house television,* and pageants call on the talents of the theatrical designer.

### TRADE SHOWS

The design approach and presentation for trade shows is basically the same as for theatre, although the goal is different. Instead of visually reinforcing a playwright's idea, the designer is called on to provide theatrical flair to the selling of a product or the promotion of a marketing technique to a captive audience of company personnel. The use of dramatic form and theatrical staging adds interest and excitement to what could be a dull subject.

**Figure 4–22**
Theatrical Design Outside the Theatre

Industrial show design by HOTOPP Associates.

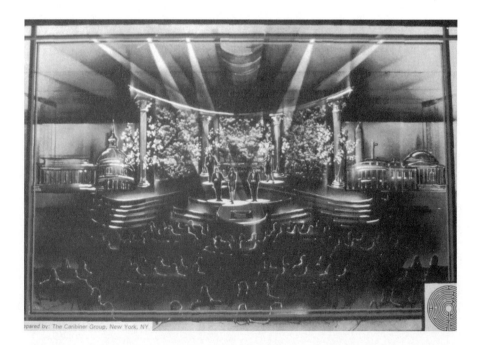

pared by: The Caribiner Group, New York, NY

**Figure 4—23**
Pageant Wagon

Another example of design outside the theatre. A design for a Mardi Gras float designed by Zhany Xiang. Photo courtesy of Brian Kern, Mardi Gras World.

## IN-HOUSE TELEVISION

In-house television is another outlet for theatre techniques. Large national and international companies use closed-circuit television as a more immediate means of maintaining contact with widespread branches than trade shows. Computer animation is also becoming a major form of communication. When television goes digital it is not too difficult to foresee the importance of the computer in the future of this means of communication.

## PAGEANTS

Usually performed outdoors in an amphitheatre or stadium, the pageant is a large-scale event. Its format is often historical or documentary in style and it uses a narrator to advance the story line.

The scene of action may be a fixed group of exteriors, interiors, or a natural setting, with the action moving from one area to the next. On the other hand, elaborate means may be employed, such as a water canal for ships or barges, tracked wagons or a treadmill for scenery or actors, and on occasion, horses. The climax of the evening may be a chase, a race, or a full-scale battle scene with pyrotechnics. The opportunities for scenery, costume, and lighting designers are obvious.

**The Pageant Wagon**     As an extension of the pageant, the pageant wagon is part of theatre history. A present-day example can be seen in the famous Mardi Gras floats in New Orleans (Figure 4–23). Traditionally part of the celebration of the beginning of Lent, the floats are a creative outlet for both costume and scene design.

# DRAFTING THE DESIGN 5

Although scene design is three-dimensional in final form, most of the presentation of the design idea in preparation for construction is two-dimensional in character. The graphics of presentation are the visual language or fundamental means of communication between the designer, stage technicians, and director. The planning of a show throughout all its phases relies on a common knowledge of simple drafting techniques to communicate technical and artistic information. The designer must give simple, clear, and accurate information so that all ideas may be carried out efficiently and accurately.

## DRAFTING EQUIPMENT

The young student designer will need to become acquainted with certain tools and materials. Drafting for the theatre is similar to architectural drafting and engineering drawing but is not as elaborate.

A good *drawing board* is made of clear white pine, cleated to prevent warping, and for most purposes is about 24 inches by 30 inches in size. A *drafting table,* the top of which is a drawing board, should be a little larger. A top of about 36 inches by 42 inches gives additional work space around the drawing board.

Drawing boards need to be padded to prevent the pencil from following the grain of the wood. The best surface is a vinyl plastic cover that is tinted pale green on one side and off-white on the other. Although expensive, it is an excellent drafting surface and will last a lifetime.

The *T-square* guides off one side of the drawing board to establish the horizontal lines in the drawing. Its accuracy depends upon the straightness of the working edge and the squareness of the head and blade. A 30-inch T-square made of hardwood with a transparent-edge blade and fixed head is

## DRAFTING EQUIPMENT

For the beginner, a list of basic drafting equipment should include the following:

1. A drawing board or drafting table
2. Drawing board padding
3. T-square or parallel rule
4. Set of triangles or adjustable triangle
5. Small set of drafting instruments
   a. 6-inch compass
   b. Lengthening bar
   c. 6-inch divider
   d. 6-inch bow compass
   e. 4-inch bow compass
   f. 4-inch divider
6. Scale rule
7. Pencils and leads
8. Tracing paper
9. Accessories
   a. Erasers
   b. Erasing shield
   c. Drafting tape
   d. Lead pointer
   e. Drawing cleaning powder

best for all-around service. A traveling parallel straightedge, which serves the same function as a T-square, is attached permanently to the top of a drafting table. Its length, of course, is determined by the longest dimension of the table top.

Two transparent celluloid *triangles* give the customary set of angles as well as perpendicular lines when they are guided off of the T-square. A 6-inch 45-degree and an 8- or 10-inch 30–60-degree triangle are the most convenient sizes.

An instrument that lends itself to drawing the many odd angles so frequently found in a stage setting is the *adjustable triangle*. It is a combination triangle and protractor with an adjustable edge that allows the selection of any angle between 45 degrees and perpendicular.

Figure 5–1 illustrates the equipment just described. In addition, the designer needs other instruments, most of which are shown in Figure 5–2. A set of drafting instruments containing a 6-inch compass and dividers with lengthening bar and inking attachments plus a bow compass and bow dividers would fulfill the average drafting requirements. When assembling drawing instruments for the first time, it is wise to invest in a good set. The accuracy and clarity of the work depends on the quality of the instruments.

The basic drafting instrument is the *compass*. It is needed to draw a circle or swing an arc. A 6-inch bow compass is a valuable asset. It holds a set very

### Figure 5–1
### Drafting Equipment

(a) Drawing board and tools.

(1) Cleated white-pine drawing board.

(2) Tinted-vinyl padding for drawing-board surface.

(3) T-square.

(4) 45-degree triangle.

(5) 30–60-degree triangle.

(b) Drafting table with adjustable tilt and height.

(6) Parallel straight edge attached to the top of the drawing table by a cable system that allows it to travel from top to bottom and remain parallel.

(7) Adjustable triangle that is able to adjust to many different angles.

(c) Detail of set-triangle.

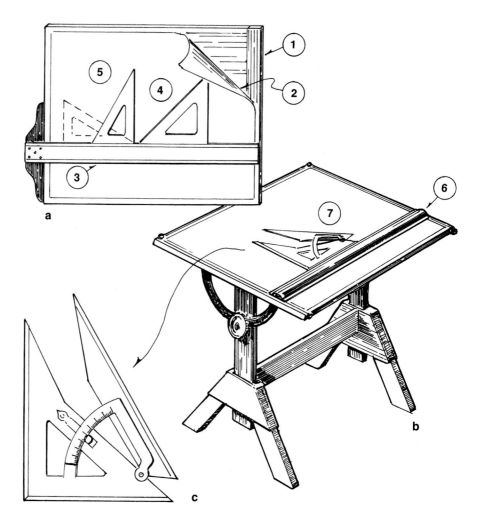

firmly and accurately for repeated use on the same arc or circle. Many small drafting sets consist only of a compass with lengthening bar and inking attachments. Extra points are also provided to turn the compass into dividers.

The *lengthening bar* is an attachment that increases the length of one arm of the compass, making it possible to swing a larger radius to make an arc or circle.

*Dividers* are used to hold or transfer a dimension. The compass can perform the same operation but with less accuracy. Bow instruments such as the *bow compass* and *bow dividers* are better for small circles and measurements and for retaining a recurring dimension or arc.

Because most scenery is too large to be represented in a drawing at actual size, it is necessary to reduce the size in regular proportions. The *scale rule* is devised to make the change in proportion as painless as possible. The most useful scale rule is the triangular form, which provides twelve different graduations. To the beginner, a confusing factor is the discovery that there are two types of scale rules: the Architect's scale, which divides the proportional foot into twelfths or inches, and the Engineer's scale, which divides the inch

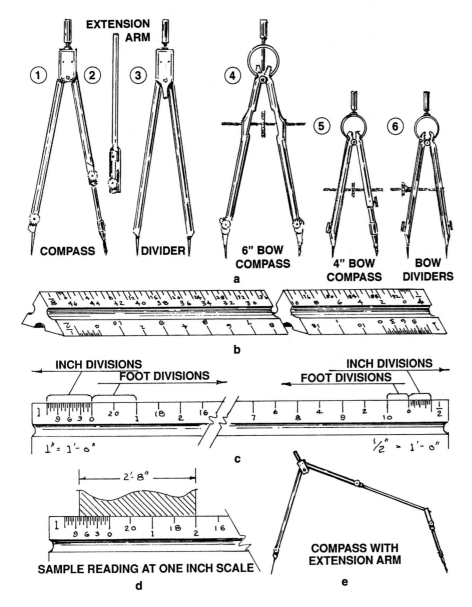

### Figure 5–2
#### Drafting Instruments

(a) The minimum set of drafting instruments.
   (1) Compass
   (2) Extension arm
   (3) Divider
   (4) Six-inch bow compass
   (5) Four-inch bow compass
   (6) Bow divider
(b) Architect's scale rule, triangular form; three edges, six faces, and twelve scales.
(c) Drawing of one face to demonstrate the method of reading a scale rule. The face shown contains two scales: 1″ = 1′0″ to the left and $\frac{1}{2}$″ = 1′0″ to the right. To read the one-inch scale, for example, inches are read to the left of zero while foot divisions are read to the right.
(d) Drawing showing a sample reading of a surface 2′8″ in dimension at the scale of 1″ = 1′0″.
(e) Compass with extension arm attached to increase radius.

into decimals or tenths, with divisions from ten to sixty. The names are trade names, not an indication of the profession using them—engineers have as much use for the Architect's scale as do architects. Inasmuch as stage sets, like houses, are built in feet and inches, the planning of scenery is done with the Architect's scale rule.

To save time and increase accuracy, the designer often uses various *templates* to quickly trace geometric shapes, eccentric curves, or furniture outlines onto a floor plan. Shown in Figure 5–3 are templates for house furnishings, circles, squares and other geometric shapes, ellipses, and a set of french curves that can serve as an edge for a clear, hard line drafting.

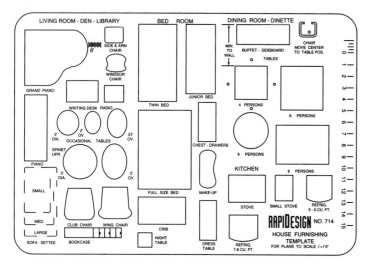

**a**

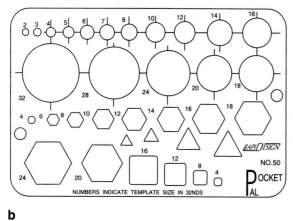

**b**

**c**

# Figure 5–3
## Drafting Templates and French Curves

(a) House furnishing template. Scale $\frac{1}{4}'' = 1'0''$.
(b) Circles, squares, triangles and hexagons.
(c) The ellipse or circle in isometric.
(d) French curves.

**d**

*Drawing pencils* and *leads* for lead holders have varying degrees of hardness and softness. Soft lead produces a blacker line than hard lead. The leads are graded by letter—from 6B, which is very soft, through HB and H, which are medium soft to firm, to 6H, the hardest lead. The combination of H, 2H, and 4H leads is generally a good combination. It should be noted, however, that everyone drafts a bit differently, some with a light hand and some with a heavier hand. Some adjustment might be needed with the specific lead being used to give the variety in line quality necessary for a good blueprint.

The choice of *drafting paper* can depend on the type of drafting being done. Almost all drafting uses some kind of *tracing paper*. There are many different kinds, so the beginner is wise to seek the advice of a competent dealer. Vellum, an excellent tracing paper although expensive, is a durable, 100% rag stock, with a nonglare surface to reduce eyestrain. It has enough tooth in the surface for pencil drafting to produce an excellent print. Very cheap rolls of thin canary yellow or white tracing paper can be used for preliminary drawings. This saves not only the good drafting paper for the finished drafting but also saves money.

The accessories that complete the draftsman's list of equipment are made up of such items as a *lead pointer* for pointing the leads of the draftsman's mechanical pencils; an *eraser* and *erasing shield* for erasing pencil-line mistakes, plus an *art gum eraser* or *drawing cleaning powder* to help keep the drawing paper clean; and *drafting tape* or dots, which are used to fasten the tracing paper to the drawing board.

## THE GRAPHICS OF DRAFTING

Drafting practices in the theatre are so numerous and loosely defined that they cannot easily be categorized. There are as many ways to draft a show as there are designers. A close inspection, however, reveals that each designer differs only in the amount of information given and in the way the material is organized. All have in common a background of engineering drawing and its basic principle—orthographic projection.

### ORTHOGRAPHIC PROJECTION

In spite of its academic sound, the orthographic projection is a simple drawing. *Orthographic* means "straight line." A straight-line projection is a method of representing the exact shape of an object in a line drawing on a plane perpendicular to the lines of projection from the object (Figure 5–4).

For example, it is easy to recognize the familiar three-step unit from a perspective drawing (Figure 5–4a). The carpenter, however, who needs more information than a pretty sketch, wants to know height, width, and depth. An orthographic projection is a drafter's way of drawing the unit to give this information. It reveals the object one view at a time and from all angles. The observer is free to move around the object to view it from front to rear and from top to bottom. Each view is seen in true dimension by straight-line projection. In certain views (rear, left side, and bottom) some outlines are hidden from the viewer. It is customary to represent hidden outlines with a dashed line, as can be seen in Figure 5–4b, c, and d.

**View Alignment**     Obviously, a series of unrelated views of an object are of little value unless they are organized in a connective manner to show the

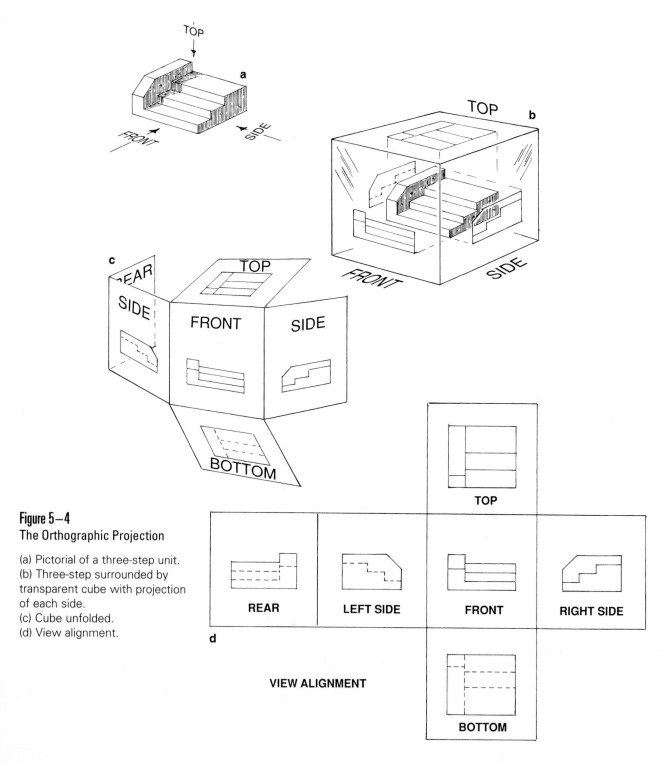

**Figure 5–4**
The Orthographic Projection

(a) Pictorial of a three-step unit.
(b) Three-step surrounded by transparent cube with projection of each side.
(c) Cube unfolded.
(d) View alignment.

VIEW ALIGNMENT

position of the object in space. Hence, a conventional arrangement of views is the basis of all drafting techniques.

To understand the method of transposing the views of the object in space onto the drawing board requires some visual imagination. Imagine, for example, that the three-step unit is in the center of a transparent cube (Figure 5–4b). Projected on each side of the cube is a line drawing of the object as it appears in each view. With the side containing the front view as the center, the other faces of the cube are unfolded to either side, to the top, and to the bottom (Figure 5–4c and d).

The front view is always the most recognizable one, showing the main characteristics of the object. It is the key view that gives the carpenter a bearing for visualizing the three-step unit in three dimensions. The top and side views are shown above and to the sides of the front view, providing the three principal views of the object. Borrowing architectural terminology, some views are referred to as *elevations*, a term that is applied to all views seen in a horizontal direction. The horizontal views include the front elevation, side elevations, and rear elevation. An academic (and less frequently used) expression refers to the views as *projections*. The front, top, and side views become respectively the vertical, horizontal, and profile projections.

Of course the carpenter does not refer to these drawings as orthographic projections. With the addition of dimensions to the three principal views, and some material specifications, the carpenter is ready to start building (Figure 5–5).

## DRAFTING CONVENTIONS

As the designer begins to make working drawings, which are flat and less descriptive than the original sketch, he or she soon discovers that the drafter has a way of making the lines speak for themselves. In the drafter's language, symbols and conventions are words. The vocabulary has lines of all types. There are thick lines, thin lines, dotted lines, dashed lines, straight lines, and curved lines. Each has a different meaning and function. The drafter's language, like any language, depends on a mutual knowledge of the symbols to correctly read a set of working drawings.

### LINE SYMBOLS

The first and simplest convention is the drawing of lines in different weights or thickness. The scene designer drafts with three weights of line. Occasionally for speed, or because of the simplicity of the drawing, only two weights of line are used. The goal is clarity of presentation and accuracy of representation. The different weights—light, medium, and heavy—are relative in thickness from one drawing to another. Because the scene designer drafts in so many scales, standardization of thickness or number of weights is impossible. A floor plan may need three weights of line, a mechanical or decorative detail two weights, and a full-scale pattern only one.

### Figure 5—5
### Scaled and Dimensioned Drawings, Problems

Designers' working drawings (a) generally show three views of the object, drawn to scale and dimensioned. Occasionally one view may be omitted or an additional view (such as a section) included, depending upon the complexity of the subject.

*Orthographic Projection Problems.*
(b) Supply missing line.
(c) Construct missing view.

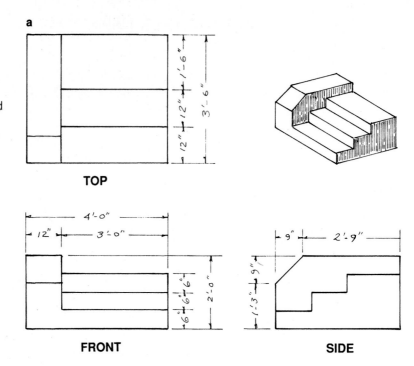

**TOP**

**FRONT**

**SIDE**

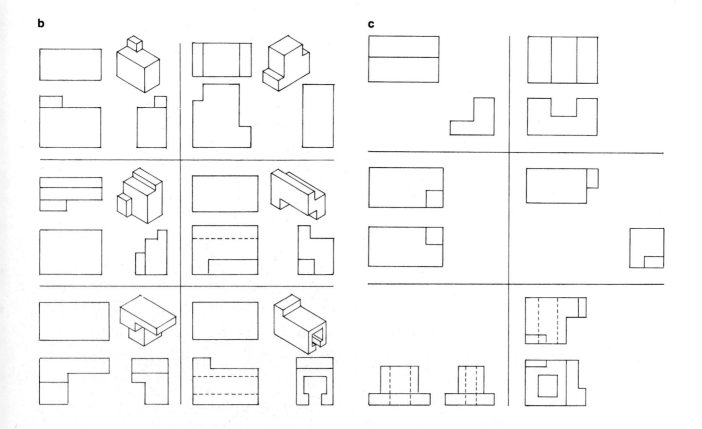

**b**

**c**

A line is made heavy or light depending on its eye-catching importance on the blueprint. Obviously, heavy lines are going to be seen first, medium-weight lines second, and lightweight lines last. The use of different weight lines gives the blueprint a feeling of depth. It is a very slight third dimension, but it is enough to make the print easier to read. The USITT (United States Institute for Theatre Technology) Graphic Standard Board recommends for drafting in pencil the following guide to line thickness: 0.3mm ($\frac{3}{10}$ of millimeter) for a thin line, 0.5mm for a thick line, and 0.9mm for the infrequent extra-thick line. Beyond the slight descriptive quality of the weight of a line, there is the meaning or symbol of the function implied in the use of certain lines that needs to be explained and that are shown in Figure 5–6.

**Medium-Weight Lines (Thick)**  It is easier to begin with medium-weight lines, for they are used the most and have already been seen in the orthographic projection of the three-step unit (Figure 5–4). They are the *outline lines* that represent the shape of the object, showing visible edges of all surfaces as they appear at the angle of view. The visible outline is a solid, medium-weight line. Occasionally a view will cover or hide a surface outline. It then becomes a *hidden outline* and is drawn as a dotted line or series of small dashes.

Frequently a drafter will want to show where an adjoining element of scenery touches a surface, or show an alternate position of the same object. The *phantom line* symbolizes the removed object by outlining its position in the view. The designer has a choice of two symbols: a dashed line or the repetition of an elongated dash and two dots. Because a phantom line should always carry a label, the choice of line depends on the complexity of the outline of the removed part. Whichever symbol is chosen should be used consistently throughout the drawing.

**Lightweight Lines (Thin)**  Lightweight lines have a variety of uses. Their function is to give additional information about the object and still not detract from the overall picture created by the outlines.

*Dimension lines*, with arrowheads at the ends, mark the extent of the surface that is being dimensioned. Figures, set into the line, show exact distance. If dimension lines are set too close to the drawing, or within the drawing, they may become confused with outlines. To keep the dimension line away from the object, the *extension line* is used. These lines are solid and are drawn perpendicular to the surface of the object. As the name implies, they extend the surface to the dimension line. Although the arrowheads of the dimension line touch the extension line, the extension line itself is held clear of the object, about $\frac{1}{16}$ inch, wherever possible.

*Leaders*, relatives of dimension lines, are made with one-sided arrowheads that touch the surface where a note or dimension applies. If the leader is always drawn slanted or curved, there is less chance for anyone to confuse it with the dimension line.

*Break lines* are space savers that denote a shortening of length or height. Occasionally, the drafter wants to draw a unit of scenery that is too long to

**Figure 5–6**
Line Symbols

(a) Lightweight lines (thin)
(b) Medium-weight line (thick)
(c) Heavy-weight lines (double thick)
(d) Types of dimensions

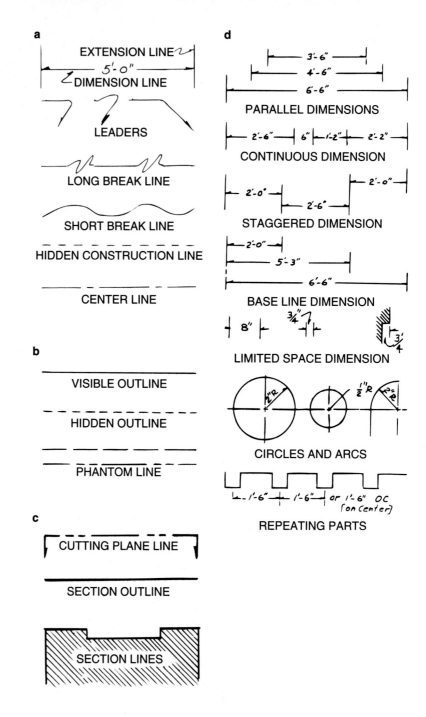

fit on the paper. A reduction of length is accomplished by taking a piece out of the center and using a break line to show that the piece is not represented in full length. The break line can also be used to indicate that the outer surface of an object has been cut away to show inner structure. The *long break line* is a straight line with spasmodic eruptions occurring at intervals, while the *short break line* is a more subtle curve with less regularity.

The *center line,* symbolized by an alternating long dash and dot, is used to establish the center of circles and to show the dividing line of symmetrical parts. The center line is also a familiar symbol in the floor plan of a stage setting, where it marks the center of the stage or proscenium opening. It is an important reference line for the location of scenery on the stage.

The final lightweight line is the *hidden construction line.* It is a dashed line used to indicate rear construction such as bracing, picture battens, or covered hinging not visible in the view.

**Heavy-Weight Lines (Double Thick)**   Heavy-weight lines are used solely to indicate the cross section of an object or the cutting away and removing of a portion to reveal the inside. The *cutting-plan line,* drawn over an adjoining view to locate the position of the cut, consists of a repeating dash and a double dot. The arrowheads point the direction seen in the sectional view.

The other heavy-weight line is the *section outline,* which appears in the sectional view. It is a heavy solid line that outlines the cut surface to emphasize it over the uncut surfaces. The cut surface is further set apart by the use of *section lines,* which are lightweight crosshatched lines drawn within the cut surface outline.

## SCALED DRAWINGS

The most important part of a set of working drawings is the dimension. A carpenter cannot begin to build without some indication of size. Scaled or dimensioned drawings are crucial for such information. Most misunderstandings that occur between the drawing board and the finished setting are over dimensions, such as the wall that is too small for the sideboard or the door that is too large for the door opening.

Many errors can be avoided if the designer uses a scaled drawing. If it is carefully drawn, it not only gives the carpenter a way to figure sizes, it also gives the designer a fairly accurate basis for studying the proportional relationship of various elements of the set.

The usual scale of a working drawing is $\frac{1}{2}$ inch equals one foot ($\frac{1''}{2}$ = 1'0"), which means that every half inch on the drawing is equal to one foot at full-scale or actual size. Decorative details that might not be clear at the small scale are frequently increased to the scale of 1" = 1'0" or larger. Any important bits of detail that the designer wants accurately reproduced—such as wallpaper patterns, scrolls, brackets, railings, and the like—are presented at full scale.

## DIMENSIONS

An unscaled drawing needs some indication of size before the carpenter can begin building. The placing of dimensions opposite a surface is done in a manner to show its exact limit and measure. Dimensions, however, are not reserved strictly for unscaled drawings. It is common practice to place dimensions on a scaled drawing to save time in the shop. A properly given dimension includes the dimension line, measurement, and extension lines.

## SECTIONS

On many occasions the designer feels the need to supplement the working drawings with another view that will add information to the normal top, front, and side views. The additional view most frequently used is the *section*. A designer often finds it easier to explain a three-dimensional piece of scenery by cutting it open to show the inner structure or exact contour. Because the section offers a more descriptive view, it is sometimes used in place of a side or top view.

### Figure 5–7
Sectional Views

(a) Revolved section, drawn directly on the elevation to indicate contour.
(b) Removed section, a revolved section that has been removed and set to one side of the elevation. Each section is labeled A–F.
(c) Cross Section B–B is a vertical section and A–A is a horizontal section, frequently called a *plan*.
(d) Half section, used on a symmetrical object combining the cross-section and elevational views.

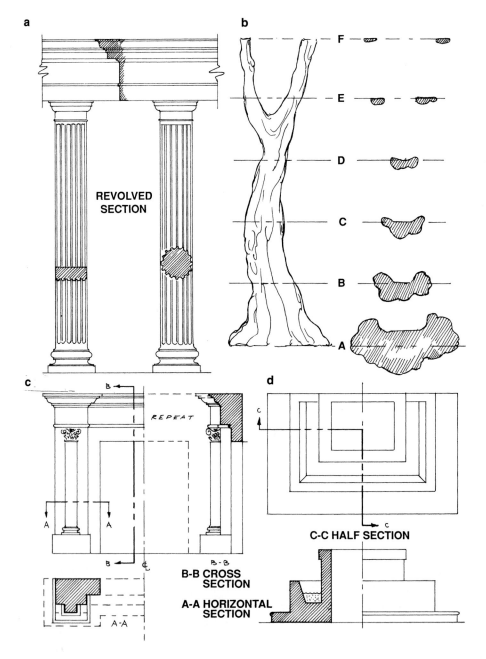

There are many types of sectional views and a variety of uses (Figure 5–7), but the two sectional views used consistently in the theatre are the floor plan and the hanging section. Of the two drawings the floor plan is more important to the designer, although the hanging section, to check technical details and vertical sightlines, is also used and will be discussed later in the chapter, in the section titled "Technical Planning."

## THE FLOOR PLAN

Long before starting the working drawings of a set, the designer must realize the importance of the floor plan. A designer continually thinks of the plan while the idea of the setting is being developed. The plan grows with the design, pushed one way for aesthetic reasons, altered another way for practical reasons, modified for staging reasons, and finally solidified into the key working drawing and information center—the floor plan.

All phases of production seek information from the floor plan. To explain the design of the set adequately, the designer finds it necessary to refer often to the plan. The carpenter consults it to lay out the construction. The director and stage manager are unable to map out the staging without understanding and studying it. The setup, rigging, and lighting depend on information in the floor plan to complete the final assembly of the set on the stage.

The floor plan is a horizontal section with the cutting plane passed at a level that shows (when the upper portion of the set is removed) the most characteristic view of the shape of the set. Because a stage set is made up of many small units of scenery, the floor plan is also an assembled view. The floor plan, then, reveals the horizontal shape of the set, locates it on the stage, shows the scenery assembled, and identifies with labels the units and pieces that make up the complete setting.

### SYMBOLS

The floor plan is usually drawn at the scale of $\frac{1}{2}'' = 1'0''$ or smaller. At this scale, it is necessary to use symbols and conventions to help explain the set with a limited amount of detailed drafting. Most of the symbols shown in Figure 5–8 are familiar ones; their use and meanings are logical enough if one keeps in mind that a plan is a sectional view.

### DIMENSIONING THE FLOOR PLAN

The floor plan is dimensioned from two reference lines: the center line of the proscenium opening and the plaster line. If a production will tour, the designer will substitute the set line, a dashed line or thin solid line drawn from the right return to the left return, for the plaster line. Figure 5–9 is a basic example of a designer's floor plan.

It is not necessary to dimension the plan in great detail because all the scenery will appear in separate elevational views with complete dimensions.

Figure 5–8
Floor Plan Symbols

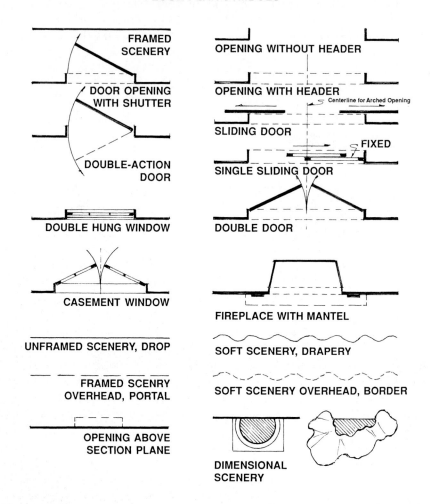

**FLOOR PLAN SYMBOLS**

FRAMED SCENERY

DOOR OPENING WITH SHUTTER

DOUBLE-ACTION DOOR

DOUBLE HUNG WINDOW

CASEMENT WINDOW

UNFRAMED SCENERY, DROP

FRAMED SCENRY OVERHEAD, PORTAL

OPENING ABOVE SECTION PLANE

OPENING WITHOUT HEADER

OPENING WITH HEADER
Centerline for Arched Opening

SLIDING DOOR

FIXED

SINGLE SLIDING DOOR

DOUBLE DOOR

FIREPLACE WITH MANTEL

SOFT SCENERY, DRAPERY

SOFT SCENERY OVERHEAD, BORDER

DIMENSIONAL SCENERY

However, sometimes certain circumstances such as a more complex, multi-level set or an unusual type of unit require additional information if the plan is to be useful.

Remember that the floor plan is also an assembled view; it will help to determine what dimensions the stage carpenter needs to know to locate and assemble the set on the stage. How wide are tormentors? How deep is the back corner of the set? Distances to the left and right use the center line as a base line, while all depth measurements are taken directly or indirectly from the set line. Any point on the stage is located by its distance right or left of the center line and its measurement upstage from the set line. After all important corners and backings are located, a few additional dimensions may be needed, such as radius dimensions of circles or arcs that may be in the floor plan.

## LABELING

Part of the function of an assembled view is to identify and label the parts that make up the whole. The floor plan gives this information in varying

## FLOOR PLAN SYMBOLS

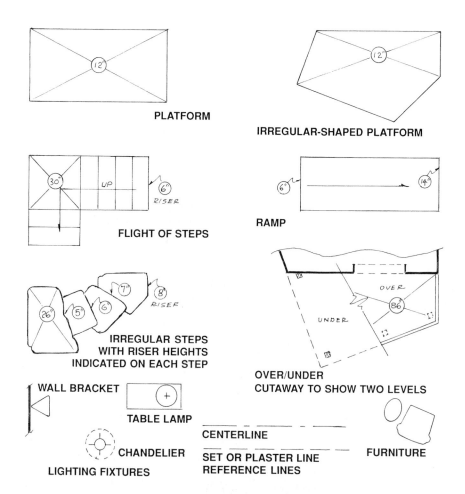

degrees of completeness depending on the working conditions and the nature of the show. Summer stock or university and community theatres, where the bulk of the structural planning falls on the designer's shoulders, may require a more specific labeling of each piece of scenery. The label becomes an easy, accurate means of identification for a single piece of scenery or assembled units of a setting.

## DESIGNER'S ELEVATIONS

Of almost equal importance to the floor plan are the designer's elevations (Figure 5–12). Compared to the floor plan, which is an assembled section showing the relationship of many parts, the elevational drawings are, in a sense, a disassembled or dismantled view of the individual parts. Because the elevation of an assembled set, as it would appear in a normal front view, has little value as a working drawing, the scene designer uses another technique. The set is taken apart, flattened out, and each piece of scenery is shown in

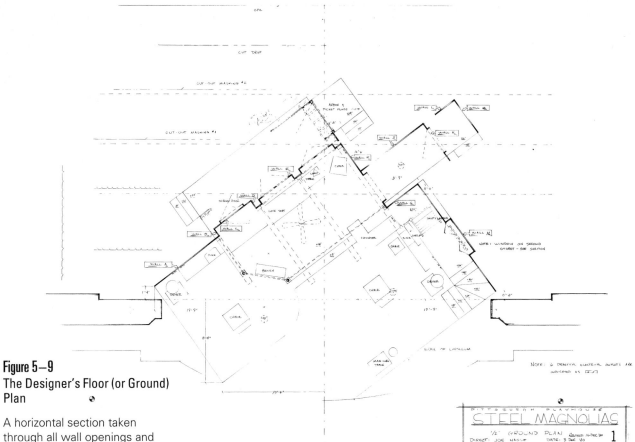

## Figure 5–9
### The Designer's Floor (or Ground) Plan

A horizontal section taken through all wall openings and above all steps and levels. The section's cutting plane is taken at a height that will give the most information. A check with the Floor Plan Symbols (Figure 5–8) will help the reader understand the plan. The dark solid lines represent a cross-section of the wall of the setting. The medium-weight lines outline the steps and levels as seen in a top view. The dotted medium-weight lines indicate openings and headers. The lightweight dimension lines locate the set on the stage as it relates to the references lines, the center line, set line, and plaster line.

## Figure 5–10
### Floor Plan Showing a Change-of-Level

A more complicated setting with a change-of-level for *Falstaff*.

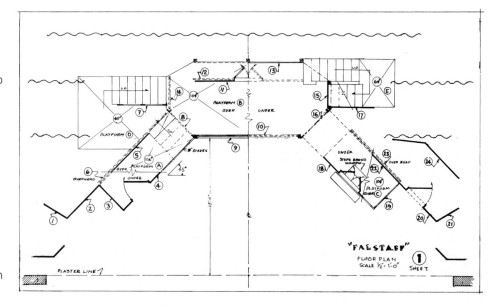

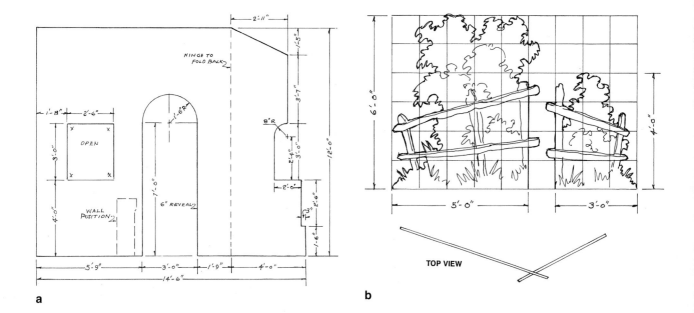

**a**

**b**

front view at a scale of $\frac{1}{2} = 1'0''$. Starting with the right return, the setting is drafted to show all pieces of scenery laid out in order, piece by piece, to the left return. All pieces are represented at $\frac{1}{2}$-inch scale in true size and shape.

Each flat wall surface or unit of scenery is outlined. A solid line or space between units marks an open joint. For design reasons, it may be necessary to indicate a covered joint on the line where two or more wings are hinged together to make up a flat wall surface. The covered joint is indicated with a dotted line and a note to hinge and to dutchman, or cover, the joint. Normally, this is not necessary because the carpenter decides just how an oversized surface will be subdivided. The decision as to how it is to be made is guided by such technical considerations as the size of the stage, the method of handling the sets, and, if the scenery has to be transported, the nature of the transportation. The old maximum wing width of 5 feet 9 inches is based on the height of a baggage-car door, through which all the scenery of a road show had to be able to pass when it traveled by train. However, if the scenery travels by truck, or is not traveling at all, the maximum standard width can vary accordingly. The designer will do well, however, to keep in mind these technical considerations, for they are the limiting features that often control the size and shape of the design.

## APPLIED DETAIL

Designers vary in the amount of detail they show at $\frac{1}{2}$-inch scale. Although the decorative trim and other details are best shown at a larger scale, it is wise to sketch at least a portion of the detail on the $\frac{1}{2}$-inch elevations. It not only shows the trim in assembled view but also gives the carpenter some idea of any special construction that may be needed. Because of the light wood frame and canvas construction of scenery, pictures, valance boxes, or lighting

**Figure 5–11**
Dimensioning the Elevation

(a) A portion of a designer's elevation illustrating many types of dimensions, such as continuous, overall radius, and so on.
(b) The irregular outline of a set piece is best dimensioned with an overlaid grid.

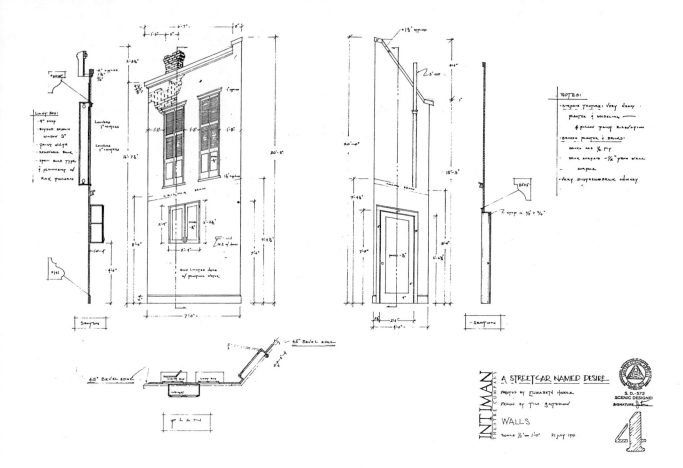

**Figure 5–12**
Designer's Elevation

The front elevation of every element of scenery is shown in a
flattened-out view. The basic
outside dimensions and interior
openings are indicated. Side
notes give specific directions to
builders.

fixtures cannot be placed in the middle of a wall without providing extra
structural support from behind. If the applied details are partially sketched
in the elevation, or indicated with the dashed-line symbol of an adjacent
part, the carpenter will know where to supply the additional construction
(refer again to Figure 5–12).

Obviously, the labels of the elevation must agree with the labels of the
corresponding units in the floor plan. The accuracy of cross-labeling is especially important when stock scenery is being used, for unless the set is
extremely simple, it is the carpenter's only guide as to how the pieces assemble. On occasion, for clarification, a portion of a floor plan may be repeated
near the elevation drawings of a complicated unit of scenery. If there is still
a possibility of misunderstanding, a pictorial drawing can be included.

## COMPUTER-AIDED DRAFTING

The adaptation of computer graphics as a drafting aid is a rapidly advancing
technique. The various software systems are designated as follows: CAD
(computer-aided design); CADD (computer-aided design and drafting); the
most sophisticated AutoCAD, with a *digitized tablet* that serves as a drawing

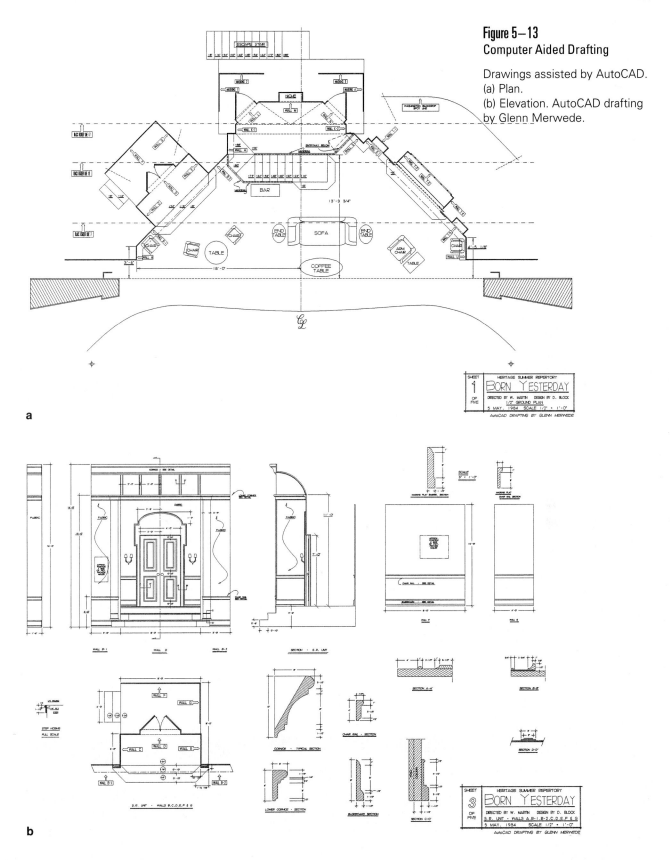

**Figure 5—13**
**Computer Aided Drafting**

**Figure 5—13**
**Computer Aided Drafting**

Drawings assisted by AutoCAD.
(a) Plan.
(b) Elevation. AutoCAD drafting
by Glenn Merwede.

surface; and a *word processor* with several fonts and letter sizes—all used in conjunction with a plotter to produce excellent line quality.

Figures 5–13a and 5–13b are examples of computer drafting. They are drawings, aided by AutoCAD, of a floor plan and one sheet of elevations. While AutoCAD is expensive and out of reach for many theatre groups it is becoming more and more common behind the scenes.

The use of a computer, however, does not replace the need for knowledge and skill in drafting. It is still necessary to study drafting techniques and to be familiar with its symbols and conventions as well as the special requirements of the theatre.

## DRAFTING THREE-DIMENSIONAL SCENERY

Architectural forms such as columns, step units, or a fireplace mantel are usually presented with at least three views: a front view, a top view, and a side or vertical section. Most of the time, a sectional view gives more information than the traditional side view.

With the addition of dimensions, all the three-dimensional forms in Figure 5–7 are suitable drafting presentations. The process is illustrated in Figure 5–14.

An irregular three-dimension, however, is more difficult to draft. The form is segmented into a series of contour pieces that will be fastened to-

**Figure 5–14**

Drafting an Irregular Three-Dimensional Form

The three-dimensional form shown of a tree trunk. The designer's elevation provides an accurate outline of the trunk and a clay scale model shows the contours of the trunk.
(1) The outline of the tree trunk is framed.
(2) The clay model is segmented at intervals that reflect the dimensions of the covering material. Each cut is a scale cross-section or contour of that interval.
(3) The contour pieces are framed and placed at the measured intervals on the framed outline of the trunk. The rest is easy. Contour pieces are cross-braced, then covered with screen or chicken wire and shaped to the contour of the tree trunk to be covered, textured, and painted.

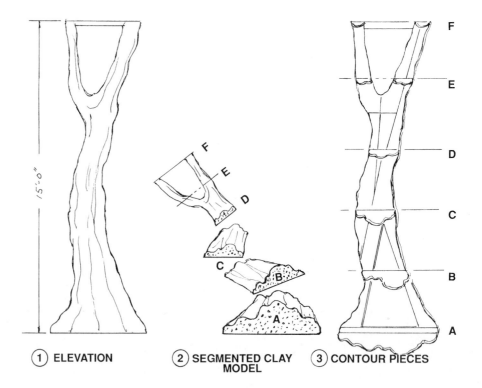

① ELEVATION    ② SEGMENTED CLAY MODEL    ③ CONTOUR PIECES

gether and covered to create the three-dimensional form. The tree trunk shown in Figure 5–7b is a typical example. The designer will get the best results if he or she also submits a scaled model sculptured in modeling clay. The carpenter can then cut horizontal sections at intervals to get an accurate contour (Figure 5–14).

## TECHNICAL PLANNING

For the most part, the scene designer is not concerned with technical planning unless to indicate the best place to divide an oversized element of scenery or to hinge two units. There may be occasions, however, when the scenery is built by unskilled hands, in which case the designer becomes the chief guardian of construction. Under these circumstances, to avoid being tied down by shop supervision when countless other details are pressing, the wise designer will provide construction drawings.

The simplest way to lay out the framed construction of scenery is to use *rear elevations*. A view from this direction looks at the scenery as it appears under construction in the shop. A rear elevation shows the framing and profiling, explains the assembly, locates the hinges, and indicates bracing and stiffening. The detail and completeness of the rear elevations must be determined by the aptitude of the shop help. An experienced carpenter might

**Figure 5–15**
**Rear Elevations**

Detailed construction drawings show the framing of each piece of scenery and indicate how each is assembled. Note the use of vertical and horizontal sections as assembled views. The numbers cross-relate units of scenery to either of the assembled views.

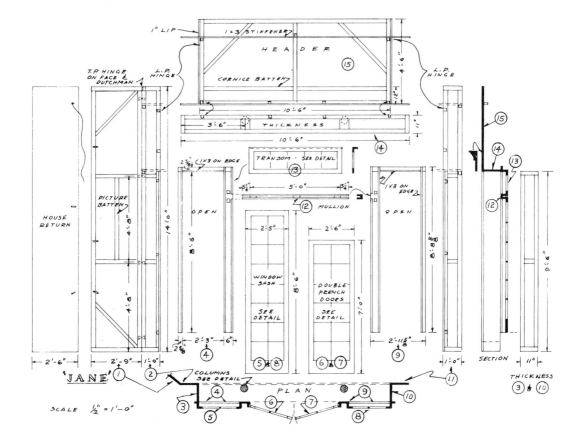

### Figure 5–16
### Technical Drafting Symbols

The drafting symbols are grouped into four areas related to the
(a) framing,
(b) joining,
(c) stiffening and bracing, and
(d) the rigging of framed scenery to fly. Flat scenery framing or rear elevations symbols include
    (1) framing layout,
    (2) brace and toggle rail,
    (3) keystone and corner blocks,
    (4) change of material.
Framed scenery joining techniques and hardware symbols include
    (5) tight pin hinge,
    (6) loose pin hinge,
    (7) stop block,
    (8) stop cleat,
    (9) lashline in corner block,
    (10) lashline eye, and
    (11) lash cleat.
Stiffening and bracing framed scenery symbols are
    (12) loose pin stiffener (horizontal 1 × 3 on edge),
    (13) stage brace cleat,
    (14) keeper hook, and
    (15) vertical LPH brace or folding jack.
Rigging framed scenery to hang symbols include
    (16) top hangers iron,
    (17) bottom hanger iron,
    (18) hinged foot iron,
    (19) rigid foot iron,
    (20) ceiling plate, and
    (21) picture hook and socket.

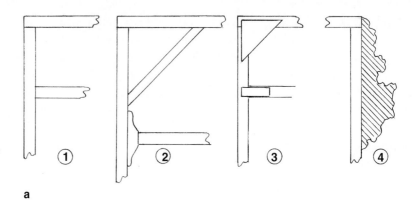

a

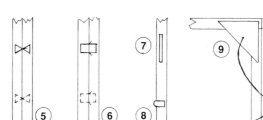

b

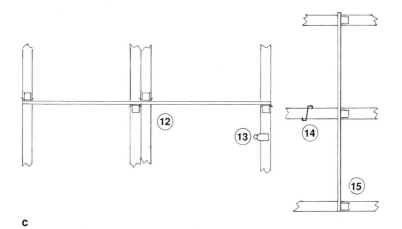

c

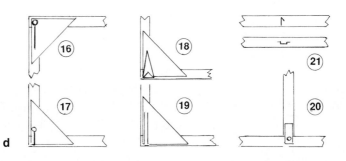

d

need a construction drawing for the occasional unusual piece of scenery, while inexperienced help would need every piece of scenery detailed (Figure 5–15). As can be seen, rear elevations employ many symbols to indicate joining hardware and hinging and bracing techniques, all of which are a part of technical planning. The symbols illustrated in Figure 5–16 will mean more after a study of scenery construction and tools in Chapters 6 and 7.

Three-dimensional pieces such as fireplaces, doors, steps, and rocks are not clearly explained in a rear elevation. They are built by combining sectional views with designer's front and side elevations. The sectional view not only shows the internal structure but helps to explain the contour of the object. Irregular forms, of course, may require many sections. Very special shapes or profiles are often drawn at full scale to serve as a pattern.

## TECHNICAL DRAFTING SYMBOLS

Line weights and symbols used in technical drafting are slightly different from those used by the scene designer. The need for accuracy and detailed information requires precise drafting and uniform standards. In an effort to conform more closely to ANSI (American National Standards Institute) standards for engineering drafting, technical drafting for the theatre is limited to two line weights: *thin* and *thick*. These thicknesses are fixed for all drawings. USITT's Graphic Standard Board recommends the following thicknesses for technical drafting with pencil: 0.3mm for a thin line, and 0.5mm for a thick line.

A concession is made for the possible need of a heavy-weight line by supplying an *extra-thick* or double-thick line for section outline. A comparison of line thicknesses and symbols can be seen in Figure 5–6. Other technical drafting symbols more specifically related to the planning of the construction and joining of scenery can be seen in Figure 5–16.

## THE HANGING SECTION AND PLAN

The hanging section is another important part of technical planning. A drawing of hanging scenery is necessary to the designer in planning a multiscene production or a heavy hanging show. The designer soon discovers that flying space is filled very quickly with lighting equipment, traveler tracks, masking curtains, and the like. To avoid a hopeless tangle in the flies, the hanging plot of a heavy show is carefully studied first in plan and section.

The hanging section, which is a sectional view taken vertically through the stage on the center line, is not a working drawing in itself. It provides information that can be used in the floor plan and elevations as working drawings. In addition to taking the guesswork out of vertical masking by checking the extreme vertical sightlines, the hanging section gives an accurate picture of floor-space problems. It shows the upstage and downstage space requirements more clearly than the floor plan that becomes the working drawing (Figure 5–17).

### Figure 5—17
### Section and Hanging Plot

(a) Cross-section of a setting locating line-sets and trim heights. The center line of the floor plan is the cutting plane.
(b) Hanging Plot. A list of working line-sets along the center line of a half plan.

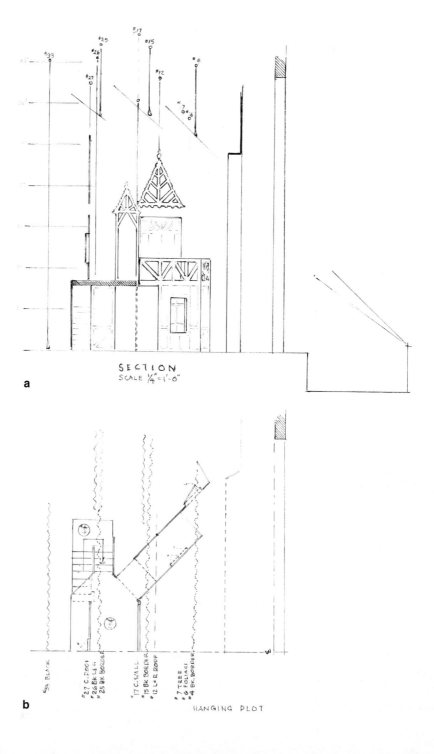

SECTION
SCALE ¼"=1'-0"

a

HANGING PLOT

b

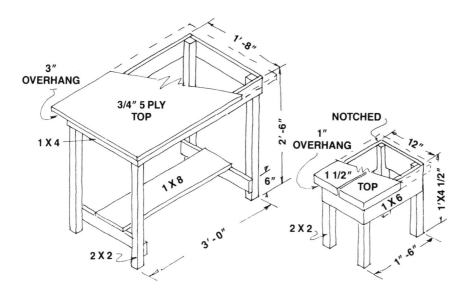

Figure 5—18
Free-hand Pictorial Drawings

Dimensioned free-hand isometric drawings and simple furniture. If an object is simple in form, a pictorial drawing with dimensions can serve as a working drawing. There is enough information provided in this type of drawing to allow the carpenter to begin building immediately. A more complicated object would need additional views.

If a show is extremely heavy it may require a separate hanging plan to indicate the disposition of all scenery that is to be flown. To keep the plan from becoming confusing, most of the scenery on the floor is not shown. The hanging plan may be very general and schematic or quite detailed, depending on the proportion of the rigging, the theatre, and the type of show. For a wing-and-backdrop type of production, for example, it is little more than a listing of drops in the order they will hang and the numbering of the act and scene in which they will work. A more complicated hanging plan would indicate the exact positions of spot lines and extra rigging.

Recent engineering developments, allowing a more flexible flying system and gridiron design than the existing pin-and-rail and counterweight methods, indicate a time in the future when the hanging plan will be a required drawing for every show.

## PLANNING PROPERTIES

The designer is responsible for the selection of properties, for the design of specially built pieces of furniture, and for the general arrangement of properties in the setting.

In planning the properties, the designer's chief concern is to coordinate design needs with those of the director. A meeting of minds can be achieved easily if the designer can show by sketches, clippings, or photographs what is planned and indicate by means of a plan the size and position of set properties as they appear in the setting.

The construction of a special prop, like any three-dimensional piece of scenery, would require some sort of working drawing. The usual plan showing front and side views can be used, or, if the piece is not too complicated, a dimensioned pictorial drawing will serve as a working drawing (Figure 5–18).

Again, the designer will find it wise to study all the important details at full scale.

## PICTORIAL DRAWINGS

The designer's sketch is a type of pictorial drawing, but because it is in perspective it cannot be used as a working drawing. But imagine a pictorial drawing with the edges of the receding surfaces not converging and the sides not foreshortened. Such a drawing can be drawn to scale and used as a supplementary view to the working drawings. The lack of perspective makes

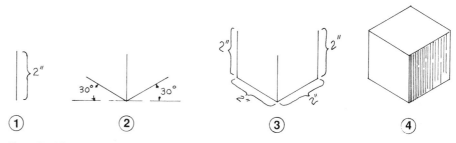

### Figure 5—19
Construction of the Isometric Drawing

The object is a two-inch cube.
(1) Vertical axis, the nearest corner of the cube.
(2) Slanted axes, right and left.
(3) Slanted lines and uprights drawn to scale.
(4) The completed isometric drawing of the cube.

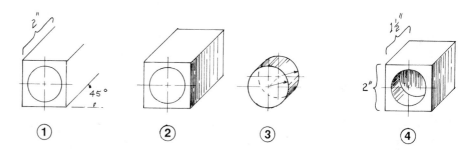

### Figure 5—20
Construction of the Oblique Drawing

(1) The principal face with slant line drawn to the right or left. All the lines are drawn to a scale.
(2) The completed oblique drawing.
(3) An oblique drawing of a circular disk. The center of the circle of the thickness is set to the right of the oblique line.
(4) A cabinet drawing. All slanted lines are drawn at a reduced scale to minimize the distorted look of a regular oblique drawing.

it possible to draw to scale, although the view may have a distorted mechanical appearance.

The two basic kinds of pictorials are the isometric and the oblique drawings. Their difference is dependent on the angle of the view. The isometric drawing represents an object seen from one corner and slightly above (Figure 5–19). An oblique drawing shows the object as seen opposite one face with the side angled off to the right or left (Figure 5–20).

The term *isometric*, meaning "equal measure" (as compared to the foreshortened distances or unequal measure of perspective), accurately describes its appearance. An isometric drawing has three axes to represent the principal planes of the object. The first is a vertical line to indicate all the upright edges; second, a slanted line to the right, 30 degrees to the horizontal, for the horizontal edges of the right plane; and third, a 30-degree line slanted to the left to represent the horizontal edges of the planes to the left. These lines, and all lines parallel to them, are known as *isometric lines*. Conversely, lines that are not parallel to any of the three axes are *nonisometric lines*. Heights and distances can be measured on isometric lines, but a nonisometric line cannot be drawn to scale (Figure 5–19).

Because irregular edges, curves, and angles are distorted in an isometric view, it may be desirable to change the direction of the view to show them at a better vantage. By moving around the object until the complicated surface is parallel to the plane of the paper, or frontal position, it is possible to see the irregular edge or curve without distortion. A view from this direction is an *oblique* drawing.

The same general pictorial characteristics are present in the oblique drawing as in the isometric, with the exception of a more pronounced distortion

**Figure 5–21**
A Cabinet Drawing

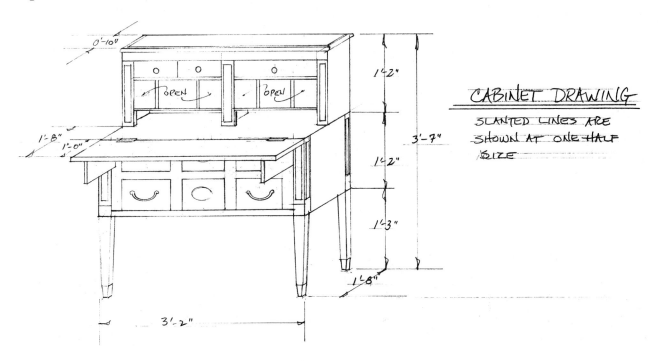

CABINET DRAWING
SLANTED LINES ARE
SHOWN AT ONE HALF
SIZE

in appearance. Because of the frontal position of one of the principal planes, two of the oblique axes are at right angles to each other. The angle of the third axis, representing the plane of the sides, may vary from 30 to 45 degrees to the horizontal. It can be drawn either to the right or left, and slanted either up or down (Figure 5–20). By placing the side that contains the irregular outlines, angles, or curves in the frontal position, drafting time can be saved and the appearance of the view made more attractive.

To reduce the distortion and improve the looks of the oblique drawing, the draftsman sometimes uses a *cabinet drawing*. It is constructed with the complicated face parallel to the picture plane—like the oblique—but dis-

### Figure 5–22
#### Pictorial Drawings

(a) An exploded isometric drawing to show how certain pieces of scenery fit together.
(b) Isometric drawing used to explain a complicated pivoting movement.
(c) An oblique drawing of a decorative bracket.
(d) An isometric drawing using a horizontal axis instead of the usual vertical axis.

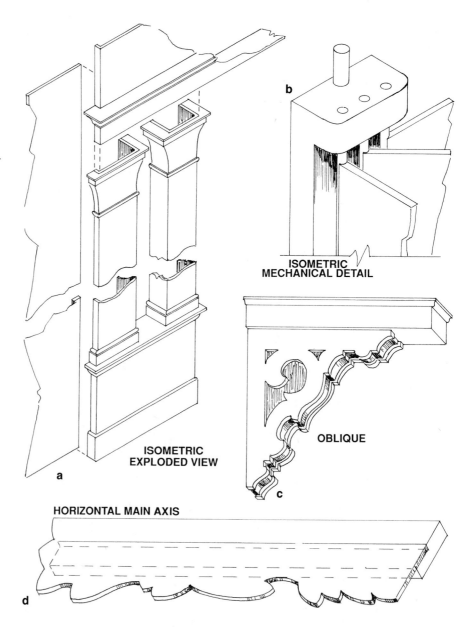

**b**

ISOMETRIC
MECHANICAL DETAIL

ISOMETRIC
EXPLODED VIEW

**a**

OBLIQUE

**c**

HORIZONTAL MAIN AXIS

**d**

tances measured parallel to the angled axis are reduced in scale. A ratio of 2:3 or 3:4 between the frontal planes and the angled axis produces a pleasing proportion. By always labeling the cabinet drawing and giving the ratio of the measurements on the angled axis, the possibility of it being mistaken for an oblique drawing is avoided (Figure 5–21).

Pictorial drawings may be dimensioned like a working drawing. The technique, however, is slightly different. Instead of being perpendicular to the surface, the extension lines are drawn as extensions of one of the isometric planes, and the dimension line is parallel to the object rather than perpendicular to the extension line. To help give the feeling that the dimension is in one of the isometric planes, the figures are slanted with the extension lines. If the object is not too complicated, a dimensioned pictorial drawing can be used as a working drawing.

Besides their use as working drawings, pictorials are frequently used as supplementary views to explain bits of complicated assembly or mechanical detail (Figure 5–22).

# PART II

# EXECUTING THE DESIGN

# SCENE DESIGN AND TECHNICAL PRODUCTION

# 6

Before the ideas of the designer can reach the stage, the designs, in the form of working drawings, have to go through a preparation or construction period. The scaled model is transformed into full-scale elements of scenery, the graded wash in the sketch becomes a carefully painted backdrop, and the insignificant spot on the elevation is fashioned into a pointed bit of detail. Step by step, all the scenery is fitted together on the stage, under lights, and in final form.

Although the study of technical production is placed here in the logical order of the development of a stage setting, it also—paradoxically—represents knowledge a scene designer should possess *before* beginning a design. For this reason a study of technical production is a necessary part of a scene designer's training and background. As the architect is familiar with building techniques and materials, so should the scene designer be acquainted with methods of constructing and handling scenery as well as the uses of theatrical materials and techniques. A logical place to begin is with a survey of the tools and materials that are used to make scenery and an examination of the working procedures of a scenery shop.

## THE SCENERY SHOP

Scenery is frequently built and painted under the adverse condition of an inadequate shop. Designers soon learn that an ill-equipped shop with sparse working space puts a limit on the kind and amount of scenery that can be built and painted. Occasionally they find themselves in the enviable position of being able to plan their own shop or at least asked to specify the space requirements of the ideal scenery shop. In preparation for such an occasion, the designer should have some knowledge of the space requirements and layout of a good scenery shop.

## SPACE REQUIREMENTS

The overall area of a scenery shop depends on four things: the size of the stage the shop is to serve; the location of the shop in relation to the stage and storage areas; the number and kinds of productions to be produced in an average season; and the nature of the shop's working procedure and personnel.

The size of the stage, or in some cases several stages, which the shop is to serve has a direct bearing on the size of the shop itself. A large stage requires large elements of scenery. A shop serving a large stage, of course, needs the space to execute the expansive proportions of such scenery. In a similar manner, the large amounts of scenery necessary to supply more than one stage would influence the size of the shop. The scale of the scenery may be smaller, but a shop serving several stages must be arranged to handle quantities of scenery.

The location of the scenery shop also affects its size. For example, a shop near the stage could utilize stage space for the construction of scenery and thereby supplement the shop area. On the other hand, a shop in a remote location needs additional space for the storage of scenery and properties as well as the necessary construction and painting areas. Although a distant shop has the disadvantage of causing the additional handling of scenery from the shop to the stage and back again, it does have the decided advantage of being able to operate free of preperformance uses of the stage. A shop adjacent to the stage is doomed to conflict with rehearsals and performances, which will render it inoperative a major portion of the time.

The number and kinds of productions also help determine the space requirements of a scenery shop. A repertory company, for example, would require enormous storage space to retain the scenery of numerous productions intact, while perhaps only building one or two new productions a year. An opera or musical-comedy production group would have a greater demand for scenery than would a company that mounts intimately scaled productions.

The final consideration that has some influence on the overall size of the shop is the shop procedure and personnel. The nature of the shop's personnel and working hours may vary from a staff of full-time professionals to scattered groups of part-time student apprentices or volunteers. A small, highly skilled staff working steadily can use building space more efficiently than large sporadic groups requiring sufficient space to do many separate jobs at once. A further evaluation of the space requirements resulting from shop procedure includes an analysis of the areas of work, tools and equipment, and materials of the average scenery shop.

## WORK AREAS

The shop is divided into areas related to the various steps in the process of building and painting. These areas are organized for the following functions:

(1) storage of materials and tools, (2) the cutting and working of lumber (boring, cutting, and so on), (3) the framing and covering of basic units of scenery, (4) the trial assembly of basic units into portions or all of the complete setting, (5) a metalworking area, (6) a plastic-working area, (7) a property preparation area, (8) and finally an area for the painting of scenery (Figure 6–1).

## Figure 6–1
### Scenery Shop Layout

Represented is a schematic plan of a scenery shop and related areas for a modest producing theatre. The basic areas are:
(1) Scenery shop including areas for the cutting and framing of scenic units as well as tool storage and technical director's office. The heavy tools are a radial saw, table saw, band saw, drill press, sander and two movable templates.
(2) Area for the construction and maintenance of set properties containing a spray-paint booth, wood lathe, work bench and low furniture work-table.
(3) Metalworking shop with forced ventilation. In the room are a welding table and electric welder, work bench with vise and emery wheel, an anvil, gas welding tanks, various cutting tools, sheet metal brake and metal lathe.
(4) Assembly and painting area which has enough space and height for a trial assembly of all or a portion of a set. There is enough floor space to stretch a drop as well as a vertical paint frame. Paint storage is in adjacent areas.
Overhead and off the balcony are:
(5) Sewing room for draperies, drops and gauzes. On the balcony are stored draperies and drops.
(6) Plastic working area which is well ventilated. Vacuum forming, blue printing and area for the construction of small properties are located here.

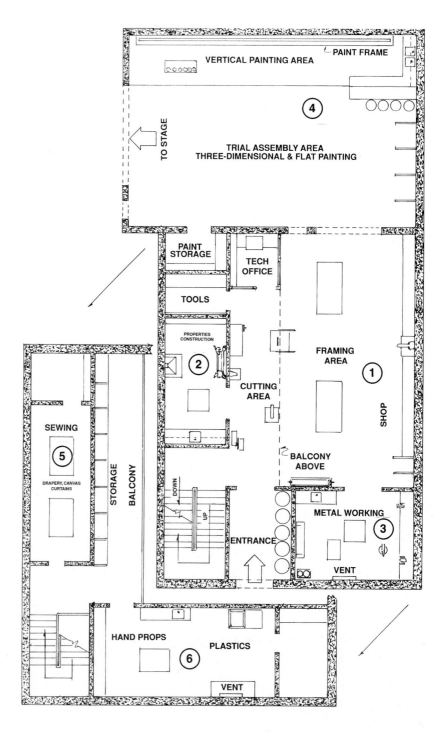

## SCENERY MATERIALS AND TOOLS

An ideal scenery shop is well stocked with appropriate materials and tools. Although some materials will be mentioned in relation to the construction of certain types of scenery, it may be wise to consider briefly all the materials that are used for making scenery. To compile a comprehensive list is, of course, next to impossible, because designers and technicians are constantly bringing new materials into the theatre every day as well as discovering new uses for old materials.

Materials can be divided and classified into the following groups of similar functions:

1. structural (lumber and metal)
2. cover stock (fabric and hard surfaces)
3. hardware (joining and stage hardware)
4. rigging (rope, cable, wire, and chain)
5. paints and related supplies (to be discussed in Chapter 9)

## WOOD AS SCENERY MATERIAL

Lumber is the principal framing and structural material, supplemented and reinforced on occasion by structural steel, pipe, and aluminum. The sharp reduction of logging on federal land in the Northwest, for environmental reasons, has reduced the national supply of white pine, resulting in higher lumber prices. Although selective cutting on private lands has partially replenished supplies, prices still remain high. Because the degree of availability and cost of lumber vary from region to region throughout the country, it is difficult to formulate a single solution for all.

*Recycled wood* is one source, although it does involve extra handling costs or a shop equipped to resize salvaged lumber. There are some successful attempts to create *synthetic wood* of recycled plastic grocery bags and salvaged wood chips (Trex, by Mobil Oil Corporation). Some shops save money by buying large quantities of random length, wide board pine, which is stored to be cut and sized for framing later; others pay the market price. Some have turned to lightweight structural steel framing. Until a nationwide solution evolves, lumber remains the chief structural material, with steel and a changing design philosophy as a future alternative.

To fill the needs of scenic construction, lumber must be lightweight, strong, straight, and inexpensive. The best combination of weight and strength is found in white pine. Although woods such as redwood and spruce are lighter, they do not have the strength and they tend to splinter and split. The hardwoods are stronger, of course, but weigh and cost too much.

Lumber selection and construction techniques vary from region to region. The use of plywood as a cover stock for framed scenery construction, for example, permits the framing stock to be of less expensive woods such as spruce or fir.

## SHOP WORK AREAS

1. *Storage.* Within all shops it is necessary to provide space for the storage of materials and small tools. This means lumber racks, pipe and structural steel racks, paint bins, and hardware cabinets. Provisions should also be made for the storage of brushes near the painting area and for small tools near the woodworking area.

2. *The woodworking area.* This second area is related to the next step in building scenery. Here the lumber is worked (bored, planed, jigsawed, and so on). Within the area there should be space for the large power tools such as table saws, band saws, drill presses, and the necessary workbenches. A large shop would include an air compressor and storage tank for pneumatic tools. A heavy-duty compressor can also serve the painting area and property shop.

   Careful consideration should be given to the lighting of the woodworking area as well as the other work areas. The location of power outlets convenient to the working positions of power tools in all areas is essential.

3. *The framing area.* The framing and covering of scenery can take place in the center of the shop on template benches (Figure 6–2), but the joining or hinging of units of scenery together must take place in a larger area.

4. *The assembly area.* This fourth space ideally should be as large as the stage area and high enough to stand the scenery upright. Besides being a trial assembly area, its floor can serve as a space to lay out or "loft" full-scale patterns of irregularly shaped scenery as well as flat painting on the floor.

5. *The metalworking area.* This area should ideally be near the assembly area, since some metal work is used for the bracing of scenery or the support of weight-bearing forms. This is where metal will be cut, bent, and joined (bolted or welded). The welding area should be well ventilated and on a concrete floor.

### GRADES AND SIZES OF LUMBER

Lumber is classified at the yard into quality groups. The straightness of grain and freedom from knots determine the quality. Hence, clear white pine is of the highest quality. It is further classified as to its expected use. A board that is to become trim or a finished surface is of a higher quality than a structural member hidden from view.

The finishing lumber or *select grades* are designated by the letters A, B, C, and D. Hence B-select or better is a high-grade pine. C-select is used in the construction of paneled doors, window sashes, turned work, and architectural moldings.

6. *The plastic-working area.* The use of plastic in all forms (foam casting, thermoplastic, and the sculpturing of foam) needs a separate space to work. Because of the fumes and dust, ventilation is important. Occasionally, plastic-working can be done in a part of the property area.

7. *Property preparation area.* The most frequently neglected area in shop planning is a space to build properties. The altering, repairing, upholstering, and finishing of furniture is a specialized operation that requires different tools, materials, and paints from those found in the scenery shop. A property shop does not need a lot of space. It should, however, be an area near but separated from the dust and confusion of the scenery shop and the splatter of flying paint from the painting area.

8. *The painting area.* Another important space in the shop, the painting area should be convenient to a sink, gas or electric burners, and the paint bins. Vertical painting, which occupies the least amount of floor space, requires overhead clearance or sufficient height to stand the scenery upright. The simplest vertical painting method is to mount the scenery on a fixed frame against a wall and paint from a rolling platform or boomerang. The most convenient method is the use of a counterweighted, vertical paint frame, which lowers into a well, or raises off the floor. The painting is done from different levels or decks (see Chapter 9).

   A more precarious method is to raise and lower a painting scaffolding in front of a fixed frame. In addition to being laborious and dangerous, the scaffolding has the added inconvenience of usually being some distance from the sink, burner, and paint supplies.

   With even the best equipment for vertical painting, it is sometimes necessary to paint horizontally on the floor. Certain painting techniques require horizontal painting. The floor of the assembly area or the stage floor (if stage use can be worked into the production schedule) often serves this purpose.

The *common grades* are numbered 1 to 5. They are not intended for a finished surface although many times 1- and 2-common are used as knotty pine paneling. In general, 2-common is the usual framing material for scenery unless the theatre is in an area of the country where the better grades of pine are available at reasonable prices. Assuming a long run, a higher quality might be used, but at considerable expense.

The *stock sizes* of lumber refer to the rough-cut size and not to the finished dimension after the wood has been dressed (planed or smooth on all sides). Thus 1 by 3 is really $\frac{3}{4}$ inch by $2\frac{1}{2}$ inches. The longest stock length is 16 feet, although longer lengths can be obtained on special order.

Because lumber is cut in a variety of widths and thicknesses, it has a unit of measurement—the *board-foot,* common to all sizes. A board-foot is a 1-foot-square unit measuring 1 inch in thickness. A piece of lumber of any size can be reduced from its linear dimensions into board-feet. A 16-foot length of 1 by 3, for example, contains 4 board-feet. Depending on the region, lumber is priced either by the board-foot or by the linear foot.

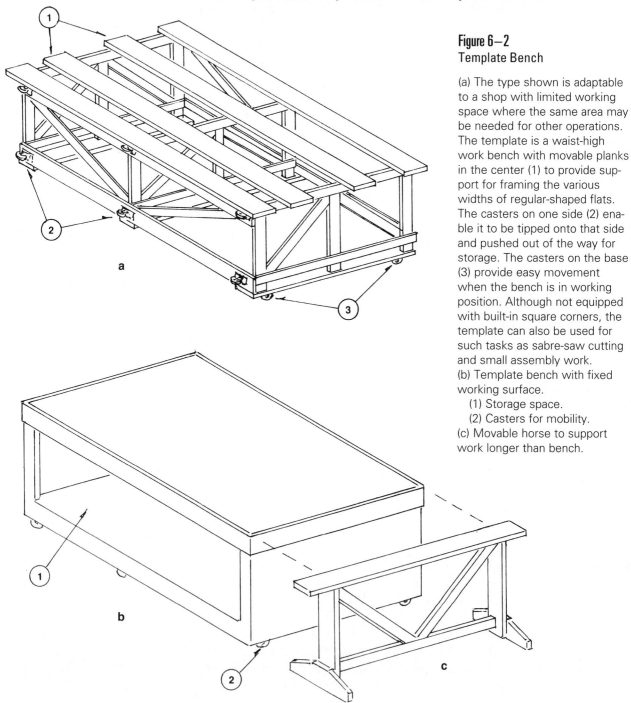

a

b

c

### Figure 6–2
### Template Bench

(a) The type shown is adaptable to a shop with limited working space where the same area may be needed for other operations. The template is a waist-high work bench with movable planks in the center (1) to provide support for framing the various widths of regular-shaped flats. The casters on one side (2) enable it to be tipped onto that side and pushed out of the way for storage. The casters on the base (3) provide easy movement when the bench is in working position. Although not equipped with built-in square corners, the template can also be used for such tasks as sabre-saw cutting and small assembly work.
(b) Template bench with fixed working surface.
   (1) Storage space.
   (2) Casters for mobility.
(c) Movable horse to support work longer than bench.

Special shapes like "rounds" are stocked in diameters from $\frac{3}{4}$ inch to $1\frac{1}{2}$ inches and sometimes as large as 3 inches in diameter. Dowel is available in $\frac{1}{8}$- to 1-inch diameters and 3-foot lengths made of maple and birch.

Other special shapes are stock moldings, which are made in a great variety of sizes and contours. Before specifying moldings, the designer should

**Figure 6–3**
Stock Lumber and Molding Shapes

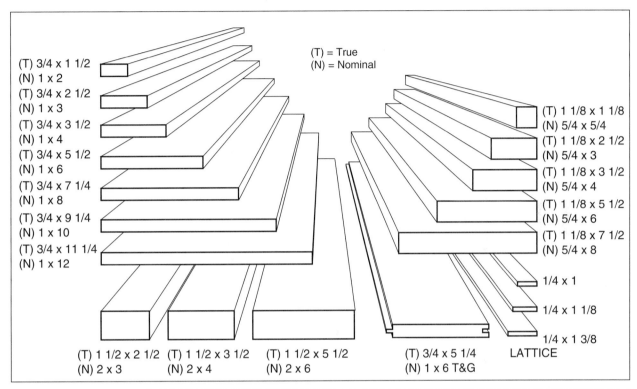

(T) = True
(N) = Nominal

(T) 3/4 x 1 1/2
(N) 1 x 2
(T) 3/4 x 2 1/2
(N) 1 x 3
(T) 3/4 x 3 1/2
(N) 1 x 4
(T) 3/4 x 5 1/2
(N) 1 x 6
(T) 3/4 x 7 1/4
(N) 1 x 8
(T) 3/4 x 9 1/4
(N) 1 x 10
(T) 3/4 x 11 1/4
(N) 1 x 12

(T) 1 1/8 x 1 1/8
(N) 5/4 x 5/4
(T) 1 1/8 x 2 1/2
(N) 5/4 x 3
(T) 1 1/8 x 3 1/2
(N) 5/4 x 4
(T) 1 1/8 x 5 1/2
(N) 5/4 x 6
(T) 1 1/8 x 7 1/2
(N) 5/4 x 8

1/4 x 1
1/4 x 1 1/8
1/4 x 1 3/8
LATTICE

(T) 1 1/2 x 2 1/2    (T) 1 1/2 x 3 1/2    (T) 1 1/2 x 5 1/2    (T) 3/4 x 5 1/4
(N) 2 x 3           (N) 2 x 4           (N) 2 x 6           (N) 1 x 6 T&G

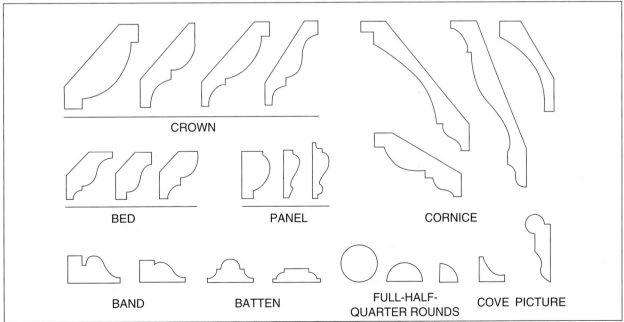

CROWN

BED          PANEL          CORNICE

BAND          BATTEN          FULL-HALF-          COVE  PICTURE
                            QUARTER ROUNDS

check local suppliers, because names and shapes vary throughout the country. A few of the most frequently used moldings are illustrated in Figure 6–3, along with the stock lumber sizes.

## WOODWORKING TOOLS AND EQUIPMENT

The tools of a scenery shop are primarily for woodworking, with limited provisions for the working of metal. To build scenery it is necessary to cut, pare or shape, bore, and join the wood. The tools to work the wood are either hand tools for limited and special work or power tools for mass production and precision work. The working and joining of wood, however, is always preceded by careful measuring and marking.

### MEASURING AND MARKING TOOLS

Tools for measuring and marking are used not only with each technique of working wood but also in every step in the construction and assembly of the completed setting (Figure 6–4). Almost all mistakes in building are directly traceable to wrong measurements or a misinterpreted mark. The importance of accurate measurements cannot be overstressed.

Some of the tools are obviously for measuring only (6-foot rule and 50-foot tape) and others are made specifically for marking (tri-square, bevel gauge, scribe, spirit level, spline, and center square). A few tools are, however, designed for both measuring and marking.

The *combination square,* with its adjustable sliding bar, is calibrated for measuring as well as establishing a marking guide for 90-degree and 45-degree angles.

The *framing square* with calibrated edges is a useful tool in marking the angle cut of a stair carriage and for establishing a right angle for framing.

The *marking gauge* is calibrated to mark for a rip cut, an operation that can be duplicated by the combination square.

Within the group of marking tools, the *tri-square* is calibrated for limited measuring although its chief function is as a marking guide for a 90-degree angle cut. The *bar* or *beam* holding the trammel points is sometimes calibrated to measure the radius of the circle or arc it is to swing. The other tools in this group serve as marking guides only.

The *bevel gauge* is designed for transferring or saving a predetermined angle or bevel.

The *scribe* can follow an irregular surface with one point and scratch or mark the outline of the surface at a fixed distance with the other point.

The *spline* or *spring curve* is used to mark an irregular curve, or to plot a curved edge in full-scale lofting.

The *spirit level* establishes a true vertical or horizontal, and the *center square* locates the unmarked center of a circle or round stock.

The *chalk line* is for snapping an extremely long straight line that may be used as a framing guide, as a reference line for full-scale lofting, or as a guide for painting.

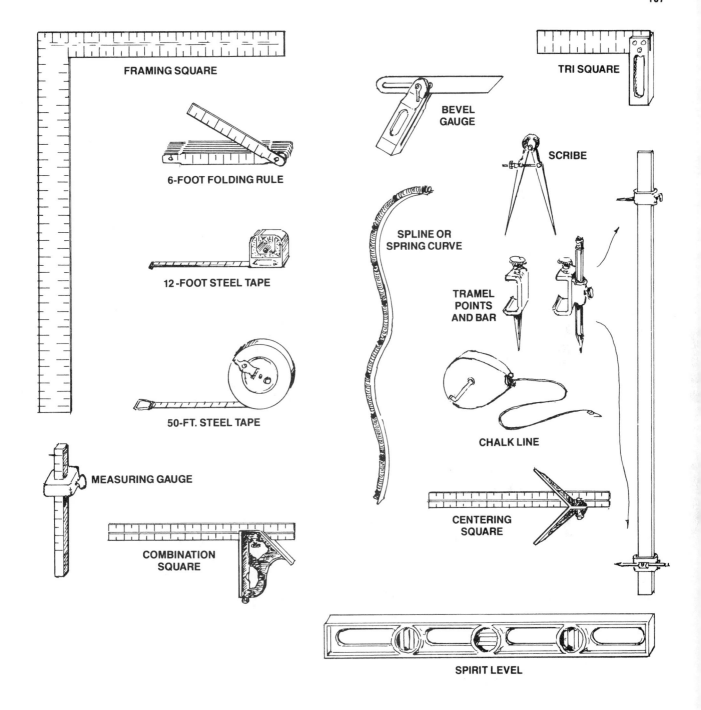

FRAMING SQUARE

6-FOOT FOLDING RULE

12-FOOT STEEL TAPE

50-FT. STEEL TAPE

MEASURING GAUGE

COMBINATION SQUARE

TRI SQUARE

BEVEL GAUGE

SCRIBE

SPLINE OR SPRING CURVE

TRAMEL POINTS AND BAR

CHALK LINE

CENTERING SQUARE

SPIRIT LEVEL

Figure 6–4
Woodworking Measuring Tools

## WOOD-CUTTING TOOLS

The chief cutting tool is the *saw*. Of the many saws in the scenery shop some are hand saws, others power saws that are hand-held, and the remaining are fixed power saws. Figure 6–5 illustrates the various types of saws as discussed on the following pages.

**Basic Hand Saws**     The specific work a saw can do depends on the shape of the tooth (pointed or chisel), the set of the tooth (flare of every other

**Figure 6–5**
Wood Cutting Tools

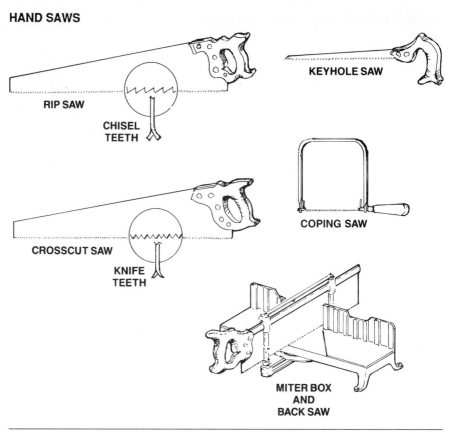

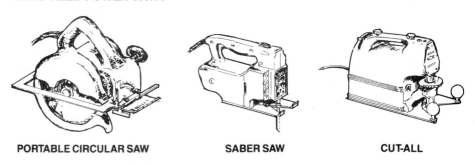

tooth in the opposite direction), and the tooth count (number of teeth per inch).

Because wood has a grain, which is the alternating density of the fibers within its structure, it requires a different kind of saw to cut *across* the grain than to cut *with* the grain. The teeth of a *crosscut saw* are sharp and straight to cut through the wood fibers, while the teeth of the *ripsaw* are angled and flat-edged like a chisel to chip the wood with the grain. The ripsaw has the widest set and the lowest tooth count (6 to 8 teeth per inch). The crosscut saw has a tooth count of 8, 10, or as many as 12 teeth per inch.

**FIXED POWER SAWS**

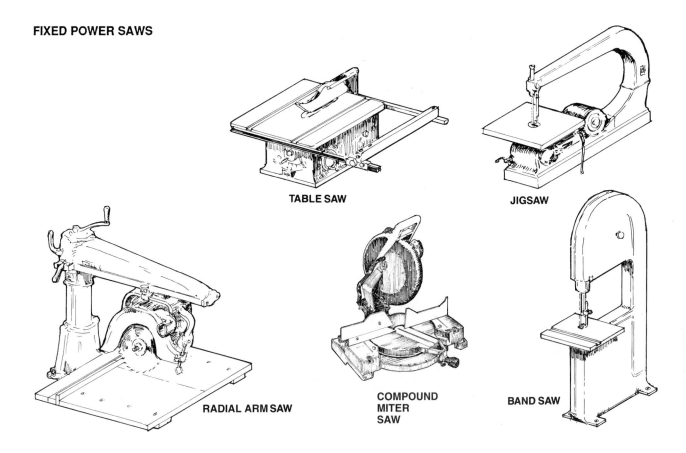

TABLE SAW

JIGSAW

RADIAL ARM SAW

COMPOUND MITER SAW

BAND SAW

The set of a saw is the degree of bend every other tooth has away from the norm of the saw blade. The set of the saw teeth keep the saw from binding because the width of the cut is wider than the blade. When a saw has lost its set, it begins to bind in the cut (see the accompanying Safety Practice box).

An angled cut or miter can be cut freehand with a crosscut saw, or it can be accurately cut in a miter box with a *backsaw*. The backsaw, with a high tooth count (10 to 12 teeth per inch), is a stiff-bladed saw with a straight back that serves as a guide in the miter box. It is extremely useful in mitering moldings for a cornice, picture frame, or panel.

**Hand Tools for Irregular Cutting**    Not all cutting in the making of scenery is straight-line cutting. As a matter of fact, a high percentage of the cutting is irregular or scroll work. Cutouts and profile edges require the greatest amount of scroll work.

A hand saw to cut on an irregular line must necessarily have a small blade to be able to turn and follow the irregular line. The *coping saw* has a high tooth count of 12 per inch to produce a smoothly cut edge. It also has a removable blade for inside cuts. The deep throat of the frame that holds the blade allows the saw to reach well into the work.

The *keyhole saw* with a tooth count of 8 to 10 is made for heavy, coarse, and fast work. The small blade, although not as small as the coping saw, allows irregular cutting beyond the limits a coping saw can reach.

**Hand-Held Power Saws**     The *portable circular saw* is designed to be brought to the work rather than for bringing the work to the saw. It can be used to advantage as a ripsaw or crosscut saw on partially completed units of scenery. Because of its light weight and small blade, it is limited as to depth of cut and accuracy. It is, however, a useful tool to have in a busy shop.

For irregular cutting, the *saber saw*, which is a portable jigsaw, does not limit the size of the work. It is a very versatile tool for scroll cutting at any stage of assembly.

The cut-awl, which is designed for light, detailed cutting, works best on profile and composition board. It also requires a padded bench or table for satisfactory results.

**Fixed Power Saws**     Power tools made for straight-line cutting are the table saw, radial arm saw, and portable circular saw. Each may be fitted with a rip, crosscut, or combination blade for specific work.

A 10-inch, tilting-arbor, 1-horsepower *table saw* with miter gauge and rip fence is a basic piece of equipment. It is a heavy enough tool to do precision work in quantity. It miters and rips with ease and accuracy.

A 10- to 12-inch 1-horsepower *radial arm saw* provides the necessary power for cutting heavy lumber. Its pullover action above the wood and long table make it an accurate crosscut and limited mitering tool. Because the guide fence becomes inaccurate from repeated crosscutting, it is not a very accurate ripping tool.

**The Power Compound Miter Saw**    A miter cut can be defined as any cut across the grain of the wood (as opposed to a bevel cut, which is in the same direction as the grain). A simple miter is a method of turning a corner with two bands of wood or molding. Each piece of wood is cut at an angle that bisects that of the corner. If the corner, for example, is a right angle (90 degrees), the molding is cut at an angle of 45 degrees.

When a molding changes planes as well as turning a corner (such as the molding on the gable end of a house that turns to follow the eaves of the side of the house), it is a *compound miter.* A simple miter can be cut on the radial arm saw, table saw, or miter box. However, to cut a compound miter, the saw blade has to be tilted as well as angled. A compound miter saw has these features.

The *power compound miter saw* is a very specialized power tool, and some models can be quite expensive. It does however, take the guesswork out of cutting a miter.

**Power Tools for Irregular Cutting**    Power tools that speed up the production of scroll work are the band saw and jigsaw. The *band saw* with its continuous blade is limited to outside cutting and to work as large as the depth of its throat. A band saw with a 20-inch throat will serve the average need of a scenery shop if it is supplemented with other equipment to do inside cutting.

The *jigsaw* with its removable straight blade and deep throat is made for both inside and outside scroll cutting.

## BASIC WOOD-PARING TOOLS

The simplest tool for freehand shaping of wood is the *chisel.* Although the hand chisel cannot compare in speed and accuracy to power tools, it can be used to do a limited amount of shaping and notching of wood. It is an excellent tool to clean up a power-cut dado, rabbet, mortise, or routed area. With skilled handling, it can, if necessary, make any of these cuts itself. A set of chisels would include a variety of widths from $\frac{1}{4}$ inch to $1\frac{1}{4}$ inches. The chisel and the other paring tools described here are shown in Figure 6–6.

The paring edge of the chisel is shown in the inset of Figure 6–6. The top bevel is forged, but the lower bevel is sharpened into a cutting edge. Note that the angle is about 45 degrees. When the edge becomes dull or nicked it can be resharpened by first reshaping the edge on the coarse emery wheel and then grinding a new cutting surface at 45 degrees. The sharpening is finished on an oil stone.

The *drawknife* is not a precision tool. It is useful to pare away waste or roughly shape a surface before planing.

The *smoothing plane* can pare a surface to an accurate dimension. It is made to smooth with the grain of the wood, in contrast to the small *block plane,*

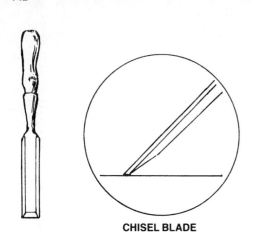

CHISEL

CHISEL BLADE

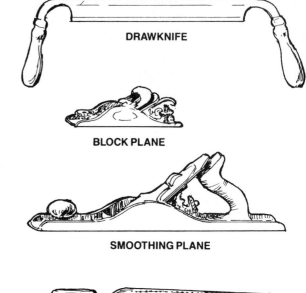

DRAWKNIFE

BLOCK PLANE

SMOOTHING PLANE

SURFORM

RASP

**HAND PARING TOOLS**

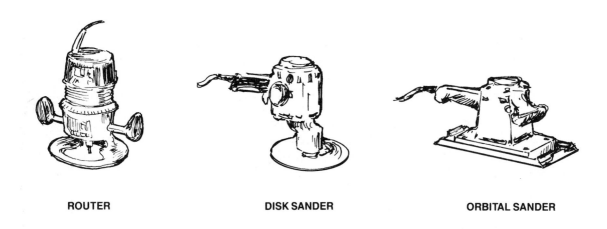

ROUTER

DISK SANDER

ORBITAL SANDER

**HAND-HELD POWER SHAPING TOOLS**

**Figure 6—6**
Wood Paring Tools

which works across the grain. The block plane can smooth or shape the end of a board and can be used to correct a bad saw cut or shorten a member to improve a delicate fit.

The *rasp* and *Surform,* a replaceable rasp blade in a holder, are also designed to work across the grain. They can do the same shaping faster than the block plane but leave a rougher finish.

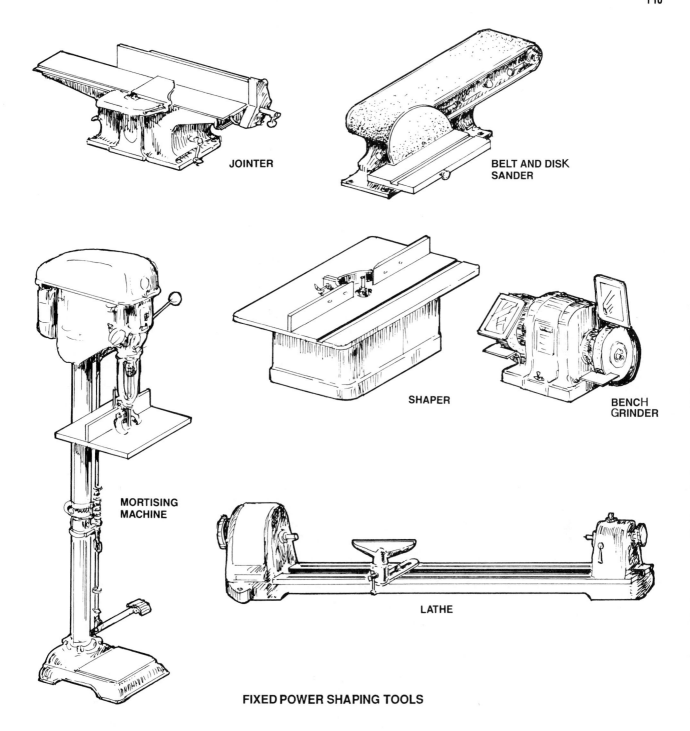

**JOINTER**

**BELT AND DISK SANDER**

**MORTISING MACHINE**

**SHAPER**

**BENCH GRINDER**

**LATHE**

**FIXED POWER SHAPING TOOLS**

## POWER SHAPERS AND SANDERS

Probably the most useful small power tool for shaping is the *router*. In addition to routing to countersink hinges, it can cut tenons, dados, and rabbets. With special bits it can also do a limited amount of molding cutting.

*Portable sanders* are handy tools at the bench or when brought to the work area. The *disk sander* is best to use when smoothing an end cut. With coarse sandpaper it can reshape or round a cut. It is less effective sanding a flat surface because it tends to leave sanding marks.

The *orbital sander* is excellent for smoothing a flat surface. It is lightweight and economical, using a half sheet of regular 9-inch by 11-inch sandpaper. There is also a small, quarter-sheet palm grip orbital sander for finish sanding.

Power tools designed to do various shaping and smoothing operations are limited mostly to special cuts. The *rotary planer* or *joiner*, for example, can smooth a board, size a board by changing the depth of cut, bevel the edge by angling the fence, as well as cut a rabbet on one side of the board.

Likewise, the *rotary shaper* is designed especially to cut moldings. It can cut a variety of moldings by changing or combining different blades.

The *mortising machine*, or mortising attachment for a drill press, with its square chisel, is limited to cutting the deep square hole of a mortise. It is a time-saving tool in a professional scenery shop where there is a lot of mortise-and-tenon joining.

Although mortise-and-tenon joint for the framing of flats is not found in most shops, the *square chisel* is a useful tool. A well-built door, for example, has mortise-and-tenon joint and inset panels.

Some shaping operations can be performed on the table saw and radial arm saw. The circular table saw can be equipped with a dado head, which is a set of special blades to cut a groove. Molding cutters can also be attached to the circular saw for simple molding cutting. The radial arm saw can also be rigged to dado, shape, and rout. Any changeover, of course, takes time and ties up the saw for other uses.

For finished smoothing, a power *belt and disk sander* quickly and accurately smooths the end, edge, or face of a board. In this same category, the *bench grinder* is used to smooth and shape metal as well as sharpen hand tools.

The *wood lathe* is a cylindrical shaping tool. A block of wood is rotated on its long axis and shaped with a chisel which is held on an adjustable rest that can be moved with the work. A baluster or spindle for furniture or stair railing can be turned on this tool.

The *jointer* is a power plane. Its rotating blades can smooth the edge or surface of a board. By setting the fence at an angle, the edge of the board can be planed with an angle.

**BORING TOOLS**

Tools with a cutting edge that revolves about a central axis to cut a circular hole are called boring tools (Figure 6–7). The tool consists of two basic parts: the bit, which is the cutting part of the tool, and the mechanism to rotate the bit.

There is, of course, great variation in the types of bit, depending on the size and depth of the hole, kind of hole (clean bore, taper, ream), and the nature of the material (hardness, thickness). Likewise, the power-providing part of the tool will vary with type of bit used and the speed of rotation necessary to do the work. The types of bit and means of rotation found in the average scenery shop are shown in the box on page 146.

The *auger bit* has a screw lead that, when rotated, pulls the cutting edges of the bit into contact with the wood. The auger bit does not need to rotate

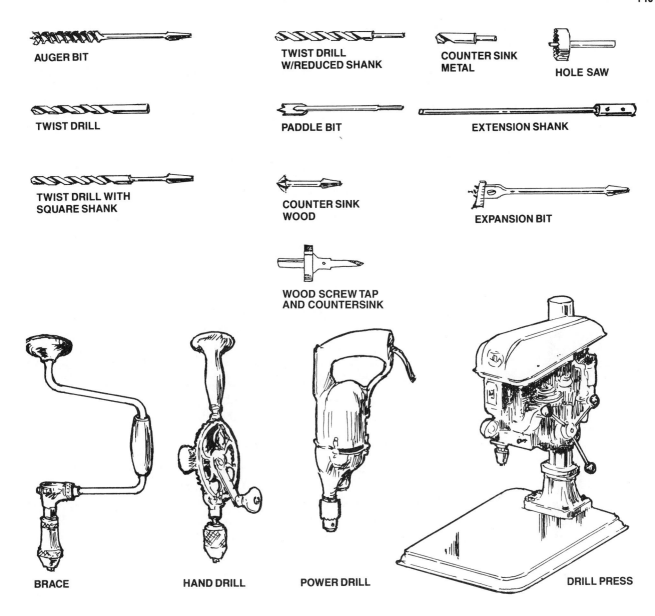

AUGER BIT

TWIST DRILL

TWIST DRILL WITH
SQUARE SHANK

TWIST DRILL
W/REDUCED SHANK

PADDLE BIT

COUNTER SINK
WOOD

WOOD SCREW TAP
AND COUNTERSINK

COUNTER SINK
METAL

HOLE SAW

EXTENSION SHANK

EXPANSION BIT

BRACE

HAND DRILL

POWER DRILL

DRILL PRESS

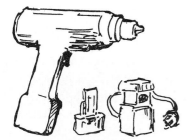

CORDLESS DRILL
W/BATTERY PACK
AND CHARGER

Figure 6—7
Wood Boring Tools

## BORING TOOLS

| Bits | Rotating Tools |
|---|---|
| Auger bit | Brace |
| Twist drill | Hand drill |
| Twist drill (square shank) | Power hand drill |
| Twist drill ($\frac{1}{4}$-inch round shank) | Drill press |
| Paddle bit ($\frac{1}{4}$-inch round shank) | Cordless drill |
| Countersink, wood | |
| Countersink, metal | |
| Hole-saw | |
| Expanding bit | |
| Extension shank | |

at a high speed. It is usually driven with the brace made to receive its square shank. The *brace* is a cranklike form designed to give the carpenter a mechanical advantage rather than to increase the speed of rotation. Augers are manufactured in size differences of $\frac{1}{16}$ inch. They are numbered by sixteenths; thus a $\frac{1}{2}$-inch auger would be a No. 8 bit.

*Twist drills* have no screw lead and depend on speed of rotation and pressure to advance into the material. The *hand drill* is designed to increase the speed of rotation as well as provide some mechanical advantage. The high-speed portable *power hand drill* is excellent for this type of work.

The *spade or paddle bit* is a wood-cutting bit made for high-speed rotation with a small round shank ($\frac{1}{4}$ inch) for the small power drill. The paddle end of the bit varies from $\frac{3}{8}$ inch to $1\frac{1}{4}$ inches in width. The chisel-like edges do the cutting and depend on high speed for accuracy.

Also in the auger bit class is the *expanding bit,* which is adjustable and can bore a hole as large as $1\frac{1}{4}$ inches to $2\frac{1}{2}$ inches in diameter.

The *countersink bit* is used on either wood or metal after the hole has been bored. It enlarges the top of the opening with a beveled cut of sufficient depth to set a flathead screw or bolt flush with the outer surface of the material.

The *hole-saw* is used to cut oversized holes ($1\frac{1}{2}$ inches and more) at high speed. Although faster and cleaner than the expanding bit, it is limited in its depth of cut.

The hex *extension shank* can lengthen the depth of cut of a paddle drill by extending its shank. It is good for drilling the length of a block of wood, for example.

The *drill press,* which is a stationary power drill, has added advantages of such controls as depth of bore and speed variation for precision work. The drill press with a mortising attachment makes a very useful tool in the scenery shop.

The *cordless drill* with rechargeable batteries is useful away from the shop. It can do light work such as drilling to set a screw in a hinge.

## BASIC WOOD CONSTRUCTION TOOLS AND HARDWARE

The fastening of wood to wood is a basic construction technique. Tools are designed to drive or set hardware such as *nails, staples, screws,* or *bolts,* to fasten wood together in a variety of surface-to-surface combinations (see Chapter 7, especially Figure 7–5). Wood is also fastened with glue, either as the primary method or to reinforce the nail, staple, or screw (Figure 6–8).

**Hammers**     The *claw hammer* is used to drive a nail or set a screw. The rounded claw is used to correct mistakes by pulling a misdirected nail.

The *straight claw hammer,* sometimes called the "ripper," provides a straight claw for prying apart joined members.

The *mallet* with a wooden, rubber, plastic, or leatherbound head is not used for heavy driving. It can be used to tap a member into place without damaging the edge of the wood. The mallet is also used with the chisel.

The *magnetic tack hammer* is used primarily in upholstering to attach heavy material and padding to a wooden frame.

**Screwdrivers**     The *ratchet* or *"Yankee" screwdriver* drives the screw by pushing down on the handgrip. It can be reversed to pull out the screw. Straight screwdrivers come in several types for screws with *slotted head, Phillips head, hex head,* or *nut driver.* There are also screwdrivers for *"Robertson"* or recessed square-head screws, which are becoming more and more popular. Their advantage is that the drive doesn't slip and destroy the screw head as it does with the Phillips head.

Most scenery shops now also use power drills or cordless drills to drive screws. These tools use a special (preferably hardened) bit for the same type screw heads as mentioned above.

**Staplers**     The *staple gun* drives the staple when the trigger is squeezed, while the *staple hammer* requires a hammering action.

**Bolt-Fastening Tools**     When wood is joined together by bolting, a tool is needed to tighten the nut. Besides the nut driver already mentioned, there are tools that grip the nut. The *plier* is a simple tool to grip the nut, although care must be taken because too much stress will damage the sides of the nut. The *cresent wrench* has adjustable jaws to fit the sides of the nut, thereby applying even pressure. The *socket wrench* with ratchet action and interchangeable wrench heads is a very efficient tool to tighten or loosen a nut. It also has an extension shaft to work in tight places.

If the joint is temporary for the easy dismantling of a scenic unit, a *wing nut* is used. The wing nut can be tightened and loosened by hand.

A *bolt cutter* is often needed to trim or shorten a bolt. The ratio of the small jaw opening to the long handles gives it greater leverage.

To correct mistakes or take apart a joint, the *crowbar, pry bar* (Wonder bar), or *nail puller* is needed. All three are strong and, because of their long handles, have a very efficient leverage. Their leverage is based on the principle of the *lever.* A long bar placed over a fulcrum or point of pivot close to

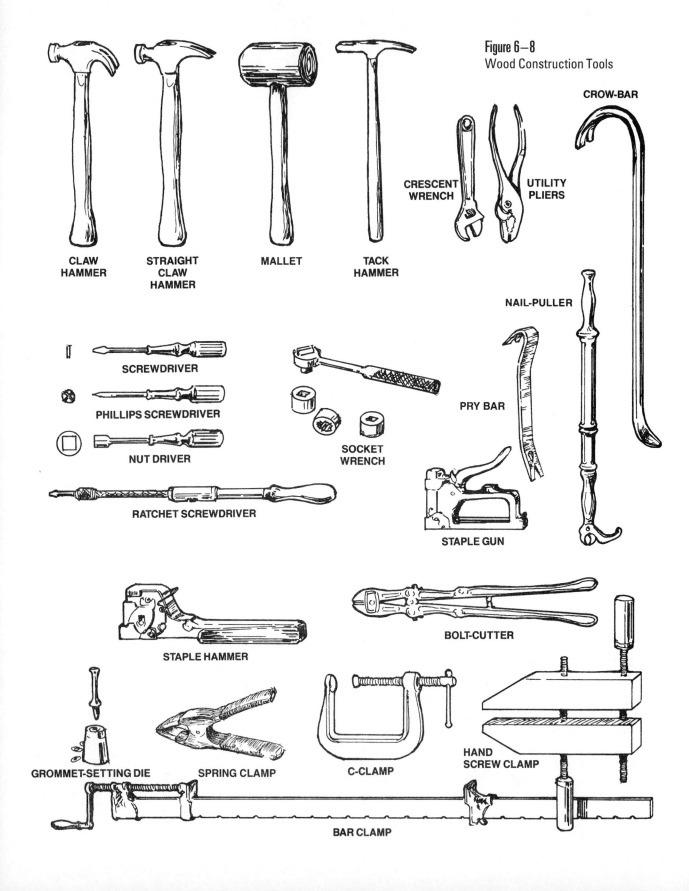

Figure 6—8
Wood Construction Tools

CROW-BAR

CLAW HAMMER

STRAIGHT CLAW HAMMER

MALLET

TACK HAMMER

CRESCENT WRENCH

UTILITY PLIERS

NAIL-PULLER

SCREWDRIVER

PHILLIPS SCREWDRIVER

NUT DRIVER

SOCKET WRENCH

PRY BAR

RATCHET SCREWDRIVER

STAPLE GUN

STAPLE HAMMER

BOLT-CUTTER

GROMMET-SETTING DIE

SPRING CLAMP

C-CLAMP

HAND SCREW CLAMP

BAR CLAMP

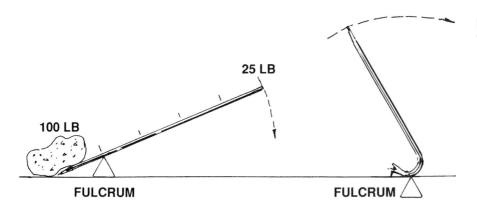

Figure 6–9
The Lever

the work (a rock to be moved or a nail to be pulled) requires less energy at the long end of the bar (Figure 6–9).

**Clamps**     The final method of wood-joining is gluing. Since glue requires time to set, the clamp holds the members firmly in place. The *C clamp* holds boards face-to-face as does the *wood clamp* (also called *hand-screwed clamp* or *Jorgensen clamp*) which, because it is made of wood, does less damage to the surfaces. The *bar clamp* is designed to hold the boards edge-to-edge.

There are a number of variations on the bar clamp. One is the *pipe clamp*, which uses a manufactured set of jaws that can be attached to any length of standard pipe. This provides an almost unlimited clamping range and a bit more flexibility than the bar clamp.

Besides being an easy-on/easy-off clamp for holding a joint, the heavy-duty *spring clamp* can serve as an extra hand to the carpenter in the shop. This type of clamp works best on face-to-face joints. While the extra-strong spring holds the joint firmly together, the polyvinyl sleeve protects the wood. A spring clamp with a 4-inch reach is best for all purposes.

## PNEUMATIC TOOLS

Tools driven by air pressure save time and energy. No well-equipped scenery shop should be without the speed and efficiency of the pneumatic nailer and staple gun (Figure 6–10). With the slightest pressure of the finger, a nail or staple is set in one stroke.

The sectional view in Figure 6–10 discloses the principle of the nailer. Shown in the cross section is the cylinder and piston to which the driver blade is attached. The piston is held to the top of the cylinder against the head bumper (3) by air from the last shot. When the trigger is released, air drives the piston, which in turn pushes the nail or staple out of the gun. The nails are stored in the nail magazine (6) and are spring-loaded to push each nail into position to be set. The nailer shown in the section is for brads and finish nails. It is designed to set 1-inch brads, as well as 4d, 6d, and 8d finish nails, which are made of a finer wire and have a smaller head than the common nail. All of the component parts of the pneumatic gun are proportional to the fastener being used. Structural nails, such as 6d, 8d, and 10d common, would be larger and the nail magazine would have to increase in size also.

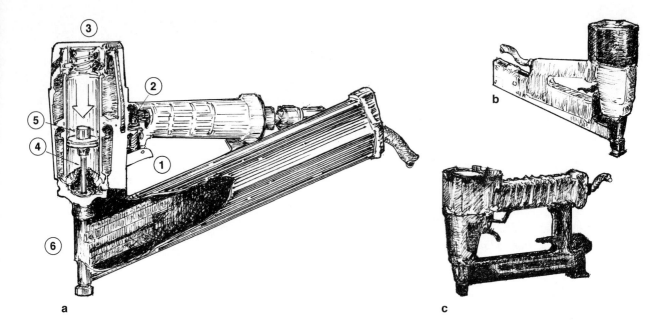

**Figure 6–10**
Pneumatic Tools

(a) Cross section of a pneumatic nailer designed to set finish nails from one-inch brads to 8d finish nails.
(b) Pneumatic nailer for structural nails 6d to 10d common.
(c) Stapler for $\frac{3}{8}$-inch to 2-inch staples. A one-inch staple is suitable for attaching corner blocks in scenery framing.

It should be noted that frequently the position of the nail magazine is different for the nailer than for the stapler. The nailer magazine is angled so that the work-contacting element can be clearly seen, allowing the operator greater flexibility in choosing the placement of the nail.

The pneumatic staple gun can drive, and clinch if needed, staples from $\frac{5}{8}$ inch to 2 inches in length. The 1-inch staple is used to fasten corner and keystone blocks in the construction of flat scenery (see Chapter 7). It should be noted that staples vary in (crown) width and wire gauge.

Because pneumatic tools require about 90 pounds per square inch of pressure to operate, the shop must have either a portable heavy-duty compressor or a built-in compressed air service with convenient connection positions throughout the shop. The same system can provide compressed air to the painting and property construction areas to operate paint spray guns.

In addition to the nailer and stapler, a large shop with an air pressure system might use a pneumatic reversible drill with socket wrench and screwdriver attachments.

## METAL AS SCENERY MATERIAL

Metal has been used in the theatre as a structural material for some time. In recent theatre there are many examples of metal being used as a design feature. For these reasons, it is important for the designer and technician to understand the many forms and techniques of using metal.

Iron is the basic metal. It is combined with carbon to make steel. A high proportion of carbon produces a harder steel. Steel can have other alloys such as chromium or nickel, but the most useful combinations for the theatre are a low-carbon steel and malleable iron.

## FORMING AND FABRICATING METAL

While the metal is still molten it can be *formed* in many ways: *rolling* to produce *plate* and *sheet* metal; *extruding* by squeezing the molten metal through a shaped aperture forming such shapes as rod, tubes, and so on; *casting* liquid metal into block forms; *drawing* the softened metal through a small aperture to make *wire*; and *forging* or stamping the metal into a prescribed shape.

Out of the forming we have the following familiar shapes: *plate*, rolled steel no thinner than $\frac{1}{8}$ inch; *sheet*, rolled steel no thicker than $\frac{1}{8}$ inch; *strip*, rolled steel narrower than plate; *strap*, narrow strip; *rod*, solid round and square; *structural* shapes such as channel, angle, and so on; *tube*, extruded round, square, and rectangular; *pipe*, round malleable iron; *wire*, drawn carbon steel that can be twisted into cable.

The *fabricating* of metal involves unique techniques and tools. The following terms are used in the fabrication of metal: *brake forming*, to bend plate or sheet metal; to *shear* is to cut sheet metal; *spinning*, sheet metal is placed into a lathe-like machine and spun (while spinning, a blunt tool shapes the metal into bowl or bell shapes); *rolling*, the cold-rolling of sheet metal into curved or cylindrical shapes; *twisting*, a square bar can be twisted into a decorative shape or wire can be twisted into cable; *blanking*, the punching of holes or a pattern through plate or sheet metal; *wrought iron*, the twisting, bending, or rolling of soft iron into decorative shapes; *joining*, the bolting or riveting together of structural steel or sheet metal; *welding*, joining by fusing metals together at a high temperature; *soldering*, the joining of sheet metal or tin with solder.

**Structural Steel Shapes**     The numerous shapes of structural steel that will be shown and discussed represent typical cross sections (Figure 6–11). In all examples, the thickness of the metal and the length of a leg can be manufactured in many combinations. The choice of the combination of size and thickness of the metal depends on the work the structural member is expected to do. In the beginning, it is wise for the designer and technician to become familiar with all the size and weight variations of any one shape.

*Strap:* If it is very thin it is called *band*. Its most frequent use is as a *silliron*, $\frac{3}{4}$ inch wide by $\frac{3}{16}$ inch thick.

*Strip:* It is a wide strap. A $2\frac{1}{2}$-inch wide by $\frac{1}{8}$-inch thick strip is sometimes cut and drilled for mending plates.

*Angle:* It is a good reinforcing shape to stiffen or brace scenery. It is a very useful cross section and comes in many sizes.

*Channel:* Its U-shaped cross section makes it stronger though not as adaptable as an angle.

*Tee:* The T shape is useful for stiffening. When it is used horizontally in a framework, it is stronger than an angle. The tee also serves as a guide for the arbor in a counterweight system.

*I beam:* As the name suggests, the I beam is best used as a beam where the major thrust or weight is on the top of the I.

*Round tube:* This is one of the many extruded forms. The larger tubes can become vertical support members while smaller diameter tubes can be bent

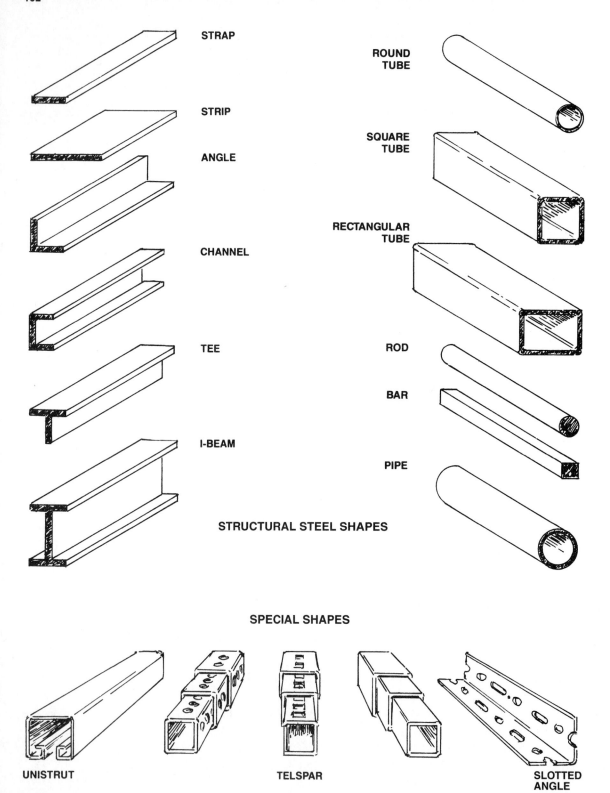

STRAP

STRIP

ANGLE

CHANNEL

TEE

I-BEAM

ROUND TUBE

SQUARE TUBE

RECTANGULAR TUBE

ROD

BAR

PIPE

STRUCTURAL STEEL SHAPES

SPECIAL SHAPES

UNISTRUT

TELSPAR

SLOTTED ANGLE

Figure 6–11
Structural Steel Shapes

into decorative shapes (see TWC in the subsection titled "Special Shapes," which follows this).

*Square tube:* This popular shape can be cut and welded into structural or decorative forms.

*Rectangular tube:* This piece is a good clean shape for design or structural uses.

*Rod:* A round solid, the rod is sometimes used as the internal member of a steel truss or is easily bent into decorative shapes.

*Bar:* A square solid, sometimes used as a spindle in a metal railing, bars can be bent and twisted into ornamental shapes found in wrought iron work.

*Pipe:* With heavier side walls than tube, malleable iron pipe can be threaded and joined with fittings (Figure 6–12). Although the outside dimensions (OD) remains the same, pipe is available in three side-wall thicknesses: standard, extra strength, and double extra strength.

**Special Shapes**     Frequently, a manufacturer's name will be commonly used in reference to a specific type of material (or tool). These names have become the "generic" reference to the material in some cases; in other instances, there is only one company that manufactures a particular material. Some of these special shapes are shown in Figure 6–11 and are described here.

*Unistrut,* a specially formed channel-shaped steel, with its fittings is a method of knockdown framing that is adaptable to platforming and trussing in the theatre. It eliminates the necessity of welding and cutting and is available in different forms.

*Thin-wall conduit* (TWC) galvanized-steel pipe has become a very popular structural and decorative material in the theatre. With walls too thin to thread and therefore easy to bend, it has many uses in scenery construction. It comes in three diameters ($\frac{1}{2}$-inch, $\frac{3}{4}$-inch, and $1\frac{1}{4}$-inch), in 10-foot lengths.

The types of telescoping square tube commonly referred to as *Telspar* are (1) solid sides, (2) punched with round holes, and (3) punched with square holes.

*Slotted angle iron,* designed to bolt together in a variety of shapes, is also made in strap and channel shapes.

**Flat Steel**     Steel plate and sheet metal have been mentioned as forms of flat steel.

*Plate* is rigid and comes as thin as $\frac{1}{8}$ inch. It can be cut to order in sizes for various needs, such as a clinch plate or pipe stand base to add weight to the bottom.

*Expanded metal plate* is steel plate that is punched with a pattern of slits and then stretched from opposite edges to expand the plate into a grille surface. Expanded metal is weight-bearing and has been used as platform flooring, allowing light to pass through in interesting patterns. Lightweight expanded metal has been used as a screen surface for light projections.

*Sheet metal* is rolled steel less than $\frac{1}{8}$-inch thickness. The various thicknesses are indicated in *gauges.* They decrease in steps of 1.5 hundredth of an inch (0.015)—hence, the larger the gauge, the thinner the sheet.

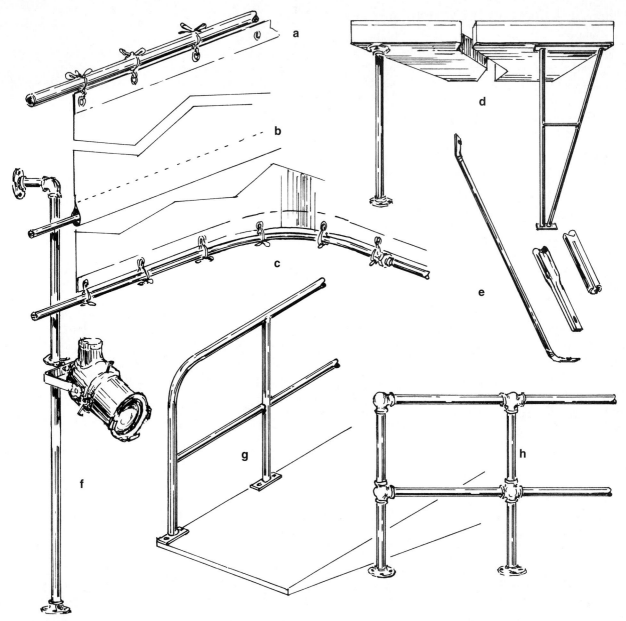

**Figure 6–12**
Various Uses of Iron Pipe

(a) Top batten for drop, cyclo-rama, or stage drapery.
(b) Bottom batten for a drop-in pipe sleeve.
(c) Curved bottom batten using tielines.
(d) Free-standing platform legs.
(e) Special bracing.
(f) Lighting booms and battens.
(g) Bent pipe and welded railing.
(h) Cut pipe and fitted railing.

Galvanized steel, aluminum sheet, tin (tinned steel), zinc, and copper have been used as scenic materials, as has highly polished stainless steel. Light pans, shadow boxes, and special effects are a few of the uses of sheet metal in scenery construction.

The *metal screening* such as hardware cloth ($\frac{1}{4}$-inch mesh), glavanized screen ($\frac{1}{16}$-inch mesh), and chicken wire (1-inch mesh) are primarily used as structural materials. Occasionally, galvanized screening is used to simulate window glass.

# METALWORKING TOOLS AND EQUIPMENT

The use of metal in the theatre requires special tools to cut, shape, and join the many forms of metal as well as ways of coping with the various methods of fabrication. Although some woodworking tools can be used on metal, most metalworking tools have special functions. The following tools are used for the measuring, marking, shaping, and cutting of metal (see Figure 6–13).

## MEASURING AND MARKING TOOLS

Most marking on metal is done with a *scriber*. Its sharp point scratches a line on the surface of the metal. (Pencil and chalk lines smudge and are not feasible.) A measuring tape is usable for long dimensions; however, a *flat steel rule* not only gives measurements, but also serves as a straightedge for marking. The large *framing square* is also useful for layouts.

The *compass scriber* will mark a circle or arc as well as scribe an irregular shape or pattern.

Both the *China marker*, often called a *grease pencil*, and *"soapstone"* are used for marking on metal or any other object with a hard, highly polished surface.

**Figure 6–13**
Metalworking Tools

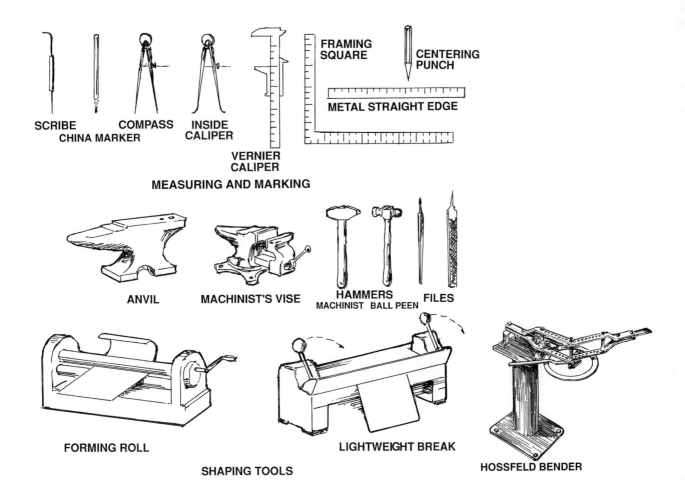

The *center punch*, as its name implies, marks the center of a circle or provides a start hole for drilling in metal.

### SHAPING TOOLS

Figure 6–14 illustrates some of the many uses in the theatre for shaped metal products. The *anvil* is the original tool for the shaping and bending of steel and malleable iron. The metal is shaped, hot or cold, by hammering on the flat or rounded surfaces of the anvil. The heavy *blacksmith hammer* and the *ball peen* hammer do the shaping.

Strap iron can be bent in a *machinist's vise* with its steel jaws and small anvil. The vise can hold metal for shaping with a file. The *metal files,* flat and triangular, can smooth a rough cut or round an edge.

Pipe and tube also can be shaped. The *conduit bender* is a hand tool for bending thin-wall conduit (TWC). Besides bending, pipe can be shaped by cutting and threaded to be joined in numerous ways (Figure 6–12).

To cut and fit pipe, several hand tools are needed. The pipe is held in a *pipe vise* and cut with a *pipe cutter.* The pipe cutter, technically a cutting tool, rotates around the pipe to make a clean cut. The *pipe threader*, with several *die heads* to fit the various pipe sizes, cuts threads on the end of the pipe. The numerous tools are shown in Figure 6–15.

Some shaping tools, although operated by hand, are too large to be hand-held tools. The *sheet-metal roll,* for example, is hand operated. Sheet metal is fed between three rollers, two fixed and one adjustable. The position of the

**Figure 6–14**
Decorative and Structural Uses of Rod and Strap.

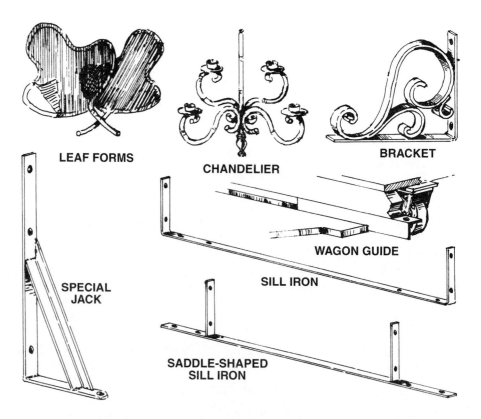

LEAF FORMS

CHANDELIER

BRACKET

SPECIAL JACK

WAGON GUIDE

SILL IRON

SADDLE-SHAPED SILL IRON

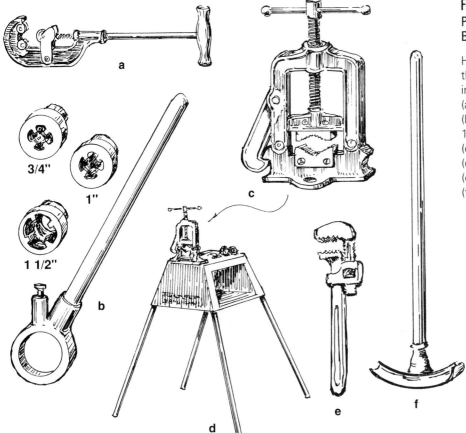

Figure 6–15
Pipe-Cutting, Threading, and Bending Tools

Hand tools used for cutting, threading and bending pipe include:
(a) pipe cutter,
(b) pipe threader with $\frac{3}{4}$-inch, 1-inch, and $1\frac{1}{2}$-inch die heads,
(c) pipe vise,
(d) portable vise stand,
(e) Stillson wrench, and
(f) pipe bender.

adjustable roller will increase or decrease the degree of curl in the shaped sheet metal.

The *brake form* is hand or foot operated to cleanly bend sheet metal to a prescribed angle.

The *Hossfeld bender* is a tool used to bend many shapes of metal—pipe, tube, rod, bar, and angle.

## MANUAL CUTTING TOOLS

The hand *hacksaw* with a fine-toothed blade is normally used to cut metal bars or bolts. The *pipe cutter* has been mentioned as a necessary tool for cutting and threading pipe. The hand tools to cut sheet metal are the *tin shears*, for cutting a straight line; *nippers*, for end cutting; and side-cutting pliers. There is also a large stationary sheet metal shear that "chops" full sheets of metal in one cut. Refer to Figure 6–16 for illustrations of manual metal-cutting tools.

## METALWORKING POWER TOOLS

To cut sheet metal or aluminum, both of thicker gauges, a *saber saw* with a metal cutting blade is a noisy but effective method. Two tools designed to

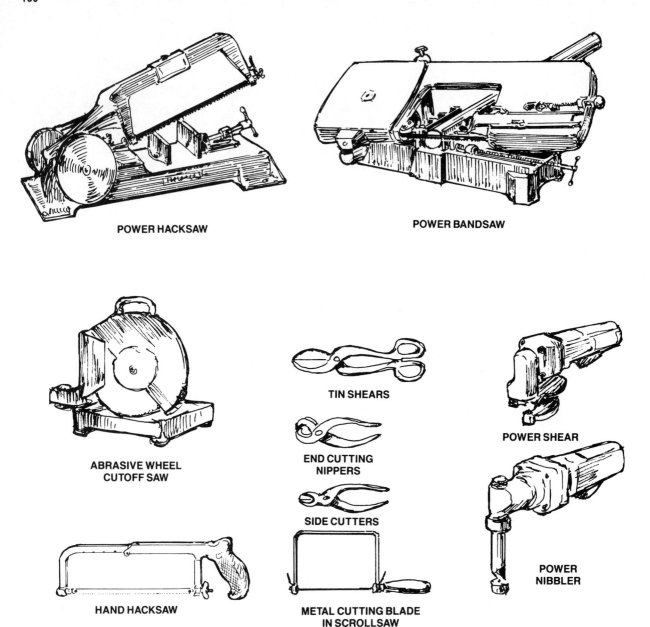

POWER HACKSAW

POWER BANDSAW

ABRASIVE WHEEL
CUTOFF SAW

TIN SHEARS

END CUTTING
NIPPERS

SIDE CUTTERS

POWER SHEAR

POWER
NIBBLER

HAND HACKSAW

METAL CUTTING BLADE
IN SCROLLSAW

**Figure 6–16**
Metal-Cutting Tools

cut sheet metal are the *power shear*, which is hand-held and will cut straight or curved, and the *power nibbler* for inside cutting. It requires an .87-inch starting hole.

The major tools to crosscut pipe, tube, or any structural steel forms are the *power hacksaw*, the *power band saw*, and the *abrasive wheel cutoff saw*.

The *power hand drill* with $\frac{1}{2}$-inch chuck capacity is a heavier tool than the wood drill. The *drill press* is a fixed tool for precision work. A *drill press vise* is used to hold the work in position. Another fixed power tool is the *bench grinder*. With one coarse and one fine wheel, the bench grinder can sharpen tools or grind down a metal edge.

The *cold saw* is a stationary saw that uses an extremely hard blade, low rotational speed, and a fluid coolant/lubricant. It is designed to make extremely accurate miter cuts.

## BASIC METAL-JOINING TOOLS AND MATERIALS

The various forms of metal can be joined with bolts, screws (sheet metal), rivets, solder, or by fusing the metals together with a weld. Pipe joining, besides the many fittings, can be accomplished on the outside. The *saddle tee* is strapped on the surface of the pipe, providing a right-angle coupling. The rotalock clamps the adjoining pipe, also at a 90-degree angle (Figure 6–17). The *Stillson wrench* (Figure 6–15), with jaws to grip and a long arm, is used to tighten the pipe into a fitting. The *vise-grip wrench*, along with other uses, can be used to tighten smaller diameter pipe.

The wrenches and screwdrivers from woodworking that can be used to join metal are the socket wrench, nut driver, and cresent wrench. The Phillips screwdriver can be used to set *sheet-metal screws*. With a small starter hole, the self-threading sheet-metal screw easily joins two or more pieces.

Sheet metal can be firmly joined with *rivets*. A hole is drilled through overlapping sheets; the rivet is inserted through the hole from the back; a washer is place over the shaft of the rivet; and, to finish the joining, the shaft is *peened* or flattened with a ball peen hammer. When the back is inaccessible, a *pop rivet* can be used. The *pop riveter* compresses the rivet in place with a squeeze or two of the handles. Figure 6–18 shows some of these fasteners.

## SOLDERING

As a method of joining metal, solder functions as a *bond*. The strength of the bond depends on the preparation of the surfaces to be joined and an even

### Figure 6–17
### Pipe Joining

Some of the screw fittings used to join sections of pipe:
(1) coupling,
(2) nipple,
(3) reducing coupling,
(4) tee,
(5) cross,
(6) union, ring end,
(7) union, screw end,
(8) cap,
(9) 90-degree elbow,
(10) 45-degree elbow,
(11) street ells,
(12) floor flange,
(13) adjustable elbow (railing fitting),
(14) pipe strap,
(15) batten inside sleeve splice,
(16) saddle tee, double strap,
(17) rotalock,
(18) pipe hanger.

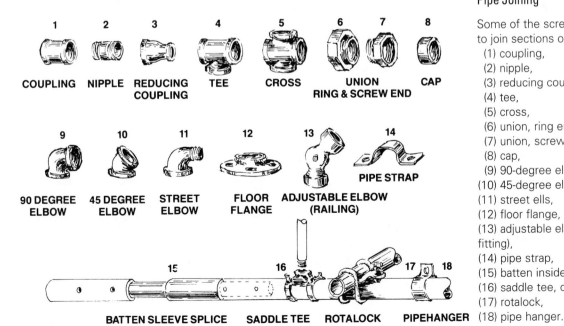

| 1 | 2 | 3 | 4 | 5 | 6 | 7 | 8 |
| COUPLING | NIPPLE | REDUCING COUPLING | TEE | CROSS | UNION RING & SCREW END | | CAP |

| 9 | 10 | 11 | 12 | 13 | 14 |
| 90 DEGREE ELBOW | 45 DEGREE ELBOW | STREET ELBOW | FLOOR FLANGE | ADJUSTABLE ELBOW (RAILING) | PIPE STRAP |

| 15 | 16 | 17 | 18 |
| BATTEN SLEEVE SPLICE | SADDLE TEE | ROTALOCK | PIPEHANGER |

Figure 6–18
Metal-Joining Tools

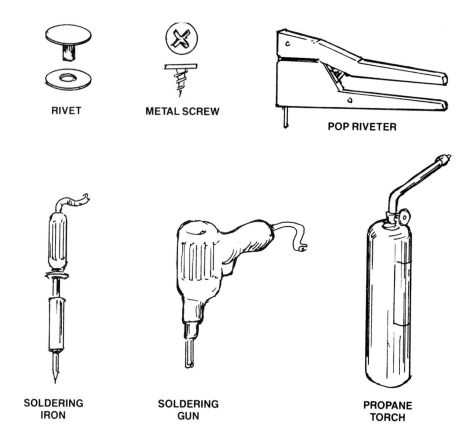

RIVET     METAL SCREW     POP RIVETER

SOLDERING IRON     SOLDERING GUN     PROPANE TORCH

application of solder. The surfaces should be cleansed of oil, paint, or oxidation (rust). A flux, borax, or rosin is applied to further clean the metal and prevent oxidation.

Figure 6–18 shows some of the tools used for soldering. An electric *soldering iron* or *soldering gun* supplies sufficient heat at the tip to melt the solder along the joint. The soldering of pipe to a fitting requires a torch. The *propane torch* supplies heat to a large area of the fitting so that when the solder is applied it is sucked into the joint. The joint surfaces are cleaned and polished with emery cloth and coated with flux before applying the heat and solder. For the soldering of electrical connections, a rosin flux is used to prevent corrosion.

## WELDING

Welding is the *fusing* of metal. It provides a more permanent joint than soldering. It is a faster method of joining but requires specialized equipment. The two most useful welding processes adaptable to the construction and designing of scenery are *gas-welding* and *arc-welding*.

**Gas-Welding Equipment**     *Oxyacetylene welding* (OAW) ignites an oxygen and acetylene mixture to produce one of the hottest flames known. Welding is possible with or without a filler metal. Gas-welding equipment can perform a wide range of work in addition to the fusing of metal. It can (1) braze, or join metals with a rod that melts at a lower temperature than the two metals;

(2) join metals with solder, a tin and lead alloy that melts at a much lower temperature than the two metals; (3) cut sheet metal with a cutting attachment that concentrates the oxygen flow; and (4) preheat metal with the torch, for reshaping on the anvil.

The chief disadvantage of gas-welding is heat warpage. Heat expands metal and, unless handled very carefully, gas-welding can cause warping of the metal near the welded point. The choice of a welding rod that will melt at the same temperature as (or slightly lower than) the melting point of the steel will minimize the amount of distortion.

The relative harmlessness of the flame is another advantage of gas-welding when used in the scenery shop or on the stage. The only exception is when the cutting tip is being used. To cut metal with a torch, a tiny jet of oxygen is directed onto the white-hot metal, producing a rather spectacular shower of sparks.

The most cumbersome parts of a gas-welding outfit are the heavy tanks containing the two welding gases, oxygen and acetylene. A tank truck is essential to make their movement easier. The methods of acquiring oxygen and acetylene vary with the suppliers. Some gas suppliers charge a fixed deposit on the tank, which is refunded when the empty tank is returned, while others rent the container on a per diem basis. If a supplier insists on the tank-rental arrangement, it pays in the long run to purchase a set of empty tanks to exchange for each tank of gas and thereby eliminate the per diem rental charge which, though small, can mount up during idle times between productions.

A listing of the parts and attachments of a gas-welding outfit, including the gas tanks, is found in (Figure 6–19).

**Arc-Welding Equipment**     The heat of arc-welding comes, as the name implies, from the arc of a high-amperage short circuit between the metal and the rod or electrode. The work has to be grounded to complete the circuit from the rod to the holder, through the electrode cable and to the transformer. *Shielded metal arc-welding* (SMAW) is the most adaptable arc-welding technique for the theatre workshop. Upon striking, the arc is enveloped in a shield of inert gas as the coating of the rod burns. This shield of inert gas keeps the oxygen in the air out of the critical metallurgical change of the welding process.

Of the two welding methods, arc-welding requires more skill. It takes practice to develop a steady hand to strike an arc and draw a good bead. Arc-welding's chief advantage is in the speed of the welding operation. Because a welding temperature is reached almost instantaneously and in such a small area, the amount of heat warpage is negligible. This is important in the welding of a preassembled part when its fit is critical to the final shape of the completed structure.

**Gas-Metal Arc-Welding**     A third welding process, which has become adaptable to theatre shop use, is the gas-metal arc-welding method commonly referred to as *metal inert gas* or MIG. The components of MIG equipment are found in Figure 6–20. Also see Figure 6–21. MIG uses a wire-fed electrode through a gas hose and gun nozzle to the work. The arc is surrounded with an inert gas shield and is automatically fed with a wire electrode in the center of the nozzle. MIG welding is a simple one-handed operation that is easy to learn. The heat of the arc and gauge of the wire can be altered

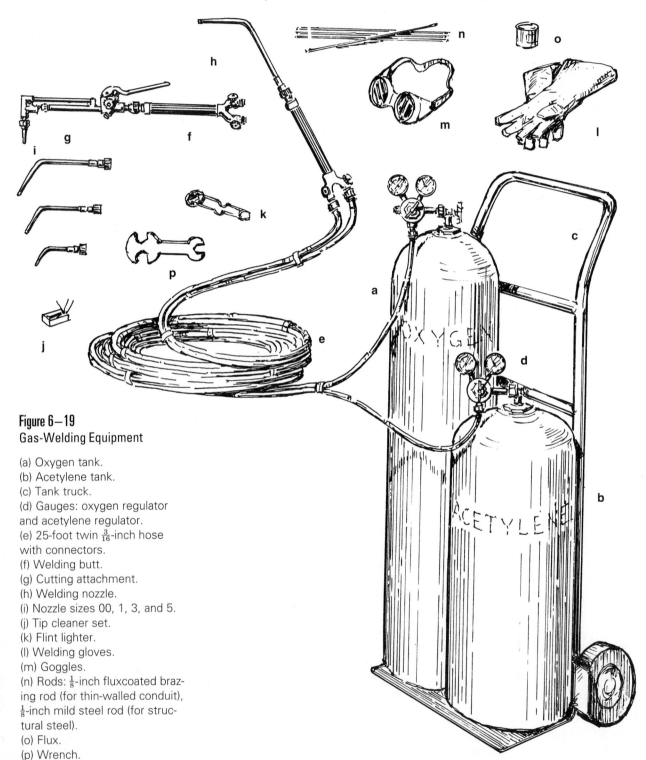

**Figure 6–19**
Gas-Welding Equipment

(a) Oxygen tank.
(b) Acetylene tank.
(c) Tank truck.
(d) Gauges: oxygen regulator and acetylene regulator.
(e) 25-foot twin $\frac{3}{16}$-inch hose with connectors.
(f) Welding butt.
(g) Cutting attachment.
(h) Welding nozzle.
(i) Nozzle sizes 00, 1, 3, and 5.
(j) Tip cleaner set.
(k) Flint lighter.
(l) Welding gloves.
(m) Goggles.
(n) Rods: $\frac{1}{8}$-inch fluxcoated brazing rod (for thin-walled conduit), $\frac{1}{8}$-inch mild steel rod (for structural steel).
(o) Flux.
(p) Wrench.

### Safety Practice

Gas welding operators should wear goggles, protective clothing, and gloves, more for protection from flying sparks than from the intensity of the flame itself. Because there are no ultraviolet rays generated in the flame by gas-welding, it does not have to be isolated or shielded from other shop activity. Precautions should be taken, however, to guard flammable materials from the sparks by using sheetrock pads under and around the work. A respiratory mask should also be worn.

Arc-welding operators require the same protection, especially from the ultraviolet rays of the arc. A welder's helmet with a ray-absorbing window should be worn to protect the eyes. If other workers are nearby, a portable shield can be used to protect their eyes.

Prolonged welding in a closed room requires forced ventilation.

### Figure 6–20
### Gas-Metal Arc-Welding Equipment

(a) Power unit MIG—160 amperes DC at 22 volts (60% duty cycle).
(b) Gas cylinder—mixture of argon and $CO_2$ or helium.
(c) Gauges—tank pressure, work pressure.
(d) Gas hose-cable.
(e) Automatic wire-feeder, built-in wire-feeder is a feature of this particular unit (AIRCO, DIP/ STICK 160).
(f) Gun and nozzle.
(g) Ground cable.
(h) Electrode cable for stick-welding.
(i) Spot-welding attachment.
(j) Helmet, fiberglass with ray-absorbing viewing window.
(k) Gloves.
(l) Apron or smock.
(m) Rods for stick-welding.
(n) Folding screen.
(o) Angled grinder to smooth weld.

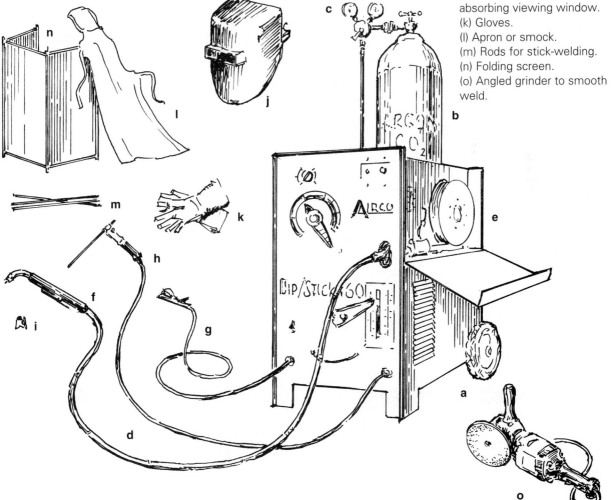

**Figure 6–21**
Gas-Metal Arc-Welding

Note the expanded metal welding table top.

**Figure 6–22**
Metal Scenery

(Below left) Sheet metal (16 to 18 gauge) over square tube structural framing. (Right) Rear view of welded frame. The Tyrone Guthrie Theatre production of *Oedipus the King* by Sophocles. Designer—Desmond Heeley. Photo courtesy Kewley.

**Figure 6–23**
**Steel Staircase**

Spiral staircase for a production of Molière's *Tartuffe* framed with 1-inch square steel tube. (Bottom left) Full assembly. (Top) Framing of tread supports. (Bottom right) Bending the sweep of the helix. Designer—Douglas Maddox. Construction—Eric Harriz and Roger Segalla. Photos courtesy Mark Baird.

**Figure 6—24**
Decorative Use of Thin-Wall Conduit

Forest scene from Shakespeare's *As You Like It*. Designer—John Kavelin. Carnegie-Mellon University. Photo courtesy Nelson.

**Figure 6—25**
Pipe-Scaffold Design

A scaffolding of black iron pipe held with rota locks and plank platforming make up the setting for a production of *'Tis a Pity She's a Whore*. Stainless steel sheet metal covers the central floor in an interesting use of metal as scenery. Photo courtesy Nelson.

to weld various metals including aluminum. A special spot-welding fitting can be attached to the end of the nozzle for temporarily tacking or permanently joining adjacent surfaces. Some MIG units can also switch to stick-welding (regular arc-welding with rod) without the use of gas. In addition, a special form of MIG wire is available with a core that negates the need for gas.

Figures 6–22, 6–23, 6–24, and 6–25 offer photographic examples of the types of scenery and set designs that can be achieved using the metal-working techniques discussed in this chapter.

## SCENERY SURFACES

### COVER STOCK

The material used to cover the structural frame of scenery, thereby providing a surface for painting, is known as *cover stock*. The frame can be covered with a fabric or a hard surface, depending on the use and handling of the particular piece of scenery. A translucent backing, for example, is framed and covered differently from a section of wall that must support the weight of an actor.

**Covering Fabrics**     The usual covering fabrics for framed scenery are 8-ounce canvas duck and 5- to 6-ounce unbleached muslin. Muslin is more frequently used as a drop material than as cover stock for framed scenery. However, almost any fabric can become a covering material to serve as a special effect or as an unusual painting surface. Burlap, velour, scrim, terry cloth, and even string rugs have been used as covering fabrics.

**Hard Surfaces**     Soft-covered flats are largely the domain of schools. Because perceptions of what is realistic have evolved and the number of intimate theatres such as the thrust has increased, what is acceptable to an audience has changed. Hard-covered flats are much more common. They are more efficient and, not insignificantly, more expensive. The most frequently used hard-surface material is $\frac{1}{8}$-inch or $\frac{1}{4}$-inch lauan (also called Philippine mahogany) plywood. It is lightweight but still strong enough to supply a hard surface with a minimum of framing.

Other hard-surface materials include $\frac{1}{8}$-inch and $\frac{3}{16}$-inch Upson board, an inexpensive board made of laminated paper; $\frac{1}{4}$-inch A-C ply, a very sturdy but heavy board (also used for keystone and corner blocks); $\frac{1}{2}$-inch Homosote, a paper-pulp board with very little strength but thick enough to be carved or textured; and Masonite, a very heavy hard surface of compressed wood pulp. Tempered Masonite is an extremely hard surface that is often used as a floor covering. Double-faced corrugated cardboard is an inexpensive hard surface for limited profiling and covering, providing the scenery is not subjected to excessive handling. Some shops also include $\frac{3}{4}$-inch and 1-inch five ply as cover stock, although its chief use is for platform tops.

Most of these materials are available at the local lumber yard in stock 4-by-8-foot sheets. Occasionally, oversized sheets—such as 5 feet by 9 feet, 4 feet by 10 feet, and 4 feet by 12 feet—are stocked.

Plastic surfaces are another type of hard-surface cover stock or applique. However, because the use of modern plastic as a scenery surface is usually related to a textured or relief-sculptured surface, it is reserved for discussion in Chapter 7, where the techniques of working plastics such as Styrofoam, urethane foam, and thermoplastics are treated.

## SCENERY HARDWARE

In the scenery shop, hardware is divided into two categories: fastening hardware and stage hardware. The first is hardware used in the construction and basic assembly of scenery; the second is for the bracing, stiffening, rigging, and on-stage assemble of scenery.

### FASTENING HARDWARE

This is an important part of normal scenery construction. It includes all the necessary nails, screws, and bolts to fasten wood to wood or metal to wood.

**Nails**    Driven with a hammer or pneumatic nailer, a nail is used for a more permanent fastening of wood to wood, such as framed scenery units or platform construction. The various types of nails serve specific purposes.

All nails are stamped out of steel wire of varying thickness, length, and shape of head. The thickness or weight is known as *penny* and is represented by the letter *d*—hence, a 10d nail is longer and thicker than an 8d nail.

A *common nail* has a flat head for easier driving and easier extracting. The wide flat head also adds strength to the joint. Useful common nails for theatre might include 8d ($2\frac{1}{2}$ inches), 10d (3 inches), and 16d ($3\frac{1}{2}$ inches). A *box nail* is a lightweight (smaller wire) common nail, 4d ($1\frac{1}{2}$ inches) or 6d (2 inches). A *finish nail* is a small wire, small-headed nail for finish work such as attaching molding or trim. A finish nail's head is set below the surface of the wood to be filled or covered with wood putty or paste, thereby concealing the nail. Finish nails in stock would begin with 1-inch wire brads (very fine wire), and would include 4d ($1\frac{1}{2}$ inches), 6d (2 inches), and 8d ($2\frac{1}{2}$ inches). The double-headed *duplex nail* is used for temporary assembly, sized 6d, 8d, and 10d.

**Screws**    The tapered advancing threads of the screw are drawn into the wood by turning the screwdriver, providing a very firm fastening of wood to wood. The diameter of a screw is indicated by number, and the length in inches. The types of heads are numerous—*flat head* with tapered sides to countersink into the wood; *round head* to set on the wood surface; *bugle head*, a flat head with silhouette of a bugle horn; *pan head*, a flattened round; and the *hex head* of the *lag screw.* The types of recesses in the screw head for the driving tool include the *slot, Phillips,* and *Robertson* square. (Refer again to Figure 6–8 and the subsection on screwdrivers.) The most common sizes to stock might be No. 8 screws: $\frac{3}{4}$-, 1-, $1\frac{1}{4}$-, $1\frac{1}{2}$-, 2-, $2\frac{1}{2}$-, and 3-inch.

By increasing the depth and pitch of the threads, a *wood screw* not only can hold better, but can be driven faster. The industrial quality wood screw is made of tempered high-grade carbon steel and is lubricated for easy installation. It has extruded threads, which means the threads extend beyond the diameter of the shank (most screws are turned from shank stock). The extruded threads give the screw greater holding power.

The *drywall screw* is of similiar quality to and can be used in place of a wood screw. The best sizes to stock might be No. 8 screws: $\frac{3}{4}$-, 1-, $1\frac{1}{4}$-, $1\frac{1}{2}$-, $1\frac{5}{8}$-, 2-, $2\frac{1}{2}$-, and 3-inch. Their flat heads have Phillips slots or square recesses.

A *lag screw* has wood screw threads. It is used in heavy assembly where a bolt is not feasible, and it is driven with a socket wrench. Sizes $\frac{5}{16}$ to $\frac{1}{2}$ inch in diameter and $1\frac{1}{2}$ to 4 inches in length are suitable for most needs.

**Tacks and Staples**      A No. 6 or No. 10 *carpet tack* will secure a carpet, padding, or ground cloth. *Upholstering tacks* in various colors and patterns aid in the construction or remodeling of furniture for properties; usual size will be $\frac{1}{2}$-inch or $\frac{5}{8}$-inch.

The size and shape of a *staple* will vary with the type and make of the stapler as well as with the nature of the work. There are, for example, hand-powered staplers, hammer staplers, electric staplers, and pneumatic staplers—each requiring a slightly different type of staple. Staples for hand or electric staplers, for attaching fabric or metal screening to wood, are usually sized $\frac{1}{4}$-, $\frac{3}{8}$-, $\frac{5}{16}$-, or $\frac{1}{2}$-inch. Staples for pneumatic staplers, for fastening wood to wood, are most commonly found in $\frac{3}{4}$-, 1-, $1\frac{1}{4}$-, $1\frac{1}{2}$-, and 2-inch sizes.

**Bolts, Nuts, and Washers**      As fastening hardware, the bolt plus nut is stronger than the nail or screw. The nut and bolt is also easy to disassemble, which is compatible with the knockdown aspect of scenery construction. Bolts commonly used in theatre are of three types: the stove bolt, the carriage bolt, and the machine bolt.

The *stove bolt* with a flat head and slotted recess is threaded its full length. In short lengths and small diameters ($\frac{3}{16}$ inch), it is used to reinforce the screws in a backflap hinge or hanger iron. Its flat fits into the countersink of the stage hardware. The slotted round head stove bolt is devised to set on the face rather than being countersunk. Both bolts are tightened using a socket wrench on the nut and a screwdriver in the slotted head. Suggested sizes are $\frac{1}{36}$-inch diameter—1, 2, or 3 inches in length; and $\frac{3}{8}$-inch diameter— 2, 4, or 6 inches in length.

The *carriage bolt* is specifically for fastening wood. The rounded head with a square shank is expected to draw into the wood surface and thereby resist turning as the nut is tightened. Since the bolt is not threaded its full length, care needs to be taken to select the right length bolt for each joint. Normal sizes to stock are $\frac{3}{8}$-inch diameter—3, $3\frac{1}{2}$, 4, and 6 inches in length.

The *machine bolt* has a finer thread, a square or hex head, and, although it can be used for wood, is manufactured for metal assembly such as slotted angle and structural steel framing. The size of bolt depends on the forms of the steel and the nature of the structure. Frequently used sizes are $\frac{3}{8}$-inch diameter—1, $1\frac{1}{2}$, 2, $2\frac{1}{2}$, 3, $3\frac{1}{2}$, and 4 inches in length; and $\frac{1}{2}$-inch diameter— 6 and 8 inches in length.

**Figure 6–26**
Types of Washers

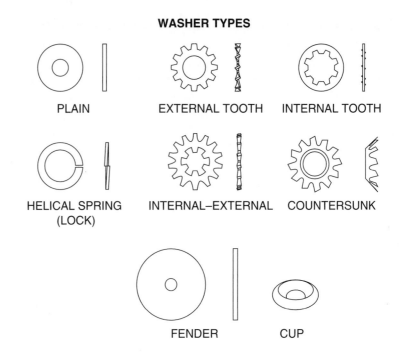

WASHER TYPES

PLAIN  EXTERNAL TOOTH  INTERNAL TOOTH

HELICAL SPRING (LOCK)  INTERNAL–EXTERNAL  COUNTERSUNK

FENDER  CUP

*Nuts* are usually hexagonal in shape with inside threading that matches the bolt. Their function is to tighten the bolt in place. Although the *hex nut* has to be tightened with a wrench, the *wing nut* is designed to be tightened by hand for easy and quick assembly. A *T-nut* has sharp prongs to affix the nut into the wood surface around a predrilled hole, thus permitting rapid fastening.

The *washer* is a flat disk of steel with the center hole slightly larger than the diameter of the bolt. It spreads the pressure of the tightened nut for a stronger fastening. The *lock washer* is a cut disk with offset ends that provide enough pressure to keep the nut locked in place. There are several other shapes of lock washers, including "star" and "wave" shapes (Figure 6–26).

### STAGE HARDWARE

The necessary portability of scenery leads to the use of many pieces of hardware made especially for the stage. Most of them are designed to brace, stiffen, and temporarily join units of scenery as well as to work with rigging for the flying of scenery (Figure 6–27).

Stage hardware has been broken down into categories that relate to their function:

**Stiffening Hardware**    The loose-pin back-flap hinge is used to attach a horizontal stiffening member to the back of two or more units of scenery. A *keeper hook* over the toggle rails of two or more units can receive a horizontal stiffener.

**Bracing Hardware**　　An adjustable stage-brace hooks into a *brace cleat* to function as a vertical brace. A *strap hinge* is used to brace and hold a door frame in position. A *hinged foot iron* and a *bent foot iron* with a *stage screw* secures the bottom of a unit of scenery for better bracing. There are two types of stage screws. The first has bolt threading to screw into a preset plug (improved stage screw). The second is the traditional stage screw or *peg*, as it is sometimes referred to. A *straight foot iron* is sometimes found on the bottom of a jack, which is a hinged brace. A *floor stay* is designed to hook over the bottom batten of a drop.

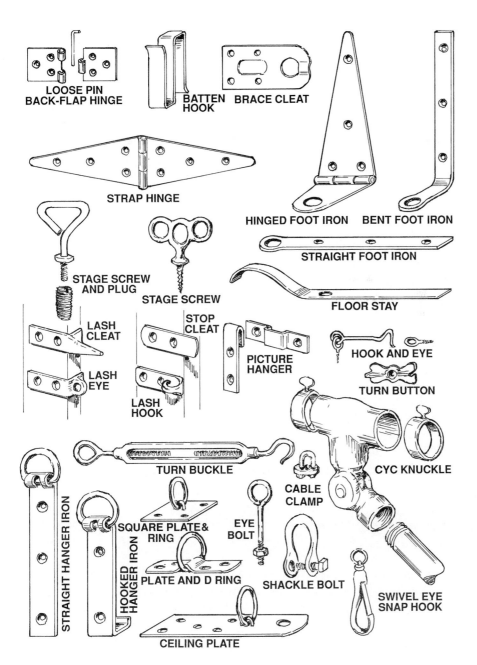

**Figure 6–27**
Stage Hardware

LOOSE PIN BACK-FLAP HINGE　　BATTEN HOOK　　BRACE CLEAT

STRAP HINGE

HINGED FOOT IRON　　BENT FOOT IRON

STAGE SCREW AND PLUG

STAGE SCREW

STRAIGHT FOOT IRON

FLOOR STAY

LASH CLEAT

STOP CLEAT

LASH EYE

LASH HOOK

PICTURE HANGER

HOOK AND EYE

TURN BUTTON

CYC KNUCKLE

TURN BUCKLE

CABLE CLAMP

STRAIGHT HANGER IRON

SQUARE PLATE & RING

EYE BOLT

HOOKED HANGER IRON

PLATE AND D RING

SHACKLE BOLT

SWIVEL EYE SNAP HOOK

CEILING PLATE

**Hardware Assembly**     To lash two flats together is one method of joining. Shown in Figure 6–27 are a *lash cleat* and a *lash eye*. Both are attached to the stile of a flat. The lash line is fastened to the eye and hooks around alternating lash cleats. The *stop cleat* holds flats together in a corner lash. A *lash hook* is used when there is not enough space for a lash cleat. The *picture hanger* and *socket* are used for fastening a picture to a toggle rail or picture batten. The *hook and eye*, although not strong, is a quick way to make a joint, as is the *turn button*. The *casket lock*, or *coffin lock*, recessed into the edge of a wagon platform, is a hidden lock that can be unlocked with an Allen wrench through a small hole in the platform top (see Chapter 10, Figure 10–16).

**Rigging Hardware**     As the name suggests, this hardware is used with rigging in the flying of scenery. Rigging hardware is essentially of three types, as follows (Figure 6–28):

1. *Hardware that attaches directly to the unit to be flown.* In traditional theatrical flats, a *straight hanger iron* (or top hanger iron) is used at the top of a framed unit of scenery, while a *hooked hanger iron* (also called bottom hanger iron) is used on the bottom. *Eye bolts* can be used as a lifting point for scenery or to guide a lift line. A *screw eye* can be used for only extremely lightweight pieces. A *square plate and ring* or *ceiling plate* can often be used for flying scenery such as a ceiling. A *D-ring and plate* can be used to hang both vertical and horizontal units and is also used to guide lines. The same plate without the D-ring, often called a *keeper plate*, is frequently used to guide cable off the top of a flat.

2. *Hardware that creates a usable termination in the cable or rope.* The *thimble* is used as a part of making an eye or loop in rope or cable. It supports the rope and prevents kinking. The loop is held in place by either a *cable clip* (also called a *Crosby*), which is temporary, or a *swage* (also called a *Nicopress sleeve*), which is permanent. The permanent sleeve is stronger and requires a special tool called a *swaging tool* or *Nicopress tool*.

3. *Hardware that connects the two above, allowing for adjustment and removability.* The *shackle* is a two-part fastener consisting of an inverted U-shape that slips through the loop of the thimble and a removable pin that passes through the ring of the attachment hardware. A *quick link* resembles a single link of chain, one side of which can open or close with a threaded fitting. The *snap hook* is a forged hook with a spring-loaded latch. The *caribiner* is a piece of rock-climbing hardware with a spring-loaded latch that is often lockable. Lightweight latchhooks, or *dog clips*, should only be used for extremely lightweight pieces, as they are not intended for lifting.

## ROPE, CABLE, WIRE, AND CHAIN

### ROPE

Constructed of spun *fibers* that are first twisted (normally to the left) into a *strand*, rope is formed by twisting three or four strands in the opposite direction (i.e., to the right). This twisting is known as the *lay* of the rope. The

Figure 6–28
Rigging Hardware

SHOULDER PATTERN
EYE BOLT

CABLE THIMBLE

CABLE CLIP

NICO STOP AND SLEEVE

THIRD CRIMP

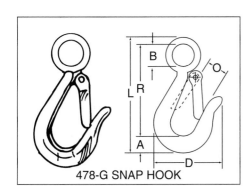

478-G SNAP HOOK

QUICK LINK

SCREW PIN
SHACKLE

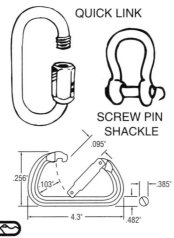

**MOUNTAIN D**

| | |
|---|---|
| Gate opening clearance | .950" |
| Weight | 2.4 oz. (68 gm) |

SMC Aluminum
mountaineering carabiners

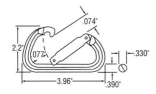

**LIGHTWEIGHT D**

| | |
|---|---|
| Gate opening clearance | .740" |
| Weight | 1.7 oz. (48 gm) |

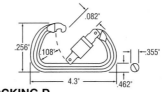

**LOCKING D**

| | |
|---|---|
| Gate opening clearance | .820" |
| Weight | 2.6 oz. (74 gm) |

opposing tensions of the lay of the rope and the lay of the strand hold the rope together.

The fibers of a rope can be from *natural* or *synthetic* sources. The most common natural fiber is manila. It is relatively inexpensive and has many uses in the theatre. Synthetic fibers such as nylon, polypropylene, polyethylene, and polyester have been incorporated into rope construction. The continuous length of synthetic fibers adds strength and flexibility to a rope. Although the cost of a synthetic fiber rope is considerably higher than one of natural fiber, its life span can be much longer.

Sizes of rope most frequently used in the theatre include these:

$\frac{5}{8}$-, $\frac{3}{4}$-, $\frac{7}{8}$-inch three-strand—used for purchase lines of a counterweight flying system and the lift or hoist line or a pin and rail system

$\frac{1}{4}$-, $\frac{3}{8}$-, $\frac{5}{8}$-inch three-strand—a lightweight rigging good for breasting and bridling (see Chapter 10)

**Rope Safety and Care**     Those who work in the theatre should observe the following guidelines for safe use and maintenance of rope:

1. Do not overload. The rope manufacturer's listed BP (breaking point) is for new rope and under a fixed load. Rope in the theatre is run over sheaves and pulleys, tied and untied, and subjected to variable loads—all of which eventually weakens the rope. To avoid overloading, it is good practice to use a safety factor of 10, or one-tenth of BP. A normal hoist line of manila rope, for example, is $\frac{3}{4}$-inch three-strand with a BP of 5,400 pounds. With a safety factor of 10, 540 pounds would be a safe load.

2. Keep a file of the installation date of all hoist and purchase lines.

3. Establish a schedule of inspection, rotation, and replacement of hoist lines, especially those of natural fiber.

4. The inspection should check for fraying or chaffing where a rope runs over the gridiron or through a sheave. Look for damage from clewing several lines together and other stress points of stage rigging.

5. Store natural fiber rope in a clean, dry area, away from excessive heat.

6. Protect ends of rope from fraying or unwinding by binding or whipping the strands together.

**Braided Rope**     Using a different technique, the strands of fiber are braided together into a very flexible rope. Cotton is the most common natural fiber used in braided rope. However, the same synthetic fibers found in stranded rope are used in braided rope. When strands of synthetic fiber are braided around a central braided core, the rope develops amazing strength. It is not, however, recommended for hoisting rope because of its tendency to stretch and lose trim. It is also very expensive. An excellent combination of fibers for theatre use is made of braided cotton strands around a central core or strand of polyester or polyethylene. Many other combinations are available.

Sizes and uses of braided rope include these:

$\frac{1}{2}$-inch (No. 10)—drawline for heavy traveler curtain

$\frac{5}{16}$-inch (No.8)—lash line and lightweight rigging

$\frac{1}{8}$-inch awning cord—lightweight window curtain rigging, trick line, and tie-lines

## CABLE

Sometimes referred to as *wire rope,* cable is made of flexible, high-grade steel wire twisted into strands like fiber rope. Six or more strands are twisted into cable. A cable is identified by its diameter, plus two numbers such as $6 \times 7$, $6 \times 16$, or $6 \times 19$. The first number indicates the number of strands, the second the number of wires in a strand. A $\frac{1}{2}$-inch $6 \times 7$, for example, would be a cable $\frac{1}{2}$ inch in diameter, made up of 6 strands with 7 wires per strand. The same factor of 10 also applies as a safe load guide for cable rigging.

*Aircraft cable* is made of flexible, high tensile strength steel. Its greater flexibility and strength allow it to pass through smaller pulleys and make it useful for special rigging and winch work.

Sizes and uses of cable are as follows:

$\frac{1}{4}$-, $\frac{3}{8}$-inch $6 \times 19$—hoist line in counterweight system

$\frac{3}{16}$-inch $7 \times 19$ aircraft cable—winch, turntable, and wagon drives

$\frac{1}{8}$-inch $7 \times 19$ aircraft cable—most flown scenery, some winch drives, and actor flying rigging

## WIRE

Single wire in various sizes is used to reinforce or guy properties or units of scenery. Some special uses are these:

Pin wire (No. 13 gauge)—used in short lengths as a temporary pin of a loose-pin hinge, to facilitate its easy removal during a quick change

Stove wire (No. 16 gauge)—very soft, flexible wire; because of its dark color, it is invisible at a short distance and can be used to stabilize decorative properties that tend to vibrate or fall during the movement of a wagon or turntable

## CHAIN

Other than to attach and trim hanging scenery, special rigging, or chain drive, chain is used to weight stage draperies. Sizes and uses are as follows:

$\frac{1}{2}$-, $\frac{3}{4}$-inch jack chain (single or double)—curtain weight

$\frac{3}{4}$-, $\frac{7}{8}$-inch jack chain (24- to 36-inch lengths)—trim chain on pipe batten of the counterweight system

# CONSTRUCTING SCENERY

# 7

Scene designers and technicians are interested in the construction of scenery, not only to become familiar with building techniques but also to become aware of the uses and limitations of various materials. The more they know about present-day theatrical materials and techniques the better they are able to introduce new materials and original methods into designs, as well as to develop a knowledgeable use of contemporary types of scenery.

The building of scenery is under the charge of the *technical director* or shop head. This is the person who is responsible for translating the designer's idea into reality. The artistry and craft of the technical director can have a profound impact on the design.

## TYPES OF SCENERY

Scenery construction may seem at first glance to be unduly flimsy and unnecessarily complicated. This is due, chiefly, to the unique demands placed on scenery by the theatre. First, it must be portable and lightweight in structure so as to move easily on the stage and from theatre to theatre. Second, scenery has to be able to assume large-scale proportions for either decorative or masking reasons. Therefore, large areas of scenery must be furnished with the minimum of structure and the maximum of portability. And last, because scenery is here today and gone tomorrow, its construction must be economical. To be economical does not necessarily mean to buy the cheapest materials. It means to balance costs against the weight and structural demands of a material. It also implies the economical use of scenery. Higher material costs can be afforded if a scenic element has more than one use or can be reused at a later date.

For the purpose of discussing construction techniques, the various types of scenery are divided into groups that are similar in construction and alike in function as well as related in handling methods. Scenery is broadly divided first into two general classifications: two-dimensional and three-dimensional.

*Two-dimensional scenery,* under this broad division, is meant to include all flat scenery with reference to its basic shape rather than to the way it is used on the stage. Although units of flat scenery, for example, may be assembled together to make a three-dimensional form on the stage, the individual pieces are still classified as two-dimensional scenery.

Two-dimensional scenery is further subdivided into two groups: framed and unframed, or soft scenery. Within these two groupings falls the bulk of the scenery that is used on the stage either in the form of wings and flats or stage draperies and drops.

*Three-dimensional scenery* obviously refers to the pieces that are built in three dimensions to be handled and used as solid forms. Three-dimensional scenery is separated into two basic groups: weight-bearing, meaning the weight of the actor, and nonweight-bearing forms.

## SOFT SCENERY

Such large unframed pieces as stage draperies, the drop, and the cyclorama, or "cyc," are counted as soft scenery. They all have the same function—to provide a large area of scenery with a minimum of construction and a maximum of portability. Being soft, they are dependent on hanging from a batten or pipe for support. As a result they can be easily folded or rolled for transportation or storage.

### STAGE DRAPERIES

The large panels of stage draperies are made by sewing small widths of materials together with vertical seams. There are three sound reasons for using vertical seams. First, because the direction of the weave or decoration is with the length of the fabric, it hangs and looks better in a vertical position. Second, a vertical seam is less conspicuous because it is lost in the folds of the drapery. Third, there is less strain on a vertical than on a horizontal seam, which carries the cumulative weight of each width of material from the bottom seam to the top.

The seams are face-to-face to present a smooth front surface. The top is reinforced with a 3- to 4-inch webbing through which are set the grommet rings at 1-foot intervals for the tie-lines. The bottom has a generous hem containing a chain that functions as a weight for the curtain. Occasionally, the chain is encased in a separate sound-deadening pocket, called a pipe pocket, that is sewn on the backside of the drapery instead of being enclosed directly in the hem.

Drapery fabrics may be sewn flat on the top webbing or may be gathered or pleated onto the webbing to give a fixed fullness to the curtain. Fixed

## Figure 7–1
### Stage Draperies

(a) Flat drapery construction. Webbing with grommets and tie-lines at top; hem enclosing chain weight at bottom.
(b) Gathered drapery. Fullness gathered on top webbing; chain pocket attached above hem at the bottom.
(c) Types of stage draperies: border, leg, panel.

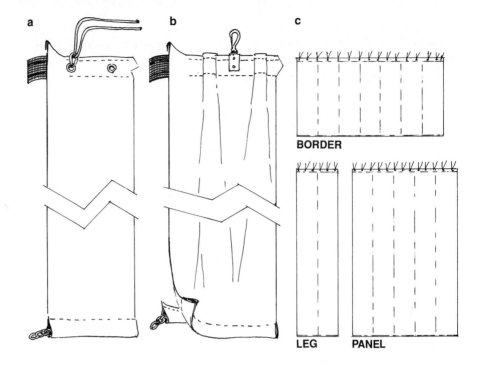

fullness is an advantage for a front curtain or traveler curtain. However, it is not as flexible as a flat curtain panel, because the latter can be hung either flat or with varying degrees of fullness in a greater variety of uses (Figure 7–1).

**Drapery Materials**     Stage draperies can be made of a variety of fabrics, depending on the specific use they are to serve and the limitations of the budget. Are the draperies to be opaque, translucent, or transparent? Are they to be pictorial, decorative, or just masking? Are they to be stock draperies or a one-shot special effect? Answering such questions helps decide the kind of material to choose and its relationship to cost and use.

Velour, although expensive, is the favored drapery material. Its pile weave has a rich texture under the stage lights that cannot be duplicated with cheaper substitutes. It hangs and drapes beautifully, is opaque, and is also easy to maintain, handle, and store. Among the more economical velour substitutes that bear mentioning are duvetyn, commando cloth, and flannel.

Commando cloth and duvetyn are almost as opaque as velour but drape poorly and lack as rich a surface quality. Flannel drapes a little better than duvetyn, and it has almost the same opacity. Its woolly nap surface has a fair texture under stage lights.

Stage draperies are made of other materials, not with the intention of imitating velour, but to create their own effect. Cotton rep and monk's cloth have enough texture to make an interesting inexpensive curtain when hung in fullness. Wide-ribbed corduroy is another drapery texture, which though semi-opaque, drapes and hangs well.

Sometimes draperies are expected to be translucent or, on occasion, transparent. Dyed muslin is the least expensive translucent fabric. It has a further advantage of coming in wider widths than such materials as satin or nylon crepe in the translucent class.

Gauze, the general term applied to all transparent materials, is available in a variety of fabrics such as cotton or nylon net, chiffon, and organdy, to name a few familiar commercial textiles. Although these fabrics are available at the local fabric store, their chief disadvantage is their narrow width, which increases the number of seams in a curtain. The seams become visible when the transparent curtain is back-lighted. There are gauzes, as well as muslins, that are woven on wide looms especially for theatre use. Bobbinet and shark's-tooth scrim, two transparent materials, are made in 30-foot widths. Bobbinet is a hexagonal net that is more sheer but weaker than shark's-tooth scrim, which has a rectangular or ladder pattern (Figure 7–2). The shark's-tooth, in addition to draping well, is dense enough to provide a dye-painting surface and still become transparent when back-lighted. Filled scrim or leno scrim can be used as a cyc, or painted drop, for a softer look.

## DROPS

Another large-area piece of scenery is the drop, taking its name from the fact that it hangs on a batten and is dropped in, as opposed to the older method of the shutter that slid on stage from opposite sides. The drop is made with horizontal face-to-face seams to create a smooth surface (Figure 7–3a). The horizontal seams, when the drop is hanging, are under enough tension from the weight of the material and bottom batten to stretch into a smooth surface.

A translucent drop is dye-painted and can be equipped with tie-lines at the top and tie-lines or a pipe pocket at the bottom (Figure 7–3b). The position of the seams of a translucent drop are important, because if they are not carefully hidden in the design they produce a distracting shadow line.

**Figure 7–2**
**Gauzes**

The three basic gauze materials: net, bobbinet, and scrim are illustrated to show their difference in weave.
Net, square weave. A larger mesh (1 inch) is knotted like a fish net. Loose, tabby-weave materials are sometimes called gauze. The fabric, which looks like surgical gauze, has very little strength.
Bobbinet, hexagonal weave. Very transparent and strong, but stretches out of shape easily.
Shark's-tooth scrim, ladder weave. Strong, not as sheer as bobbinet; best for dye painting.

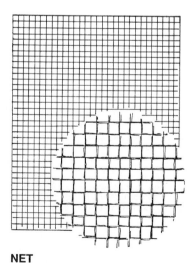

**NET**

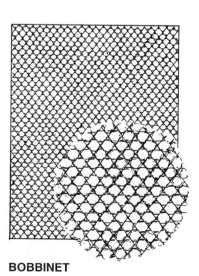

**BOBBINET**

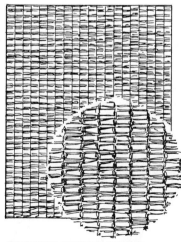

**SHARK'S-TOOTH SCRIM**

### Figure 7–3
#### Drop Construction

(a) Rear view of a roll drop.
  (1) Top batten, double 1 × 4.
  (2) Face-to-face horizontal seam.
  (3) Bottom batten, doubles 2 inches half round.
(b) Rear view of a folding drop.
  (1) Top webbing with grommets and tie-lines.
  (2) Netting glued over openings or cut edges to support loose ends.
  (3) Drop bottom with pipe sleeve for the removal of bottom batten.
  (4) Drop bottom made with grommets and tie-lines.
(c) Types of drops:
  (1) Plain back drop.
  (2) Cut border.
  (3) Cut drop, netted.
  (4) Leg drop.
  (5) Also referred to as leg drop or leg.

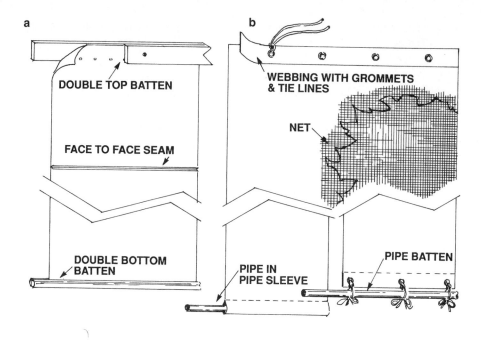

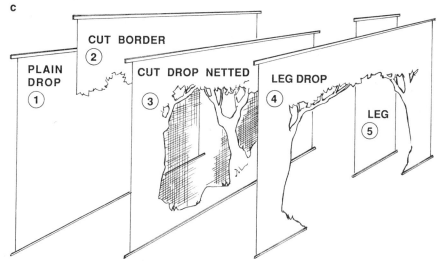

For this reason, translucent drops are sometimes made with vertical seams and with irregular spacing, or, if the budget permits, they are made seamless by using 30-foot-width muslin.

For transportation, drops are made to fold. Acrylic and latex paints are flexible enough to withstand folding *only* if the paint application is kept thin and is kept to one layer. Even then, eventually the paint will crack.

Drops are commonly made of muslin because it is available in wide widths and is an excellent, inexpensive translucent material. Drops are sometimes made of other materials, frequently for an unusual textural quality, such as burlap, velour, and terry cloth. And, of course, drops can be made of the gauze materials. Shark's-tooth and bobbinet are used more often than other sheer fabrics because they come in wider widths.

A cut drop such as in Figure 7–3c is often backed with bobbinet, opera net, or scenery net. The cut edges of a drop can be supported with a lighter material, often with a 1-inch square mesh. When the net is dyed to match the background, it becomes nearly invisible. A plastic netting of $\frac{3}{4}$-inch mesh, originally manufactured to protect farm crops, is another option that works well.

## THE CYCLORAMA

The largest single piece of scenery in the theatre is the cyclorama, or "cyc." The cyclorama's most familiar use is as a sky or void, backing a setting or elements of scenery placed in the foreground. Most commonly, the cyc is hung flat across the back of the setting, although it can also extend downstage in a gentle arc on either one or both sides of the set.

The cyclorama presents the greatest problem in the necessity to create a large, uninterrupted, smooth surface. It is ideal to have a seamless cyc, but that can be prohibitively expensive. With a seamed cyc, the direction of the sewn seams becomes important. Because the cyc material is hung flat, the tension from horizontal seams will pull the surface smooth.

Vertical seams round the corners better than the horizontal seams, but they do not present as smooth a finished surface. In both cases the seams are sure to show under a high level of illumination. This can be corrected by hanging a large flat panel of dyed (very light blue) shark's-tooth scrim directly in front of the canvas cyclorama, using the same batten. Because it is a wide material, the number of vertical seams can be reduced to two on the normal cyclorama. The scrim becomes the reflecting surface and the canvas acts as a backing.

## FRAMED SCENERY

The structure of framed scenery is planned to support itself in a standing position. Although a framed piece may be aided by hanging support, or may be flown altogether, the basic framing principle remains the same. Framed scenery, as a construction technique, does not lend itself easily to the framing of a large area. It is possible to develop the framing for a large area, but to do this it has to be hinged to fold into a smaller size or be dismantled into smaller parts to move in and out of the theatre. Most framing, then, deals with relatively small modules when compared to the large sizes of unframed scenery.

### WOOD SCENIC CONSTRUCTION

The traditional material for scenic construction is wood. The various wood joints are derived from the many ways of combining lumber surfaces. The surfaces of lumber are described as its face (flat surface), edge, and end. The

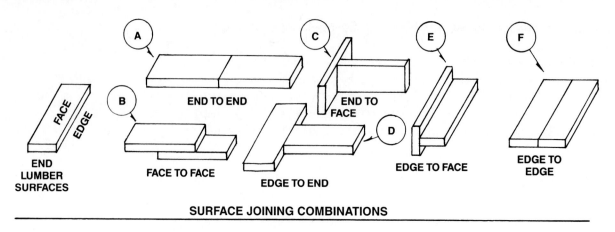

**SURFACE JOINING COMBINATIONS**

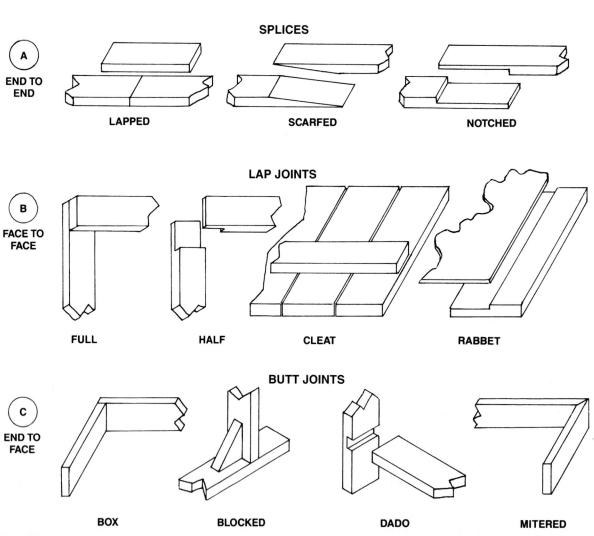

**Figure 7–4**
Typical Wood Joints Used in
Scenery Construction

## BUTT JOINTS

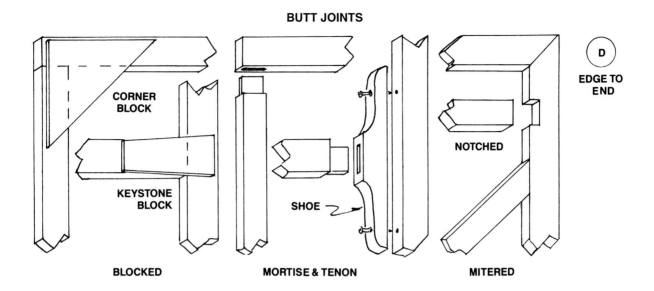

CORNER BLOCK

KEYSTONE BLOCK

SHOE

NOTCHED

**BLOCKED**

**MORTISE & TENON**

**MITERED**

D

**EDGE TO END**

## BUTT JOINTS

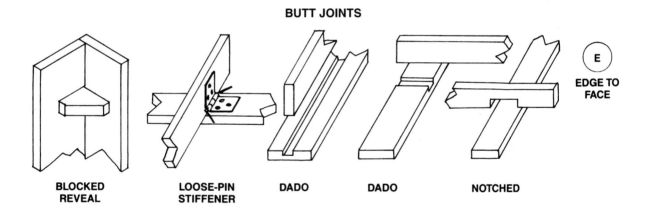

**BLOCKED REVEAL**

**LOOSE-PIN STIFFENER**

**DADO**

**DADO**

**NOTCHED**

E

**EDGE TO FACE**

## PLANKING

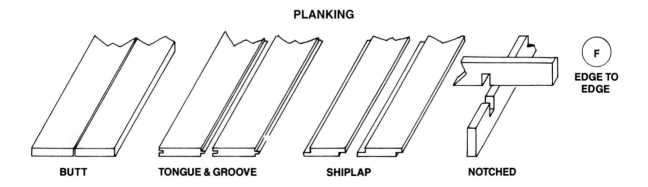

**BUTT**

**TONGUE & GROOVE**

**SHIPLAP**

**NOTCHED**

F

**EDGE TO EDGE**

surface-joining combinations are classified as end to end, face to face, end to face, edge to end, edge to face, and edge to edge, as illustrated at the top of Figure 7–4.

The making of a joint has two steps: first, the cutting and fitting of the joint; and second, the securing of the joint with hardware or glue. Fixed or permanent joints are used in constructing individual units of scenery. A temporary joint is used to construct individual pieces to make a larger unit.

In Figure 7–4, the numerous joints used in scenery construction are classified in groups that combine the same surfaces. Fixed joints are secured

**Figure 7–5**
Framed Scenery

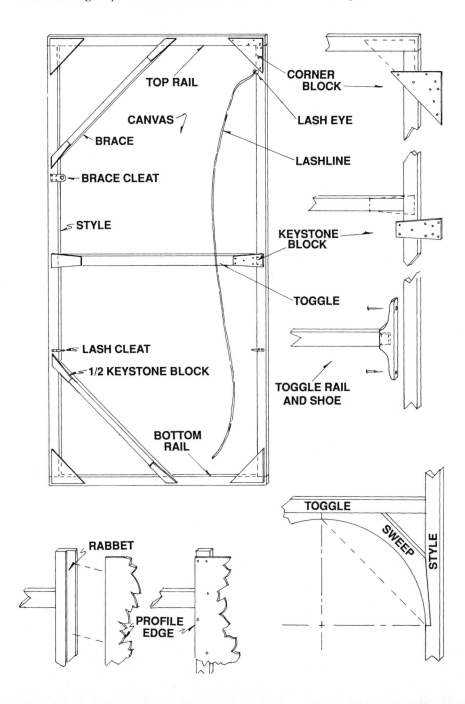

with nails, staples or screws, and glue. Knockdown or temporary joints are held with bolts, loose-pin hinges, keeper hooks, and turn buttons.

The framing of a traditional theatrical flat such as in Figure 7–5 illustrates the basic technique that is applied to any size or shape. The end to edge joint is strengthened most commonly with a $\frac{1}{4}$-inch plywood plate called a *corner block* or *keystone*. In the past, these joints often used a mortise and tenon connection, as illustrated. The time-intensive nature of this kind of construction has made it obsolete. In fact, time constraints have even reduced the traditional keystone to a simpler rectangular shape.

The top and bottom horizontal framing members are called *rails*, while the vertical framing members are *stiles*. Internal horizontals or verticals are referred to as *toggles* and are generally spaced at 4- to 5-foot intervals.

**Figure 7–6**
**Types of Framed Scenery**

(a) The framing of a set-piece with profile edges of three ply.
(b) Detail of sill iron used across the bottom of a door opening in a flat.
(c) Detail of canvas-covering technique. Note that tacks or staples are set on the inside edge of the external framework. The loose outside edge of canvas is then pasted to the flat surface of the frame.
(d) Flat with profile edges, of three ply.
(e) Door flat.
(f) Window flat.
(g) Two-fold flat with double-door opening. Note hinged sill iron.

The *diagonal braces*, the remaining internal framing members, function to strengthen and hold square the rectangular shape. A rectangle is basically a weak structure and can be very easily racked out of shape. The triangle, on the other hand, is very rigid and resists a change of shape. Hence, two diagonal braces off one side of the rectangle, as shown in Figure 7–5, will resist a change of shape. Bracing on opposite corners, however, is not as strong and can be racked out of shape.

Figure 7–6 shows several examples of framed scenery.

### HARD COVERED SCENERY

It is now more common for flats to be covered with a hard sheet material such as lauan, as discussed in Chapter 6. In some instances, the framing technique is the same as for soft covered flats. The hard cover, however, negates the need for diagonals and often corner blocks and keystones.

Another common variation is known as the *Hollywood flat,* in which the faces of the framing members are perpendicular to the face of the flat.

The advantages of hard covered flats are greater structural integrity as well as the ability to accept a wide range of textural surfaces. However, whenever possible, the flats should be covered with muslin to provide a better paint surface than lauan (Figure 7–7).

### FRAMING CURVED SCENERY

The framing of a curved surface requires a similar technique to the Hollywood flat. All framing members are on edge rather than flat. The toggles are sweeps, most often of plywood, cut to the curve of the surface. The surface

**Figure 7–7**
**Hard Covered Scenery**

Scenery for intimate theatre such as the Black Box frequently use hard covered scenery because of the smaller scale and the closeness of the audience when compared to the proscenium theatre. Stiles and toggles are framed on edge to stiffen the $\frac{1}{8}$-inch plywood cover, which can be used as a flat or curved surface.
(a) Flat surface.
(b) Flat surface with opening.
(c) Curved surface.

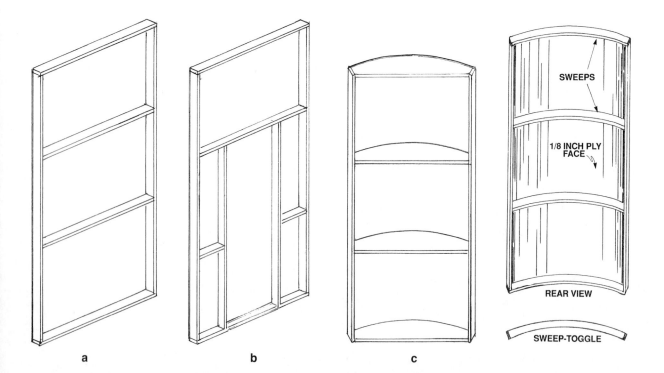

a     b     c

covering must be firm yet able to bend, such as lauan or $\frac{1}{8}$-inch ply. Scenery canvas or muslin is glued to the finished form to provide a surface matching the rest of the scenery (Figure 7–7).

## DOORS

Doors and windows are those important details that are often neglected in the haste of preparing a set. A door, in a sense, is a moving piece of scenery that is used by the actor. In a split second, its malfunction cannot only give away the scenic illusion but can also break up the carefully built mood of a scene.

The building and hanging of a door is a skilled and time-consuming job. For these reasons, the average amateur group is better off to make or have made a set of good stock door casings that can be used in a variety of ways.

In the making of a door the normal scenery-framing techniques are often too lightweight. There was a time when the audience would accept a canvas door painted to look like oak planking but sounding and handling like a screen door. The modern audience, schooled by years of movie and television realism, is jarred by this obvious theatricality. There is a limit, however, to the weight of a door that can be supported in framed scenery that does not have the solidity of the stud framing or masonry it is simulating. Hence, it is necessary to reach a compromise in a construction technique that will keep the door portable and lightweight enough to shift while at the same time achieving a degree of solidity and sturdiness for the action.

A door unit is made up of three basic parts: (1) the actual door, sometimes called "shutter"; (2) the reveal, comprising the jambs (vertical members), header (top), and sill (bottom); and (3) the trim, which forms the decorative frame around the door opening. The door is always hinged to the reveal. The trim, however, is constructed in one of two ways: It may be attached to the reveal, or it may be kept as a separate member and applied to the face of the flat. The first method, called a *cased door*, is independent of the scenic unit. With the trim permanently attached to the reveal, the reveal of the cased door assembly slides through a prepared opening in the flat which is considerably larger than the size of the door itself (Figure 7–8a).

The second method, referred to as a *scene door*, is dependent on the unit to which it is attached. The trim is not attached to the reveal, which is built to the exact size of the flat opening. The reveal, containing the shutter, "butt fits" to the opening from behind (Figure 7–8b). The scene door provides a great deal more flexibility in the ways the trim can be handled. It can, for example, be completely painted or attached and set away from the opening to increase the apparent size of the doorway (Figure 7–9a).

The action of a door affects its construction. For example, a door that swings onstage requires double facing; a double-action door (kitchen door) takes special hinging, as does a Dutch door; sliding doors involve tracking; and additional rigging becomes necessary for the trick door that, as if by magic, opens and closes by itself.

A contemporary-styled door could be a manufactured door from a lumber yard. The flush, hollow core door is the most adaptable and can be easily

**Figure 7–8**
Stock Door Construction

(a) Cased-door unit.
(1) Door reveal and trim built as one unit.
(2) Flat with a standard door opening.
(3) Detail of door construction.
(4) Angled strap hinge on jamb to hold door unit in the opening.
(5) Blocks to hold trim in place.
(6) Cross section of door unit through the header.
(7) Plan of the cased-door unit showing the hinging.
(8) Butt hinge on door.
(b) Scene-door unit.
(1) Separate trim.
(2) Flat with a standard door opening.
(3) Door and reveal.
(4) Corner blocks to hold reveal frame square.
(5) Rim lock. Attached on back side of door.
(6) Tubular latch. Sets into edge of door.

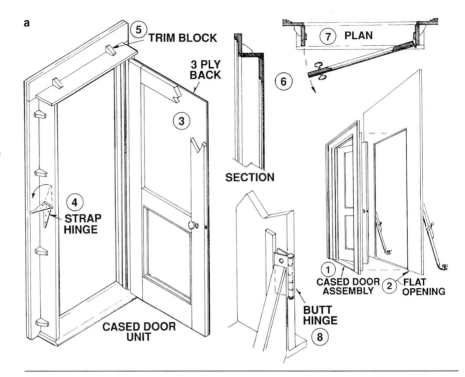

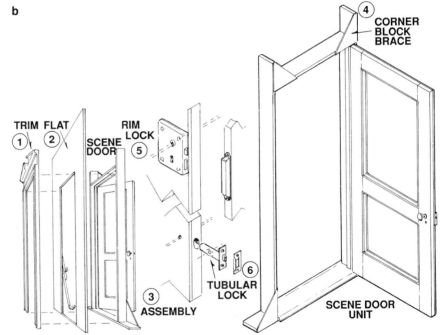

modified to fit a design. Paneled doors are usually quite expensive and are frequently too small in scale for the stage.

## WINDOWS

Similar to the door, a window has a reveal and trim, but the window sash takes the place of the door. The arrangements of panes within the sash varies

**Figure 7–9**
Variations in Door Trim and Paneling

(a) Various methods of handling the trim around the same-size door opening, possible with a scene-door unit. (1) Wide-set trim. (2) Close-set and high trim with transom. (3) Painted trim.
(b) Door paneling. The paneling for (2), (3), and (4) are constructed within the basic paneling of a stock door (1). (5) The flush side of a stock door painted and cleated to look like a planked door.

with the style of the window. Because the window sash is more open than a door, it is difficult to build. The pattern of the thin mullions often becomes too fragile for normal stage framing unless the window is far enough upstage to fake them in profile board. Delicate tracery is frequently reinforced by a backing of screening that passes for glass and strengthens the mullions at the same time.

To simulate glass, panes are sometimes left clear or backed with netting. The net, although nearly invisible, has enough density to give the feeling of glass. It is more apparent by contrast if the window is opened during the action of the play.

Real glass is too dangerous to use on the stage, and plexiglass is difficult to work with because it reflects the many stage lights; when the window background is darker than the on stage lights, the window becomes a perfect mirror. Also, to avoid a plexiglass "shimmy," it has to be at least $\frac{1}{8}$ inch in thickness, which then becomes expensive. (The use of plexiglass windows in TV and movies, on the other hand, is common practice. Reflection problems are minimal because there is only the one eye of the camera and not the 500 or more pairs of eyes of a theatre audience.)

Window action, like that of the door, involves sliding or swinging on hinges. A window may have the vertical sliding action of a double-hung window, or may slide horizontally. It may have the vertical hinging of a casement window or the horizontal hinging of the awning-type window.

It is a little more difficult to plan a set of stock windows than doors because of the greater variation in sash styles. Certain often-used, conventionally styled windows can be standardized and put into stock. Also the casing (reveal and trim) may be kept in stock to be used with interchangeable or new sashes for each show (Figure 7–10). As with doors, manufactured windows can be used where practicable.

## TRIM

Decorative trim appears in a set in places other than around door and window openings. Some additional areas of trim, painted or practical, are baseboards, chair rails, wainscoting, cornices, and overmantel decoration. Trim that is attached in these areas might need to be removable for handling or shifting.

The attached trim requires additional framing within the flat for support. Chair rails and baseboards are easy to attach, but the construction and hanging of a cornice is more complicated. Although trim details are slightly oversized for the stage, the average cornice can be made up of stock moldings. To keep the framing lightweight, the molding is nailed to blocks set at about 2-foot intervals and backed with 3-ply or longitudinal framing strips. The whole assembly is attached to the wall flats with bolts or turnbuttons (Figure 7–11).

Architectural and decorative trim, of course, can be duplicated in lightweight materials such as carved Styrofoam or vacu-formed shapes (see the section titled "Textured and Sculptured Surfaces" later in this chapter).

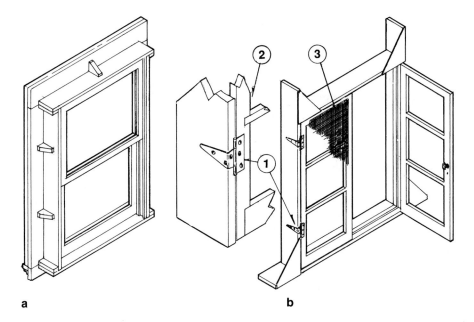

a                                    b

### Figure 7–10
### Window Construction

(a) Double-hung window. Trim is attached to reveal in the same manner as the cased door.
(b) Casement window. The reveal is constructed in the same way as the scene door with hinged sashes.
 (1) A bent T-strap hinge in place of the butt hinge.
 (2) Notched mullions.
 (3) Galvanized screening to strengthen the sash and simulate glass.

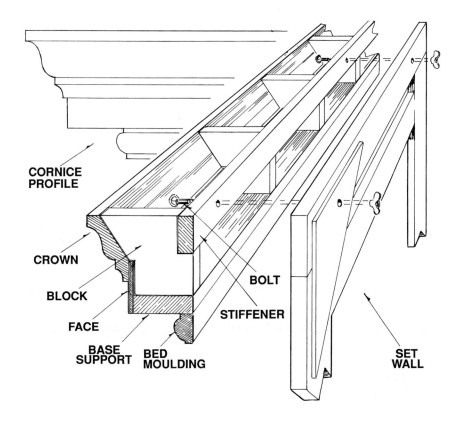

CORNICE PROFILE

CROWN

BLOCK

FACE

BASE SUPPORT

BED MOULDING

BOLT

STIFFENER

SET WALL

### Figure 7–11
### Cornice Construction

A cornice is a lightly framed three-dimensional element of trim designed to attach along the length of a wall. The perspective view shows the block-framing technique and a method of attaching the cornice to the scenery.

## THREE-DIMENSIONAL SCENERY

### WEIGHT-BEARING STRUCTURES

Certain elements of scenery cannot be reduced to flat planes. Others, because they are so small, are more practically built as three-dimensional forms. This is especially important if the form is to bear the weight of a sitting or standing actor. Weight-bearing structures are present in such architectural forms as steps, ramps, and raised levels; in the irregular forms of rocks; and in the free form of an abstract design. The raising of a large portion of the stage floor and the use of steps and ramps brings excitment to the design composition, variation to the staging, and headaches to the stage technician. In the absence of any mechanical means of raising sections of the stage floor, the problem becomes one of creating a second floor at a specific distance above the stage floor. The level must be structurally sound enough to support actors and furniture with a minimum of deflection and, at the same time, be portable and economical. A large expanse of platforming is subdivided into smaller units for ease of handling. A single unit is made to knock down into even smaller parts.

**Platform Construction**    Any platforming technique can be resolved into the three structural members that are always present in some form or other: the top, rail, and post. The top, which is the actual bearing surface, is directly supported by the rails. Crossrails run parallel to the shortest dimension of the level. Their interval is linked to the material and thickness of the top. The average top, $\frac{5}{8}$-inch or $\frac{3}{4}$-inch 5-ply board, should be supported at 30-inch intervals. The span, however, can be increased by use of cleats or stiffeners on the underside and thereby, in effect, increase the thickness of the top material. The rail is, in turn, supported by the post. The interval of posting is dependent on the size of the rail. A 1 by 3 rail (on edge) should be posted at not more than 3-foot intervals, and at 4-foot intervals for a 1 by 4 rail.

The most common form of platform construction in use today is the "rigid" platform. This typically consists of a lumber frame of 2-by-4s or 1-by-6s covered with a $\frac{5}{8}$-inch or $\frac{3}{4}$-inch plywood lid permanently attached. The platform is then elevated to any variety of heights using simple lumber legs, typically 2-by-4s bolted to the frame. There are several variations including steel and aluminum frames on legs. This style of construction is applicable to regular or irregular shapes of platforms.

A more efficient method of platform support is the use of "stud walls." Taking the idea from house construction, this is an all 2-by-4 frame consisting of two horizontal members joined by a series of vertical members. The advantages of this method are quick installation, very rigid support, and the ability to create raked decks easily.

**The Parallel**    One way of providing a raised level for the stage is the parallel method. The parallel is a hinged trestle structure that opens to support a top and folds into a flat pack when not in use (Figure 7–12).

As a stock platforming method, the parallel has the advantage of being lightweight, easy to assemble and transport, and fairly sturdy. It also can be adapted to irregular shapes as well as to the conventional rectangle. Its chief disadvantage is a storage problem. To maintain any variation in levels, duplicate sets of parallels of different heights have to be kept in storage.

A convenient stock size for regular-shaped parallels depends first on general handling and storage conditions; second, on the construction of the top; and last, on the riser heights of stock steps that work with the platforms. If the top is to be made of $\frac{3}{4}$-inch 5-ply, a 4-by-8-foot top is the most economical size. Stock parallel heights, obviously, should be at intervals related to

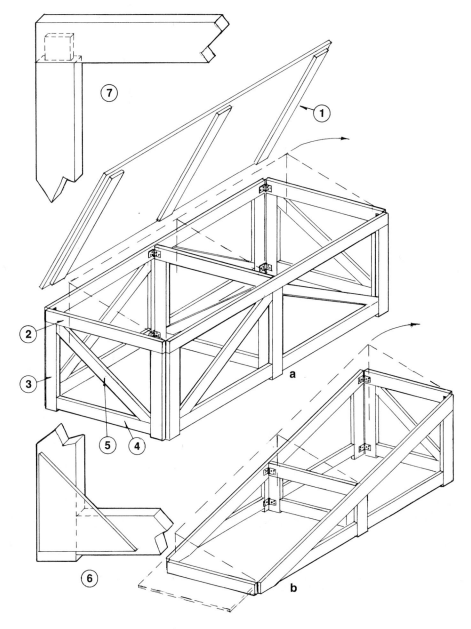

**Figure 7–12**
**The Parallel Platform**

(a) Basic parallel construction with open-corner hinging.
 (1) Top $\frac{3}{4}$-inch 5-ply with cleats. Typical trestle framing includes (2) top rail bearing on (3) the post, tied by (4) the bottom rail, and strengthened by (5) the diagonal brace. The framing may be joined either by (6) corner blocks or (7) by mortise-and-tenon joints.
(b) The parallel technique used on a slanted platform or ramp.

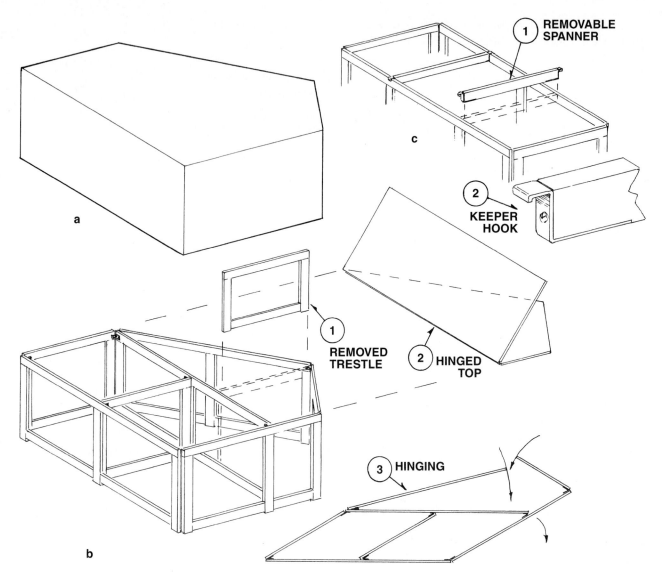

**Figure 7–13**
The Irregular-shaped Platform

(a) The hinging and assembly of an irregular-shaped platform are solved individually.
(b) To fold: (1) Loose-pin-hinged internal trestle is detached after top (2) has been removed. (3) By unpinning the hinges of one corner, the parallel will fold into a flat pack.
(c) The use of a ''spanner'' allows the removal of internal trestles in cases where it is necessary to keep the area under the top clear. (1) Spanner is of heavy enough stock, usually 2 × 4 or 2 × 6, to make a strong span. (2) Detail of keeper-hook on end of spanner.

riser heights of the steps, 6- or 7-inch intervals being normal. Parallel heights usually vary at double-riser intervals such as 12-, 24-, and 36-inch, or 14-, 28-, and 42-inch intervals.

The framing of a single trestle or "gate" of a parallel employs the post-and-rail technique. In Figure 7–12a, note that the top rail is borne by the two vertical members, or posts, which carry through to the floor. The bottom rail is merely a tie-rail that completes the rectangle. The diagonals are necessary to hold the gate square and eliminate side sway or "rack" in the finished platform. The single gate, though lightweight, gathers strength when it is hinged to the other members of the parallel. To fold flat, the parallel must hinge as shown.

Any irregular shape that can be reduced to flat planes may be constructed by the parallel method. The gates can be loose-pin-hinged together rather than folded, for many times the pattern of the supports is so irregular the parallel cannot fold flat (Figure 7–13).

**Other Platform Techniques**    There have been various other attempts to standardize platforming construction, aiming to cut down the size of stored parts, to reduce the amount of internal framing (by using material other than wood), and at the same time to provide a sound structure. The post-and-rail and scaffolding methods (Figure 7–14) are ventures in this direction. Both succeed in reducing the storage space of spare parts and each provides a very sturdy platform with a minimum of framing. The techniques, although very practicable for regular shapes, do not lend themselves readily to irregular shapes. The limits placed on design, however, are minor when compared to the stage-space and sightline limitations imposed by some theatre buildings.

Steel pipe and aluminum tubing have been used as platforming materials in two different methods. The first method involves the adaptation of construction scaffolding for stage uses. Each scaffold unit is made out of aluminum tubing and at heights of 1 to 3 feet at 1-foot intervals. Figure 7–14c illustrates how the various heights of scaffolds interlock, or stack, one on top of the other. Each set has its own system of cross bracing.

A more recent use of pipe for platforming is an adaptation of the parallel method (Figure 7–14d). The unique feature of the design is the making of the corner into its own hinge. The unit takes a 4-foot-square top that is overhung 1 inch for a facing flat.

Other examples of steel in platform framing involve the use of manufactured shapes of structural steel. The shapes are designed to interlock and bolt together. Figure 7–15 illustrates the use of the Unistrut channel, Telspar, and slotted angles as platform. The slotted flat angles offer ample surfaces for combining wood with steel in platform construction. It should be noted that the use of these manufactured steel shapes is expensive.

Regardless of whichever type of platforming is favored, the parallel method is, like the framing of a plane flat, an example of basic structural framing. With this basic knowledge the carpenter can modify or embellish the technique to fit all special needs.

## Figure 7–14
### Other Platforming Techniques

(a) Post and rail or rigid framing.

(b) Detail of top construction.

(c) Scaffold method.

(1) Tubular steel or aluminum scaffold unit.

(2) Spacer to interlock units.

(3) Foot.

(4) Cross braces to space and stabilize scaffold units.

(5) The stacking of one scaffold unit upon another to gain height.

(d) Steel parallel method. A smaller moduled tubular steel and angle iron-framed parallel.

(1) Top overhangs unit to allow for facing flat.

(2) Spacer to interlock and stack units.

(3) Corners become hinges.

(4) Pin attached to top to lock it in place.

(5) Internal pin of hinge corner made up of (6) opened-end trestle and (7) closed-end trestle.

(8) Foot.

(9) Extended foot.

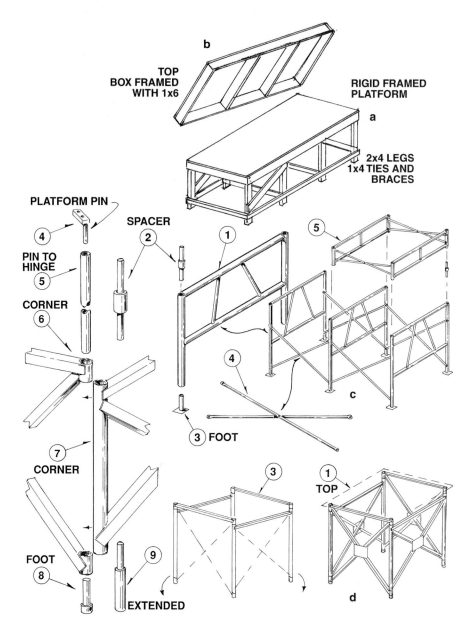

**Truss vs. Beam**    Before discussing truss construction, it is necessary to define some basic structural terms. The four types of stress a structure is subjected to are (1) *compression*—forces pushing against each other, (2) *tension*—pulling, (3) *shear*—offset pushing, and (4) *torque*—a twisting force (Figure 7–16a).

A *beam* is a horizontal structural member that bridges a long span between vertical supports. In the theatre, beams and cross-beams support the stage floor to provide a pattern of trap openings. Because of its necessarily heavy weight, a beam is not very suitable for scenery construction. By framing a beamlike structure with a network of cross-bracing, the resulting lightweight

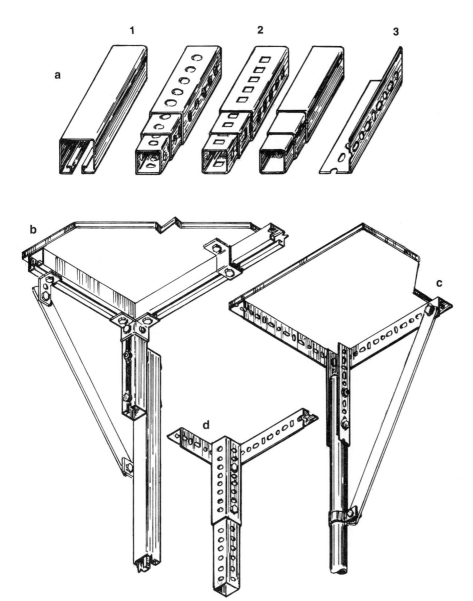

**Figure 7—15**
Platforming Techniques Using Preformed Steel

(a) Commercial preformed steel shapes.
   (1) Unistrut channel.
   (2) Three types of Telspar, a telescoping square pipe shape manufactured by Unistrut Corporation.
   (3) Dexion, a slotted angle iron also made in bar and channel shapes.
(b) A corner view of a platforming technique using Unistrut channel as the basic corner post. Longer extensions of optional lengths are attached with stock Unistrut fittings and cross bracing.
(c) Slotted angle framing with a basic post of slotted channel. Iron pipe is used as the extension.
(d) Slotted angle framing with a slotted channel or Telspar basic post. The extension is Telspar.
Drawing after designs by Philip Eck and Ned Bowman

structure (a *truss*) can function as a beam. The truss, although larger in size, weighs less while providing the same structural support.

Truss framing involves two long horizontal members, top and bottom, and a series of vertical posts spotted at intervals to hold the members apart. The framing is completed by inserting a diagonal at each interval.

The stress-forces on a beam or beam-type structure can be illustrated with an exaggerated stress condition by placing the beam in an unstable condition. As the beam sags, the top face is under compression while the bottom face is in tension (Figure 7—16a). The stress-forces within a truss are similar. When the top member is compressed in a horizontal direction, the

**Figure 7–16**
Truss Construction

A lightweight framing designed to function as a beam or joist.
(a) A beam in an unstable condition to illustrate the direction of stress forces and to identify the various types.
(b) Simple truss showing direction of stress-forces.
(c) Truss technique for steel joist.
(d) Bridge truss hidden in the railing of a scenic bridge.

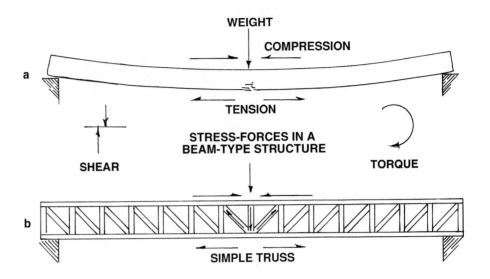

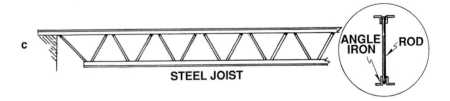

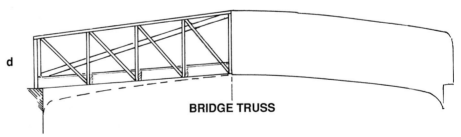

bottom member is in tension. The vertical members are compressed and the diagonals are also in tension.

A long single truss has a tendency to torque or twist. As a result, a long span has to be stiffened with a second truss, forming a box truss. Repeated trusses, when used as a joist, are bridged or cross-braced.

**Stress-Skin Panels**    The stress-skin construction technique produces a panel of great rigidity and structural strength. Typical stress-skin construction consists of two plywood sheets that sandwich an internal structure, often wood or a honeycomb core (Figure 7–17). In essence, the "skins" resist the forces of compresion and tension in the same manner as the top and bottom

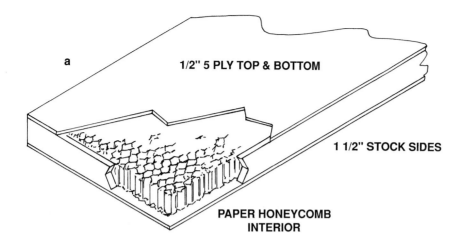

a

1/2" 5 PLY TOP & BOTTOM

1 1/2" STOCK SIDES

PAPER HONEYCOMB
INTERIOR

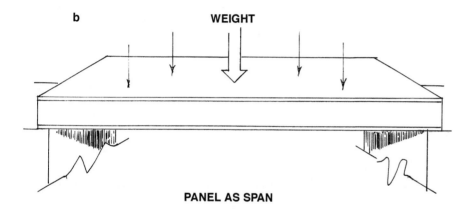

b

WEIGHT

PANEL AS SPAN

**Figure 7–17**
**Stress Skin Panel**

(a) Construction of panel.
(b) Stress skin panel as bridge. Its honeycomb interior spreads the load to support a relatively heavy weight over a limited span.

of a truss. The more rigid nature of a stress-skin panel generally reduces the amount of substructure support required.

**Free Forms**     The irregular surfaces that cannot be reduced to a series of flat planes have to be constructed as a three-dimensional unit. Rock pieces and abstract forms that have to bear weight are examples of this type of irregular surface.

The framing of an irregular surface is, of course, more or less extemporaneous and dependent on some final sculptural touches by the designer to complete the form. For this reason the design drawings of a free form should be accompanied by a scaled model. The form usually suggests the manner of construction; nevertheless there is a basic method that can be adapted to most irregular shapes.

One method of construction of a rock piece, demonstrated in Figure 7–18, goes through the following steps: (1) The exact shape of the base of the rock is framed in the conventional flat-scenery technique. (2) Across the shortest dimension of the base is set a series of contour pieces that follow

**Figure 7–18**
Construction of Rock Forms

(Right)
(1) Shape of form on floor.
Conventional framing.
(2) Contour pieces.
(3) Cross bracing.
(4) Wire screening.
(5) Burlap.
(Photo, left) Three-dimensional
shape before covering with
burlap.
(Right) Same shape covered.

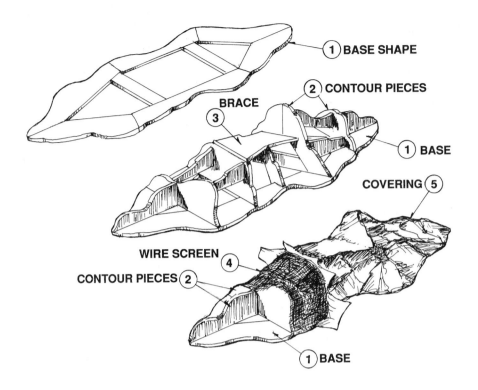

1 **BASE SHAPE**

2 **CONTOUR PIECES**

**BRACE**

3

1 **BASE**

**COVERING** 5

**WIRE SCREEN**

**CONTOUR PIECES** 2

4

1 **BASE**

the contour of a section taken at that point (see "Sections," Chapter 5). (3) The contour pieces are stiffened with cross-bracing and all bearing surfaces are reinforced. (4) Over the contour pieces is placed 1-inch chicken wire or $\frac{1}{2}$-inch screen wire, which is pinched or stretched in the desired shape. (5) The final surface is applied to the screen wire. The kind of covering material depends on the nature of the texture that is desired. The best results are usually obtained with fabric. It is applied by first dipping it into a mixture of strong glue size and base color. The fabric is then draped over and tacked to the framework and allowed to harden. A form made in this manner is lightweight, inexpensive, and surprisingly sturdy.

For additonal techniques see "Textured and Sculptured Surfaces," later in this chapter.

**Ramps**     Ramps can be executed in the same manner as any of the above mentioned platforms. For one example, see Figure 7–12b.

**Steps**     Whereas the ramp is a gradual change of level, the step is more direct, dividing the change into a series of intermediate levels. A flight of steps is made up of risers and treads. The *tread* is the bearing surface and the *riser* is the interval of change in level. The rule of thumb guiding the size relationship of the tread to the riser is based on the ease of movement up and down the steps. The sum of the riser and tread in a continuous flight of steps is kept about 18 inches. For example, a 6-inch riser would require a 12-inch tread, an 8-inch riser a 10-inch tread. Any rise lower than 4 inches and higher than 9 inches is problematic.

Obviously the low-riser and wide-tread combination is more desirable for the onstage steps, permitting the actor to move easily and gracefully up and down.

A flight of steps can be built for the stage in any number of ways. One method is a modified platform trestle construction with each tread supported by a complicated post-and-rail framework (Figure 7–14a). This way, however, the steps are a part of a bulky three-dimensional platform that is difficult to store and move.

Steps can be made to knock down into more easily handled parts by the use of the cut-carriage method of construction (Figure 7–19b). The pattern of the riser and tread is cut from a wide board running parallel to a line drawn through the nosing of each step. The nosing is at the intersection of the top of the riser and the outside edge of the tread. A carriage is cut from a wide enough board to retain at least 3 inches of uncut board along the bottom edge. The thickness of a carriage depends somewhat on its unsupported length. Frequently $\frac{5}{4}$-inch pine stock is used, chiefly for its lightness as well as strength. Sometimes 1-inch pine stock is substituted for lightweight construction, while 2-inch stock is used for a heavier structure. The use of a *metal carriage* can be seen in Figure 6–23.

The choice of carriage stock is also affected by the nature of the riser material. Is the riser made of 1-inch pine, $\frac{1}{4}$-inch 3-ply, or is it left open? As

## Figure 7–19
## Stair Construction Techniques

(a) Trestle method.

(1) Trestle with the top edge framed to riser-tread pattern.

(2) Three ply used as riser stock.

(b) Cut-carriage method.

(1) Carriage cut to riser tread pattern. Step unit leans on platform for support.

(c) Closed-carriage method.

(1) Closed carriage can only be used on the outside of stair unit, hence this type of construction limits the width of the stairs.

(2) Cleat to hold tread. Note that no riser is used.

(d) Cut-carriage method used on an irregular-shaped flight of steps.

(1) Carriages with same riser height but varying tread dimensions.

(e) Stair facing, framed out of $1\frac{1}{8}$-inch baluster stock (1) which is pin-hinged to steps (2). If both faces are covered with 3 ply (3), the facing unit becomes reversible with minimum alterations.

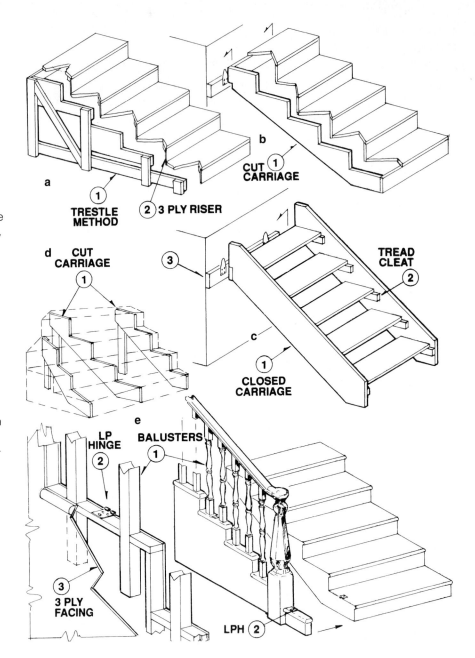

the riser material becomes lighter, the carriage stock should increase in thickness.

A flight of steps would have, typically, two carriages. Additional carriages would depend on the thickness of the tread and the width of the steps. For example, a $\frac{3}{4}$-inch-thick tread would need a carriage at least every 30 inches of width.

The lower step of the carriage sits on the floor and the top is either attached to the front of a platform or is supported by legs.

The understructure of a stair unit (or platform) is often hidden by a facing. One method of doing this is seen in Figure 7–19e. In this method, the stair railing, balcony, stringer, and newel post are incorporated into the facing. The carriage supports the bottom ends of the balusters. It can be an "open carriage," revealing the profile of the tread and risers, or it may be a "closed carriage," masking the ends of the steps.

## NONWEIGHT-BEARING STRUCTURES

Columns, tree trunks, and any other objects that have dimension but do not bear weight comprise the last type of scenery. Since these kinds of structures need only be strong enough to hold their shape, framing is lightweight in comparison to weight-bearing structures.

An irregular shape may be built in three dimensions by the use of two structural elements: the basic silhouette of the object and numerous contour pieces. In a tree trunk, for example, the basic silhouette is the vertical outline of the trunk and branches. The contour pieces are spaced at intervals perpendicular to the silhouette frame (Figure 7–20). After sufficient bracing and stiffening, the form of the trunk is rounded into shape by attaching chicken wire or wire screening over the contour pieces. The chicken wire is covered with burlap or canvas for the finished surface.

Figure 7–20
Construction of Columns and Tree Trunks

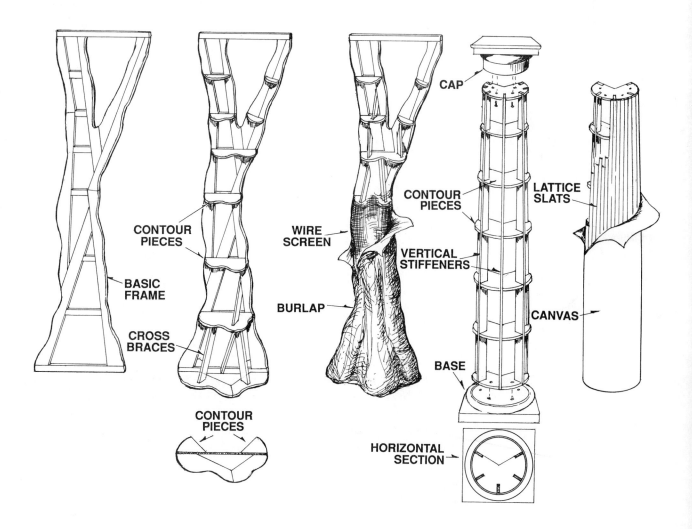

In a rock, the basic silhouette is horizontal and the contour pieces are vertical, which, as has been mentioned, can become structural if the rock has to bear weight.

Columns have regular shapes and lend themselves to a slightly different construction method. It is not necessary to use a silhouette piece. The circular or semicircular contour pieces can be attached to a central core or be held at intervals by slats on the outer surface (Figure 7–20). The exterior surface of the column can be handled in two different ways: 1) The surface can be made up of thin vertical slats (best for a column with a taper) that are covered with canvas after all of the slats have been rounded with a plane or rasp, or; 2) the column can be covered with a flexible paperlike $\frac{1}{8}$-inch lauan or other thin sheeting material. Columns can also be made of Sonotube, or can be shaped as a box column with square sides.

## TEXTURED AND SCULPTURED SURFACES

Designers are always fascinated by a deeply textured surface. It reacts well under stage lights and gives the scenery a feeling of authenticity and stability. A deeply textured surface like the stone wall in Figure 7–21 can be accomplished by using the laborious technique of applied papier-mâché. New plastic foams and forming techniques have made it easier to texture a surface or to create sculptural relief, architectural details, and many three-dimensional forms. Figure 7–22 provides some examples.

### PRE-MANUFACTURED FOAMS

The demand for greater perfection in the design and construction of decorative details on both properties and small elements of scenery, which grew out of the intimacy of the thrust and arena theatres, has led to easier methods of simulating a sculpture form. The closeness to the audience, the increased amount of handling, and the change of design focus from scenic background to set properties are the basic influences on new theatre forms.

*Styrofoam*, the trade name of Dow Chemical's low-density, rigid polystyrene foam (RPF), has been used successfully as a lightweight material that is easy to carve into three-dimensional details or textured surfaces. Blocks of Styrofoam can be glued together or to a scenery surface for convenient carving.

Regular Styrofoam is low-density and therefore very porous. This limits detailed carving and reduces its strength. *Urethane* is a high-density, rigid foam (RUF) that, because of its high density, is easier to carve in detail or turn on a lathe. It also has greater strength than a low-density foam.

Sections of rigid or flexible foams can be glued to reinforcing wood or an adjacent surface with a variety of adhesives. Manufacturer's recommendations are *very important* in the selection of appropriate adhesives.

Sculpture surfaces of foam need to be sealed or primed to provide a usuable surface for paint. A flexible glue alone or a layer of cheesecloth adhered with the glue are possible methods for sealing the surface.

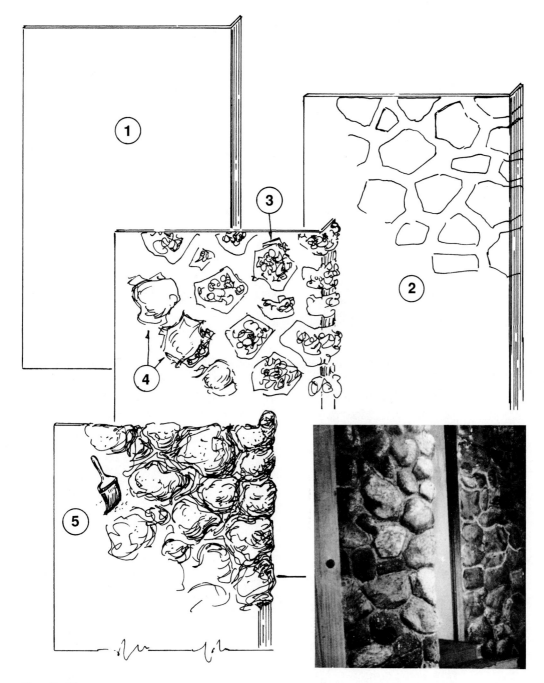

**Figure 7–21**
Three-dimensional Surface

Shown are the steps in the construction of a highly textured surface such as a stone wall.

(1) Hard undersurface, either $\frac{1}{8}$ plywood, upson board, or double-faced corrugated cardboard, shellacked to reduce warpage.

(2) Surface is diagrammed into areas representing the shape of each stone. Cutout appliqués of corrugated board are helpful in reaching a desirable composition.

(3) Each stone surface is built up with glue-soaked newspaper or rough-hewn Styrofoam.

(4) Individual stone is covered with a square of cheesecloth to give it its final form.

(5) After the covering has dried, the entire surface is covered with a thick coat of texture paint and then painted.

## Figure 7−22
## Carved and Turned Rigid Foam

(a) Turned rigid urethane foam: left, baluster with wooden core: right, turned finial.
(b) Relief carving, Styrofoam, sealed with flexible glue, finished with casein paint.
(c) Sculptured Styrofoam and mulched wood embedded in polyurethane foam with welded iron cyclone fencing. *Oedipus Rex* by Stravinsky/Cocteau. Final ritual masks were each 9 to 12 feet high. The set measured 54 feet at the highest point. Designer—John Ezell.

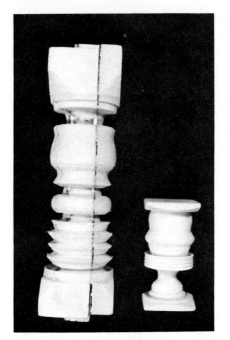

a

b

c

Foams, of course, are very lightweight and many times have to be counterweighted or attached to heavier units of scenery to maintain stability and the illusion of reality. Nothing is more disconcerting than a supposedly quarter-ton Greek statue bouncing like a ping-pong ball if knocked over.

*Ethafoam rod* is a commercial insulation material. It is a flexible, closed-cell foam extruded in various diameters of $\frac{1}{2}$ inch to 2 inches. It can be easily cut with a band saw or knife into half-rounds or quarter-rounds and glued to a surface as a decorative relief or curved molding. Similar forms in sheets and other shapes are available.

## TWO-PART FOAM

Some foams are manufactured and sold as a two-part kit. Proper mixing of the two components yields either a rigid or a flexible foam, depending on the particular ingredients. This is useful, for instance, in cases where a mold can be prepared for a sculptural element or decorative detail that recurs several times on a set. The choice of a rigid or a flexible foam is determined by its use onstage. For example, the application of relief detail on a curved or flexible surface requires a flexible foam. Figure 7–23 illustrates another use for this material.

It is critical to follow the manufacturer's instructions and recommendations when working with foams, both for ease of use and for safety.

## THERMOPLASTICS

Another method for the shaping of three-dimensional details such as arabesques, props, masks, armorplate, or the duplication of real objects is the vacuum forming of sheet plastic. Formerly a manufacturing technique that was out of reach of the average scenery shop, it is fast becoming an important construction method for those hard-to-execute details.

The chemical structure of a thermoplastic is such that when heated it loses its rigid state and becomes ductile. While it is in this pliant condition it can be reshaped or stretched over a positive (or negative) mold, then allowed to cool and return to a hardened state. The fact that a true thermoplastic can be reheated and reshaped without a discernible change in its physical properties makes it economically feasible for theatre use.

## Figure 7–23
## Foam Casting

Demonstrating one of the many forms plastic foam casting can take. Drawings show the steps taken to duplicate various forms of bakery goods.

(1) Mixing IASCO's Prepolymer "A" with a Resin-Catalyst "B" in equal parts.

(2) Mixture is stirred vigorously for about 30 seconds.

(3) Mixture poured into hollow mold prepared with parting agent.

(4) Mixing tool and a visual reminder of mixing precautions, disposable surgical gloves and respirator mask.

(5) After liquid foam expands into the mold (about 20 minutes) the casting is removed from the mold. With the excess foam cut away, the foam is ready for painting.

Photo: bakery shop full of foam cast bakery goods, *Cyrano de Bergerac*, Guthrie Theatre. Designer—John Jensen. Photo courtesy Kewley.

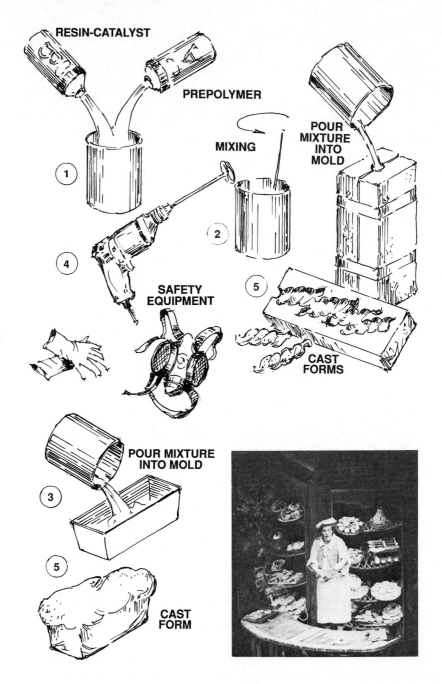

RESIN-CATALYST

PREPOLYMER

MIXING

POUR MIXTURE INTO MOLD

SAFETY EQUIPMENT

CAST FORMS

POUR MIXTURE INTO MOLD

CAST FORM

Of the many thermoplastics available there are three that seem best suited for use in the theatre. They must be opaque, translucent, or transparent, have a selection of color or take paint and dyes, be noncombustible, and be strong enough to withstand normal handling onstage and the mechanics of fastening (nailing, stapling, and so on). The three thermoplastics meeting these requirements are high-impact polystyrene, low-density polyethylene, and cellulose acetate. The working thickness need not be greater than .004″

(4 thousandths of an inch); it depends on how rigid or flexible the final form is meant to be.

*High-impact polystyrene*, as the name implies, has a high impact strength, great flexibility for intricate forming, a wide range of colors, and is obtainable in opaque or translucent sheets.

*Low-density polyethylene* is also tough and flexible. It is normally milky white (no colors) and opaque, but turns translucent when heated and formed.

*Cellulose acetate* is a well-known plastic with excellent forming characteristics. It is also very sturdy, with the distinct difference of being completely transparent.

**Vacuum Forming**     The heated thermoplastic sheet, in order to take an accurate impression copy of the mold, must be tightly drawn or sucked by a vacuum around the form. The process is called vacuum forming. The basic steps of vacuum forming are as follows: (1) Heat the plastic sheet uniformly to the temperature that renders it flexible (750–1000°F). (2) Transfer it quickly to a forming table where it is stretched over the mold and its edges clamped to the table in an airtight seal. (3) The air is removed through the forming table by a vacuum tank and pump, thereby sucking the heated plastic sheet over the mold. (4) Allow the plastic to cool and harden into its new shape. (5) Break the seal and remove the plastic form for trimming, painting, and attaching to scenery, costume, or any other formed unit.

The use of a reservoir tank permits the rapid vacuuming action that is necessary or the plastic will cool and return to a rigid state. The pump then recovers the vacuum in the tank while the next sheet of plastic is being heated. Figure 7–24 illustrates the various components that make up a vacuum forming machine.

**Figure 7–24**
**Thermoplastic Vacuum Forming**

The cut-away drawing of a vacuum-forming machine suitable for a scenery shop.

(1) The oven has slanted metal sides with sheetrock lining. The floor of the oven is covered with a pattern of coiled resistor wire forming a heating element.

(2) Plastic sheet in angle-iron frame.

(3) Frame is hinged to swing off of the oven and onto the mold and forming table when the plastic sheet is ductile.

(4) Forming table. Floor is pierced with $\frac{1}{8}$-inch holes spaced at 1-inch intervals to vent the vacuum chamber underneath.

(5) Mold.

(6) Vacuum chamber.

(7) Bleed valve; can be rigged for pedal action.

(8) Gauge reading inches of mercury.

(9) Air hose or pipe to reservoir tank.

(10) Vacuum pump.

(11) Reservoir tank.

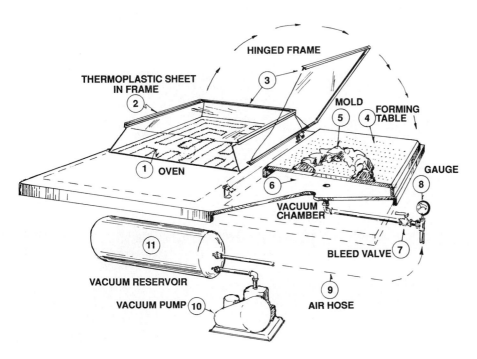

**Heat Gun** There are some additional tools that are useful accessories to the thermoplastic-forming process. The heat gun, which is capable of delivering a blast of hot air (750–1000°F) from an enclosed heating element and turbo fan, is used at close range to soften portions of the plastic sheet that may not have taken to the mold accurately.

**Welding Gun** Similar to the heat gun, the hot-air welding gun produces a fine jet of hot air (400–700°F) that, when directed at a seam or thermoplastic welding rod, can weld plastic sheets or plastic forms together. Because the welding gun needs a jet flow of air, it has to operate from an air compressor.

**Figure 7–25**
**Hot Wire Cutters**

Table and hand hot wire cutters for sculpting rigid foams.
(1) Nichrome resistance wire.
(2) Low-voltage, high-amperage transformer (about 16 amperes).
(3) Adjustable arm to facilitate the cutting of large blocks of foam.
(Left drawing) Table hot wire cutter rigged to shape molding.
(4) Nichrome wire bent into the shape of the molding.
(5) Strip of styrene foam or rigid urethane foam.
(6) Fence guide clamped to table top. Photo: hand hot wire cutter.

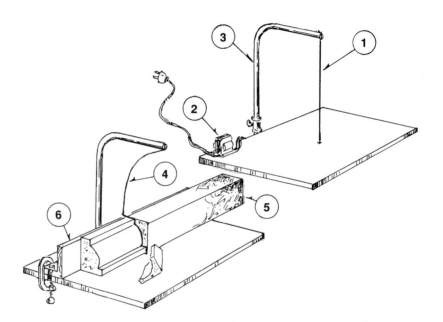

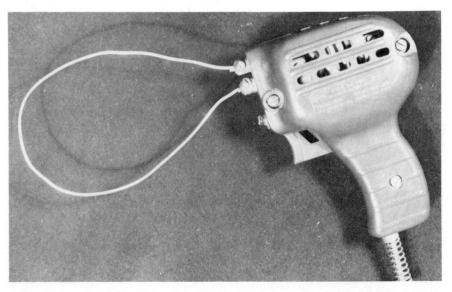

a

b

c

**Figure 7–26**
Thermoplastic Forms

A few of the many architectural and decorative details that can be vacuum formed for use on the stage setting.
(a) A cornice section. In this category, column capitals and bases, pilasters and panel molding can be included.
(b) Open grill work, split baluster, and decorative details.
(c) Low relief panel decoration. Additional thermoplastic forms can be seen in Figure 11–14.

**Figure 7—27**
**Fabrication of Rigid Foam**

Armor has fiberglass under form. A one-to-one mix of 16-pound density IASCO rigid foam to build pea-pod form, caskets, gauntlets, and details. Latex and graphite surface with paper-doily appliqué as decorative detail. Armor and photo courtesy Jim Bakkom.

**Figure 7—28**
**Cast Plastics**

This altar for *Oedipus the King* was designed to look like an oversized, polished half of a geode. The top surface is made of layers of tinted Clear-cast, a clear polyester available at local craft shops, supported on a hollow frame of wooden ribs with a Celastic covering. The crusty edge is modeled fiberglass resin and Cab-o-sil (formed silica), an inert powder that gives the mixture body for modeling. Photo courtesy Bakkom.

**Hot-Wire Cutter** Although not used in the actual thermoplastic process, the hot-wire cutter is a handy tool for cutting and shaping rigid foam. Both the table hot-wire cutter and the hand cutter using the flexible wire loop (Figure 7–25) are useful to cut large blocks and to carve small forms. The wire loop is made of a high-resistance wire conductor. (Chromel or Nichrome resistor wire). The wire's resistance generates enough heat to melt the rigid foam, thus enabling it to cut the block cleanly and quickly.

Other three-dimensional forming techniques such as fiberglass, Celastic, and the like are discussed in Chapter 11, because they relate to properties, furniture, and costume accessories. Figures 7–26, 7–27, and 7–28 show some of the pieces that can be made using the techniques discussed here. Figure 7–29 illustrates a sophisticated vacuum forming process for theatre usage.

## MIRROR SURFACES

Highly reflective surfaces and optical mirror surfaces have always fascinated the scene designer as a theatrical effect. Until the mylar surface entered the

a  b

c  d

e  f

**Figure 7–29**
**Commercial Vacuum Forming of Stage Products**

Shown are process pictures of the more sophisticated vacuum-forming equipment developed in the Tobins Lake Studios for the mass production of stage properties, armor, and architectural elements. Although this special equipment is capable of producing more than the average scenery shop, the studio's output is still far short of commercial manufacturing production.
(a) View of forming table. Note overhead oven.
(b) Plastic sheet in place over molds.
(c) After the "pull" with the oven raised.
(d) The making of a permanent mold to withstand the heat and pressure of numerous pulls. A fresh pull from the prototype is used as a negative mold. It is backed with sand for stability.
(e) The negative mold is filled with epoxy resin sometimes loaded with aluminum to save weight. The final mold is drilled with a pattern of small holes to improve the suction of the pull.
(f) Storage shelves of permanent molds.

**Safety Practice**

Any method of shaping foams—whether hot-wire cutting, sawing, or sanding—can release toxic gases. The operator must therefore wear a respirator and work only in a well-ventilated space.

theatre, large mirrors were heavy and awkward to handle. A mylar mirror surface, when rigidly mounted or tightly stretched, provides the reflection optics of a real mirror, yet is lightweight and easy to handle.

### SILVER SHRINK MIRROR

This technique utilizes a vinyl-backed reflective surface designed to be tacked to a frame and then shrunk with heat to a smooth mirrorlike surface. The heat source can be a normal portable electric heater or a heat gun. The 54-inch width of the material, however, limits the size of the individual frame. A full stage mirror, for example, would have to be made of several frames. However, if the planes of the frames are parallel, the divisions are not noticeable.

### SCRIM-BACKED MIRROR

This form of stage mirror is backed with a scrim instead of vinyl, and thus has the added advantage of being transparent when lighted from behind. When stretched and heat-shrunk, it serves as a mirror surface, transparent scrim, or a rear projection screen.

### MIRRORED PLEXIGLASS

Although expensive and limited in large sizes, mirrored plexiglass has been successfully adapted for a large surface by repeating small mirrored squares (Figure 4–5c). The joints are not visible at a distance.

# 8 COLOR IN THE DESIGN

The final step in the execution of the design, the painting of scenery, has not been discussed. It is imperative to examine first the use of color in the theatre, however, as it relates to painting, lighting, and the designing of scenery and costumes. This might begin by asking the question "What is color?"

"Color is *light*," says the physicist when referring to the small visible portion of the electromagnetic spectrum. "Color is *paint*," replies the artist, "light merely reveals it." "Color is in the *eye*," says the physiologist, "for no two people see color in the same way and some are color-blind." "Color is in the *mind*," the psychologist insists, to explain why some experience color with their eyes closed or in their dreams. All these attributes, of course, are present in any color experience. To these, the artist in the theatre might add—as a part of its creative use, critical analysis, and emotional response— the *philosophy* of color.

Although scenery, costume, and lighting designers desire this knowledge of color to the same degree, they have slightly divergent interests in its use. The lighting designer, for example, is more involved with the physics of color, while the scene and costume designers are interested in the painting and dyeing of color as well as the manipulation of colored materials. Whatever the final use of color may be, each designer has need of the same knowledge of color, for all areas of design eventually must come together onstage to form the total visual effect. The beginning designer in the theatre must be aware of the separate uses of color and seek a color explanation that satisfies the use of color both as light and as paint.

It can be seen that any explanation of color in the theatre must, therefore, involve not only the separate study of color in light and color in pigment, but also the integration of the two in an inclusive definition.

It is important that all workers in the theatre understand at least the basic terminology of color to be able to communicate in the language of color. It is good to be aware that not only do no two people "see" color in exactly the same way, but no two *respond* to color the same way. Color inevitably elicits an emotional response. It is certainly the strongest element of design and is therefore the most difficult (if not the most important) element to understand.

## THE LANGUAGE OF COLOR

It is always difficult to talk or write about color, for words trigger individual images and do not convey accurate information. There are, however, a few terms that are so much a part of the description of a color that it is impractical to converse without knowing their meanings.

The three variants of color—*hue, value,* and *chroma*—are the most familiar terms used to describe a specific color. All will be discussed and illustrated in detail later, but briefly one can describe a color by hue identification (red, yellow, and so on); value level, or the black-to-white relationship of a color; and the degree of chroma or freedom from neutralization by mixture with another hue.

Within the framework of these variants, an elusive color can be described in simple semiscientific terms by referring to its hue, degree of chroma, and value level. In normal communication their use brings to mind a more consistent image of a specific color than would the use of such emotionally charged labels as "blushing pink" or "passionate purple." Because descriptive labels are so firmly a part of the advertising and merchandising of color in fabric, paint, and the light-color medium, a designer soon learns to translate them into more communicative terms. A "chocolate" shade, for example, might be described more precisely as a spectrum orange neutralized to one-half chroma but retaining its normal low-light value position.

## COLOR IN LIGHT

A basic knowledge of color begins with its presence in light. Without light there would be no color. Everyone has seen in some form or other the breaking up or refraction of sunlight into a spectrum of color. The refraction of sunlight through a bevel-edged window or in a rainbow are simple examples. The physicist with more precise laboratory prisms can produce an accurate spectrum with wavelength values for each hue and can explain the existence of these hues, from infrared to ultra-violet, as a visible part of the electromagnetic spectrum. This is the beginning of *hue,* the first variant of color (Color Plate 8–1).

### HUE

The position of a color in the spectrum determines its hue. The number of hues that can be separated or identified as principal hues in the spectrum is arbitrary. Six easily identified hues are *red* (R), *orange* (O), *yellow* (Y), *green* (G),

Figure 8–1
Spectrum and Six Basic Hues

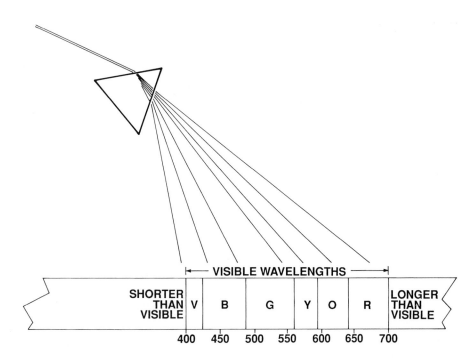

blue (B), and *violet* (V) (Figure 8–1). The expanding of the number of discernible hues depends on their ultimate use or application in a color theory or system of color notation. The use of color by the artist, for example, is linked to a medium such as paint or dye. Light, on the other hand, is colored by passing it through some kind of colored filter. Because of the purity of the color mediums in light, it is possible to establish primary hues in light.

The primary hues, within the six basic hues of the spectrum, form the basis for the mixing of color in both light and pigment. Red, green, and blue are the light primaries (see "Additive Mixing" a little later in this chapter). The intermediate hues, or secondaries, are produced by mixing any pair of primary hues.

It is important to mention at this point that mixing of paint as a color medium is not as accurate as the mixing of colors in light. It involves a different physical process, hence the painter requires a finer separation of spectrum hues to creatively mix and use color (see "Color in Paint" later in the chapter).

## VALUE

The light-to-dark relationship of a hue or mixed color is its value. The lighter values, nearer white, are known as *tints* and the darker values, approaching black, are referred to as *shades*. Both represent a variation from the true hue.

The use of value as a color variant or control is more the tool of the painter than of the lighting designer because of the necessarily greater range in pigment mixing. Subtle value differences are easier to accomplish in paint, particularly in the darker ranges, because in the use of colored light there is no black.

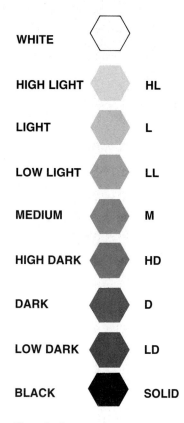

| | |
|---|---|
| WHITE | |
| HIGH LIGHT | HL |
| LIGHT | L |
| LOW LIGHT | LL |
| MEDIUM | M |
| HIGH DARK | HD |
| DARK | D |
| LOW DARK | LD |
| BLACK | SOLID |

Figure 8–2
Value Steps

The number of steps in a value scale is arbitrary. The limiting factor is usually the ability of the eye to distinguish the difference between adjacent steps. Seven steps between black and white seem to be a comfortable number (Figure 8–2).

The value in the center of the scale is referred to as *medium* (M). The steps above M towards white are *low light* (LL), *light* (L), and *high light* (HL). Below M towards black is *high dark* (HD), *dark* (D), and *low dark* (LD). Within this range the artist can create form without the use of color.

**The Value Sketch**    Visual artists frequently use the values of a single color or black-to-white tones to model forms with simulated light in a sketch technique. The interplay of high light, shade, and shadow can be very expressive. The simple example in Figure 8–3a is a value sketch developed from a middle gray background using a black and white prismatic pencil.

Many old masters applied monochromatic underpainting, using the values of a single hue to express form and light before overpainting in full color.

Values can be expressed in a pen and ink technique. The openness or density of the cross-hatching can create a range of light and darkness in either a dramatic or subtle manner (Figure 8–3b).

**Value and Hue**    Some hues come from the spectrum with a natural value difference. The light-to-dark difference of yellow and violet is the most extreme example. Other hues have less value difference and some, of course, are about equal (Color Plate 8–2). Hues that have little value difference, such as RO and BG, contrast each other with another force. They are *hue opposites*, or complimentary colors. When certain hue opposites like RO and BG are placed side by side, the color contrast is so high that it produces an apparent vibration in the eye. This phenomenon involves both the physics and optics of color and will be discussed later, after all the aspects of color have been examined.

Hue opposites, however, do perform another function. When mixed in equal parts they tend to neutralize or offset each other. Hue opposites in light produce white, while their mixture in paint results in neutral tones. This change in the purity of a hue is the third variant of color, *chroma*.

**CHROMA**

The instant the purity of a principal hue is modified, the change is referred to as a change of its chroma. The degree of pureness, or freedom from neutrality, like the value scale, can be measured in steps. The number of steps from pure hue to complete gray varies according to color theories. A very precise measuring and mixing method can produce a great number of steps. The artist, however, can see and work easily in quarter portions, moving from a fully saturated hue to one-quarter neutral, through one-half, then three-quarters to full neutrality. This serves merely as an explanation of chroma, and the artist is free to use more steps for a more subtle change.

It is interesting to note in Color Plate 8–3, which shows the value and chroma changes produced by the mixing of orange and blue hues, that when

the value of either orange or blue is raised or lowered, its chroma is also changed as the tint or shade becomes more neutral. On the other hand, the quarter steps on the direct horizontal line to the value scale represent a chroma change without a value drop. This is accomplished on the orange side by the proportional mixing of blue (the hue opposite or complement of orange) after it has been raised to the matching value of orange. In other words, it is possible to change the chroma of a hue without affecting its value, but it is impossible to change the value of a hue without modifying its chroma.

All neutralization can be accomplished, theoretically, by the use of black or white paint. It is possible under scientifically controlled conditions of paint manufacturing, but the scenic artist knows that certain opaque colors do not respond to mixing with black. The use of a complementary color to neutralize a hue gives the painter a chromatic neutral that has a little more life under the stage lights. The neutralization of a pigment hue or its modification by another color is due to the particular method of mixing colors in paint. When painters mix colors on the palette or in the bucket they are using *subtractive mixing*.

## COLOR MIXING

Although hue, value, and chroma are theoretical variables of color, a designer must understand them also as a means to describe a color and use them to create new shades and match old ones. Color is varied by mixing. The two methods are *additive mixing* and *subtractive mixing*. While both methods effect hue changes, additive mixing also noticeably alters value, and subtractive mixing modifies chroma.

**Additive Mixing**     The blending of colored *light* from two or more sources is additive mixing. It is best demonstrated by the three overlapping fields of the light primary hues in Color Plate 8–4a. The additive mixing of the light

**Figure 8–3**
Value Sketch

(a) Black and white Prismatic pencil over a medium value background.
(b) Pen and ink sketch technique.

primaries red, green, and blue produces, first, the secondaries. Green and blue cross to make a turquoise (*BG*), red and blue produce the light secondary magenta (*RV*), and red and green make an amber (*YO*). The white in the center is the additive mixing of all three primaries. Note that the additive mixing of two hues raises the value of the mixed color.

Figure 8–4 diagrams the physics of additive mixing of red (*R*) and blue (*B*). A single red color filter, for example, absorbs all other hues from the spectrum and transmits only red. When red rays overlap with light from a blue filter (see diagram) the colors are "added," resulting in a red-violet or magenta hue. The most spectacular example of additive mixing is the combination of two contrasting colors, for example red and green. Their mixing produces a yellow or amber. (Note that the yellow and orange hues fall between red and green in the color spectrum.) The additive mixing of a secondary and primary hue, or of all three primary hues, results in a synthetic white. Remember that all colors resolve into white before being refracted into the color spectrum.

Primary and secondary hues are frequently used to light the actor. The favorite combination of lavender and bastard amber, for example, uses tints of primary blue and secondary amber. Medium straw and steel blue, for example, are tints of complementary hues, blue and orange. The additive mixing of the two colors models the actor's face in a flattering white light that can be warmed (more red) or cooled (more blue) by changing the intensity of one of the spotlights (Color Plate 8–4b).

**Subtractive Mixing**     The opposite of additive mixing is subtractive mixing—the crossing or combining of color mediums in front of a single source of light. Color Plate 8–5a illustrates the effect of combining two color mediums, blue-green and yellow, in front of a light source containing all the spectrum hues. The green color that is transmitted is the only hue not sub-

**Figure 8–4**
Additive Mixing

Light represented in its primaries—red, green and blue—is passed through a blue filter. Red and green are filtered out, resulting in a blue-colored light. Red filter absorbs green and blue, passing red. The fields of red and blue light overlap and additively mix a third, magenta. Magenta is red-violet raised in value because additive mixing raises the value of the mixed color.

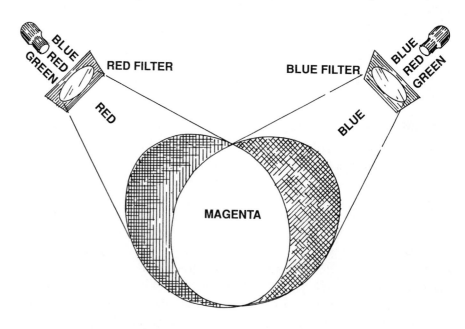

tracted or filtered out of the light by the combined color mediums. It is not as visually apparent, but the same subtractive results are present when the artist mixes blue-green and yellow in paint (Color Plate 8–5b).

Subtractive mixing in paint and light is characterized by a move toward neutrality and darker shades. This is particularly evident when the hues are complementary colors. It is understandable that the closer the color mediums are to hue opposites, the less light can be transmitted until a block or point of negative transmission is reached.

In theory, the mixing of complementary colors in paint results in a nearly black neutral for the same reason. The reality is that, due to the impurities of manufactured color in pigment, although mixing complementary colors will indeed lower its chroma, the color will more likely result in a gray. Scenic artists often refer to this as "graying down" or "neutralizing" a color.

## COLOR IN PAINT

Color in paint, of course, depends on light to realize its physical properties. The color of a surface reaches the eye by the reflection of the light that is illuminating it. Just as a light color medium transmits a color by absorbing some spectrum hues and letting through others, so a colored surface reflects only the colors of the paint (Color Plate 8–6). These are the physical properties of a paint surface that begins with its coloring agent, pigment.

### PIGMENT

The term *pigment* is an inclusive term that refers to the coloring agent in paints, dyes, and nature. It can be best explained as the chemical properties of color that create hue. At first, pigments came from natural sources; the indigo and madder plants are familiar examples. Minerals and semiprecious stones were also pulverized and made into pigments. The crude chemistry of the past established many of the traditional names of colors still used today, such as madder lake and indigo blue.

Colors other than those found directly in nature were often made synthetically from known minerals and their compounds. In the mid-nineteenth century, organic colors made their first appearance as organic dyes. Although present-day pigments are a product of inorganic chemistry producing synthetic colors, many still bear the name of their chemical origin, such as chrome green, alizarin crimson, and calcium red.

Because the mixing of pigments is subtractive (see "Subtractive Mixing" earlier in this chapter), to attempt the creation of intermediate hues from the mixing of pigment primaries is impractical compared to the ease of the additive mixing of light primaries. Hence, the painter prefers to begin with a larger palette that might include all the principal hues of the spectrum. While a small palette made up of the six principal colors already mentioned is usable, the scenic artist favors a palette of twelve principal colors for reasons of flexibility and economy.

**Twelve Principal Hues**    Beginning with the six original hues (red, orange, yellow, green, blue, and violet) six additional hues may be created through intermediate steps (refer again to Color Plate 8–2). Each new hue thus formed takes its name from the two original hues on either side. The hue between yellow and orange, for example, would be *yellow-orange* and so on around the color wheel (Color Plate 8–7).

The new intermediate color is not thought of as a paint mixture of the two adjacent colors but as a full chroma hue from the spectrum. The result is a working palette of twelve full-intensity hues that will reduce the degree of neutralization from subtractive mixing that might have occurred with a smaller palette. Some scenic artists even prefer a palette with more than twelve hues. Also, in certain situations such as the commercial or industrial use of color, the number of principal colors may be expanded to twenty-four or more. In any event, the expansion is based on the twelve principal hues that become a basis of reference for individual use.

## THE COLOR WHEEL

To better show the physical relationship of spectrum hues, most color notation systems use a color wheel (Color Plates 8–7 and 8–8). The circular arrangement of colors brings into view the diametric and adjacent correlation of the twelve spectral hues and thus provides designers a schematic view of primary and secondary hue relationships as well as pairs of complementary colors that appear diametrically opposite each other around the wheel. A knowledge of complementary hues is not only necessary for mixing both light and pigment, but is also important in composition. This is apparent in the choice of tints and shades in a production color scheme for both costumes and scenery. Because color in light and pigment are constantly brought together in the theatre, they must be aligned in a compatible arrangement so that both have the same complementary colors.

**Integrating Light and Pigment**    The attempt to bring color in light and pigment into one system of notation is best illustrated in the color wheel. The light primaries and secondaries are represented in the pigment primaries. The complement of blue in light, for example, is yellow, while its opposite in pigment is orange. To integrate light pigment into one wheel, the light primaries have been moved slightly to fit into the pigment wheel. Light primary red becomes red-orange (*RO*), green becomes a yellow-green (*YG*), and blue becomes a blue-violet (*BV*). The maneuver also more accurately represents the light primary hues.

**The Pigment Color Wheel**    In addition to showing a contiguous relationship of the twelve principal colors, the pigment color wheel (Color Plate 8–7) also emphasizes hue opposites of complementary colors. The hues are full chroma and represent the basic pigment colors of the painter's palette.

Because most pigment mixing is subtractive, the gray tone in the center indicates the neutralizing effect of any pair of complementary colors. The many tints and shades resulting from the mixing of one pair of complementary hues (orange and blue) was shown in Color Plate 8–3, where the flexible relationship between *chroma* and *value* was demonstrated. The subtlety of neutral shades and almost unlimited combinations of hues is the major advantage of subtractive mixing in pigments.

**The Light Color Wheel**     Although the conception is different, the arrangement of the twelve principal colors in the light wheel is the same as the pigment wheel. The primary, secondary, and intermediate colors are developed from the additive mixing of the light primaries. As the additive mixing of colored light tends to move toward white, the secondary and intermediate colors are therefore lighter in value than their companion colors in the pigment wheel.

The light color wheel in Color Plate 8–8 represents the interrelation of the colors in light with the twelve principal hues more than it indicates a complete range of colors in light. A full range of saturated color mediums of all spectrum hues is available for selective use.

## COLOR VISION

The source of color can be scientifically explained; the mixture of color can be diagrammed; and all the variants of color can be arranged in a system of notation. However, what the eye sees and the brain interprets is an individual color experience. Although the eye functions very much like a camera, it is not a scientific instrument. It receives light through its lens, which focuses the image or impression onto the layers of the retina in the inner eye. The innumerable nerve endings (rods and cones) of the retina culminate in the optic nerve, which carries the impression signal to the brain for interpretation. The impression is registered in terms of color and intensity (brightness), which, in a sense, is another way of saying hue and value. The eye sees value differences (intensity) through the *rods* and hue variations through the *cones*. A few people can only distinguish value differences and not variations of hue. Because the greatest difference in hue falls in the middle of the value scale, most color-blind individuals cannot see the difference between red and green.

### INTENSITY AND COLOR OVERLOAD

The retina of the eye assimilates light energy. When it is saturated (isomerized), it is said to be *bleached*. Hence, after any sudden change of intensity or color, the retina has to regenerate itself. This process takes place over a noticeable period of time. Since the rods are sensitive to *intensity* and the cones are sensitive to *color*, there is a difference in the time it takes the eye to readjust from a sudden intensity change than to a color change. It takes the eye about one to one and a half minutes to adjust in a blackout, for example (rod regeneration); a color change (cone regeneration) may take as long as five minutes.

The time lag the eye experiences after a sudden change of color explains *after image*, a phenomenon of color vision. Until the eye has recovered, it retains an image of the object and a color impression long after the object has been removed or changed. The after-image, however, is in the *complementary hue* of the original image color.

An ingenious demonstration of after-image was immortalized in Diaghilev's Ballet Russe production of *Le Coq d'Or* with decor by Natalya Concharova. The first scene, a garden, was dominated by a brilliant red-orange tree. During twenty minutes of dancing, the eye was saturated with an unbalanced color scheme; upon changing to the next scene, the audience was reportedly plagued by a blue-green after-image of the first-scene tree floating ethereally about the stage. The impression, of course, was in the eyes of the beholders.

The phenomenon of after-image, or the color-balancing tendency of the eye, is present in another form. It was first referred to in 1886 as the *simultaneous contrast of color* by M. E. Chevreul, an early color theorist. In 1960, Joseph Albers called the same effect *interaction of color*.

**The Interaction of Color**     How a color reacts to an adjacent hue or to its background is known as the interaction of color. Certain reactions are painfully obvious while others are extremely subtle. The degree of color interplay is a critical element in the use of color by all stage designers. Aside from the mixing and creating of colors itself, the designer's choice and arrangement of colors become one of the most forceful elements in stimulating an emotional or intellectual response on the part of the audience.

The interaction of colors affects all variants of color. The *value* of a color can seem to change by juxtaposition; a neutral can be influenced by a surrounding color and appear to take on a *hue*; and the *chroma* of a color can be sharpened or deadened by its background. Color Plates 8–9, 8–10, and 8–11 show a few classic examples of obvious color interactions that have an influence on the designer's use of color or choice of a color scheme.

## COLOR SENSATION AND SUBJECTIVE RESPONSE

The experience of color includes elements of sensation or emotion as well. Designers in the theatre must be aware of the scope of this emotional response on the part of the audience (which is often subconscious) when they choose colors, in both pigment and light, to establish a mood or specific atmosphere on the stage. The psychological effect of color on an audience, however, is difficult to measure. To some extent the designer must depend on a measurable individual response and hope it will multiply.

Most emotional response to color is conditioned by a lifetime of reaction to colors in nature and under natural light. We are repulsed, for example, by strong colors in light that produce unnatural flesh tones or discolor our food.

## EMOTIONAL COLOR

With these psychological influences in mind—the natural, traditional, and symbolic sensations of color—we will attempt to describe the general emotional connotations attached to the six basic spectrum hues.

| | |
|---|---|
| *Yellow* | Radiant, light-giving, golden, saintly; in light values near white, virginal |
| *Orange* | Festive, earthy, peasant colors; in neutral shades, nature in the fall |
| *Red* | Active, passionate, full of inner warmth, fiery, strong, forceful |
| *Violet* | Royal, piety; in deeper shades, shadows, terror, chaos, a reddening color |
| *Blue* | Passive, receding, deep, cool, purity, icy tints |
| *Green* | Tranquility, compassion, nature in the spring and summer |

We are also influenced by centuries of social and religious conventions that are buried deeply in the subconscious. Finally, we react to symbolism in color, some primal and others more contemporary (such as traffic lights and color-coded road signs).

The psychological description of a hue is, at best, very general. The emotional response to a color can be countered or modified by adjacent colors, as well as the color of the background. The intercolor experience, which involves both the psychological response and the physiological limitation of the eye, can also be tricked by an optical illusion. This phenomenon of fooling both the eye and the mind is dependable enough to be considered an important part of the impact of color on a theatre audience.

## COLOR MANIPULATION

Some designers have an intuitive sense of color. The colors they put together seem right for the specific dramatic moment or atmospheric scene. A designer in the theatre, however, frequently has to suppress personal preferences to bring a color scheme into harmony or contrast with the colors in the show. To ensure the chances of a unified color solution, all designers—scenery, costume, and lighting—rely on advance color schemes to coordinate the final color impression.

### THE COLOR SCHEME

The development of a production color scheme may be as simple as deciding on the overall tonality of a single hue, or it may involve selecting a number of related or contrasting colors. The *harmony* or *contrast* of hues becomes the basic control of a production color scheme. The mood of the production is often expressed in the interrelationship of the colors in the scheme. Although the basic control is established in full chroma on the color wheel, all the variants of color (hue, value, and chroma) are called on to provide interest and flexibility to the final colors in the composition. Aside from the obvious harmony of a *monochromatic* color scheme, which relies on the manipulation of the value and chroma of a single hue, various schemes can be created in terms of *chords* on the color wheel.

**The Geometry of a Color Scheme**     One way to develop a color scheme is to draw chords from color to color on the circumference of the wheel. A short chord system, of course, furnishes a closer interval between hues than a scheme of longer chords. As the interval grows longer, hue contrasts will increase until hue opposites, or a complementary scheme, is reached.

To show a few of the unlimited color combinations enclosed in the geometry of the chords, Figure 8–5 demonstrates all of the possibilities on a single axis (yellow and violet). They vary from the close *harmony* of one hue to the vibrant *contrast* of a pair of complementary colors, as follows:

1. A *monochromatic* scheme. The natural high value of yellow limits its range. It can be neutralized into ochres, warmed with orange, and cooled with green to add variety to a one-color control.
2. An *analogous* scheme combines neighboring hues with the shortest chord into a harmonious scheme. The three hues in this example are yellow-orange, yellow, and yellow-green.
3. A *third interval* triad of hues derives from a triangle including yellow, orange, and green. The chord has lengthened, thereby increasing the interval between colors and providing slightly more contrast to the scheme.
4. The *fourth interval* scheme is first illustrated as a three-color combination—yellow, red-orange, and blue-green. A fourth interval chord always involves one pair of complementary colors, which increases the contrast of the scheme.
5. A *fourth interval* scheme is shown involving four colors. The quadrate of chords includes two pairs of complements when violet is added to the triad of yellow, red-orange, and blue-green. The designer can soften the contrast of the scheme by varying the value and chroma of one or all of the hues.
6. A *fifth interval* triad. The equilateral triangle of chords takes in the pigment primaries red, yellow, and blue as a scheme. The fifth interval scheme is not as obvious when the axis is between intermediate colors such as yellow-orange, red-violet, and blue-green.
7. *Split-complement* is a rather arbitrary selection of chords. It is usually used to soften the high contrast of a complementary scheme. In this example, yellow is in combination with red-violet and blue-violet, which flank the complementary hue, violet.
8. *Complementary* hues offer the highest contrast as a color scheme. The two colors, yellow and violet, also have a high value contrast. The most vibrant pair of complementaries is red-orange and blue-green.

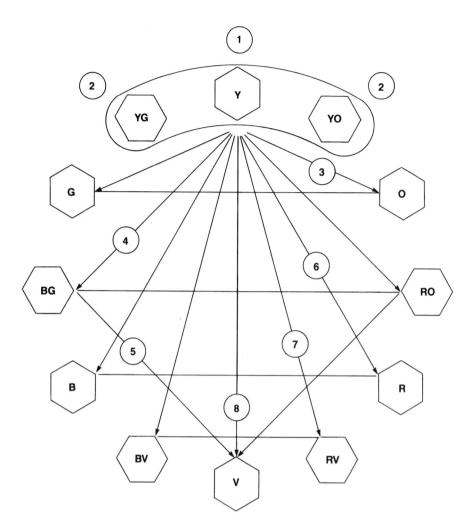

**Figure 8—5**
**Color Chords**

Various color schemes related to color wheel. Shown is one of the six complementary areas, yellow to violet. The various schemes are:
(1) monochromatic;
(2) analogous or neighboring colors;
(3) third interval triad;
(4) fourth interval triad; one pair of complementaries;
(5) fourth interval quadrate; two pairs of complementaries;
(6) fifth interval triad, primaries or secondaries;
(7) split-complement triad; and
(8) complementary.
Although this chord is on the yellow-violet axis, it can be rotated to any of twelve other possibilities.

The various color schemes are a guide to color composition within a design or throughout a production. The geometry of color, besides providing a means of *color communication* between collaborating designers, is also a device for *explaining* or *teaching* color relationships and is often used to *analyze* the dramatic use of color in a favorite or classical design. It is important to remember that, ultimately, any color scheme that proves satisfying is directly related to the expertise of the designer.

**THE COLOR PLOT**

The control of color within a composition is only a portion of the color planning that occurs in designing for the theatre. The color scheme for each setting of a multiscene play must also be considered in the content of the *whole* production.

Some scene designers use some form of a *color plot* to make preliminary studies of the entire production. Although it is a view of the show the audience will never see, it does serve as a color guide for the lighting and costume designers. Through the color plot, the overall development of color can be studied. The functional relationship of connecting colors and hue accents is clearly visible. The progressive unfolding of color change within a scene or throughout a production, as well as moments of high contrast or subdued uniformity, can be demonstrated in the color plot.

The color plot is very important to the costume designer. It shows the overall relationship of all costumes in the production and enables the costume designer to plot small scenes and families of color that may help to visually define sympathetic characters and rival groups or individuals. The focus or center of attention in a large group scene can be planned, as well as the control of the overall emotional impact or mood within the scene. The color plot also establishes the progression of colors from scene to scene and act to act.

A character's age and position in society (deacon, servant, master, and so on) can enter the color plot in the broad, symbolic statement of a single color note. The costume designer, however, frequently uses more than one color to note a single costume as a means of studying color accents and harmonies between characters.

## COLOR MODIFICATION

We have seen how color can be changed by mixing, can be influenced by interaction with other colors, and can be created by optical illusion. Surface color can also be modified by colored light. The constant use of colored light on a colored surface is unique to the theatre. Designers in the theatre not only have to consider the colors of a painted background, costumes, and other materials of a set, but also the colors of the lights that will reveal them. This is especially true if the lighting for the scene is unusual, such as a romantic moonlit scene or the flooding of the stage with red or green hues to provide an unnatural effect.

Fortunately, color modification is not quite as complicated as it seems. The effect of colored light on a colored surface is a result of subtractive mixing. In other words, if a red light is thrown on a yellow surface, the yellow is modified into orange tones.

The modification of a color in a costume or on scenery by colored light is a theatrical example of the joining of two color mediums, pigment and light (Color Plates 8–12a and 8–12b). Designers in the theatre are constantly aware of how colored light and pigment influence each other. They are always prepared to compensate in either medium to create a natural effect or to deliberately cause dramatic reversals of color.

# 9  PAINTING SCENERY

Scenery painting is a highly skilled and specialized portion of creating a setting. It is also a very interesting and fascinating part of scene design and technical production. Most of the methods and techniques of handling scene paint are familiar to anyone with visual arts training. The main difference between scenery painting and easel painting is one of scale. Instead of painting at a small drawing board, the scenic artist paints at life-size or larger.

Because the scale of scene painting is so large, the scenic artist uses a broad technique, sometimes so broad that what appear to be slaps and dashes up close do not take form until viewed from a distance. Learning to paint on a large scale and with a broad technique is an easy adjustment for the visual artist. The uninitiated, however, should first become accomplished in handling watercolors in sketch form before attempting large-scale painting. Sketching and painting from still life or landscape not only improve the student designer's drawing and painting ability, but also increase his or her perception of light and color in nature. These processes also serve to underscore the significance of color as an element of design.

## PAINT AND COLOR

The design of a setting can succeed or fail on the strength of the painting. Hence, the designer should carefully plan how the scenery is to be painted. The most important consideration is the use of color. A scene designer must be familiar not only with the mixing and use of pigments, but also with the use of colored lights.

The prominence and forcefulness of color as an element of design was mentioned in Chapter 3. The attributes of the color experience and the philosophy of the use of color in the theatre were discussed in Chapter 8.

The scenic artist or scene designer employs the same philosophy, terminology, and mixing procedures in the use of color for scenery as would any other visual artist.

## SCENIC PAINT

The scenic artist's first act is to create a working palette of scene paint that will relate to the twelve principal hues of the spectrum. The size of the palette will vary, depending on the individual artist's tastes and working methods; on the pureness of hue and mixing behavior of the available pigments; and finally, on the relative cost of individual colors.

Most scene paints are bought ready-mixed, although unmixed dry pigment is still on the market. The mixture in this case refers to the presence of all or part of the properties of paint as a medium, which will be discussed separately under "Mixing Procedures" a little later in the chapter.

Designers need to know the wide range of types of paint available. In choosing the type of paint to use, they must determine the types of surfaces to be painted. Some paints are general purpose while others are designed to be used in very specific situations. The most commonly used paints for scenery are *casein* (milk-based), *latex*, and *acrylics*. Whenever possible, it is wisest to use a water-based paint such as those previously mentioned because they are generally safer and easier to use. There are so many new products on the market that there is a water-based paint made for almost any given circumstance, even painting plexiglass. When using one of the many paints that are not water-soluble, such as enamels, lacquer-based, or acetone-based, it is important to note the solvent required and to carefully follow safety precautions in order to use the paint safely.

The designer must also make a judgment as to how the pigment color of a paint compares to the corresponding spectrum hue. If the paint sample does not match favorably in hue, value, and chroma, the designer may have to compensate by choosing colors on either side of the spectrum and stock two pigments instead of one. The pigment yellow is a good example. Because a true spectrum yellow is not obtainable, two yellows are usually stocked— one that will mix easily with blue or green, and the other with orange.

In preparing a list of stock scenic colors, it is natural to compare the quality of the pigments' hues to the twelve principal colors of the color wheel. A good scene-painting palette would include them as well as some special colors and the earth colors.

**Dry Pigment**    Dry pigments are ground for theatrical use and therefore are available only at supply houses specializing in scenic paints and supplies. While dry pigment once was industry standard, it is only occasionally used today. Many shops will use what remains from years past, but few shops stock these pigments on an ongoing basis.

**Ready-Mixed Paints**    With ready-mixed paints, the pigment, color, binder, and vehicle are premixed in proper proportions into a creamy paste. Caseins often have too little binder, and under a series of washes (painting with little pigment and much water) an undercoat of color has a tendency to come off. It is sometimes advisable to add binder such as a clear acrylic or a polyvinyl acrylic (PVA) to the paint. Rosco Laboratories produces a number of different brands of scenic paint that vary in quality and potential use. The least expensive is "Off-Broadway" acrylic scene paint, although it is generally low-quality in terms of color richness. "Iddings Deep Colors" is a casein scenic paint. It is more expensive and good in quality of color richness. "Supersaturated" is another vinyl scenic paint. It is the most expensive and has excellent color richness. It also has the ability to be diluted to a very thin mixture while retaining its depth of color.

Latex and acrylic paints can be used almost interchangeably. Although as wide a range of color as the caseins is available, they both tend to be chalkier and stickier. They also can take longer to mix when matching a color. Latex paints are often used as a cheap substitute for caseins but in general they are less intense in color. Colors very high in chroma can be bought, but they tend to be as expensive as caseins.

**Mixing Procedures**      Scene paint is composed of three basic components: *pigment* (color), *binder*, and *vehicle*. The pigment and binder are suspended in a liquid that allows the paint to be brushed or sprayed onto a surface. The vehicle then evaporates and the binder holds the pigment to the surface. Most of the paint that is used for scenery is ready-mixed and requires only the addition of water.

When dry pigments are used as scene paint, the pigments are suspended in a water vehicle with a water-soluble glue as a binder. A filler such as whiting (an inexpensive chalk, sold in powdered form) is frequently added to the mixture to give the paint body and opacity. Because whiting affects the value of the color, it is not used when a pure full-chroma hue is desired.

The binder used for dry pigment is called "size." Traditionally, the size was made from a casein, gelatin, or animal glue that was manufactured in granular form and required a process of soaking and then boiling in water. It is common practice now to use other glues, such as a flexible glue, as a binder for dry pigment. Once prepared, the size can be mixed directly with the dry pigment. Certain colors, such as Prussian blue and Van Dyke brown, will not suspend if mixed directly with the size. They must first be soaked in denatured alcohol. Once mixed into a paste form, the size can be added slowly.

To match a specific shade of color, the scenic artist often mixes various colors dry before adding the size. While this may achieve an accurate match, it is a harzardous process. The fine powder of dry pigment can easily become airborne and then inhaled. It is vital that the user wear a dust mask while mixing. This is important to remember while mixing any form of powder.

Although large-scale painting with dry pigment has fallen into disuse, generally because of its time-consuming preparation, it is sometimes a convenient medium to have in the shop. Dry pigment can be mixed in small quantities with other binders such as shellac, flat varnish, or clear acrylic for a semigloss effect or for wood-graining.

## ANILINE DYES

Aniline dyes are available in almost all the standard colors. They are used for inking in outlines, thin wash glazes, translucencies, and for dip-dyeing fabrics.

Dyeing or painting with dyes is a different process than painting with scene paints. Scene paint changes the color of a surface by covering it with a pigment that is held in place by a binder. Dyeing, on the other hand, is a chemical process. The dye color becomes a part of the material it is dyeing. it is important that the dye and material have an affinity for each other, or a complete chemical action will not take place.

To dye cotton duck or muslin, it is sometimes necessary to add a small amount of acetic acid or vinegar to the dye solution. The acetic acid increases the affinity of the cotton for the dye, causing the fabric to absorb more color from the dye bath. The addition of a small quantity of salt also helps to increase the amount of absorption. Salt counteracts the tendency of dyestuffs to go into solution, making it easier for the dye color to be absorbed by the material. However, the presence of too much salt in the mixture, possibly from salted dyes or flameproofing compounds frequently mixed with the dye bath, can keep the dye from going into solution. All crystals must dissolve, or streaks of concentrated color will appear on the surface of the canvas. If the dye separates, the addition of some alcohol will ensure a complete solution. Normally, the crystals go into solution in hot water without any trouble.

For extensive *dye-painting*—when painting a translucent drop, for example—the muslin is prepared with a starch size (see "Size Coats" later in this chapter). If the painting is being done on a fabric that cannot be starch-sized, such as velour or silk, a small amount of starch can be added to the dye mixture to keep it from spreading on the fabric.

Dip-dyeing is used mostly on small pieces of fabric, such as window drapes or tablecloths. Occasionally, large gauze pieces are dipped with excellent results.

The preparation of the dye for dip-dyeing is the same as for dye-painting except, of course, larger in quantity. It is important to be sure that enough dye has been mixed, for to run out of dye mix in the middle of a dipping is disastrous. The color of the mix should be checked by dipping a sample of the fabric before preparing it for dipping.

In preparation for dip-dyeing, the fabric is first soaked in water. If it is new material, it should be washed to remove the size. After wringing, the still-damp fabric is dipped into the dye mix. If it is a stage gauze, after squeezing or wringing out the excess dye, it should be stretched to dry, or hung in place and stretched back into shape as it dries.

An important thing to remember is that dip-dyeing will take out any flameproofing that might have been in the material. It has to be reflameproofed later, or better still, flameproofed directly by a mixture added to the dye. The regular sal ammoniac and borax mixture can be cut to half strength by adding water and still give a satisfactory result. It is best, however, to run some test experiments under dipping conditions before taking a chance with a large piece.

## THE TOXICITY OF PAINT AND DYE

The daily contact of paints, dyes, and their solvents—all of which often contain toxic chemicals—can become a health hazard unless handled carefully. Toxic chemicals can enter the bloodstream in many ways: They may be ingested, entering the body through the stomach; inhaled into the lungs; or absorbed through the pores of the skin.

Although the paints and dyes discussed in this text are relatively safe, individual tolerances can vary. Some people have a multiple chemical sensitivity (MCS), while others are allergic to the touch and smell of paints.

**Solvents**    Used as a vehicle to put pigment into a solution, a solvent is basically a paint thinner. Water is the principal solvent for scenic paints, although an occasional chemical solvent is used on a stubborn mixer or in the manufacturing of ready-mixed paints.

Some familiar solvents used in the theatre are *alcohol* (methanol or wood alcohol), *turpentine, mineral spirits* (a substitute for turpentine), *ammonia,* and *formaldehyde* in ready-mix acrylic paints. All these solvents are considered toxic, and if allowed to enter the respiratory tract or bloodstream, can cause damage to the central nervous system, kidneys, or bladder. Any contact with the eyes should also be avoided.

Most solvents are by nature volatile and will evaporate quickly in a well-ventilated shop. However, if the painting is in confined quarters and for a prolonged time, the eyes should be protected with goggles, the hands with gloves, and the lungs with an air-purifying respirator.

**Pigments**    The color or hue of a paint is its pigment. The source of a pigment frequently helps to establish its degree of toxicity. Most pigments used in theatre are either inorganic or synthetic organic in origin.

*Inorganic* pigments come from the earth or minerals. Earth colors—such as ochre, burnt and raw sienna, ivory black, Prussian blue, and titanium white—are considered nontoxic. Pigments from mineral sources—such as cadmium yellow, raw and burnt umber, and cobalt blue—may have some lead content and should be treated as toxic.

*Synthetic organic* pigments are man-made color from organic materials. Although the organic source may not be toxic, toxic chemicals are often used in the pigments' manufacture. Such pigments as chrome yellow, chrome green, and molybdate (moly) orange should be used with extreme caution.

**Dyes**    Most of the bulk dyes used in the theatre are referred to as aniline dyes. In their original organic state they were very toxic. Present-day aniline dyes are synthetic and are prepared especially for cotton (duck and muslin). Although considered nontoxic, they are hazardous in the powder or crystal state. Extreme care should be taken to avoid inhaling dust when handling dye crystals before they are put into a liquid state. As with dry pigment, when mixing dyes it is wise to wear a dust mask. Some shops keep dyes in a concentrated liquid state that was prepared earlier, rather than during the pressures of a heavy work schedule. When painting with dyes, avoid skin and eye contact. Protect an open cut with rubber gloves.

Frequently materials other than cotton—such as rayon, wool, or silk—have to be dyed. There are commercial dyes available in small quantities and for all fabrics. Package or household dyes may be potentially hazardous. Read the directions and handle with extreme caution.

For additional and more detailed information about solvents, pigments, and dyes, write to the center of Occupational Hazards, 5 Beekman Street, New York, New York 10038. Literature on most aspects of painting can be obtained. Enclose a stamped, self-addressed envelope.

## PAINTER'S ELEVATIONS

Designers must thoroughly prepare for scene painting even if they plan to do their own painting. Painting ideas are expressed in painter's elevations, which, unlike sketches, remove all the atmosphere of stage lighting to show true colors and exact form. This is the point in the process when the designer must think through the appropriate painting technique and procedure for a design. The painter's elevation is a scaled drawing showing in detail the cartooning (or line drawing), the actual color, and a clear indication of the technique to be used. The scale of the elevation varies with the designer. The larger the scale, however, the more accurately it can be interpreted. The painter's elevations for most settings can be done at $\frac{1}{2}$-inch scale.

The paint elevation can also provide clear information to the costume designer and especially the lighting designer, so that they have a full picture of what the set will be.

Working from the painter's elevations, the scene painter can proportionally enlarge the drawing to full-scale. A grid of horizontal and vertical lines is placed over the drawing, spaced, in the scale of the drawing. A 2-foot grid is common, but every situation is different and the decision of grid size should be determined by the complexity of the painting. Sometimes a 4-foot grid is enough; it is possible that a 6-inch grid might be needed (for details on a face, perhaps). Whatever the size, a similar grid, at full scale, is drawn on the priming coat of the surface to be painted.

Ways of numbering or lettering the grid vary. In Europe, for example, the artists prefer to number the spaces (Figures 9–1a and 9–1b), while in the United States the numbering of the lines is favored (Figure 9–1c). Proceeding square by square, the painter transposes the small-scale elevation into a full-scale layout of the design.

## PAINTING PROCEDURE

The three steps toward preparing a surface for decorative painting are the size, prime, and base coats of paint. Their individual use or omission varies in accordance with the complexity of the design, the nature of the surface, and the painting technique. Figure 9–2 illustrates the basic painting procedure, from the painter's elevation to the finished piece.

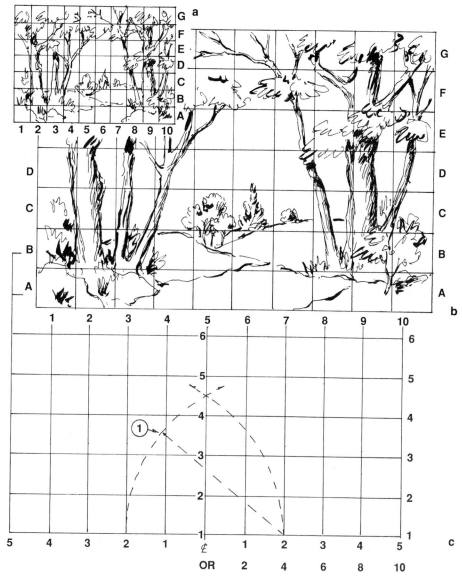

## Figure 9–1
### Methods of Proportional Enlarging

(a) The designer's elevation with a grid of two- or three-foot squares. Spaces are numbered from left to right and lettered from bottom to top.
(b) Full-scale layout of the drawing with the same labeling method.
(c) Full-scale grid with the lines numbered from the center line in opposite directions and from the bottom to top. The base line and center line are established first. (1) A perpendicular center line is constructed off the base line through the intersection of two arcs swung from centers equidistant from the center point.

## SIZE COAT

When working with soft covered flats and muslin drops (or any piece of scenery that is covered with canvas or muslin), the first step in the painting process is preparing the surface. This is done with a size coat, which shrinks the fabric and glazes the surface without filling it. One commonly used method is the *starch size*. The starch size is used to prepare a canvas or muslin for dye-painting or very thin opaque paints. It can also serve as a surface for opaque paints, especially if the opaque coat is not completely covering the surface but is applied to leave areas of unpainted background. Starch size can be made by adding a cup of cooked Argo starch to a 16-quart bucket of hot water at about a 20-to-1 proportion. It is important to remember, however, that the actual temperature of the water and the amount of humidity in the

a

## Figure 9—2
Scenery Painting Procedure:
Painter's elevations to finish scenery

(a) Painter's elevation of an oleo drop prepared by the designer. The drawing has been gridded with 2-foot squares in preparation for enlarging.

(b) Proportional enlarging. The muslin has been sized and the drop has been gridded with charcoal and snap line to full-scale dimensions. The design is sketched in with charcoal so that mistakes and construction lines can easily be "flogged" or dusted off.

(c) Inking the cartoon. The charcoal drawing or cartoon of the design is fixed to the muslin with a thin dye outline.

(d) Painting into the cartoon. Wash backgrounds and detail painting can proceed without fear of losing the cartoon since the dye will bleed through the paint and be visible as guide lines.

(e) Finished drop. An oleo drop for *Under the Gas Lights* by Augustin Daly. Designer—Glenn Gauer. Photo courtesy Nelson.

b

c

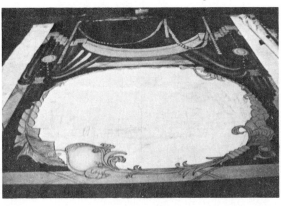

d

e

air will affect the strength of the starch size. Also, every scenic artist has his or her own preferences as to how thin or thick to mix the starch size. (This comes with experience). A touch of dye can be added to make the size coat more visible for brushing onto the fabric. The resulting coat is a taut, slightly glazed surface that is excellent for dye as well as paint.

## PRIME COAT

The second step in preparing new canvas is the prime coat, which has the function of filling the canvas. When painting on new canvas it is necessary to have it filled or the colors will "strike in" and lose brilliance. This phenomenon is very noticeable when old canvas is used beside new canvas on a flat.

The type of prime coat used will depend on the kind of paint that will be used on top and how the piece of scenery is to be used on stage. A translucent drop will most often be prepared with a thin layer of starch. White latex is often used for flats. There are primer coats manufactured specifically for metal (for use after the metal is cleaned off) and for plastics. If using dry pigment, a prime coat is made of working size and whiting with a touch of color to facilitate the application. Whatever is used as a prime is kept thin in order not to overload the muslin. Most prime coats tend to be opaque and therefore cannot be used over areas that are to be translucent or dye-painted.

All cartooning or layout drawing is done in charcoal on the prime coat. After the drawing is completed, key points or portions of the cartoons are "inked" in using an industrial marker supplied with replaceable felt tips, a fine line of dye, or indelible pencil. The rest of the charcoal is "flogged" or dusted off the surface in preparation for the base coat. The inked-in portions of the design will bleed through the base coat and serve as a guide for later detailed painting.

## BASE COAT

The base coat is the underpainting for the final decorative painting and texturing. The application and color of the base coat depend on what is to follow. For example, a base coat may be one tone as a basis for a slick, modern paneled wall; it may be a scumbling of two or three tones in preparation for an antiqued, weather-beaten surface; or it may become a graded wash under a stenciled wallpaper design.

As a mixture, the base coat is kept thin in order not to overload the canvas.

## DETAIL AND DECORATIVE PAINTING

The final step in scene painting is the definition of form, or the illusion of form, through the various painting techniques or lining, texturing, and stenciling. We will also discuss the designing and painting of trees and the technique of pouncing.

**Lining**      The technique of lining, with straightedge or free hand, is to represent in two dimensions the complicated surfaces of the moldings in a cornice, chair rail, panel, or door trim (Figure 9–3).

Careful lining, in addition to local color, is done to establish highlight, shade, and shadow. The specific choices of color for both highlights and shadows are completely dependent on the design, generally employing the idea of working with complementary colors. More than two shadow or highlight tones might be used, again determined by the complexity and nature of the design. Highlights are by definition lighter in value than the local color, the shadows darker. Cooler colors are more frequently used for shadows because they tend to recede, but very successful shadows can also be painted in warm tones.

The order of lining for a panel or cornice is determined after first studying a cross section of the molding and the direction of the light that would reveal the molding if it were real. The position of a window or artificial light sources are clues for fixing the general direction of light for each wall in the set.

**Texturing**      To avoid the starkness of a single tone and to bring more depth to a flat surface, the painter uses various texturing techniques. Because stage lighting is from many sources, most natural shadows and reflected-light

### Figure 9–3
Lining Techniques

(a) Profile of cornice to be painted.
(b) Lining of cornice.
(c) Lining of a raised panel molding.
   (1)  Assumed direction of light.
   (2)  Local color.
   (3)  Highlight.
   (4)  Shadow, darkest tone.
   (5)  Shade.

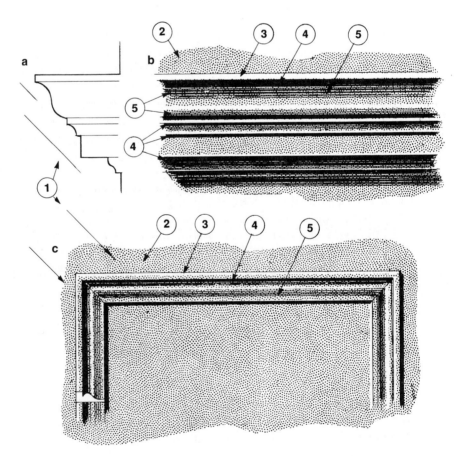

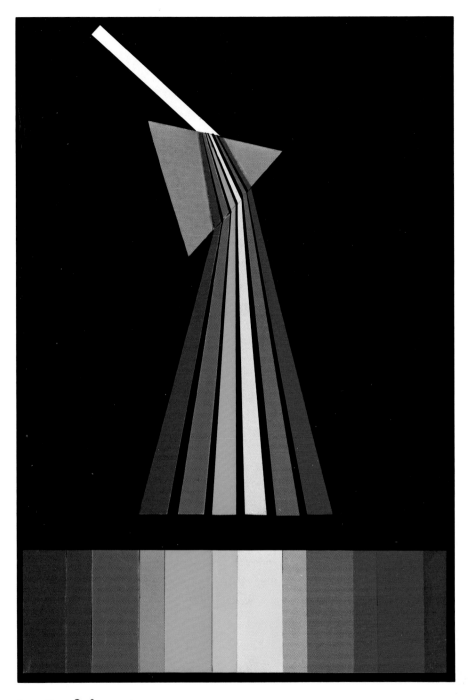

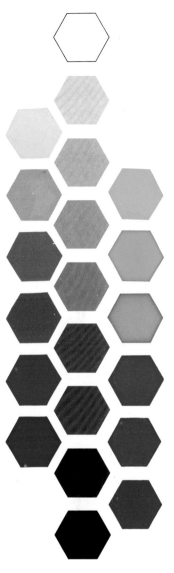

**COLOR PLATE 8–1**
**SPECTRUM HUES**
The breakdown of sunlight through prism refraction into first six, and then twelve, spectrum hues.

**COLOR PLATE 8–2**
**HUE VALUE RELATIONSHIP**
The twelve principal spectrum hues are arranged next to the value scale in their natural light-to-dark relationship. The middle value of the seven steps between black and white is referred to as medium value while the three steps above are known as lowlight, light, and highlight. The lower value steps are called highdark, dark, and lowdark.

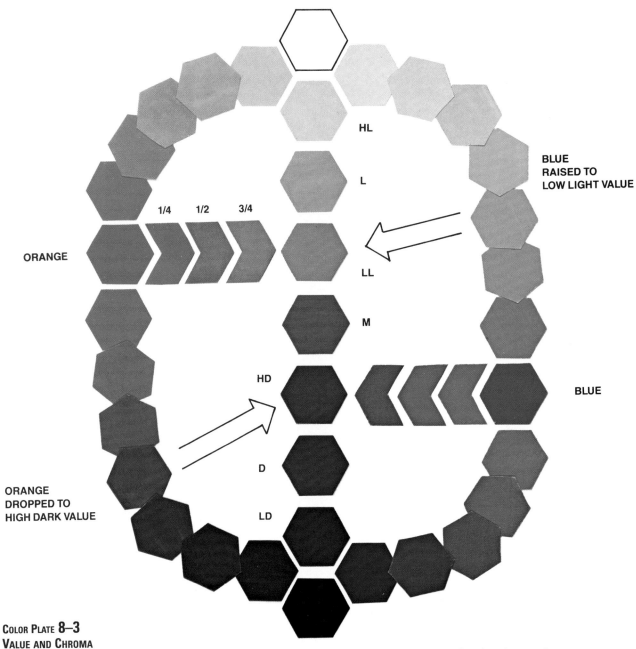

**COLOR PLATE 8–3**
**VALUE AND CHROMA**

The complementary hues, blue and orange, are subjected to value and chroma changes first by alternately mixing each color with white and black in the outside ring to effect a value change. Chroma changes at a fixed value are accomplished horizontally by mixing the color with its complementary hue after it has been raised or lowered to the same value (arrow). Note that to change the value of a hue automatically alters its chroma without necessarily affecting value.

It is possible, of course, to alter chroma at each value step and completely fill the circle with a variety of tints and shades. This mixing procedure (although impossible to reproduce accurately), applied to any set of complementaries, is important to the stage designer as a method of creating new and unusual colors, as well as in matching existing shades.

**COLOR PLATE 8-4a**
**ADDITIVE MIXING**
The additive mixing of light
primaries by the crossing of
three spotlight rays. Note that
the secondary hues formed by
the mixing of two adjacent primaries are lighter in value, and
that the mixing of three primaries results in white light.

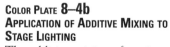

**COLOR PLATE 8–4b**
**APPLICATION OF ADDITIVE MIXING TO**
**STAGE LIGHTING**
The additive mixing of a primary hue with its complementary
will also produce white light.
Tints of blue-green and light
amber in opposing spotlights,
for example, can be used to
light an acting area. The white
light of the area can be toned
to a warm or cool shade by
altering the intensity of one
side or the other.

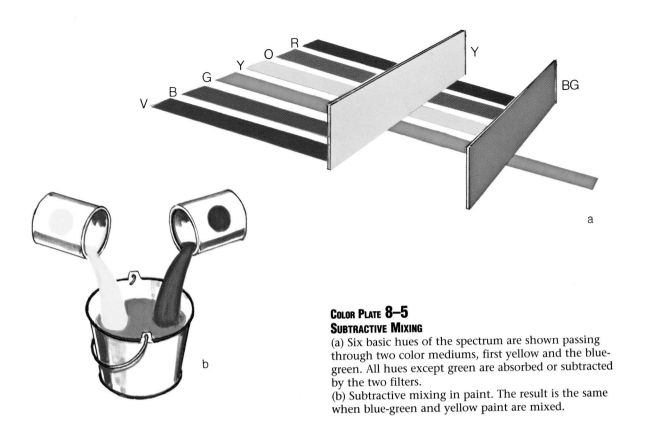

**COLOR PLATE 8–5**
**SUBTRACTIVE MIXING**
(a) Six basic hues of the spectrum are shown passing through two color mediums, first yellow and the blue-green. All hues except green are absorbed or subtracted by the two filters.
(b) Subtractive mixing in paint. The result is the same when blue-green and yellow paint are mixed.

**COLOR PLATE 8–6**
**COLOR REFLECTION**
The horizontal orange strip represents an orange-colored surface. It appears orange under sunlight because only red, yellow, and orange hues of the spectrum have been reflected. The other hues have been absorbed.

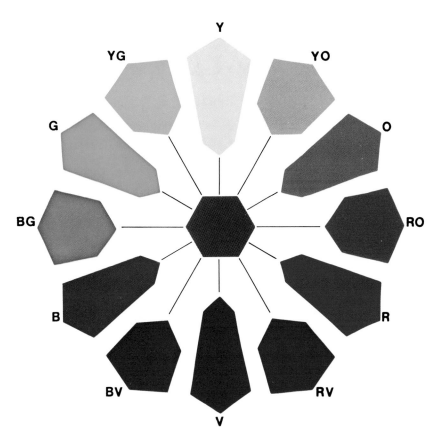

COLOR PLATE **8–7**
**PIGMENT COLOR WHEEL**
Twelve principal hues of the spectrum arranged in a circle. Diagonals are color opposites; their subtractive mixing would produce a neutral shade similar to the gray lozenge in the center.

COLOR PLATE **8–8**
**LIGHT COLOR WHEEL**
The light color wheel is centered on the light primaries. The large lozenges are the light primaries YG, BV, and RO. Two adjacent primaries mix to form intermediate secondaries that become complementary hues. The secondaries are lighter in value due to the additive mixing of the primaries. The additive mixing of all primaries is symbolized by the white lozenge in the center. The light color wheel also represents the interrelation of color in light and the twelve principal hues of pigment.

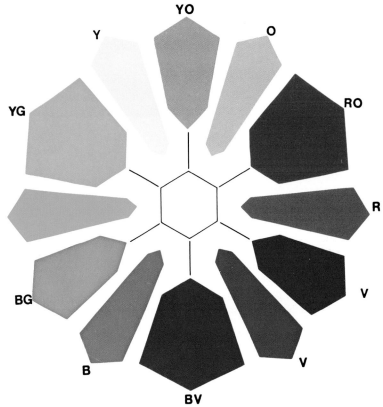

**COLOR PLATE 8–9**
**INTERACTION OF COLOR HUE REACTION INFLUENCING A NEUTRAL**
A small neutral figure is influenced by the color of the ground that surrounds it. The neutral in each of the six basic spectrum hues appears to be tinted with the complementary color of the background. The influence can be noted in each case when compared with the same gray tone to the right of each hue.

COLOR PLATE **8–10**
**INTERACTION OF COLOR CHROMA REACTIONS**
The chroma of the six basic hues appears to take on more brilliance as the background is darkened.

COLOR PLATE **8–11**
**INTERACTION OF COLOR VALUE REACTION**
The value of the center of each area of color is the same. It appears to be lighter or darker as it is influenced by the surrounding color.

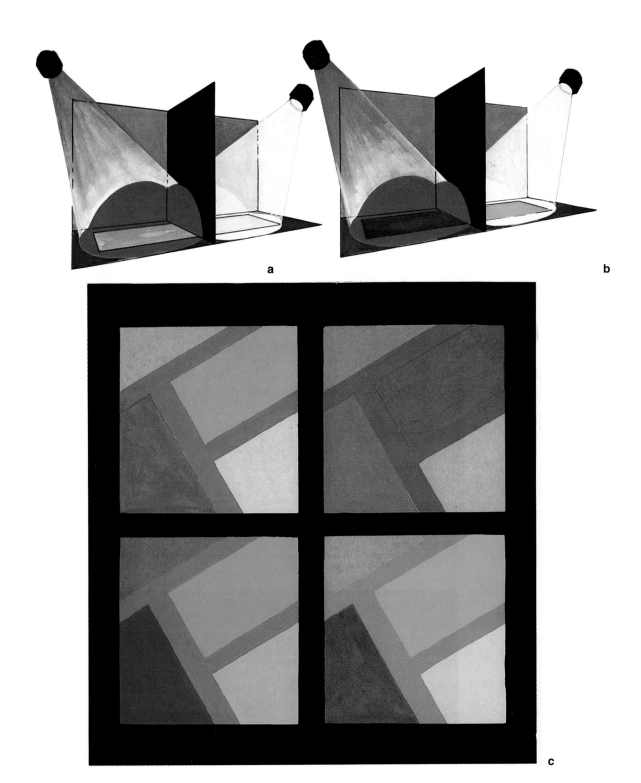

**COLOR PLATE 8–12**
**COLOR MODIFICATION**

A demonstration of the subtractive mixing effect when a colored surface is modified by a colored light. (a) Yellow surface under red light. (b) Green surface under red light. (c) A multi-colored design is seen under three different colors of light. The color of light on the two upper squares (left) clear, (right) medium-red. On the lower squares (left) sky-blue, (right) moss green.

tonalities are eliminated. Much of this natural variation of tonality has to be painted into the set through the use of texturing techniques.

One of the simplest texturing techniques is to wet-blend three or more tones of a color on a surface. Using three brushes, one in each bucket, the three tones are brushed or blended together on the canvas while the paints are still wet. The result is an impression of one color with more depth and quality than is found in a single flat tone. This technique is usually handled on a broad scale with subtlety or obviousness depending on the contrast or harmony of the tones.

A blending technique can also be done over a dry surface by blending the tones together with dry-brushing or feathering. Dry-brushing, as the name implies, is done with the tip of a relatively dry brush in order to cover the under-surface only partially and thus let it show through. Feathering refers to the direction of the brush stroke. The brush is drawn from the wet surface toward the dry so that the stroke ends in a featherlike pattern.

Other texturing techniques on a smaller scale include sponging, stippling, spattering, combing, use of a paint roller, and spraying. Each technique creates an individual feeling of texture as well as blending the tones into a vibrant surface (Figure 9–4).

All these techniques can be used to simulate the textural qualities of a specific material such as stone, plaster, wallpaper, and the like. Some materials, however, require texturing techniques that border on decorative painting; wood and wood graining are prime examples (Figure 9–5).

The painting of wood graining employs the same movement of color found in the other techniques. The grain pattern, of course, will vary with the type and use of the make-believe wood. Is it to be matched-grain walnut veneer on a late Empire breakfront secretary, or knotty pine vertical paneling? Any attempt at realistic representation of wood graining on the stage should be preceded by a careful study of the real wood's color and grain characteristics.

If the wood is a door or door trim and should appear as a varnished finish, the graining can be glazed. Glazing, however, not only reduces the contrast between colors but also lowers their value. This must be taken into consideration in the preparation of the grain colors.

The glazing of grain that has a varnished finish can be accomplished in a number of different ways. One method is to grain the surface first, then apply a shellac, clear acrylic, or flat-varnish glaze.

If it is dry pigment, a safer and easier approach is to put something with the paint that will give a gloss and eliminate the necessity of glazing the surface at all. Scene paint can be mixed directly with flat varnish, which serves as a binder as well as giving the paint a slight sheen. Shellac mixed with scene paint produces the same effect as does clear acrylic. Clear acrylic and acrylic varnish are easier to mix than varnish or shellac. Either method can be brought into a higher luster by polishing with paste wax later. Glazed surfaces must be handled with caution, however, for there is always the danger of creating a surface that is too reflective; it then becomes annoying to the actors and audience.

### Figure 9—4
### Texture Painting Techniques

(1) Wet blending or scumble.
(2) Dry scumble.
(3) Spattering.
(4) Combing or dry brushing.
(5) Rag rolling.
(6) Spraying.
(7) Feather duster.
(8) Paint roller.
(9) Taped paint roller to add a pattern to texture.
(10) Foam-rubber stamp.

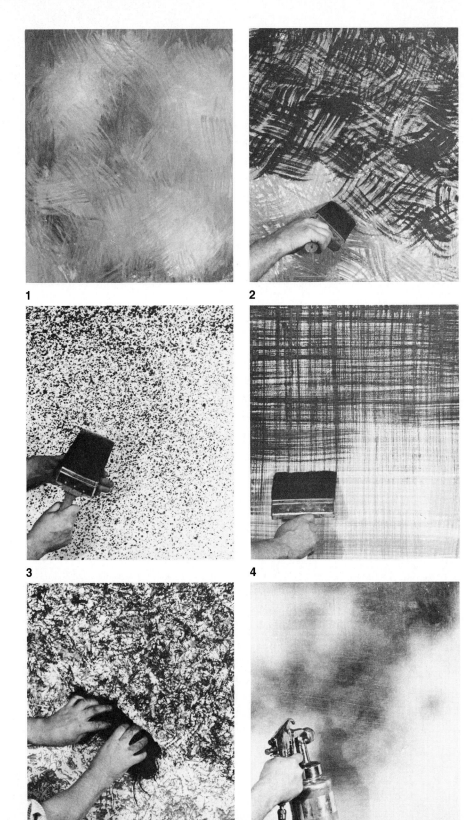

**Foliage**    The designing and painting of trees and foliage requires practice and a study of natural forms. The designer should first study trees in their natural state, perhaps painting them in watercolors. A designer will soon learn to see the overall mass of foliage, then the subdivisions of smaller units relating to the branches of the tree's structure, and finally the detail of a single leaf. It is interesting to see how light reveals the forms, passing through translucent areas. Some branches catch light while others are silhouetted.

The conceptual treatment of a tree on stage can assume many forms. Stage foliage can be translucent, opaque, or textured. The tree style may be real or stylized, or it may even be suggested with light patterns. Foliage can be carefully painted leaf by leaf or boldly painted in block areas loosely suggesting the organic form.

A landscape artist often starts with the darkest tones. Leaf masses in the shadow or silhouette are blocked in first. The lighter shades and highlights

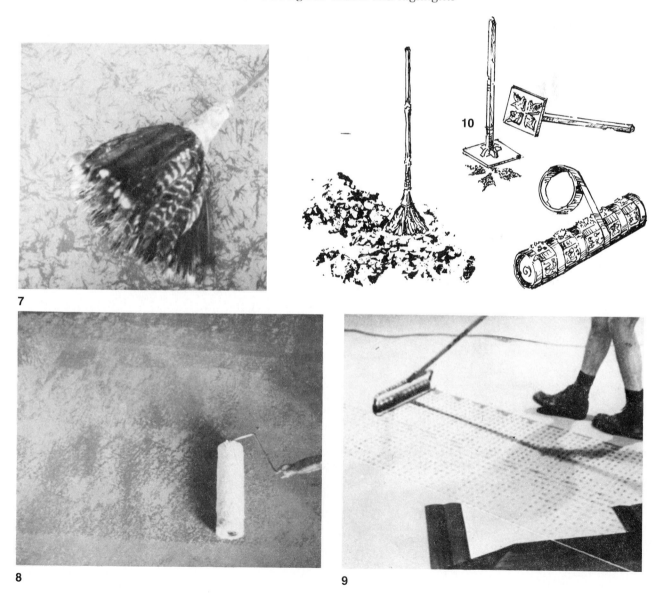

7

8

9

10

a

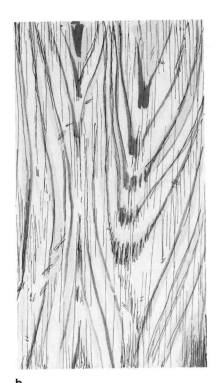

b

c

**Figure 9–5**
Wood-grain and Marble
Texturing

(a) Pine grain.
(b) Oak grain.
(c) Marble.

are painted last in opaque paint. If the foliage of the tree is to be translucent and painted with dyes, the technique is reversed: The lighter tones are painted first and the darker shades last.

There are, of course, an infinite number of ways to paint foliage. The particular method will, as always, depend on the needs and style of the design (see Figure 9–6).

**Stenciling**  The chief use of stenciling is for a painted wallpaper (or something similar) in which a design motif is repeated in an interlocking overall pattern. The cutting and printing of a stenciled design is the fastest and most effective method of repeating a small motif. After the means of interlocking the motif has been carefully figured out in relation to the size of the wall area, the motif is traced upon a sheet of stencil paper. Stencil paper is a tough, oil-impregnated paper especially for stencils. It is readily available in art shops or paint and wallpaper stores, or can be made by applying a half-and-half mixture of linseed oil and turpentine to heavy kraft paper. Oak tag is a cheaper and thinner substitute for stencil paper. It must be treated the same way and is good only for light usage, as it wears out quickly.

A well-planned stencil has at least one full motif with portions of adjacent motifs to key the stencil into an interlocking scheme. The size of the motif and the amount needed for interlocking the design more or less determine the size of the stencil sheet. Care should be taken not to create too large a stencil that might become awkward to handle. The motif is cut out of the paper with a sharp knife, razor blade, or X-acto® knife. Be sure to leave some

tabs within the open parts to support the loose ends and strengthen the
stencil as a whole. Two or more stencils can be cut at one time, for it is wise
to have more than one stencil, especially if there is a large area to cover.
They can be alternated in use so as to minimize the tendency of a stencil to
become damp and misshapen from hard use.

After the stencil is cut, it is framed at the outside edges with 1-by-2 on
edge to further strengthen it and at the same time provide a sheild to the
spray if the paint is being applied with a spray gun. The stencil is coated on
both sides with clear shellac or any water-repellent plastic spray as an additional protection from the water-soaking effect of scene paint.

The stencil print can be made by three different methods: by spray gun,
by brush, or by sponge. The spray gun is fast but sometimes messy. Stenciling
with a brush is slower. The brush should be kept fairly dry and stroked toward
the center of the openings to avoid dribbles. The use of a sponge or soft
cloth to apply the paint works best on an open stencil, for the print is purposely textured and not clean cut (Figure 9–7).

**Pouncing**     Pouncing is another method of transferring and repeating a
design motif. It is generally used when the motif is either too large for a
stencil, does not repeat enough times for one to bother cutting a stencil, or

## Figure 9–7
### Stenciling Techniques

(a) Unframed stencil for dry-brush application.

(b) Framed stencil for spray-gun application. Note how the stencil is keyed at the top and bottom. Because this stencil follows a vertical line it is not necessary to key it horizontally.

(c) Pouncing:
  (1) Pounce, or perforated design.
  (2) Pounce wheel.
  (3) Pounce bag.
  (4) The pounced design transferred onto the canvas.

(d) Border stencil.

(e) Brick stencil.

(f) Lining and spattering the stencil pattern.

(g) Finished brick pattern.

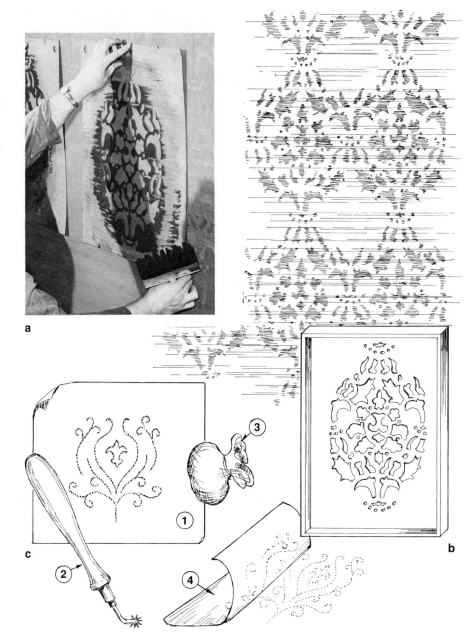

is repeated in reverse. Pouncing differs from stenciling in that only the outline or cartoon of the motif, instead of a painted print, is transferred (Figure 9–7c).

The pounce pattern is made by first drawing the design on a piece of brown kraft paper and then perforating the outline with a pounce wheel. The best type of pounce wheel has a small swivel-mounted perforating wheel. It works better on a padded surface, such as a blanket or fold of canvas, than on a hard tabletop or floor.

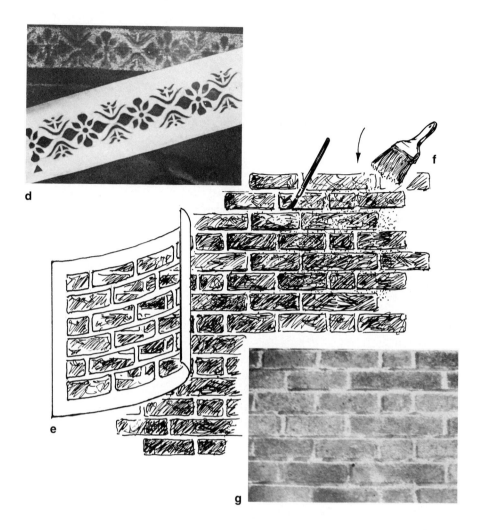

After the design is perforated and the back-side rough edges are lightly sanded, the paper is laid on the canvas in the desired position. The pattern is rubbed with a pounce bag made of a thin material such as cheesecloth filled with charcoal dust. The outline is strengthened after the pouncing with charcoal, paint, or dye, depending on the painting technique to follow.

## TEXTURED SURFACES

Although their value on the stage is debatable, textured surfaces are sometimes desirable. Important points to consider before texturing a surface include these: (1) A textured surface cannot be reclaimed for a different use without re-covering the piece of scenery. (2) Deeply textured surfaces will not stand excessive handling or wear. (3) Unless the texturing is in a position on the stage to get the proper lighting, it may as well be painted. Figures 9–8 and 9–9 illustrate two techniques for creating a textured surface.

 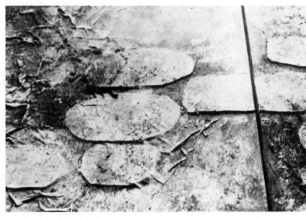

a               b

**Figure 9–8**
**Textured Surfaces**

(a) Preparation for textured surface. Burlap, muslin, and random shapes of upson board glued to the surface of scenery units.
(b) Appliquéd surface is covered with a mixture of joint cement and sawdust. After it is dry, the surface is painted in dark tones and then higher surfaces are dry brushed with lighter tones.

**Sawdust Coat** Sawdust or wood chips can be mixed directly with scenic paint and applied as a texture coat. The binder should be stiffened a little to adhere the sawdust firmly. A sawdust coat requires less preparation and dries quickly but does not have a deep texture.

**Water Putty** Durham's Water Putty, a commercial surface repair mixture in powder form, can be used as a texture coat. It works best on a hard surface (3-ply or wood) and can be combed or stippled into a deep texture. Although it dries off-white, it can be colored either with dye during the mixing or with paint after it has dried. When hardened it is tough, but still subject to chipping.

**Joint Compound** A compound developed commercially to cement tape over drywall joints in house construction, joint cement will hold a deep texture if a little white glue is added to the compound before application.

**Marble Coat** A texture paint made of marble dust sets up extremely hard. This marble coat takes a deep texture, can be colored when mixing, and when hardened it can be handled with a minimum of chipping. It is the hardest of the prepared texture coats.

**SURFACE MATERIALS**

Surface materials used mainly for textural purposes exist in a variety of forms. Each has its special handling and individual effect.

**Irish Linen** Irish linen has, of course, long since disappeared from the U. S. theatre as the standard covering for framed scenery. Its durability and excellent texture, however, have not quite been replaced by the scene canvas in common use.

**Canvas** Canvas, which is 8-ounce cotton duck, has been discussed as a painting surface. Professionally, it is the standard and most frequently used

a

## Figure 9—9
## Textured Details

Decorative details such as this rinceau pattern are often in slight relief.

(a) A cut-out of the border pattern is prepared in upson board. Thick texture paint (J. C. Penney) is applied with a cake decorator to the cutout, which is then glued to the architrave position of the entablature.

(b) When dry, all recessed surfaces are stained dark and later brushed with metallic gold paint.

(c) Final assembly.

b

c

painting surface for all framed scenery. All other surfaces are limited in use to a special effect.

**Muslin**     Unbleached muslin is the next most frequently used covering material. Although it lacks the texture and durability of canvas, its lightweight weave is useful for other purposes. As was mentioned, muslin is an excellent dye-painting surface for translucencies.

**Scrim**     Scrim can be used as a painting surface in addition to its general use as a dye-painted transparency. It can also be used as a covering material if backed by canvas or some other opaque fabric. Unbacked scrim can also be painted (dry-brushed) with thin scenic colors. They are not as good as dyes, for they tend to stiffen the scrim, which is a disadvantage if it has to fold or roll. If large areas of scrim must be painted, it is best to use a spray gun to avoid stretching the scrim out of shape.

The open mesh of a scrim can be filled to create opaque areas. One means of doing so is to squeeze pure undiluted clear latex mixed with a casein color in a paste consistency onto the scrim to fill the mesh. A table-mustard squeeze bottle is a good applicator. If the scrim is to be filled while it is on the floor in a horizontal position, steps should be taken to prevent the latex from sticking to the floor. Vis-Queen, a clear transparent plastic, is a good separator. More expensive premixed fillers are also available (for example, Roscofiller).

**Burlap**     Burlap is frequently used as a covering material chiefly for its texture. Burlap should be backed or fastened to a firm surface, for it is made of jute and may stretch or sag under a heavy coat of paint. Sometimes it helps to paint and dry burlap horizontally. Burlap needs to be heavily sized to keep the color from "striking in." However, this may be a desirable effect if it is to be an old tapestry or wall hanging.

**Wallpaper**     Occasionally the scenic artist will be expected to hang wallpaper. Figure 9–10 illustrates the proper technique.

### METHODS OF PAINTING

Scenery is painted in two different positions, horizontally and vertically. The various methods of painting are devised to facilitate either way of painting.

#### HORIZONTAL PAINTING

Painting on the floor is the oldest and simplest method and requires the least mechanical assistance. Long handles on the brushes, charcoal holders, and straightedges help to take the backache out of horizontal painting. The most essential requirement is lots of smooth floor space (preferably wood) and good overhead illumination (Figure 9–11).

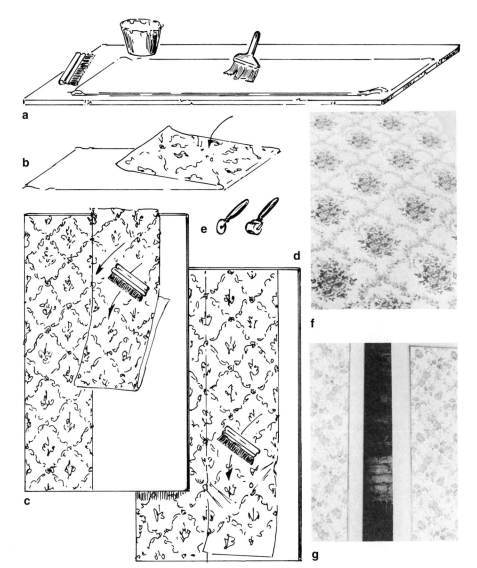

### Figure 9–10
Wallpapering

Occasionally the scenic artist is expected to hang wallpaper. The surface, if canvas, should be sized and based with casein or latex paint. If the wall surface is hard a size coat is sufficient.

(a) Wallpaper strips of approximate length face down on pasting board. Wheat paste is used for regular wallpaper, or vinyl paste on vinyl wallpaper.

(b) Paste-covered strip is folded one third as shown.

(c) Exposed portion of pasted strip is smoothed onto wall, being careful to match the pattern. Bubbles are smoothed out with wallpaper brush.

(d) Strip is unfolded and brushed flat.

(e) Cutting wheel and roller. Edges are trimmed and, if paper is being applied to a hard surface, the edges are rolled.

(f) Wallpapered unit of scenery.

(g) Wallpapered panels.

Although some painting techniques are best employed horizontally, others are accomplished more easily in a vertical position.

## STATIONARY FRAME AND BOOMERANG

It is easy to fasten scenery against a wall or on a stationary frame along a wall, but it is not so easy to paint all areas without using a ladder. A rolling platform, or *boomerang*, as it is called, provides the painter with two or three painting levels (Figure 9–12).

## MOVING FRAME

The moving paint frame that raises or lowers past the working level brings the greatest flexibility to vertical painting (Figure 9–12). The frame lowers

**Figure 9–11**
Painting on the Floor

Extensive floor painting is made easier with the use of proper tools and the right type of brushes.
(a) Individual paint-bucket carrier.
(b) Long handles for the brushes.
(c) Paint cart with palette area for mixing paint.
(d) Straight edge with handle.

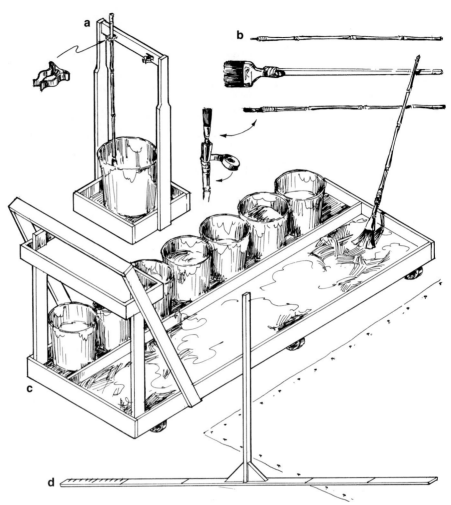

into a well or to a second painting level. Some unusually high frames often have two or three decks so that the painters can work at different levels at the same time.

## BRUSHES AND OTHER EQUIPMENT

The painter's most important tool is, of course, the *brush*. A good brush should have long bristles and a full shape. (Avoid hollow centers.) Pure bristles are so expensive, especially in the larger sizes, that many painters have turned to nylon brushes. A nylon brush with sandblasted tips is about half the price of the pure-bristle brush of the same size. The difference in price is offset by the slight disadvantage of nylon, for watercolor tends to run off nylon, causing it to hold less paint than a pure-bristle brush.

Because scene-painting brushes are used predominately in watercolors, the bristles should be rubber set. Some brushes set in glue are suitable for oil paint but will break down with continued use in watercolor.

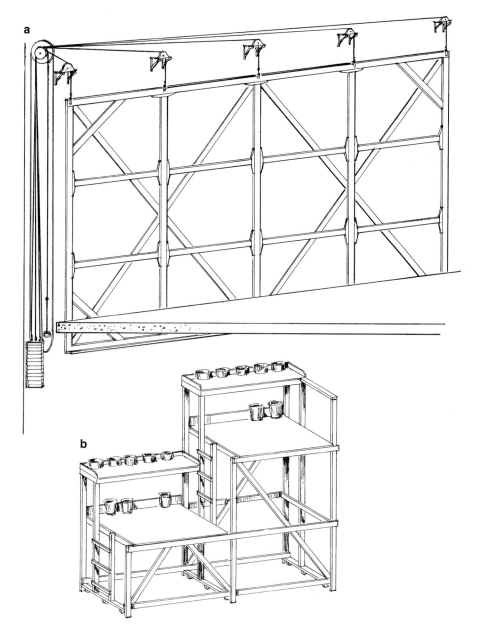

**Figure 9–12**
Vertical Painting Methods

(a) The moving paint frame raises and lowers into a well extending below the main working-deck level. Scenery is attached to the frame and is painted in a vertical position by raising and lowering the frame.
(b) The boomerang, a stepped-level platform on casters, provides a variety of working levels for the painter.

## TYPES OF BRUSHES

The types of brushes for scene painting are classified by the work they do, such as priming, base-coating or "lay-in," decorating, and lining (Figure 9–13a).

The *priming brush* is the widest brush (6 to 8 inches). It holds a large quantity of paint, which makes it good for spreading size and prime coats quickly and efficiently.

The *lay-in brush*, about 4 inches wide, is used for the more careful painting of a base coat, blending, spattering, and similar techniques.

## PAINTING TOOLS

In addition to brushes and paints, the painter uses other necessary painting tools, including these:

1. Beveled straightedge (6 feet)
2. Rule or steel tape
3. Snap line (50 feet)
4. Bow snap line (6 to 8 feet)
5. Plumb bob
6. Charcoal stick and holder
7. Large compass (36 inches)
8. Tank sprays
9. Spray gun and compressor
10. Pounce wheel
11. Buckets (14 and 16 quarts)
12. Small pots or cans (No. 10 cans)
13. Burner and double boiler for cooking starch
14. Flogger
15. Paint roller

The *fitch* is a flat brush with a long handle, varying in width from $1\frac{1}{2}$ to 3 inches. It is used for decorative painting such as architectural details or the foliage of a tree. The fitch brush is a pure-bristle brush made especially for scenic painting and can be quite expensive. A *sash tool*, which is a flat, long-handled brush for painting window sashes, can be used as an inexpensive decorative painting brush. The sash tool, however, is not made any wider than 2 inches.

*Liners* are also long-handled brushes varying in width from $\frac{1}{4}$ to 1 inch. Liners should have long, pure bristles to perform well. A 1-inch sash tool can do limited lining, but there is no substitute for the smaller brushes.

### HOW TO CLEAN BRUSHES

Water-based paints "set up" quicker than most oil-based paints. This is an advantage while painting, but a disadvantage when cleaning brushes. Also, latex and acrylic paints are water-repellent when they are dry. To keep brushes from building up paint in the heel, an unclean brush should not be allowed to dry. An uncleaned brush not in use at the moment is usually kept in a pail of clean water.

When brushes are cleaned at the end of a workday, attention is focused on getting all paint out of the heel of the brush. A wire brush is useful to comb out stubborn paint. After washing, the bristles of the brush should be shaped while damp and left to dry.

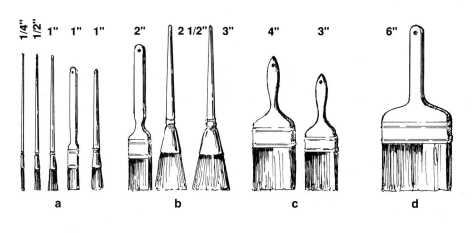

a    b    c    d

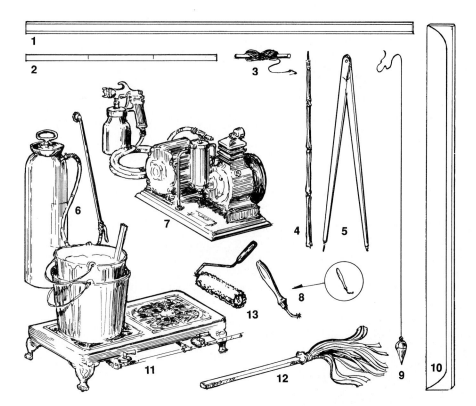

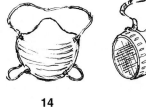

**Figure 9–13**

**Brushes, Tools, and Safety Equipment**

Scene-painting brushes:
(a) Lining brushes, flat and oval.
(b) Decorating brushes.
(c) Lay-in brushes.
(d) Priming brush. Painting tools and accessories:

  (1) Beveled straight edge.
  (2) Yard stick.
  (3) Snap line.
  (4) Charcoal and holder.
  (5) Large compass.
  (6) Tank spray.
  (7) Spray gun and compressor.
  (8) Pounce wheel.
  (9) Plumb bob.
  (10) Bow snap line.
  (11) Burner and double boiler for starch size.
  (12) Flogger.
  (13) Paint roller.
  (14) Dust mask.
  (15) Air-purifying respirator mask.
  (16) Goggles.
  (17) Rubber gloves.

## ADDITIONAL PAINTING SUPPLIES

| | |
|---|---|
| *White shellac* | For glazes, water-repellent finishes, binder and hardener |
| *Alcohol* | Solvent for shellac; speeds the dissolving of colors that are poor mixers |
| *Flat varnish* | Glaze finish and paint binder |
| *Turpentine* | Solvent for varnish and oil paints |
| *Liquid wax* | Glaze finish and paint binder |
| *Metallic paints* | Powder mixed with strong size or clear acrylic for metallic surfaces; all right for scenery, but not for props; spray cans (Krylon) have harder finish, good for props, more expensive |
| *Glycerin* | Added to paints for slow drying |
| *Lysol* | Preservative |
| *Alum* | For alum-size preparation |
| *Sal ammoniac* <br> *Borax* | Flameproofing chemicals: Formula—1 lb. borax, 1 lb. sal ammoniac, 3 qts. of water |

If the brush has been in dye, it may need to be soaked overnight in a mixture of whiting and water to draw out all the dye.

### OTHER PAINTING TOOLS AND SUPPLIES

In addition to brushes and paints, the painter uses other implements to prepare, lay out, and paint scenery. These tools include measuring devices, buckets, rollers, and so forth. Many of them are pictured in Figure 9–13, and they are highlighted in the box above as well.

Painters also use other supplies that supplement dry colors, glue, and dyes that are directly associated with scene painting. Some have already been mentioned in relation to a particular painting technique, but for your reference they are highlighted in the box above.

### FLAMEPROOFING

Canvas and muslin can be purchased already flameproofed, but if the scenery has been washed for reuse the canvas will have to be flameproofed again. A mixture of 1 pound of sal ammoniac, 1 pound of borax, and 3 quarts of water is an inexpensive flameproofing formula. It is brushed or sprayed onto previously dampened material for the best results. Sheer materials, such as scrim or bobbinet, should be dipped to ensure successful flameproofing.

Because the flameproofing mixture is highly corrosive to metals, brushes and spray cans should, after use, be washed thoroughly in cold water. A small

amount of acetic acid in the water helps to counteract the corrosive action. Also be aware that the fumes of the flameproofing mix can be toxic to some individuals. Therefore, any prolonged exposure during the flameproofing procedure requires good ventilation and the use of an air-purifying mask.

## TESTING FLAMEPROOFING

The term *flameproofing* does not mean that a treated fabric will stop a flame, but that it will *not support* a flame. Hence when an obscure section of a drop or flat is *tested*—by bringing a lighted match to the surface—it will burn a hole, but it will stop burning when the flame is removed signifying that the fabric is flameproof.

Testing and other fire regulations vary over the country. It is wise for the designer and technician to become familiar with local regulations before beginning production.

# HANDLING SCENERY

**10**

Confronted with a multiscene play, a designer has to consider, early in the planning, a method of handling the settings. A production scheme is developed from the numerous ways of moving scenery, and this scheme frequently influences the design concept. Consequently, the more designers know of the mechanics of the modern stage and of theatrical techniques for moving scenery, the closer they can come to fully realizing their design concept. In those venues where the designer has to be clever enough to overcome limited funds and poorly equipped stages, this is especially true. Thus, technical knowledge can help a designer solve scenery-shifting problems with an ingenuity that often becomes inventively original.

## FACTORS INFLUENCING THE HANDLING OF SCENERY

The basic methods of handling scenery, in the order of their increasing complexity and additional construction, are (1) the manual running of scenery on the floor; (2) the flying of scenery; (3) the moving of scenery on casters, including such large units as wagons and revolving stages; and (4) the handling of scenery through the stage floor by elevators.

How scenery is to be handled is influenced by four major factors: (1) the *play*; (2) the *theatre*, its stage, and available personnel and resources; (3) the *design* of the production; and (4) the *budget*.

### PLAY STRUCTURE

The form of the play and its plot structure are the primary influences on the handling of scenery. A play, for instance, may have many unrelated episodic scenes, a flashback technique, several simultaneous scenes with continuous action, or the conventional three-act form. The structure of the play, in addition to determining the number of scenes or locale changes and their order of appearance or reappearance, also establishes the *kind* of change.

The most common interval for a change of scene is between acts. The act change, which can be very short (one minute is not uncommon, depending on the particular circumstances) or as long as fifteen minutes or more, presents no great problem under optimum conditions, assuming the stage has adequate flying and offstage space. Even under limited stage conditions, an act change usually allows enough time to maneuver the scenery, although it may require more ingenuity and hard work.

A change within the act, or a scene change, can be almost instanteous or considerably longer than one minute. A scene change, by necessity a fast change, can be handled in several different ways. It may be a *hidden* change, taking place behind a curtain, or without a curtain but hidden by a blackout. It may be a *visible* change (avista) made in full view of the audience with a display of theatrical magic, or by actor-stagehands openly moving elements of scenery as a part of the action. In contrast to the other kinds of changes, the avista becomes a part of the play by calling attention to the movement of the scenery. As a theatrical technique, it obviously fits only certain types of plays and production schemes.

## THEATRE AND STAGE

The shape of the theatre and the size of the stage have an important influence on the movement of scenery. The amount of flying space and equipment; the placement, number, and size of any existing traps; the extent of offstage and wing space; the size of the proscenium arch and sightline conditions— all obviously help determine the way scenery can be handled.

Some stages have more elaborate mechanical aids or stage machinery for shifting scenery, such as a built-in revolving stage, tracking and offstage space for full stage wagons, or elevator stages. The existence of one or more of these mechanical aids often will influence scenery-handling techniques.

Touring productions have other scenery-shifting considerations. Instead of one theatre and stage, the designer has to consider the size and sightline conditions of many stages and auditoriums as well as the physical limitations and extreme portability expected of scenery for a road show. Elaborate scenery-moving devices such as turntables and treadmills are sometimes duplicated in order to reduce the setup time in each theatre.

## DESIGN AND SCHEME OF PRODUCTION

The scene designer reconciles the needs of the play and the stage and adds a third control, the scheme of the production. The designer's production scheme stems from the kind of scene or locale change inherent in the play, the physical limitations of the stage, and the production concept (Chapter 4). A designer cannot design a large production without thinking through, at least in basic terms, a method or scheme for handling the changes.

## BUDGET

The influence of budget on the handling of scenery is felt directly through the control of the scale of the set designs and general size of the production. Although the operational budget has little direct effect on the form of the physical stage, it does influence its operation through the provision of funds for an adequate production staff. A large stage with a small technical staff, for example, would limit the amount of scenery that could be efficiently handled.

Several factors affect the operational budget. A Broadway show with a prolonged run, for example, can reduce its operational costs by spending more money on costly mechanical aids to shift the scenery, thereby cutting down the number of stagehands on the weekly payroll. In venues such as universities or community theatre, labor can be paid or volunteer. People-intensive solutions are often used when labor is free. Material costs, labor costs, and reusability all must be balanced against each other.

## BACKSTAGE ORGANIZATION

Anyone who has seen a fast change from a backstage vantage point has been amazed by the teamwork and precision with which the large pieces of scenery, properties, and actors seem to move. This is due, to some extent, to careful rehearsing, but largely it is the result of normal backstage organization and its division of responsibility. Under the coordinating management of the stage manager, a production has two major divisions: acting and technical. The technical responsibilities are divided between the scenery, electrical, property, and costume departments.

### STAGE MANAGER

The stage manager is the conduit through which information flows among the entire company, although there is more direct contact with the director and the actor. The stage manager officiates at the first technical rehearsal, sometimes without actors, to allow all hands to become familiar with the timing of shifts, light and sound cues, and the placement of properties.

Once the production is on stage, the stage manager becomes fully responsible. The stage manager starts each performance, gives all cues, calls the actors, posts all daily calls, and is charged with maintaining both the production standards set by the director and designers and onstage company discipline.

### STAGE CARPENTER

Although taking cues from the stage manager, the stage carpenter is in charge of the shifts, the rigging, and the general condition of the scenery. The crew, which is made up of deckhands (stagehands) and flymen, reports to the stage carpenter.

## MASTER ELECTRICIAN

The responsibilities of the master electrician include the hanging and focusing of lighting instruments, the maintenance of all electrical equipment, and sometimes the operation of the control console for the lighting cues.

## PROPERTY MASTER

The property master's duties include the care and maintenance of the set and hand props and supervising the handling of props during a shift, helped by crew assigned to the property department.

## SOUND TECHNICIAN

A typical production usually involves one or more of the three types of sound support: (1) the reinforcing of live voice, (2) recorded music or sound as background or accompaniment, and (3) recorded or live sound effects. The sound technician is responsible for the placement of microphones and speakers as well as the operation of the sound mixer during the performance according to the specifications of the sound designer. The sound technician is often responsible for rigging the audio communication system, providing all department heads instant communication.

## WARDROBER

The care and maintenance of all costumes is the responsibility of the wardrobe supervisor (and, during a fast costume change, of the actors as well). The backstage organization of community and university theatre often places the supervision of makeup in the costume department.

## MANUAL RUNNING OF SCENERY ON THE FLOOR

As mentioned at the beginning of this chapter, manual running of scenery is the simplest handling method and requires the least additional construction. If the units are strong enough to support themselves, usually the only additional support that is needed is horizontal stiffening, the vertical bracing of the piece in an upright position, and a quick and easy method of joining together the various parts of the set. Occasionally the extreme height of scenery combined with its traditional thinness makes it difficult to move for anyone not experienced in handling scenery.

Some of the many ways of handling single flats, two-folds, and partially assembled units of scenery on the floor are illustrated in Figure 10–1.

Figure 10–1a illustrates how a large unit of scenery is raised. The stagehands on the backside are *footing*, or holding, the bottom edge with their feet while the other two stagehands "walk-up" the piece by pushing on solid surfaces, such as the stiles.

## Figure 10–1
### Manually Handling Scenery

The running or "gripping" of scenery is the simplest handling method although, occasionally, the awkward shape or extreme size of a piece may require experience to handle it successfully.
(a) "Walking-up" a stiffened two-fold.
(b) "Edging-up" a single flat.
(c) Running or "gripping" a single flat.
(d) Making a lash.
(e) Running a two-fold.
(f) Three stagehands running a top-heavy piece.
(g) "Floating" down a single flat.

To "edge-up" a single flat is a similar maneuver (Figure 10–1b). With the flat on edge, one stagehand is holding the point down while the second is walking-up the unit by pushing along the edge.

To "run" a single flat (Figure 10–1c), the stagehand has one hand low and the other high for balance. By lifting the lead corner slightly off the floor, the stagehand handles the flat in perfect balance.

Lashing is a method of joining two flats in their playing position with lightweight rope (Figure 10–1d).

### STIFFENING, BRACING, AND JOINING

Because scenery has to travel in units of relatively small, lightweight size to get in and out of theatres, the joining or unfolding of these smaller units into larger shapes is necessary. The new larger shape requires stiffening to be safely handled in a shift.

A stiffener is usually a horizontal member (1-by-3 or 1-by-4 on edge) that is loose-pin-hinged into place as the set is assembled. A "brace jack" (often shortened to "jack") is a triangular form with a small base providing maximum bracing. A jack can be loose- or tight-pin-hinged to the scenery it is bracing.

Bracing and stiffening can take a variety of forms depending on the shape and size of the scenery being reinforced (Figure 10–2). The three categories of joining are related to the portable nature of scenery and the degree of permanence of the joint. Elements of scenery may be joined together (1) by fixed or permanent joining, (2) by assembly joining, or (3) by temporary joining. The kind of joint and its location are often important to the design, for the designer and technical director will seek ways to avoid a crack or open joint in a conspicuous area of the setting.

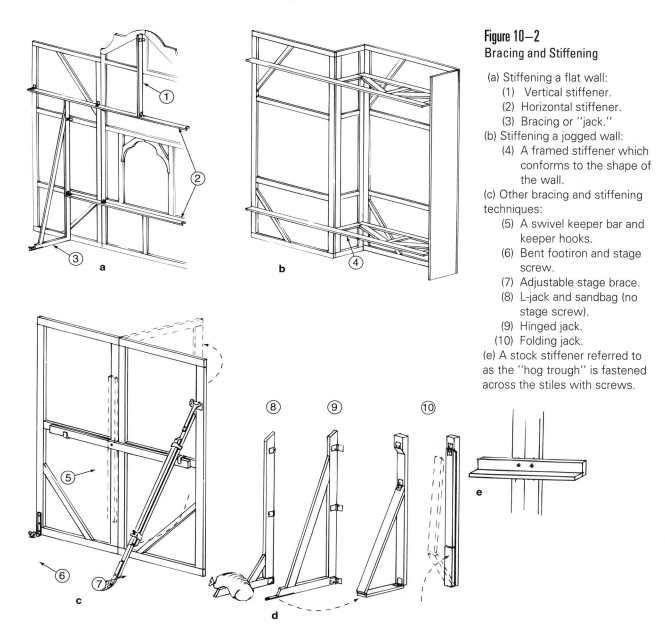

**Figure 10–2**
**Bracing and Stiffening**

(a) Stiffening a flat wall:
   (1)  Vertical stiffener.
   (2)  Horizontal stiffener.
   (3)  Bracing or "jack."
(b) Stiffening a jogged wall:
   (4)  A framed stiffener which conforms to the shape of the wall.
(c) Other bracing and stiffening techniques:
   (5)  A swivel keeper bar and keeper hooks.
   (6)  Bent footiron and stage screw.
   (7)  Adjustable stage brace.
   (8)  L-jack and sandbag (no stage screw).
   (9)  Hinged jack.
  (10)  Folding jack.
(e) A stock stiffener referred to as the "hog trough" is fastened across the stiles with screws.

Fixed joining occurs as the scenery is being built (with use of nails, screws, staples, and so on). A fixed, hinged joint is made with tight-pin hinges so that larger units composed of several small pieces may unfold into larger sizes. A *dutchman* is a thin strip of fabric (same as that covering the flat) glued to the face of a flat in order to cover the tight-pin hinges installed in the face. The smaller pieces remain fixed together and travel or move folded

### Figure 10—3
### Fixed and Temporary Scenery Joints

A few methods of fastening scenic elements together for either easy handling or for a quick scene shift. Fixed joining:
(a) Tight-pin hinge and dutchman.
(b) Two-fold, two flats tight pin-hinged together.
(c) Three-fold, two jogs, and a flat hinged together.
(d) Three-fold and "tumbler" to hinge three full-width flats together.
Assembly joining:
(e) Loose-pin hinge.
(f) Picture hanger.
(g) S-battern hook.
(h) Lashing, flush and around corner. Note stop cleat.
(i) Bolting Hollywood flats with bolt and wing nut.
(j) Turn buttons.

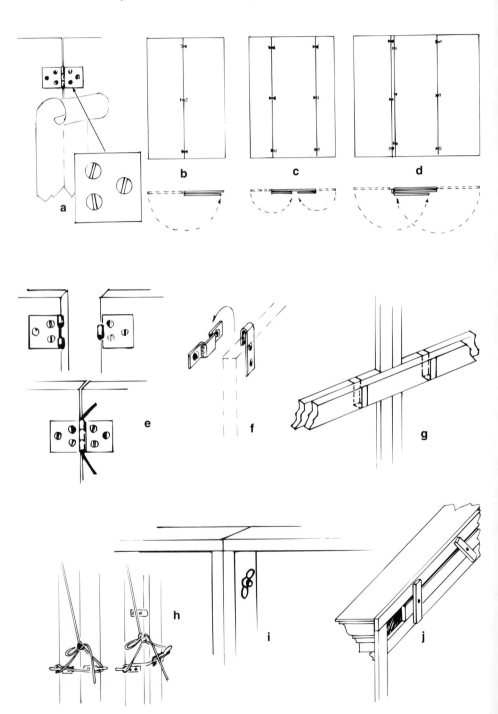

from shop to stage, to be unfolded and stiffened into their final shape in the theatre (Figure 10–3a, b, c, and d). The typical joining of Hollywood flats uses either bolts or screws through the stiles.

On the other hand, large areas of scenery may be made in separate small pieces to be assembled in the theatre. Loose-pin hinges, screws, bolts, wing nuts, and turn buttons are also frequently used. Larger units are stiffened and braced.

The joining of scenery during an act change commonly uses loose-pin hinges, coffin or casket locks, lashing, and stage screws.

## FLYING SCENERY

The designer is always interested in the size of the stage house and type of flying system, if any, over the stage. A good stage house that is designed to handle scenery in the air will have an adequate flying system and a generous amount of hanging space, which means a high and wide loft. The two common methods of flying scenery are the *hemp* and the *counterweight* systems. Both are based on the presence of a gridiron over the stage to support the sheaves or pulley block and the extended control of the line-sets to one of the side walls. They differ in complexity of the rigging, cost of installation, and flexibility of use. Other systems have also been developed to meet ongoing changes in the theatre over the years.

### GRID

As the name implies, the grid is an open floor of iron high over the stage. The average grid has three to seven openings, or *wells*, that run up- and downstage. Across each opening, usually 6 to 8 inches wide, are the loft blocks through which each liftline runs toward the stage floor.

The space between the wells is typically floored with strips of 3-inch channel iron running parallel to the wells. The channel iron strips are set far enough apart to allow the placement of additional sheaves for special spotlines (Figure 10–4c).

Recent gridiron designs employ the use of loft blocks, suspended above the gridiron floor from beams over each well. This keeps the grid floor clear for the placement of additional spotlines.

### LINE-SETS

A line-set refers to the grouping of three or more lines into a set to be handled as one unit. The sheaves of a line-set are usually placed over each well and are all the same distance from the proscenium, thus forming a line parallel to the plasterline.

The number of lines in a line-set depends on the number of wells in the individual grid. A stage with a wide proscenium opening might have as many as five lines in a set, while a smaller stage usually has only three lines to a set.

**Figure 10–4**
Flying Systems

(a) Pin-and-rail or "hemp" system:
  (1) Short line.
  (2) Center line.
  (3) Long line.
  (4) Tandem head block.
  (5) Double pinrail on fly door.
  (6) Sandbag counterweight.
  (7) Clew or "sunday" on a line-set.
(b) Counterweight system:
  (1) Pipe batten, a fixed line set.
  (2) Hoisting cable for liftlines.
  (3) Head block, multi-grooved.
  (4) Trim chains at top of arbor.
  (5) "T" track.
  (6) Purchase line.
  (7) Lock and safety line on lock rail which may be on a fly floor or the stage deck.
  (8) Idler pulley
(c) A demonstration of the flexibility of the pin-and-rail system:
  (1) Spot sheaves used to fly a drop at an askew angle. The spotlines use the same or adjacent head blocks.
  (2) The separation of a single line from a line-set to use in a spot-sheave.

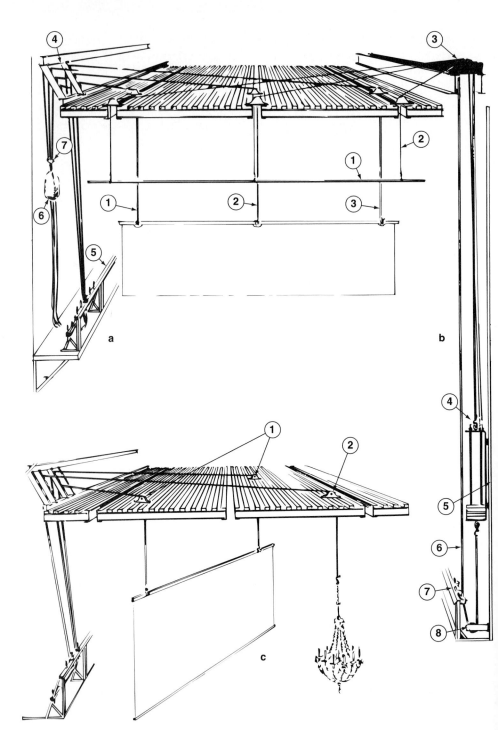

The lines are named by their length and position on the stage. The line nearest the control side (pinrail or lockrail) of the stage is called the *short line* and the line to the far side of the stage is the *long line*. The line in between is the *center line*. A four-line set would have two center lines (a long center and a short center), and so on.

## THE HEMP SYSTEM

The hemp system is the older and more flexible of the two flying systems. It is less costly to install but does require more skill and more people to operate. The hemp system typically uses $\frac{3}{4}$-inch manila rope for liftlines. As illustrated in Figure 10–4a, the individual line in a line-set (1, 2, and 3) comes up from the stage, passes through the loft block, and travels horizontally to one pulley in the head block (4) located on the left or right stage wall. From the head block, in which the pulleys are mounted in tandem, the lines are brought together as a set and tied off at the pinrail (5). The lower rail of the pinrail is usually the trim tie for the drop in its "in" or working position, and the top rail receives the tie for the "out" or stored position. A line-set can be bound together (7) and sandbagged (6) to counterweight a heavy piece for easy handling using a trim clamp. The trim clamp is also used to adjust the level of a batten.

As can be seen, the hemp system has great flexibility in its ability to use only part of a line-set, add a spotline to a line-set, or in some instances cross line-sets. The adding of a spotline employs a single rope and loft block occasionally placed in a remote position on the grid, to fly a raked or angled piece of scenery (Figure 10–4c).

The chief disadvantage of a hemp house is in the number of hands required to run a show, as well as the professional skill necessary to rig and safely counterweight heavy pieces of scenery.

## THE COUNTERWEIGHT SYSTEM

Unlike the hemp system, which can separate lines or add a single line to the line-sets, the counterweight system uses fixed line-sets. Although the counterweight system was born in an era of box settings and raked scenery as theatrical styles, it is, paradoxically, rigidly based on wing-and-backdrop staging. It keeps the lines in sets fixed to a pipe batten parallel to the footlights.

The system, as illustrated in Figure 10–4b, begins at the pipe batten (1) and the permanently attached wire-cable liftlines (2). Lifting the batten, the lines pass through the individual loft blocks at each well, then over a multigrooved, single-pulley head block (3) and attach to the top of the counterweight arbor (4). The arbor is guided by a "T" track (5), or guy wire, and controlled by a separate purchase line. The purchase line (6), typically made of manila or synthetic rope, is also attached to the top of the counterweight arbor and passes through the large groove in the head block. It then turns toward the floor and, after going through the lock (7) on the lock rail and around the idler pulley (8), fastens to the bottom of the arbor.

Pulling down on the outside purchase line lifts the arbor and lowers the scenery hanging on the batten. A corresponding amount of weight placed on the arbor balances the weight of the scenery. Although the counterweight system is easy to run with parallel scenery, it is less flexible because of the fixed line-sets. Most of the rigging time used to hang an angled or raked piece is spent in overcoming rather than using the system.

Typically the counterweight system includes a mechanism for adjusting the level or trim of the batten relative to the stage floor. These mechanisms generally consist of either turnbuckles or trim chains that connect the liftlines to the batten or the arbor.

## WINCH SYSTEMS

There have been attempts in the past to electrify a flying system—for example, by using a single, electric motor-driven winch to lift a battened line-set. In this system, all the lines in the set are wound upon a single drum that turns in only one direction to lift the batten. A mechanical clutching and braking device disengages the drum from the motor, allowing the weight of the attached scenery to bring the batten back down to the stage floor. Its only advantage over the counterweight system is that it requires only one person to run the remote-control operation. The slow, fixed speed and insensitivity of the system combined with the rather hazardous braking operation has caused the "electric batten," as it was once called, to fall into disuse.

**The Motor-Driven Spotline System**    In an attempt to bring to the counterweight system the flexibility of the hemp, George Izenour and Associates developed the motor-driven spotline system (Figure 10–5). It seems apparent from the drawing that the basic concept of the system is to use an individual driver motor on a specially designed double-purchase counterweight line-set.

The driver, which is a variable-speed $\frac{3}{4}$-horsepower DC electric motor, is placed either under the stage floor or behind the stage wall to minimize noise. It is attached to the lower portion of the purchase line by a sprocket and roller chain drive and utilizes both dynamic and electromechanical braking.

The top of the arbor is not connected to the conventional fixed line-set arrangement but utilizes new spotline and trim adjustment features. The head block, although in a tandem-mounted position, is made up of individual caster-mounted swivel pulleys, which increase the possible "fleet angle" or spread of the lines in the set. The swivel head block, while allowing a wide spread to the pattern of the loft blocks in the line-set, is dependent on the adjustable length of each line in the set to be completely flexible. The length adjustment of an individual line is accomplished by taking up each line on a trimming winch at the trimming gallery position. This small hand winch is located at what would normally be the end or "dead tie" of a single liftline in a double-purchase system.

To base the motor-driven arbor on a double-purchase counterweight system, however, gives the flyman cause for concern because of the tremendous demand for counterweights. The nature of the rigging produces a mechanical disadvantage of 2:1, thereby creating a counterweight load twice the weight of the scenery it is lifting. The storing of counterweights and the endless job of loading and unloading an arbor are tasks that are not eliminated, but are *doubled* when the double-purchase system is employed.

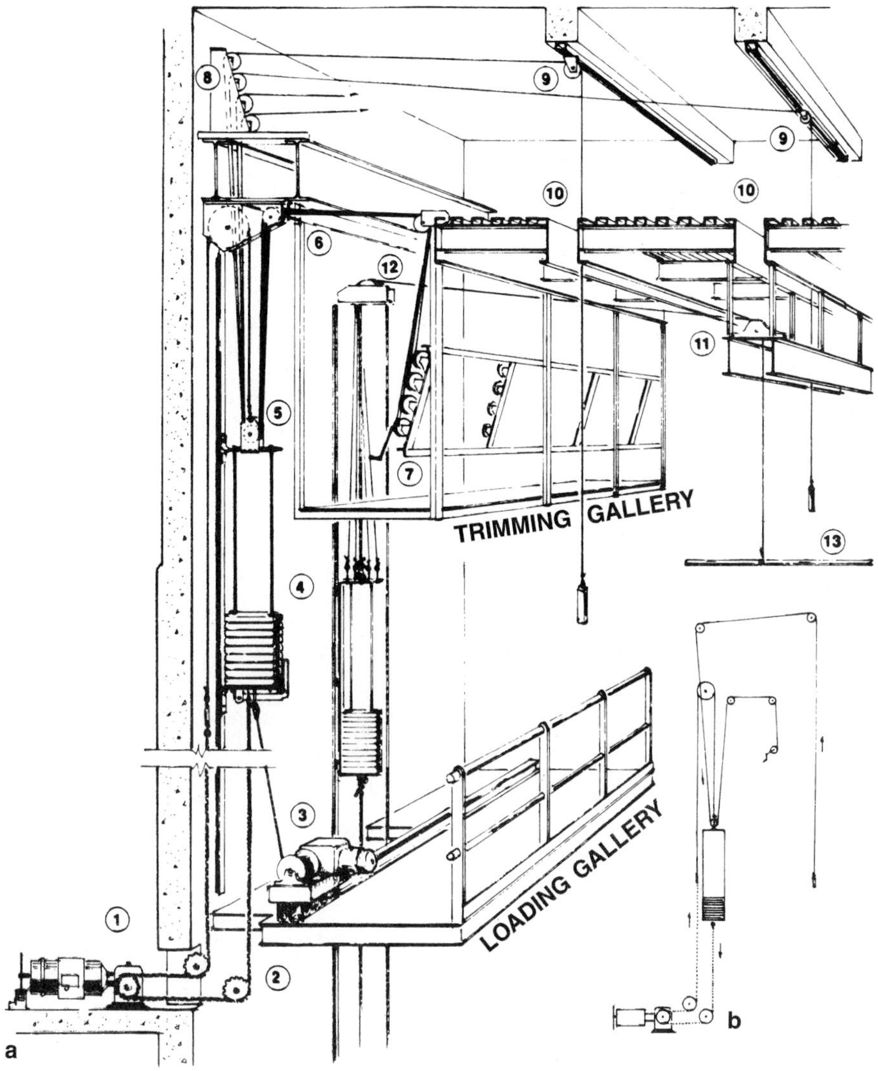

**Figure 10—5**
**Motor-driven Spotline System**

(a) A pictorial drawing of the rigging for one line-set:
  (1) Driver motor, a $\frac{3}{4}$ horsepower, variable speed DC motor.
  (2) Sprocket and roller chain drive.
  (3) Moveable bull-winch to retrieve empty arbor for loading.
  (4) Arbor.
  (5) Grooved pulleys to return the four liftlines.
  (6) Grooved muling pulley, the normal dead-tie position on the regular double-purchase counterweight system.
  (7) Trimming winches to adjust the length of each liftline.
  (8) Swivel head blocks in tandem mount.
  (9) Swivel loft blocks.
  (10) Channel openings at about 4-foot intervals.
  (11) Underslung channel supporting loft blocks for rigid line sets.
  (12) Head block for rigid line-set.
  (13) Pipe batten.
(b) Schematic diagram of the motor-driven spotline system.

The advantages of the motor-driven spotline system are threefold. First, the number of lines to each motor is quadrupled; second, the synchronizing problem within a line-set is eliminated and improved between line-sets; and last, by using the double-purchase rigging, the top speed is doubled from 2 feet per second to 4 feet per second.

The motor-driven spotline system in its present form is not intended to be the sole method of flying scenery. An installation including 12 to 24 motor-driven arbors interspersed with several counterweighted rigid line-sets, as well as the always flexible hemp line-sets, would be considered ideal.

**The Hydraulic Flying System**      The general principal of the hydraulic system is to use the power generated by an hydraulic cylinder and ram to provide the lift. The *piston* in the hydraulic cylinder, which is mounted vertically on a side wall of the stage, is double-faced and can be driven by fluid pressure from either side. Because of the short stroke of the ram in the cylinder, the system relies on a complicated rigging to reduce the ratio of the travel of the batten to the length of the ram stroke.

The $\frac{3}{16}$-inch plastic-coated lift cables run horizontally over each loft block to a pair of head blocks that reverse the direction to meet a running pulley block or double-purchase rig. This maneuver not only shortens the distance of the lift cables by half but also provides a mechanical advantage of 2:1. The pulley block is moved by a single $\frac{5}{16}$-inch flexible lead cable to a second moving pulley block. The second moving block, which is attached to the top of the ram, however, is doubled. The double moving block reduces the run of the lead cable by a 4:1 ratio.

The combination of the two double-purchase rigs, the first 2:1 and the second 4:1, reduces the ratio of the ram stroke to the batten travel to an 8:1 ratio. Figure 10–6 diagrams the rigging of a four-line batten system. A single cylinder can be isolated for a single spotline rig.

### RIGGING

Regardless of which system is used, there are several flying and rigging techniques common to all systems. While many of the routine problems inherent in the older systems are eliminated in a winch system, certain specific problems pertaining to the movement of scenery in relationship to its hanging position and grid height will be forever present.

Stage rigging begins with the relatively simple process of hanging scenery and includes the more complicated maneuvers of breasting and tripping

**Figure 10–6**
Hydraulic Flying System

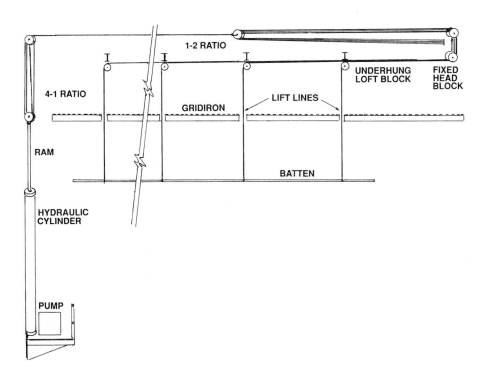

scenery elements. The handling of stage curtains (such as the traveler, tableau, and contour curtains) and the unframed drop are also a part of stage rigging.

**Hanging Scenery**     An early and critical step in rigging is the preparation of scenery to hang by providing hardware or some other means of attaching the liftlines. Hanger irons or D-rings, which are used on framed scenery, should be bolted to a vertical member of the framing for greater strength. On extremely tall or heavy pieces two rings are used, the one at the top serving as a guide for the liftline that is attached to the bottom. Lifting the load from the bottom is not only a safer procedure, but it also provides a convenient position to trim each line (Figure 10–7a,b).

**Cable Clamps**     Often, framed scenery is hung a distance below the batten on a thin cable and attached to the scenery with special hardware. Although the cable may be very flexible, it is important not to allow a kink to form in the method of attaching, or the cable will lose its strength.

Figure 10–7d illustrates cable clamps and thimbles used to secure the cable to the batten and the scenery. Cable clamps are used on cable as small as $\frac{1}{8}$ inch. Alternatively, the *Nicopress* clamp is a very secure, though permanent, fastener. The soft-metal tubes are designed to slide over the cables and are crimped into place with a Nicopress tool (Figure 10–7d).

Unframed pieces of scenery, such as drops and borders, are hung from their top battens and can be fastened to a pipe batten or can be picked up by a set of lines in many ways (Figure 10–7c). The long thin batten requires numerous pickup points about every 6 feet (see "Bridling," also in this section) to keep it from sagging and thereby spoiling the trim of the drop.

**Knots**     Safe stage rigging requires the use of a modest number of knots, and the technical director and anyone who supervises rigging should be skilled in the use of at least a few of the knots and hitches that appear in stage rigging. Some of the most frequently used knots are illustrated in Figure 10–8 along with notations of their uses for stage rigging. A more detailed and comprehensive manual of knots and splices can be found in the catalogues of cordage companies (see "Additional Reading" at the back of this book).

**Breasting Scenery**     Regardless of which flying system is being used, two pieces of scenery cannot occupy the same space at the same time, although the designer may wish they could. Consequently, it sometimes becomes necessary to hang a unit away from its working position and rely on breasting lines to bring it to its proper location. A breasting line (sometimes called a *checkline* or restraining line) is usually dead-tied at one end to the gridiron or side-stage position and fastened to the scenery at the opposite end. When the piece is in its flown position the breasting line is slack, but as the piece comes into its working position the breasting line becomes taut and breasts

## Figure 10–7
### The Hanging of Scenery

(a) Hanging hardware:
  (1) Top hanger iron, straight.
  (2) Ceiling plate and ring.
  (3) Bottom hanger iron, hooked.

(b) Trim adjustments:
  (1) Trimming hitch using hemp rope or sash cord.
  (2) A snatch line. The snap hook on the end of the lift-line makes it possible to unhook a flown piece of scenery.
  (3) Turnbuckle on wire cable, another way to adjust the trim of a flown piece of scenery.

(c) Various methods of hanging a drop:
  (1) Tie around top batten.
  (2) Tie through batten.
  (3) Drop holder.
  (4) Tie lines to pipe batten.
  (5 and 6) Floor stays.

(d) Cable Clamps and Nico Press.

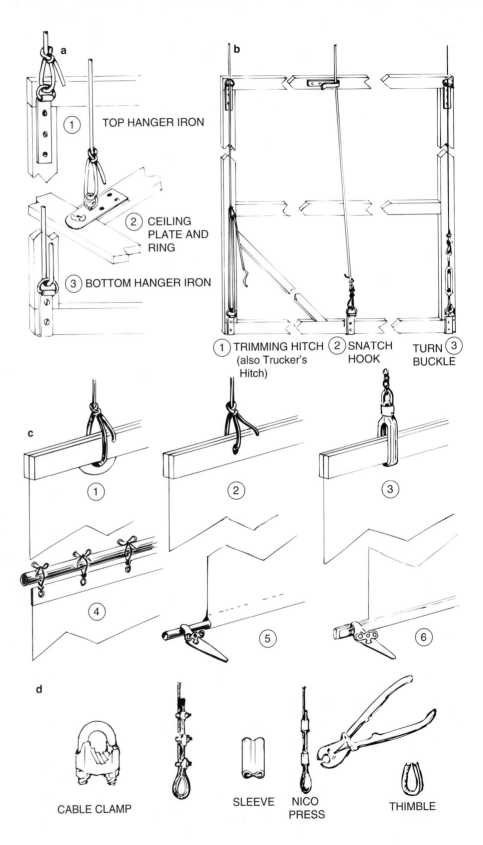

TOP HANGER IRON

CEILING PLATE AND RING

BOTTOM HANGER IRON

(1) TRIMMING HITCH (also Trucker's Hitch)
(2) SNATCH HOOK
(3) TURN BUCKLE

CABLE CLAMP    SLEEVE    NICO PRESS    THIMBLE

the unit off dead-center hanging. (Several breasting maneuvers are illustrated in Figure 10–9c, d, e, and f.)

**Bridling**     The bridle is a simple rigging used to spread the load picked up on one line (Figure 10–9a,b). The number of lines in a set can be reduced, or the number of pickup points increased, by the bridling technique.

**Tripping Scenery**     Many rigging problems result from too low a grid or the complete absence of one. Tripping, which can only be used on soft or semisoft scenery, is one way of flying scenery in a limited space (Figure

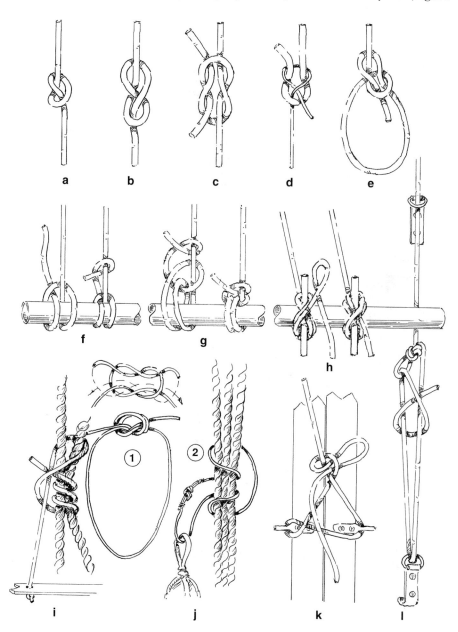

## Figure 10–8
### Knots Used in Stage Rigging

(a) Half hitch or overhand knot.
(b) Figure eight, used to put a knot in the end of a line to keep it from running through a pulley or eye.
(c) Square knot, for joining ropes of the same size.
(d) Sheetbend, for joining ropes of different sizes.
(e) Bowline. A fixed loop used on end of liftline through ring.
(f) Clove hitch on a batten, finished with a half hitch. It grips firmly under tension, but is easy to adjust or untie.
(g) Fisherman's bend. Excellent for a tie onto a batten. Not as easy to adjust as the clove hitch.
(h) Half hitch over a belaying pin. Used as tie-off on pinrail.
(i) Stopper hitch, made with a smaller line in the middle of a larger rope. The safety line on the counterweight lock rail uses a stopper hitch on the purchase lines.
(j) Sunday:
   (1) A method of joining the ends of a small loop of wire cable without putting a sharp kink in the cable.
   (2) The loop is then used to clew a set of rope lines together so as to counterweight them with a sandbag.
(k) Lashline tie-off.
(l) Trimming hitch, to adjust the trim of a hanging piece of scenery.

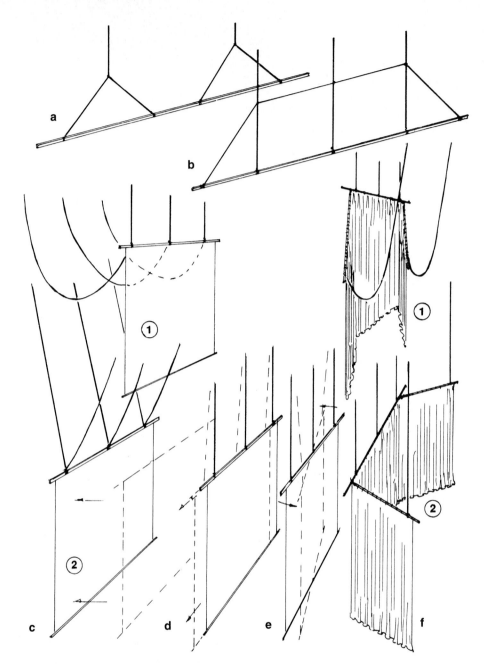

**Figure 10–9**
Bridling and Breasting Techniques

(a) A simple bridle.
(b) A bridle of a set of lines to suport the overhang of an extra-long batten.
(c) Breasting a drop up- and downstage:
    (1) Stored position.
    (2) Working position.
(d) Breasting across stage.
(e) Twisting a batten into an angled position.
(f) Breast lines on the side-tab arms of a drape cyc:
    (1) Stored position, arms hanging down.
    (2) Working position, arms pulled by breast lines into spread position.

10–10d, e, and f). By picking up the bottom of a drop as well as the top, it can be flown in half the height necessary to clear a full drop. The height can be further reduced by picking up the drop a third of the height off the floor and thereby tripping it in thirds.

An extreme variation of tripping is to roll a drop on its bottom batten or drum at the bottom edge (Figure 10–10a, b, and c). The old opera house "oleo" drop was rigged in this manner, and it still is a good way of flying a drop on a stage with reduced flying space.

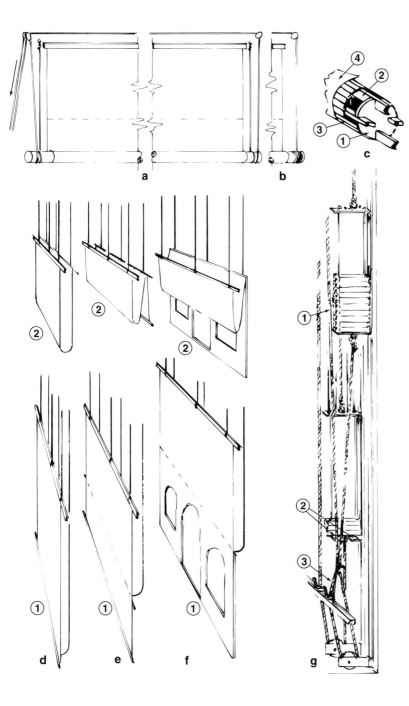

a    b    c

d    e    f    g

### Figure 10–10
### Tripping Techniques

(a) The "oleo" drop, which rolls on the bottom batten or drum. Note: the rigging of the rope gives operator a mechanical advantage of two. Drop is made with horizontal seams to make it roll flat.

(b) An alternate rigging. Liftline has equal turns on the end of drum, in reverse direction of drop. When liftline is pulled, it unwinds as the drop winds onto the drum and thus rises.

(c) Detail of drum construction:
  (1) Contour pieces.
  (2) Linear stiffeners.
  (3) Lattice slats.
  (4) Padding and final cover.

(d) Tripping a drop; back set of lines is attached to bottom batten:
  (1) Working position.
  (2) Stored or tripped position.

(e) Tripping in thirds. Upstage batten is attached at one-third height of the drop off the floor:
  (1) Working position.
  (2) Tripped position.

(f) Tripping a drop which has the lower portion framed.
  (1) Working position.
  (2) Tripped position.

(g) Carpet hoist, handling a variable load:
  (1) Free arbor (no batten attached) carrying counterweights.
  (2) Working arbor with batten that handles the variable load.
  (3) Free arbor is locked off at top position allowing working arbor to run free of counterweight after load has been removed from batten (rigging is only usable on light loads of 100–150 pounds).

**Levitation**    The flying of objects or persons, as if in defiance of gravity, requires special rigging. Any circumstance that requires the flying of a human being is best performed by an expert. In fact, there are companies that have made a specialty of flying actors. To create a workable setting for flying actors or objects, a designer should be familiar with the spatial requirements for a flying effect. The right kind of background, properly planned exits and entrances, and atmospheric lighting can serve to mask or camouflage any exposed support wires and highlight the illusion.

To create the illusion of floating in space, an object must be supported on as fine a wire as possible so that the support will disappear from view at a distance. Lightweight objects such as a bat or bird can be supported on fishing line (20-pound test), which becomes invisible at a very short distance. The size and strength of the support wire to fly an actor, however, is more critical. The kind of wire used depends on whether or not it has to go over a pulley. Wire rope, such as aircraft cable, is extremely flexible and strong for its size: $\frac{1}{16}$-inch aircraft cable has a breaking strength of 500 pounds and has a safe load of 50 to 100 pounds; $\frac{1}{8}$-inch aircraft cable is standard for most flying apparatus. Although it is slightly more visible, it is much safer, having a breaking strength of 2,000 pounds with a safe working load of 200 to 400 pounds.

**Flying Apparatus**    A flying apparatus begins with a harness for the actor. It is made of strong webbing and is fitted about the legs and chest like a parachute harness. The ring, to which the wire is attached, is placed approximately in the middle of the back, a little above the actor's center of gravity. The harness, of course, is worn under the costume with only the ring protruding. This type of harness works best when the action of flying is preceded or followed by free movement of the actor on the stage. Brief exits are planned into the offstage wings to permit the hookup or unhooking of the flying apparatus. If the actor's weight is counterweighted, when he or she is off the flying rig it creates an unbalanced condition. The rigging shown in Figure 10–11d uses the mechanical advantage of the "wheel and axle" to compensate for the weight of the actor. The liftline for the actor is wound around the axle, while the purchase line for the operator encircles the wheel. Distance or length of rope is sacrificed, however, which means the operator will pull 3 feet of rope to lift the actor 1 foot off of the floor.

For lateral movement, the rig employs a pendulum technique, which means that if the actor is airborne a certain distance from the center he or she will swing, on a diagonal, to a equal distance opposite of center. With rehearsal this technique can be used to fly from one part of the stage to another. Similarly, the actor can fly in large circles by running circles on the stage before being airborne. For diagonal or transverse movement, the pulley of the center drop line can be rigged to move on a track.

If the flying actor stays in the air and the direction is fixed, the rigging is different. Since the actor is in the air longer, the harness should provide more support, such as a lightweight framing and a higher center of gravity for the point of suspension (Figure 10–11e).

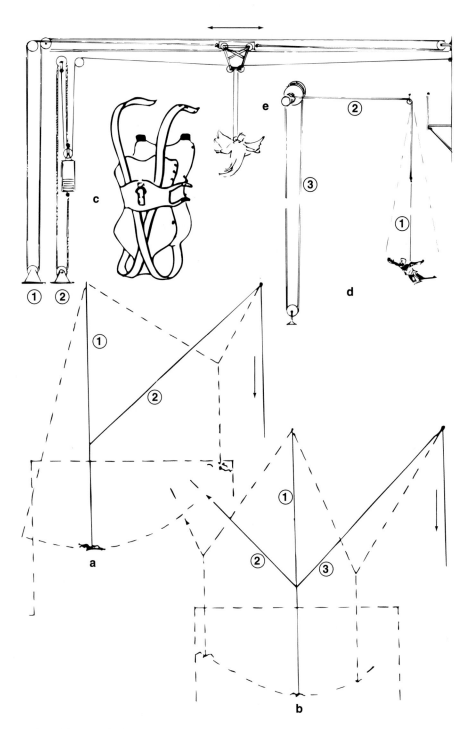

**Figure 10–11**
Levitation

Types of rigging for flying objects or persons:

(a) Pendulum and breast line:
  (1) Pendulum line, placed off center, has long arc when it is swinging free of breast line.
  (2) Breast line shortens arc and lifts object up and out of sight.

(b) Pendulum and double breast line:
  (1) Pendulum line.
  (2) First breast line.
  (3) Second breast line.

(c) Harness for actor.

(d) Schematic diagram of a flying rig using the wheel and drum for lift-control.
  (1) $\frac{1}{8}''$ aircraft cable lead to the actor.
  (2) Rope or larger cable feeds through swivel sheave at grid to the drum.
  (3) Operating line around the wheel. The ratio of the drum's smaller radius to the larger radius of the wheel provides a mechanical advantage for the operator. Because a counterweight is not involved, the actor is free to detach the rig when on the floor.

(e) Flying rig for limited pattern. The actor can fly a lateral pattern across the stage.

## VARIABLE LOAD

Of the many rigging problems experienced with conventional flying systems, the most annoying is the variable load or unbalanced condition resulting from the removal of part or all of the scenery load from a set of lines. The *deus ex machina*, descending with a live cargo of gods or goddesses and then ascending to the heavens empty, is an example of a variable load.

If the weight variation is not too great (100–150 pounds), the carpet hoist is one way of compensating. The counterbalancing weight to the variable load is not directly attached to the load-bearing batten but is handled on a separate purchase line. Figure 10–10g shows a carpet hoist rigging on a counterweight system. The counterbalancing weight is on the first arbor (1), which is a "free arbor," meaning that it is not attached to a batten or line-set.

The second arbor (2), which carries only enough weight to bring the arbor down, is attached to the batten handling the variable load. The extending hooks on the bottom of this arbor pass under and engage the first arbor to utilize its weights. Note that when the first arbor is locked or tied off in an up position at the moment the variable load is being removed, the second arbor is free to disengage and return to a down position. The counterbalancing weight can be returned to the second arbor by reversing the procedure and unlocking the first arbor.

Any larger weight variation has to be handled by an electric floor winch or a hand winch, which provides a mechanical advantage to offset the unbalanced load condition.

## CURTAIN RIGGING

The actions or movements of a stage curtain, other than raising or lowering on a batten, are many and varied. The most common movements are drawn horizontally from the sides, tripped diagonally into a tableau shape, or tripped vertically into the varied patterns of a contour curtain.

**Traveler or Draw Curtain**    The conventional action of a traveler curtain is the drawing together of two curtain halves on two overlapping sections of track. The track guides the carriers, which are attached to the top edge of the curtain at about 1-foot intervals. The drawline is fastened to the first or lead carrier, which pushes or pulls the rest of the carriers to open or close the curtain. The many track and carrier designs and the rigging of the drawline are illustrated in Figure 10–12.

Sometimes a one-way traveler is needed, which means that instead of coming from opposite sides of the stage, the curtain is drawn onstage from one side on a single long track (Figure 10–12b). Also illustrated is a rear-fold device that causes all carriers to move at once rather than being pushed or pulled by the lead carrier (Figure 10–12c).

**Tableau Curtain**    Like the traveler, the tableau curtain is made up of two curtain panels hung, with a center overlap, from a single batten. Each panel is lifted or tripped by a diagonal drawline attached to the central edge, about a third of its height off the floor, that runs through rings on the back of the curtain to a pulley on the batten (Figure 10–13a). The tableau has a quicker action than a traveler, but does not lift completely out of sight unless the batten is also raised at the final moment. Because of its picturesque quality, the tableau curtain drape is frequently left in view as a decorative frame for the scene.

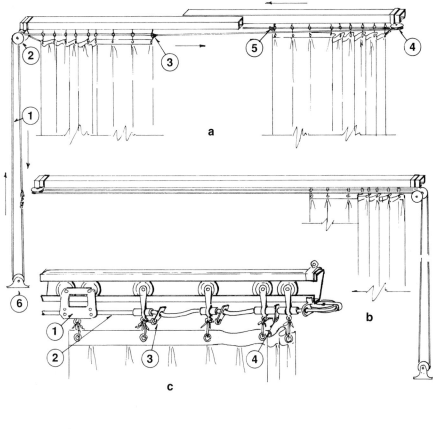

a

b

c

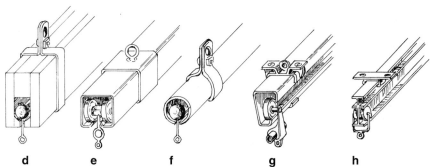

d    e    f    g    h

**Figure 10–12**
Traveler Curtains and Tracks

(a) Rigging of a draw curtain or two-way traveler:
   (1) Draw line.
   (2) Head block.
   (3) Lead carrier on downstage curtain, fastened to drawline.
   (4) Change-of-direction pulley.
   (5) Lead carrier on upstage curtain also fastened to drawline.
   (6) Floor block.
(b) One-way traveler curtain.
(c) Detail of rear-fold attachment. All carriers move at once with drawline and curtain folds offstage rather than bunching onstage.
   (1) Lead carrier.
   (2) Drawline.
   (3) Rear-fold attachment grips drawline until it is straightened up by bumping into the next carrier.
   (4) Drawline now passes through the rear-fold attachment.
Various Types of Traveler Tracks and Carriers:
(d) Wooden track with ball carriers.
(e) Square steel track with double-wheel carrier.
(f) Round steel track with ball carriers.
(g) Triangular steel track with side opening and single-wheel carriers.
(h) I-beam track.

**Contour Curtain**    The contour curtain is made in a single panel with great fullness, usually about 200 percent of the curtain width. The curtain, which is made of material that drapes well, is tripped by a series of vertical drawlines attached to the bottom edge of the curtain and running through rings on the back to pulleys attached to the batten. By varying the lift on certain lines, the bottom edge of the curtain takes on many different contours (Figure 10–13b).

**Brail Curtain**    The front curtain in a no-loft stage is sometimes rigged as a brail curtain to achieve a faster and more desirable lifting action than the slower side motion of a traveler curtain. In this case the amount of lift on

**Figure 10–13**
Front Curtain Riggings

(a) Tableau curtain.
(b) Contour curtain. The lift lines
are numbered 1–6. The lines are
paired 1–6, 3–4, and 2–5.
(c) Brail curtain.

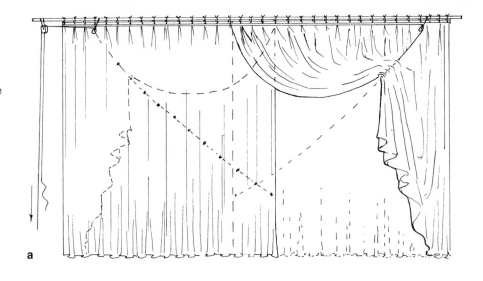

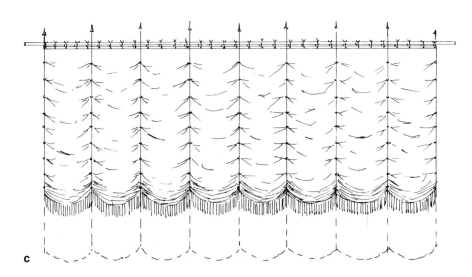

each drawline is equal, eliminating the need for the abnormal fullness of a regular contour curtain. To add a decorative quality, the curtain may have the horizontal fullness that is obtained by gathering material on the vertical seams, thereby producing a series of soft swags (Figure 10–13c).

## SCENERY ON CASTERS

Moving a three-dimensional piece of scenery on the floor is made easier and faster if it is mounted on casters. Such mounting can vary from a single caster on the edge of a hinged wing to the large castered platform or wagon to move an entire set. In between are such techniques as castered tip and lift jacks and outrigger wagons for rolling.

### CASTERS

The stage places special demands on casters. A good stage caster should first of all run quietly, which requires a rubber wheel or a rubber-tired wheel. The rubber-tired wheel is a better long-time investment because the tires can be replaced as they wear.

Secondly, the caster wheel should have as large a diameter as possible ($3\frac{1}{2}$ to 4 inches). A wagon on 4-inch-diameter caster wheels rolls with little effort and is not easily stopped by small obstructions such as rugs, padding, ground cloth, or lighting cables.

Casters are of two general types: those made to move freely in any direction, and those made to move in a fixed direction. The *swivel caster* has a free action that allows it to move in any direction, while the *fixed caster* is limited to one direction. A refinement of the typical swivel caster incorporates a mechanism that locks the swivel action, thereby creating the equivalent of a fixed caster.

### LIFT AND TIP JACKS

Mounting scenery on casters in order to make it move easily creates a paradoxical problem of anchoring, preventing the unit from moving at an undesirable moment. Lift and tip jacks are methods of lifting or tipping a piece of scenery from a standing position onto casters to move (Figures 10–14d and 10–15e,f). The scenery, however, sits firmly on the floor when it is in its working position.

Another way to anchor a castered platform or a bulky three-dimensional piece of scenery is to attach it to units that are sitting on the floor or by tipping the piece onto casters mounted on its offstage or upstage edge (Figure 10–15d).

### OUTRIGGER WAGONS

An outrigger wagon is essentially a pattern of castered jacks or braces around the outside of a set or portion of a set. The scenery remains on casters. It is

**Figure 10–14**
**Castering Techniques**

(a) Single caster mounted on rear of flat.

(b) Single caster mounted in corner.

(c) Outrigger wagon.

(d) Tip jack:

   (1) Scenery tipped back to rest on casters.

   (2) Scenery upright, blocked-off caster in working position.

(e) Castered jack:

   (1) Side view showing how scenery is held clear of floor.

   (2) Caster jack on a hinged or "wild" piece of scenery.

(f) Flat-top swivel caster.

(g) Flat-top fixed caster.

(h) Stem-type swivel caster for furniture.

(i) Small stem-type ball caster for furniture.

(j) Large stem-type swivel caster. Mounts into bottom of scaffolding pipe.

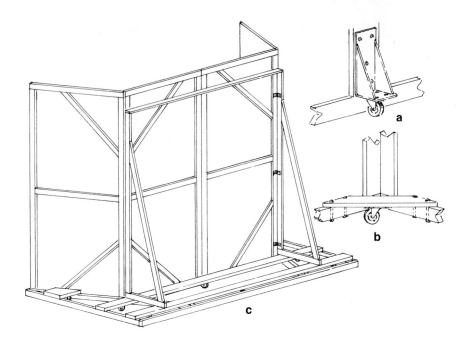

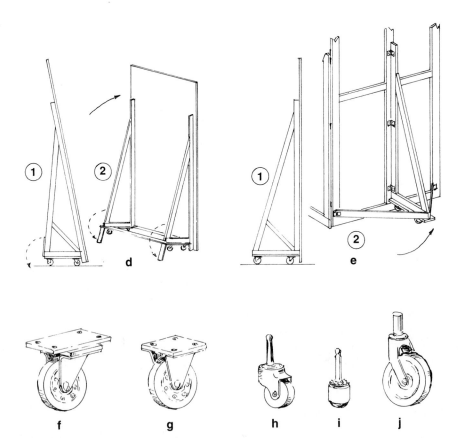

a skeleton wagon intended to brace and caster the scenery. The action of the scene is played not on a wagon but on the stage floor (Figure 10–14c).

## WAGONS

The low-level platform (6 to 8 inches) on casters or wagons can carry a large portion of a setting including the set props. Large wagons often carry an entire setting, which can swiftly and easily move into place for a scene change. Although requiring ample floor space, the wagon is a flexible and efficient method of handling scenery.

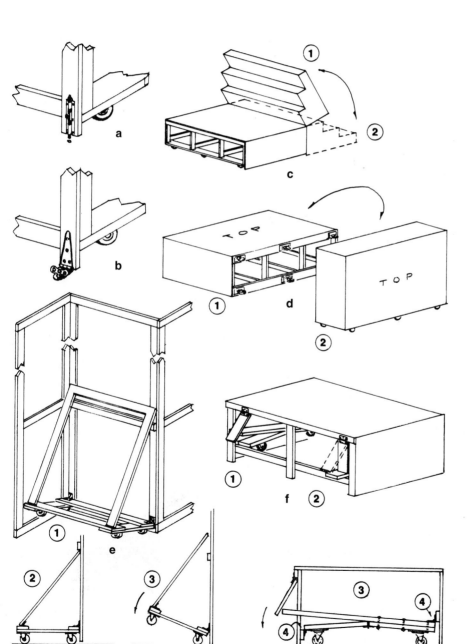

### Figure 10–15
#### Methods of Stabilizing Castered Units

(a) Barrel bolt fits into hole in stage floor.

(b) Hinged footiron and stage screw.

(c) Portion of platform not on casters:

    (1) Steps hinged to castered platform folds on top for easy movement.

    (2) Unfolded and resting on the stage floor, the steps stabilize the platform unit.

(d) Casters on offstage edge of platform:

    (1) Platform in working position, casters on back edge.

    (2) Platform is tipped onto casters to move.

(e) Lift jack:

    (1) Pictorial view of lift jack.

    (2) Side view showing jack lifting scenery.

    (3) Jack released, scenery rests on floor.

(f) Lift jack under a platform:

    (1) Jack released.

    (2) Jack depressed to lift platform on casters.

    (3) Sectional view.

    (4) Note eccentric hinging.

Wagon construction is basically the same as platform construction. The caster in a sense becomes the leg of the platform. If the casters are mounted on caster planks, the minimum span between supports can be increased. The caster plank, in addition to providing a sturdy mount for the caster, serves as a support for the top to increase the overall strength of the wagon. Normally, unless the wagon is to carry an extremely heavy load, such as a piano, the spacing of casters at 3-foot intervals is sufficient to remove any noticeable deflection.

Stock wagon units made in a convenient size (3-by-6-foot or 4-by-8-foot modules) for handling are joined to make larger units (Figure 10–16). Although stock wagons use more casters than are necessary for the total area, the flexibility of arrangements and handling and ease of storage justify the module system.

**Figure 10–16**
The Wagon Unit

(a) Construction of a stock wagon:
   (1)  4-inch swivel casters.
   (2)  2 × 6 caster planks.
   (3)  2 × 3 frame.
   (4)  4 × 8-foot, $\frac{3}{4}$-inch 5-ply top.
(b) Cross section.
(c) Large wagon made up of stock units:
   (1)  Stock unit.
   (2)  Units pin-hinged together.
   (3)  Facing boards.
(d) A different shape made of three stock wagons and two special corner pieces.
(e) Casket Lock. A unit to lock together wagons.

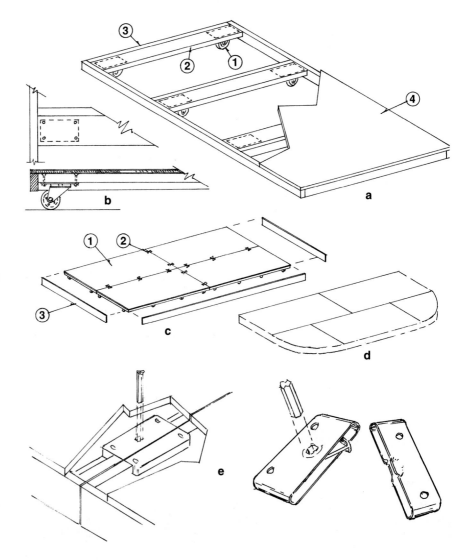

**The Casket Lock**     Wagon modules can be fastened together to make up a larger wagon unit with a hidden fastener, the casket lock. The two halves of the lock are mounted opposite each other in countersunk slots. Through an access hole in the top, the two halves of the fastener are locked together with an Allen wrench-type key (Figure 10–16e).

## THE AIR BEARING CASTER

To literally float on air, the air caster lifts a wagon or heavy unit of scenery on a film of air for the easy movement on- or offstage. The air supply can be from one of two sources, a low-pressure air blower or a high-pressure air compressor. The low-pressure air blower delivers an even flow of air at a constant pressure and is more economical, although it does entail a larger air caster unit. The air compressor can use a smaller lift unit, but it is more expensive and requires a storage tank to maintain an even pressure. Many shops, however, have a fixed air compression system with hookup positions in the scenery shop for pneumatic tools, in the paint shop for spray gun painting, and on the stage for setup and touch-up. To avoid a loss of pressure in the prolonged use of the air caster, an extra storage tank can be added to the system.

**Preparing the Floor**     The floor surface is critical for air casters. It must be smooth and level. The average stage floor is soft wood, pierced with floor traps. Since the clearance of an air castered unit is only $\frac{3}{4}$ inch, there cannot be dips or abrupt rises on the floor of more than $\frac{1}{8}$ inch in ten feet. Surfaces like linoleum, vinyl, or smooth-side masonite boards are recommended. All joints and cracks should be sealed so as not to lose air pressure.

**Positioning the Air Caster**     The manufacturer recommends a perimeter placement of the air caster, partly for easy access to the caster for maintenance and replacement. For large units, this may complicate construction of the wagon. The internal structure must be strong enough to bridge the width with minimum deflection. If internally placed air casters are to be used, access through the platform floor should be planned.

Shown in Figure 10–17 are two types of air casters from different manufacturers. The round-pad unit has an off-air support built into the unit, while the square-pad unit's off-air support is built into the platform. The round-pad is a more visible caster and is better adapted for moving scaffold-type structures or a pipe-sculptured scenic unit.

## WAGON MOVEMENTS

Aside from the free movement of a wagon carrying a full or partial set, there are several controlled movements that can become a scheme of production for handling scenery entirely on casters. These involve the construction of guiding "tracks" either above or recessed into the stage floor (Figures 10–18, 10–19, and 10–20). The scheme is sometimes based on a pair of alternating

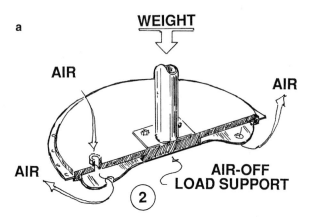

WEIGHT

AIR

AIR

AIR

AIR-OFF
LOAD SUPPORT

2

### Figure 10–17
### The Air Bearing Caster

Shown are two types of air casters. First, the round-pad with built in air-off support.
(a) Section.
(b) Photo of a single pad.
(c) Distribution of casters. Photos courtesy of Rolar System Inc., Santa Barbara.
(d) Theatrical use of round-pad air-caster in a production of *The Tempest* at the Tyrone Guthrie Theatre. The arrow indicates one of several air-casters placed at strategic points on a giant wire sculpture, which pivots and rotates to indicate the many locations on Prospero's magical island. Photo courtesy James Bakkom.
(e) Square-pad air-caster. The off-air load-support has to be built into the platform structure.
(g) A perimeter placement of casters is recommended for easy access. Air Caster Corporation, Decatur, Ill.

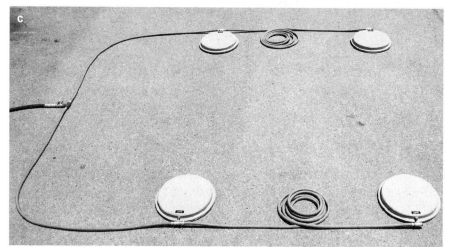

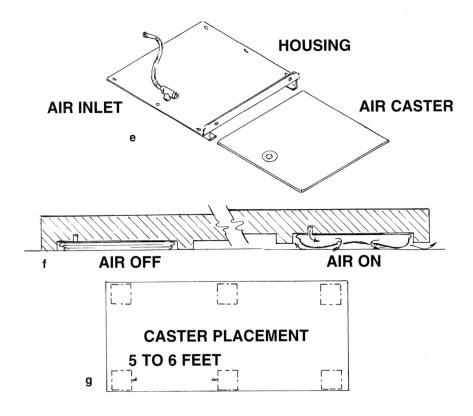

HOUSING

AIR INLET      AIR CASTER

e

f    AIR OFF        AIR ON

CASTER PLACEMENT
5 TO 6 FEET

g

wagons, allowing the scenery and props to be changed on the offstage wagon while the alternate wagon is in the playing position. The transverse, jack-knife, and split-wagon movements operate on this principle.

When there are small sets in a production, it is sometimes desirable to keep each set intact on separate wagons. The stage then becomes packed with wagon sets and the shifting is accomplished by shuttling each wagon into position. The pattern of movement varies with the size and shape of the sets and their order of appearance in the play.

## THE REVOLVING STAGE

Another controlled movement is that of a castered unit around a fixed pivot: a revolving stage. Such a stage, which is not permanently built into the stage floor, is similar to the wagon in structure. To remain portable, a turntable is made in smaller sections that are fastened together (Figure 10–21). The fixed casters are mounted in a pattern to properly support each unit and are fixed in a position in which the axle of the caster is on a radius line drawn from the pivot point. If the casters are carefully mounted, the turntable will revolve about its pivot point with very little effort.

Another method of assembling a turntable is to reverse the normal position of the casters under the table and place them upside down on the stage floor (Figure 10–21c). The casters are placed in concentric circles as bearing points on a prepared rolling surface on the underside of the table. Each caster is shimmed to the same height to ensure a level turntable floor. This compensates for any irregularities in the stage floor. Although the assembly time is longer and the table is a little higher off the stage floor, the result is a smooth-running, quiet turntable. Figure 10–22 illustrates the assembly steps as well as the cable-drive and motor method of powering a revolving stage.

### Figure 10–18
Tracked Wagon Movement

(a) Tracks on top of the stage floor.
  (1)  Steel angle irons.
  (2)  Beveled wood which though subject to wear is quieter than steel on steel.
(b) Section detail.
(c) Section showing track cut into the stage floor. In an elaborate tracked-wagon scheme such as those diagramed in d, e, and f, a temporary stage floor is installed with space beneath the track groove for cables to drive the wagon unit by hand winch from an offstage position.
Types of Tracked Wagon Movements:
(d) Transverse movement.
(e) Split transverse wagons and a large single wagon moving up- and downstage.
(f) Multimovements: transverse, diagonal, as well as up- and downstage.

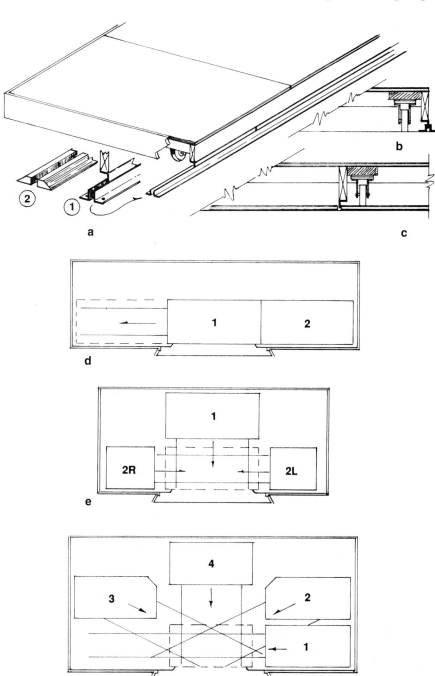

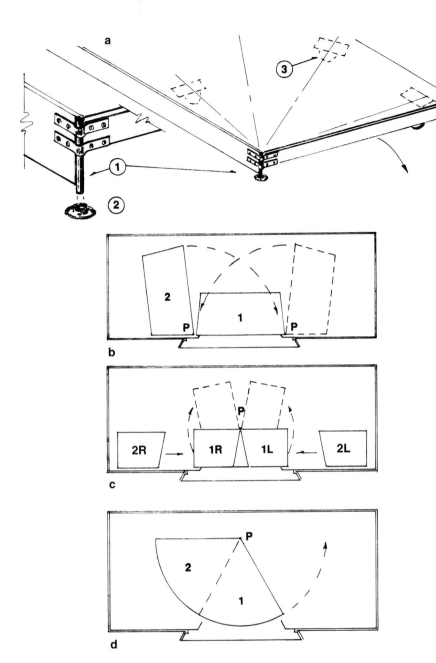

b

c

d

**Figure 10—19**
Pivoted Wagon Movement

(a) Pivot mounted on the corner of the wagon:
   (1) Pivot detail.
   (2) Socket fastened to the floor at the pivot point. Although the pivot and socket positions are often reversed in a turntable installation, it is best under the illustrated conditions to place the socket on the floor. A corner pivot, besides being an awkward mounting position, may also have to bear weight because the nearest caster is usually about four feet away.
   (3) Fixed caster set perpendicular to radius.
(b) Jackknife wagons.
(c) Type of jackknife in combination with split wagons.
(d) Pivoting a segment of a circle, semi-revolving.

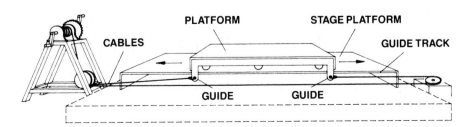

**Figure 10—20**
Cable Drive for a Moving Wagon

A schematic drawing showing the drive cable, hidden from view under a raised stage floor, and attached to wagon guides, right and left. The cable turns on the drum of the winch to pull the wagon to the right or left.

## Figure 10–21
## The Revolving Stage

A portable revolving stage or turntable can be built many ways. Shown here are two methods.

(a) Turntable made up of stock wagon units with special-shaped wagons to form the curve of the outside edge:
   (1) Stock wagon.
   (2) Special wagon to complete circle.
   (3) Casters blocked perpendicular to radius.
   (4) Section.

(b) Turntable made of wedge-shaped units around cental core. Fewer casters are used, creating less noise:
   (1) Basic wedge-shaped unit.
   (2) Top removed showing the position of casters.
   (3) Central core.
   (4) Section.

(c) Turntable construction, reverse castering.
   (1) Basic wedge-shaped unit.
   (2) Central core, ball-bearing pivot.
   (3) Single unit viewed from underneath to show framing.
   (4) Bearing surface in path of casters, $\frac{3}{4}$-inch 5-ply or particle board.
   (5) Casters mounted on the stage floor in patterns that are the same circumference as the caster-bearing surface on the underside of the turntable.
   (6) Spirit level and rotating bar to check the level of each caster mount to ensure a steady, level rotation. Although the reverse caster turntable takes longer to assemble, it is quieter and easier to turn than the conventionally castered unit.

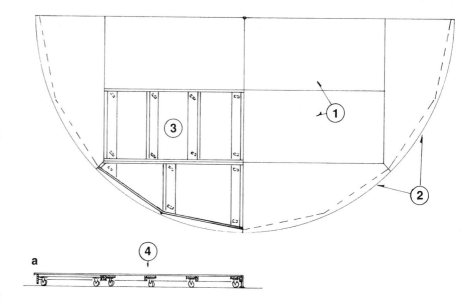

a

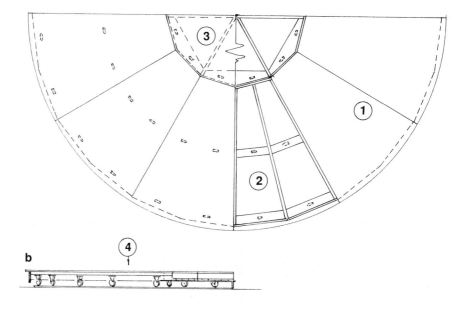

b

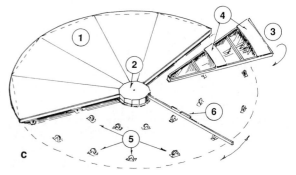

c

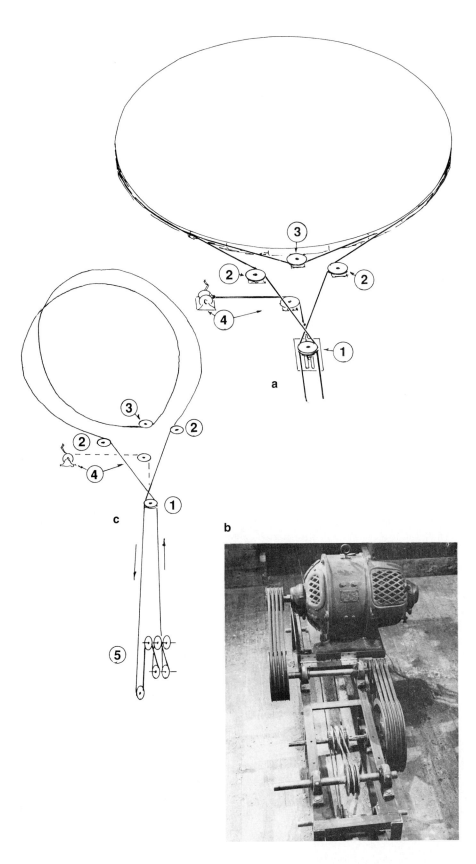

### Figure 10—22
Motorized Cable Drive for a Single Turntable

(a) Sketch shows:
  (1) Tension idler.
  (2) Mule pulley to change direction of the cable.
  (3) Centering pulley, it keeps cable from creeping and binding as it winds and unwinds on the edge of the turntable.
  (4) Winch to control the tension on the cable.
(b) Motor and reduction pulley system. The drive is a 2.5 horsepower, variable speed, reversible, 230-volt DC motor. Instead of a drum, a system of pulleys is used to keep the cable from binding and still provide enough friction to move the turntable.
(c) A diagram of the threading of the cable, which is one-quarter inch of flexible steel long-spliced into a continuous loop. Photo courtesy Tom Eaton.

**Single Turntable**    The revolving stage as a basic device can have a variety of sizes and uses. The most familiar is the large single turntable. Figure 10–23 illustrates the methods used to power these structures. Unless the stage is especially designed for a large turntable, its diameter is limited by the depth of the stage. If the stage happens to be shallow in proportion to the proscenium opening, a single turntable will leave an awkward corner in the downstage right and left positions. Attempts to fill the area with a

**Figure 10–23**

Methods of Powering a Single Turntable

(a) Cable and winch:
   (1) A spliced cable with one turn around the outside edge of the turntable is held taut by
   (2) a tension idler and powered by
   (3) a hand winch.

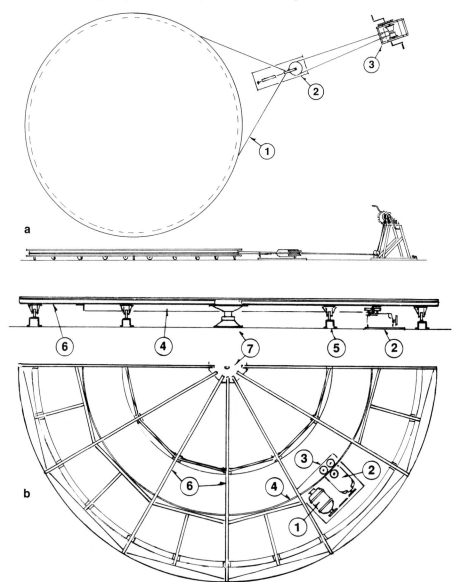

(b) Motor-driven turntable: A reversible and variable-speed electric motor underneath a highly mounted turntable.
   (1) Motor.
   (2) Reduction gear box.
   (3) Spring loaded friction drive wheels, or bevel gears.
   (4) Drive ring for friction drive, or gear ring for bevel gear drive.
   (5) Raised, fiber-padded track for fixed casters.
   (6) Steel channel-beam framework.
   (7) Roller-bearing pivot. It should be noted that both a and b turntables are usually surrounded by a raised temporary stage floor flush with the top of the turntable.

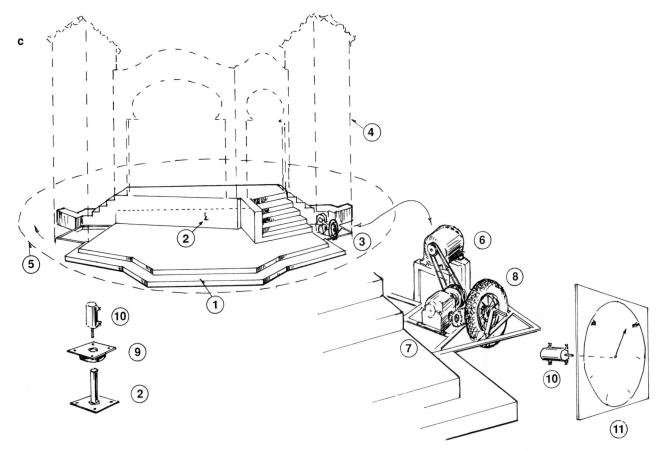

(c) Drive wheel power unit. An example of a turntable on top of the stage floor with an eccentric pivot position making the use of the ring drive or cable drive impracticable:

(1) Basic platform structure on fixed casters perpendicular to radius.

(2) Pivot located off the center of the platform.

(3) Wheel drive power unit hidden by

(4) superstructure of the setting.

(5) The path of rotation.

(6) Components of the power unit: 5-horsepower, reversible DC motor linked to

(7) gear reduction box.

(8) Drive wheel which turns the platform by friction drive off of the stage floor. It is connected to the gear box by a sprocket and roller-chain drive.

(9) Ball-bearing socket fixed to the platform.

(10) Turn indicator. A self-synchronizing motor (SELSYN) mounted on the wagon with its shaft fixed to the pivot and wired to a companion motor mounted offstage. An arrow attached to the shaft of the second "selsyn" becomes a pointer to indicate the exact position of the turntable.

(11) Dial face of the turn indicator. (Original installation designed and constructed by George B. Honcher and Pat Mitchell.)

show portal or with hinged pieces on the turntable that unfold and mask the corner more or less negate the basic function of the single revolving stage (Figure 10–24a).

**Two Turntables**    A shallow stage is adaptable to the use of two turntables that either touch in the center or are held slightly apart. This method removes the awkward corners of the single turntable, but it creates a design problem—that of joining all the sets in the center (Figure 10–24b).

### Figure 10–24
Turntable and Ring Combinations

(a) Single large turntable.
(b) Two small turntables.
(c) Two small turntables with rings.
(d) Single turntable in a transverse wagon.

(e) Large turntable with two small disks.
(f) Large turntable with ring.
(g) Semi-revolving ring-segment and small turntable.
(h) A pair of rings.

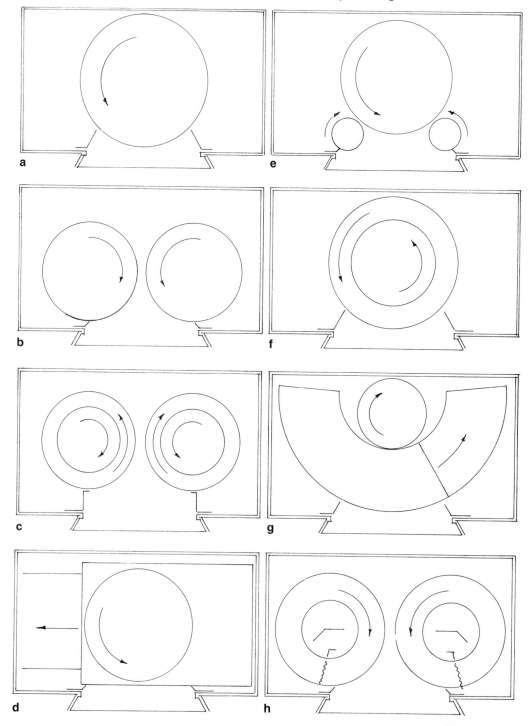

**Three Turntables**     Occasionally, a large turntable is combined with two small disks in the downstage right and left positions. The small disks either carry scenery related to the large set in the center or are small independent sets. The production scheme for *I Remember Mama*, designed by George Jenkins, used this technique (Figure 10–24e).

**Ring and Turntable**     A great deal more variety of movement is achieved using a ring and turntable combination. The ring and turntable are individually powered so that they can turn in the same direction at identical or different speeds, or they may revolve in opposite directions. The possible combinations of fixed units on the ring and turntable are almost endless. If the changes are made avista, it becomes a delightful scheme of production. The settings for *Protective Custody*, designed by Peter Larkin, were handled in this manner (Figure 10–24f).

**Two Rings and Two Turntables**     Although less adaptable to revolving fixed units than the single ring and turntable, two rings around two turntables provide a very flexible method of changing elements of scenery and properties. This was demonstrated in the production of *Lady in the Dark*, designed by Harry Horner. With the help of flown pieces of scenery, the settings were able to blend from one scene to the next in full view of the audience (Figure 10–24c).

**Semi-Revolves and Combinations**     The remaining variations of the revolving technique are the semi-revolving stage and combination of a turntable and a wagon.

The semi-revolving stage is a portion of a ring or turntable tracked to swing in half an arc and then return to its original position (Figure 10–24g). The semi-revolving stage may be large or small, used singly or in pairs, or, in some cases, combined with a turntable.

A combination of revolving and lateral movements can be accomplished by building a turntable into a full-stage transverse wagon (Figure 10–24d). This combination works best when a portion of one set is reused many times during the show. The lobby of *Grand Hotel*, for example, was saved in this manner. Most of the lobby settings remained on the left side of the wagon while a portion moved on the turntable. The smaller rooms and other scenes in the hotel occupied the remainder of the turntable and were moved into better sightlines by sliding the wagon to the left. The scheme can be varied by setting the turntable into the center of the wagon and having elements of scenery on both sides instead of one side.

**The Air Caster for the Revolving Stage**     It is possible to use air casters on a turntable or any pivoting motion. A semi-revolve is not a problem, but if the motion is a complete revolve the air hose may become tangled. Portable air compressors and air blowers can ride on the revolve. Although they are equipped with noise suppressers, they still need to be covered with music or cleverly motivated bedlam. If the theatre has a trap room, the air hose can feed through an enlarged center pivot.

**Figure 10—25**
Elevator Stage

A backstage view of the elaborate elevator installation at the Metropolitan Opera House, New York.

Conventional drive systems such as cable or rim drive can be used on the air caster. An air-castered wagon is able to be tracked and driven by cable, or just pushed.

## ELEVATOR STAGES

As a means of moving scenery, the permanent elevator stage requires sophisticated stage machinery. Unless the theatre is in the position to make constant use of the equipment, or the elevators have a second function such as a scenery and property lift to remote storage areas, the installation is extravagant. With few exceptions (the Metropolitan Opera, Radio City Music Hall, and similar presentation houses), the normal legitimate theatre in the United States has little use for the elevator stage as a method of changing scenery (Figure 10—25).

The financial organization and scale of production of numerous state theatres in Europe make the elaborate elevator stage a more feasible method of handling scenery than could be supported by the unsubsidized theatres of the United States.

### SMALL ELEVATORS AND TRAPS

Although the average stage may not have an elevator system, it usually has a portion of the floor area made in sections of "traps" that may be used to raise small elements of scenery through the stage floor. The traps can be removed to give access through the stage floor into the trap room below. Entrances by stairs or ladder can be made from below through such an open-

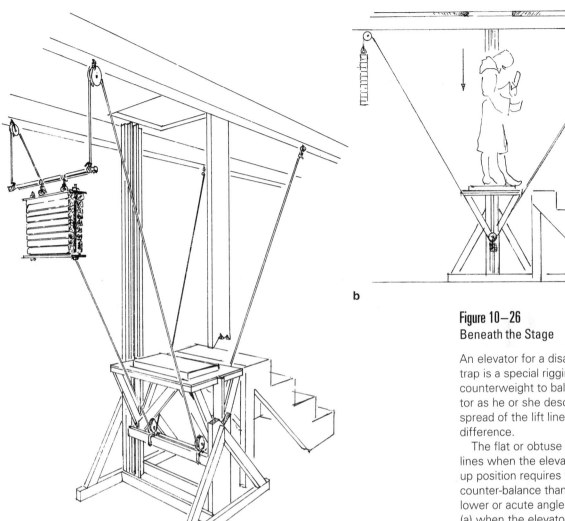

**b**

**Figure 10—26**
**Beneath the Stage**

An elevator for a disappearance trap is a special rigging of a counterweight to balance an actor as he or she descends. The spread of the lift lines makes the difference.

The flat or obtuse angle of the lines when the elevator is in an up position requires more counter-balance than at the lower or acute angle. Hence in (a) when the elevator is at the top, the weights just balance the empty elevator. The weight of the actor will unbalance the load until near the bottom (b) when the counterweight slows the descent to a stop. The actor steps off and the elevator returns to fill the trap. A little smoke and fire helps the effect.

Warning! When the elevator is off cue in the up position—it should be wedged or otherwise locked or the wrong actor might get an unexpected ride.

ing. Trap openings are made between structural beams supporting the stage floor. The designer must be aware of the specific position of the traps in a given theatre.

The construction of a temporary lift that can be used for scenery or actors is shown in Figure 10–26a. The example illustrated is a small unit. Elevator platforms can vary greatly in size, but a larger elevator would require more guides and liftlines.

## THE ELEVATOR FLOOR

Some performance spaces incorporate elevators whose primary function is to shape the stage floor. In this instance, sections of the stage floor can be raised or lowered by elevators to make levels or pits, but are generally not used to move scenery. They can, however, be considered as a means of changing the appearance or form of the stage floor, thus creating a new scene without moving scenery.

## THE COMPUTER BACKSTAGE

The influence of the computer on scenery-moving technology has advanced markedly in the last decade. Blockbuster shows like *Cats, Phantom of the Opera,* and *Miss Saigon* have advanced state-of-the-art backstage technology. The computer can be used to control hydraulic and scissors lifts, electric winches, flying, and various other scenic effects. In addition, theatre technicians have applied the computer to more mundane tasks such as maintaining an inventory of all units of scenery, platforms, and lighting equipment, with instructions for assembly and strike. When computer control is reinforced with a television monitor, it can provide the operator a situation report as to accuracy or completion of a tricky scenery maneuver. The basic acting area for *Miss Saigon,* for example, is framed on three sides with panels of oversized rustic shutters. Each panel is flown individually, providing considerable flexibility of arrangement of openings. The liftlines of each panel are motor-driven and computerized. A TV monitor allows the operator to verify the final position of each screen.

The computer has allowed the scenic designer considerably more flexibility in terms of complex movement of scenery. It has radically altered the body of knowledge necessary for the technical director and the stage technician. This capability, in combination with the popularity of spectacle, can provide a backstage show as exciting as the one the audience is experiencing.

# 11 STAGE PROPERTIES AND THE DESIGNER

In addition to large scenic background elements of the stage setting, the designer is responsible for the design and selection of stage properties and smaller bits of scenery used by the actors. This may vary from finding a marble-topped Louis XV console table to making an exotic sofa for a Turkish cosy corner, or from borrowing a Victorian tea set to fashioning tree leaves. Whether borrowed or constructed, each property must be carefully coordinated into the design composition and adjusted to the production scheme, and must also be checked for size and ease of use by the actors.

Stage properties are in essence the design details of the overall visual composition. Although the visual significance of properties applies more specifically to a realistic interior setting than to an exterior or abstract scene, their contribution cannot be overemphasized. Stage properties are, many times, the accent or artistic touch that makes or breaks the effectiveness of a stage setting.

Perhaps a more significant use of properties occurs on the thrust and arena stages, both of which are almost entirely dependent on properties to set the scene visually. Because of the close audience–stage relationship in both cases, the finished detail and quality of all properties are subject to closer inspection than they are on the proscenium stage.

Another important visual consideration of a stage property is its "rightness" for the play. The designer has to continually ask such questions as these: Is this chair in the right historical period and nationality? Is the sideboard the kind Mama would choose? And so on. The selection and designing of furniture and properties is done in close collaboration with the director in order to ensure their appropriateness for the play and to check how they fit into the staging of the action. For example, large furniture may hinder movement, or a high-backed chair may block off a view of upstage action.

Real furniture is, of course, used in the modern theatre, although it is often altered to become stageworthy. Scale and color are sometimes changed to improve the relationship to the stage composition. Because of these alterations, even real furniture may take on a theatrical look. It becomes a stage property suggesting, sometimes faintly, sometimes openly, that it is no longer real. The name *property*, or "prop," is often synonymous with the unreal or theatrical.

Properties of a setting should be planned and built simultaneously with the rest of the scenic elements. Their importance to the design and production scheme is sometimes overlooked in the planning period. In theatres that are fully staffed, there will be a prop master who is in charge of seeing that all of the properties necessary for the production are built, bought, borrowed, or in some other fashion make it to the stage. If instead it is the responsibility of the designer, it is often started too late, or too many decisions in the selection of furniture or decorative features are postponed until the final hectic rehearsals. This often occurs when the designer, overworked and pressed for time, places the responsibility of organizing the properties on the shoulders of a willing but not-too-able apprentice.

To make better use of their time, designers should have a competent background in historical furniture styles and period decorations and should be thoroughly acquainted with the traditional uses of properties in the theatre. They must also be able to evaluate a property in terms of its importance to the action of the play and its sheer decorative qualities.

## PROPERTIES vs. SCENERY

What is a prop? When does a small piece of scenery become a property or a large property become scenery? The decision of when a small piece is a prop or scenery (or costumes, for that matter) often depends on the staffing of the particular theatre and who is best qualified to provide what is necessary. Few shops have hard and fast rules. Indeed, often pieces can easily fall into several categories. The traditional categories that follow are no more than a guide.

Stage properties are traditionally defined as (1) all objects carried or handled by the actors; (2) separate portions of the set on which the actors may stand or sit, such as rocks, stumps, or logs; (3) decorative features not permanently built or painted on the scenery, such as pictures, draperies, and so on; (4) the ground cloth and rugs; and (5) all sound and visual effects that are not electrically powered, such as a gunshot or door slam.

In the average show, the categorical division of properties is based for the most part on these traditional definitions of a property. Exceptions or collaborations are made all the time with the agreement of all concerned. Hence, a tree trunk may be scenery and foliage a property; a pair of glasses discovered on the stage is a property while those brought on stage by the actors are considered costumes. Heavy properties often become scenery because of their size or necessity to be fastened to the scenery for movement.

Properties may also be classified according to their size and use. Properties can be designated as either hand, set, or dress properties, or as visual or sound-effect properties.

## HAND PROPERTIES

The small objects handled by the actor on the stage are hand props. They include such items as teacups, books, fans, letters, and many more similar articles.

## SET PROPERTIES

As the name implies, set properties are the larger elements more closely related to the scenery but still used by the actors. This group often includes furniture, stoves, sinks, rugs, ground cloth, and any domestic object. Exterior set props consist of small rocks, stumps, bushes, foliage, real dirt (*Tobacco Road*), grass mats, and so on.

Set properties are in the care of the property person, who supervises the placing of the set prop on the stage and its removal to a stored position offstage.

## DRESS PROPERTIES

Dress properties are more closely related to the setting. Their chief functions are decoration and to help establish the atmosphere of the environment through detail. Dress properties consist of all the elements not specifically used by the actors that serve to fill in and complete or *dress* the set. Window curtains, pictures, wall hangings, and flower groupings are a few typical dress properties.

As a class, dress properties are not necessarily superficial. They can become a strong decorative feature in a setting. Because they are not used by the actors, they can often be faked in order to be handled more easily or in a different way from the normal set property. Bookcases, for example, may have faked books and be attached to the scenery. A saloon back bar is often dressed with fake plastic or papier-mâché bottles to cut down the weight. A period piano or spinet, which is hard to find and harder to borrow, can be easily built and faked as a dress prop (Figure 11–1). These are, of course, just a few of the many, many types of faked dress properties, which although often not easy to construct are in fact possible.

## SELECTING SET AND DRESS PROPERTIES

The designer is responsible for the compositional unity, period continuity, and color relationships of the set and dress properties. Their first notation appears in the designer's sketch, which may or may not be clear as to the indication of the real form. Once the general idea of the design has been accepted, the designer can turn to a more careful study of period line and availability of each piece.

**Figure 11–1**
**Dress Properties**

(a) Fake spinet piano.
(b) Dummy books in book case.
(c) Papier-Mâché bar bottles.

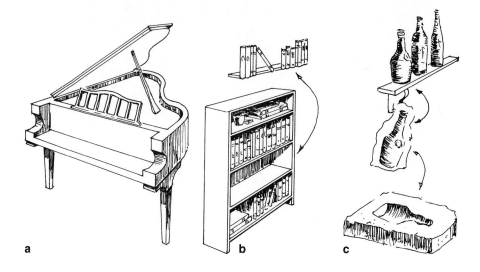

a                                        b                      c

The final decision on each piece of furniture is made by the designer with the director's approval. To help reach this decision at an early stage in the planning, the designer uses individual sketches or illustrational clippings. The selection of set properties can be further facilitated by the use of a furniture plot, which gives exact references to the size of an individual piece in relation to its surroundings.

## PERIOD STYLE AND DECORATIVE FORM

It is important for a designer to have a full understanding of period architecture, interior design, and furniture style. The realistic interior, although perhaps not as popular or ubiquitous as it once was, is still common. A suggestion of an interior may appear in the thrust and arena stages or on the proscenium stage. A period style can be established in the furniture of the setting or by a suggested doorway and window. A simple set with only one or two pieces had best have the right pieces.

The more familiar the designer is with the historical background of a period style, the easier it will be to design the setting (whether realistic or not), select the set and dress properties, and create the appropriate environment. (This applies to the costume designer also.)

A period style is a reflection of its times. It is evident in the architecture, interiors, and furniture of each period in history. Most changes in form, from period to period, are logical transitions, although some are reactionary. Occasionally a style is eclectic in form, borrowing from a period in the past. Of all furniture, the chair is a most noticeable example.

The form of a chair, through periodic changes, is at first functional, which then gives way to more decorative form, and eventually, to a greater degree of comfort.

In Figure 11–2 you see an abbreviated representation of the chair form from ancient times to the near present, in an attempt to illustrate the effect of period style and decorative form. The examples begin with the ancient periods: Egyptian (1), Assyrian (2), Mycenean (3), the Greek klismos chair (4), and Roman throne chair (5). Out of Romanesque, the heavy armchair (6). The figure shows a Gothic high-back chair (7) with linen-fold carving and crowned with pinnacles and tracery of Gothic architecture. The Renaissance of Italy is represented by the Dante chair (8), and the Renaissance in France by the "Caqueteuse" chair (9).

Next, the French styles: Louis XIII (10) showing a Flemish influence, Louis XIV French baroque (11), Louis XV rococo (12), and Louis XVI neoclassicism (13).

From England: English Renaissance wainscot chair (14), Restoration (15), Queen Anne (16), and the cabinetmakers of the Georgian periods—Chippendale (17), Hepplewhite (18), and Sheraton (19).

Napoleon's Empire style returned to classic Greek and Roman for inspiration, as seen in the Empire side chair (20), based on the Greek klismos chair. The mid-Victorian armchair (21) was called, in its time, French Antique and was an English revival of the Louis XV style.

More recent examples include Eastlake (22), an American chair inspired by a Gothic revival; art nouveau (23) out of France and into the twentieth century; the mission-styled Morris chair (24), a part of the Arts and Crafts movement; the cantilevered chair (25) by Breuer of the Bauhaus, the first chair to be designed for mass production; and a bent plywood chair by Eames (26).

## DRAPERIES AND WINDOW DRESSINGS

Draperies are one of the main decorative details that bring character to an interior setting. Their elegance or cheapness, period, style or lack of style, or even their complete absence contributes immeasurably to the visual expression of the kind of place and people in the play.

From historical references, the designer can plan to use draperies—which, depending on the period, may include window, door, fireplace mantel, picture, and mirror draperies. The designing of draperies is based on a knowledge of the look of the period, the way the material drapes or hangs, and the methods of cutting and assembling the material into the desired effect.

A designer needs to prepare a carefully scaled or dimensioned drawing of the assembled drapery, specifying the material and the action, if any. Window curtains, for example, may have to be opened or closed for a tableau during the action of the play. As with the rest of the set, the designer is expected to guide the execution of the draperies and therefore needs to know something about drapery patterns and assembly techniques.

Although draperies may occur in many positions other than the windows of a setting, the fundamental parts making up the decorative portion are the same. The basic parts of a window dressing, which may or may not be used at the same time, are the *blind* or *shade*, the *curtain* (or glass curtain, as it is sometimes called), the *overdrapery*, and the *valance* (Figure 11–3). The over-drapery and valance are the frame, so to speak, while the glass curtain diffuses the outside light, and the blind cuts off the view into the room from the outside.

**The Blind or Shade**     Early blinds were shutters, both outside and inside the window. They were a protection from weather as well as break-in. A more special type of shade for a grand window is the festoon-draped shade. It is pulled up from the bottom by a series of vertical liftlines that have been threaded through rings on the back of the curtain, like the rigging of a brail curtain (Figure 11–4).

**Figure 11–2**
Period Style and Decorative Form

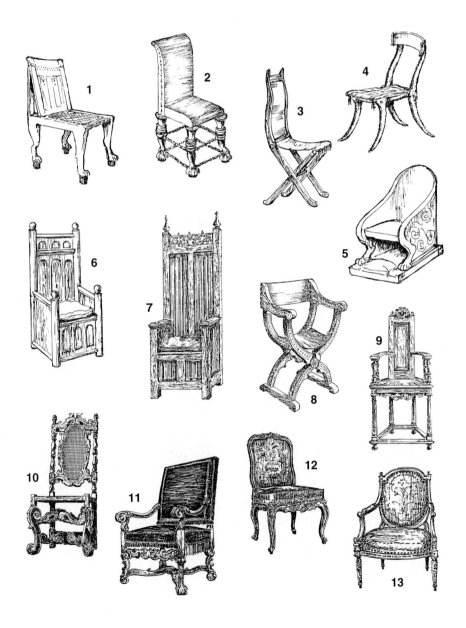

**The Curtain**　　Usually made of a translucent material or lace, the curtain is used to diffuse the outside light. It may be rigged to draw closed or may tie back in a soft drape. On some occasions, the curtain might be the final decorative feature, omitting the overdrapery. A half curtain is often used on a smaller window.

**The Overdrapery**　　As the vertical frame of the window, the overdrapery is made of a rich and heavy material. It is the decorative and color accent of the room. An overdrapery may have the same action as the curtain, such as drawing from right to left, or be draped to a hook or tieback. If it is a fixed overdrapery, it can be made to a pattern that will improve its drape.

## Figure 11–3
### Window Dressing

The basic details of dressing begin with:
(a) The proportions of the window.
(b) Window with decorative blind.
(c) Blind and lace curtain.
(d) Over drapes (sides) and decorative valance.
A window may be dressed with one, two or all of these details as shown below.

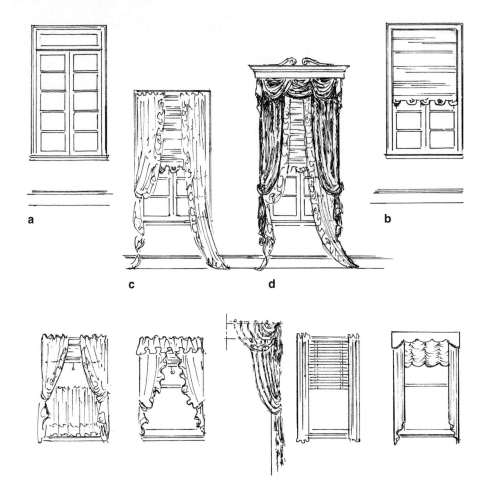

a

b

c

d

**The Valance**   The decorative emphasis of the window dressing is in the valance, and therefore requires a greater variety of draping techniques. A valance is made up of swags, plaits, tails, and wing pieces—sometimes incorporated into one drape, such as the festoon valance (Figure 11–5a). More often, though, the valance is made of separate swags and wings that are joined together to look like a single piece of fabric (Figure 11–5d, e).

A valance may be boxed and crowned with a cornice or an architectural feature, or the swags are sometimes padded or stiffened into a fixed silhouette. Figure 11–6 illustrates a few options.

**Drapery Materials**   The materials for window draperies are divided into three groups: (1) the transparent or sheer fabrics for glass curtains and some types of draped shades; (2) the translucent materials for the shade, unless it is opaque; and (3) the opaque materials of the overdrapery and valance. The sheer materials may be chiffon, organdy, net, or theatrical gauze, to name a few. Muslin, silk, and handkerchief linen are examples of translucent fabrics. Though the opaque materials for overdraperies are numerous, they usually are made of a fabric that will drape well, such as velour, velveteen, corduroy, or monk's cloth.

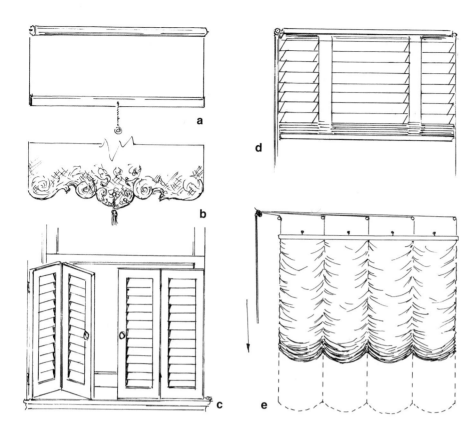

**Figure 11—4**
Blinds, Shades, and Shutters

Types of blinds:
(a) Roller blind.
(b) Decorative roller blind.
(c) Shutters.
(d) Venetian blind.
(e) Festoon shade.

## BORROWING OR RENTING PROPERTIES

Nonprofessional and professional producing groups alike must rely on renting and borrowing furniture or else maintain in storage a collection of stock period furniture for continuous use. Storing select period pieces is by far the most satisfactory method of securing properties for a repertory or stock company. Stock furniture can be varied with new upholstering and painted for reuse in future productions. However, this practice is not always feasible.

A producing group that depends on borrowing furniture and other articles must make an effort to maintain goodwill with the community. It pays to be businesslike when borrowing properties. Unfortunately, many a property room has been furnished with unreturned props—which is obviously not the way to build goodwill. A few simple rules for borrowing will help create a friendly, businesslike way of handling a loan:

1. Make a list of each borrowed article, including the name and address of the owner, date borrowed and date to be returned, estimated value, description noting condition (scratches, cracks, or parts missing), and remuneration (cash, complimentary tickets, or program credit). Request a signed receipt from the owner upon return of the article.
2. Centralize all borrowing by one person rather than by different people for each production.
3. Never borrow priceless heirlooms or irreplaceable antiques.

**Figure 11–5**
Types of Draperies and Valances

(a) Festoon valance and pattern.
(b) Eccentrically draped festoon valance.
(c) Crossed festoons as valance.
(d) Valance of swag and wing pieces.
(e) Festoon valance and side draperies showing pattern for side drapery.
(f) Swag pattern.
(g) Draping swag.
(h) Pattern of wing piece or tail.
(i) Draping or folding a wing piece.
(j) A double or central tail.
(k) Pattern of a central tail.

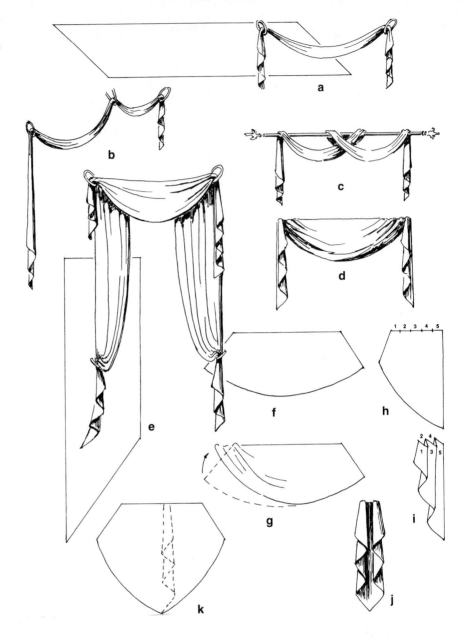

**Figure 11–6**
Types of Valances

(a) Café-curtain as valance.
(b) Boxed festoon.
(c) Draped rope or braid.
(d) Rigid valance covered with velvet and appliqued with silk and brocade.

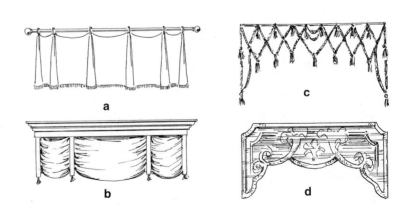

4. Take special care of all borrowed properties on the stage, using dust covers and padding to prevent damage from movement of the scenery.
5. Return borrowed pieces promptly on the date promised and in the borrowed condition.
6. Secure and file a receipt. Records become an excellent source for quickly locating and reborrowing for another production.

## MAKING AND REMAKING FURNITURE

Although difficult and time-consuming, prop shops are often called on to build pieces of furniture. Not all shops have this capability. There are several styles and rustic pieces of furniture that may more easily be made than found or borrowed. Some of the unupholstered, carpenter-style pieces shown in Figure 11–7 can be made. Although not necessarily easy to do, these do not

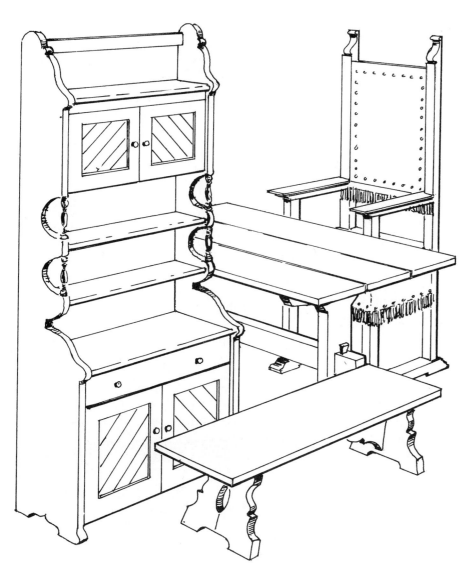

Figure 11–7
Examples of Carpenter-style
Furniture That Are Easy to Make

### Figure 11-8
### Making New Furniture

(a) A hard-to-find tête-à-tête is constructed in the property shop. Frame and webbing ready for padding and upholstering.
(b) Finished settee.
(c) Plexiglass seat and back give a side chair a new look. On the left, rigid urethane foam with wooden core carved into legs for a console table. In the right background, turned rigid foam baluster.

require extremely fine furniture-building skills. The newly-constructed pieces in Figure 11–8 require somewhat more expertise.

Furniture can sometimes be altered, especially if the alteration involves a reduction in size rather than an increase. Of course, it all depends on the piece at hand and what is desired by the designer. The practiced eye of the designer or prop person will be able to see in an otherwise hideous late-Victorian "masterpiece"—after a little painting, reupholstering, and trimming away excess parts—a Louis XIV side chair that would fool Molière. Given enough time, patience, and skill, a props artisan can turn a secondhand furniture store into a treasure house of "antiques" (Figure 11–9).

## UPHOLSTERING

When sundry set properties are brought together on the stage for the first time, some or all may have to be upholstered for either color or compositional reasons. Extensive reupholstering is not recommended on borrowed pieces, although it is possible to cover the existing surface with a new material by catching it lightly with a needle and thread. This should not be attempted on antiques, however, which might have weak upholstering. Bright colors or

**Figure 11–9**
Remaking Furniture

Remodeling a sofa:
(a) The original sofa before alterations.
(b) Back removed, reupholstered, and freshly painted.
Reupholstering, tufting:
(c) Tufting a sofa.
(d) Rear view of ties used to form tufts.
Photos courtesy Gene Diskey.

a

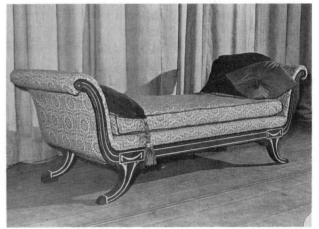

b

c

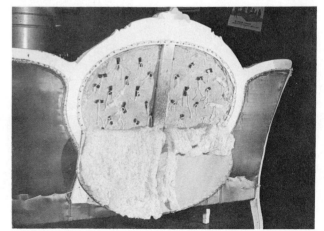

d

### Figure 11–10
#### Upholstering Techniques

(a) Tacking: (1) Hidden tacking. (2) Tacking covered by a panel. (3) Tacking kept on an unexposed surface. (4) Decorative tacking. (5) Tacking covered with gimp braid. (6) Tacking covered with fringe. (7) Upholstering tacks, 4, 6, 12, and gimp tacks, 3, 4.
(b) Fringes and braid: (1) and (2) Ball fringes. (3) and (4) Tassel fringes. (5) Bullion fringe. (6) Braid. (7) Gimp braid. (8) Ruffle.
(c) Plaits: (1) Pinch plait. (2) Box plait. (3) Accordion plaits. (4) Gathering.

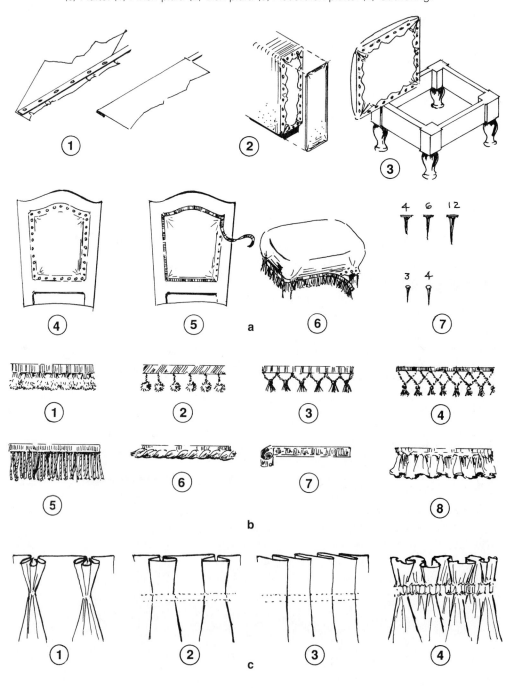

shiny materials on a borrowed piece can be dulled by covering them with a black net.

To reupholster furniture that belongs to the theatre, it is best to follow the same method of covering used originally. If the old covering is removed carefully, the pieces can serve as a pattern for cutting the new material. While the upholstering is off, repairs can be made to the springs, webbing, and padding, and the piece can be painted. If the furniture is going to be kept in stock, the padding can be covered first with muslin, which serves as a base for any future changes in upholstering.

Expert upholstering will hide or cover the tacking. This may be accomplished in many ways. The material can be tacked on a hidden edge in back or underneath, or tacked to a surface that is later hidden by a covered panel. Exposed tacks can be covered with a decorative gimp braid or fringe. Sometimes tacks may be studded and left exposed as a decorative feature in themselves (Figure 11–10).

## FLOOR COVERING

Traditionally, all floor covering (such as rugs and ground cloth) was handled by the property department. In present-day theatre, however, with its greater emphasis on floor design, floor covering has become more and more a part of scenery (Figure 11–11). Many modern proscenium theatres have an increased seating gradient that allows the audience to see more of the floor; on the thrust and arena stage, the floor is an important part of the overall design. As a result, the modern designer must be conscious of the floor covering as a means of unifying the stage composition. A floor design might involve painting a ground cloth (although that is a rare occurence) or a built stage deck to simulate wood or mosaic, or creating a related hue to help anchor the design to the floor. Any stage setting on an unrelated or contrasting floor seems to float in space. When this occurs, it should be an intentional effect and not an accident of design.

A built-up or sloped stage floor will often be made of real materials, such as a planked floor that has the look and sound of wood. Such a floor can also be marbleized by using paint on a tempered masonite or particleboard to create the highly-polished surface of marble.

Latex and acrylic-based paints are durable enough to use on rigid surfaces, especially when they are later glazed with clear latex or acrylic. Such a surface can be damp-mopped and polished to perfection for each performance.

There are many examples of unusual floor coverings that go beyond conventional ground cloth or painted floor: the real dirt in *Tobacco Road,* for example, and the artificial snow in *Ethan Frome.* An unusual Spanish production of Aristophanes' *Lysistrata* comes to mind. The entire stage floor and scenery were covered with free-form overstuffed canvas, which obviously encouraged very unconventional movement.

**Figure 11–11**
Floor Covering

Close up of the ramped floor for a production of *Macbeth*. The wood frame and cover is textured with fiberglass. Designer—Albert Filoni. Photo by Filoni.

## FUNCTIONAL FLOOR COVERING

A stage floor may have to be covered for purely technical reasons. An entire stage, for example, may have to be built up to surround a turntable or to provide slots to guide wagon movements. Stage floors are also notorious for their poor condition, a situation that bothers dancers the most. To correct this, most ballet companies and dance groups prefer to cover an imperfect floor with one of several available vinyl coverings. Some dance companies even carry their own portable floor. D'Anser, the trademark name of a portable modular floor, is transported in 4-by-8-foot units. This floor is 3 inches thick, with offset wooden supports that allow for the "bounce" dancers want. The units connect with interlocking hardware and can cover the entire stage area. D'Anser was designed by Ronald Bates and Perry Silvey of the New York City Ballet.

## FABRICATING AND CASTING TECHNIQUES

Properties often require decorative details or bold relief at an exaggerated scale beyond that of conventional furniture. These and other forms (such as architectural details, costume armor plate, small properties, and various free forms) are often made in the shop to obtain the exact shape and dimension the designer seeks. The forms may be fabricated or cast from a real object or from the prepared mold of a three-dimensional shape. These same techniques can be used to adapt a "found" object.

## PAPIER-MÂCHÉ

The term *mâché work* has grown to include all techniques and materials used to mold or fake carved relief detail on furniture or scenery. The original papier-mâché technique used paper or paper pulp, which was either modeled directly on the surface or, in order to duplicate a large number, was fashioned from a plaster mold.

When modeling directly with papier-mâché, a porous paper is used, such as tissue, paper toweling, or newsprint. The paper, after being torn into convenient strips and dampened in water, is dipped into binder consisting of wheat paste and strong glue size. Any excess binder is lightly squeezed out of the now near-pulp mass, which is then applied to the furniture surface to be modeled into the desired shape. If the relief is high, some preliminary modeling can be done with wire screening, to which the mâché is applied as the final surface. The technique is very similar to that described in Chapter 5 for construction of large irregular shapes.

To duplicate identical forms, the same process can be applied to a greased positive or negative mold. In molding mâché there is a noticeable amount of shrinkage in the size of the final shape that has to be taken into consideration.

## CELASTIC

Because papier-mâché is fragile, a sturdier substance may often be needed. The industry standard for this kind of work used to be Celastic, a cheesecloth material impregnated with cellulose nitrate and a fire retardant. When softened in acetone, this rather stiff fabric becomes pliable and can be shaped or molded in a negative or positive mold. As the solvent evaporates, the Celastic hardens into the new shape (Figure 11–12). It is rarely used now because it requires the use of acetone, which is a highly volatile solvent (and one that sets off allergic reactions in many people). Acetone can also cause a serious rash if left on the skin. If absolutely no other product will work,

### Figure 11–12

#### Celastic

(a) Fabric is softened in special solvent.
(b) Softened fabric is draped over prepared understructure.
(c) Final form after Celastic has hardened.
(d) Celastic used in negative mold.
(e) Over a positive mold.
(f) Greek statuary. Celastic No. 411 (lightweight) over an armature, spray-enameled white, then antiqued. Statue and photo courtesy Jim Bakkom.

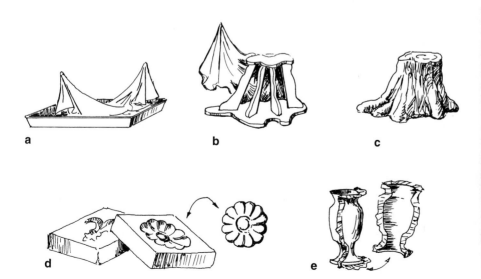

a          b          c

d          e

proper protection must be used—gloves and mask are the minimum—and work should only be done in a well-ventilated room.

There are several products on the market today that will serve just as well and are much safer. "Friendly Plastic" is one. This is a plastic that becomes pliable when immersed in hot water. It then can be molded any way desired.

### STYROFOAM

Architectural detail, sculptural pieces, and out-of-the-way dress props may often be fashioned out of Styrofoam. However, Styrofoam is fragile and its surface needs to be protected or hardened. Either a seal of flexible glue alone or cheesecloth adhered with glue will work, but one must still be careful. The user also needs to be aware of the high flammability of Styrofoam (and all other foams) and its property of releasing toxic gas when heat is applied.

### FIBERGLASS

Fiberglass is easily adaptable to three-dimensional details on scenery or properties. The technique, like the papier-mâché and Celastic procedures, shapes a fiberglass cloth over a positive form or into a negative mold after first coating the mold with a releasing agent. The pieces of fiberglass cloth are saturated and cemented together with a solution composed of a fabricating resin and a hardener. Because the hardener is the catalytic agent of the mixture, the amount present controls the degree of hardness of the final form. The proportion of resin to hardener is usually about 5:1 but, because the strength of these plastics may vary from dealer to dealer, any mixture should be tested for its finished hardness before beginning extensive fabrication. Acetone, which is the solvent for the plastics, is used to clean brushes.

There are many types and weights of fiberglass cloth. Woven glass cloth is available in light, medium, and heavy weights. The woven glass cloth is not suitable for making objects with opaque surfaces that are to be painted. The medium and heavy weight cloths work very well for making costume armor plate and helmets. The matted glass cloth is generally lightweight and quite translucent and is often used for fabricating shapes like lamp globes or similar translucent forms such as floor covering (see again, Figure 11–11).

Again, fiberglass is used only rarely in the theatre. Because of its expense, toxicity, and inherent danger (working with tiny pieces of glass fiber), extreme precautions must be taken. It should be used when no other product will work.

### BODY ARMOR AND MASK MAKING

Some of the mâché techniques can be applied to the making of full or partial masks, or, in some cases, to appear as decorative details on scenery. Figure 11–13 illustrates the designing and making of masks. In general there are three basic forming techniques for mask making: papier-mâché, Celastic, and

a

## Figure 11–13
## Mask-making Techniques

(a) An example of a full face mask and its negative mold. Ritual or larger decorative masks can be reproduced in quantity by using the vacuum forming technique if water clay is used in place of plasticine to make the mold. Designer—Pat Moser. (Below) Positive mold technique using Celastic.

(b) Plasticine clay original.

(c) Foil covering the clay mold as a parting agent.

(d) Softened Celastic strips applied to the mold. The hardened form is then cut off the mold and sealed together to complete the raw mask.

(e) Finished mask with a velour covering and applied hair. Designer—Louise Krozek.

b

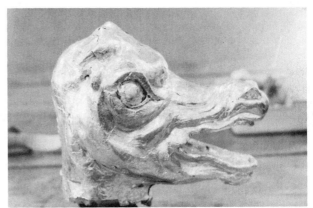

c

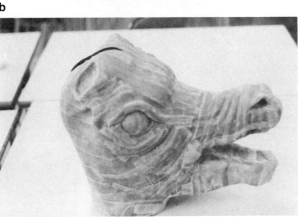

d

e

**Figure 11–14**
Properties and Armor

A few of the innumerable vacuum-formed articles for theatre
use from Tobin Lake Studios.
(Right) Prop telephone, architectural details, armor breastplate,
and other articles are shown in
various stages of assembly and
surface finish. (Below) Full armor
and shields vacuum-formed
from vinyl plastic sheets. The
swords in the display are made
of tempered steel.

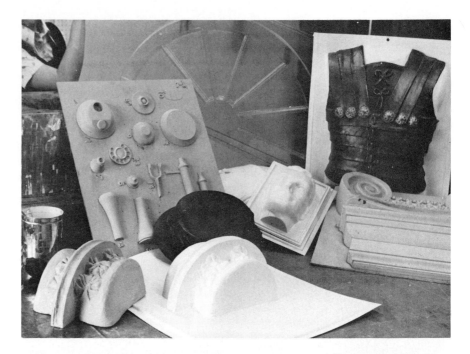

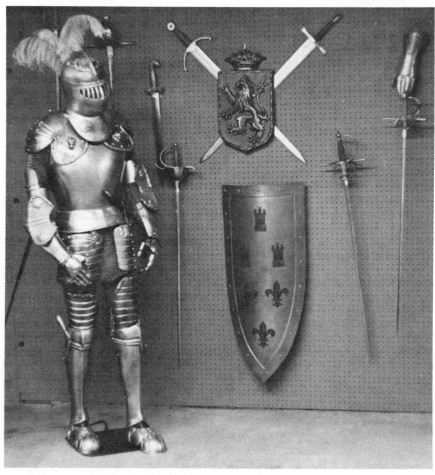

rubber latex. Fiberglass and thermal plastics lend themselves to the forming of body armor, such as breastplates and helmets (Figure 11–14).

## LAMINATED FELT

Another method for constructing small set or dress properties is the laminated-felt technique. It is a process that works best for hollow forms, such as vases, goblets, and body armor. It can also be used to make open filigree or oversized costume jewelry.

Working over a position form covered with aluminum foil to ensure its "parting," the shape is built up with laminated strips of felt coated with Elmer's or polyvinyl glue. Decorative detail is appliquéd in the same manner. Once the shape is hardened, it is painted with a glaze made up of shellac cut one-half with thinner. The glaze is applied in successive coats to build up a hard surface. Aniline dye may be added to the glaze to serve as an undercolor or as an antique effect if it is the final coat.

If the surface is to be metallic (to simulate silver, gold, or bronze) dry metallic powder is brushed into one of the glaze coats as highlights. A metallic surface developed in this manner has a very authentic look on the stage.

Felt can be kept flexible by using a flexible glue rather than Elmer's. A flexible glue made by Swift and Company, Adhesive Division, is a transparent polyvinyl that can, with dye staining, make felt look and feel like leather. The same flexible glue is also an excellent sealer for Styrofoam and Artfoam prior to painting.

## EFFECT PROPERTIES

Although some visual effects have become electrified, most are still produced mechanically. Smoke, fire, and flash explosions are usually electrically controlled; however, smoke also can be made nonelectrically by combining solid carbon dioxide (dry ice) and water.

Some familiar visual effects that are mechanical are the snow cradle and rain pipes, which are shown in Figure 11–15, along with other special effects that call on the ingenuity of the stage technician and property person to rig and trigger on cue.

## BREAKAWAYS

Many times pieces of furniture, dishes, or other objects have to break onstage. The chairs that collapse and the flagpole that falls down in *Cockadoodle Dandy*, or a railing that breaks during a fight scene are a few examples of properties or scenery breaking on cue and in a predetermined manner.

In Figure 11–16, a railing breakaway is prebroken and lightly glued together. Thin strips of wood are tacked to the back of the repair to give a convincing splintering sound as the railing breaks again. The pattern of the break is carefully planned in order to control the fall of the pieces in the same manner for each performance.

**Figure 11–15**
Visual Effects

(a) Snow cradle.
(b) Rain pipe.
(c) Water reflection.

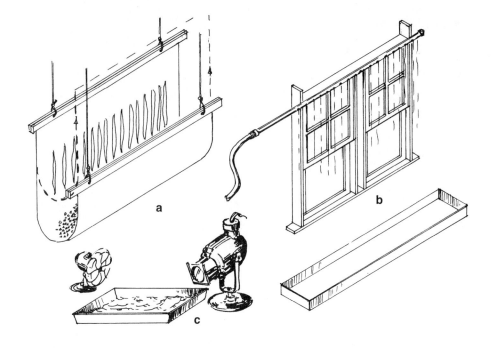

**Figure 11–16**
Breakaway Railing

(a) Railing prepared for breaking:
   (1) Prebroken spots, lightly glued.
   (2) Loose spindles, lightly glued.
(b) Railing after breaking:
   (1) Prepared hinge points.

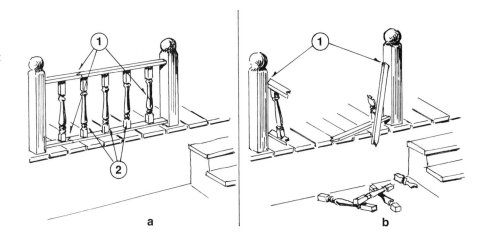

**Breakaway Windowpanes and Mirrors** Breaking real glass onstage is dangerous and is to be avoided! Flying glass and broken glass left on the floor can be a hazard. If an actor must be close to breaking glass, it is always desirable to use other materials. One familiar substitute used often in the motion picture industry is candy glass. Candy glass, or hardened sugar and water, is prepared like old-fashioned rock candy. After a supersaturated solution of sugar and water is brought to about 260 degrees Fahrenheit, it is poured on a smooth surface into a thin sheet. The sheet hardens into a clear, transparent solid. Candy glass, however, has a low melting point and may soften under stage lights or excessive handling. There are now also plastic resins that can be used.

**Pottery Breakaways**     Opaque shapes such as teacups, dishes, or small objects of art are much easier to make into breakaways. Because they are not transparent, inexpensive pottery or china pieces may be prebroken and lightly glued together again to ensure their breaking onstage. As the second breaking usually shatters the piece beyond reclaiming, a breakaway should be prepared for each preformance.

If the authenticity, both in sound and looks, of the breakaway object is extremely important to the play, a replica can be made by slipcasting. A clay slip or solution of powdered water clay and water is poured into a mold of the object and, after setting a few minutes, is poured out. A thin shell of clay adheres to the mold, making a hollow casting of the object. After drying thoroughly (48 hours) the raw-clay casting is fired in a ceramic kiln to bisque hardness. A great number can be prepared this way.

## FOLIAGE

Artificial flowers and the foliage of hedges, bush pieces, and small trees are considered properties, as are live flowers, potted plants, and sprays of real leaves used to dress the setting. The expression *prop bush* means that the bush is not real, but also implies that it is shaped in three dimensions, as opposed to a flat, painted set piece.

Lifelike artificial flowers can be obtained easily from display houses, local variety stores, or the home decoration section of a department store. (Although they are more expensive than real flowers, with proper care they can be used over again.)

Stylized or caricatured blossoms have to be specially made. Their scale and design determine the material used. Exotic tropical flowers in a musical comedy, for example, have been made of velveteen or satin, with leaves made of wire loops covered with sheer chiffon.

Banks of blossoms and box hedges can be made of shaped 1-inch mesh chicken wire with ruffle-edged colored crepe paper or silk pushed into the

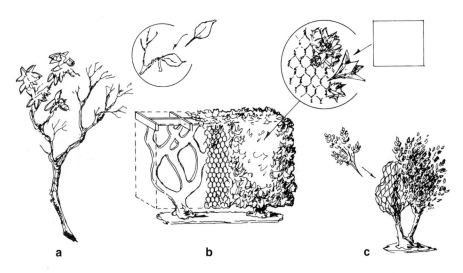

a               b               c

**Figure 11–17**
Foliage

(a) Artificial leaves wired or taped to real tree branches or section.
(b) Trimmed boxwood hedge made of frame covered with inch-mesh chicken wire. Crepe-paper or fabric squares are pushed into openings (color is more convincing if two or three shades of green are used).
(c) Untrimmed box or ilex bush; chicken wire shaped over basic frame and filled with sprays of artificial boxwood or ilex.

openings. A more realistic box hedge can be made of chicken wire holding sprays of artificial boxwood or ilex leaves (Figure 11–17). Large-mesh chicken wire can be used to support clumps of leaves on a tree branch, or as a hanging border related to a tree trunk. The leaf material, which can be either paper or fabric, should have sufficient stiffness to hold a leaflike shape, or it will have to be stiffened with wire. Window-shade stock, which comes in several shades of green, makes a good leaf fabric to staple onto a branch or chicken-wire frame.

## SOUND EFFECTS

There was a time in theatre history when visual and sound effects were the major concern of the property department. Before the advent of high-fidelity

**Figure 11–18**
**Mechanical Sound Effects**

(a) Wind machine.
(b) Rain, shot in rotating drum.
(c) Rain, shot in tray with wire-screen bottom.
(d) Thunder sheet.
(e) Rumble cart.
(f) Falling rubble after an explosion.
(g) Wood crash.
(h) Gun shots.
(i) Slap stick.
(j) Horses' hoofs.

recording, many sound effects were created mechanically by the property person. Most of these old machines are now gathering dust in the property room.

An adequate sound system can bring any effect to the audience with a truer quality and a more sensitive control than any mechanical sound effect. There is one possible exception: the effect of offstage gunfire. The recordings of distant battle scenes are fairly convincing, but close rifle or revolver shots are better when a starter's gun with blank cartridges is fired backstage. More and more, it is getting difficult to find firearms that can be used on the stage. Each state, and some cities, has very strict laws requiring permits for even a starter pistol or a gun that will shoot only blanks. Although generally harmless when used properly, they can pose a real danger. It is necessary to check with the local police to determine what the local laws are and how a prop gun can be legally obtained.

More as historical record than as modern practice, Figure 11–18 shows some of the mechanical sound effects that are a part of the property department. Directors, on occasion, have requested old mechanical sound effects for their theatrical quality rather than having the movielike realism of electronic sound.

# PART III

# STAGE LIGHTING AND SOUND

# DESIGNING THE SOUND 12

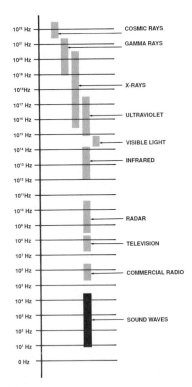

**Figure 12–1**
**The Electromagnetic Spectrum**

The normal range of human hearing is generally considered to be between 20 and 20,000 hertz (cycles per second).

**S**ound is the most recent element to become a member of the theatrical design team. Not so many years ago, theatre sound was primarily comprised of mechanical effects supervised by the properties department, while things requiring electricity, such as bells and buzzers, were relegated to the lighting and electrics department. With the advent of high-fidelity recording and playback equipment in the 1960s, sound reproduction became a practical theatre tool. The next decade brought about more sophisticated equipment for recording and playback. The synthesizer, a revolutionary electronic keyboard developed by Robert Moog, could reproduce a multitude of musical sounds. Digital technology followed with compact discs, DAT (digital audio tape) recorders, sampling, CD-ROM discs, hard disk recording, and digital audio workstations. Today we find ourselves in the midst of a technological audio revolution that is destined to reshape the way we think about and use sound in the theatre. So much potential and opportunity makes it an exciting time for theatrical sound designers. Design collaboration now involves another powerful element—not visual, but auditory.

## FUNDAMENTALS OF SOUND

Whether it be familiar music and talk from a radio station, the environmental sounds of an afternoon spent in the park, or background chatter from an unwatched television, we are surrounded by sound. Our brain has the capacity to focus on a particular sound or reject all in order to concentrate on something else. Music affects us emotionally. It can heighten or relieve tension. And, due to its temporal nature, music has the power to alter our perception of time. The responsibility of the theatrical sound designer is to manipulate sound in such a way as to enhance the effect of dramatic action.

## THE PHENOMENON OF SOUND

We are most familiar with sound as air waves or vibrations existing within a certain range of wavelengths of the electromagnetic spectrum (Figure 12–1). However, nearly all of us have experienced hearing under water, an occurrence that illustrates the fact that sound moves more or less easily through nearly all materials. In fact, sound moves very slowly through air compared to most other mediums—only about 1,130 feet per second under usual conditions of altitude, humidity, and temperature (approximately 1 foot per millisecond). Sound cannot travel through a vacuum due to the fact that nothing exists from which waves can be created.

Sound can be thought of as pressure waves moving in all directions from the source. As the sound waves move, they diminish in height (loudness or *amplitude*), but the wavelength itself (*frequency*) does not change (Figure 12–2). Sound bounces off some hard surfaces with little absorption; and, if this reflection happens several times before being absorbed, *reverberation* occurs. Finally, the sound may reach a receptor, like our ears.

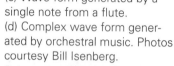

## Figure 12–2
### Various Sound Waves

These four photographs are from an oscilloscope display of various sound waves.
(a) A simple sine wave.
(b) A sine wave illustrating higher frequency with equal amplitude.
(c) Wave form generated by a single note from a flute.
(d) Complex wave form generated by orchestral music. Photos courtesy Bill Isenberg.

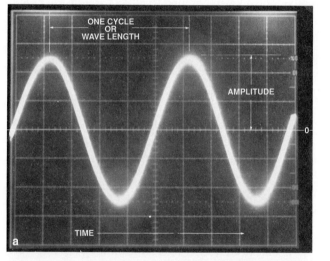

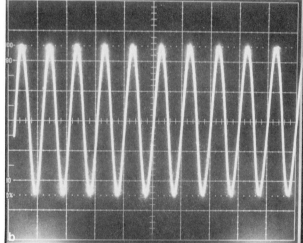

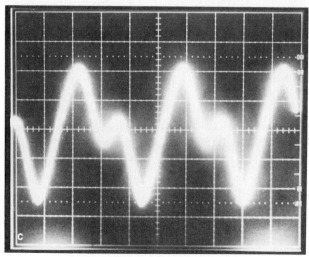

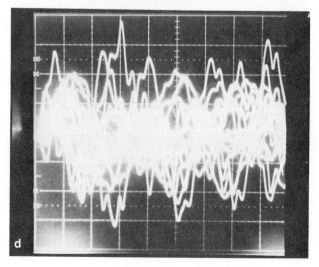

Figure 12–3
The Human Ear

Sound is gathered by the outer ear or pinna and directed down the ear canal to the ear drum or tympanum. Virbrations of the ear drum are conveyed through the hammer, anvil, and stirrup (the ossicles) of the middle ear to the fluid-filled inner ear or cochlea. Here tiny hair cells stimulated by traveling waves send nerve impulses to the brain via the auditory nerve.

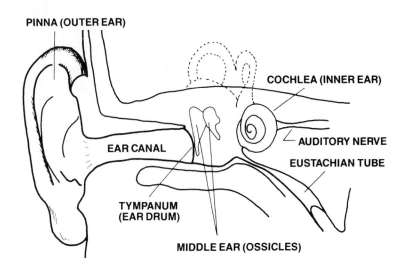

**The Ear**     As can be seen in Figure 12–3, the ear is made up of several parts. The *pinna,* or outer ear, acts like an antenna to collect sound waves and direct them into the *ear canal.* The pinna is also instrumental in the location of sound direction. The ear canal terminates at the *tympanum,* or ear drum, which vibrates in reaction to the sound waves. The middle ear contains three tiny bones that take up and intensify the vibrations. The fluid-containing *cochlea,* or inner ear, houses the many nerve endings that receive pressure from the vibrations. Responding to the pressure, these nerves send electrochemical signals to the brain for interpretation. Much important input concerning loudness and frequency is gathered in the spiral tube we call the cochlea; however, it is the brain that has the primary power of selectivity and analysis.

**MEASURING SOUND**

In order to describe a certain sound we must have a technical vocabulary that defines the components specifically enough to be meaningful. While very few sounds are made up of a single frequency, they all can be broken down into their various component frequencies and amplitudes.

**Frequency**     The length of a sound wave is defined according to its *frequency* in time and is measured in cycles per second or *hertz* (Hz). There is a direct relationship between *pitch* and frequency: The high-pitched sounds from a flute have high frequencies; the low-pitched sounds from a cello have low frequencies. Frequency is the prime means we have for discerning one sound from another. The normal human ear can hear frequencies from 20 Hz to 20,000 Hz (these frequencies represent wavelengths from approximately 56 feet to $\frac{2}{3}$ inch long!). Figure 12–4 shows some common frequency ranges.

**Amplitude**     The height of a sound wave is called its *amplitude,* which is synonymous with the volume or intensity of sound. The most common meas-

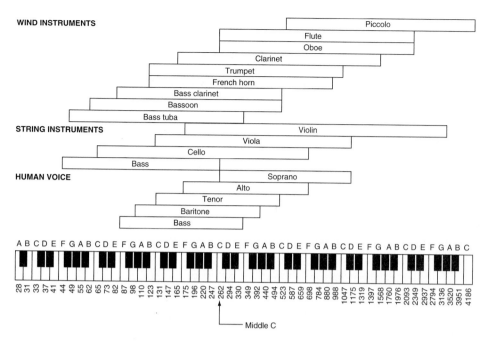

**FREQUENCY IN CYCLES PER SECOND (HZ)**

## Figure 12–4
### Frequency Ranges

A comparison of some common sounds and their frequency ranges.

ure of amplitude is the *decibel* (dB), with 1 dB being the smallest difference that can be distinguished by the normal human ear. The decibel measurement is not on a linear scale, however; it is technically a ratio of two intensities. Further information on decibel levels will be found in the next chapter.

The following are important terms and concepts concerning the volume of sound. *Sound pressure level* (SPL) is a standard measurement of loudness that uses decibel values (Figure 12–5). *Threshold of hearing* refers to the quietest sound we can hear, or 0 dB SPL. The *dynamic range* of a sound is the difference between its smallest and greatest sound pressure levels. Finally, it is important to remember that sound intensity drops off by the square of the distance from the source (*inverse square law*).

**Timbre and Harmonics**     As stated earlier, very few sounds are pure (containing a single frequency and amplitude). Most sound is made up of a combination of frequencies and amplitudes, perceived as a single sound. The relationship between the various frequencies and amplitudes determines the quality, or *timbre*, of the sound. Timbre is the distinction in sound between two different musical instruments playing an identical note at the same volume. A determining factor in timbre is *harmonics*, a musical term for frequencies that are multiples of a primary or fundamental frequency. Harmonics are present in all complex sounds.

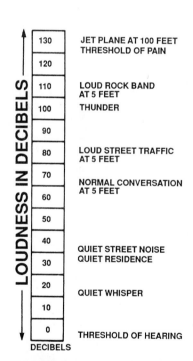

## Figure 12–5
### Sound Pressure Levels (Loudness)

A sound pressure level (SPL) chart illustrating various common sounds with their loudness measured in decibels (dB).

## PERCEPTION

Sound and vision are the tools we use to recognize our surroundings. Vision is unidirectional, while sound perception is omnidirectional. The two work together to determine our environmental sensitivity. By a process of triangulation, our two ears give us the ability to generally locate the sound of a bird chirping. We then look in the direction of the sound to discover more detailed information. Because of the placement of our ears, locating a sound on the horizontal axis is easier than doing so vertically.

The theatrical sound designer must be acquainted with additional principles of sound perception concerned with distance, loudness, masking, recognition, and reverberation.

**Distance**    The inverse square law tells us that the loudness of a sound decreases significantly over distance. In addition, air absorbs sound energy. The higher the frequency, the more absorption takes place. As a result, distant sound is not only perceived as softer, it is also lacking in higher frequencies.

**Loudness**    An important feature of loudness was verified by two men named Fletcher and Munsen while working for Bell Laboratories. They experimented with the perceived loudness of sound frequencies over varying sound pressure levels. It was discovered that the frequencies we hear best are between 2,000 and 4,000 Hz, and that this apparent midrange acuity becomes more pronounced as loudness decreases. Consequently, distant and quiet sounds are perceived as having limited dynamic range. Lower and higher frequencies are not heard as well. Our brain's most accurate indication of the distance of a sound is through frequency identification.

**Masking**    The phenomenon of *masking* occurs when one sound or event demands our attention to such a degree as to negate other sounds or events. The theatrical sound designer must realize that a sound is too obvious the moment it unintentionally takes dramatic focus.

It has been discovered that if all else is equal, low frequencies will mask higher frequencies. This is significant especially when a designer considers the sound to be used in *underscoring* (playing music under dialogue). Masking occurs if the underscoring frequencies are lower than those of the dramatic dialogue.

**Recognition**    It has been pointed out that decreasing the amplitude of a sound does not by itself give the sound a sense of distance. Likewise, merely increasing the amplitude will not necessarily allow us to hear better. *Recognition* of a sound is dependent on the interaction of its duration, familiarity, and volume. A sound must last long enough to be understood. Familiar sounds are more easily recognized. And, to a point, a louder sound is more readily perceived. All three of these factors must be taken into account by the designer when making sound choices.

**Reverberation**    Creating a prolongational effect by the reflection of sound waves is known as *reverberation*. A primary source of environmental recognition is the relationship of reflected sound to direct sound. For instance, if the delay between direct sound and reflected sound is great, our environment is felt to be cavernous. A sound is perceived as "rich" if it contains a certain degree of reverberation; it is dull or flat if it doesn't. The sound designer can manipulate the mood of a sound or a piece of music through frequency as well as reverberation control.

## ACOUSTICS

Acoustical measurements of a room or a theatre refer to how that specific space responds to sound. While the study of acoustics is a subject of its own, there are several factors that are of such significance to the sound technician and designer that they shall be discussed here.

**Acoustical Reverberation**    A major element in acoustical study, reverberation must be controlled in order for sound to be heard well. Too little reverberation makes a room sound "dead," lacking in richness and fullness; too much causes complete lack of intelligibility. The key to good sound parallels the reflective qualities of a room; however, the matter is complicated by the fact that ideal reverberation time for speech is not the same as for music. Between .8 and 1.4 seconds of reverberation time is preferable for the speaking voice. Musical instruments require more time for their sounds to blend well—from 4 to 5 seconds.

**Reflective Surfaces**    Because sound emanates in all directions from a source, it is reflected by a number of different surfaces in the typical theatre. Scenery on stage, as well as the walls, floor, and ceiling of the auditorium, all reflect sound. If the side walls of an auditorium are parallel to each other, sound is bounced back and forth between them, creating reverberation that may destroy intelligibility. A hard flat ceiling can act as a valuable sound reflector, but a convex ceiling serves better because it disperses the sound more evenly (Figure 12–6).

In order to control reverberation, acousticians treat walls and ceilings with absorptive materials. They carefully design the shape and interrelationship of walls and the ceiling and pay close attention to the rake (slope) of audience seating, the seats themselves, and floor treatment. Larger multipurpose auditoriums are built with adjustable ceilings and side walls that either increase or decrease reverberation time in order to accommodate both speech and musical instruments.

## SOUND IN THE THEATRE

In addition to the performer's natural voice, sound in the theatre can be divided into four functional categories: (1) reinforcement, (2) live music, (3) communications, and (4) production design/playback.

**Figure 12–6**
Sound Distribution

These drawings illustrate how building architecture can affect the distribution of sound. Not only does this apply to ceilings, but to side and back walls as well as the floor. As indicated, concave reflectors focus the sound and can cause echo.

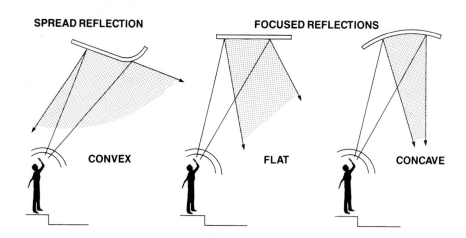

SPREAD REFLECTION    FOCUSED REFLECTIONS

CONVEX            FLAT            CONCAVE

## REINFORCEMENT

Perhaps the most difficult of sound tasks, reinforcement is the process of amplification and/or processing of any live sound. In the theatre such sounds are most often, but not restricted to, a performer's voice or a musical instrument. What makes this endeavor difficult is the usual desire to maintain as natural a quality as possible. Reinforcement is typically necessitated by either poor acoustics or the desire to balance two or more sounds. Balancing an orchestra and a singing voice, for instance, is a common necessity in today's musical theatre.

**Amplification**    We determine the source direction of a sound by distinguishing either the sound heard first or the loudest of several sounds. Reinforcement requires the use of microphones and speakers, which introduces the problem of timing when the sound will reach an audience member. If live sound arrives slightly before reproduced sound, the audience will recognize the live sound as the source. However, in large auditoriums or in situations where speakers are closer to the audience than performers, the sense of source direction is distorted. Sound sent electronically to a speaker moves significantly faster than live sound travels through the air and therefore must be delayed. Digital delay processing allows reinforcement systems to maintain the apparent source onstage.

In addition to the need for delay of amplified sound, the requirements of a reinforcement system for the musical theatre will most likely change for each and every production. The design of such systems involves speaker selection and placement, microphone selection and placement, and a sophisticated mixing control console that must be located in the auditorium. The mixing console operator must hear what the audience hears.

A final reinforcement concern is that of amplification not *of* the performer, but *for* the performer. Such an arrangement is called a *foldback system*. It consists of speakers that allow performers to better hear recorded or live music as well as themselves. Individually controlled speakers, called either foldback or monitor speakers, are located backstage so as to direct their sound to the performers.

**Sound Processing**     The act of treating sound with electronic equipment in order to change its quality is called sound processing. Extremely valuable in both production design and reinforcement, processing involves routing the sound through equipment such as a *digital effects processor* or an *equalizer* (Figure 12–7). Although certainly a matter of opinion, both the female and male voice, as well as most musical instruments, can benefit from proper and judicial equalization—a process of electronically boosting or cutting selected frequencies. Due to the nature of their particular acoustics, many auditoriums require equalization in order to control undesirable resonant frequencies. An equalizer will often be found as an integral part of the reinforcement system.

### LIVE MUSIC

While live music in the theatre is certainly not limited to the musical theatre orchestra, electronic sound requirements tend to be most elaborate when contending with a full orchestra. The live orchestra is an important part of the magic and attraction of musical theatre, an art form having its roots in the theatre of the United States. There are occasions when the live musical requires no electronic treatment of sound at all, but these tend to be the exception rather than the rule.

**The Orchestra**     Traditionally found in a pit located at the front of the stage, the musical theatre orchestra of today may just as likely be found backstage behind a scrim, or on a side stage, or even on the stage itself. Such changes have been brought about by the healthy desire to break with the traditional structure of the American musical, as well as an increased interest in stages other than the proscenium. However, moving the orchestra is often fraught with numerous problems including sound. Individual musical instruments, instrumental sections, or even the entire orchestra may need to be

a

b
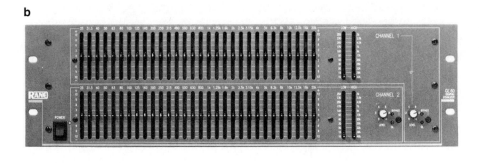

### Figure 12–7
Processing Equipment

(a) A Yamaha SPX990 digital multi-effects processor that allows for a wide selection of pre-set effects including delay, echo, and reverb, along with multiple programmable effects. Photo courtesy Yamaha Corporation.
(b) A $\frac{1}{3}$ octave stereo Rane GE60 graphic equalizer that breaks the full frequency range into 30 separate controllable sections per channel. Photo courtesy Rane Corporation.

covered by microphones in order to provide sound that is properly balanced with that of the performers. Even a small orchestra requires a great deal of physical space that must include room for music stands and lights, details that might fall under the auspices of the sound department.

**The Conductor**     An orchestra's conductor usually has no special sound requirements with the possible exception of necessary communications (discussed below). However, the conductor must be able to see the stage and the orchestra; and the performers must be able to see the conductor. These seemingly obvious details can require extensive treatment, often demanding closed-circuit television. A single camera set up to cover the stage can suffice for the conductor equipped with a small video monitor. A second camera focused on the conductor, along with several large monitors situated about the stage or on a balcony rail, may be necessary to enable the performers to see the baton. If this is the case, sufficient light must be provided on the conductor to accommodate a television signal.

### AUDIO COMMUNICATIONS

The necessity for a number of people scattered all over a theatre to be in constant touch with the stage manager and each other during a performance requires a flexible and reliable system of audio communication. Usually such a system is built into the theatre. If this is not the case, a portable system is necessary, and the sound technician may have to attend to such details. Headsets are the most common and useful system, and several companies manufacture a sturdy and reliable product (Figure 12–8).

There are certain locations in the theatre that are best served by speaker stations as well as headsets. These include the fly rail and loading dock where stagehands cannot wear headsets, and perhaps soundproof booths such as the lighting control booth.

**Figure 12–8**
Headset System

Shown are a single and double earphone headset, belt pack, and the CS222 main power station manufactured by Clear-Com. Photo courtesy Clear-Com Intercom Systems.

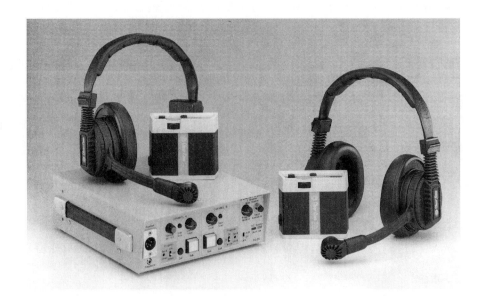

## HEADSET SUGGESTIONS

1. A system with more than one channel is often very useful, sometimes imperative.
2. Use headsets with one earphone rather than two, so that live sound can be heard also (an exception might be in high-volume sound situations such as rock concerts.)
3. Always have working spare headsets and the belt packs that power them available and readily accessible.
4. Treat headsets with the care and respect they deserve—they are fragile instruments.
5. Know what to do if headsets fail—have a backup system.

## PRODUCTION SOUND DESIGN

Design of music and audio effects for theatrical production is certainly the most creative and perhaps the most important function of sound in the theatre. Such design requires that a person have a strong background in general theatrical production, a good knowledge of sound equipment, as well as an interest in and familiarity with music and sound. In addition, music composition skills are a big plus. The manner in which sound design may contribute to theatrical production can be broken down into three categories:

*Evoking* a specific atmosphere or mood

*Reinforcing* the action of the play

*Commenting* on the action of the play

**Evoking Atmosphere or Mood**     The most familiar way sound can evoke a specific atmosphere or mood is by using environmental sounds in a realistic manner. Examples are abundant: the bright chirping of birds for a cheerful morning scene, the ominous rolls of thunder preceding a storm, or the sad notes of waltz music coming from a nearby dance hall. While it must be handled with some degree of caution, realistically motivated sound is one of the easiest to use due to an audience's inclination to readily accept such sound.

Nonrealistic or unmotivated (lacking any apparent source) sound created by the designer for a specific effect can also be used to evoke a feeling of atmosphere or mood. *Musical underscoring*, the process of playing music or sound effects under a performer's dialogue, is a good example. Such usage is more difficult for an audience to accept, but can be extremely effective. A subtle touch is recommended.

A designer must never forget the power of silence! The artful process of establishing an atmospheric sound, such as crickets chirping, and suddenly cutting off the sound can be more dynamic and effective than any other device.

Further examples of the use of atmospheric sound are pre- and post-show incidental music, as well as musical "punctuations." Punctuation effects are most often used for entrances or exits of characters or at the end of scenes. They may be realistic, such as a clap of thunder; or stylistic, such as musical fanfares; or frankly presentational, such as the abstract grinding of stones together upon each entrance of a particular character as a leitmotif. Once again, subtlety should be the watchword.

**Reinforcing the Action**     Using sound in a realistic manner to reinforce the action of a play helps to keep the audience informed of current or upcoming events. Sound coming from a television just switched on is an example, as is the ringing of a telephone or the sound of an approaching delivery truck. Such sounds are not chosen arbitrarily, for the designer must remain faithful to the period and style of the production. And, even though the sound is primarily reinforcing the action of the play, there is often room for comment: The sound from the television may have a sharp and nagging tone; the telephone ring may be insistent; or the delivery truck's parcel may be urgent. These sounds usually fall into the category of effects. In addition, offstage voices or "voice-over" effects might be used to reinforce a central action.

**Commenting on the Action**     The designer can comment on an action by using sound in a more symbolic manner. Such usage may or may not be motivated, and a wide variety of approaches might be taken. For example, a tympani roll on the entrance of a character might be either comic or sinister depending on its treatment; and comic music playing under a very straight and serious scene will certainly affect the audience's reaction to the scene. In every case, however, the designer must be extremely sensitive to the stylistic approach of the production and be sure that the sound is in every way appropriate to that style.

## ELEMENTS OF SOUND DESIGN

The tools with which the designer works are the building blocks of any sound design. Choices are made based on the script and the production concept as arrived at by the design team. At the designer's command are the following elements: music (live or recorded), sound effects (live or recorded), synthetic or processed sound, and speaker placement.

### MUSIC

Most of today's productions use either live or recorded music to enhance the performance.

**Incidental Music**     Pre-show music may be played as an audience enters the theatre. Selection of this *incidental* music is never left to chance, for the designer would be wasting a great opportunity to put audience members in the proper frame of mind for the upcoming performance. Pre-show music can establish the period of the ensuing production, comment on the action that is about to take place, or give the audience a hint as to the style of the production. In addition, a special type of sound (electronic music, for instance) specifically selected by the designer for the production can be introduced at this time in order to acclimate the audience to the sound.

In making selections from existing music, the designer must proceed with great caution. Music carries with it associative memories that stick with people for a very long time—sometimes, if it is a strong enough association, all their lives. The *William Tell Overture* (used as theme of "The Lone Ranger"), *Also Sprach Zarathustra* (used in 2001), and the much-played *1812 Overture* are just a few examples of music selections that obviously would have to be used with great care. Most designers like to work with original music in order to avoid the possibility of such associations. Using a composer is highly recommended in situations where music is intended to play a major emotive role in the production.

**Change Music**   Music accompanying a well-choreographed scene change can make pleasurable a potentially painful experience. Yet, music used solely for covering changes and nowhere else in the production may appear obvious and out of place. Of course, so-called *change music* must be as carefully selected as any other. The designer may select the music to be reflective of the scene just past or perhaps set the tone for that yet to come. Always remember to allow for greatly varying scene change lengths from performance to performance.

**Underscoring**   As mentioned earlier, the powerful technique of *underscoring* involves playing music or other sounds during character dialogue. It is perhaps the trickiest of ways to use music in a production. The danger lies in competing with the spoken word to the extent of distraction or masking. In addition, the technique itself, which is used more favorably in television and film production, has the potential of becoming obvious and ridiculous. The camera focuses attention of an audience to a much greater degree than in the theatre, where the normal field of focus is considerably broader. Therefore, underscoring, while not to be avoided, must be approached with great care and consideration by the designer. Many stage directors may at first find underscoring distracting to the point of being unacceptable as a technique. However, it can be used effectively if the sound designer introduces the music at low levels using limited dynamic range, and remembers the principles of masking.

**Effect Music**   When music is necessitated as an *effect* (motivated by a phonograph playing, a radio, a piano in the sitting room, an orchestra, or a jazz combo across the street), selections require careful attention as to their appropriateness. Not only is style and period important, but being true to the *source* of the music is critical. A live jazz combo onstage will have a great deal of dynamic range, sounding very different from that same combo heard on the radio or even across the street.

## SOUND EFFECTS

While it is possible that any use of sound in a stage production could be labeled an effect, it is convenient to consider most music and processed sound as separate from effects. Sound effects may be found prerecorded, they can be self-recorded, or they may be created. Sources of sound effects are only as limited as the designer's imagination.

**Prerecorded Sound**     Prerecorded sound can be found on records, tapes, or compact discs. Several of the better sound effect libraries from which prerecorded effects may be purchased include the following:

> *BBC Sound Effects Library*—forty CDs (four sets of ten) grouped into general categories; reasonably priced
>
> *Dimension Sound Effects*—a smaller collection of ten CDs
>
> *Hollywood Edge Sound Effects Library*—twenty CDs
>
> *Network Sound Effects*—more than fifty CDs; computer index available
>
> *Sound Ideas*—more than eighty CDs broken down into five series, including the Lucasfilm library
>
> *Valentino Sound Effects Library*—more than thirty-five CDs available in groups of ten

Various small collections can be found at record stores and, while quality varies, they are the least expensive. Although the purchase of an effects library is a significant investment, the ready availability of effects is an absolute necessity for even the modest production studio. While synthesizers and samplers have elevated sound production to new heights, they have yet to reduce the value of an effects library. When investing in a library, remember that compact discs are far superior to alternative storage media.

Other sources of prerecorded effects might be local radio stations or a professional recording studio, where both the quality and cost will be high. Become familiar with the studio nearest you; its personnel are usually audio experts and can be of great assistance.

**Self-Recorded Sound**     Recording sound yourself, from either environmental sources, musical instruments, or the human voice, constitutes the second category of sound effects. Recording on location can be fraught with problems that range from special equipment demands to the need for sound isolation. While not to be totally avoided, this technique of sound gathering should never be left to the last moment, and a backup plan is advisable. Studio work is much safer, and a wide range of recordings can be accomplished in a well-equipped studio space.

In an effort to keep unwanted noise at a minimum, live recording is often done with a microphone placed close to the sound source. In doing so, attention must be paid to a phenomenon known as *proximity effect*. Due to the fact that various frequencies can differ greatly in wavelength, a directional microphone placed less than two feet away from a source will exhibit an increase in low-frequency response. The results can be balanced by using an equalizer.

**Figure 12–9**
Digital Audio Workstation

Shown is a digital audio production system manufactured by Digidesign. It is a Macintosh-based system for recording directly to a hard disk. It allows visual editing of wave forms and playback of multiple tracks. Photo courtesy Digidesign Inc.

In addition, close-up recording accentuates sounds which otherwise would be indistinguishable. A good example of this effect is the squeak of a guitar string as the musician's finger moves. Such sounds are nearly impossible to process out of a finished recording. Special consideration must be given to this problem by the recording engineer.

**Created Effects**     Created effects are by far the most interesting and offer the most potential for exciting design results. Found objects such as pieces of metal, noise-making machines, and everyday things such as squeaky screen door hinges all have possibilities for interesting effects. Investigate objects made up of as many different materials as possible (tin interacting with fiberglass, metal tubes striking glass, for example) and imagine how each sound might be used—keep a written record of your findings.

The possibilities for creating sound by using samplers and digital audio workstations are endless (Figure 12–9). A sound can be recorded into a sampler and then electronically treated. Digital audio workstations have tremendous capabilities for editing sound—without tape!

## SYNTHETIC AND PROCESSED SOUND

Some of the greatest potential for creating exciting music and effects falls under the categories of synthetic and processed sound. Production and manipulation of sound as a design tool has been made possible by technological advances resulting in equipment such as *synthesizers, samplers,* and *digital effects processors* (Figure 12–10).

**Synthetic Sound**     The most common type of *synthesizer* comes in the form of an electronic keyboard that has the ability to simulate an array of sounds, including those of various musical instruments. They are available in a variety of types and price ranges, one type being primarily intended for performance and another for production. Due to the fact that a basic analog synthesizer is made up of a number of components such as sound oscillators, amplifiers, and filters, it can be used to process as well as produce sound. *Digital synthesizers,* currently the most sophisticated and versatile type available, can also have the capability of sampling sound.

*Sampling keyboards* closely resemble synthesizers and have many of the same functions. Additionally, they are able to receive and store audio data in digital form. After the sound is converted to digital data it can be manipulated in any manner, combined with other sound or sounds, and played back with no loss in quality. Possibilities are endless as the sound designer learns to use this equipment to produce and/or alter sound to fit the mood or style of a production.

*Samplers* have the potential to record, store, and manipulate sound without the addition of a keyboard. Sampling capacity is currently limited by the amount of memory and storage available. As RAM and large-capacity hard disks become less expensive, the sampler or some variation of it will likely take the place of tape recorders in theatre production.

**MIDI**    A further advantage of digital technology is the ability to interface between different pieces of equipment. However, in order for this to be possible, various manufacturers had to agree on a common digital "language." *Musical Instrument Digital Interface,* or MIDI, was born out of this need. MIDI is the accepted standard protocol for digital communication between one component and another. As the name implies, MIDI was originally developed for musical instruments, but today is experiencing a much broader application. *MIDI Show Control* involves computers with MIDI ports "speaking" to lighting control consoles, sound systems, and automation devices.

**Processed Sound**    Samplers, as well as equipment with more specific functions such as the *digital effect processor,* offer ways to alter sound in order to create a particular effect.

One of the most popular is *speed distortion:* the process of speeding up or slowing down a recorded sound in order to change its quality. As a sound is

**Figure 12–10**
Synthesizer

Shown is the Yamaha VL1 Virtual Acoustic Synthesizer. It uses a computer model or "algorithm" instead of oscillators and function generators to recreate an instrument "virtually" within the synthesizer. Photo courtesy Yamaha Corporation.

slowed, its pitch is lowered, resulting in a "bigger" sound; for instance, a small engine can be made to sound like a huge turbine by slowing the playback speed. This has always been the primary reason for a variable-speed tape machine in the sound studio.

Other valuable techniques are mixing *sound on sound;* playing back in the *reverse direction; filtering* using an equalizer; adding *echo* or *reverberation;* and *pitch shifting* (altering frequency). Sound-on-sound mixing through the use of a sampler or a multitrack tape machine can be very subtle, just adding a "richness" to the sound; or its effect can be quite abstract and bold. Using an equalizer to filter sound can reduce or eliminate low frequencies, allowing a piece of music to better perform as underscoring. It can add as well as subtract hiss and noise in a recording, and subtly adjust the quality of a music selection or sound by attenuating (turning down) or boosting certain frequencies. The last three techniques (echo, reverberation, and pitch shifting) can all be achieved with a sampler or the use of specialized equipment such as a *digital reverb unit.*

## SPEAKER PLACEMENT

The final tool available to the sound designer is control over how the sound will reach the audience. While the selection of speaker type (discussed in the next chapter) has a significant effect on a sound's quality, the placement of speakers is of primary concern to the sound designer. It is important to remember that the location of our ears gives us greater horizontal (as opposed to vertical) sensitivity to the direction of a sound source. Therefore, principles of sound *reinforcement* state that speakers should be located above the stage in order to maintain a proper directional sense of the performer. This is a good rule to remember but may not always apply to performance music and sound effects.

For effects that have a distinct source (for example, a gutted radio prop located onstage), the speaker should be located inside or as close as possible to the object. Speakers come in a variety of sizes, and good sound is being reproduced from some very small speakers these days—so do not hesitate to locate the speaker right onstage if possible. Distant effects can often be helped by speakers aimed in some direction other than at the audience. The theatre's grid and auditorium ceiling are also valuable speaker positions.

Many sound designers like to hang their speakers above the stage. This is desirable for a variety of reasons: clearing valuable deck (stage floor) space, keeping sound cable in the air (off the floor), and source direction. If plans include hanging speakers, the scenic and lighting departments must be advised well in advance; they also need that air space and, if consulted, will less likely place a black border immediately downstage of your hanging position.

Finally, it must be realized that flexibility of speaker placement is absolutely necessary to good production sound. While not true for reinforcement, playback requires that the designer have the ability to place speakers in any position.

## DESIGNING SOUND FOR THE THEATRE: STEPS AND CONSIDERATIONS

### THE SOUND DESIGNER AND THE DESIGN TEAM

Several earlier references have been made to qualities that a designer of sound for the theatre should possess: a working knowledge of theatre production in general and sound production specifically; a passion for music, with interest in all types and periods; a technical knowledge that provides understanding of the equipment involved in sound production; and a keen environmental awareness that will facilitate design creativity. In addition, a trait that is essential for every designer in the theatre is the ability and desire to share in the design process—to be a member of a design *team*. Being a collaborative art is the most significant aspect of theatrical design, making it unique from the rest of the arts. Relating to other designers and their ideas in a positive manner is not only exciting but is the very basis of collaboration.

The sound designer is involved with the production and the production team from their inception. A production *concept* is the result of script analysis and design meetings with all the designers, the director, and perhaps the playwright. This concept will be the product of much thinking and input, and must suggest in what direction the production will go—including, but not necessarily limited to, the period, thematic elements of the script being emphasized, and the production style. From this information will grow design ideas that will be unified by the fact that each stemmed from a single concept. Only then will the sound designer be ready to begin the exciting process of making specific choices.

### DESIGN STAGE

Design for the theatre always begins with the script, for it embodies the playwright's ideas, on which all production choices are based. The first time the designer reads a script, it should be read as if it were a novel. Subsequent readings will allow the designer to begin formulating a sense of the sound for the production. After meeting with the collaborative team, a *sound score* will be developed.

**The Sound Score**     The early sound score (Figure 12–11) is a visual representation of what the sound eventually might be like. It embodies a preliminary presentation of ideas of mood, style, and period, which may or may not include specific cues. This valuable paperwork can aid in the presentation of a sound designer's ideas to the rest of the production team and acts as an initial outline of the final sound design. While there are no set rules concerning what information the score should contain, some things that should be included are these:

1.  The *name* of the sound cue or idea
2.  Script *location*

3. A *description* of the cue in terms of its content, mood, style, and other information including special treatment
4. The *purpose* for the cue (could be as simple as the telephone ringing, or as complex as underscoring intended to affect the audience psychologically)

**Research**     A great deal of thought goes into the creation of a sound score, with all decisions being based on the script and production concept. The period the production is set in will undoubtedly affect the ultimate style and quality of the sound. Period research, an essential step toward any good sound design, must take place as soon as possible, for a sound score cannot be developed without proper research. Of course, films and actual period music are good research sources—but do not ignore reading about the period, reading books from the period, looking at art of the period, and looking at photographs from the period. Photographic records of architecture, clothing, and interiors will be a tremendous aid in discovering the feel of the times.

## PREPRODUCTION STAGE

Once the sound score is complete, the designer may start to collect the required music and effects as well as begin the recording process. The time required for this work varies greatly depending on the complexity of the design. At least three weeks must be allowed before technical rehearsals begin, while complex production designs may take several months to complete.

**The Master Tape**     As sounds are found they should be recorded onto a *master tape,* which will later be used to produce the show tape(s). This master

**SOUND SCORE**
**12TH NIGHT**

SOUND DESIGNER: JEFF LADMAN

| NO. | PAGE | DESCRIPTION |
|-----|------|-------------|
| 1 | 1 | Extension of boat entrance as Viola leaves the boat and steps foot onto the Illyrian sands |
| 2 | 1 | Viola moves further onto Illyrian soil |
| 3 | 2 | Strain of music from Orsino's group in the distance. It is coming from the portable gramophone, but will open out more generally as they come onto the stage. Will need to be timed to end. Something excruciatingly romantic |
| 4 | 3 | Orsino's "love" music; repeat of section of previous |
| 5 | 3 | Exit of Orsino as group moves away and exits. In the same vein as preceding. Might be the beginning of the piece to which we only heard the later part. |
| 6 | 4 | Pull down on Viola/Orsino motif that runs through the show. |
| 7 | 15 | Toby entrance music with cart, et. al. ("Arise, Arise"?) Music is coming from the jukebox on the cart, then opens up to a more general sound. |
| 8 | 15 | Olivia mourning music (interrupts or overlaps the preceding). A kind of dirge which needs to cover a cross-over by Olivia and her entourage. Will be interrupted by a large belch from Sir Toby in the middle of it. So, may need to be constructed in two parts. |
| 9 | 21 | Live dance cues |

**Figure 12–11**
Sound Score

Shown is an example of what form a sound score might take. It is intended to aid the designer in formulating and presenting early sound ideas to the director and fellow designers. Material courtesy Jeff Ladman, resident sound designer, Old Globe Theatre.

must be of the highest quality possible. Recording tape is available in different thicknesses directly related to playing time (more thin tape fits on a reel). Since thinner tapes tend to stretch, the master must be 1 or $1\frac{1}{2}$ mil thick. Recording speed should not be any slower than $7\frac{1}{2}$ inches per second (i.p.s.) because the higher the recording speed, the better the reproduction quality. Each copy of a master is called a *generation*, so a copy of the master would be labeled "second generation" (the master itself being "first generation"). Since the quality of analog sound production decreases with each generation, it is wise to plan carefully to need as few generations as possible. A side note: The fact that digital technology eliminates concern about tape generations is one of several reasons for its warm welcome into the world of sound processing.

**The Director's Tape**    As soon as a significant amount of sound has been collected, the designer must produce a special cassette tape for the director containing representative selections of music and sound effects. The purpose of this *director's tape* is to gain imperative feedback concerning the style and mood of the selections as well as their appropriateness to the production. This is also a good time to attend rehearsals in order to get a better feeling for atmospherics created by the actors, pace of the production, and overall directoral intent. Keeping in close contact with the director and stage manager of a production in rehearsal just makes good sense.

**The Rehearsal Tape**    A director may need a *rehearsal tape* well in advance of the actual show tape in order to coordinate actor timing or familiarize the actors with particular sounds. Such a tape should be recorded onto a cassette for ease of playback and should contain sound that is as close to the final product as possible. Preparing a rehearsal tape can prove to be of great advantage to the sound designer, often cutting hours off a technical rehearsal.

Sound processing such as equalization or digital reverberation treatment should happen next, followed by the editing and building of the show tape. However, before the show tape can be created, the designer must produce a *sound plot*.

---

### RECORDING TIPS

1. Always record the master tape with more than enough of each sound required for the production.
2. Be sure to keep careful track of what and where each effect is on the tape.
3. Do not process sound on the master tape; save processing for the second generation.
4. Record hot—keep record levels high so that adjustments can be made later.

## THE SOUND PLOT

Another planning tool for the designer, the sound plot is similar to the sound score—but much more detailed and technical (Figure 12–12). The components and format vary with requirements, but important information includes sound cue number; script page number; cue description and length; deck, track, and speakers in use. This is the time when the designer plans exactly how the production sound will be run—how many decks are necessary; exact speaker requirements and control; how long cuts should be on the show tape; and how many cues there will be. Often the stage manager can be of help and should at least be consulted for last-minute changes. The formulation of the sound plot will give the designer enough information to intelligently proceed with the making of the show tape, but a tape must never be attempted without this paperwork. In addition, if sound requirements are complex with many overlapping cues, it is advisable to do additional charts (sometimes referred to as *work sheets*) detailing in time line form each track of each tape.

## PRODUCTION STAGE

Whether the production period begins with a sound rehearsal or technical rehearsals, the sound designer needs to have several details taken care of prior to this time. Cues should be written into the stage manager's script several days before the technical or sound rehearsal. The director may wish to be present at this session, so it should be scheduled well in advance. Each of the stage manager's cues should have a very specific call placement so that changes made later can be done in an exact manner.

**Cue Sheets**     Running *cue sheets* must be written for the sound operator(s). The sound plot will serve as their basis, making them very easy to write. Cue sheets should be arranged in columns headed as follows:

1. Cue number
2. Action ("fade up," for example)

---

### DESIGN STEPS

1. Script reading and collaborative meetings with director and design team to determine production style, period, and mood
2. Research and study resulting in sound score
3. Collection and recording of music and sounds
4. Creation of a director's tape and attendance at rehearsals
5. Creation of a rehearsal tape, if necessary
6. Development of the sound plot
7. Recording of the show tape(s)

3. Fade time
4. Cue length
5. Deck in use
6. Track(s) in use
7. Volume (usually mixer level)
8. Speaker selection
9. Comments or notes ("visual cue," for example)

**System Check**   It is very wise for the sound designer to take a quiet moment in the theatre before the first sound or technical rehearsal and set preliminary sound levels for each cue, checking speaker functions at the same time. This is also a good time to brief and check out the operator(s) on the

**Figure 12–12**
Sound Plot

Shown is the first page of the sound plot for a production of *Twelfth Night* at San Diego's Old Globe Theatre, with sound designed by Jeff Ladman. The sound plot aids the designer in making and communicating operational decisions.

**SOUND PLOT**
**OLD GLOBE THEATRE**

PRODUCTION: TWELFTH NIGHT                      PAGE: 1 OF 10
SOUND DESIGNER: JEFF LADMAN                     ISSUE: #1
DIRECTOR: LAIRD WILLIAMSON                       SM: VANDYKE

| PAGE | CUE # | TIME | DESCRIPTION | A | B | C | D |
|---|---|---|---|---|---|---|---|
| 1 | 5 | 1:12<br>7:50 | MUSIC + F/X  BOAT ENTRANCE<br>TK 1 MUSIC, TK 2 WATER, TK 3,4 WAVES | X | | | |
| 1 | 5.5 | ---- | TK 1 - A DECK - MUSIC FADES OUT<br>        WITH ACTION | | ↓ | | |
| 1 | 6 | 1:12 | MUSIC: VIOLA MOVES INLAND<br>TK 1,3 | | | X | |
| 2 | 7 | M :40<br>F/X:48 | MUSIC: GRAMOPHONE<br>TK 1,3 MUSIC   TK 4 NEEDLE | | X | | |
| | 7.1 | AUTO | BLOSSOM INTO HOUSE | | ↓ | | |
| 3 | 7.5 | ---- | ON NEEDLE REMOVE - DUMP B DK | | ↓ | | |
| 3 | 8 | F/X:01<br>M :21 | MUSIC: GRAMOPHONE        @ TOP DROP<br>TK 1,3 MUSIC   TK 4 NEEDLE | | | X | |
| | 8.1 | AUTO | BLOSSOM INTO HOUSE | | | ↓ | |
| 3 | 8.5 | ---- | DUMP OUT C - DK | | | ↓ | |
| 4 | 9 | :40 | MUSIC: GRAMOPHONE        @ TOP DROP<br>TK 1,3 MUSIC   TK 4 NEEDLE | | X | | |
| | 9.2 | AUTO | AUTO FADE OUT LONG | | ↓ | | |
| 5 | 11 | :24 | MUSIC: JUKEBOX - TOBY ENT.<br>TK 1,3 MUSIC           (P.O.) | | | X | |
| | | | WITH CUE 11: FADE OUT OF A DK | ↓ | ↓ | | |
| 5 | 12 | :30 | MUSIC: OLIVIA ENT.<br>TK 1,3 MUSIC           (P.O.) | | X | | |
| 5 | 13 | ---- | F/X: BELCH<br>TK 1,3             (P.O.) | | | | X |
| 5 | 14 | :29 | MUSIC: OLIVIA EXIT<br>TK 1,3 MUSIC | | | X | |
| | 14.2 | AUTO | FADE OUT W/ EXIT | | | ↓ | |
| 7 | 14.5 | :01 | F/X: POP<br>                    (P.O.) | | | | X |

equipment, being sure to allow plenty of time for problem solving. If the headset communication system is the responsibility of the sound department, the sound designer should find out what is required from the stage manager and prepare and check out the equipment. Leaving these details for the day of the technical rehearsal is a serious mistake and will waste much time. Good preparation and planning is never more evident than at the technical rehearsal; every effort should be taken to make this experience a painless one.

**Sound Rehearsal**     The sound designer should arrive a bit early for the sound or technical rehearsal and be sure that the sound operator(s) and the equipment are ready to begin on time. Every sound cue should be run under performance conditions so that length and level can be properly judged. (Be aware that an audience, when you have one, will absorb roughly 3 dB of sound.) Sit at the "tech" table and make sure that both the stage manager calling the cues and the operator(s) take careful notes of all changes. Nothing is more frustrating than mistakes being repeated because changes were not properly noted. Remember to give yourself and your crew proper breaks.

**Dress Rehearsals**     Often the designer will need to make adjustments after the technical rehearsal and before the dress rehearsals begin. These changes will usually be minor if everything has gone well, but may require a great deal of studio time if there are problems. It is imperative that the corrected tape be ready for the first dress, so planning ahead is important. Once the dress process has begun, sound problems must be dealt with while the run goes on. The sound designer may not stop a dress rehearsal for a problem unless it is an emergency. Make sure to touch base with the director, stage manager, and operator(s) after every rehearsal. Be sure that a backup recording of the final tape is readily available in case of emergency.

**The Run**     Before each performance the sound operator will need to check the entire system to ascertain that everything is in proper working order. It is good practice to record a series of pre-show tests at the beginning of the show tape, which can be used for this purpose. Each speaker should be tested individually and a show cue should be run to check volume levels.

# SOUND SYSTEMS AND EQUIPMENT 13

As in the other design areas, mastering the art of theatrical sound involves not only artistry but also technology. The functions of various pieces of equipment and how they interrelate is of primary importance to the sound designer/technician. The evolution of theatrical sound design has been driven by technology—what follows is a closer look at that technology.

## THE SOUND SYSTEM

Sound plays several different roles in the theatre and the requirements of a sound system vary with each.

The *reinforcement system* comprises microphones, a mixer, amplifiers, and speakers, with most systems also having in-line signal processing that is located between the mixer and the amplifier. The *playback system* is used to create music and effects during a production. Tape decks, DAT recorders, and CD players are necessary components. This system may also need additional processing or control equipment and requires speakers of different types and in different locations from those best suited for reinforcement. The *recording system* adds input sources such as a turntable, compact disc player, synthesizer, and sampler. In addition, specialized remote recording equipment may be necessary. The type of microphones used for recording will differ from those of the reinforcement system, and there is less need for multiple amplifiers and speakers. It is possible for the recording system to be located in a studio rather than the production sound booth. Such an arrangement, while more desirable, is expensive due to the need for duplicate equipment.

Figure 13–1 illustrates a *combination system* typical of most moderate theatre facilities. This system introduces a *patch panel,* which provides flexibility in connecting one piece of equipment to another. The following overview of individual components carries this system in mind.

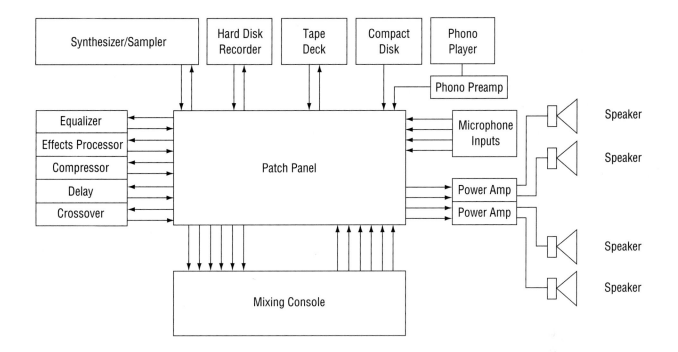

**Figure 13–1**
**Block Diagram of a Combination Sound System**

A system such as the one shown is typical of most theatre sound systems in that it combines reinforcement, playback, and recording possibilities.

## INPUT SOURCES

Anything that sends a sound signal to the system is considered an input source. Two commonly used methods of transmitting and storing a source's signal are *analog* and *digital*. While they cannot be used interchangeably, an analog signal can be converted to digital and vice versa.

Analog signals have been with us for a long time. They are electrical waveforms carried through wires that duplicate sound waveforms. A microphone is a piece of equipment categorized as a *transducer* because it changes acoustic waveforms into the electrical waveforms of an analog signal.

The fairly recent development of digital technology has offered a solution to some of the inherent problems of analog signals. In the digital process, an analog signal is converted to a rapid series of on-or-off (binary) pulses. These pulses can be read, recorded, and manipulated with great precision, resulting in more flexible and accurate storage and reproduction.

Major input sources are microphones, tapes, records, compact discs, synthesizers, and samplers.

**Microphones**     As stated above, microphones convert sound waves into electrical energy for transmission to another location. As can be seen in Figure 13–2, they come in a variety of sizes and shapes. The vocal microphone shown in Figure 13–2a is a good choice for multipurpose use, although most tasks are performed best with specialized types.

General area reinforcement uses surface-mounted or *boundary microphones* placed along the front of the stage. Two types of boundary microphones manufactured by Crown International are the pressure zone microphone or

PZM (Figure 13–2b) and the phase coherent cardioid or PCC (Figure 13–2c).

Specific reinforcement of selected performers is accomplished by using *personal microphones*, either hand-held or miniature (Figure 13–2d). The popularity of wireless miniature microphones has grown as they have become more dependable and cost-effective. If used properly, modern wireless microphones in combination with boundary microphones work very well for most stage reinforcement applications.

**Tape**    Recording tape functions as an input source due to its ability to store sound and play it back. The tape's film is coated with ferrous oxide particles, which can be magnetized, allowing the storage of either analog or digital signals. A tape deck receives the electrical signal and transfers it to the tape by means of a small electromagnetic "head." A second head is capable of "reading" the signal stored on the tape with the purpose of transmitting it to other pieces of audio equipment such as amplifiers and speakers. The standard tape used in analog theatrical recording comes on an open reel, is $\frac{1}{4}$ inch wide, and is played at speeds of $7\frac{1}{2}$ or 15 i. p. s. (inches per second). Assuming that the signal is analog, fast recording speeds provide higher quality sound because the magnetic information is spread over more tape.

## Figure 13–2
### Microphones

Four commonly used types of microphones:
(a) A hand-held cardioid vocal mike, the Shure SM58. Photo courtesy Shure Brothers.
(b) The Crown PZM (Pressure Zone Microphone), a boundary microphone with an omnidirectional pickup pattern.
(c) The Crown PCC (Phase Coherent Cardioid), a boundary microphone with a cardioid pickup pattern for rear sound rejection.
(d) The Crown GLM 100, a miniature personal microphone that can be part of a wireless system. Photos courtesy Crown International.

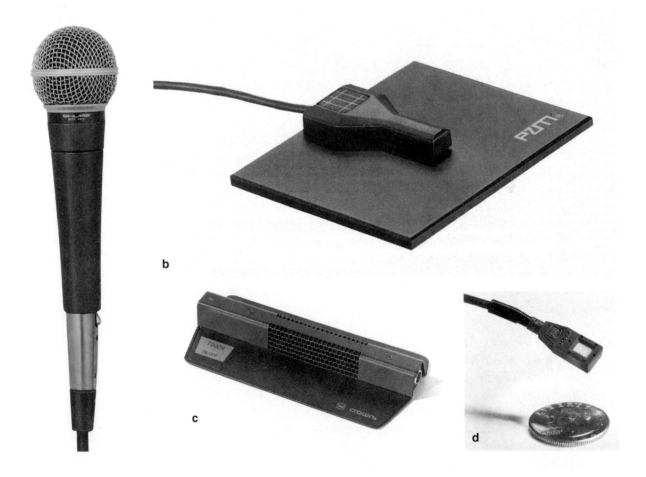

Currently two tape formats are common for DAT or digital audio tape recording: a two-track tape that comes in a small cassette and a larger eight-track version. MDM (modular digital multitrack) machines record the eight tracks onto tapes such as those commonly used for 8mm or VHS-C video recording.

Be aware that tape quality varies. Poor recording tape can stretch in playback and/or "print through" when stored. Print-through occurs when there is a transfer of magnetism from one layer of tape to the next and can render a production tape useless. To minimize print-through, tape should be stored "tail out" (end of tape first) in a cool, dry location out of direct sunlight. Being magnetic, recording tape is sensitive to all magnetic fields. An entire reel or cassette of tape may be erased by using an electromagnet called a *bulk eraser*.

**Records and Compact Discs**     Although there remains some music that can only be found on records, the compact disc is clearly a superior input source. Today's recording studios still have both turntables and disc players for input to a tape deck. Seldom will either be used in live playback—rather, the contents will be stored on tape or in the memory of a digital sampler and then edited for playback as necessary. Sound effect libraries are expensive and should be handled with care. Like tape, discs should be stored properly and kept out of direct sunlight.

**Synthesizers and Samplers**     Synthesizers and samplers can be used to create a vast array of sounds. In addition, digital samplers can record and store these sounds for subsequent manipulation or playback. Both pieces of equipment act as input sources but, like discs, they are not traditionally used in live theatrical playback.

**SIGNAL PROCESSING**

Various pieces of equipment are used to manipulate the sound from an input source before it moves on to the amplifiers and speakers. This is referred to as *signal processing*. The most simple system might be composed of a microphone, a preamp or mixer, an amplifier, and a speaker. However, the theatrical combination sound system must be as flexible as possible.

**The Patch**     The patch or interconnect panel provides convenient routing of sound signals from one component in the system to another. It is made up of a confusing-looking collection of jacks that allow an operator to connect any input source into any signal-processing unit (Figure 13–3). Depending on the needs of the job at hand, a tape deck's output could be patched into the equalizer or into the mixer or into another tape deck. The patch bay is made up of single $\frac{1}{8}$- or $\frac{1}{4}$-inch diameter jacks that are labeled by function. For instance, "MIX 3 IN" translates to "mixer channel number 3 input." Once the purpose of a patch panel is understood and the various pieces of equipment in the system are known, using the patch becomes a fairly easy task.

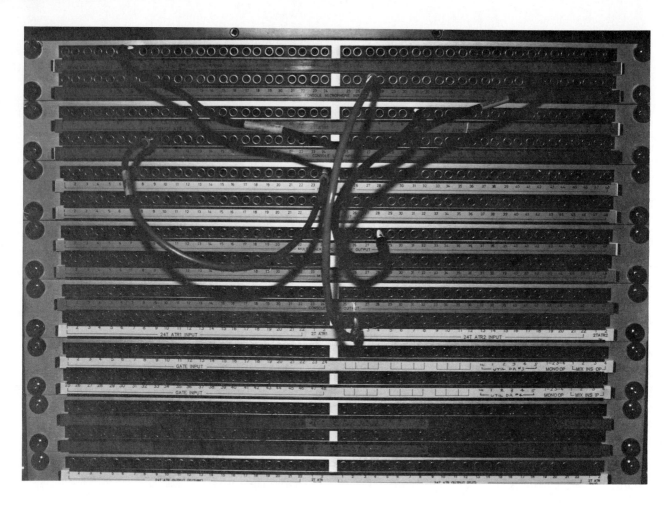

**Figure 13–3**
Patch Panel

A patch panel such as the one shown allows interconnection of one component of the sound system with another. Photo courtesy Charles Weeks.

**The Mixer**  The primary function of a mixer (Figure 13–4) is to combine a large number of input signals into one or more output channels. In addition, a mixing console provides volume control as well as equalization for each of the input signals. A mixer is useful in reinforcement, recording, and playback situations.

In reinforcement, when various performers are using microphones, the mixer and its operator are located in the house and will "ride" the sound levels. That is to say, the operator will bring up a mike when needed, take it out when not required, and balance the sounds from more than one microphone.

Since the power of a microphone's signal is relatively slight, the analog mixer contains preamplifiers that take these *low-level* signals and increase them to an acceptable power. This higher power is referred to as *line-level*.

The digital mixer (Figure 13–4b) receives an analog signal and immediately converts it to digital, thereby eliminating the need for signal amplification. Being digital, the signal processing and routing is more sophisticated, and MIDI control is possible (see Chapter 12).

In recording and playback, the mixer will be used to accept several input sources, balance them, and mix them into one or more output channels. The signal will then be sent on to the next piece of equipment, very possibly an equalizer.

**The Equalizer**     While the mixer provides some degree of equalization through its tone controls, an equalizer allows for much more precise adjustment of specific frequencies. Two main types of equalizers exist: *graphic* and *parametric*. The graphic type shown in Figure 12–7 has sliding faders permanently assigned to frequency bands that are typically between one-third and one octave in width. The parametric type allows the operator to select specific frequencies for control and to individually adjust the band width. Like the mixer, the equalizer is a valuable component for reinforcement, recording, and playback.

a

b

**Figure 13–4**
Mixers

Shown are two mixers from Yamaha:
(a) The M2000 Mixing Console with 40 inputs, 8 sub-group outputs, an auxiliary mix matrix, and a stereo main output.
(b) The Pro Mix 01 digital mixer with 16 inputs, digital signal processing, digital patch bay, and MIDI dynamic-automation. Photos courtesy Yamaha Corporation.

**Specialized Equipment**    A great variety of specialized sound-processing equipment exists including delay units, compressors, and pitch shifters. One particularly versatile and useful unit for theatrical sound is the *multi-effects processor.* It can alter a sound in varying degrees—from making it richer by adding a slight amount of reverberation, to the creation of an echo (repetition of a whole sound). In addition, it will provide pitch shifting, flanging, auto-pan, and so on.

## OUTPUT SOURCES

Other than live sound, the amplifier and the speaker constitute the only output sources used in theatrical production.

**Amplifiers**    Line-level voltage is not enough power to make a loud-speaker work (in technical jargon, to "drive" the speaker). Therefore, an amplifier matched to the loudspeaker's power rating is assigned to each speaker. Rack-mounted amplifiers are commonly placed in the ceiling of an auditorium between the sound control booth and the majority of speakers. The amplifier receives a line-level signal from the control booth, amplifies it to *speaker-level,* and sends it on to its assigned speaker.

**Loudspeakers**    Like microphones, loudspeakers are specialized and come in a wide range of sizes, types, and prices. They receive the sound signal from the amplifier and transduce it back into pressure waves that we can hear. The more accurately a speaker performs this task, the better it is for theatrical use; but quality varies greatly.

## THE EQUIPMENT

The sound designer or technician must have enough knowledge of how and why a piece of equipment works to make intelligent choices about using or specifying equipment. The following section describes, in greater detail, the functional aspects of input, processing, and output equipment.

### MICROPHONES

Most microphones are categorized in two ways: (1) by how they perform the task of changing sound into electrical energy, and (2) by the various pickup patterns available. While there are a number of different microphone types, in the theatre we are concerned with only two—the dynamic microphone and the condenser microphone.

**Microphone Types**    The *dynamic* microphone, short for dynamic moving coil, uses a diaphragm that is similar to our eardrum to receive sound waves. The diaphragm causes movement of a metal coil inside a magnetic field, which in turn generates an electrical signal—an analog of the sound waves. Probably the most common microphone, the dynamic can be designed with any sound pickup pattern. It is the least fragile of types and can be of excellent quality.

The *condenser* microphone receives sound waves on electronic plates that generate a signal. However, so little initial power is created that a small amplifier must be located nearby. The amplifier housed in the microphone may be powered by a DC (direct current) power supply in the form of a small battery, or more likely by an electrical supply from the mixing board (called "phantom" power). While being the highest quality available, this microphone is also more delicate and expensive than the dynamic. A condenser microphone is normally chosen for more demanding or critical sound tasks.

**Microphone Pickup Patterns**    A microphone without a restricted pickup pattern will receive sound equally from all directions. For instance, a microphone located on the floor at stage front will receive direct sound from a performer's voice, bounced sound from the floor, as well as sound from the orchestra and audience. Restricted pickup patterns help the microphone be more selective. Figure 13–5 illustrates four common pickup patterns: *omnidirectional, bidirectional, cardioid directional,* and *supercardioid directional.*

As the name implies, an omnidirectional pattern microphone receives sound from all directions. This pattern is used for body mikes, monitor mikes, the pressure zone microphone (PZM) shown in Figure 13–2b, and in situations such as group recording where all sound is required. *Feedback,* a condition where sound from a speaker is picked up by a microphone and continuously reamplified, can be a particular problem with this pattern.

A bidirectional pattern looks like the figure eight. It works well in recording two-person interviews or in any other situation where the desired sound comes primarily from two opposite directions.

A cardioid pattern is the most useful for general theatrical applications. Rejection of sound increases as one moves around the microphone and is nearly total at the rear, lessening the possibility of feedback.

For long-range directional pickup, the supercardioid pattern is desirable. This pattern is used by the phase coherent cardioid (PCC) microphone (Figure 13–2c), which is commonly placed along the downstage edge of the apron and used for general vocal pickup.

**Wireless Microphones**    A microphone without the nuisance of a cable is very desirable, particularly for vocal reinforcement. The wireless microphones shown in Figure 13–6 are actually miniature FM radio stations. The tiny body mike is wired to a low-power transmitter worn by the performer. This transmitter sends a radio signal of specific frequency to a receiver located offstage. The receiver picks up only that frequency and sends the analog-converted signal through a wire to the sound system for amplification. The transmitter and receivers can be made to operate on a variety of matched frequencies in order to isolate one microphone from another when several are in use. Care must be taken in selecting these frequencies to avoid interference from other broadcasting. A good solution is to use vacant VHF (30

**Figure 13–5**
Microphone Pickup Patterns

The choice of pickup pattern is determined by the specific task.

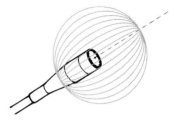

**OMNIDIRECTIONAL**

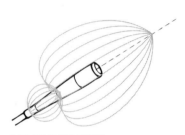

**SUPERCARDIOID**

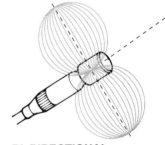

**BI-DIRECTIONAL**

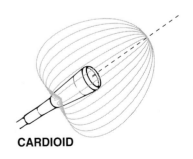

**CARDIOID**

## MICROPHONE CARE

Microphones are pieces of equipment that need to be cared for in order to perform well over their life span.

1. Never blow into a microphone to test it.
2. Store microphones in a cool, dry cabinet on a padded shelf or in their cases.
3. Don't thump or bang microphones on a hard surface.

to 300 megahertz) or UHF (300 to 3,000 megahertz) television channel frequencies. The batteries that power the transmitter often require changing before every performance.

This type of system is fairly delicate and good ones are expensive. However, the negatives are outweighed by the convenience of the system and the quality of its sound reproduction. Performers often wear the tiny microphone on the forehead at the hairline, with the wire running through the hair and down the back. This technique avoids noise from clothing and prevents variation in sound level as the head turns from side to side.

**Figure 13–6**
Wireless Microphone

Shown is a RAMSA wireless microphone system with diversity receivers and both "hand held" and "body pack" transmitters. Photo courtesy RAMSA/ Panasonic Professional Audio Systems.

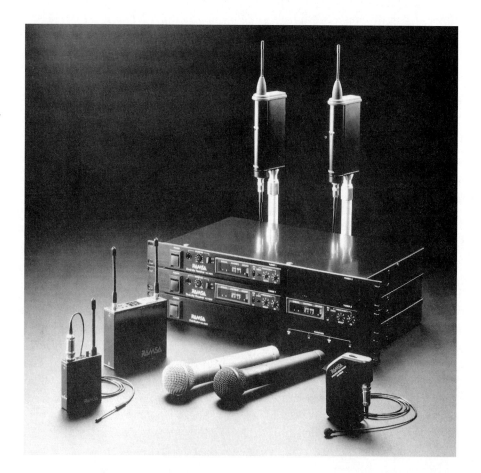

## TAPE MACHINES

A *tape recorder* is a machine primarily intended for home or portable use that contains an amplifier and possibly speakers. A *tape deck* is a professional machine, more durable and capable of reproducing higher quality sound than a home tape recorder. Two types of tape machines exist: analog and digital.

**The Basic Analog Tape Deck**   The tape deck (Figure 13–7) has long been a very important piece of equipment in the theatre. Unless music or a sound effect is to be performed live, it is usually recorded and then played back on the tape deck. In recent years alternative methods of storing sound— offering great advantages over tape—have become available. However, the tape deck is not destined to go the way of vinyl recordings quite yet.

A sound studio tape deck has three magnetic heads that perform the functions of *erasing* or demagnetizing, *recording* or magnetizing, and *playback* or reading the encoded tape (Figure 13–8).

**Figure 13–7**
Tape Deck

Shown is a professional 2-track stereo analog tape deck. Photo courtesy Studer Revox America, Inc.

The erase head is first in line as the tape runs (left to right). Active when recording, the erase head provides a clean tape for the record head to magnetize. The record head forms magnetic paths, called *tracks*, along the length of the tape. Two tracks running in the same direction are capable of reproducing stereo sound. While there exist a multitude of track formats and widths, a two-track stereo arrangement is by far the most common and useful for theatre applications. Third and last in line, the playback head is also active during recording. This makes it possible for the operator to monitor what was just recorded on the tape. In playback mode, both the erase and record heads are automatically shut off.

A desirable feature for a deck used in the preparation of tapes is an edit function. This will allow the operator to precisely locate a sound by rolling the tape by hand past the playback head while monitoring the signal. Better decks will have a three-motor transport—one motor for each tape reel and one for the *capstan* (Figure 13–8), which has the important responsibility of precisely controlling the speed of the tape as it travels past the heads. One final feature, very valuable to sound processing, is continuously variable speed.

**Tape Deck Electronics**     While features vary from machine to machine, some general comments are in order:

Function control switches (play, fast-forward, and the like) should be electrical or solenoid-operated. This will provide for better start-ups, protect the machine from inexperienced operators, and ensure compatibility with remote control devices including computer control.

Most machines provide a *monitor select switch*, which gives an operator the option of monitoring either the actual input signal or the recorded signal from the playback head, allowing a comparison of the two signals.

Volume controls will be found for both input and playback channels. Two important volume-monitoring features found on most machines are the *VU meter* and a *peak reading LED* (Figure 13–9).

## Figure 13–8
### Tape Deck Heads

This illustration shows how recording tape passes by the three heads of the analog tape deck. The tape is pulled past the heads by the action of the capstan and pressure roller.

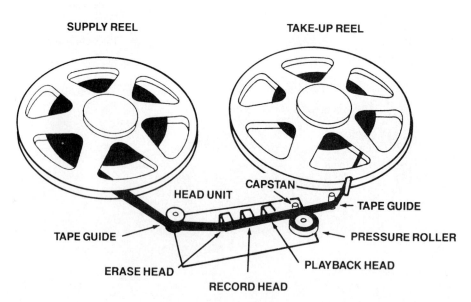

SUPPLY REEL    TAKE-UP REEL

CAPSTAN
HEAD UNIT
TAPE GUIDE
TAPE GUIDE
PRESSURE ROLLER
ERASE HEAD
PLAYBACK HEAD
RECORD HEAD

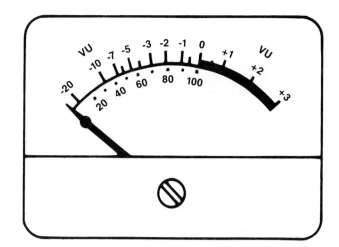

**Figure 13—9**
Volume Monitoring

An illustration of a VU (Volume Unit) meter used to indicate volume of an analog tape signal. The volume units of a digital signal peak at 0.

The VU (volume unit) meter measures electrical signal in decibels, but on a scale called dBm, which is different from the more familiar dB SPL scale. The basic difference is that 0 dB SPL is equated with the threshold of hearing, while 0 dBm is considerably louder (electrical value of .775 volt into 600 ohms). Little else matters as long as the operator understands that both negative and positive dB readings are routine on the dBm scale. The VU meter indicates sound levels from −20 dB to +3 dB for each channel or track (a quadraphonic machine will have four VU meters). In most situations no distortion will occur if the sound peak levels are kept at or below +3 dB. Most sounds and music benefit from being recorded near maximum level. Because a VU meter is rather slow in reacting, many machines will have peak indicator LEDs. These register quickly when a volume peaks over +3 dB.

Many tape decks are provided with a noise reduction system (i. e., "dBX" or "Dolby") that reduces or eliminates unwanted tape hiss introduced during the recording process. The electronics of the system adjust the sound's dynamic range before recording and then return it to its original value during playback. Care must be taken that a tape recorded with noise reduction is played back on an identical system.

A tape machine should be protected from dust with a proper dustcover, and the heads must be cleaned on a regular basis (see "How to Clean and Demagnetize Tape Heads" at the end of this chapter).

**DAT Machines**     As mentioned earlier, there is a new generation of equipment that is designed to record a digital rather than analog signal on magnetic tape. Advantages are ease of editing and improved sound quality due to significant reduction in tape noise. Disadvantages, compared to other storage systems such as digital samplers, are slow random access when editing and, until recently, start-up delay. As stated earlier, tapes come in cassettes and can be multitrack, although two-track is most common for theatrical use.

DAT machines as well as self-recorded compact discs seem destined to be the two major input sources of the future. The machine shown in Figure

**Figure 13–10**
DAT Machine

Shown is a DAT (Digital Audio Tape) machine manufactured by Panasonic. It features a 3-second RAM buffer for instant start capability. Photo courtesy Panasonic Professional Audio Systems.

13–10 provides a RAM (random access memory) buffer for instant-start capability.

## TURNTABLES AND COMPACT DISC PLAYERS

A good turntable cartridge is a must; and the stylus should be cleaned and checked frequently. The proper way to clean a stylus is with a fine brush and alcohol, moving the brush over the stylus from back to front only.

The audio world has received the compact disc with open arms for a variety of reasons. Disc players are easy to use, may be controlled remotely, and allow easy access to tracks. The compact disc as a storage device is superior in that it eliminates the scratch and pop of records as well as tape hiss associated with recording tape. Sound quality from a compact disc is superior in dynamic range and frequency response to that of a vinyl disc or recording tape; and a disc will maintain that quality indefinitely.

## DIGITAL SAMPLERS

Three types of digital samplers exist today: sampling keyboards, digital hard disk recorders, and digital workstations. *Sampling keyboards* sample a sound into RAM, allowing instant access to the sound for editing and processing. The length of the sample is limited by the amount of random access memory. *Digital hard disk recorders,* such as the one shown in Figure 13–11, sample a sound directly onto a hard disk and normally have expanded capacity. *Digital workstations* are computer-based systems that allow visual editing and processing of sound waveforms. All three systems offer the advantages of digital processing and storage.

## MIXERS

Mixers (Figure 13–12) are available digital and analog, and in a wide variety of styles dependent on function. As mentioned earlier, theatrical mixers may

**Figure 13–11**
Digital Hard Disk Recorder

Shown is an Akai DR4d hard disk recorder offering 4-channel simultaneous recording and play-back as well as workstation-like editing functions. Photo courtesy Akai Digital.

need to serve several purposes—in-house reinforcement mixing, studio recording, and show playback. Mixer capacity is specified in terms of input and output channels: six to eight channels in and two channels out is a minimum requirement; twelve to twenty-four or even thirty-two inputs, with six to eight output channels is more normal.

**Sound Path**     The mixer is a complex piece of equipment. It must control a large number of inputs and direct them to various output channels. In an analog mixer, such as the one shown in Figure 13–12, each input channel has a line-level as well as a low- or microphone-level input. The low-level input is wired directly to a preamplifier located within the mixer. The sound signal then travels to an input attenuator or "trim pot" used to adjust the volume level, and on to equalizer controls. Next is another fader called a "pan pot" that determines how much volume will be routed, by switches, to the selected output channels. Yet another fader will master the level of the selected output channel. Finally, the VU meter registers the resulting sound.

An operator can monitor the sound either completely mixed just before the VU meter, or unadulterated just before the input fader (called PFL or prefade listen).

Auxiliary feeds for processing equipment are standard on many mixers and a mixer can be custom designed for particular use.

**Digital Technology**     A digital mixer receives an analog signal and immediately converts it to digital. The digital signal is subject to more sophisticated equalization and less equipment noise than if it was analog. The signal path is much the same as described above. A further advantage of digital mixers is the possibility of MIDI control.

## EQUALIZERS

The equalizer serves two basic functions for theatrical sound. This piece of processing equipment can (1) adjust selected frequencies of an output signal

## Figure 13–12
Mixer Sound Path

(a) The input section of a Sound-craft Delta DLX mixing console showing the preamplifier section, equalizer, auxiliary sends, routing/panning, and fader.
(b) The output section of the Soundcraft shows the four group outputs, auxiliary outputs, and the stereo main outputs.
(c) A simplified block diagram illustrating the signal path through the Soundcraft mixing console.

in accordance with room acoustics or for the control of feedback, or (2) alter voice, music, or sound frequencies in order to improve tone quality.

The exact location of equalization in the sound's path from input source to output source is made adjustable by the patch panel. If an equalizer is used only to adjust room acoustics, it should be of the parametric type and left alone to do its job. However, equalizers used to control tone quality will need adjustment with each task. In this case, an easily accessible graphic equalizer is preferable.

## AMPLIFIERS

Power amplifiers such as the one shown in Figure 13–13 have come a long way since the days of a metal box filled with glowing tubes. However, something that has not changed is the important fact that amplifiers and speakers must be compatible. Proper matching involves *impedance* (similar to resistance in an AC circuit, measured in ohms) as well as *RMS power rating*. RMS (root mean square) is a way of describing power or wattage capacities of amplifiers

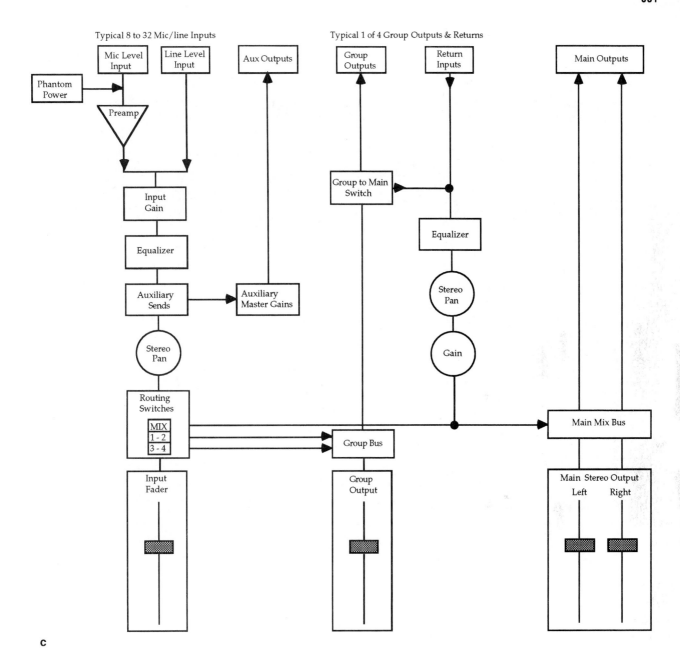

Typical 8 to 32 Mic/line Inputs   Typical 1 of 4 Group Outputs & Returns

Simplified System Block Diagram

and speakers. Under most conditions, an amplifier's RMS power rating (measured in wattage) must never exceed that of the speaker. While loudspeakers can have impedances varying from 2 to 30 ohms (most common are 8 and 16 ohms) and amplifiers usually are designed for loads of 4, 8, or 16 ohms, they must be matched for proper sound reproduction. It is highly recommended that a theatrical sound system have compatible amplifiers permanently assigned to each speaker.

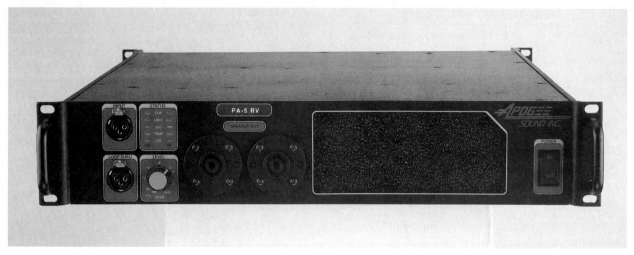

**Figure 13–13**
Amplifier

Shown is an Apogee PA-5 RV 400-watt processor-amplifier that incorporates both specialized signal processing and power amplification into one unit. Photo courtesy Apogee Sound, Inc.

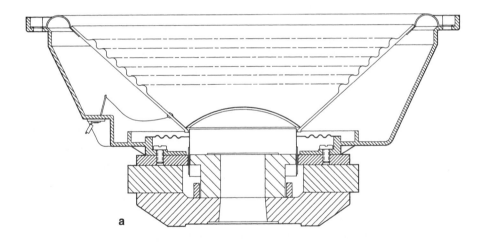

a

**Figure 13–14**
Sectional Drawings of Two
Speaker Types

(a) Cone-type driver.
(b) Compression driver without
its horn. Drawings courtesy
JBL Inc.

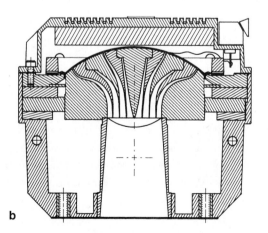

b

## LOUDSPEAKERS

Two general speaker types exist: the *cone speaker* (Figure 13–14a) and the *compression driver speaker* (Figure 13–14b). In both cases a moving diaphragm generates pressure waves. The larger cone speakers have a plastic or paper diaphragm, while compression drivers have a diaphragm made of a stiff material such as aluminum or titanium. A metal diaphragm has the advantage of being more able to produce sounds in the higher frequencies. A horn such as that shown in Figure 13–15 is usually coupled to a compression driver to control the sound dispersion. The extent of directionality is dependent on the shape and size of the horn, which can be designed for specific tasks.

Most speakers will be enclosed in a cabinet that plays a significant acoustic role in the sound production. Sometimes housed in or attached to the cabinet will be a *crossover network*. This electronic device receives the sound signal from the amplifier and separates the frequencies into ranges that are acceptable to the individual speakers. Low frequencies are handled by the *woofer*, a large cone whose size is determined by the sound volume it is required to generate—the more volume, the larger the cone diameter. While the presence of a mid-range speaker is possible, the middle and high frequencies are usually handled by a single compression driver. These horn-type speakers are normally attached to a cabinet, as shown in Figure 13–15.

**Power Ratings**     As noted above, speakers have an RMS power rating usually measured at 8 ohms. The RMS rating serves as a guide to the speaker's

### Figure 13–15
Speaker Systems

(a) A horn-loaded compression driver mounted on a cabinet containing two cone-type woofers. Photo courtesy Electro-Voice.
(b) An Apogee cabinet speaker and its processor. Photo courtesy Apogee Sound, Inc.

a

b

performance in terms of volume. However, it must be realized that some speakers are more efficient than others. Do not rely on RMS figures alone, but compare them with the sound pressure levels published by the manufacturers (SPL at 1 meter with 1 watt input).

**Phasing**   Proper electrical phasing is important in hooking up speakers. This simply means that one must always pay attention to the positive and negative connections from amplifier to speaker, never crossing them. Doing so will cause the diaphragm of one speaker to move in, while that of another moves out. The result is a cancellation of sound.

**Selection**   Speaker selection is determined by application. Theatre speakers should be able to produce 115 dB of sound pressure level without distortion; they should have as wide and flat a frequency response as possible; and they should be kept to a minimum physical size. All this translates into money. Be prepared to pay top dollar for your speakers. They are the weakest link in the reproduction system and must be of the highest quality to make up for this fact.

## WIRING AND CONNECTORS

The power of sound signals varies in voltage from low-level microphone signals (less than 1 volt) to high-voltage speaker lines carrying 70 volts. There are two types of wiring used to connect one piece of audio equipment to another: *balanced* and *unbalanced* lines. Connections from amplifiers to speakers deserve special attention because of the relatively high voltages used.

**General Audio**   An unbalanced line is a cable made up of a single conductor with a shield of metal wrapping around it (Figure 13–16a). The single conductor is the positive wire, while the shield acts as both the negative and ground. A balanced line has two conductors with a shield (Figure 13–16b). These negative and positive conductors carry the signal, while the shield simply acts as a ground.

Unbalanced lines are less expensive but are subject to electrical interference. They are typically used from one piece of equipment to another. Balanced lines are used for microphone lines and other long runs of cable. It is most desirable to have the entire system balanced.

Even with a completely balanced system, it is best to keep audio cable away from higher voltage electrical lines (such as lighting cables), which produce a significant magnetic field resulting in interference.

**Speaker Lines**   If the distance from amplifier to speaker is short, one only need be sure that the wire is adequate in size. However, if the run is long or several speakers are being driven, a voltage increase may be necessary to ensure that the speaker or speakers receive adequate power. Many amplifiers will have connections that allow for 4-, 8-, or 16-ohm normal voltage or for an increase to either 25 or 70 volts. If using higher voltage, a small transformer located at the speaker steps down the voltage from the amplifier to normal speaker-level.

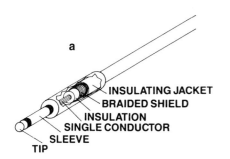 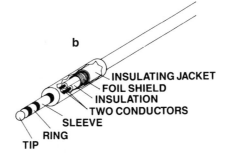

**Figure 13–16**
Balanced and Unbalanced Lines

(a) An unbalanced line with a matching jack plug.
(b) A balanced line with matching jack plug.

## COMPUTERIZED SOUND CONTROL

The idea of using the power of a computer to expand the potential for complex, theatrical sound design and operation has been resisted just as it was in the field of theatrical lighting. It is high time to reverse such thinking. Equipment such as that shown in Figure 13–17 is being installed in major theatrical sound facilities throughout the country.

Computerized control allows for memory storage and playback of highly complex sound cues with the press of a single "GO" button by the operator. Interface with existing equipment is routine, operation is as simple as a lighting control system, programming is by keyboard or a standard mouse, and cost is not prohibitive. Just as the lighting computer has freed the designer from hardware restrictions, so will the sound computer allow theatrical sound the opportunity to reach its full potential.

## HOW TO . . .

The following sections give practical information on how to make a tape—including recording and editing; hints for placing speakers; how to select and place microphones; and how to clean and demagnetize the heads of a tape deck.

### HOW TO MAKE A PRODUCTION TAPE

Once the sound designer has located the necessary music and sounds for a production, the next step is recording, and then editing the tape for playback during the performance. Handle the recording tape as little as possible. And keep good records—be sure to document what was recorded, where, and the length of each segment. One sensible guideline is always to record more music or effect than you think you will need. It is easy to edit sound out, but much more difficult to add in.

**Dubbing**     The simplest of recording processes, dubbing refers to tape-recording the prerecorded sound from a record, compact disc, or another tape. The steps are outlined in the box that follows.

a

## Figure 13–17
### Computerized Control

(a) Shown is the Richmond "Command/Cue" computerized control system. Photo courtesy Richmond Sound Design Ltd.
(b) A cue sheet printed by the Command/Cue for the production of *Twelfth Night* at the Old Globe Theatre. Sound designer—Jeff Ladman.

b      Richmond Sound Design COMMAND/CUE PLUS Sound Cues

12th Night

| | | | | | |
|---|---|---|---|---|---|
| 1. | Viola Entrance @ Top | A Dk | x000 | PRESS F10 | Y |
| 2. | Mirror Rise | B Dk | x000 | PRESS F10 | Y |
| 2.1. | Fade OUT A Dk | | x000 | 00:00:00.1 | Y |
| 3. | Feste Entrance | C Dk | x000 | 00:00:07.0 | Y |
| 4. | The Storm | B Dk | x000 | PRESS F10 | Y |
| 4.1. | Lose C Dk | | x000 | 00:00:00.1 | Y |
| 4.8. | Fade Storm DOWN | | X000 | PRESS F10 | Y |
| 4.9. | Call to Illyria/Storm OUT | D Dk | x000 | PRESS F10 | Y |
| 5. | Boat Entrance | A Dk | x000 | PRESS F10 | Y |
| 5.5. | Music OUT/Amb. fade | | x000 | PRESS F10 | Y |
| 6. | Viola move Inland | C Dk | x000 | PRESS F10 | Y |
| 6.9. | Viola move Inland Fade OUT | | x000 | 00:00:12.9 | Y |
| 7. | Gramophone Duke Ent. | B Dk | x000 | PRESS F10 | Y |
| 7.5. | Gramophone Needle DUMP | | x000 | PRESS F10 | Y |
| 8. | Gramophone reprise | C Dk | x000 | PRESS F10 | Y |
| 8.1. | Gramophone Blossom | | x000 | 00:00:01.5 | Y |
| 8.5. | Gramophone DUMP | | x000 | PRESS F10 | Y |
| 9. | Gramophone Duke Exit | B Dk | x000 | PRESS F10 | Y |
| 9.2. | Gramophone fade Away | | x000 | 00:00:05.0 | Y |
| 11. | JukeBox/Toby Entrance | C Dk | x000 | PRESS F10 | Y |
| 11.2. | JukeBox Blossom | | x000 | 00:00:02.0 | Y |
| 12. | Olivia Entrance | B Dk | x000 | 00:00:21.9 | Y |
| 13. | Belch | D Dk | x000 | 00:00:26.1 | Y |

## HOW TO MAKE A DUB

When dubbing the prerecorded sound from a record, compact disc, or another tape, follow these steps:

1. Place a reel of blank tape on the left spindle of the tape deck and thread it past the heads onto a take-up reel.
2. Prepare the deck by making sure that the power is on, the speed correct, the monitor switched to "source," the counter at zero, and the "record" volume up.
3. Check to make sure the source machine's playback volume settings are up.
4. Play the source sound and adjust the deck's record volume as necessary according to VU meters (see "Record Levels" below).
5. When satisfied with levels, begin recording deck, wait a few seconds to allow tape to roll and reach speed, and then begin source sound. Switch the monitor to playback and listen off the playback head.
6. When source sound is ended, allow the tape to run a few seconds before stopping.

**Record Levels**   While a general rule for recording is to keep the volume as high as possible without distortion, it is wise to remember a few suggestions for specific situations. Normal speech should be recorded between $-5$ and 0 dB. Music with a wide dynamic range such as classical must be carefully monitored so that the peaks hit, but do not exceed, $+3$ dB.

**Live Recording**   Live recording of a synthesizer is simply a matter of patching its output into the recording deck, but recording sounds with a microphone is another matter entirely. The mike input will want to go through a mixer and then into the recording deck, allowing the operator volume and mixing control. In most instances, it is safest to record "flat" (without equalization) and make adjustments later. The recording studio normally should be quite "dead," with walls and floors covered with absorbent material (carpeting works fine); and ambient sound must be eliminated.

There should always be ample time allowed for any recording session. Before the "talent" arrives, all equipment should be checked out to be sure it is in good working order. Make a recording of the room to see what you hear. Do not be afraid to experiment; mistakes often reveal the best of techniques. Try a variety of different microphones as well as placements. Remember that microphones (especially omnidirectional microphones) pick up *everything,* including the sound of the tape machine (which should be in another room).

**Selecting and Placing Microphones**   When recording the speaking voice, a directional or an omnidirectional microphone may be used. The directional mike eliminates more ambient sound, while the omnidirectional provides more "presence" and is less likely to "pop." Place the microphone 6 to 12 inches away from the person being recorded and run a series of tests with him or her talking into the mike. The effect of distant sound is best achieved with the person off-axis or to one side of a directional mike; or, it can be added later with equalization and reverberation.

Recording a group of voices can be done with a single omnidirectional mike. If stereo is necessary, try a stereo microphone or two directional mikes crossed as in Figure 13–18.

### HOW TO EDIT TAPE

Editing a tape for production playback is as important as any other step in the design process. Editing should only be attempted after the sound plot is complete, so that the designer knows precisely how the operator will perform the various functions of running the show.

**Determining the Sound Plot**    Working closely with the script, the director, and the stage manager—and by attending rehearsals—the sound designer will determine exactly how each production sound tape will be compiled. Perhaps this will be as simple as determining the order of effects and music on one reel of tape. But, more likely, it will involve figuring out the use of each track on several tapes playing simultaneously.

**Building a Show Tape**    A standard show tape will have a 5-foot piece of leader tape at the beginning or "head" and the same at the end or "tail," with recording tape in between. The head and tail are carefully marked as such, and the show name and deck number should be included. Between each

Figure 13–18
Stereo Microphone
Arrangement

Illustration showing crossed microphones to achieve stereo pickup.

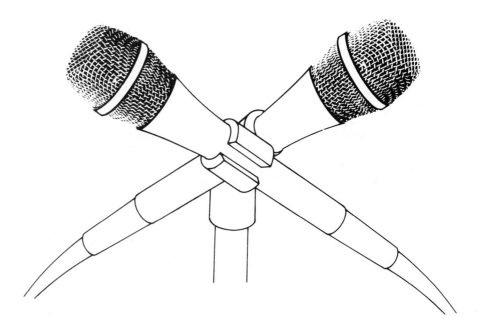

cut, more leader tape (approximately 2 feet long) will be inserted with the cue number clearly marked on the tape just preceding that cut.

Never force a sound operator to return to a cue by rewinding. If a sound is repeated, a second cut should be made and placed in order within the show tape.

Every sound studio will have one tape deck that is used for editing show tapes. This deck should be mounted flat with a splicing block (illustrated in Figure 13–19) permanently fixed to the tabletop in front of the deck.

## HOW TO SPLICE

A splice is necessary for attaching leader tape to recording tape. The equipment necessary for splicing are a metal splicing block (EdiTall), splicing tape, a single-edge razor blade, a china marker or grease pencil, and leader tape. Read carefully the instructions that come with the EdiTall splicing block.

1. Locate the sound to be spliced by rolling the tape at normal speed. Once found, engage the deck's editing mode and roll the tape by hand until the sound is exactly located. Mark the location of the sound with your grease pencil. Do not mark directly on the playback head; devise a system of marking a set distance from the head and measuring that distance.
2. Transfer the tape from the deck to the splicing block. Handle the recording tape by its edges and place the tape in the block with the nonmagnetic back side up.
3. Assuming that you are attaching leader tape to the beginning of a sound cue, place your sound location mark $\frac{1}{2}$ inch to the left side of the splicing block's 45-degree cutting groove (Figure 13–19a). Lay the leader tape in the splicing block directly on top of the recording tape with its end just overlapping your sound location mark (Figure 13–19b).
4. Draw the *demagnetized* razor blade along the 45-degree cutting groove, cutting through both recording and leader tapes (Figure 13–19c). Remove the excess leader tape to the left of your cut and pull out the unwanted recording tape from the right of the cut.
5. Slide the splice to one side of the cutting groove and carefully butt the two ends together. They must not overlap, but meet perfectly.
6. Apply a $\frac{3}{4}$-inch length of splicing tape across the splice, pressing it down to eliminate any air bubbles (Figure 13–19d). It is best to use tape that is $\frac{7}{32}$ inch rather than $\frac{1}{4}$ inch wide, for the splicing tape must never overlap the edges of the recording tape. Many designers prefer "Editabs," a brand of precut splicing tape.
7. *Do not pull the tape straight out of the block!* Remove the tape by holding it by the edges and turning it out of the block's grove.
8. Check your splice by running it by the heads at proper speed and with proper tension.

**Making a Tape Loop**     Sound that continues for long periods of time, such as a foghorn or the chirping of crickets, is easy to record if you "loop" the sound. While the best method is using a sampler and loop the sound, an endless loop cassette offers another solution, as does building your own loop. The length of the loop depends on the effect, but tension must be maintained on the loop at all times while dubbing—running the tape around a home-made jig of uncoated nails works well. The loop's splice must be absolutely silent, otherwise the audience will hear a "pop" every time the splice passes the record head. Also, be careful that no moment on the loop is terribly discernible unless repetition is desired, as in the foghorn example. Never attempt to use a tape loop for live playback—only for recording the effect—and make sure that the length of your recording is more than sufficient.

## HOW TO PLACE SPEAKERS

Elementary speaker placement for reinforcement and general sound was discussed earlier. It is best to place reinforcement loudspeakers above and just in front of the performer. However, other locations may be necessary if the designer wishes to approximate the direction of a sound source. Physical limitations of the performance space may also compromise speaker placement.

If stereo sound is required, two speakers separated by some distance will be necessary. This can be achieved by placing speakers above and to each side of the performer, perhaps with a fill-in center speaker. Be aware that this arrangement may be fine for sound effects and music, but will cause the spoken word to be less intelligible.

Speakers for the arena stage should be located as close as possible to center, above the performance space, pointing out toward the audience. The dispersion pattern of the high-frequency horns should be narrow enough to direct the sound to the audience and not into the acting area. If such an arrangement causes feedback, the speakers will have to move toward the audience until the problem is alleviated. Cabinet-type speakers may work well for the small arena.

## HOW TO SELECT AND PLACE PERFORMANCE MICROPHONES

There are two categories of microphone use pertinent to this discussion: vocal reinforcement and musical pickup.

**Vocal**     Other than body mikes, the best solution for vocal microphone selection and placement in the reinforcement system is floor mikes placed downstage in the footlight position. The best microphone for this task is the supercardiod PCC-type with rear sound rejection. Position the mikes about 10 feet apart, keeping in mind that an odd number is best so as to provide a center position. They will be effective approximately 15 to 20 feet upstage.

Difficult-to-reach positions often require some theatrical ingenuity. Mounting a PCC- or PZM-type microphone on the scenery can effectively

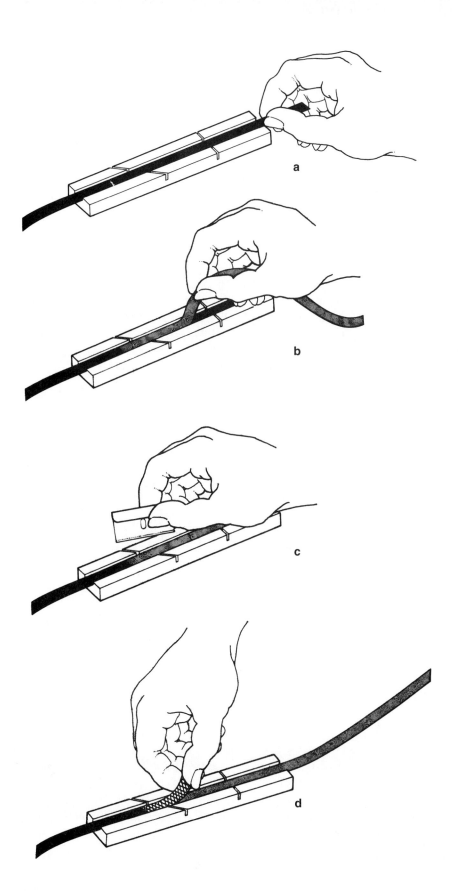

**Figure 13—19**
**Four Steps in Splicing Analog Recording Tape**

(a) Placing the tape in the splicing block.
(b) Placing leader tape in the block.
(c) Cutting the tape.
(d) Placing splicing tape over the cut.

solve a tough reinforcement problem. Suspending a small condenser mike above the playing area is another possible solution.

Keeping the number of microphones in use to an absolute minimum is an important rule to follow. As the number of live microphones increases, the possible volume before feedback decreases significantly. A good operator will never have a microphone pot open if it is not needed.

**Musical** The sound from any electronic musical instrument should be fed into the mixer by means of a *direct box.* Sometimes referred to as a DI box (direct injection box), this small electronic circuit makes it possible for the signal from the instrument to go directly into the microphone input of the mixer.

Most other instruments can best be miked by placing a directional microphone as close to the sound source as possible. In addition, special microphones are manufactured specifically for musical instrument pickup. Some are standard microphones and others, called *contact microphones,* react to sound vibrations. A PZM mounted inside a partially closed piano lid produces good sound. Manufacturer's catalogues will provide additional information on the various microphones made for musical pickup.

### HOW TO CLEAN AND DEMAGNETIZE TAPE HEADS

Oxide from magnetic recording tape builds up on the heads, capstan, and tape guides of the tape machine. This residue will reduce recording fidelity and eventually may result in tape spillage. Cleaning is a simple process that should be done periodically and after every heavy use of the machine. Use denatured alcohol and a clean cotton cloth or cotton swab. Rub the damp swab over contact surfaces and allow to dry.

The heads should be demagnetized with the inexpensive machine made for just this purpose after every 25 to 30 hours of use. Be sure not to leave recording tape in the vicinity of the demagnetizer.

# 14 INTRODUCTION TO STAGE LIGHTING DESIGN

While each one of us reacts to our environment in a unique manner, it is generally true that we take light and lighting for granted. Like a veterinarian who will be aware of things in an animal that even its owner does not notice, the lighting designer is acutely aware of the presence of light: its quality, color, shadow and direction, warmth or coolness, texture, and movement. The first thing a student of lighting seeks to develop is such an awareness—not for theatrical lighting, for that will come later, but for the light that surrounds us each and every day.

The design of lighting begins with an *idea*. In the theatre, this idea results from interpretation of the script by the director and the production design team (lighting, scenic, costume, and sound designers). In dance, the idea comes from the choreographer and the movement and the music. In concert lighting, it begins with the music. In advertising, it is inspired by the product. It matters not whether the lighting designer is found working in a theatre or a museum or a restaurant or a film studio or an exhibition hall—the design will be based on a collection of impressions, an idea.

The following material will primarily focus on stage lighting design, for the theatre has historically been the source of lighting design and continues to be the prime training ground for today's lighting designers.

## STAGE LIGHTING

What is the magic of stage lighting? The demands upon it are many. The costume designer, while considering period, silhouette, color, and character in choosing the fabric for a costume, also wonders how it will look *under the lights*. The scene designer, in selecting the colors of draperies and upholstery or deciding the scale of detail on the scenery, hopes they will show well *under the lights.* The actor in the dressing room ponders if makeup will look right *under the lights.*

The primary concern of stage lighting is, and will always remain, *visibility* (a rule that the designer must never forget). Yet, visibility is much more than simple intensity or brightness of light. Good lighting ties together the visual aspects of the stage and supports the dramatic intent of the production. The lighting designer is also concerned with revelation of form, mood of the scene, and composition of the stage picture.

Scripts may call for effects such as a hearth fire, a bolt of lightning, or a flashing sign—all of which fall under the auspices of the lighting designer. Most often, however, the concern is with lighting the actor: a moving target that can be illuminated in an endless variety of moods and degrees of visibility. Herein lies the real challenge and excitement of stage lighting design.

## THE SCENE DESIGNER

Scene design, unlike the other visual arts, is deeply dependent on the use of light as a part of the final composition—the dramatic picture. Stage lighting holds such importance in contribution to the total visual effect that every designer should be familiar with its techniques.

The design of lighting may begin with the scene designer's sketch, which presents a suggestion of the light that will illuminate the scene. It may appear to be coming from such natural sources as the sun, the moon, or a fire, or from artificial sources such as table lamps or ceiling fixtures. In contrast, the sources may be frankly arbitrary and depend on the position and color of the instruments that are used to build the composition. The sketch or rendering, as opposed to the model, is the scene designer's only means of conveying a sense of mood (Figure 14–1).

Such sketches, however, are only a start in the planning of stage lighting. A sketch represents an artistic vision that must be technically sound to be properly realized. The floor plan and section that accompany the sketch give the first clues as to the credibility of the designer's lighting ideas. Many a beautiful sketch as been based on a floor plan that revealed, on closer study, impossible lighting angles and insufficient space for the lighting instruments.

A single person designing the scenery, costumes, lighting, and sound for a production would be most able to achieve a unified approach or concept. However, today the production design team is generally made up of several designers and the director. Diverse ideas and views must be brought together into a single outlook or concept by active and open communication among the members of this collaborative team as well as strong leadership from the director.

## THE LIGHTING DESIGNER

In contemporary theatre, the lighting designer is the newest member to join the visual design team. Except for a few scene designers who enjoyed lighting their own scenery, the lighting of most Broadway productions in the first half of this century was neglected and became, by default, one of the innumerable duties of the stage manager or stage electrician. It was inevitable

### Figure 14—1
### Scene Designer Sketches

The planning of stage lighting may begin with the scene designer's sketches where the kind of illumination, its distribution, color and general atmosphere are indicated. These two sketches were done for a production of *Follies* designed by Beeb Salzer. See color plate 15—1 for a production photograph.

that lighting specialists would eventually move into this neglected field and demonstrate with startling results what could be done if one person devoted his or her sole attention to the planning of lighting. This trend continued as lighting designers developed their art and craft, inspired by the work of people like Stanley McCandless, Jean Rosenthal, and Abe Feder.

The lighting designer must understand and have compassion for the total design effort, particularly since he or she is the only design member who does not submit, in advance, a visual statement of what is intended. The costume and scene designers present a multitude of sketches, material samples, and models as visual examples of their intent. The lighting designer, on the other hand, may submit sketches of light in the form of a *storyboard*, but most often relies on verbal exchanges until the time comes to draft the light plot. Fortunately, the lighting designer commonly has the advantage of attending rehearsals before the final plot is completed.

Setting aside the technical aspects of electricity, instrument and control design, and details of plotting, the lighting designer is concerned first with the aesthetics of light. To develop a sense of composition and taste in color, a lighting designer must start with qualities and limitations of the medium itself.

## QUALITIES OF LIGHT

Once light is created, whether from the sun or from an artificial source, it has certain inherent qualities that become characteristic of the medium itself. Just as paint has traits particular to its medium, so light conforms to its own set of attributes. The physical characteristics of light in relationship to scenery are discussed in Chapter 3. The separate study of light as applied to stage lighting involves these same qualities: intensity, distribution, color, and movement.

### INTENSITY

The first and most obvious quality of light is its intensity or brightness, which may be actual or comparative brightness. The actual brightness of the sun, for example, can be contrasted to the comparative brightness of automobile headlights at night. Spotlights in a darkened theatre offer the designer the same comparative brightness under more controlled conditions. The entire composition of a stage picture is dependent on varying intensities of light. In addition, intensity has a strong effect on mood and atmosphere of a scene.

Varying the intensity of a light source is most often achieved by means of a dimmer. Groups of dimmers working together can direct audience focus as well as alter stage composition. Intensity is commonly measured in *foot-candles.*

### DISTRIBUTION

Most often we see light as it is reflected off various surfaces. The manner in which it is distributed upon these surfaces is dependent on the source's *direction* and *quality*. The lighting designer is in complete control of the source and, therefore, of its direction and quality.

**Direction**   Visibility of an object is highly dependent on the direction of the light striking it. A change in lighting direction can radically alter the perception of size and/or shape of any form (Figure 14–2). Highlight and especially shadow are the best indicators of direction. A theatre audience feels most at ease with light coming from the natural direction of above and in front of the performer. Like intensity, direction has a strong effect on mood and atmosphere.

**Quality**   The concept of "quality" is very closely related to texture and is dependent on a source's intensity and diffusion. A highly diffuse light tends

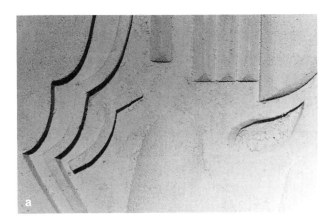

to have divergent rays, while a less diffuse light has coherent and parallel rays. Diffuse light is perceived as soft and lacking in intensity. More coherent light is harsher, more intense, and creates harder edges.

Creative use of the direction and texture of light introduces highlight, shade, and shadow into the stage composition.

## COLOR

The third property of light is its ability to transmit and reveal color. Color, a forceful element in all areas of theatre design, is often considered the most effective and dramatic quality of light. The use of colored light to enhance the mood of a scene is a common theatrical technique. The lighting designer may use color in a theatrically realistic way to convey time of day or atmospheric conditions. On the other hand, color choices may be heightened or exaggerated in order to stylize the look of a production.

The ability of colored light to alter the color of the surfaces it strikes makes it a powerful design tool. Modification of the natural color of a scenic form or costume by colored light is a design technique unique to the theatre. Color modification and the additive mixing of colored light are two rather basic concepts of color as a quality of light that must be understood by all designers in the theatre.

## MOVEMENT

While not an intrinsic quality of light, movement is an extremely important characteristic of stage lighting. It implies a change in intensity, distribution,

**Figure 14–2**
Distribution

Demonstrating the effects of distribution of light on a highly textured surface or low-relief carving.
(a) A low-relief sculptural form lighted with a single source from the front.
(b) The same form lighted with two side-angle sources of different intensity or color.

LIGHT QUALITIES

Intensity
Distribution
Color
Movement

or color that might be as subtle as a slow progression from predawn to daybreak or as blatant as a blackout. Most light movement is controlled by means of dimmers. A lighting *cue* in the form of a shift from one "look" to another involves movement. Movement can take and control focus. Movement alters composition.

## STAGE LIGHTING AND THE ELEMENTS OF DESIGN

The principles of *composition* are the same for the lighting designer as they are for the scene designer or any graphic or visual artist. Composition is the organization of the visual elements of design into a unified form or arrangement of forms. Lighting is the unifying and fluid force of the stage composition.

The role of the lighting designer as a member of the design team demands that he or she be acutely aware of the elements of design affecting the creative process of the scenery and costume designers. The elemental factors that make up any visual form or arrangement of forms, as discussed in Chapter 3, can be listed in the order of their importance to the creative process:

Line

Dimension

Movement

Light

Color

Texture

### LINE

As an element of design, line defines form. Its force is present in a composition in many ways. Line can enclose spaces as an outline creating shape (two-dimensional form), or as a contour line suggesting three-dimensional form. Strong back-lighting, for example, emphasizes the silhouette or outline of a form, while directional side-lighting reveals its contour. Light has the power to deny, alter, or accentuate line (Figure 14–2).

Line can appear in a composition as a *real line* in many different modes (straight, curved, spiral, and so on), or as a *suggested line* that is simulated by the eye as it follows a sequence of related shapes.

When line creates a path of action, it also frequently assumes a direction. A strong beam of light revealed by smoke in the air cannot help but establish direction. The *linear shape* of the beam coupled with a concentration of brightness creates a strong focus in the composition (Figure 14–3).

### DIMENSION

The size of a form is an important part of its dimension. However, as an element of design, dimension is concerned not only with the size of an

**Figure 14–3**
Light as Line

A beam of light made visible in the air creates a sense of direction and focus as is evident in this production of *King Lear* directed by Jack O'Brien for the Old Globe Theatre, San Diego in 1993. Scenery design—Ralph Funicello, lighting—David Segal, and costumes—Robert Morgan.

individual shape or mass, but also with the contrasting relationship of the size of one shape to another—large to small, large to large, and so on. Accordingly, the size of the space between two objects has a definite effect on their apparent mass. Control of light on either the object or the space influences the dimension of one or the other.

By accentuating vertical surfaces, light can make an object look taller. Lighting from directly above, or "top-lighting," may cause an object to appear squat. Light can reverse the feeling of dimension by making a two-dimensional shape look three-dimensional and vice versa.

## MOVEMENT

The action of form is movement. It is the kinetic energy of composition. Motion within a stage composition can be either real or optical.

*Optical motion* is the movement of the eye through a composition. When a form or group of forms is static, optical motion is dependent on the sequential arrangement of those forms. Since a form is seen only as well as it is lit, lighting plays an important role in optical motion. Note the movement of your eye through the painting by Rembrandt in Figure 14–4.

Movement of the eye can easily be altered by changing the composition through a selective shift in light intensity on one or more forms. Strong directional light rays or the sequential arrangement of light sources are examples of the use of light as optical motion.

## LIGHT

Form can only be revealed under light. Due to the dominant presence of light in all areas of stage design, it is imperative that light be discussed as a basic influence in the beginning of the creative process. Awareness of the

**Figure 14—4**
Optical Motion

Artists use light to cause eye movement through a painting, thereby increasing visual interest. Rembrandt Harmensz van Rijn (or follower), Dutch, 1606–1669, Young Woman at an Open Half-Door, oil on canvas, 1645, 102.5 × 85.1 cm, Mr. and Mrs. Martin A. Ryerson Collection, 1894.1022. Photograph copyright 1994, The Art Institute of Chicago, all rights reserved.

significance of light as a design element is as important to the scenery and costume designers as the appreciation of all the elements of design is to the lighting expert.

## COLOR

Form can be altered by color. As an element of design it is a powerful stimulus within the composition. Color can change the dimension of form, reverse the direction of line, alter the interval between forms, and generate optical motion. Color in the theatre comes from two basic sources: pigment or dye present on the surface of the form, or colored light that affects the color of the form.

## TEXTURE

The tactile aspect of form is referred to as texture. Textural treatment of surfaces is of great interest to the lighting designer. Surfaces that are highly polished, rough-hewn, or rusticated will each reflect light differently, casting interesting shadows. Three-dimensional texture is best revealed by directional side-light, while painted or simulated texture appears more real under a wash of light that has no strong sense of direction.

In its simplest form, texture in light is the product of a specific type of lighting instrument. One of the considerations in selecting an instrument involves the textural quality of its light. In addition, the designer can create texture in light by adjusting focus, using diffusion media, or breaking up the light with specially designed patterns called *gobos*. (Look ahead to Figures 14–6b and 14–8 to see the use of gobo patterns in light.)

## STAGE LIGHTING AND THEATRICAL FORM

Several factors have a great effect on the development of a lighting idea and the subsequent light plot. The *production concept* and resulting *scenery and costume designs* will influence color palette as well as style. The *scenery* may affect specific placement of lighting instruments. The *style* of the production as well as the *script itself* guides the lighting designer toward an approach. Finally, *budget* and the *physical form of the theatre* will impact the lighting design.

### PRODUCTION AND LIGHTING STYLE

While the term *style* is subject to overuse and misunderstanding (see Chapter 3), we use it here in its broadest sense. In a recent conversation with a gathering of students, scenic designer Ming Cho Lee made the comment: "I don't know what style is. I think Howard Bay referred to it as a peculiar way of drawing." An individual artist's work possesses a unique look—a particular flair or technical approach referred to as a *signature*. A landscape painted by Monet and the identical landscape painted by van Gogh would look quite different—the difference being a collection of techniques comprising the artist's style. In the professional theatre, like the art world, designers are known and often hired for their particular style.

In order to complicate matters, a theatrical production also has a style of its own. A production's style (earlier in this book defined as "degree of reality") is related to and often a result of its *concept*. Concept and style are arrived at through a collaborative interaction of the designers and director. After analysis of the play, the director and designers agree upon an approach that includes a style for the production. The designers then contribute their own techniques to this style, resulting in a unique interpretation of the dramatic work.

**Figure 14—5**
Motivational Lighting

(a) The documentary style of Brecht's *The Measures Taken* illustrates a highly motivational approach to the lighting. Design—Frederic Youens. Photo by Nelson.

A designer's style evolves over a period of time and is always shaped by the work (techniques) of others. Style in lighting is evidenced by a unique interaction of the qualities of light: intensity, color, distribution, and movement. A particular methodology may have a strong influence on style. For instance, the well-known lighting designer Paulie Jenkins claims that she always considers back-light first when thinking about how to light a scene. This would certainly affect the choices she makes and would be an important element of her style.

Two very basic techniques that contribute to style are *motivational* and *nonmotivational* lighting. Motivational lighting is based on the desire to duplicate a specific source of light such as the sun, a candle, a window, and so on. Environmental conditions such as time of day, weather, time of year, and

a

locale are all taken into consideration (Figure 14–5). Nonmotivational light-ing ignores the above rationale as a basis for color selection, instrument choice, and lighting angle. Instead, the lighting designer makes these choices in response to a desired mood, a compositional requirement, or simply a "feeling" about the scene.

The beginning lighting designer should start by concentrating on mo-tivational lighting, but must realize that a nonmotivational approach can be quite as valid and sometimes more expressive and exciting. The production style helps the designer select an approach that will employ one or perhaps both of these basic lighting techniques (Figure 14–6).

(b) Motivational lighting is often required to support realism, as indicated in this production pho-tograph of *Tartuffe* directed by Dan Sullivan for Seattle Reper-tory Theatre in 1988. Scenery design—Ralph Funicello, light-ing—James F. Ingalls, and costumes—Ann Hould-Ward.

## PHYSICAL PLANT

The physical theatre itself has great influence over lighting potential in terms of distribution. Where lighting instruments may be placed and how their light strikes the actors and scenery are chiefly determined by the space's architecture. Beginning with the *proscenium theatre* and its traditional audience and stage arrangement, lighting, for the most part, is essentially shadow-box illumination that caters to theatrical realism or illusory theatre. Lighting in-struments are traditionally concealed behind masking legs and borders on-stage and in "ports" or "beams" front-of-house. In older theatres,

## Figure 14–6
### Lighting Style

(a) Highly stylized motivational lighting is shown here from a production of *You Can't Take It With You*. Set design—Craig Wolf. Lighting design—Doug Grekin. Photo by Mountain Mist. (b) Abstract non-motivational lighting is appropriate for this production of *A Midsummer Night's Dream* with scenery designed by Michael Yeargan and lighting by Pat Collins. Copyright The Hartford Stage Company. 1989. Photo courtesy T. Charles Erickson.

front-of-house positions are often limited, possibly to only a balcony rail. Worth noting is the fact that, scenery permitting, the proscenium stage is the most versatile form for side-lighting possibilities.

The *thrust stage*, with its audience on three sides, minimizes the use of scenery and makes illusion a greater responsibility of the lighting designer. This new-old form of theatricality (popular in the sixteenth century) relies chiefly on lighting, costumes, and properties for its visual composition. Additionally, in most thrust houses the stage floor becomes very prominent due to audience viewing angle. In some cases the floor is more of a background to the actor than are any upstage scenery or properties. The lighting designer must keep this in mind when choosing color and texture of the light. Thrust staging requires full-coverage (360 degrees) lighting. An exciting and challenging theatre form, modern thrust theatres provide flexibility in lighting positions both front-of-house as well as overstage.

*Arena staging* surrounds the stage area with audience. The arena theatre form increases the demands on stage lighting and virtually eliminates scenery. Like thrust, the arena requires 360-degree coverage but is often a bit more restrictive in terms of lighting possibilities. A good arena theatre will be equipped with a lighting grid that covers the entire space and allows total flexibility in hanging position.

*Theatre of total environment*, the most recent form, not only brings back scenery elements, but also expands the use of lighting to even greater dimensions by surrounding or immersing the audience in the atmosphere or environment of the play. The circle has been completed by returning to a proscenium form. The production, however, is not contained behind the frame, but is allowed to spill out and surround the audience.

*Flexible* or *black box staging* should not be neglected, for it is capable of achieving, on a small scale, any of the aforementioned audience–stage arrangements and even more. It is, by its sheer flexibility, a frankly impromptu form with its exposed lighting instruments and temporary seating arrangement.

## FUNCTIONS OF STAGE LIGHTING

The basic obligation of stage design is to give the actor or performer *meaning* in his or her surroundings, providing an atmosphere in which the role may be logically interpreted. Through the manipulation of light in all its aspects— intensity, color, distribution, and movement—the lighting designer assists in creating an environment for the play by achieving *selective visibility*, appropriate *composition*, and *revelation of form;* and by *establishing mood* and *reinforcing the theme.*

### SELECTIVE VISIBILITY

It is important to understand that the actor must be seen in order to be heard. Visibility cannot be defined as a fixed degree of brightness or an established angle of distribution. It is the amount of light needed for a moment of recognition deemed appropriate for that point in the action of the play. "To see what should be seen" may mean revealing only the silhouette of a three-dimensional form, the solidity of its mass, or the full decorative and textural detail of all surfaces.

## COMPOSITION

Stage composition begins with the scenic design and floor plan, is developed by the placement and movement of actors, and is completed when lit by the lighting designer. More than any other design element, light is able to direct the audience's eye and control what is and is not seen. Points of visual focus are determined by the blocking and the action. Since light possesses the

**Figure 14–7**
**Composition**

The work of Giorgio de Chirico emphasizes the significance of light as an element of composition. Giorgio de Chirico, Italian, 1888–1978, The Philosopher's Conquest, oil on canvas, 1914, 125.1 × 99.1 cm, Joseph Winterbotham Collection, 1939.405. Photograph copyright 1994, The Art Institute of Chicago, all rights reserved.

additional quality of incredible fluidity, stage composition can be altered with relative ease.

Much can be learned about composition through study of art. For instance, cast shadows and highlights have significant influence on the composition of *The Philosopher's Conquest* by Giorgio de Chirico (Figure 14–7). Although light can have composition of its own (projected patterns, for example), its chief function is to selectively reveal stage forms in the proper relationship to other forms and to the background. And here the complexity of compositional lighting begins.

Compositional lighting means lighting one form and not another; controlling shadows, keeping them off the background; lighting three-dimensional forms to make them look three-dimensional (not as easy as it seems); and other similar problems, including the most significant: lighting the actor (Figure 14–8).

**Figure 14–8**
**Compositional Stage Lighting**

These photographs from a production of *A Christmas Carol* at San Diego Repertory Theatre illustrate the use of compositional lighting to create focus, as well as to enhance both mood and locale. Lighting design—Peter Maradudin, scenery—Kent Dorsey, and costumes—Nancy Jo Smith.

## REVELATION OF FORM

Figure 14–9 illustrates that a form can be revealed in a variety of ways. The three-dimensional form of the actor must be shown in a consistent and predictable manner while moving through space—something best not left to chance. Even in the proscenium theatre with the audience viewing from principally a frontal angle, the lighting designer focuses light upon the sides and backs of actors in order to enhance their dimensionality. However, form is often best revealed if the various sources of light playing upon it have some degree of contrast—either in intensity or color. Altering form is one of light's greatest powers.

**Figure 14–9**
Selective Visibility

Illustrating the effect of four different kinds of visibility.
(a) An object visible in silhouette only.
(b) With front light added, the object is visible as a three-dimensional form.
(c) With the addition of another direction of light, the object's detail becomes visible.
(d) An example of detail and form becoming less visible as a result of too much light.

## ESTABLISHING THE MOOD

The lighting designer begins with a feeling for the overall mood of the play or scene. A color impression comes from the mood as well as a suggestion of the intensity and distribution of light. The word *mood* tends to suggest dark and gloomy surroundings, but bright comedy or nonsensical farce also indicate a type of mood.

Occasionally a lighting designer will allow concern for mood or atmosphere to override all else, sacrificing other functions, including visibility. Unfortunately, this has happened frequently enough for directors to have become wary of "mood lighting" and shy away from any such discussion. Two things must be understood:

1. Mood and atmosphere are *unavoidable* features of light, and to ignore that fact is as dangerous as overstating the mood.
2. Mood is only one of five equally important light functions; to slight any one for another *must* be a conscious decision made by the entire design team and director.

Although an abstract or dramatic mood is more impressive and eye-catching than the realistic visibility of a conventional interior setting, it is also far easier to accomplish with light.

## REINFORCING THE THEME

The key word here is *reinforcing.* The lighting of a scene must support the action. Because the visual expression of theme depends on the designer's interpretation of the playwright's message, the lighting designer is concerned with compositional revelation of the thematic forms of the setting. The theme-dominated play by Tennessee Williams, *A Streetcar Named Desire*, offers a good example of how various light qualities can support thematic action (Figure 14–10).

In the more extreme theme-oriented or documentary plays of Bertolt Brecht, the theme is often stressed by eliminating the theatricality of stage lighting by showing the play under a clear, uncolored wash of light. Lighting reinforces the theme visually through the use of projections that take the form of propaganda pictures or subtitles.

## LIGHT FUNCTIONS

Selective Visibility

Composition

Revelation of Form

Establishing Mood

Reinforcement

## Figure 14–10
### Reinforcing the Theme

Tennessee Williams' *A Streetcar Named Desire* is an example of a theme-dominated play. The lighting designer supports the theme of the play through the use of various qualities of light. This production was directed by John Hirsch in the Avon Theatre for the Stratford Festival, Ontario in 1984. Scenery design—Ralph Funicello, lighting—Michael J. Whitfield, and costumes—Debra Hanson.

## ROLE OF THE LIGHTING DESIGNER

Each designer in the production team functions differently according to the demands of the separate areas. The scenic and costume designers must begin their work well in advance of the production in order to allow sufficient time for purchase of materials and construction. The lighting and sound designers have the pleasure of more time to assimilate and observe the production process unfold, but must accept the added responsibilities that are implicit in that knowledge.

It has been made clear that *all* designers are involved in the creative development of a production concept. This collaborative process is the only time that ideas are shared among the members of the production team. It is the time when the lighting and scenic designers work closely together in order to anticipate any lighting requirements that may affect scenery (adding an onstage follow spot position after the scenery drawings have gone into the shops is terribly expensive if not impossible). It is the time when the style of the production is determined and critical design choices are made. It is the time when all of the designers can discuss color palette and the desired "look" of the show.

**Preparation**     The designer must first and foremost know the script. The number of readings will depend on the individual designer as well as the script, but we emphasize: At the very least, three readings are necessary. The first is simply to enjoy the play as a piece of literature (it should be read as one would a novel); the second identifies technical concerns, such as time of day, effects, and specific lighting action; and the third develops characterization and thematic elements of the script.

Good, solid research is as important to the lighting designer as it is to the other members of the production team. The various works of the playwright, as well as critical reviews, should be studied in order to discover more about point of view and style of working. The play's time period and locale must be carefully researched—primarily for atmosphere, but also for technical details. Any music involved in the production should be investigated for style and mood qualities. A knowledge and appreciation of music as well as art of the period will greatly enchance the lighting designer's creative work. The simple fact is that good research results in a superior creative product— every time.

**Rehearsals**     Attending rehearsals is richly rewarding for the lighting designer and must be taken advantage of if at all possible, for here the true depth and dimensions of a production are discovered through the interaction of director and actors. Attend rehearsals early on to witness the development of characters as well as later to study timing and movement patterns. Be sure to speak with the director beforehand about attending rehearsals, if for no other reason than as a courtesy.

The various reasons for attending rehearsals may seem obvious, but many directors believe that blocking is the lighting designer's only concern. While blocking and space usage are important, other benefits include increased awareness of the director's intent, deeper understanding of how the director works, and a feeling for both mood and pace. Planning for compositional lighting is extremely difficult without prior knowledge of blocking; however, every rehearsal need not be a run-through to satisfy other equally important lighting needs.

**Preproduction**     The light plot, which has been developing in the designer's head for a period of time, is usually put on paper (or into a CADD program) one or two weeks before the lighting move-in day. While every designer has individual ways of working, most who draft their own plots create at the same time. After initially drawing the theatre and scenery, lighting areas are determined. Next, specific instrumentation and distribution methods are chosen. Finally, color is solidified and control choices are made.

Good and thorough preplanning is of the utmost importance. Lighting cues are written and conveyed to the stage manager who will call them during performances. The designer or an assistant is present to answer questions during the put-in, but crews are supervised by a master electrician who is well acquainted with the theatre facilities and equipment. A focus session follows the put-in and hopefully the designer will have the theatre to himself or herself for the several hours required to aim and adjust the beams of light from the various instruments.

**Production**     Dimmer readings for each lighting cue may be put on paper by the designer before lighting rehearsals begin. This information is given to the light board operator to feed into the computer and is then adjusted visually during the acting rehearsal previous to technical rehearsals. This procedure allows the technical rehearsal to be just that—a *technical* rehearsal rather than a *lighting* rehearsal. If the designer prefers to build the show visually or if the production is complex enough to require a separate lighting rehearsal, it should be scheduled to take place before the technical. During subsequent dress rehearsals the lighting designer watches from the auditorium and makes level and timing changes, a procedure that may continue through previews.

### THE ASSISTANT LIGHTING DESIGNER

As the art of lighting became more complex, many designers turned to young people who were interested in the craft to act as their assistants. In this way both parties benefited, as novice lighting designers learned by observing the work of those more experienced and established.

While duties vary with different designers and situations, paperwork is nearly always the responsibility of the assistant. Some designers may hire an assistant to draft the light plot, in which case a solid working knowledge of CAD is important; some will place their assistants in charge of paperwork such as shop orders, instrument schedules, focus charts, hookups, and the like, requiring familiarity with a good software program; and some designers will expect an assistant to call channels during the focus and take notes during

### Figure 14–11
#### Compositional Lighting and the Lighting Lab

In addition to the training advantages of actual production lighting, the well-equipped lighting lab offers a parallel experience. The student lighting designer can reconstruct lighting angles and direction for any stage form—proscenium, arena, or thrust—and experiment, in a hands-on manner, with compositional properties of light. In this example the scenic form purposely contains a variety of surfaces. Sweeping curves, sharp corners, openings, and texture lend interest. The photographs show some of the effects.

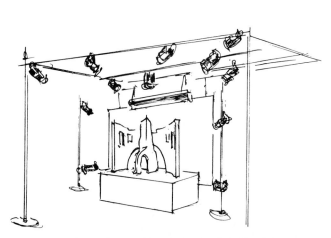

technical rehearsals. No matter what the duties, the assistant is able to closely observe the designer's work as well as that of the entire production machine.

Every beginning designer should seek work as an assistant. It is advisable to assist several different designers, in a variety of theatres, in order to meet different people and learn various ways of working. A good assistant is a silent observer, but also should not be afraid to ask questions when necessary. In this way, the assistant will learn what to expect and how to be flexible. The assistant should not be intimidated by the designer—he or she enjoys and appreciates the assistant's contribution.

The proper way to obtain an assistant position is to submit a resume to the designer, along with a cover letter indicating when you are available.

## THE LIGHTING LABORATORY

More and more institutions that are genuinely committed to training lighting designers are seeking and finding the space and equipment for lighting labs. The light lab comes in many sizes and forms; most exist in found spaces that have been equipped by students and faculty with a limited budget. The available equipment is often ancient and may be less than useful in an actual production. However, the lab is also the place for experimentation with state-of-the-art instrumentation; many facilities select for purchase one or two new pieces of equipment each year to be used in the lab.

Ideally the light lab will be on a human scale, with a grid somewhere between 12 and 15 feet high. It should have its own control system and circuitry, although neither need be elaborate. An intelligent arrangement is to combine the lighting lab with a makeup classroom, for makeup instruction often requires stage lighting. Lab exercises vary from reproduction of light in a painting to demonstrations of color, angle, and quality of light. A variety of laboratory exercises are available in a publication by U. S. I. T. T. (United States Institute for Theatre Technology), titled *Practical Projects for Teaching Lighting Design, A Compendium.*

It is an observable fact that today's student learns better in a lighting laboratory than in any other environment. The student is less intimidated by scale and equipment when working in the lab as opposed to the theatre. The hands-on experience of laboratory work accelerates learning and solidifies conceptual material received in the classroom. And, if students have free access to the lab, they can learn at their own pace.

An excellent example of the use of a large-scale model for demonstration in the lighting lab is seen in Figure 14–11. Note the various uses of light angle for texture and composition.

## DEVELOPMENT OF A LIGHTING DESIGNER

Designing for the theatre requires a great deal from an individual. Not only must one have artistic talent and technical know-how, but the designer must also be able to communicate. The next few chapters will instruct the young designer in the nuts and bolts of lighting, but it must never be forgotten along the way that a *designer* is being nurtured. The importance of "learning to see"—of establishing visual memory—must always be in the forethought of the reader. Experimentation is essential: lighting instruments should be examined, dimmer systems operated, and colors mixed. The lighting designer can learn only so much from theory and example; he or she must have opportunities to put theory into practice. Since production space is always in great demand, a lighting laboratory becomes a tremendous aid to practical training.

But always remember, while wandering through the maze of technical information, pause now and then—and *look*.

# COLOR AND LIGHT

## 15

*C*olor, as one of the four characteristics of light (see Chapter 14), is a powerful force in a stage composition. It can be subtle or dramatic, decorative or atmospheric, or, by its very absence, call attention to itself. Color in light animates the scene. The energy of light reveals, brightens, and adds color to actors and scenery, thereby increasing their vitality.

Several basic color observations are important to the lighting designer:

1. An object has a particular color of its own—its surface color.
2. Light is colored—even if its color is white.
3. The color of light affects the color of objects.
4. Certain perceptual factors influence how we see color.

Of the design elements, color often seems to be the most complex. It is for this reason that it was first discussed at length in Chapter 8 and again here, early in our study of stage lighting. No pressure must be felt to "master" the subject of color usage, for it will take time and experience. The beginning lighting designer must learn basic principles of color physics, physiology, and psychology. Attention must be paid to color in dye and pigment as well as in light, for most often they interrelate.

### COLOR IS LIGHT

Color would not exist without light. Breaking up white light into spectral hues by means of a prism is a common illustration of the fact that such light is actually made up of a variety of colors. If we perceive a light as white, the receptors in our eyes are actually receiving a mixture of colors that our brain interprets as white. The color receptors in our eyes (*cones*) are most sensitive to three color wavelengths: red, green, and blue. The combination of these *primary colors* creates white light.

## THE VISIBLE SPECTRUM

The visible wavelengths of the electromagnetic spectrum provide color and light (Color Plate 15–1b). Every color has a different spectral wavelength. These wavelengths are measured in *nanometers*, with one nanometer being equal to one-billionth of a meter. The visible portion of the spectrum is a minute section with wavelengths falling in the vicinity of 400 to 700 nanometers in length (Figure 15–1). The shortest, 390 to 430 nanometers, produces what we call violet light. The next length is blue, followed by green, yellow, orange, and finally (between 630 and 700 nanometers) red light. The wavelengths shorter than 390 nanometers are called *ultraviolet* (beyond violet) and those longer than 700 nanometers are *infrared* (below red).

## THE LANGUAGE OF COLOR

In describing a color, it is important to use a common language that will be understood by other designers and coworkers. The three variants of color in pigments and dyes (discussed in Chapter 8) are hue, chroma, and value. The lighting designer uses these variants as a basis of color terminology. A color can be described in simple terms by referring to its hue (blue, yellow, and so on), its chroma or saturation (purity), and its value (lightness or brightness).

## HUE

The position of a color in the spectrum determines its *hue*. Hue is the quality that allows us to differentiate one color from another or from a gray of the same value (brightness). Six easily identified hues are red, orange, yellow, green, blue, and violet. As mentioned earlier, the cones in our eyes respond most strongly to the three hues of red, green, and blue. The lighting designer often finds it useful to think of any hue as a mixture of these three primary colors in light.

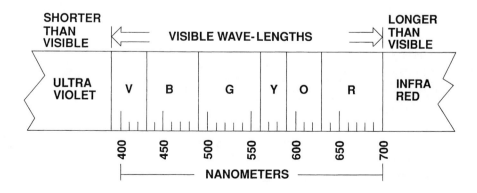

**Figure 15–1**
The Electromagnetic Spectrum

The six principal colors are violet, blue, green, yellow, orange, and red. Their wavelengths are measured in nanometers, equal to one-billionth of a meter (*See* Color Plate 15–1b).

### CHROMA OR SATURATION

In the context of lighting, the term *saturation* is preferred to that of *chroma*. Saturation refers to the amount of pure spectral hue present in a color. Primary blue for example is a highly saturated color. Lee Filters No. 110, middle rose, is less saturated than Lee No. 111, dark pink. (See "Plastic Media" later in this chapter for a discussion of color filters.) The instant the purity of a spectral hue is modified by mixing, the result is a difference in saturation. Unsaturated colors, referred to as *tints*, possess a large admixture of white to the spectral hue.

### VALUE OR BRIGHTNESS

In paint or dye the term *value* refers to the amount of white or black added to the color hue. In light, value is more difficult to define, for it relates to the brilliance or *brightness* of a color. A tint has higher value (is brighter) than a primary color. Yet, in light, brightness also refers to those particular colors that tend to more highly excite the receptors in the eye's retina. Yellow and yellow-green are two such colors.

### KELVIN TEMPERATURE

The lighting designer has yet another concern: the color of the source of light itself. We tend to think of light emitted from the sun and almost any incandescent lamp as being white. In reality, the actual color of light given off by various sources can be quite different. The method we have of identifying the exact color makeup of any light source is called *color temperature*. Its measurement is in degrees Kelvin (after the British physicist, William Lord Kelvin.)

Unlike literal temperature, a higher Kelvin temperature indicates a cooler-colored source—one that is higher in blue content. A source with low Kelvin temperature is rich in warmer colors such as red and amber. Candlelight, which tends to be a warm, yellow-red, is rated at 1,800 degrees Kelvin (K); light from a standard incandescent household lamp is close to 3,000° K; and daylight is surprisingly blue at a cool 5,700° K. Color Plate 15–2a illustrates the approximate color of each of these sources. More detailed information about Kelvin temperature will be found in Chapter 22, but the idea of a scale to measure the color of a light source is important to understand at this point.

### COLOR FILTERING

Most stage lighting instruments produce a light that we consider "white," rated at approximately 3,200° K. Currently, the only practical means of significantly altering this color is by interrupting the beam of light with a filter. Placed in front of candles, clear glass vessels containing red wine and other colored liquids were once employed as filters. Modern stage lighting uses the same technique with filters of colored plastic or dichroic glass.

**COLOR PLATE 15–1a**
**FOLLIES**
A photograph from the production of *Follies*, designed by Beeb Salzer, whose sketches are seen in Chapter 14, Figure 14–1. The projections were achieved by using multiple projectors, making sketches even more necessary in order to achieve the desired background look. Lighting design—Bette Ogami Ellithorpe.

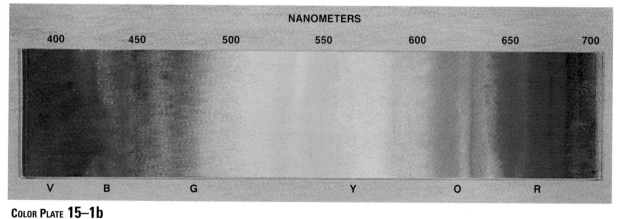

**COLOR PLATE 15–1b**
**THE SPECTRUM**
Shown are the spectral hues and their respective wavelengths measured in nanometers.

**COLOR PLATE 15–2a**
**KELVIN TEMPERATURE**
These three lights illustrate the visual difference between a source at 1800°K, such as candelight; a source at 3200°K, such as stage lighting; and a source at 5700°K, such as daylight.

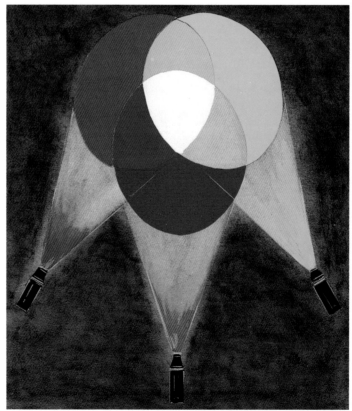

**COLOR PLATE 15–2b**
**MIXING OF PRIMARY COLORS**
When the three primary colors of light are mixed, white light is the result. Any two primaries mix to form secondary colors.

**COLOR PLATE 15–3a**
**BLUE-GREEN FABRIC UNDER WHITE AND AMBER LIGHT**
White light side-by-side with amber light (R16) on the same blue-green fabric.

**COLOR PLATE 15–3b**
**THE EFFECT OF AMBER DRIFT**
Shown is an instrument with a blue filter (R68) at a dimmer reading of 100 percent, and the same filter at a dimmer reading of 70 percent.

**COLOR PLATE 15–4**
**COLOR ON A SCENE**
Two photographs from a production of *As You Like It* illustrate the strong effect color has on a scene.

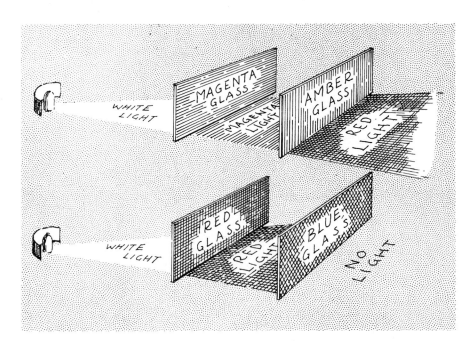

**Figure 15–2**
Color Filtering

(top) White light, when filtered through two secondaries such as magenta (violet) and amber (yellow), results in red, the secondaries' common primary. (bottom) White light, when filtered by two primaries, is completely absorbed so that no light whatever emerges.

As the name implies, a filter placed in front of a light source causes selected colors to be filtered or blocked from passing through. This is an important concept to understand. When white light is shone through a blue filter, the red and green wavelengths are blocked; only the blue wavelengths are allowed to pass. In theory, if a pure blue light is shone through a pure red filter, no light at all will be allowed to pass (Figure 15–2).

## COLOR INTERACTION

Color in light and pigment can be varied by mixing. When two lights of different colors strike a white surface, the result is a mixture of those colors. If the surface is itself colored, mixing still takes place, but the reflected color is altered by the surface color. This is called *color modification*.

### THE COLOR TRIANGLE

A good way to illustrate color mixing is by using a color triangle such as the one illustrated in Figure 15–3. Each of the three primary colors is located at one of the points of the triangle. The center of the triangle represents the mixture of all three primaries to create white light.

**Secondary Colors**    If any two of the primary colors are mixed along the edge of the triangle, a *secondary color* is the result. Mixing primary red and primary blue results in *violet*. Mixing primary green and primary blue results in blue-green or *cyan*. Mixing primary red and primary green results in *yellow* or amber. If mixed together, these three secondary colors create white light.

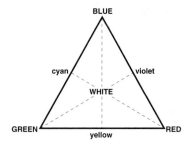

**Figure 15–3**
The Color Triangle

The color triangle illustrates how the three primary colors (red, green, and blue) mix to secondary colors and to white.

**Complementary Colors**    Directly across the triangle from any color is located that color's *complementary*. Violet is the complementary of green; cyan is the complementary of red; and yellow is the complementary of blue. As the triangle indicates, mixing a color with its complementary results in white light.

## COLOR MIXING

Mixing colored light is commonplace in the theatre. Overlapping beams of light combine in a variety of ways, filling each other's shadows with rich and vibrant hues that enliven a scene. The results of mixing are predictable by thinking in terms of the primary colors and keeping the color triangle in mind.

Primary and secondary hues in lighter values (tints) are frequently used to light the actor. Tints of the complementary colors yellow and blue, for example, may be used from opposite sides of the stage or in pairs from a single direction. The mixing of the two colors models the actor in flattering white light that can be warmed or cooled by changing the intensity of the spotlights (Color Plate 15–2b).

## COLOR REFLECTION

Just as light allows us to see an object, it also reveals the object's color. The eye sees the color of a surface by *reflection*. A colored surface lit by white light reflects its own color while absorbing all others (Figure 15–4). So a colored surface acts somewhat like a color filter except that it selectively reflects color rather than allowing it to pass through. For example, if an actor wearing a blue costume is lit by unfiltered white light, the costume absorbs all red and green wavelengths while reflecting only the blue. This is why it is cooler to wear white clothing than black: Black absorbs all color, turning the light energy into heat.

**Color Modification**    When colored light strikes a differently colored surface, *color modification* takes place. This means that the surface color of the object being lit is altered to some degree. Ideally, color modification is used to the advantage of the lighting designer. It is a well-known fact that certain warm tints are complimentary to skin tones, making an actor's face appear pink and healthy.

Once more using the example of a blue costume, examine what happens when it is lit with yellow or amber light. If the fabric is any color other than primary blue, it will contain some degree of red and green. Let us assume that the blue is actually a cool blue, containing more green than red. Yellow light is made up of red and green. Therefore, under yellow light, the cool blue costume will appear more green than it would under white light (Color Plate 15–3a).

Color modification of scenery or costumes can present a problem, or it can be used to the benefit of a scene. It is simply a matter of knowing how colored light will react on a colored surface. Once again, thinking in terms of the primaries is beneficial.

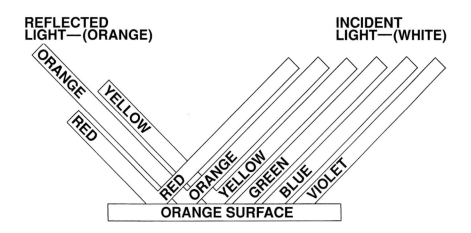

**REFLECTED LIGHT—(ORANGE)**

**INCIDENT LIGHT—(WHITE)**

ORANGE

YELLOW

RED

RED ORANGE YELLOW GREEN BLUE VIOLET

**ORANGE SURFACE**

**Figure 15—4**
Selective Color Reflection

The horizontal orange strip represents an orange-colored surface (a costume, for instance). It appears orange under white light because only the red, yellow, and orange hues of the spectrum are reflected. The other hues are absorbed by the surface.

## COLOR VISION

The source of color can be scientifically explained; the language of color can be notated; and the mixture of color can be diagrammed. The eye functions very much like a camera. However, what the eye sees as interpreted by the brain is an individual and personal color experience.

### COLOR PHYSIOLOGY

The lens of the eye is capable of focusing on objects between distances of approximately eight inches and infinity by changing the curvature of its surface—in effect, changing its own focal length. The iris contains the pupil, located just in front of the lens, that opens or closes to allow more or less light into the eye (Figure 15–5). As a protective device, it is able to close quite a bit faster than it opens.

Two types of nerve endings located in the retina area of the eye detect light intensity and color: the rods and the cones. Rods are sensitive to intensity or brightness only. As noted earlier, the color-sensitive cones are of three types: one most sensitive to colored light in the red range, the second most sensitive to blue, and the third to green light. Rods and cones send an electrochemical signal to the brain that varies in frequency with the intensity of the light. It is important to realize that the brain then *interprets* the signal. This interpretation is affected by many factors including viewer expectation and need.

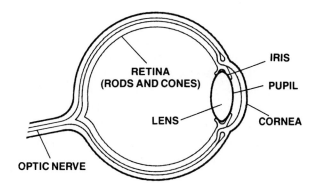

RETINA
(RODS AND CONES)

IRIS

PUPIL

LENS

CORNEA

OPTIC NERVE

**Figure 15—5**
The Eye

The rods located in the retina are sensitive to brightness. The cones are most sensitive to color.

## COLOR PERCEPTION

Knowledge of *how* we see color is perhaps of greater interest to the lighting designer than to other designers in the theatre. An understanding of the physiology of the eye as it relates to color vision gives the designer some indication of how an audience may react to both intensity and color.

### INTENSITY AND COLOR

The eye's sensitivity to high or low levels of illumination affects the color we see. The *rods* of the retina, which produce most low-intensity or night vision, are most sensitive to wavelengths in the green–blue range. This sensitivity adds a greenish-blue cast to all hues seen under low levels of light. Moonlight appears to have a blue tint, even though it is the reflection of the sun greatly reduced in intensity. As far as the brain is concerned, "blue tint" is a color impression that the designer has to consider within a stage composition.

Color-receptive *cones* function best under moderate to high levels of illumination. This accounts for our reduced color vision at night. At very high levels of illumination, the cones are more sensitive to red and green wavelengths of light. The sun at noon, although a brilliant white, appears to have a yellowish tint (combination of red and green). Stage conventions such as "night is blue" or "sunlight is yellow" are often based on audience expectations.

### RETINAL FATIGUE

The retina of the eye assimilates light energy. When it is saturated the effect is twofold: (1) color impressions become weaker, and (2) intensity appears to be lower. Regeneration takes place over a noticeable period of time. Intensity-sensitive rods take roughly one and a half minutes to return to normal. The color-sensitive cones may take as long as five minutes to regenerate.

**Intensity Fatigue**     Visual fatigue becomes a factor when stage pictures remain static for long periods of time. For example, if a scene has little visual contrast over a period of ten minutes, fatigue may cause viewer discomfort. It becomes difficult to see well. Light levels appear to be low. The lighting designer may be required to slowly boost intensity levels in order to achieve visual parity with the earlier scene.

**Color Fatigue**     The classic example of color fatigue as it occurs in the theatre is the annoying predominance of yellow light in a day scene that has immediately followed a night scene. The night scene, lit with an abundance of blue light, causes the retina's blue receptors to fatigue. The "white" day scene appears too yellow because the red and green cones are much more responsive than the blue. Color contrast in the blue scene can help to reduce the effects of retinal fatigue. Likewise, shifting the color of the daylight toward blue can cause that scene to look more natural.

**After-Image**     Another phenomenon of color vision, *after-image* is the time lag of an image well after the actual object is gone. If color fatigue has had time to set in, the after-image appears to be the complementary color of the original object.

In a similar situation, the shadow cast by a colored light source can appear to be its complementary color. This is due in part to color fatigue, but also to the color-balancing tendency of the eye. If the shadow from a red light source is faintly illuminated with a colorless light, it will appear to have a blue-green cast.

## INTERACTION OF COLORS

How we perceive a color in relationship to an adjacent hue or to its background is known as *color interaction*. Knowing how to use contrasting colors is a valuable tool for the lighting designer. The working knowledge of color interaction becomes a basic element of color selection.

For example, hue opposites such as blue-green and red-orange seem virtually to vibrate in contrast to one another. Their use in close proximity creates tension. Such colors might be considered when a strong separation between actor and background is desired.

Due to differences in wavelength, certain colors appear to recede while others accede. When viewed next to each other, cool blues and greens seem to be more distant than warmer reds and yellows. A designer may chose to create an artificial sense of depth by a subtle layering of color from warm to cool.

## DESIGNING WITH COLOR

Numerous color choices are made in the course of our everyday lives, but the average person makes most of them on a subconscious level. The interior designer, fashion designer, and theatre designer must force such choices to the conscious level, analyzing how and why specific color determinations are made.

Before examining color usage in greater detail, several points should be made. First of all, the term *white light* is most often used to describe the color of unfiltered light. The fact is that the color makeup of white light can be highly variable. Our eye accepts an astonishing range of colored light as "white," depending on circumstances. For this reason, the term *no color* (abbreviated N/C) is preferable to "white" when one discusses color and filtering. Understanding the previously mentioned concept of color temperature (measured in degrees Kelvin) is also important to a discussion of color.

### AMBER DRIFT

The lighting designer must always keep in mind the effect of dimming on the color of a light source. In almost every case the intensity of a theatrical lighting instrument is controlled by means of a dimmer. Dimming lowers or alters the electrical flow sent to the instrument's lamp. As a result, the lamp's filament burns less brightly.

As a lamp is dimmed, it radiates a warmer color of light, a phenomenon known as *amber drift*. The further a lamp is dimmed, the greater the shift in color. By the time a dimmer reaches 50 or 60 percent of original intensity, the color of light has changed significantly. This effect is particularly harmful to colors in the blue range. A blue filter in front of an instrument burning at 100-percent intensity emits a very different color from that of the same filter in front of an instrument burning at 70-percent intensity (Color Plate 15–3b). Like many other lighting phenomena, this quality can either present a problem for a designer or be used to advantage.

### MIXING ON A SURFACE

Mixing occurs anytime two different-colored lights are used on the same area. The resultant color depends on several variables:

1. The colors of the light sources
2. The direction of the light sources
3. The contour shape of the surface being lit
4. The natural color of the surface being lit

If two light sources strike a surface from different angles, and if the surface is three-dimensional and sculpted (an actor's face, for example), many interesting things happen. First of all, one source will cast shadows that are filled or partially filled by the other source's light and color. Second, an overall even color mix will not be achieved because the sources are coming from different directions. What will be seen instead is a heavy coloration from one source that merges gradually to an even mix with the second color and finally moves into the color of the second source. Such coloration adds three-dimensionality to a figure on stage and can help in establishing a direction of light (Figure 15–6).

### MIXING IN THE AIR

Another form of color mixing involves placement of two or more light sources very close to one another, effectively acting as a single source. The most common example of such mixing in the theatre is use of striplights or cyc lights on a cyclorama or backdrop. This technique is also employed for area lighting, using spotlights placed very close to one another. The purpose is to allow the designer a large range of color options through mixing, while only using two lighting instruments. Of course, this type of mixing depends on dimming, and therefore each instrument must be under separate control.

### CHOOSING COLOR

The designer chooses colored light for one of four reasons:

1. The light is motivated by a specific source (the sun, a lamp, the fireplace), and colored light helps convey the motivation.

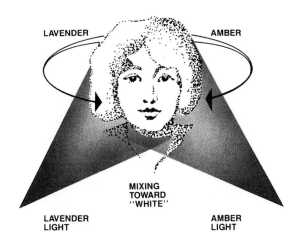

LAVENDER AMBER

MIXING
TOWARD
"WHITE"

LAVENDER
LIGHT

AMBER
LIGHT

**Figure 15—6**
Color Mixing

Two complementary colors striking a three-dimensional object (such as an actor's face) from different directions will gradually mix toward white.

2. The mood of a scene is reinforced by the light; color heightens the effect.
3. A visual contrast between light sources is desirable; color increases that contrast.
4. Change or dramatic effect for its own sake is desired.

Most often the dilemma is not whether to use color, but which color to choose. The lighting designer's job in this respect is made easier by the fact that most design teams determine a production's *color scheme* early in the design process. The scenic and costume designers will have made their color choices based on these earlier discussions; the lighting designer should follow suit.

## A METHOD OF USING COLOR

Successful designing with color depends on taste, knowledge, and experience. One important technique was developed by Stanley McCandless, a man who more than any other might be considered the founder of lighting design in the United States. McCandless suggested that one way to achieve the most *natural* look when lighting the actor onstage is to position lighting instruments to each side of the actor at an angle of approximately 45 degrees, and 45 degrees up from the horizontal (Figure 15–7). Two complementary colors are then placed in the instruments—such as a light blue in one and a warm amber in the other. The amber acts as a *key* or primary source light, while the blue reads as *fill* or reflected light. The colors mix with each other on the actor's face and body front to a shade of white. This technique has formed a basis for color use in modern lighting design.

Note in the example above that two complementary colors are used to mix toward white light. In addition, it is stated that one color acts as a key and the other as fill. An audience views the warmer of two equally intense light sources as primary; the cooler source serves as shadow.

**Figure 15—7**
45-degree—45-degree Mixing

A stage-left blue fill source and a stage-right amber key source will mix toward white light at the center of the actor's body (*See* Color Plate 15–2b).

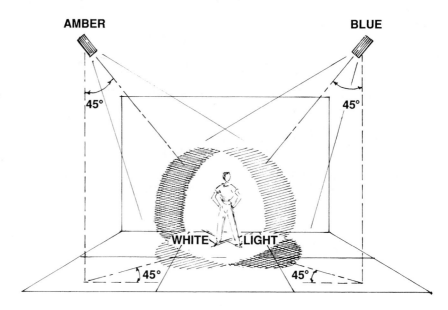

AMBER

BLUE

45°   45°

WHITE   LIGHT

45°   45°

## WARM AND COOL COLORS

Most people consider the color red as bloodlike, typifying violence, anger, and perhaps war. Amber is likely to be perceived as sunlight, warm and comfortable. Blue typifies restraint and coolness, while green may be seen as restful. These and similar identifications are taken into consideration when a designer selects stage colors. However, it is a mistake to place too much emphasis on the psychological effects of color. The personal nature of color perception causes color symbolism to be fraught with conflicting theories.

There is one psychological aspect, however, that should not be ignored: the matter of the relative warmth and coolness of colors. Few people would deny that bright red-orange suggests warmth; most would agree that brittle blue-white gives an impression of coolness. Color Plate 15–4 is a good example of the warmth and coolness of colors being used in a literal manner to convey temperature. Color warmth and coolness used in a more abstract manner can also have a strong effect on the mood of a scene.

Given samples of twenty different tints and shades, rarely will two people list them in exactly the same order from warm to cool. But in general the reds, oranges, and ambers are considered in the warm group, while the cool group consists of blues, violets, and greens. Some mixtures of hues from the opposing groups seem to be on the borderline. The particular effect they give at any moment is dependent on what color is viewed in relationship to them (color interaction and contrast).

**Color Contrast**     Without contrast, a stage picture appears dull and lifeless. In lighting, contrast is achievable either through intensity differences or through color differences.

The precise feeling given by most tints is purely a matter of comparison. A pale blue that seems positively icy next to a bastard amber appears quite warm when placed adjacent to a stronger shade of blue-green. Pink and lavender are frequently used on the stage as freewheeling tints whose effects can be reversed merely by changing the hues used in association with them.

Unfiltered light may also appear to be warm in one situation and cool in another. Opposite a cool color, such as the palest of blues or greens, uncolored light appears quite warm. But in comparison to a pink or pale amber, white light will definitely be on the cool side.

Some designers enjoy using the palest of tints or perhaps no color at all to lend a certain stylistic look to a production. In this situation, the effect of dimming on the color of the light becomes particularly significant. A clear light source at full dimmer reading is not only brighter than one reading at lower dimmer levels, but it is also cooler and harsher in color. Intensity as well as color contrast is achieved—without the use of filters!

## USING COLOR MODIFICATION

Designers in the theatre not only have to consider the colors of a painted background, costumes, and other materials of a set, but also the colors of the lights that will reveal them.

Fortunately, color modification is not quite as complicated as it may seem. The effect of colored light on a colored surface is the result of mixing. If a red light is thrown on a yellow surface, the yellow is modified into orange tones.

The modification of a color in a costume or on scenery by colored light is a theatrical example of the joining of two color media—pigment and light. Designers in the theatre are constantly aware of how colored light and pigment influence each other. The lighting designer may enhance the mood of a scene by *washing* the stage with pale blue light. Perhaps this effect alters the brown walls or floor of the set, resulting in a cooler, gray feeling. The reverse could be achieved by using a pale pink tint upon the scene.

## COLORED LIGHT AND THE ACTOR

A later chapter will suggest specific colors to use in various specific situations, but the designer must always consider the general effects that are desired for various portions of the stage picture. For the acting area front-lighting, for example, it is best to avoid saturated and unnatural shades that will adversely affect the faces and costumes of the actors. Tints of blue or yellow containing green can be detrimental to skin tones.

**Costume Color**      Preserving color integrity of costumes can be a difficult task. Often the acting areas are lighted with tints of pinks and ambers, flattering enough to the human face but deadly to green costume materials. Because the scene may definitely call for such colors in the light, the lighting designer must at all times keep abreast with the costume designer's color palette.

Knowing what will happen to a given costume under colored light is simplified by breaking down the colors into primaries. For example, assume a yellow dress is lit by a cool blue light from one angle and a straw or cool amber from another. The cool blue light contains a mix of green and blue. The cool amber is made up of red and green. The yellow dress reflects red and green. The conclusion, reached by simply noting the preponderance of green, is that we are probably going to be in trouble. A warmer blue or lavender and a warmer amber light would be a better choice.

If a scene seems to call for strong color, using it in back-light should be considered. Colored back-light does not affect the costumes or faces of the actors and can tone the floor in an effective manner. A strongly contrasting back-light color acts to separate performers from their background.

## COLORED LIGHT AND THE SCENERY

Unless otherwise informed, always operate on the assumption that the scene designer has painted the settings the way they should appear. Thus, for a lighting designer to attempt to improve on the scene designer's artistry would be impertinent. Enhance it, yes, but strictly in accordance with the scene designer's wishes. Close collaboration between scene and lighting designers is crucial. The result will usually be that nearby scenery, such as the walls of an interior setting, will receive acting area tints of light only.

A good rule of thumb for a lighting designer to begin with is this: If you are debating whether or not to light the scenery—don't. Generally, light on scenery such as flats and drops will cast unwanted shadows and possibly create a situation where the walls and the actors are competing for focus.

On the other hand, color washing the scenery (including the floor) can help to create some very nice and useful effects. Nearly any scenic or costume color can be made to appear warmer or cooler—more or less inviting—through the use of colored light. A scene designer may, in addition, actually paint the set in several different colors that can be selectively accentuated or deemphasized by colored light.

## COLOR ON THE SKY

Lighting designers are frequently called on to use color on a sky-drop or cyclorama. The term *sky-drop* refers to a large expanse of cloth that may be lightly colored but is not painted with any kind of sky or landscape. A *cyclorama* is a curved sky-drop.

Careful consideration and experimentation must be given to choosing sky colors. If at all possible, colors under consideration should be examined by projecting them onto the actual drop. The color of the drop itself will affect the lighting choice, for sky-drops can vary from numerous shades of white to blue. If the drop is unavailable, experimentation on a similar surface in the lighting lab is recommended.

Is it better to select a single color medium that gives the exact hue desired, or is a blending of several colors preferable? Of course, if there is to be a color change during the scene, then more than one color must be provided. More delicate and precise shadings can also be achieved if several different colors are blended into one.

Mixing of the three primaries is a traditional, but often wasteful, method of achieving variable color on a sky-drop. Light transmission from primary colors, particularly blue, is extremely low. This presents a problem because near-primary blue is an important sky color. A possible solution is to double the output by using two circuits of blue and mixing it with other secondary colors.

Tints are seldom useful as sky color. They are too pale and tend to do nothing but muddy a sky. Unlike acting areas, more saturated colors are called for in lighting sky-drops.

## SELECTING COLOR

As we have seen, color choice is a complex issue. A number of factors might enter into the equation: mood, time of day, motivational source, dramatic effect, color contrast, scenery, costumes, or actor skin tone. One thing is certain—experimentation is a key element in good color selection.

Experimenting with color mixing is especially important for the beginning lighting designer. Colors projected by stage lighting instruments can

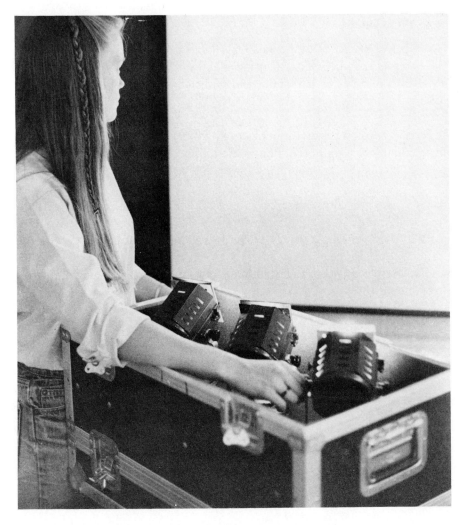

**Figure 15—8**
**The Color Mix-Box**

Three Fresnels on dimmers allow the designer freedom to mix colors in a space other than the theatre.

be examined in the theatre or in a lighting laboratory—in fact anyplace that has dimmers.

**The Color Mix-Box**     A particularly useful tool for color experimentation outside the theatre is the mix-box (Figure 15–8). Three-inch Fresnels and three common household dimmers are used in the mix-box shown. The box is portable and can be plugged into any household circuit. In order to use a mix-box, a lighting designer must have available a file box of color media that contains a frame-size cut of every color the designer may need.

### COLOR MEDIA

It is common in the theatre to refer to color filters as *gels*, being short for "gelatin," the first material to be manufactured as a color medium. However, except for very special applications, gelatin is no longer in use. There are three kinds of color media in general use today: plastic, colored glass, and dichroic glass.

### PLASTIC MEDIA

Two types of plastic color media are available: acetate and Mylar. Acetate is less expensive than Mylar, but it fades and may even change color over a period of time. Mylar is durable and withstands fairly high temperatures, making it the most widely used medium.

**Acetate**     Rosco Laboratories makes Roscolene, the only acetate color medium commonly used in the United States. Roscolene is available in a wide range of colors that are numbered in the 800 series.

**Mylar**     Mylar filters were developed a number of years ago for use with the hotter, quartz stage lighting instruments. Like acetate, Mylar is available in sheets that measure 20 by 24 inches. It can also be purchased by the roll (24 inches by 50 feet). It is durable and may be reused. Three companies supply Mylar filters in the United States: Great American (GamColor), Lee (Lee Filters), and Rosco (Roscolux).

GamColor is conveniently arranged in color-order, using numbers in the 100s through 900s. Basic Lee Filters are numbered in the 100s, while their special application colors use the 200s, and Broadway Colors are numbered in two digits. Roscolux is arranged in color-order and begins its numbering at 001 and goes into the 100s. In adding new colors, Roscolux found it best to insert a color number between two others. The inserted colors are numbered in the 300s. For example, Rosco added a new color, pale violet, between existing color No. 55, lilac, and color No. 56, gypsy lavender. The new color's number is 355.

To avoid confusion caused by different manufacturers using the same numbers, the following is suggested for designers when designating a color:

Use an "R" or "X" prefix before Roscolux numbers.

Use an "L" prefix before Lee Filter numbers.

Use a "G" prefix before GamColor numbers.

**Handling Plastic Media**     Cutting sheets of color media down to size is easily accomplished by using a large paper cutter. The color frame size of most 6-inch lighting instruments is $7\frac{1}{2}$ by $7\frac{1}{2}$ inches. The frame size of an 8-inch instrument is 10 by 10 inches. Always make sure of proper frame size before cutting.

A new piece of plastic (particularly acetate) may, when placed in the heat of a light beam, give off considerable steam for a period. This effect, which appears to be smoke, can be quite distracting, if not alarming, to the audience. It is wise, therefore, to test new plastic well before curtain time; if it smokes, leave the instrument on until all is well.

When acetate is used as a color medium, it is good practice to perforate the sheet with numerous small holes. This procedure allows the heat from the lighting instrument to pass through the filter. The holes will not affect the performance of the plastic in any way, except to prolong its life. Nor will the holes appear in the beam pattern. An ice pick or awl may be used for this purpose, but the neatest and easiest method is to run a pounce wheel several times over the full sheet before cutting it to size.

## COLORED GLASS

Colored glass filters are expensive and break when dropped. While plastic may be cut to any size or shape desired, glass must be ordered for exactly the purpose required. It comes in few colors, is heavy, and is bulky to store. Glass does have three advantages: It never fades; it is heat resistant; and it can be molded like a lens in order to spread light.

Colored glass roundels can be obtained with the following features:

*Plain*     For color filtering only

*Stippled*     For color and also to diffuse the beam

*Spread*     For color and also to spread the beam laterally, so that the various colors will blend more readily

*Stripped*     Very thin glass in narrow strips to color the light from extremely hot-beamed instruments.

## DICHROIC GLASS

Thin pieces of glass treated with a dichroic coating can act as superb color filters. Currently being used in automated fixtures, several dichroic filters in combination are able to produce a wide range of colors (Figure 15–9). Remarkable for its purity, the quality of color from dichroics is unobtainable with colored glass or plastic. The major drawback of dichroic filters is their expense. The cost of a 6-inch filter is prohibitive except for theme parks and architectural applications where alternatives are equally expensive.

## Figure 15–9
### Dichroic Color Wheel

Shown is the color wheel from an Intellabeam 700HX automated fixture. One circle is open while the other eleven hold a range of dichroic glass color filters.

### AUTOMATED COLOR CHANGERS

Remote control of color projected by a stage lighting instrument is a valuable design tool. The theatrical use of automated color changers has become widespread due to the fact that one lighting instrument serves the color purposes of several.

Figure 15–10 shows one of the various systems in use today. Most employ a series of plastic colors fixed end-to-end to form a roll. A metal box containing the color, two rollers, and a motor slides into the lighting instrument's color holder. An electrical cable (DMX) runs from the unit to the lighting control console, which instructs the motor what to do. Changers hold from seven to twelve different colors. Over the past few years they have become reliable and fairly quiet.

The use of color changers offers great flexibility, but a designer must alter the way light cues are normally written. Up to three lighting control channels are necessary to independently operate each changer. Color changes are written into the memory of the lighting control board just like light cues. However, an instrument is unable to imperceptibly fade from one color to another without first going to black. Additional "dark set" cues are often necessary before changing to a new color.

### DIFFUSION MATERIAL

Diffusion material, often called *frost*, diffuses light from an instrument and softens or even eliminates a shutter cut or beam edge. Although not a color medium, it is manufactured by the same companies that produce color media. Frosts are listed in the "swatch" or sample books and are commercially supplied in sheets.

A wide range of diffusers are available—from a very light frost, which just barely takes the edge off a sharply focused instrument, to a heavy frost, which makes a beam edge all but disappear. In addition, several densities of

**Figure 15–10**
**Remotely-controlled Color Changer**

Shown is a Coloram color changer manufactured by Wybron. It can provide up to thirty-two colors and is able to move from one end of the gelstring to the other in two seconds. Photo courtesy Wybron, Inc.

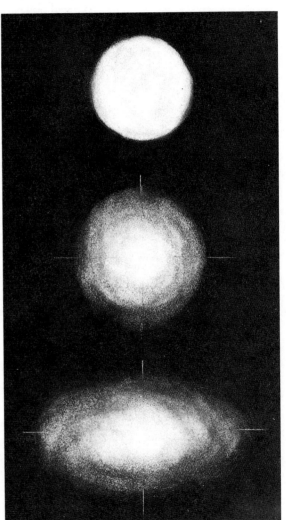

**Figure 15–11**
**Diffusion Material**

The effect of three different diffusion materials:
(top) A light frost such as Rosco's "Hamburg Frost" No. R114.
(middle) A heavy frost that keeps a hot center similar to Rosco's "Tough Frost" No. R103.
(bottom) A spread frost such as Rosco's "Tough Silk" No. R104.

"silk" are available, which cause the beam of light to spread in two directions only (Figure 15–11).

It should be noted that diffusion material has limited application in front-of-house positions due to the amount of unwanted spill light that is produced. While any use of frost reduces light intensity to some degree, some heavy frosts cause nearly as much light to come out of the side of the filter as the front. The variety of frost media available provides a lighting designer with many options and is an important tool of the trade.

**Figure 15–12**
Color Swatch Books

Color sample books, called "swatch books" are available from the three major manufacturers. Photos courtesy Rosco Laboratories, Inc., Lee Colortran, Inc., and The Great American Market.

## OBTAINING COLOR SAMPLES

To obtain color swatch books, contact your local color media supplier or write the following manufacturers:

*GamColor*   The Great American Market
            826 N. Cole Avenue
            Hollywood, CA 90038

*Rosco*      Rosco Laboratories Inc.
            36 Bush Avenue
            Port Chester, NY 10573

*Lee*        LeeColortran Inc.
            1015 Chestnut Street
            Burbank, CA 91506

## COLOR MANUFACTURERS

It is good practice to replace swatch books every two or three years, avoiding faded color samples and keeping abreast of newly added colors. Never trust the names that the various manufacturers assign to their colors. Names are given to individualize the color, making it easier to remember. However, their descriptive accuracy is suspect. One need only compare GamColor's "light steel blue" (G720) with Roscolux's color of the same name (R64) to fully understand why such labels are meaningless.

# STAGE LIGHTING PRACTICE: DISTRIBUTION

# 16

The four qualities of light, as mentioned earlier in this book, are color, distribution, intensity, and movement. *Distribution* relates to how the actor will be seen. It involves choices of direction, angle, and quality of light. *Direction* refers to whether the light is coming from the front or the side or the back. *Angle* relates to the height of the light source (e. g., is the light coming from low on the horizon, or is it high like the noonday sun?). *Quality* is concerned with the texture of the light (is it harsh or soft, broken up or smooth?).

In the study of distribution, it is best to begin with motivational lighting. Accordingly, the early part of this chapter includes a discussion of types of light from familiar sources such as daylight, night-time light, and artificial light.

## LIGHTING THE ACTOR

The primary concern of a stage lighting designer is lighting the actor. The actor must have good visibility. The actor must be lit in a manner appropriate to the play. The actor must be seen in proper relationship to the background. Distribution is of primary importance because it involves the angle, direction, and quality of light that reveals the actors, especially their faces, in natural form.

### NATURAL LIGHTING

The expression *in natural form* is the designer's clue. It means the actor's face should be seen as it appears under natural lighting. In imitating nature, theatre uses reality as a basis from which to deviate. Accordingly, the lighting designer must be keenly aware of the various attributes of natural lighting.

Our eyes have been schooled by a lifetime of seeing one another under sunlight or interior lighting coming from above. We are so accustomed to

seeing the features of a face disclosed by light from an overhead direction that to light it from below, for example, produces an unnatural look (Figure 16–1).

It has long been the practice of artists and architects to render their drawings as though light were falling on the subject from over the artist's shoulder at an angle of roughly 45 degrees. Following the lead of Stanley McCandless, theatre lighting designers adopted this same practice. Light at a 45-degree angle enhances visibility and appears natural. At the same time, this angle of light creates interesting highlights and shadows on the actor's face. Intentional deviation from this angle in order to heighten an effect or create a particular mood is common design practice in today's theatre.

### HIGHLIGHT AND SHADOW

The primary way to determine the angle and direction of a light source is by the *highlight* and *shadow* created. Time of day is determined by the length of shadows cast by trees and buildings. The shadow of an object lit at an angle of 45 degrees is the same length as the height of the object.

It is the shadow in Figure 16–1 that makes the subject look unnatural. Highlight and shadow, which give dimension to a form, are controlled by source angle and direction. Figure 16–2 further illustrates the relationship of

**Figure 16–1**
**Lighting the Actor**

Upward angle from the footlights or apron. An unnatural, though dramatic, angle.

## LIGHT FROM BELOW        ## LIGHT FROM ABOVE

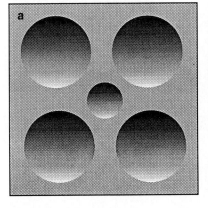

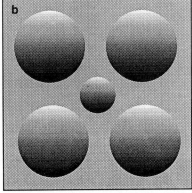

**Figure 16–2**
**Perception as Influenced by Lighting Angle**

An illustration of how we assume the direction of light to be from above is shown in Figures a and b, identical rectangles each containing five convex domes. With lighting from below, as in Figure a, the domes appear to be concave; while with lighting from above, as in Figure b, they appear convex.

highlight and shadow to perception. We are so accustomed to light from above that changing this angle has the power to alter appearances.

Highlight and shadow offer interest to scenic objects as well as to an actor's face. In addition, they often become important parts of the stage composition. Shadowless illumination is uninteresting and reduces visibility.

## ANGLES AND DIRECTION OF LIGHT

*Angle* of light is commonly measured in degrees. The horizon is considered 0 degrees and light from directly above is at 90 degrees. *Direction* of light can also be measured in degrees, but is most often referred to as front-, side-, or back-lighting. Each direction of light possesses its own attributes, with visibility being the most important attribute of front-light.

### FRONT-LIGHT

Theatrical front-lighting is seldom directly front-on to the performer. Such light, especially if it is low-angled, flattens facial features and lacks interest (Figure 16–3).

Moving the light to one side of the performer creates a much more interesting sense of directionality. Shadows are produced and the actor's face suddenly has dimension. However, while highly theatrical, a deep shadow on the opposite side of the face reduces visibility (Figure 16–4). A second light is often necessary to fill in this shadow.

**45-Degree/45-Degree System**    Returning for a moment to the teachings of Stanley McCandless, it was his opinion that two front-lights were desirable, with the beam of one spotlight directed at a 45-degree angle above and to the right of the actor, and that of the second spotlight directed 45 degrees above and to the left of the actor (a total of 90 degrees between lights). You will remember from Chapter 15 that placing a warm tint in one spotlight and a cool tint in the other has a pleasing, natural effect. Varying the color or intensity of these spotlights creates a sense of directionality. The primary source or *key-light* comes from the warmer or more intense spotlight,

### Figure 16–3
Lighting the Actor

Low angle, full-front light. Note lack of definition.

### Figure 16–4
Lighting the Actor

Front light from stage-left only at a 45-degree angle. Note the lack of visibility on the dark side of the face.

### Figure 16–5
Lighting the Actor

Front light from the left and right at a 45-degree angle. The stage-right side of the face has a higher-intensity light, suggesting the direction of the motivating or "key" source.

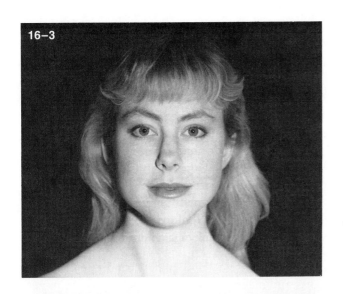

16–3

16–4

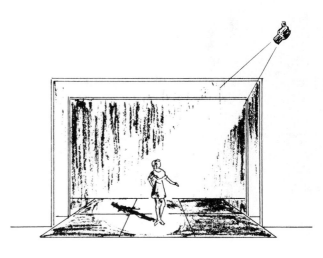

16–5

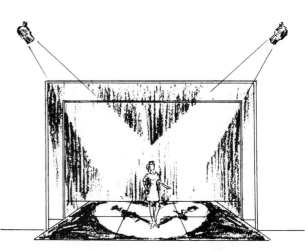

and the shadow or *fill-light* comes from the cool or dimmer light (Figure 16–5). In the 1930s, McCandless felt that this was the most natural way to light an actor with good visibility. And it was.

**Jewel Lighting**    In the early days of Broadway, New York theatres were not equipped to place lighting instruments at an angle of 45 degrees to the performer. Lights could be hung off a pipe running along the front of the balcony (balcony rail), but the angle was terribly low. Lights could be hung on pipes over-stage, but that angle was too steep. So Broadway designers convinced their producers to let them use the closest audience box on either side of the auditorium as a lighting position. While these seats offered poor visibility for patrons, the lighting angle to the stage was fairly good. However, the direction was much more from the side than front.

The performers acting downstage were lit with three lights: one from each box boom, creating good highlight and shadow, and one from the balcony rail, filling shadows and making eyes sparkle (hence, the term *jewel lighting*). Although lighting positions have improved, one can still see the roots of this system in the work of today's Broadway designers.

**Altering Angle and Direction**    The most interesting kind of stage lighting employs many angles and directions of light. Over the years designers have demanded an increasingly great number of lighting instruments for their productions. Total number of units in a light plot has doubled and tripled. The principal motive behind this increase has been the desire for more varied angles and directions of light. Today we are on the brink of an automated fixture revolution. With moving lights (or moving mirrors), one light serves the purpose of many: It changes color, beam quality, and texture—but most importantly, it changes angle and direction.

The only rule of visibility lighting is that there be at least one source somewhere from the front. It can be filled by a source from the side or by a second front-light. A creative lighting designer determines angle and direction based on the desired effect. If a natural effect is desired, a 45-degree angle with a direction somewhat to the side of the performer might be chosen for the key-light. If a harsher or more severe effect seems appropriate, the angle might increase to 60 degrees or the direction might move more to the side. If a softer, less angular feeling is the goal, the angle might be lowered to 30 degrees or the direction might change more to the front.

Altering the look of a scene through lighting was once primarily done by changing color. Today, it is just as likely that new looks are achieved through changes in angle and direction. Designers should be aware that in order for a change to be noticeably different, the new lighting angle or direction must be roughly 30 degrees from that of the old.

## BACK-LIGHT

Light coming from behind an actor creates dimensionality. It separates performer from background. It color-tones the stage floor and adds contrast to the scene. Compare Figures 16–5 and 16–6; the difference is a result of back-light.

The use of back-light allows the lighting designer to put a brighter light on the background than would otherwise be possible. It permits scenic and costume designers to use colors without fear of the actor blending into the background. Because the color of back-light does not affect an actor's skin tone or costume color, stronger colors than those used in front-lighting may be considered. Creative use of back-light color can help to establish an overhead motivational source or simply color and texture the stage floor for a specific effect.

**Angle and Direction**    Just as with front-light, back-light need not be directly behind the performer. Light from a back—side direction wraps around the figure to a greater degree. In doing so, it strikes a more visible surface area and becomes more apparent. Two back-lights, one from each side, offer a greater degree of visible light and more intensity.

The ideal angle for back-light is between 45 and 60 degrees (Figure 16—7). An angle steeper than 60 degrees appears more like top-light (Figure

**Figure 16—6**
Lighting the Actor

Three directions of light: right and left front light at 45-degrees, and back light.

**Figure 16—7**
Lighting the Actor

Backlight providing a halo or ''rim'' effect. Note shadows.

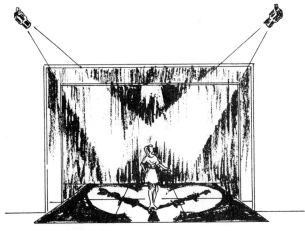

16–8). In many situations, care must be taken to prevent back-light from shining into the audience. The temptation might be to increase the back angle, creating more of a top- or down-light. But the designer must remember that top-light is not at all the same as back-light, for it tends to "squash" rather than edge an actor.

**Intensity**     Because back-light strikes so little visible surface, its intensity normally needs to be roughly one and a half times that of front-light. If it is too bright, however, a halo effect will be created on the head and shoulders of the performer. When back-lighting is kept in proper balance with the front-lights, the actor is etched clearly against the background.

### SIDE-LIGHT

The most important attribute of side-light is revelation of form. Side-lighting gives the designer additional flexibility. Both color and angle add variety as side-light is used in combination with frontal sources. Using side-light as a key source is a highly dramatic and effective technique. Like back-light, side-light can be used to establish a motivational source through color, angle, and intensity. Compared to back-light, the amount of visible surface lit by side-lighting is considerably greater.

**Low Side**     Dance lighting designers like to use side-light coming from a low angle to sculpt the figures of the dancers. Such light is hung on floor stands called *booms* located in the wings or tormentor positions. Low side is angled from 0 degrees to about 30 degrees (Figure 16–9). The best direction for dance side-light is straight to the side, neither in front of nor behind the performer.

Low side used in a stage play can create very dramatic effects, but it is often fraught with problems. Assuming that an adequate hanging position is available, the designer must be concerned with the light striking scenery in an undesirable manner. Its use is often reserved for special effects such as casting large shadows on the scenery.

**Figure 16–8**
Lighting the Actor

Downlight or toplight at a 90-degree angle (straight top). Normally not a complementary angle.

**Figure 16–9**
Lighting the Actor

Side light from the right at a 30-degree angle.

**Figure 16–10**
Lighting the Actor

Side light from the right at a 45-degree angle.

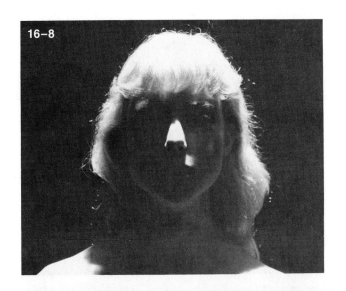

16—8

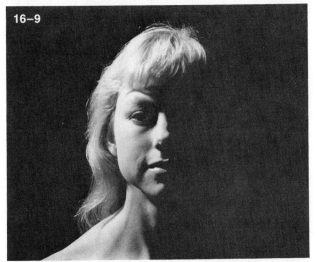

16—9

16—10

**Figure 16–11**

**Lighting Positions in the Proscenium Theatre**

(1) Ceiling beams or ports.
(2) Box booms or coves.
(3) Balcony front or balcony rail.
(4) Apron or footlights.
(5) First electric pipe or bridge.
(6) Boom.
(7) Second electric pipe (mid-stage backlight position).
(8) Ladder.
(9) Third electric (backdrop or cyclorama lighting).
(10) Ground row (backdrop or cyclorama lighting).
(11) Translucent drop backlight.
(12) Followspot.

**High Side**    A more practical angle for dramatic productions, high side is usually angled between 45 and 60 degrees (Figure 16–10). As with back-light, an angle higher than 60 degrees begins to act like top-light, beating down on the performers. It can be hung from the top of booms, from lighting *ladders* located in the wings, or from the ends of over-stage pipes. Its direction can be any from front side to straight side to back side, depending on the desired effect.

## LIGHTING POSITIONS

The proscenium theatre offers numerous possibilities for varying the angle and direction of a light source. Figure 16–11 shows various standard positions available in a simple proscenium house. Those positions on the audience side of the proscenium arch—referred to as "front-of-house" (FOH)—present the designer with a good variety of angles from the front. In terms of more extreme angles, the backstage positions offer even greater variety, including lights from side, top, and back as well as front. Most of these positions are equipped with electrical circuits for convenient instrument plugging.

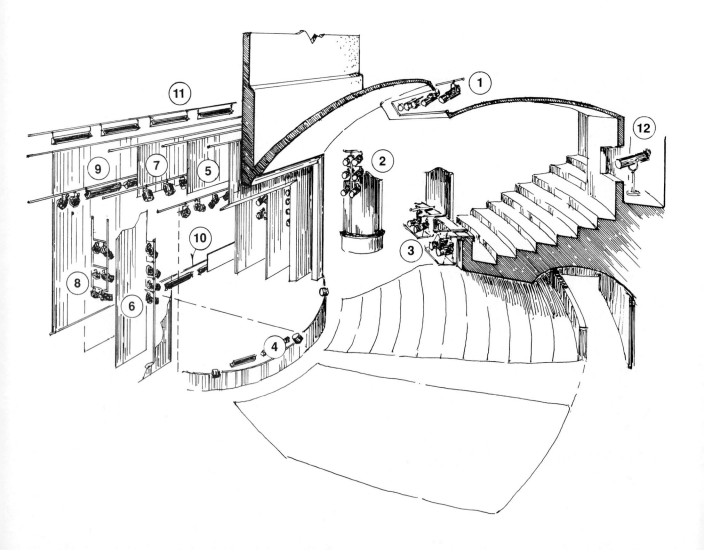

*Position 1* in Figure 16–11 is the ceiling beam or port. This is a primary visibility position for front-light. Many theatres have multiple beam positions to allow for a variety of angles onto the stage. A close position such as the one illustrated might be used to light midstage. A position further back in the auditorium would light downstage, and the first electric (position 5) would light upstage. High-angled follow spots can be used with good results from most ceiling port positions.

*Position 2* is the box boom or cove position. As mentioned earlier, this position offers a good front side-light that can be used in conjunction with front sources. It also can sculpt actors playing downstage with side-light.

*Position 3* is the balcony rail. This is a low angle, but can be valuable when used in conjunction with more extreme angles. Projections and color washes work well from the balcony rail.

*Position 4* is the footlight position. This position's lighting equipment can still be found in older theatres. Low-angled effect lighting can be placed in the footlight position. Color washing from this position is also possible.

*Position 5* is the first electric pipe. This is the furthest downstage lighting position. As such, it is usually heavily hung with front-light aimed upstage, back-light aimed downstage, and high side shooting across the stage. Occasionally a focusing bridge hangs in this position, making it valuable for high-angled follow-spotting.

*Position 6* is the side-lighting boom. It is a floor stand that can go as high as 16 feet. Such a boom provides hanging positions for both low and high side-light. It is especially valuable for dance lighting.

*Position 7* is the second electric pipe. It provides a good back-light angle as well as a location for midstage high side-light.

*Position 8* is a ladder located in the wing. This is used for high side-light and has an advantage over a boom in that it doesn't take up valuable floor space. It also can trim higher than a boom.

*Position 9* is the upstage third electric pipe. One pipe in this position is used for upstage back-lighting and a second to light the cyclorama or backdrop. Three electric pipes are a minimum, with larger theatres having as many as seven or eight.

*Position 10* is called the ground row. It is used to light the cyclorama or backdrop from the bottom. Sunsets and special sky effects are created from this position.

*Position 11* is used only if the scene designer provides a translucent backdrop. Lights in this position, upstage of the drop, shine through the fabric making it appear luminous.

*Position 12* returns front-of-house to the traditional follow spot position. This position provides the low-angled light that is the trademark of traditional musical theatre. If subtlety is desired, a higher angle should be chosen.

## LIGHTING THE ACTING AREA

Lighting someone from various positions and angles is easy if the subject remains in a fixed position. An actor, however, usually moves. In order to produce the identical lighting angle and direction as on a stationary figure, the lighting designer must constantly duplicate the focus of spotlights on many similar areas over the entire playing space. The *area lighting method* assumes that the stage should be evenly lit in a consistent manner.

## THE AREA LIGHTING METHOD

Dividing the acting space into convenient areas and then lighting each area with the same number of spotlights provides a balanced illumination. The area method of lighting the actor, first developed by Stanley McCandless in the 1930s, has proved a very efficient and systematic technique. It permits the designer to view the stage as a grid of overlapping lighting focus areas.

As scenery styles have changed and lighting instrument design has improved, the area method has been modified and expanded. Today, numerous instruments are assigned to each area, providing great color and distribution flexibility. The resulting number of lighting instruments used in some shows is staggering. Although the area method was first developed for the proscenium theatre, it has been readily adapted to other theatre forms such as thrust and arena (see Chapter 23).

**Area Alignment**    In using the area system, one of the things a designer learns is that areas must overlap considerably. If not, the actor will pass through dark spots ("dips") in lighting when moving from one area to another. A properly focused stagelighting instrument shines a light that has maximum intensity along the centerline of its beam and falls off in brightness toward the edge. If light beams are overlapped so that the fall-off of one beam is compensated by that of an adjacent light, a smooth and even coverage is achieved (Figure 16–12).

**Focus**    Television and film designers often check intensity variation by using a light-sensitive meter. Readings are taken at head height throughout the playing space. If meter readings indicate that intensity levels are uneven, the designer adjusts the focus or adds instruments to fill in the gap. The acceptable degree of variation is determined by camera sensitivity or film stock.

**Figure 16–12**
Beam Alignment

For smooth and even coverage of the acting area, light beams must be overlapped as shown. The percentage numbers represent intensity figures.

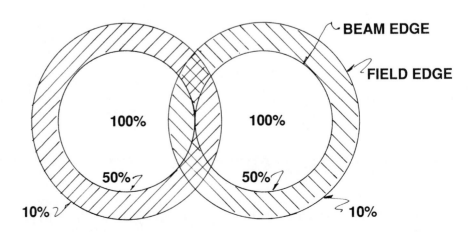

Live-audience designers (for theatre, concerts, industrials, and the like) visually check instrument focus for even coverage, relying on experience and their personal perception of design requirements. While being less precise than studio focus, this method promotes a higher level of intuitive design during the focus process.

In either case, focus techniques and procedures are passed along from designer to designer; the apprentice or assistant system is very much alive and well in the relatively small world of lighting design. A beginning designer is wise to observe focus sessions of as many experienced designers as possible, for each will exhibit individual methods and techniques.

**Area Size**    Lighting instruments are manufactured so that their intensity is appropriate for stage lighting when their beams of light are approximately 10 feet in diameter. Lighting areas vary from 8 to 12 feet in diameter, with 10 feet being a good average.

Most lighting instruments give off a predetermined size beam of light. Being cone-shaped, this beam may be measured either in degrees or diameter of its circle of light. As is apparent in examining Figure 16–13, the diameter of a light beam when it strikes a surface is determined by throw distance as well as beam angle or spread.

Normally using front-light as a basis, the designer first determines optimum lighting area size. Specific instruments are then chosen that will provide the proper coverage.

**Area Placement**    The placement and choice of the number of areas is the lighting designer's decision. It is based on the size and shape of the playing area as well as the amount of control desired. Here the term *control* refers to the ability to alter light on one portion of the stage independent of others. The more lighting areas, the greater the control possibilities. Figure 16–14 shows some examples of lighting area placement.

The action of the play and the staging of the production also help to determine number and placement of lighting areas. Attending rehearsals and paying particular attention to blocking is of immense benefit to the designer when the time comes for assigning areas. In a multiscene production some

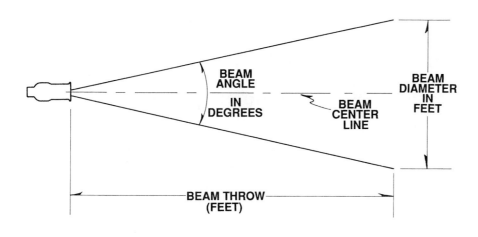

**Figure 16–13**
Light Beam

As the light beam spreads, its diameter increases and its intensity decreases.

**Figure 16–14**
Lighting Areas

(a) A conventional box setting. Note the numbering of the areas from down-stage left to up-stage right. The total number of areas varies with the size of the proscenium opening, the shape and number of settings in the production, and the desired tightness of control.
(b) An irregularly shaped interior setting. Some designers prefer to designate the areas with Roman numerals to avoid confusion with other numbers on the plot.
(c) A complicated set. Various levels often require the use of more lighting areas.

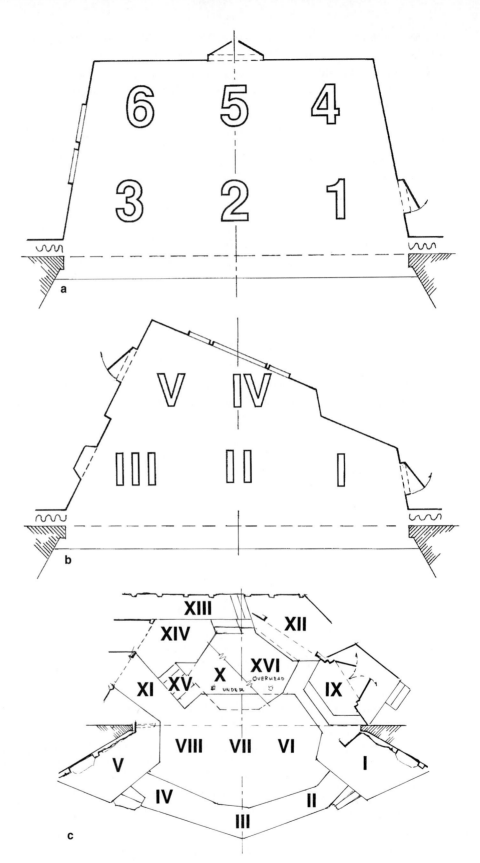

of the areas can be planned for use in more than one set, providing the floor plans are close to the same configuration.

One bit of advice: most actors have a tendency to gravitate toward center stage, so the prudent lighting designer will be sure to have a controllable center area.

**Front-Light Placement**     We will use, as illustration, a simple 45-degree two-front-light area system. Looking at area 2 in Figure 16–15, note that it is being lit by the two lights numbered 2-L and 2-R. Each is placed at an angle of approximately 45 degrees to the area and the two have similar, but opposite, directions to the performer. This procedure is repeated for each lighting area until all are covered in a similar manner. The three downstage areas are lit from the beam or ceiling port position. In order to keep a similar angle, the three upstage areas are lit from the first electric position.

Ideal lighting angles and direction often must be compromised. An example particular to lighting the proscenium stage is illustrated by the placement of instruments 1-L and 3-R. Since the desired 45-degree angle of direction is impossible to maintain because of the proscenium arch, these instruments must be shifted toward center until they adequately cover the area.

**Back- and Side-Light Placement**     Back and side angles are normally determined and instruments are plotted based on front-light areas. However, coverage from side-light does not duplicate that of front-light (Figure 16–16). Light projected at an angle to a surface produces an oval-shaped beam. Front- and back-light ovals run upstage and downstage, while side-light ovals run across the stage. Normally this presents little problem unless the side-light is being used as a key source. In this case, it is advisable to develop a second area layout exclusively for side-lighting angles.

**Figure 16–15**
Lighting the Acting Areas:
Front Light

Illustrations show the area system with a minimum of front lighting. The beam or ceiling positions (1) cover the downstage areas while the first electric position (2) lights the upstage areas.

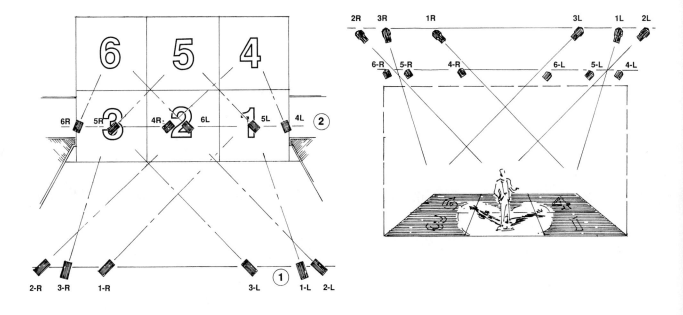

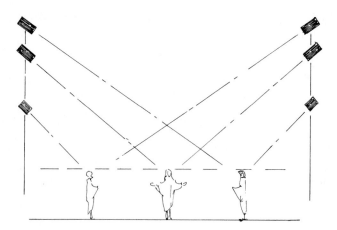

**Figure 16–16**

**Lighting the Acting Areas: Side Light**

Illustrations show three side lights from both right and left lighting across the stage in a "zone." Side light areas will not correspond in shape to those of front light due to the elongation of the light beams.

## THE WASH METHOD

Area lighting is a popular, but not exclusive, method of lighting the stage. There are a variety of other techniques that are often used in combination with area lighting. One such approach is *wash lighting.*

The term *washing* refers to the use of general illumination to cover the entire playing space. Normally coming from a single direction, wash light is excellent for color-toning the stage and actors. Various angles, directions, and colors of wash light are used in conjunction with higher intensity *accent lights* to achieve variety, interest, and good visibility.

**Single-Source Lighting**     A variation on wash lighting, *single-source lighting* attempts to recreate the feeling of one distinct source of illumination. The sun, after all, is a single source. However, it is so far away that its rays of light are nearly parallel by the time they reach us. Single-source stage lighting has diverging rays. It is normally achieved by clustering several lighting instruments and focusing them to cover the entire playing area. The effect is unique, as lighting angles change while an actor moves from place to place on the set.

## LIGHTING FLEXIBILITY

As the demands on stage lighting increase, so do the demands of designers for greater flexibility. The ability to change angle, direction, and color is solely dependent on equipment. Designers in the past have answered this need by specifying greater and greater numbers of instruments. Rather than depending on quantity, however, today's designer instead tends to specify more technologically advanced equipment.

**Double and Triple Hanging**     To improve the limited flexibility of two-instrument front-lighting, designers hang more instruments to use as additional lights for each area (Figure 16–17). By duplicating the area coverage on each side, several possibilities for color control are created. The designer

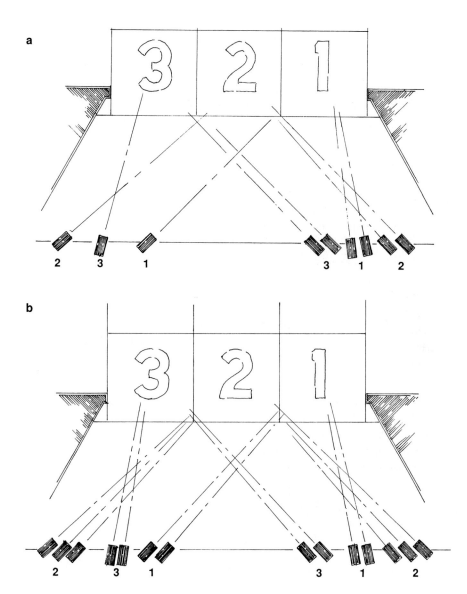

**Figure 16–17**
**Double and Triple Hanging**

Triple hanging on area 2 with double hanging on areas 1 and 3. The center area has tight and more open focus while all areas provide a selection of color and direction of key and fill sources.

can (1) change the warm–cool accent from left to right, (2) change the area color by independently mixing the colors from either the right or left, or (3) flood the stage with only one of the two area colors.

Notice also that a third spotlight has been added to area 2 in Figure 16–17. This unit can adjust focus and intensity in the all-important center stage area.

**Color Changers**     Double and triple hanging allows for greater color flexibility and can provide some degree of focus control. However, a better solution might be remotely controlled *color changers* placed in the area instruments. Back- and side-lights can also be double-hung or equipped with color changers (Figure 16–18).

**Figure 16–18**
Color Changers and Automated Fixtures

Two photographs of side-lighting towers in use for a Kenny Loggins concert. Shown are remotely controlled color changers and an Intellabeam 700HX automated fixture.

**Automated Fixtures**     Recently made available and practical for stage use, *automated fixtures* provide the ultimate in flexibility (Figure 16–18). Concert and special event lighting has provided a valuable testing ground for these remotely controlled lights: They are now quiet enough; they are reliable enough; and their price is getting low enough for theatrical use. Most automated fixtures can be controlled by today's consoles. But designing with them requires a slightly different approach from that of nonautomated fixed instruments.

Like any other instruments, automated fixtures must be focused on a particular area. The coordinates of that focus are then stored in computer memory for recall when needed. Two systems currently exist for automated fixture focus: a grid system and a "special" system. The grid system is nearly identical to the fixed-instrument area method. A grid of focus areas is determined and each automated fixture is programmed to focus on each one of the grid points or areas. The "special" system identifies heavily used areas of the stage where automated fixtures are likely to be needed. Each light is then programmed to those selected areas. While the "special" system is fine for concert lighting, the grid system is best for most theatrical applications.

Focus is only one attribute to be considered when designing with automated fixtures. Many lights offer control over color, pattern (gobos), beam size (iris), intensity (mechanical douser), and beam quality (diffusion). One or more control channels must be assigned to each attribute. Channels can be arranged in groups for ease of operation. Lighting looks, most likely including both fixed and automated lights, are assigned cue numbers, with extra cues called *dark sets* required to change an attribute, so that the change will not be visible.

Placement of automated fixtures depends on the effect desired and number of instruments available. As they are introduced in the theatre, automated fixtures work alongside fixed instruments as specials and as key-lights. High-angled front- and side-lighting are currently the most popular applications. As they become more readily available and accepted, uses will expand.

## SPECIALS AND SPECIAL VISIBILITY

*Specials* are instruments that are used in addition to regular area lighting. Their normal function is to emphasize a part of the setting or an actor in a specific location. Examples include a door special (a light carefully framed to brighten an actor standing in the doorway), a couch special (extra illumination where an important scene takes place), or a pin spot (the narrow beam of light that is held a moment longer on an actor's face during a final fade-out). Specials influence composition by attracting the eye to a desired center of attention.

*Special visibility* involves light following the moving actor. This can be achieved in one of two ways: The actor may be lit by a series of spotlights focused along the path of movement, with each light dimming, up or down at the proper moment. Or, the actor may be lit with a follow spot.

**Follow Spots**     Actor movement is followed by a single, freely mounted spotlight. The *follow spot* has long been used for musical comedies, revues, and other presentational productions where realism is of minor importance. It usually appears as a sharply defined, hard-edged circle of light that is brighter than all other stage lights. Its use in this manner is frankly presentational.

A more subtle method of follow-spotting is called "European follow-spotting," referring to the practice of placing lights and operators on the first light bridge. A soft-edged incandescent follow spot is used to unobtrusively highlight the action. An angle close to 60 degrees is preferable in order to keep the light off the scenery and minimize shadows around the actor. With good operation, European follow-spotting can be an extremely effective lighting technique.

## LIGHTING THE BACKGROUND

Except for special occasions, area lights provide the major portion of scenery illumination. In the case of a conventional interior or box setting, area lights are usually sufficient to light the walls. However, several precautions are necessary. Too often a box set's stage-right walls seem to be a totally different color from its stage-left walls. This mistake is a result of poor color mixing from the front area instruments. It is corrected by making sure that all frontal colors hit the walls with relatively equal intensity. Instruments lighting the walls of a box set should be softly focused in order to blend well and reduce shadows.

Shadows on the walls from actors or furniture can be a difficult problem. The best solution is to change the angle of light causing the shadow, but at

**Figure 16–19**
Lighting the Background

A painted backdrop, sky drop, or cyclorama lit from above and below (a) and only from above (b). When lighting from below, a masking "ground row" is necessary. Lighting with strip lights from above often requires two sets of lights, one aiming high and the other low.

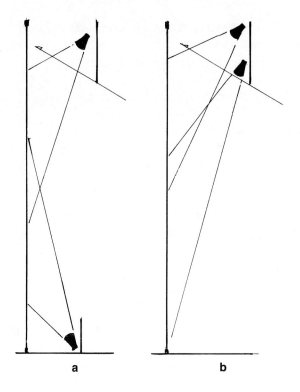

a          b

**Figure 16–20**
Lighting the Background

(a) A translucent drop (1) illuminated by backlight reflected off a reflecting drop (2) lit from above and below. In addition, the translucency is lit from the front with a set of lights from above.
(b) A translucent drop (3) positioned upstage of a scrim (4). The drop has both front and back lighting to change effect and the scrim is also lit from the front to add depth and atmosphere.

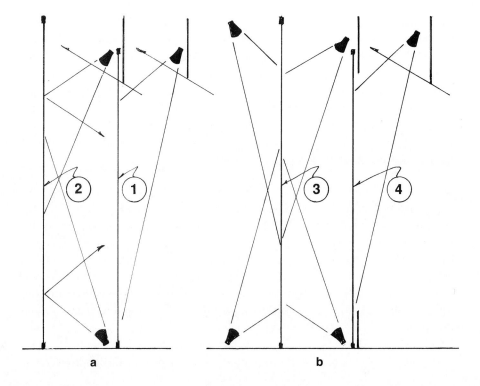

a          b

times this is impossible. A wall wash comprising lights specifically hung, focused, and colored for this purpose may help. Fresnel-type instruments are a good choice.

Background areas and backings, however, are a different matter. Many times the lighting problem is small—such as the backing behind a doorway, rarely seen for more than a moment, and then not directly by most of the audience. Not very elaborate equipment is needed to give these backings adequate illumination. The objective is to provide enough light so that an actor, when leaving the stage, does not seem to be retiring into a dark closet. Such attention to detail can make the difference between an adequate and a good design.

## BACKDROPS

Backings can assume greater proportions. An example might be a painted exterior seen through a large window. Rooftops or the exterior walls of an adjoining building may be visible in a more detailed backing. Such scenic elements demand greater attention to distribution and color control than does the simple doorway backing.

For the most complicated backgrounds, such as vast areas of sky, large backdrops or cycloramas are usually used. These require lighting instruments specially designed to provide the proper amount of light as well as even distribution and blending of color over the entire surface. Such instruments are hung in rows above the drop and often placed on the stage floor as well (Figure 16–19). The mixing of several colors may be required if the mood of the background is expected to change.

**Translucent Backings**     A translucent backdrop allows for the possibility of changes in distribution from front- to back-lighting. Scrim is a particularly useful material because of its capability to appear either opaque or transparent. A scrim hung in front of an opaque backdrop or cyclorama adds a hazy quality of distance to the backing. The scrim itself can be lit, or, better yet, the drop behind the scrim may be illuminated (Figure 16–20).

Scrim may also be used by itself as a drop. In this case the designer must pay close attention to the light that falls directly on the scrim as well as behind it. Using high-angled top-light is the best way to opaque a scrim. To make a scrim transparent, keep as much light as possible off the scrim itself while illuminating objects behind it.

**Hanging Space**     Successful background lighting depends on the close cooperation of the lighting and scene designers. For instance, all too often the scene designer does not leave enough space between ground rows and the backdrop or between borders and the cyclorama for proper lighting. No matter how good the equipment, a certain distance is required for colors to mix and blend well on a backdrop. Or sometimes backgrounds representing distant fields are so close to a window or door that it is impossible to avoid shadows from area lighting. Any illusion created by good painting is then destroyed. Most of these and other potential problems can be avoided by consultation and careful study of the scene designer's floor plan.

# INTENSITY CONTROL

*Intensity*, the third property of light to be explored here, refers to the brightness of a source. It is controlled by dimmers and is measured either in *lumens* or in *footcandles*. Dimming a lighting instrument is normally achieved by reducing the electrical current sent to the lamp. The result is that the lamp's filament glows less brightly and gives off a warmer colored light. The process of dimming up one group of lights while dimming out another group is called a *cross fade*.

## PRINCIPLES OF DIMMING

In the theatre, where aesthetics are a concern, subtle fading of light is often more appropriate than abrupt switching on or off. An audience's attention can gently be shifted by fading the light down on one scene and up on another. Time change can be indicated with the help of dimming. The mood of a scene can be altered by a cross fade from one color to another. Dimming speed can be either fast or slow, depending on the desired effect.

A dimmer is the lighting designer's paintbrush. Broad strokes are accomplished by controlling several lighting instruments with one dimmer or by grouping dimmers together. Detail work requires individual control over lighting instruments. The lighting designer must determine exactly how instruments will be controlled well before getting into the theatre.

Throughout theatre history, lighting designers have always wanted more dimmers than were available. In fact, many have felt that lack of control was the most limiting factor in a production's design. Difficult and time-consuming choices have had to be made as to which instruments would be controlled independently and which would be ganged together. A mistake made in dimmer assignments was always costly.

Finally, in the 1970s, a revolution in lighting control took place. The electronic dimmer was developed and became affordable and practical for use in the theatre. Soon after, computerized control consoles became a reality. The lighting designer was now free to create as never before.

## ARCHAIC FORMS OF DIMMING

In order to place a bit of perspective on modern lighting control, a brief examination of the history of dimming is in order. The demand for dimming in the theatre began as soon as productions moved indoors. On seventeenth-century stages, cans suspended by cords were lowered over candles to vary the light. In the eighteenth century, candles in the wings were mounted on vertical boards that could be revolved to turn the light away from the stage or back toward it.

Light fueled by natural gas was introduced in the nineteenth century. *Gas tables* were the first vestiges of modern lighting control systems. A series of valves located backstage controlled the flow of gas to various jets arranged about the playing space. Rubber tubes connecting gas jets to control valves made the location of the jets flexible. Theatre fires were commonplace.

With the advent of the incandescent lamp came crude forms of electrical dimming. All utilized the principle of dimmming by means of variable electrical resistance: The dimmer created resistance to the flow of electricity, and the amount of resistance could be varied. The carbonpile and saltwater dimmers were among these early forms. But the most popular and long-lasting was the resistance dimmer.

### RESISTANCE DIMMERS

Most commonly found in the form of a large disk, the resistance plate consisted of lengths of wire used to create electrical resistance. When properly loaded, these dimmers could fade a light source or sources in an even and smooth manner. A "road board," such as that shown in Figure 17–1, consisted of several plates mounted next to each other. It was typical for several of them to be arranged backstage, close to the power supply. A jungle of stage cable ran from the dimmers to lighting instruments located over-stage and front-of-house. As many as six or eight electricians operated the switches and dimmer handles on cue from the stage manager. To be replaced only by the electronic dimmer, road boards remained a part of rental house stocks well into the 1970s.

**Disadvantages**  In order to reduce the flow of electrical current, a resistance dimmer had to convert electrical energy into heat. Not only did this process waste electricity, but the heat generated was overwhelming. In addition, resistance plates were heavy and bulky. The greatest disadvantage from an artistic point of view was their fixed capacity. Without going into unnecessary detail, it is enough to say that the plate's capacity was dictated by the length of wire it contained. Accordingly, a lamp or lamps plugged into a resistance dimmer had to be of the same wattage as the dimmer. Otherwise, the dimmer could not dim the light(s) completely out. In order

**Figure 17—1**
Resistance Dimmer Board

Example of an early switch-board, built into a box for travel. At the right end of the row of dimmer handles is the long interlock handle and beyond it is the master switch. Photo courtesy Strand Lighting.

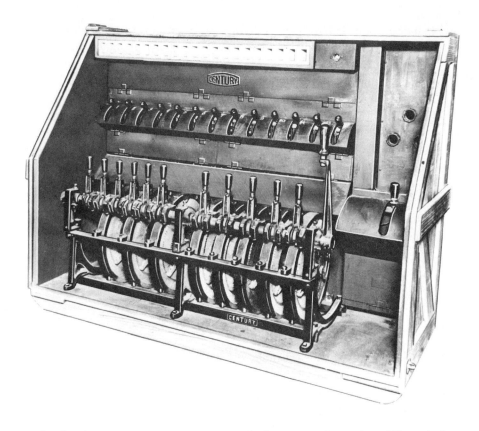

to load a dimmer to its capacity, extra lights were plugged in. These lights were often placed out in the alley behind the theatre. Called "ghost loads," they faded up and down in unison with the lights onstage.

## AUTOTRANSFORMER DIMMERS

Many of the problems with resistance dimming were solved by the autotransformer dimmer put into use in the 1940s. This device consisted of copper wire wound around a doughnutlike core made of iron. In order to know how an autotransformer works, it is necessary to understand that a magnetic field is created by electricity flowing through a wire. Wire in the autotransformer is wound in such a manner that adjacent magnetic fields work against each other, restricting the flow of current. This phenomenon is called back-electromotive force (back-EMF) or back-voltage. When the wire is arranged properly, a variable current is available along the coil. A sliding contact called the "brush" makes an electrical connection with the bare wires of the coil. As the brush moves along the coil, it conducts a variable flow of electricity to the lamp.

The autotransformer is not load-sensitive. Any wattage lamp within the capacity of the dimmer can be dimmed smoothly and effectively between full out and full up. Little heat is created and autotransformers are not quite as bulky as resistance plates.

**Package Boards**    The most common housing configuration for the autotransformer was the *package board* (Figure 17—2). The "package" usually consisted of six dimmers, circuit breakers, and a plugging panel. The board shown in Figure 17–2a includes a large-capacity dimmer that can be used to "master" the others. The model shown in Figure 17–2b has dimmer handles that can interlock with each other, allowing one person to run all six dimmers. Although heavy, these boards were transportable and were a popular means of control for a number of years. In the early 1980s, the final package board rolled (or lumbered) its way off Superior Electric's assembly line—as the electronic dimmer had finally and rightfully taken over the entire market of intensity control.

## PRESET SYSTEMS

The first truly electronic dimming system was put into operation by George Izenour in 1947 at Yale University. The two-scene *preset console* shown in

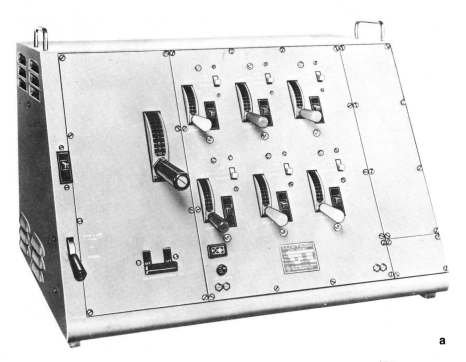

**a**

**b**

### Figure 17–2
### Autotransformer Package Boards

(a) A package containing six 1,300-watt autotransformer dimmers and a master of 6,000-watt capacity. By means of the white switches, one or more of the small dimmers could be put under control of the large one, thus providing proportional dimming for up to a total of 6,000 watts. (b) A package with six 2,500-watt dimmers and an interlock handle to which several or all of the other dimmer handles could be connected. Photos courtesy Superior Electric.

**Figure 17–3**
An Early Two-Scene
Preset Console

The transparent disks with the white handles are the controllers for the thirty dimmers, one apiece for each preset. Below is a row of on/off switches for each circuit. At the right end of the white plate is the cross-fade handle. Photo courtesy George Izenour.

Figure 17–3 was built by Izenour in 1955. It served as a model for preset systems throughout the next two decades.

**Remote Control**    With the electronic dimmer came the possibility of *remote control*. Control consoles were developed that allow operators to be located front-of-house where they can see all the action onstage. Low-voltage cables connect the control console to dimmers located backstage or in the basement. Each dimmer is represented at the control console by a small rheostat or controller. When the controller is set at 50 percent intensity, the dimmer responds in kind.

**Preset Consoles**    In addition to control of each dimmer from the console, preset systems provide one or more additional sets of controllers. The Izenour console shown in Figure 17–3 controls thirty dimmers. Since it is a two-scene preset board, it has two rows of thirty controllers each. While the controllers in the active row are communicating with the dimmers, the inactive controllers can be preset by the operator for the next lighting look. The looks are numbered, and each one is called a *preset*. A single lever, the cross-fader, is then used to fade from one preset to the next.

A limitation of the two-scene preset is the time it takes an operator to arrange the controllers for the next preset. To overcome this difficulty, manufacturers developed multiple-scene preset systems. Figure 17–4 shows a ten-scene preset system capable of controlling forty-five dimmers. Such a system often required several operators and took up a good deal of space. Due to

their low cost, two-scene preset consoles today still maintain their popularity with small facilities. However, the larger multiple-scene preset systems are things of the past, having been replaced by computerized control.

## Figure 17—4
### An Early Ten-Scene Preset Console

To the left is the preset panel with ten rows of forty-five controllers, one for each dimmer. The operator's console at the right contains another forty-five controllers across the top with preset selector buttons and a cross-fader below. Photo courtesy George Izenour.

## ELEMENTS OF ELECTRONIC CONTROL

Under older methods of control, a simple shift of emphasis in stage lighting required the designer to direct several operators who probably could not even see the results of their actions. If the desired effect was achieved once in five times, the designer was considered fortunate.

Electronic control has changed all that. The principal advantages of electronic control are these:

1. *Remote control*—allowing the operator full view of the stage
2. *Computerized control*—providing computer memory storage of presets and other specialized control functions
3. *Lower dimmer cost*—allowing for more control and the possibility of dimmer-per-circuit
4. *Smaller, lighter dimmers*—providing space for more dimmers and improving portability

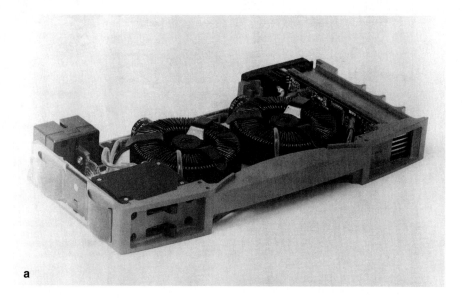

### Figure 17–5
### SCR Dimmer Module and Rack

(a) Shown is one of Colortran's *i* series dimmer modules. This is one of a new generation of "intelligent" dimmers that contains electronics allowing it to control its own processes.
(b) A dimmer rack containing forty-eight *i* series dimmer modules. The hand-held terminal shown provides feedback and control at each rack, or remotely. Photos courtesy Colortran, Inc.

The basic component of electronic control is its dimmer—the silicon controlled rectifier.

## SILICON CONTROLLED RECTIFIERS

Usually referred to as the *SCR dimmer*, its name should be interpreted to mean "a silicon rectifier under control." A silicon controlled rectifier is the actual electronic component that does the dimming. This dimmer controls the flow of electricity to the lamp in a unique manner. It quickly switches on and off—120 times per second! The electrical current actually reaches the filament of the lamp in bursts, occurring so rapidly that they cause no visible reaction. The longer the SCR remains on before switching off, the greater the electrical flow to the lamp and the brighter it burns. One point of interest: This switching action does not result in reduced voltage to the lamp. Therefore, SCR dimmers, unlike autotransformers, cannot be set to drive low-voltage devices.

Two SCRs are required for each dimmer, but the actual SCR is only the diameter of a nickel and $\frac{3}{4}$ inch thick. These little "buttons" are mounted in metal finlike devices called "heat sinks," which dissipate the heat generated by the rapid switching. Early SCR dimmers were the size of a shoe box but now are less than half that size (Figure 17–5). The other major components are a circuit breaker provided to protect the SCR, an electric choke that regulates the power flow, and a printed circuit card.

One or two dimmers are enclosed in modules that fit into racks of various sizes. The twelve-dimmer rack shown in Figure 17–6 is a standard portable size. The dimmer module can normally be slid out of its rack for servicing, making electrical connection by virtue of plugs located at the rear. Always remember to turn off the circuit breaker(s) in the front panel of the module before removing or replacing the dimmer. Miniaturization of components has allowed the creation of high-density dimmer racks containing hundreds of dimmers in a relatively small space (Figure 17–7).

**Figure 17–6**
**Twelve-Dimmer Rack**

Shown is the ETC "Sensor" portable dimmer rack. Photo courtesy Electronic Theatre Controls, Inc.

**Figure 17–7**
**High-Density Touring Dimmer Rack**

Shown is the ETC "Sensor" rolling dimmer rack. Photo courtesy Electronic Theatre Controls, Inc.

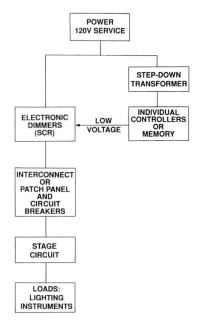

## Figure 17–8
### Typical Theatrical Power Flow

A block diagram illustrates the flow of power from the service entrance through control and to a lighting instrument. A dimmer-per-circuit system would eliminate the interconnect or patch panel.

## THE INTERCONNECT SYSTEM

In the days when SCR dimmers were large and expensive, a flexible system was necessary to allow the connection of any stage circuit to any dimmer. The major component of this system is called the *patch panel.*

Figure 17–8 illustrates the flow of power from the service entrance of a theatre to a lighting instrument using an interconnect system with a patch panel. In all but the smallest theatres it was normal to have many more stage circuits than dimmers. A patch panel allows the connection of any lighting instrument to any dimmer. In addition, it provides for the possibility of plugging multiple instruments into a single dimmer. This flexibility is an important tool for the lighting designer.

Several types of patch panels exist, but the simplest and most common is the plug-patch. All of the stage circuits terminate in numbered plugs at the end of retractable cables, much like an old-fashioned telephone switchboard (Figure 17–9). The dimmer connections, also numbered, end in jacks mounted in the panel. Any plug may be pushed into any jack. Accordingly, any instrument may be controlled by any dimmer. Several jacks are assigned to each dimmer, providing a simple way to gang more than one instrument onto a single dimmer. The only precaution is to make sure that the total instrument wattage does not exceed that of the dimmer.

## Figure 17–9
### Telephone-Type Interconnect or Patch Panel

Single plugs representing each circuit in the theatre are plugged into one of several receptacles assigned to each dimmer. Circuit breakers for each individual circuit are located on the face of the panel. Repatching during a show is often accomplished by throwing the proper circuit breakers.

## THE DIMMER-PER-CIRCUIT SYSTEM

By the early 1980s the cost of SCR dimmers had fallen to the point where it became reasonable for a theatre to provide a dimmer for each and every circuit (outlet) in the house. Although patch systems remain common in older facilities, the majority of today's well-equipped theatres have adopted dimmer-per-circuit. Just as its name implies, this system allocates an individual 2,000- or 2,400-watt dimmer to each circuit. Dimmer numbers and circuit numbers are one in the same. No longer is the lighting designer limited by lack of individual control over lighting instruments—every instrument in use can have its own dimmer.

**Soft Patching**   As noted above, dimmers are permanently assigned to circuits in the dimmer-per-circuit system. Control flexibility is achieved by means of an electronic patching feature of computer control called *soft patch.* The familiar rheostat or controller found in the preset system is now called a *channel.* By virtue of the soft patch, any channel can be assigned to any dimmer/circuit. In addition, an unlimited number of dimmer/circuits may be assigned to a single channel.

Figure 17–10 shows the electronic patch display of Colortran's "Prestige 2000" lighting control console. Selecting a new patch configuration is simply a matter of several keystrokes.

## TYPES OF ELECTRONIC CONTROL

For all practical purposes, only two types of electronic control exist: the manual system and the memory system. Memory systems are computer-based; manual systems are not. Manual systems always consist of at least one

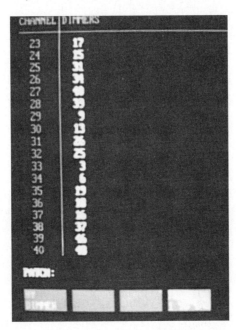

**Figure 17–10**
**Electronic Patch Screen**

Shown is the dimmer-to-channel arrangement of the Colortran Prestige 2000 electronic patch display, called "soft patching."

controller per dimmer as well as a master controller. They may be quite sophisticated and flexible, offering several presets, masters, submasters, and group masters.

## MANUAL SYSTEMS

The simplest and least expensive of the manual electronic control systems provides one controller per dimmer and might very well be contained in a single housing (Figure 17–11). Although these systems are inexpensive and portable, they are also inflexible and can be poorly built. When purchasing such a control system, it is advisable to consider the following points:

1. Are the dimmers themselves easily accessible for repair?
2. Have the dimmers been properly protected from power surges?
3. Is proper dimmer ventilation provided?
4. Are chokes installed to prevent excessive lamp filament vibration?
5. Is a master controller provided?
6. Do the controllers work smoothly and seem sturdy?
7. Finally, can the system be expanded?

The only advantage these systems provide over the older autotransformer package boards are in compactness, lightness of weight, and electronic mastering.

Of value to the very small facility is the system shown in Figure 17–12. From Dove Systems, it provides six dimming channels and an optional two-scene preset (shown). What makes it unique is that it plugs into two normal, household, electrical outlets. Care must be taken to plug into two different circuits and not to exceed the capacity of those circuits.

**Control Features**     Manual control systems can offer numerous features that add flexibility and increase the potential for complex lighting effects. Most common are features like these:

*Electronic mastering:* A single controller acts as a proportional master over all active controllers. This is useful for fading all dimmers to black.

*Submastering:* A single controller acts as a proportional master over all controllers assigned to it. Any number of controllers can be assigned to a submaster. Submasters offer additional flexibility to a standard preset system.

*Split cross-fading:* In a preset system, the cross-fader is a single controller that lets the operator fade from one preset to another. A split cross-fader consists of two faders, one for each preset, allowing the fade time of one preset to be different from that of the other. The most common application is to fade up an incoming preset more quickly than an outgoing one.

*Timed fades:* A timing device automatically executes a cross fade at a predetermined rate set by the operator. The fade is initiated at the press of a "go" button.

*Effects:* A limited number of prewritten effects (such as a channel chase) are available.

## Figure 17—11
### Portable Control

Shown is a six-dimmer controller with master and circuit breakers. Each dimmer has a capacity of 2,400 watts. Circuit plug-ins are located on the rear panel. Also shown is a remote control unit. Photo courtesy Electronics Diversified, Inc.

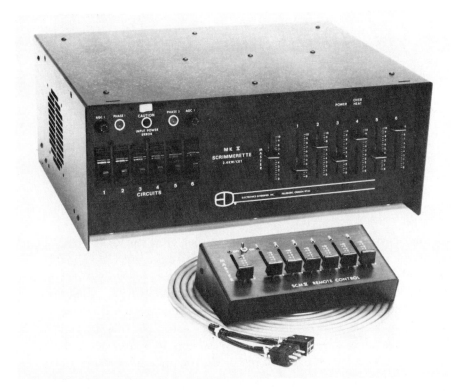

## Figure 17—12
### Small Capacity Dimming

Shown is a portable two-scene, six-channel control system unique in its ability to be powered by two normal household circuits. Photo courtesy Dove Systems.

**Figure 17–13**
Concert Lighting Control

Shown is the Avolites Rolacue *Pearl* control console. It has 512 channels, 450 memories, 30 pages, 60 channel faders, and 15 simultaneous playbacks. It can simultaneously control 30 automated fixtures, 60 color changers, and fixed instruments. Photo courtesy Avolites America Inc.

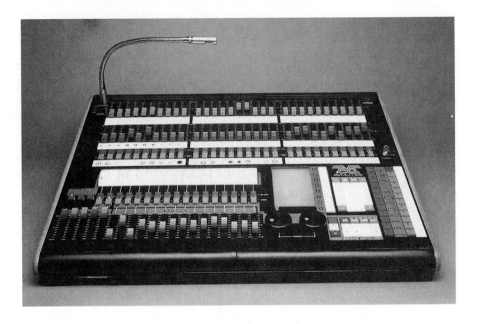

**Group Mastering**     A control console that grew out of the specialized needs of concert lighting is the *group master* board (Figure 17–13). It divides a manual console into various groups and subgroups, each with its own master control. As in a submastering system, lighting channels are assigned to group masters. The groups may be used independently of each other similar to presets, or they may be combined to create a multitude of effects.

This system is a favorite of concert designers who often act as their own operators. It offers the flexibility required in many concert situations when the lead performer decides to add a new number or change an existing one. It lends itself to creativity; each performance can be lit a bit differently. However, such systems are too complex to operate if many changes are needed in rapid succession. It is not ideal for theatre because there are too many things for an operator to keep track of during a swiftly moving play.

**Combination Systems**     The most desirable manual system combines the virtues of presetting with those of group mastering and submastering. A large variety of such control systems exist today, each with its own idiosyncrasies. Having evolved from earlier preset systems, most combination systems offer presetting with many extra features. The system shown in Figure 17–14 is equipped with a two-scene preset or 120-cue memory, submastering, timed split cross-faders, and soft patching. Combination systems are economical, portable, and offer a good alternative to small, computer memory control.

## EARLY COMPUTERIZED MEMORY SYSTEMS

Concurrent development of the SCR dimmer and the computer led inevitably to computerized control of lighting. The computer's ability to store and rapidly retrieve information made it an ideal replacement for manual preset systems. With computerized memory, cue and preset information may be

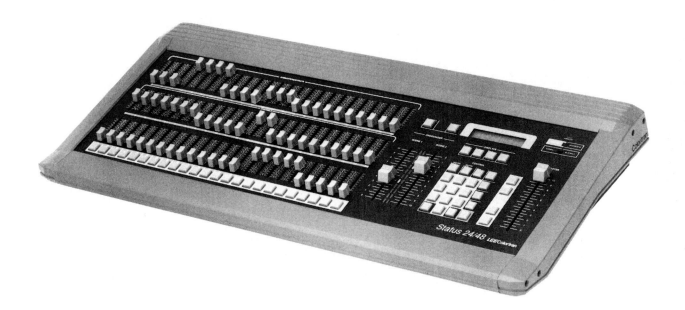

randomly recalled with push-button speed. These systems made it easy to keep track of the numerous control channels in a dimmer-per-circuit system. Current-day control of automated fixtures would be impossible without computer assistance.

Compared to those being manufactured today, early memory systems were large and bulky. They often had a single set of manual controllers as well as a keyboard; preset information could be entered into memory by setting levels on the controllers or by typing levels in by means of the keyboard. A split fader, often a timed fader, and possible group and/or submasters were standard equipment. The primary memory storage was either disc or core. (Only later was disc or magnetic tape library storage added as a standard feature.) The control signal was a low-voltage analog signal sent from the console to the dimmers. The dimmers were designed to respond to varying electrical voltages. However, voltage ranges were not standard from manufacturer to manufacturer, so one manufacturer's control console could not run another manufacturer's dimmers.

Q-File, developed jointly by Thorn Electrical Industries, Ltd. of Great Britain and Kliegl Brothers in the United States, was one of the first systems to eliminate a full set of controllers and add library storage (Figure 17–15). Autocue, manufactured by Skirpan Lighting Control Corporation, introduced the video monitor (a standard television screen) to the world of control systems. Although more complex than necessary, Autocue was the forerunner of modern state-of-the-art equipment.

Kliegl took Q-File off the market and replaced it with its popular Performance system. Colortran introduced Channel Track, a bulky system that has since been replaced by the Prestige series of consoles. Strand Lighting developed Multi-Q and Micro-Q, predecessors of Strand's popular Light Palette. And a new company, Electronic Theatre Controls (ETC), introduced a

**Figure 17–14**
**Two-Scene Preset Control**

Shown is Colortran's "Status 24/48" control console. Most modern consoles provide either manual preset or memory control. This model offers twenty-four two-scene preset channels, forty-eight manual channels, or 120 memory cues. Photo courtesy Colortran, Inc.

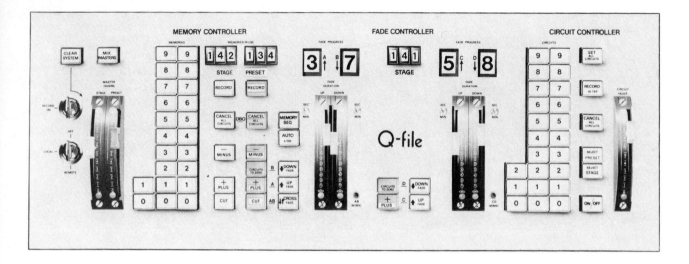

**Figure 17–15**
An Early Memory
Control Console

Shown is a "Q-File" console,
the first successful preset memory system. Originally developed
for television, it was designed
and manufactured by Thorn
Electrical Industries, Ltd. Photo
courtesy Kliegl Brothers.

line of user-friendly control systems that placed more competitive pressure
on the market.

## STATE-OF-THE-ART MEMORY SYSTEMS

While the design of early memory systems varied a great deal from manufacturer to manufacturer, current consoles are much more similar to one another. Trial and error has determined which features and functions designers
and operators prefer in a control system. Modern systems are less complex
to operate. An operator can learn the necessary skills in a short amount of
time. Designer interface with the system has been made easier and continues
to improve. Size and cost have generally been reduced. However, the most
significant advantage of modern control systems is their reliability. In the
not-so-distant past, system failure was commonplace. The computer would
"go down," often loosing all its memory. Countless hours were spent repro-
gramming shows. Those designers who failed to keep accurate "hard copy"
were never seen again. Thankfully, today's computers are more robust.

A digital protocol called DMX is currently used for communication between control console and dimmers. This standard digital signal allows any
manufacturer's equipment to "speak" to that of any other manufacturer.

Four categories of theatrical memory control systems currently exist: (1)
the nondedicated computer system, (2) the small-capacity dedicated system,
(3) the large-capacity dedicated system, and (4) the automated fixture control
system.

**Nondedicated Computer Systems**     The term *nondedicated* refers to a
computer system that is able to perform other functions in addition to lighting control. WestStar Corporation captured the nondedicated control market
with software designed to work with IBM and Apple computers. One need
purchase only the software from WestStar, although optional control features
such as a manual cross-fader and mouse controller are available. Figure
17–16a shows the complete ProStar system used with an IBM computer. The

**Figure 17–16**
**Nondedicated Memory Control**

(a) Shown is the "ProStar" system, that can be expanded to control up to 192 channels. Photo courtesy WestStar Corporation.
(b) The cue sheet display from a "ProStar" system.

operator is able to select on-screen displays of patch, channel levels, or a cue sheet used during playback. Figure 17–16b is a close-up of the system's cue sheet. The main body of the screen is dedicated to a sequential list of cues, fade times, and channel levels for the active cue. Above and below are listed operational functions from which the operator can choose.

The advantages of the nondedicated system are low cost and the fact that the computer can be put to uses other than stage lighting. Bookkeeping, box office, and a host of other software programs can all be run on this single computer. Disadvantages of the system are lack of functions, limited channel capacity, and relatively difficult operation.

**Small-Capacity Dedicated Systems**    The systems illustrated in Figure 17–17 are typical small-capacity dedicated systems. These systems offer all the standard operational features as well as some specialized ones depending on the manufacturer. They are categorized as small systems due to their limited channel and cue storage capacity. A good example is Vision, the fine and inexpensive system from ETC. This console operates a maximum of 100 control channels and has a memory capacity of 200 cues.

**Figure 17–17**
**Small Capacity Memory Control Systems**

(a) The ETC "Vision," which can control 100 channels and hold 200 cues. Photo courtesy Electronic Theatre Controls, Inc.
(b) Depending on the model, the GAM "Access" controls forty-eight or ninety-six channels and allows for 104 or 232 cues. Photo courtesy The Great American Market.
(c) Strand's "Mantrix MX," which can control 12, 24, or 48 channels with 48, 96, or 192 memories. Photo courtesy Strand Lighting, Inc.
(d) Colortran's "Encore 24/48," which controls 24 channels in two-scene preset mode or 144 channels in memory and offers 300 cues. Photo courtesy Colortran, Inc.

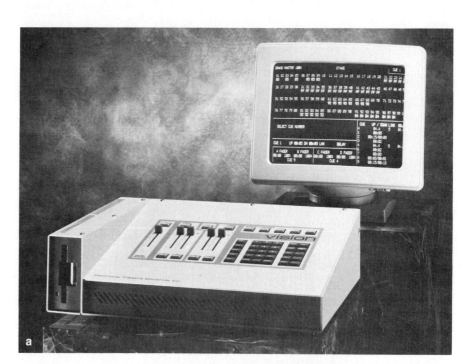

a

b

Small systems normally have one video monitor that displays various information according to operational needs. Features necessary in a quality system are a reliable battery backup, an easy-to-use entry keyboard, a video monitor for the operator, and the possibility of a remote monitor for the designer. Important functions include the ability to insert additional cues into an existing cue list, soft patching, the ability to link one cue to the next, split time fades, and a help display for the operator.

c

d

**Large-Capacity Dedicated Systems** As lighting control is called on to perform more and more functions, larger capacity systems become necessary. In the 1980s the need to control more than 100 channels was unusual. Today, with the control demands of color scrollers and automated fixtures, more than 1,000 channels may be necessary. Several such large-capacity systems are shown in Figure 17–18. As a means of comparison with the smaller systems, ETC's Obsession console is included. This system has a capacity of 1,000 cues per show and can handle 1,536 control channels. In addition, this larger system offers submasters and groups as well as a number of more sophisticated functions.

Nearly all of the larger systems have two monitors with selectable on-screen displays. During normal operation, the cue sheet is displayed on the

## Figure 17–18
**Large Capacity Memory Control Systems**

(a) Shown is the ETC "Obsession" control console which can control 1,536 channels with 1,000 cues per show. It has forty-eight overlapping submasters, 250 groups, and can operate 128 simultaneous fades.
(b) The "Obsession" designer's remote console and remote focus unit. Photos courtesy Electronic Theatre Controls, Inc.
(c) Colortran's "Encore XL/2" control system can control 1,024 channels and have 600 cues. It has forty-eight submasters and provides ten programmable macro keys. Photo courtesy Colortran, Inc.
(d) Strand's "LP90" control system controls up to 1,728 channels and allows for 600 cues. It has up to forty-eight overlapping submasters and can operate 128 simultaneous fades. Photo courtesy Strand Lighting, Inc.

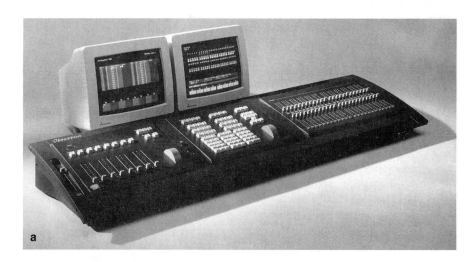

a

b

primary screen, with channel levels or other information as needed on the second screen.

The displays shown in Figure 17–19 are from a Strand Light Palette '90 control system. The cue sheet display includes cue number, time, and other playback information such as cue parts, delays, and effects. The channel display lists each control channel along with its assigned level in the designated cue (in this case, the live cue onstage).

One of the major functional advantages of the larger and more sophisticated control systems is programmable effects. Several systems offer "effect packages" that allow a limited number of effects such as a forward chase or a random flicker (useful for fire effects), but only a few allow for operator-designed effects. To be most useful, such a program must be easy to write

c

d

**Figure 17—19**
"LP90" Displays

(a) The cue sheet display.
(b) The channel display.

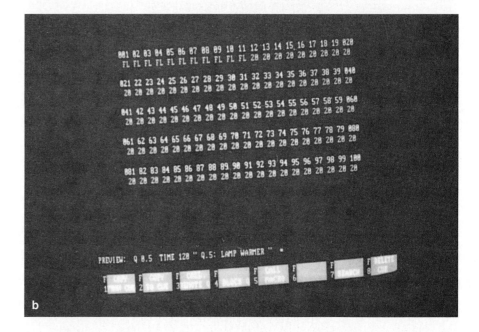

and operate as well as flexible enough to accommodate any kind of effect desired.

**Automated Fixture Control Systems** Automated fixtures, sometimes erroneously referred to as moving lights, come in a huge range of types and sizes. Their variety is reminiscent of early computerized control systems. Each manufacturer has created its own version, with nearly all of them having unique and valuable features. Until recently, control over these fixtures has also been exclusively the domain of each individual manufacturer. For instance, when a Vari*Lite system was rented for a concert tour, both the control console and the operator were part of the package. When Intellabeams were rented, a control unit designed and manufactured by High End Systems had to be included. Such proprietary activity is no longer acceptable to users. There is too much competition and the demand for automated fixtures is growing by leaps and bounds.

Automated fixtures have a number of remotely controlled features that may be labeled "parameters" or "attributes." For instance, a color wheel that provides variable color selection is one of several attributes. Each of a light's attributes requires one or more channels of control. The Cyberlight, recently developed by High End Systems, needs twenty-one control channels to operate all attributes. A bit of simple math tells us that a great number of channels are necessary to control modern automated fixtures. While a system's capacity is an important factor, ease of operation is equally significant. Early control systems were extremely complex and cumbersome to operate. In some cases, only manufacturer-trained operators were capable.

A new generation of computerized control systems is on the horizon. A control board manufactured by Celco, called Navigator, is popular because it doesn't require the operator to be a specialist. High End Systems and Lightwave Research recently introduced Status Cue (Figure 17–20a). The ideal system will control everything: moving lights, color scrollers, and conventional fixed lighting instruments. The Wholehog, manufactured by AC Lighting, is such a system (Figure 17–20b). Features include 6,000 control channels, twenty master controllers, and easy access to all attributes. An interface between a standard lap-top computer and moving lights called Firefly has been developed by the Secor Group (Figure 17–20c). It is expected that theatrical control manufacturers will soon follow with powerful systems able to control moving as well as fixed lights.

## DESIGNING WITH ELECTRONIC CONTROL

In 1975, when designer Tharon Musser insisted on a Light Palette control system for her Broadway production of A Chorus Line, it became obvious that even New York was going to accept memory lighting control. There is no doubt that lighting designers have achieved a higher level of artistry as a result of computerized control. Cue writing is simplified, the potential for more complex and sophisticated cues is greatly increased, and changes are made quickly and accurately—every time.

### CONTROL CONSIDERATIONS

Well before a production goes into the theatre, a designer must consider *control*. If not working in a dimmer-per-circuit situation, the designer faces the task of assigning instruments to dimmers. Color control is normally a

## Figure 17—20
## Moving Light Control

(a) The "Status Cue" control console from High End Systems. Manufacturers are beginning to develop moving light control systems that can control all types of equipment and are user-friendly. This system has the capacity for 6,000 "scenes" and can control up to 128 Cyberlights or 256 Intellabeams. Photo courtesy High End Systems, Inc.

(b) The "Wholehog" control console from AC Lighting allows for forty-eight parameters per fixture and 6,000 channels per cue. It can be operated as a concert console with separate looks and effects on individual masters, or as a theatre console with the entire show sequence programmed into memory. Photo courtesy CW Productions.

(c) The "Firefly" is a new device that acts as an interface between a personal computer and moving lights, color changers, fixed lights, and other equipment that utilizes DMX protocol. Photo courtesy Martello Associates, Inc. and The Secor Group, Inc.

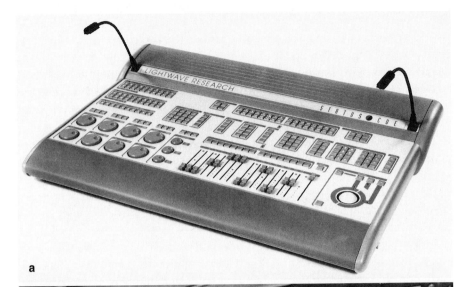

a

b

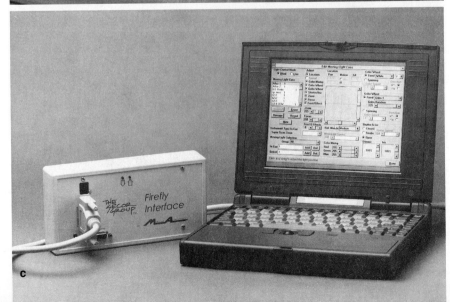

c

high priority. Seldom is it desirable to have two instruments of differing colors on the same dimmer. Area control is the next priority: Which stage areas should be controlled individually and which should be "ganged" or grouped together? The latter is a critical decision, for the designer must work with the chosen control flexibility throughout the production. Before a choice is made, the designer should view rehearsals and discuss control-related questions with the director.

Although there are no absolute rules of control priorities, the following guidelines are suggested as a beginning:

1. Control of front-of-house "visibility" area lighting is most important.
2. Area control of side-light, although of secondary importance, is still significant.
3. Area control of back- or top-light is of least importance unless the stage floor and its composition are visible to the majority of the audience.

Most specials require their own control channel, but can be repatched during intermission in many instances. Do not forget to assign control for practicals, house lights if necessary, and curtain warmers or stage toners. It is always very difficult, but good practice, to reserve two or three dimmers as spares. These will save the day in case of a dimmer failure or the discovery that additional control is required.

## PATCHING

Before the days of electronic control, dimmer board layout was a critical operational concern for the designer. It was necessary to anticipate the best way to aid the various operators in performing their sometimes octopuslike maneuvers. Today these concerns are less critical, but dimmer layout is still important to the designer for the following two reasons:

1. Channels that are frequently controlled together should be grouped together. Operationally it is much faster and easier to keystroke channels 23 through 31 than a random series of nine channel numbers.
2. Channels should be assigned in a logical order so that the designer can access them quickly. If, for instance, front-of-house lights are always assigned lower channel numbers, the designer is able to identify them more easily. Board layout is then transferred to an easily read designer's "cheat sheet" or "magic sheet" for quick reference (Figure 17–21).

**Soft Patch Capability**    The computer's electronic patch system makes logical dimmer/circuit-to-channel assignments an easy task if the designer follows basic guidelines. If using an area lighting method, assign all the instruments lighting a given area to a logical sequence of channels. For example,

**Figure 17-21**
Cheat Sheet

Shown is the "Lightwright" version of the cheat sheet for the Broadway production of *Tommy* designed by Chris Parry.

all instruments lighting area 1 should be assigned to channels 1, 11, 21, 31, 41, and so on. The front-light for area 2 is assigned to channel 2, the side-light for area 2 is assigned to channel 12, the back-light for area 2 is assigned to channel 22, with other assignments following in the same manner.

Most soft patch systems include a useful feature called *proportional patching*. This simply means that if two dimmers/circuits/instruments are ganged on a single control channel, one of them can be assigned a proportional intensity

```
========================                ===========
TOMMY - BROADWAY - CUT                  CHEAT SHEET                              Page    1
========================                ===========
                                                                                05-28-94
Lighting By: Chris Parry                                      Venue: St. James Theatre - NYC
Associate: David Grill                               Prod. Electrician: James Maloney, Jr.
================================================================================================

  Chn    Purpose                      Position         Type                    Color
-------   -------------------------   -------------   --------------------   --------------------
(  1 )   Frts Ap L.................   FOH HIGH TRUSS   6x16 w/TH              L203+R119
(  2 )   Frts Ap LC................   FOH HIGH TRUSS   6x16 w/TH              L203+R119
(  3 )   Frts Ap C.................   FOH HIGH TRUSS   6x16 w/TH              L203+R119
(  4 )   Frts Ap RC................   FOH HIGH TRUSS   6x16 w/TH              L203+R119
(  5 )   Frts Ap R.................   FOH HIGH TRUSS   6x16 w/TH              L203+R119
(  6 )   Frts DL...................   FOH HIGH TRUSS   6x16 w/TH              L203+R119
(  7 )   Frts DLC..................   FOH HIGH TRUSS   6x16 w/TH              L203+R119
(  8 )   Frts DC...................   FOH HIGH TRUSS   6x16 w/TH              L203+R119
(  9 )   Frts DRC..................   FOH HIGH TRUSS   6x16 w/TH              L203+R119
( 10 )   Frts DR...................   FOH HIGH TRUSS   6x16 w/TH              L203+R119
( 11 )
( 12 )
( 13 )   Frts UC...................   1 ELECTRIC       6x12 w/TH              L203+R119
( 14 )
( 15 )
( 16 )
( 17 )
( 18 )
( 19 )
( 20 )
( 21 )   Box L Ap L................   3 BOX BOOM L     6x16 w/TH              L202
( 22 )   Box L Ap Ctr..............   3 BOX BOOM L     6x16 w/TH              L202
( 23 )   Box L Ap R................   3 BOX BOOM L     6x22 w/TH              L202
( 24 )   Box L DL..................   2 BOX BOOM L     6x16 w/TH              L202
( 25 )   Box L DC..................   2 BOX BOOM L     6x16 w/TH              L202
( 26 )   Box L DR..................   2 BOX BOOM L     6x16 w/TH              L202
( 27 )   Box R Ap L................   3 BOX BOOM R     6x22 w/TH              L202
( 28 )   Box R Ap Ctr..............   3 BOX BOOM R     6x16 w/TH              L202
( 29 )   Box R Ap R................   3 BOX BOOM R     6x16 w/TH              L202
( 30 )   Box R DL..................   2 BOX BOOM R     6x16 w/TH              L202
( 31 )   Box R DC..................   2 BOX BOOM R     6x16 w/TH              L202
( 32 )   Box R DR..................   2 BOX BOOM R     6x16 w/TH              L202
( 33 )
( 34 )
( 35 )
```

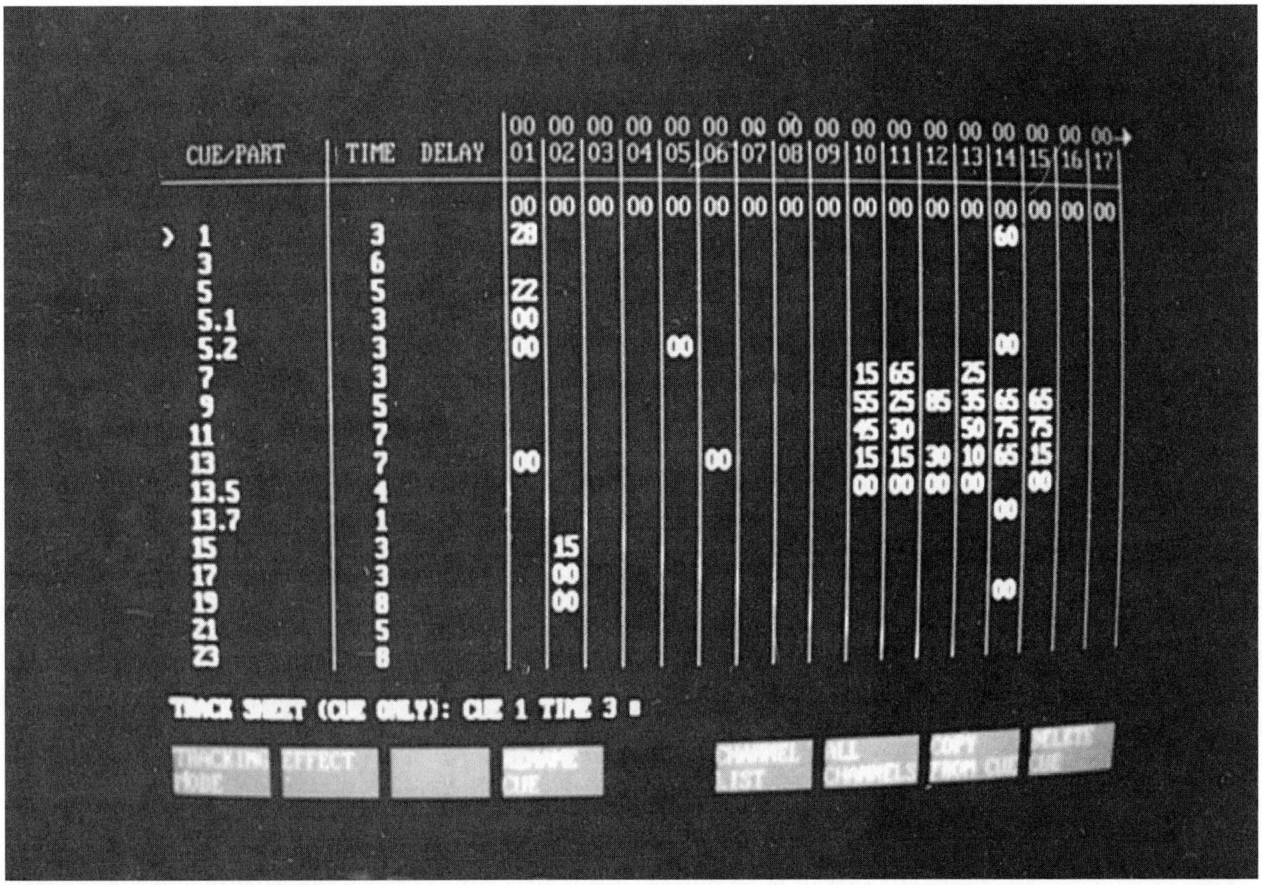

| CUE/PART | TIME | 00 01 | 00 02 | 00 03 | 00 04 | 00 05 | 00 06 | 00 07 | 00 08 | 00 09 | 00 10 | 00 11 | 00 12 | 00 13 | 00 14 | 00 15 | 00 16 | 00 17→ |
|---|---|---|---|---|---|---|---|---|---|---|---|---|---|---|---|---|---|---|
|  |  | 00 | 00 | 00 | 00 | 00 | 00 | 00 | 00 | 00 | 00 | 00 | 00 | 00 | 00 | 00 | 00 | 00 |
| ❯ 1 | 3 | 28 |  |  |  |  |  |  |  |  |  |  |  |  | 60 |  |  |  |
| 3 | 6 |  |  |  |  |  |  |  |  |  |  |  |  |  |  |  |  |  |
| 5 | 5 | 22 |  |  |  |  |  |  |  |  |  |  |  |  |  |  |  |  |
| 5.1 | 3 | 00 |  |  |  |  |  |  |  |  |  |  |  |  |  |  |  |  |
| 5.2 | 3 |  |  |  |  | 00 |  |  |  |  |  |  |  |  | 00 |  |  |  |
| 7 | 3 |  |  |  |  |  |  |  |  |  |  | 15 | 65 |  | 25 |  |  |  |
| 9 | 5 |  |  |  |  |  |  |  |  |  |  | 55 | 25 | 85 | 35 | 65 | 65 |  |
| 11 | 7 |  |  |  |  |  |  |  |  |  |  | 45 | 30 |  | 50 | 75 | 75 |  |
| 13 | 7 | 00 |  |  |  |  |  | 00 |  |  |  | 15 | 15 | 30 | 10 | 65 | 15 |  |
| 13.5 | 4 |  |  |  |  |  |  |  |  |  |  | 00 | 00 | 00 | 00 |  | 00 |  |
| 13.7 | 1 |  |  |  |  |  |  |  |  |  |  |  |  |  | 00 |  |  |  |
| 15 | 3 |  | 15 |  |  |  |  |  |  |  |  |  |  |  |  |  |  |  |
| 17 | 3 |  | 00 |  |  |  |  |  |  |  |  |  |  |  |  |  |  |  |
| 19 | 8 |  | 00 |  |  |  |  |  |  |  |  |  |  |  | 00 |  |  |  |
| 21 | 5 |  |  |  |  |  |  |  |  |  |  |  |  |  |  |  |  |  |
| 23 | 8 |  |  |  |  |  |  |  |  |  |  |  |  |  |  |  |  |  |

TRACK SHEET (CUE ONLY): CUE 1 TIME 3 ■

[ TRACKING MODE ] [ EFFECT ] [ ] [ RENAME CUE ]     [ CHANNEL LIST ] [ ALL CHANNELS ] [ COPY FROM CUE ] [ DELETE CUE ]

**Figure 17–22**
Channel Track Screen

Shown is the Channel Track Screen from Colortran's "Prestige 2000" control console.

level. For instance, if lighting instrument A is assigned a proportional level of 90 percent while instrument B is assigned nothing (default being a level of 100 percent), the intensity readings of A will always be 90 percent of those of B.

Part of the setup procedure before beginning to write a show is the creation of patch assignments. If the system's patch is left unassigned, dimmer-to-channel will assume a one-to-one relationship. Patch assignments never need to be touched during playback—a good reason for using the "record lock" key switch found on many control consoles.

## FEATURES OF ELECTRONIC SYSTEMS

As noted earlier, available functions vary from one system to another. However, the designer can normally depend on a number of fairly common operational features. Among these are split time fades, a cue copy function, and the ability to insert and/or link cues. Other features—which may or may not exist on a given system but deserve comment—are groups, tracking channels and "channel track," follow cues, a level/rate wheel, simultaneous cue playback, and direct dimmer access.

**Common Features**     Movement of light is greatly enhanced by the previously discussed *split time fade.* Rather than be restricted to a simple linear cross fade, the designer can customize a fade to perfectly coincide with action onstage.

Probably the most time-saving feature in writing cues live is *cue copy.* Called by a variety of names, this feature allows the designer to exactly copy the dimmer levels of an existing cue. To write a progression of cues, the operator copies one into the next, makes level adjustments, and repeats the procedure.

When making corrections and additions, *cue insertion* is a must. Most control systems allow "point cues" to be inserted between whole-number cues. For instance, cue #3.5 could be inserted between cues #3 and #4.

*Linking* one cue to another is also handy and can be used in some cases to form effect "loops" (link cue #6 to cue #10, then cue #10 back to cue #6).

**Specialized Features**     The concept of *groups* originated with the preset type of control and, as noted earlier, is popular for concert lighting control systems. Any number of selected channels can be labeled a "group" and accessed as such with a single command. This tactic is valuable for the rapid building of various stage looks. For instance, all the blue side-light channels could be grouped together for easy access.

The operational concept of *tracking channels* is a holdover from the days of resistance dimmers. When a dimmer level was set at a certain reading, it remained there until the operator was instructed to change it. In a tracking system, such as the Light Palette, a channel assigned to a level in a cue retains that level in all subsequent cues until told otherwise. While making perfect sense, tracking can sometimes be confusing, with channels apparently popping up out of nowhere. Many newer systems provide the designer with the option of working in either a tracking or a nontracking mode.

*Channel track* is a useful feature offered by some systems. It allows the operator to view the levels of a single channel throughout all the cues in the show. Figure 17–22 shows the channel track screen from a Colortran Prestige 2000 control console.

The action of one cue automatically following another is normally not desirable for live performance. If the timing onstage changes, the timing of the light cues must follow suit. However, *follow cues* can be valuable for a sequence effect or for timing to something other than live action.

The operational term *delay* has different meanings depending on a system's manufacturer. The *delay function* usually provides a preset time delay between the execution of one cue and the execution of the following cue.

With proper use the *level/rate wheel* can be of great assistance both in writing cues and in playback. Anything from a single channel to an entire preset can be assigned to this wheel. If a group of dimmers is "put on the wheel" and the wheel is rolled down, the intensity levels of all channels in the group are lowered. If an active fade is suddenly assigned to the wheel ("captured"), the speed of the fade in progress can be altered. In other words, the operator is able to seize control of any fade speed by using the rate wheel. An experienced console operator performs a great number of operations with the aid of this wheel.

*Simultaneous playback* of several cues is a valuable feature that most control systems provide. The slow sunset can now continue undisturbed while any number of other lighting movements take place.

Finally, *direct dimmer access* is a feature that is not used very often, but is extremely helpful when needed. In the event of several dimmers being soft patched onto a single control channel, this option allows the operator access to any one of the individual dimmers.

Every control system comes with an operation manual which, despite the fact that some are very poorly written, should be read by both the designer and operator. Systems vary enough that the designer will discover new and exciting possibilities by reviewing the manuals of unfamiliar boards.

## THE OPERATOR AND REMOTE CONTROL

As we have pointed out, the low amperage and low voltage used by modern control systems permit the operator to be placed at any distance from the stage and in any location that seems appropriate. Of the practical places, the rear of the main floor of the auditorium is unquestionably the best. It is a desirable location from which to run a show because the view of the stage is good. During rehearsals, the operator and lighting designer are in easy and direct communication with the director, stage manager, and other designers.

Operation of a memory control system is a very different task from that presented to an electrician standing backstage manipulating several large and heavy handles. Often the control apparatus is delicate and complex, not at all like a bank of simple and rugged resistance or autotransformer dimmers. An error could very well result in every light on the stage assuming the wrong reading. While a good memory control system will lessen the chances of operational error, a highly competent operator is still essential.

All computer memory control systems provide a backup disc for library storage. It is extremely important for the operator to keep this copy of a production's cues and dimmer levels up-to-date. If changes are being made, periodic copying to disc is good practice, but something the designer may forget.

A good operator will have confidence, a cool head, and enough understanding of the control system to rectify an error before it gets out of hand. The operator must know the show and fully understand the lighting designer's intentions. He or she *must watch the stage.* Cues may be taken from the stage manager, but if the show is being called from backstage, the operator should take sight and sound cues from the stage action itself.

Perhaps, most of all, the operator requires a sensitivity and sense of timing akin to an actor's. In a very real sense, the operator is also an actor. An operator does not merely snap lights on—but dims in gently, with feeling, perhaps at a varying pace to best suit the action on the stage. If the actors are fast in their pace one night, an adjustment must be made to the new tempo. A large part of the success of a production depends on the operational skills of the stage manager and light board operator.

# 18 DISTRIBUTION CONTROL: LIGHTING INSTRUMENTS

Recall that the term *distribution* refers to quality of light as well as angle and direction. Is the desired light soft or harsh? Is it textured and broken up or coherent and smooth? Does it have sharp, linear edges or a soft, rounded shape? A lighting designer matches an instrument's properties and capabilities with the specific design requirements of a production. In order to do so effectively, the designer must be familiar with the sometimes subtle differences between stage lighting instruments.

## CHOOSING THE RIGHT INSTRUMENT

Assuming the designer has an image of what is desired, the next step is to determine which type of lighting instrument is most capable of producing that specific quality of light. Several factors affect this determination:

1. Instrument inventory and/or budget
2. Physical (theatre) restrictions
3. Quality of light
4. Beam shaping and control

### INSTRUMENT INVENTORY AND/OR BUDGET

If a production's lighting equipment is being rented, the designer has free choice of instrumentation. However, rental expenses must remain within an allocated budget. Detailed information concerning rental of equipment can be found in Chapter 24. At the moment, suffice it to say that budget considerations may limit instrument choice.

Many designers work with a fixed instrument inventory. Such inventories can vary from all new equipment to a variety of types and styles purchased over the years when funds were available. Seldom does a theatre's instrument inventory provide everything a designer requires for a production. Compromises often must be made. The success of mixing and matching various pieces of equipment depends on familiarity with the instruments and begins with a basic knowledge of the types of instruments. It is wise to confirm the accuracy of an equipment list, particularly when working with older inventories.

## PHYSICAL RESTRICTIONS

The physical features of a theatre invariably affect lighting possibilities. Throw distances (distance from lighting instrument to target) vary greatly from theatre to theatre. The type and amount of offstage space for side-lighting positions may influence design decisions. Space limitations in front-of-house beam and cove positions dictate maximum instrument size as well as number. The number of hanging positions front-of-house and over-stage has a significant influence. And finally, control and circuit limitations may be a factor in instrument usage and selection.

## QUALITY OF LIGHT

A designer always considers the quality of light provided by a specific type of instrument. It is a chief determining factor of mood. Ellipsoidal reflector spotlights and some automated fixtures offer variable light qualities. On the other hand, the quality of light from Fresnels and PAR instruments cannot be altered.

A Fresnel delivers a soft beam of light with fuzzy edges and an even field. Light from a PAR has fuzzy edges, but the light itself is harsh and the field is uneven. The beam from an ellipsoidal reflector spotlight has hard edges that can be softened by various means. Its quality of light in terms of harshness is between that of a Fresnel and a PAR.

## BEAM SHAPING AND CONTROL

The possibility of altering the shape and size of a light beam is an important design consideration. Each type of stage lighting instrument is considerably different in this respect.

Ellipsoidal reflector spotlights are the most flexible of lighting instruments in terms of beam shaping and control. The light from a Fresnel and an automated fixture can be shaped and the beam size altered. The beam of a PAR is oval in shape and is nearly impossible to alter.

## THE PHYSICS OF REFLECTION AND REFRACTION

Quality of light from an instrument is determined by two things: (1) the light source itself, and (2) the manner in which the light is manipulated after it leaves the source. The latter factor is controlled by the *optics* of the lighting instrument. Understanding the laws of reflection and refraction is an important step in learning how to use light.

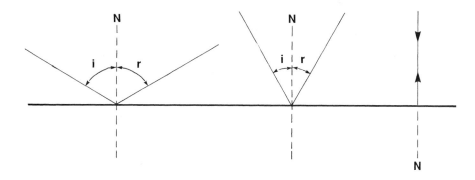

Figure 18–1
Specular Reflection

i = incident light
r = reflected light
N = the normal (a perpendicular drawn to the surface)

The angle of incidence is equal to the angle of reflection.

When a beam of light passing through air encounters anything in its path, three things can happen: (1) the light may be absorbed, (2) the light may be bent or refracted, or (3) the light may be reflected. Actually, none of the above will happen completely. Even a mirror or a lens absorbs a small portion of light, and the blackest of materials still reflects some light.

All stage lighting instruments use reflectors to increase the efficiency of their light source. Most use lenses to gather and redirect the light, focusing it into a usable beam.

## SPECULAR REFLECTION

The law of *specular reflection* explains what happens to a light beam when it strikes a smooth, shiny surface such as a mirror. It is reflected at an angle equal to the angle at which it struck, but in the opposite direction. The law actually reads: The angle of incidence is equal to the angle of reflection. If the beam strikes a specular surface head-on, it will be reflected directly back over the same path (Figure 18–1). Variations of specular reflection are spread reflection, diffuse reflection, and mixed reflection. Figure 18–2 illustrates these three phenomena.

**Spread Reflection**     If a beam of light strikes a surface with slight irregularities (such as textured paint or metallic fabric), the above rule applies. However, because the light encounters various small surfaces set at different angles to each other, the reflected rays are somewhat scattered. While maintaining the basic reflected direction, the rays diverge. This phenomenon is known as *spread reflection.*

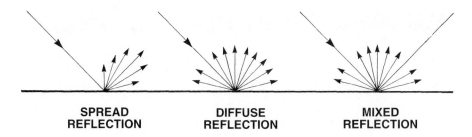

**SPREAD REFLECTION**          **DIFFUSE REFLECTION**          **MIXED REFLECTION**

Figure 18–2
Types of Reflection

Illustrated are variations of specular reflection.

**Diffuse Reflection**    Highly textured surfaces or soft cotton fabrics cause *diffuse reflection* of light. Such surfaces have many small reflectors placed at varied angles to each other, resulting in reflected light that exhibits no single direction. The entire surface appears very much the same regardless of the angle at which it is viewed.

**Mixed Reflection**    A combination of specular and diffuse reflection is known as *mixed reflection.* A piece of pottery with a high glaze produces this type of reflection. The rough ceramic surface creates diffusion, while the shiny glaze acts like a mirror.

### TYPES OF REFLECTORS

Early stage lighting instruments used reflectors that were molded glass mirrors, some of which can still be found in carbon arc follow spots. In the 1950s, reflectors began to be constructed of a lightweight spun metal. After fabrication, this metal shell is given a highly reflective and durable surface treatment referred to as *Alzak processing.* The Alzak reflector became an industry standard. Recently, a new dichroic-coated glass reflector has been put to use in some lighting instruments (Figure 18–3). The advantage of a dichroic reflector is that it can be designed to allow ultraviolet and infrared light rays to pass through the back, reflecting only visible light. This results in a light beam of significantly cooler temperature.

Stage lighting instruments use one of the following three reflector types or shapes:

1. *Spherical*—used in Fresnels, follow spots, and many automated fixtures
2. *Parabolic*—used in beam projectors and PAR-, MR-, and R-type lamps
3. *Ellipsoidal*—used in ellipsoidal reflector spotlights and automated fixtures

**Figure 18–3**
**Dichroic Reflector**

Shown is the glass dichroic-coated reflector of a ''Source Four'' ellipsoidal reflector spotlight, manufactured by Electronic Theatre Controls.

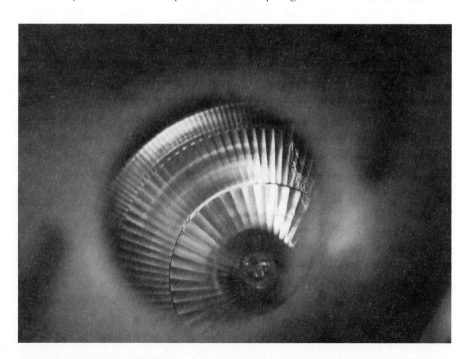

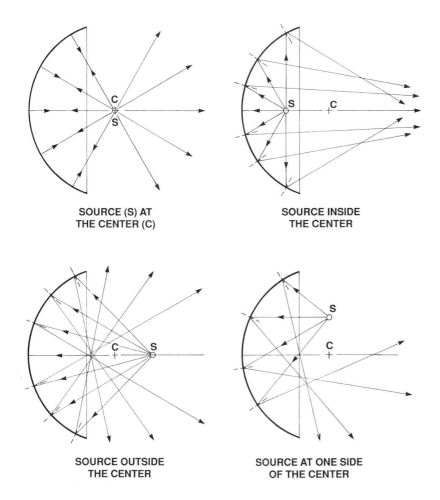

**SOURCE (S) AT
THE CENTER (C)**

**SOURCE INSIDE
THE CENTER**

**SOURCE OUTSIDE
THE CENTER**

**SOURCE AT ONE SIDE
OF THE CENTER**

**Figure 18–4**
The Spherical Reflector

If a light source is placed at the focal point or center of a spherical reflector, the reflected rays are returned directly to the focal point.

By redirecting light coming out of the back of a lamp, a reflector increases the amount of usable light from any source. The shape of a reflector determines the manner in which the light is redirected. Every reflector has a specific point where a light source must be placed in order to achieve the desired reflective pattern. This location is called the reflector's *focal point.*

**Spherical Reflectors**    The spherical reflector is made of glass or polished metal constructed in the shape of part of a sphere. The exact center of the imaginary sphere is the focal point of the spherical reflector. If a light source is placed at the focal point, its rays will be reflected squarely off the surface. The reflected light rays bounce directly back to the source itself and continue to spread from there (Figure 18–4). Light output from a lamp is nearly doubled.

**Parabolic Reflectors**    A parabolic reflector is unique in that it produces parallel rays of light. Geometrically resembling the spherical reflector, the parabolic reflector is constructed in the shape of part of a parabola. If the light source is placed at the parabola's focal center, rays striking the reflector bounce off parallel to one another (Figure 18–5). The result is a concentrated and harsh beam of light.

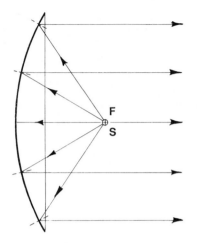

**Figure 18–5**
The Parabolic Reflector

This drawing illustrates parallel light reflection from a parabolic reflector, with the source (S) placed at the focal point (F).

Moving the source away from the focal point toward the reflector spreads the light. Moving it away from the focal point further from the reflector causes the light rays to converge.

**Ellipsoidal Reflectors**     An ellipsoidal reflector is more efficient than either spherical or parabolic reflectors. As you may have surmised, it is constructed in the form of half an ellipsoid. By mathematical definition, an ellipsoid has two focal points. The focal point nearest the reflector and where the source is placed is called the *primary focal point*. The more distant focal point is called the *conjugate focal point*. If a light source is properly positioned at the primary focal point, the rays striking the reflector are redirected to converge through the conjugate focal point (Figure 18–6). Using this reflector, a large percentage of the light from the source is gathered into a concentrated beam.

### REFRACTION OF LIGHT

Refraction refers to the bending of light. This phenomenon can be observed by looking into a pool of water and noticing how a straight stick seems to bend sharply as it passes beneath the surface. The law of refraction states that when a ray of light passes into a denser medium (for example, from air into glass) it is bent toward a perpendicular drawn to the surface at the point of entry. When it reemerges into the less dense medium, it is bent away from a perpendicular drawn at that point (Figure 18–7).

The two surfaces of the piece of glass illustrated in Figure 18–7 are parallel. In such an instance, the emerging ray of light is slightly offset but continues parallel to its original course. Lenses have nonparallel surfaces, causing light to bend in a predictable manner.

**The Plano-Convex Lens**     Light from a stage lighting instrument must be intensely concentrated in the shape of a cone. A lens is used to redirect

**Figure 18–6**
The Ellipsoidal Reflector

This drawing illustrates light reflection from an ellipsoidal reflector, with the source at the primary focal point.

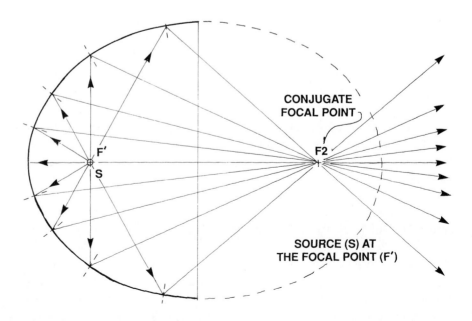

CONJUGATE
FOCAL POINT

F2

F'
S

SOURCE (S) AT
THE FOCAL POINT (F')

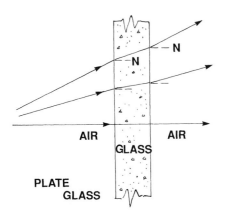

**Figure 18—7**
Refraction of Light

This drawing illustrates the refraction (bending) of rays of light
passing through a sheet of
glass. "N" = the normal (a perpendicular drawn to the surface).

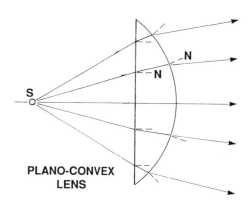

the spreading rays of light coming from the source and the reflector. The principal lens used in stage lighting instruments is *plano-convex*. It has one flat (plano) surface and a second outwardly curved (convex) surface. It is the simplest and least expensive lens for concentrating spreading rays into a compact and bright beam of light (Figure 18—8).

**Figure 18—8**
The Plano-Convex Lens

This drawing illustrates the refraction of diverging rays of light
passing through a plano-convex
lens, such as that found in an
ellipsoidal reflector spotlight.

**Focal Point and Focal Length**    Like reflectors, every lens has a *focal point*. If parallel light rays (such as those from the sun) strike a lens, they will be bent to converge at the focal point. Conversely, if a source of light is placed at the focal point of a lens, all the rays of light that emerge from the lens will be parallel to one another (Figure 18—9a). Moving the source away from the focal point causes the light rays to either diverge or converge as illustrated in Figures 18—9b and 18—9c.

The distance from the focal point to the center of the lens is called its *focal length*, and is measured in inches or millimeters. Lenses are identified by two numbers. The first indicates the diameter of the lens in inches and the second the focal length in inches. Thus, a 6-by-9-inch lens (6 × 9) has a diameter of 6 inches and a focal length of 9 inches. The greater the curvature of the convex face, the greater the bending power of the lens. Therefore, a thick lens has a shorter focal length than a thin one.

It is usually desirable to know the focal length of a lens. However, be-cause this information is rarely marked on lenses, a quick method of deter-mining focal length is valuable. If the sun is shining, the lens may be taken outside and held, plano side down, so that the sun's rays are concentrated on the ground. Using a ruler, measure the distance from the ground to the lens. Focal lengths of lenses used in stage lighting instruments are measured in even inches.

## THE PLANO-CONVEX SPOTLIGHT

The first theatrical spotlight, and for many years the only kind, was named after its plano-convex lens. It consisted of a simple metal housing containing a spherical reflector, a lamp, and a lens. The lamp and reflector could be

**Figure 18–9**
Refraction

These drawings show the refraction of light passing through a plano-convex lens under different conditions.
(a) Source (S) at the focal point (F). Note the focal length of the lens.
(b) Source inside the focal point.
(c) Source behind the focal point.

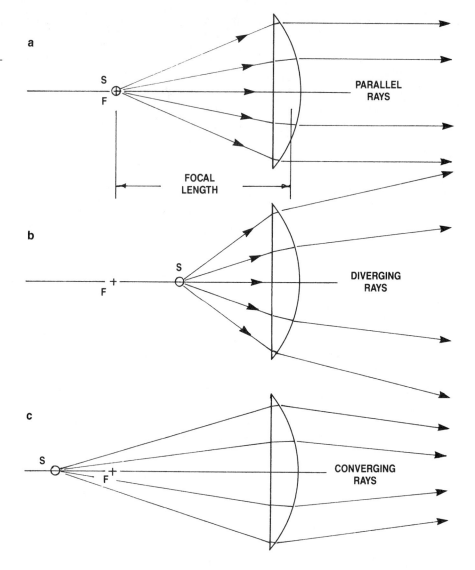

moved forward or back in order to increase or decrease the diameter of the beam of light.

In the United States, the P-C (as the plano-convex spotlight was called) has been replaced by the ellipsoidal reflector spotlight. However, in many European countries it remains the standard stage lighting instrument. Built and operated much like a Fresnel spotlight, the modern P-C gives off a high-quality, sharp beam of light that is adjustable in size (Figure 18–10).

## THE ELLIPSOIDAL REFLECTOR SPOTLIGHT

The ellipsoidal reflector spotlight (ERS) is by far the most important lighting instrument on the modern stage. Figure 18–11 illustrates several features of the ERS that are common to all stage lighting instruments. The instrument is attached to a lighting batten by means of a *C-clamp*. The C-clamp is bolted to the instrument's *yolk*. Loosening this bolt allows the instrument to be turned from side to side (called "swivel"). The yolk is attached to the instrument's *housing* by means of two handles that may be loosened to allow for tilt adjustment. At the front of the instrument are holders that accommodate a color frame and color filter.

Moving to a cutaway view of an ERS, Figure 18–12 shows how the ellipsoidal-shaped reflector receives light from the lamp and redirects it to the conjugate focal point. Here is located a metal baffle with a circular opening called the *gate*. This cuts off stray rays, allowing only the useful light to continue on to the lenses. It is an image of the opening in this gate, called the *aperture*, that appears as the sharp, round beam typical of an ERS. Four beam-shaping *shutters* are positioned immediately adjacent to the gate. If used, a *gobo* as well as an *iris* are found here as well. The lenses illustrated are examples of a *fixed lens* system, meaning that the diameter of the beam of light cannot be significantly changed. The barrel can move back and forth only enough to soften or sharpen the beam edge. A *zoom ellipsoidal* offers variable-focus lenses that allow for a range of beam sizes.

## ERS BEAM SHAPING

One feature that makes an ERS unique and valuable as a stage lighting instrument is its beam shaping capability. The beam of light from an ERS is naturally round, but its shape can be altered by means of shutters, an iris, or a gobo.

**Shutters**    The ellipsoidal's four shutters located at the gate are standard equipment. They are metal plates with heat-insulating tabs or rings attached to the part extending out of the housing. One or more shutters can be pushed

**Figure 18–10**
Modern P-C Spotlight

Pictured is Strand's "Alto PC" 2,000-watt plano-convex spotlight. It provides beam spreads from a narrow 4-degrees to a wide 57-degrees. Photo courtesy Strand Lighting, Inc.

**Figure 18–11**
Parts Common to All Lighting Instruments

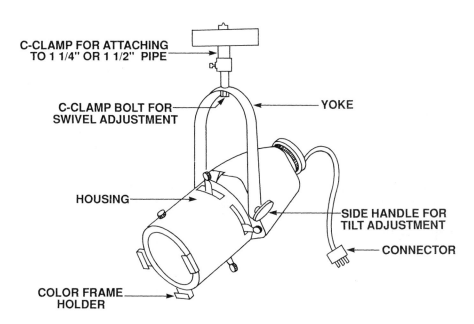

C-CLAMP FOR ATTACHING TO 1 1/4" OR 1 1/2" PIPE

C-CLAMP BOLT FOR SWIVEL ADJUSTMENT

YOKE

HOUSING

SIDE HANDLE FOR TILT ADJUSTMENT

CONNECTOR

COLOR FRAME HOLDER

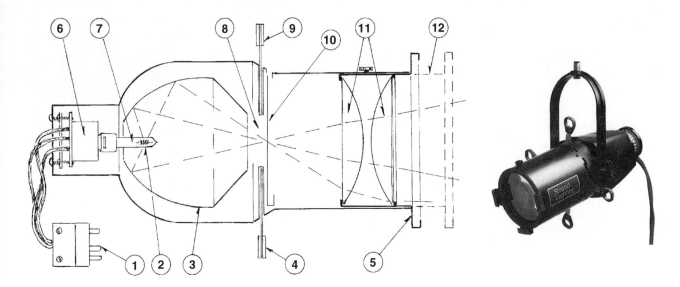

**Figure 18–12**
Ellipsoidal Reflector Spotlight

(a) Illustration showing the parts of an ERS.
  (1) Three-wire pin connector.
  (2) Lamp filament (light source).
  (3) Ellipsoidal reflector.
  (4) Bottom shutter, which shapes the top of the beam.
  (5) Color frame holder.
  (6) Axially-mounted socket.
  (7) Tungsten-halogen lamp.
  (8) The aperture or "gate" with typical reflected rays crossing at the conjugate focal point.
  (9) Top shutter.
  (10) Gobo slot and holder.
  (11) Double plano-convex lenses mounted belly to belly.
  (12) The lens barrel in alternate positions.
(b) A 6-inch "Leko." Photo courtesy Strand Lighting, Inc.

into the aperture, cutting the beam of light in a linear fashion. Light beams crossing at the gate create high temperatures that cause even the best shutters to bend and warp; therefore, it is good practice to completely open the shutters of an ellipsoidal as soon as the instrument is hung in order to avoid overheating. Some instruments are equipped with a rotating shutter assembly that allows virtually any angle of cut to be achieved.

**Irises**    An iris is an optional feature of a standard ERS. Its metal leaflike fingers act to reduce the diameter of the beam in a circular manner. Like shutters, the metal iris gets extremely hot and can warp to the point of being unusable. Some brands of ellipsoidals have irises that are permanently fixed near the gate. Others offer a drop-in slot at the top of the instrument for an iris assembly. An iris is a necessity in the event of the ERS being used as a follow spot.

**Gobos**    All ellipsoidal reflector spotlights have a slot in the top of their housing that is made to receive a template commonly called a gobo. This template, available from a number of distributors, is a metal plate with a pattern cut in it. It fits into a holder that positions the pattern near the aperture and squarely in the center of the light beam. When positioned, this simple plate turns the ERS into a shadow projector. Images of an endless variety of words or patterns can be projected onto scenery, actors, or the stage floor. By moving the lens barrel, the pattern can be either sharply focused or turned into soft, indistinguishable texture. Instruments equipped with a slot big enough for a drop-in iris can accommodate a gobo spinner capable of rotating a standard pattern. More specific information concerning the gobos themselves will be found in the next chapter. In using gobos, remember that the pattern image is inverted due to the crossing of the light rays. Consequently, the gobo should be placed upside down in its holder.

## ERS LENSES

There are currently three types of ERS lens systems:

1. *Fixed lenses* allowing an adjustment in beam edge but not in size (diameter)
2. *Interchangeable lenses* usually providing three different beam sizes
3. *Zoom lenses* providing a variable beam spread within a fixed range

All three of the above systems use a combination of plano-convex lenses and each has its own distinct advantages.

**Fixed Lenses**    This system uses two plano-convex lenses mounted belly-to-belly in a barrel. Two lenses are used rather than one, because they are lighter and less likely to crack from the heat of an instrument. A fixed lens system is the least expensive of the three systems. It produces superior quality light with a smooth and even field.

**Interchangeable Lenses**    An interchangeable lens system allows for movement of lenses in relationship to one another or the substitution of one focal-length lens for another. In either case, the size of the light beam is changed. An example of an ERS with this capability is the Colortran Mini-ellipse shown in Figure 18–13. The lens barel is removed from the instrument's housing, and by loosening four screws the lenses are exposed. Moving the front lens to one of three different positions provides field spreads of 30 degrees, 40 degrees, or 50 degrees. The flexibility of interchangeable lenses is very attractive. Lack of convenience as compared to zoom ellipsoidals is compensated by lower cost.

**Zoom Lenses**    One of the first practical zoom ellipsoidals was the Par-ellipsphere manufactured by Electro Controls of Salt Lake City (Figure 18–14). Rather than two plano-convex lenses, this instrument uses a large plano-convex lens in combination with a smaller bi-convex lens. Each of the lenses moves forward and back to achieve variable beam spreads. Several years ago Electro Controls was purchased by Strand Lighting and the Par-ellipsphere was discontinued. However, the market for zoom ellipsoidals had been established and a number of manufacturers have responded with their own versions.

   The example shown in Figure 18–15 is a modern $4\frac{1}{2}$-inch zoom ellipsoidal. It uses a 500-watt lamp and has variable field spreads from 25 to 50 degrees. A zoom ellipsoidal is more expensive than comparable fixed lenses or interchangeable lens instruments. In certain applications, the convenience and flexibility is well worth the extra expense.

## ERS BEAM AND FIELD ANGLES

When an ellipsoidal reflector spotlight is properly aligned, its cone-shaped beam of light is most intense along the center line of the beam. Moving out

**Figure 18–13**
The "Mini-ellipse"

An efficient short-throw 4-inch ERS developed by Colortran. Photo courtesy Colortran, Inc.

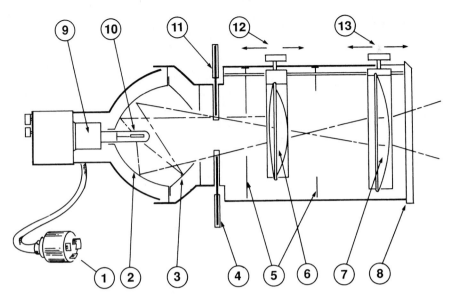

## Figure 18—14
### The Parellipsphere

(a) The Parellipsphere was the forerunner of the modern zoom ellipsoidal. Photo courtesy Electro Controls, Inc.
(b) Illustration showing the parts of the Parellipsphere.

(1) Three-wire twist-lock connector.
(2) Parellipse part of the reflector. The apex is parabolic in action.
(3) Kickback reflector with slight spherical configuration.
(4) Bottom shutter.
(5) Baffles.
(6) Nonsymmetric bi-convex lens.
(7) Plano-convex lens.
(8) Color frame holder.
(9) Prefocus medium base socket.
(10) Quartz lamp.
(11) Top shutter.
(12) Lens adjustment knob to change focal length of objective lens system.
(13) Lens adjustment knob to change beam spread.

from center to the edge of the beam, intensity drops off in an even manner. The point at which the light's intensity drops to 50 percent of maximum is called the *beam edge*. Continuing outward, the place were light intensity drops to 10 percent is called the *field edge*.

As noted earlier, lenses are traditionally identified by two numbers: diameter in inches and focal length in inches. In the theatre it is most convenient to classify spotlights by the diameter of their light beam. This is done in degrees, and the figure used is actually the angle of the *field* (Figure 18–16). For example, a 6-by-12 ellipsoidal is called a "30-degree," referring to the instrument's nominal field angle of 30 degrees.

The table that follows lists typical beam and field angles as well as appropriate throw distances for various sizes of ellipsoidal reflector spotlights. Note that these figures are approximate and may not correspond exactly to the performance of any specific instrument. Consult manufacturer specifications before using.

**Beam Adjustment**    Many modern ellipsoidals allow for adjustment of the light source in respect to the focal point of the reflector. By moving the lamp either in or out, an electrician is able to change the distribution of light from an extremely "hot center" to a "flat field." The hot center concentrates a greater amount of light into the center of the beam. The flat field evens the intensity throughout the beam. This adjustment does not alter the effective field angle, but changes the beam angle considerably.

### ERS BEAM CHARACTERISTICS

The ellipsoidal reflector spotlight throws a powerful beam of light capable of creating harsh and sharp shadows. Yet, this instrument offers the flexibility of altering the quality of light in nearly any manner.

The ellipsoidal is truly a theatrical spotlight. Stage lighting requires a tightly controlled beam of light. Stray light illuminating the architecture of the theatre or unintended scenery is both distracting and unacceptable. The ERS is by far the most successful of conventional instruments in controlling light. The precise nature of the ellipsoidal reflector coupled with clear plano-convex lenses accounts for this control. The addition of gobos can texture the light in endless ways. Frost diffusion placed in the color frame can achieve a variety of softening effects. There is no better instrument for providing flexibility as well as control of light.

**Figure 18–15**
The Zoom Ellipsoidal

The 4½-inch instrument shown has a variable focus, which allows field spreads from 25- to 50-degrees. Photo courtesy Strand Lighting, Inc.

## BEAM AND FIELD ANGLES

If the intensity of light from an ellipsoidal is considered in terms of percentages and the beam's illumination along the center line is 100 percent, the beam and field angles are defined as follows:

*Beam angle* is the point where the illumination falls off to 50 percent.

*Field angle* is the point where illumination falls off to 10 percent.

| Lens Type | Beam Angle | Field Angle | Approx. Throw |
|-----------|-----------|-------------|---------------|
| 4½ × 6 | 33° | 50° | 12–20 feet |
| 6 × 9 | 24° | 40° | 15–30 feet |
| 6 × 12 | 18° | 30° | 25–40 feet |
| 6 × 16 | 15° | 20° | 35–55 feet |
| 6 × 22 | 8° | 15° | 50–75 feet |

### ERS SIZES

Ellipsoidal reflector spotlights are available in several sizes for different applications. In general, the smaller instruments use lower wattage lamps and are designed for short-throw applications. For instance, Colortran's "Mini-ellipse" has a 500-watt lamp and even with lenses set at 30 degrees, it isn't very effective for throw distances beyond 25 feet.

By far the most popular size is the 6-inch ellipsoidal. As can be seen on the preceeding table, field spreads are available from a narrow 15 degrees up to a wide 50 degrees. Modern 6-inch ellipsoidals use lamps ranging from 500

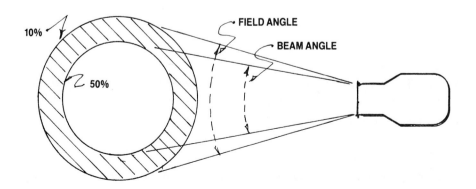

**Figure 18–16**
Beam and Field Angles

In a typical ellipsoidal reflector spotlight, 100 percent intensity is found at beam center. The beam and field angles are designated in degrees.

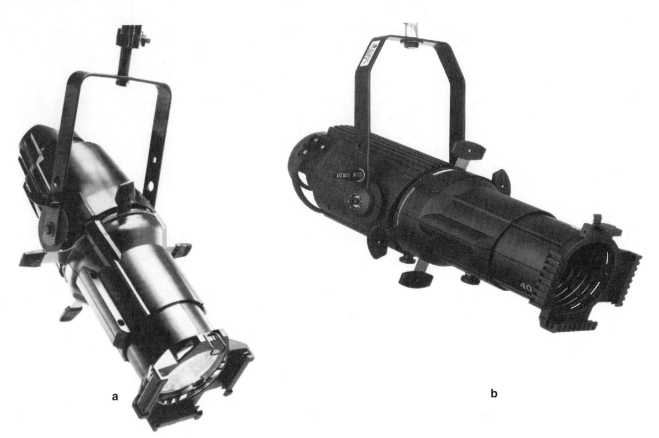

a

b

**Figure 18–17**
Modern 6-inch ERS

(a) The "Source Four" 6-inch ERS from ETC. It burns a 575-watt quartz lamp (HPL) having a color temperature of 3,250° K. It has a rotating shutter assembly, a dichroic ellipsoidal reflector, and a slot for drop-in iris. Interchangeable lens tubes offer a choice of 19-, 26-, 36-, and 50-degree field angles. Photo courtesy Electronic Theatre Controls, Inc.
(b) The "Shakespeare" Series 600 6-inch ERS from Altman. It takes a HX600 quartz lamp (FLK) and has features similar to ETC's Source Four. Lens barrels are available with field angles of 20, 30, 40, and 50 degrees. In addition, two zoom ellipsoidal models are available with field angle ranges from 15 to 35 degrees and 30 to 55 degrees. Photo courtesy Altman Stage Lighting Co.

to 1,000 watts and are valuable for throws up to 70 feet (Figure 18–17). The recent Source Four line of ellipsoidals from Electronic Theatre Controls was designed around a new high-intensity 575-watt lamp. They have a "cool mirror" dichroic reflector and rotating shutters. Altman's Shakespeare series offers similar features and uses a compact 600-watt lamp.

Larger 8- and 10-inch ellipsoidals are available for throw distances in the range of 100 feet. They take 1,000-watt lamps and have narrow field spreads from 5 to 15 degrees. They are fairly bulky compared to the 6-inch version.

## THE FRESNEL SPOTLIGHT

The Fresnel (pronounced Fré nel) gets its name from the inventor of its unique lens, Augustin-Jean Fresnel (1788–1827). The instrument is simpler than an ERS, consisting of only a spherical reflector, a lamp, and the Fresnel lens.

As shown in Figure 18–18, the Fresnel's spherical reflector returns the light back to the filament of the lamp. The light then travels on to the lens where it is redirected into the cone-shaped beam typical of spotlights.

### THE FRESNEL LENS

The thick glass of a plano-convex lens with a short focal length has a tendency to crack due to excessive heat from the source. As we have seen,

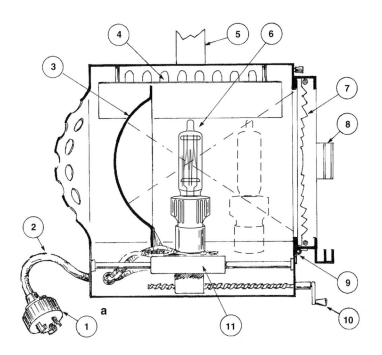

ellipsoidal reflector spotlights compensate for this deficiency by using a combination of two lenses rather than one. Another solution is to reduce the thickness of the lens by removing unnecessary glass.

The important parts of a plano-convex lens are the two surfaces, one flat and the other curved. Fresnel knew that if the curve of the convex surface was retained while "steps" were cut into the glass to reduce thickness, the lens would work like a plano-convex (Figure 18–19).

In fact, such a lens (called a "step lens") was used in ellipsoidal reflector spotlights for a short period of time. Unfortunately, disturbing ring patterns from the step risers were apparent in the light beam. In addition, the quality of light was not as sharp and crisp as that from plano-convex lenses. Use was quickly discontinued.

In order to avoid similar difficulties, the plano surface of a theatre Fresnel lens is broken up by either a light frosting technique or by a series of dimples

**Figure 18–18**
The Fresnel Spotlight

(a) A cut-away view of a typical Fresnel showing:
 (1) Three prong twist-lock connector.
 (2) Rubber coated lead wires.
 (3) Spherical reflector.
 (4) Ventilation holes.
 (5) Yoke.
 (6) Quartz lamp with a prefocus base.
 (7) Fresnel lens.
 (8) Color frame holder.
 (9) Hinged lens front for interior access.
 (10) Worm-screw drive for movable lamp and reflector carriage.
 (11) Movable carriage.
(b) A 6-inch Fresnel from Strand. Photo courtesy Strand Lighting, Inc.

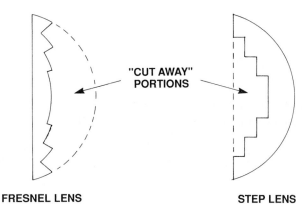

**"CUT AWAY" PORTIONS**

**FRESNEL LENS**          **STEP LENS**

**Figure 18–19**
The Fresnel and Step Lenses

These simplified diagrams show how the Fresnel and step lenses are derived from the plano-convex lens.

molded into the glass. This slight diffraction results in the very smooth and soft illumination distinctive of the Fresnel spotlight.

### FRESNEL OPERATIONAL FEATURES

The Fresnel spotlight has variable beam-spread capability. As shown in Figure 18–18, the lamp and reflector are both mounted on a sliding carriage that can be moved closer or further away from the lens.

**Spot Focus and Flood Focus**      When the lamp is moved all the way forward, the light beam achieves its largest diameter. This is referred to as *flood focus*. As the lamp is slid back away from the lens, the light beam becomes narrower. All the way back is called *spot focus*. Movement of the carriage is accomplished by means of a worm screw or a simple thumbscrew extending from the bottom of the instrument. The following table lists field angles for typical 6- and 8-inch Fresnels at both spot and flood focus:

### FRESNEL FIELD ANGLES

|  | Spot Field Angle | Flood Field Angle |
|---|---|---|
| 6-inch Fresnel | 16° | 60° |
| 8-inch Fresnel | 14° | 50° |

**Beam Shaping**      While internal beam shaping is not possible, an accessory called a *barn door* can be added. Placed in the color frame holder of the instrument, a barn door effectively shapes the beam by cutting it in a linear manner from any of four sides (Figure 18–20). Most barn doors can be rotated to allow cuts of any angle. The well-equipped theatre has barn doors for every Fresnel in its inventory.

Many newer Fresnels are provided with a top locking device as part of the color frame holder. Even so, it is wise to "safety" a barn door to the pipe or yoke of the instrument by means of a small chain or wire rope. This is particularly important for larger Fresnels, whose barn doors are heavy and easily dislodged by scenery flying on an adjacent batten.

Another accessory, useful for any instrument but particularly valuable with a Fresnel, is the *top hat* or *snoot*. A top hat is nothing more than a tin can, open on both ends and attached to a rectangular metal frame sized to fit into the color holder. Painted flat black inside and out, the top hat controls lens flare by absorbing stray light refracted by the risers of the Fresnel lens. If a lens is in audience sight, light flare from it can be quite distracting.

### FRESNEL BEAM CHARACTERISTICS

The beam of light from a Fresnel is soft in quality, with a smooth, even field. The light appears to wrap around a figure, and shadows are soft-edged and not very harsh. The Fresnel is useful in "washing" walls and drops with smooth

**Figure 18—20**
**A Fresnel with Barn Doors**

The four-way barn doors at the front of the instrument allow beam shaping. This unit, designed especially for film and television applications, allows remote spot and flood focus by turning the knob at the side. Photo courtesy Colortran, Inc.

and even coverage. It is excellent in short-throw applications blending one acting area with another.

Being a spotlight, the light from a Fresnel exhibits a good sense of direction. It can be used to simulate the soft quality of candlelight, an overcast sky, or any other diffuse source. In a proscenium theatre the Fresnel's usefulness is generally limited to over-stage, because its scattered beam characteristics cause too much illumination in the auditorium.

## FRESNEL SIZES

Fresnel spotlights come in a number of sizes, the smallest of which has a 3-inch lens and burns up to a 150-watt lamp (Figure 18—21). Fondly called an "inky," this little instrument, although not possessing much punch, is very handy for tucking into small corners.

The most common Fresnel is the 6-inch, burning 500- to 1,000-watt lamps. Short to medium throw distances of 15 to 25 feet are best suited to

**Figure 18—21**
Fresnel Sizes

(a) A 3-inch "inky," which takes a 150-watt lamp and can hide in a small space.
(b) A 10-inch 5,000-watt studio Fresnel. Photo courtesy Colortran, Inc.

b

the 6-inch instrument. This spotlight is valuable for lighting upstage acting areas where its soft-edged beam fades away on the scenery.

For larger stages and longer throw distances, the 8-inch Fresnel is recommended. It burns up to a 2,000-watt lamp and delivers a powerful beam with the typical smooth Fresnel pattern.

The Fresnel spotlight is also available with lenses from 10 to 20 inches in diameter and lamps of 5,000 or even 10,000 watts. These instruments, primarily intended for television and film use, deliver a vast amount of soft illumination.

## THE PAR FIXTURE

The heart of the PAR lighting fixture is the parabolic aluminized reflector lamp. Invented by Clarence Birdseye, the pioneer of frozen foods, this lamp in its PAR-64 version became the mainstay of concert lighting. The PAR lamp is itself a self-contained instrument, lacking only a housing and conventional plug. Its extruded-metal housing sometimes called a "PAR can" secures the PAR-64 lamp in place by means of a large spring ring. It also acts like a top hat, absorbing some of the abundant flare caused by the built-in lens of the lamp (Figure 18–22). The butt of the housing hinges open to allow access to the lamp and socket. Color frame holders including a top safety clip are fixed to the front of the fixture.

## THE PAR LAMP

PAR-type lamps are available in many sizes, but the 8-inch PAR-64 is the theatrical standard. Due to its parabolic reflector, reflected light leaves the lamp in parallel rays. A lens is necessary only to redirect those nonparallel rays of light emanating from the front of the lamp. A unique feature of the PAR-64 lamp is its oval-shaped beam, which is more than twice as long as it is wide. PAR-64 lamps are available with four different beam sizes, as shown in the following table:

### PAR-64 BEAM SIZES AND SPREADS

The PAR-64 lamp is rated at 1,000 watts and is available in the following beam spreads:

| Beam Sizes | ANSI Code | Beam Angle | Field Angle |
|---|---|---|---|
| Very narrow | FFN | $6° \times 12°$ | $10° \times 24°$ |
| Narrow | FFP | $7° \times 14°$ | $14° \times 26°$ |
| Medium | FFR | $12° \times 28°$ | $21° \times 44°$ |
| Wide | FFS | $24° \times 48°$ | $45° \times 71°$ |

**Figure 18–22**
**The PAR-64 Fixture**

(a) Illustration of the parts of the PAR fixture showing:
  (1) Color frame holder.
  (2) Light baffle.
  (3) PAR-64 lamp, 1,000-watts.
  (4) Three-wire cord and pin connector.
  (5) Yoke.
  (6) Lamp socket.
  (7) Rear hinge allowing access to lamp.
(b) A PAR-64 fixture. Note flare from the lamp on the inside of the housing.

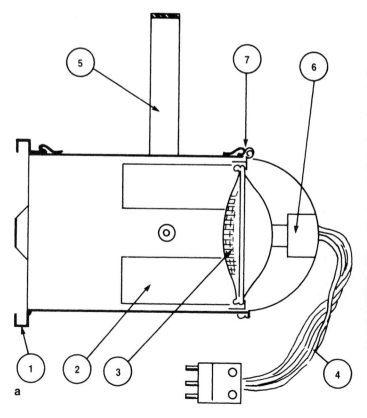

a

b

## PAR-64 CHARACTERISTICS

The oval-shaped beam of light from a PAR fixture cannot be effectively altered or adequately controlled. The use of barn doors tends to dim rather than shape the beam of light. However, the direction of the oval can be changed by simply rotating the lamp within its housing.

Because of its parabolic reflector, the quality of light from a PAR fixture is very harsh. In contrast, the beam edge remains quite diffuse due to the action of the lens. PAR fixtures deliver a very bright light and subsequently make good back-lights. However, it is difficult to blend several PARs with one another in an even manner. Like the Fresnel, the use of PAR fixtures is normally limited to over-stage.

Relative to other stage instruments, the PAR fixture is nearly indestructible, making it ideal for touring. Lamp life is long and the lamp itself is fairly inexpensive.

## AUTOMATED FIXTURES

It would not be surprising if theatres in the twenty-first century were equipped totally with automated fixtures. The lighting equipment for a recent concert tour by the singer formerly known as Prince was composed solely of automated fixtures. While the trendy popularity of moving light may wane, the potential offered by the technology cannot be denied.

The minimum requirement of an automated fixture is that it must accurately and repeatedly reproduce a focus assignment. To do so, remotely controlled tilt and swivel motors receive a signal from the control console. Normally, a single channel of control is assigned to each of the fixture's functions. Sophistication varies greatly, but the most advanced instruments change focus, intensity, color, beam size, gobo pattern, and light quality.

There are two basic types of automated fixtures: (1) a fixed instrument whose light moves by virtue of a *moving mirror*, and (2) a *moving fixture*, often called a "moving head."

### MOVING FIXTURES

There is little dispute that the leader in moving fixture design has been Vari*Lite. Several companies manufacture moving fixtures, but Vari*Lite has controlled the concert lighting market. Its two primary lighting fixtures have been the VL2B Spot Luminaire and the VL4 Wash Luminaire (Figure 18–23). Both use a 400-watt arc lamp that produces an extremely bright light with a color temperature of 5,000 degrees Kelvin (see Chapter 22). Each offers a wide variety of dichroic colors and has built-in mechanical dimmers. The VL2B Spot Luminaire uses an ellipsoidal reflector and, with the aid of an iris, offers a variable beam spread from 5 to 24 degrees. The designer has a choice of nine built-in gobos as well as the capability of changing beam edge from soft to hard focus. The VL4 Wash Luminaire has a parabolic reflector. Changing the position of the lamp within the reflector results in variable field

spreads from 12 to 18 degrees. Textured glass panels offer a unique variable degree of diffusion.

In the early 1990s Vari*Lite introduced what many consider to be its first theatrical fixture, the VL5 Wash Luminaire (Figure 18–24a). It is convection-cooled and, therefore, quiet. It uses a dimmable 1,000-watt tungsten halogen lamp with a color temperature of 3200° K. Internal dichroic color filters provide a very wide range of colors. Interchangeable front lenses in conjuction with a beam diffuser similar to that in the VL4 offer a variety of beam shapes, sizes, and qualities. Recently introduced was the VL6 Spot Luminaire (Figure 18–24b). This fixture uses an arc-lamp light source and provides a limited range of colors and gobos. It has an iris and offers hard to soft beam-edge control. Perhaps the most important feature of the VL5 and VL6 is the fact that they can be controlled by any DMX-512 control console.

These moving lights are highly sophisticated and remain fairly expensive—although prices are coming down as demand increases. The best news is that previous difficulties with control consoles are being addressed. The biggest problem with moving "heads" is noise. When several units move at the same time, the noise is too loud for a quiet moment in the theatre.

**Figure 18–23**
**Vari*Lite VL2B and VL4**
**Automated Fixtures**

The VL2B Spot Luminaire (a) and the VL4 Wash Luminaire (b) are Vari*Lite's primary concert lighting instruments. They both have bright arc lamps that burn at a high color temperature. Photo courtesy Vari*Lite.

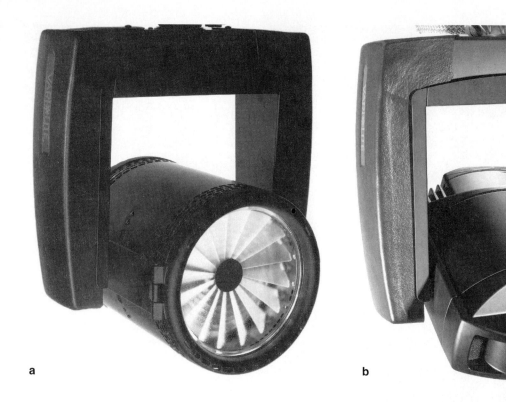

a

b

## Figure 18–24
### Vari*Lite VL5 and VL6 Automated Fixtures

The recent VL5 Wash Luminaire (a) and the VL6 Spot Luminaire (b) are Vari*Lite's first instruments suitable for theatrical applications. Photo courtesy Vari*Lite.

## FIXTURES WITH MOVING MIRRORS

A number of manufacturers are concentrating on fixtures with moving mirrors. High End Systems and Lightwave Research has established itself in the market with the Intellabeam 700HX automated fixture. Likewise, Clay Paky's line of Golden Scan automated fixtures have proven themselves to be powerful and dependable moving mirror light sources (Figure 18–25).

None of these fixtures are small. The Intellabeam is three feet long and weighs in at a hefty sixty-two pounds. It uses a 700-watt arc lamp with a color temperature of 5,600° K. Features include a gobo wheel with twelve patterns, a dichroic color wheel providing eleven colors, a mechanical iris, and a mechanical dimmer. The fixture can be used with one of three different lenses—a 10-degree, a 12.5-degree, or a 16-degree.

The Golden Scan "3" comes in two models. The smaller fixture uses a 575-watt arc lamp, while the larger has a bright 1,200-watt arc source. Both lamps produce a color temperature of 5600° K. An 11-degree lens is standard, with a 16-degree lens available. Golden Scans offer twenty-four colors, four changeable gobo patterns that can rotate, a mechanical iris, and mechanical dimming. Six DMX-512 control channels can operate a Golden Scan, as follows:

1. One controls the iris and gobo rotation.
2. A second controls the color wheel.
3. A third controls gobo selection.
4. A fourth controls color temperature, prism, and frost.

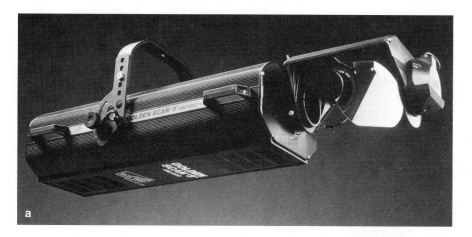

**Figure 18–25**
Moving Mirror Automated
Fixtures

(a) The Golden Scan "3", manufactured by Clay Paky, has a
bright 1,200-watt arc lamp and
an internal prism for the creation
of effects. Photo courtesy Clay
Paky SRL and Group One.
(b) The Intellabeam 700HX from
High End Systems has established itself as a reliable and
high-performance automated fixture. It is seeing more and more
use in theatrical situations.
Photo courtesy High End
Systems.

5. A fifth controls pan.
6. A sixth controls tilt.

Clay Paky does offer a smaller fixture called the MiniScan. It uses a
300-watt arc lamp with a color temperature of 5,600° K. Features include
a variable-speed color wheel with seven dichroic filters, five gobo patterns,
a mechanical dimmer, and a strobe effect. It is about two feet long and weighs
only twenty pounds. It can be controlled by four channels of analog signal
or DMX-512.

Both Clay Paky and High End Systems have recently introduced even
more powerful and sophisticated moving mirror fixtures: the Super Scan

**Figure 18–26**
The Follow Spot

(a) Illustration showing the major components of a long-throw follow spot.

(1) Lamp and reflector adjustment assembly.

(2) Spherical reflector.

(3) Arc lamp source.

(4) Dimming control (dowser).

(5) Horizontal shutter.

(6) Iris.

(7) Lens system.

(8) Zoom track.

(9) Rear pan/tilt handle.

(10) Pan lock.

(11) Tilt lock.

(12) Lock-down stabilizer.

(13) Front pan/tilt handle.

(14) Six-color boomerang.

(b) The Strong Super Trouper with a xenon arc lamp. Photo courtesy Strong Electric.

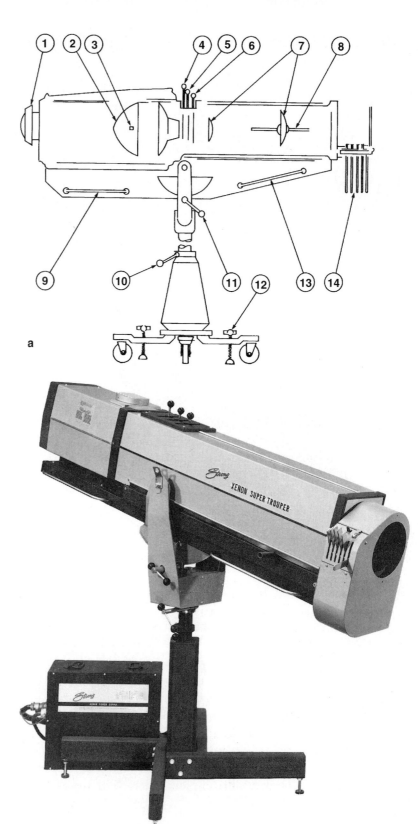

a

b

Zoom and the Cyberlight. This new generation of automated fixtures offers options that are quite remarkable. They are actually effects projectors that, incidently, can light a performer. As such, they will be discussed in the following chapter on projection and effects.

## DESIGNING WITH AUTOMATED FIXTURES

It is certainly true that a single automated fixture can do the job of several fixed instruments. While automated fixtures are a valuable tool, it remains to be seen how completely the theatre will embrace this technology. Successful designing with light requires as much control as possible over color, angle, distribution, and movement. In many ways automated fixtures offer much more control than is currently available. However, unless used in great quantities, the angle of light remains dependent on a fixed source. In this way, several conventional fixed instruments are more flexible than one automated fixture.

## FOLLOW SPOTS

The traditional follow spot is a specialty instrument intended to produce a very bright and concentrated beam of light over a long throw distance (Figure 18–26). A necessary element of a certain style of Broadway musical, the instruments and their operators are most often situated at the very rear of the auditorium in the uppermost balcony. In concert situations, multiple follow spots are used to highlight lead singers and musicians. In large venues, with some audience members several hundred feet away from the performers, extremely high levels of illumination are required for visibility. Sometimes as many as six or eight follow spots are concentrated on one performer.

A spherical reflector is used to help direct the light to an aperture similar to that of the ERS. An iris used to control beam size and a mechanical dimmer called a "douser" are located near the aperture. Also in this vicinity is a mechanism called a "damper" or "curtain shutters" that chops the beam of light in a horizontal manner. Mounted in a long barrel in front of the aperture is a lens, or lenses, that can be moved to adjust beam size and sharpness. A device called a "boomerang," which normally holds six color filters, allows for rapid changes.

The design of a follow spot is dependent on its function and throw distance. Some follow spots such as the Lycian Starklite II and the Phoebus Mighty Arc II-S are designed for truss-mounting (Figure 18–27). They are primarily used in concert situations where the fixture and an operator work from a truss located above the performance space. The Starklite II uses a 1,200-watt arc lamp and will accept a gobo and gobo rotator. The Mighty Arc II-S uses a 400-watt arc lamp and is recommended for throws from 25 to 150 feet.

Long-throw follow spots must be able to deliver a high-intensity light. Carbon arc, the original source, has been replaced by metal halide or xenon

## Figure 18–27
**Truss-Mount Follow Spot**

Several manufacturers have developed smaller follow spots that can be mounted on concert trusses. Shown is the Starklite II from Lycian Stage Lighting. It uses a 1,200-watt arc lamp, accepts a gobo and rotator, and is only three feet long. Photo courtesy Lycian Stage Lighting.

a

b

### Figure 18–28
### Long-Throw Follow Spots

(a) Lycian's Superarc-400 uses an arc lamp with a color temperature of 5600° K. It is rated for throw distances up to 500 feet. Photo courtesy Lycian Stage Lighting.

(b) The Long Throw Ultra Arc Follow Spot uses a G.E. Marc 350 projector lamp for high intensity and is one of the lightest follow spots available. Photo courtesy Phoebus Mfg.

arc lamps. The first Strong Trouper carbon arc follow spot was introduced in 1948. The xenon arc Super Trouper was placed on the market in 1975. Today, Strong International manufactures a line of eight follow spots recommended for throw distances from 30 to 460 feet (Figure 18–28). Clay Paky, the manufacturer of Golden Scan automated fixtures, recently introduced a remote control follow spot called Shadow. Depending on required throw distance, the Shadow uses either a 575- or 1,200-watt arc lamp. The control panel is normally rear-mounted and allows the operator push-button control of intensity, color, and beam size. The Shadow uses a variable-speed dichroic filter color wheel instead of the conventional color boomerang.

## CYCLORAMA AND BACKDROP LIGHTING FIXTURES

Lighting large surfaces such as cycloramas or scenic drops requires specialized equipment. The lighting instrument must be able to project a "wall" of light over considerable distances while maintaining a smooth and even field. Drops are most often lit from above, although occasionally from both above and below.

## STRIPLIGHTS

One form of stage lighting instrument that predates electricity is the striplight. A line of light is created by a number of sources—formerly candle or gas, but now electric—placed adjacent to each other.

Striplight lamps are usually wired in three or four color circuits. In a three-circuit, twelve-lamp striplight, the first and fourth lamps and the seventh and tenth lamps operate together. A great variety of color can be attained by placing different colored filters in each circuit and mixing them by controlling their respective intensities. The lamps must be spaced closely together so that their various colored beams will blend.

For many years the most common style of striplight was the 6-foot section containing twelve PAR-36 or R-40, 150-watt lamps (Figure 18–29). With their common screw bases and built-in reflectors, these lamps adequately served the purpose of producing a broad and relatively smooth sheet

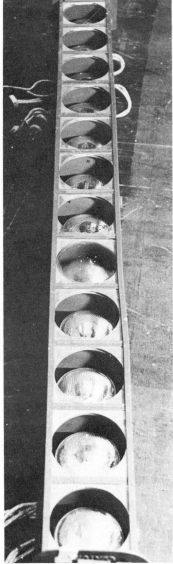

**Figure 18–29**
Reflector-Lamp Striplight

Shown is a three-circuit striplight with PAR-36 spot lamps for a longer throw. The R-40 flood lamp is normally used for short to medium throws.

**Figure 18–30**
Modern Striplights

(a) The Altman "ZipStrip," which takes MR-16 lamps. Photo courtesy Altman Stage Lighting.
(b) The Strand Coda, shown here in its single-cell version, takes a 500-watt quartz lamp. Photo courtesy Strand Lighting, Inc.

of light. The R-40 floodlight was used for short throws and the R-40 or PAR-36 spot provided a longer throw. While it is still possible to purchase striplights designed to use these lamps, other light sources have proven to be more efficient.

Modern striplight sections use one of two light sources: *quartz strips* that burn elongated 500-watt quartz lamps that throw a bright and even beam of light, and *ministrips* that use concentrated filament MR-16 lamps. Both offer superior intensity with a smooth field (Figure 18–30).

### CYC LIGHTS

With the advent of the quartz lamp came a new design in cyclorama and drop lighting fixtures. Colortran was the first manufacturer to develop what they called the Far Cyc. Although each manufacturer uses a different trade name for its particular fixture, they all burn 1,000- to 2,000-watt quartz lamps and are available with one to four lamp compartments per section. As can be seen in Figure 18–31, the reflector is curved in an inverted "J" shape so that more light is projected to the bottom of a backdrop or cyclorama.

**Figure 18–31**
The Far Cyc

A modern four-window cyclorama light developed by Colortran. Photo courtesy Colortran, Inc.

## OTHER FIXTURES

Several other types of lighting instruments with specialized functions exist. They are the beam projector, floodlight, and borderlight.

### BEAM PROJECTORS

The beam projector is basically a searchlight adapted to the theatre. Like a PAR fixture, the beam projector uses a parabolic reflector to throw parallel rays of light. Lacking a lens, the beam projector must contend with the diverging light rays that come out of the front of the lamp. Several solutions have been attempted, none of them completely successful. A very small Fresnel lens has been placed in front of the lamp to create parallel rays of light. A spherical reflector has been positioned in front of the lamp to bounce light rays back to the parabolic reflector. Baffles or louvers have been arranged so as to absorb the diverging rays.

The PAR fixture has replaced the beam projector for most applications. However, Strand Lighting recently came out with a new Beamlite beam projector (Figure 18–32). It uses a low-voltage lamp in order to reduce the filament size, making the source more optically precise. It can be lamped up

**Figure 18–32**
**Beam Projector**

Strand's Beamlite is a modern low-voltage beam projector. It takes a 1,000-watt 24-volt lamp and has a built-in transformer. It produces a bright and narrow beam of light. Photo courtesy Strand Lighting, Inc.

to 1,000 watts and has a built-in transformer. It produces a very bright, harsh and narrow beam of light for special applications.

## FLOODLIGHTS

A floodlight, as its name suggests, is a fixture designed to throw a broad wash of light over a wide area. For many years the "scoop," an ellipsoidal reflector floodlight, has been the standard instrument for such a purpose (Figure 18–33a). It has a reflector with a matte finish that distributes light smoothly and without a sharp edge to the beam. Most scoops are 16 to 18 inches in diameter and burn lamps of up to 2,000 watts. A single instrument can be valuable for lighting a fair-sized window backing. Banks of scoops have been used to light a drop and are especially useful for washing a curved surface.

The "broad" is a floodlight borrowed from television and film lighting. It contains a quartz lamp up to 1,500 watts and produces a wide field with even light distribution (Figure 18–33b).

## BORDERLIGHTS

The borderlight is a striplight lamped with 500-watt PAR-56 or 1,000-watt PAR-64 lamps. Such fixtures are frequently used over-stage to produce a bright wash-illumination. They can be colored with glass filters.

### Figure 18–33
Floodlights

(a) An Ellipsoidal Reflector Floodlight, often called a "scoop," can take a 1,000-watt lamp and provides a soft and even wash of light. Photo courtesy Altman Stage Lighting.
(b) The "Broad" was developed for film and television use, but is a handy floodlight for certain theatrical applications. It takes a 1,000- or 1,500-watt quartz lamp and comes equipped with barn doors as shown. Photo courtesy Strand Lighting, Inc.

a

b

### Safety Practice

*The best way to prevent accidents from happening is to keep equipment in good operating order.*

Sticking shutters, bent bolts, and missing knobs or handles all frustrate an electrician and encourage mistreatment. A conservative estimate would be that 25 percent of all lamp "burnouts" are caused by an angered electrician attempting to free a stuck part by giving it a tap with the old wrench.

Some houses require that lighting equipment mounted overhead be secured to the pipe with a safety chain or wire in addition to the C-clamp. While the likelihood of an instrument falling during a performance is slim, nothing could be more unnerving for a theatre patron than to have a 10-inch Leko fall from 30 feet and land nearby. To prevent accidents, the safety cable should ideally be attached to the instrument itself (as opposed to the yolk) and then around the pipe. A second cable clipped to the color frame will ensure that it stays with the instrument. Other theatres may require that a wire mesh separate all instrumentation from the auditorium.

## CARE AND HANDLING

While standard practices naturally vary from one situation to another and from one locality to another, there are good practices that should be observed everywhere. By far the most important concern should be with maintenance of equipment. Instrument hanging, circuiting, and focusing are made much simpler if equipment is in good condition.

Older instruments can be valuable if they are used properly and taken care of. Do not attempt to increase light output of an older instrument by exceeding the recommended lamp wattage. These older instruments simply do not dissipate heat as well as newer equipment and they were made for lower wattage lamps—use them that way.

The single most important factor in instrument maintenance is keeping everything clean. Lenses can be washed in mild soap and water or with a good glass cleaner. Reflectors should be wiped with a soft cloth or washed with vinegar and water. Keep body parts as free of dust as possible. A clean spotlight dissipates heat better, thereby increasing lamp life and decreasing warpage. It also delivers more light!

Commonly needed spare parts such as shutters, knobs, and lenses should be kept on hand so that repair is not delayed by waiting for a parts order. Be advised that most instrument manufacturers require a fairly large minimum charge for parts orders and, adding insult to injury, take forever to fill the order.

# PROJECTION, PRACTICALS, AND EFFECTS

# 19

This chapter covers several diverse subjects, the most significant being the use of light as a scenic element. When light is used as scenery its design normally falls under the auspices of the scenic designer; execution is the responsibility of the lighting department. The lighting designer's input into such matters is critical. Whether it be as simple as a pair of sconces on the wall of a realistic box set or as complex as multiscreen projection, the lighting designer must be involved from the beginning. It is not unusual for a projection specialist to be part of the staff of an extremely complex projection show such as the recent production of *The Who's Tommy* (see Chapter 24).

## LIGHT AS SCENERY

Light begins to be a scenic element the moment a light source is visible to the audience. Motivating sources such as candles and chandeliers add a sense of mood and style to a production. Exposed lightbulbs in signs or strung about the stage creating a carnival-like atmosphere are decorative and theatrical in their impact. Concert lighting with beams of moving light revealed in the air is one of the more recent manifestations of light as scenery. Exposed stage-lighting instruments themselves become a scenic element. All of the above examples make a strong visual contribution to the total design. However, they are a supporting element and normally not the basic scheme of production.

### THE DEVELOPMENT OF LIGHT AS SCENERY

Designer-directors like Robert Edmond Jones (1887–1954), Edward Gorden Craig (1872–1966), and Adolphe Appia (1862–1928) envisioned using light

as a central production scheme in their work. But technology of the time could not support their imagination. It took the genius of Czech scenographer Josef Svoboda (1920–   ) to show the theatre world what could be accomplished with light. An example of his work is illustrated in Figure 19–1, a photograph of the scenery for Wagner's *Tristan und Isolde.* At his theatre in Prague, Svoboda experimented extensively with low-voltage light sources. He was the first to develop, on a large scale, electrostatically charged particles in the air to act as reflectors of light. His use of projected images has pioneered new ways of thinking about scenic projection.

New technology in brighter light sources, projection screen design, and automated fixtures continues the trend toward greater use of light as scenery.

## LIGHT AS A SCHEME OF PRODUCTION

Light used as a scheme of production has been most common in the more abstract presentation of modern dance and performance art. As early as the late 1800s, dancer Lois Fuller created lighting instruments and effects in order to heighten the dramatic impact of her dance performance. Not only do we see light being projected on actors and dancers, but moving light is used as a character itself.

The modern-dance/performance-art piece illustrated in Figure 19–2, called *First Light,* was choreographed only after a lighting "score" was developed. The air is filled with fog (see "Special Effects" at the end of this chapter)

**Figure 19–1**
Light as Scenery

A column of light created by high-intensity, low-voltage light sources. The light is reflected off a special aerosol spray of minute, electrostatically charged oil-emulsion droplets capable of staying suspended in the air for a prolonged time. This early use of "cracked oil" was developed by Josef Svoboda for Wagner's *Tristan und Isolde.* Photo reprinted from *The Sceneography of Josef Svoboda* by permission of Wesleyan University Press. Copyright 1971 by Jarka Burian.

497

## Figure 19—2
### Light as a Scheme of Production

These photographs of a production of *First Light* performed by Nancy Karp + Dancers, a San Francisco based modern dance company, illustrate the use of light as a scheme of production. Choreography—Nancy Karp, visual design—Wolfram Erber, costumes—Sandra Woodall, and lighting—Craig Wolf.

to accentuate the narrow beams of side-light. The dancers move with and react to the intense beams of light, which change the composition of the space by turning on and off throughout the dance. Costumes and support lighting were designed after the piece was conceived.

Another quite different but equally effective use of light and projection is shown in Figure 19–3. These illustrations and photographs are from the English National Opera's production of Britten's *The Turn of the Screw*. Expanded metal screens shown in Figure 19–3a were reception surfaces for both front- and rear-projection. Kodak Carousel projectors, Pani 5,000-watt projectors, and Strand Patt 752 projectors were used from front-of-house positions, the stage-left and stage-right wings, and from backstage. The production photographs of Figure 19–3c illustrate the use of projected backgrounds in an abstracted style appropriate to the medium. Note the effective use of texture on the stage floor as well as the screens.

## PROJECTED SCENERY

The most familiar and accepted application of light as scenery is through the use of projections. Projections and projected scenery (usually backgrounds) are not new to the theatre. They are as old as the "magic lantern," which entered the theatre in the 1860s, predating the incandescent lamp. Early experiments with the projection of moving images, first as crude animations and then later as motion pictures, are well-known events in theatre history. The resurgence of projections in modern theatre is the result not only of improved equipment design but also of a change in attitude toward their use.

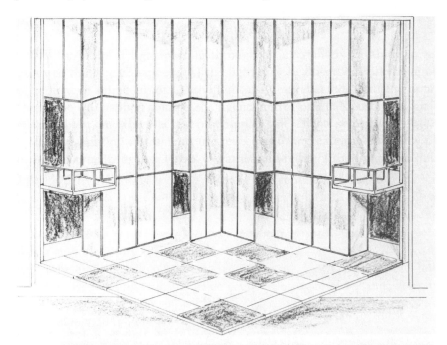

### Figure 19–3
### Projection as a Scheme of Production

Bly, a gloomy Victorian country house, is the locale for the English National Opera's production of *The Turn of the Screw* by Benjamin Britten. The eerie mood of the opera lends itself to the extremely effective use of projected scenery as the action moves rapidly through fifteen variations.
(a) Line drawing shows the arrangement of screens that form the basic setting.

a

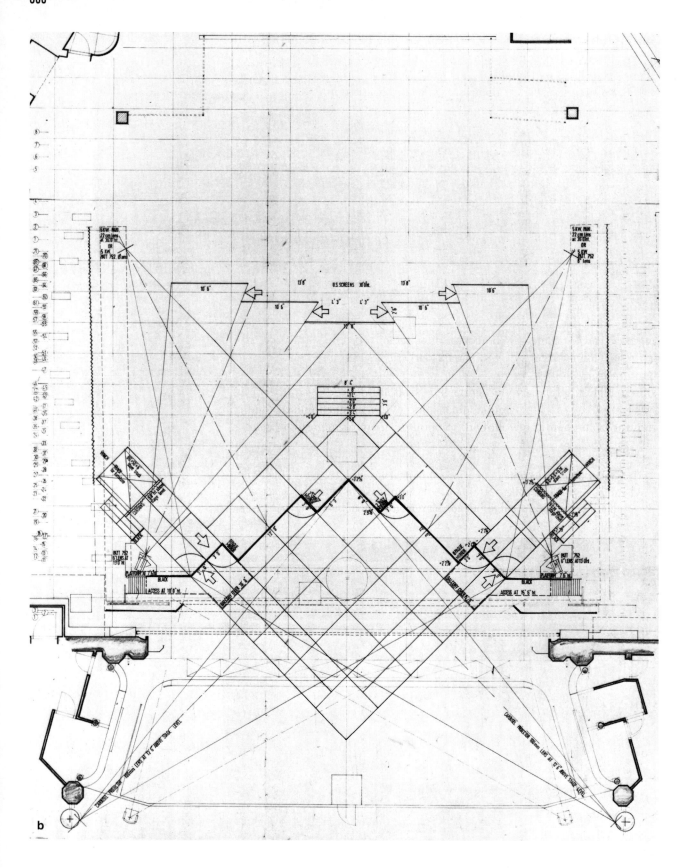

**Figure 19–3** (continued)

(b) Floor plan showing the relationship of screens and location of projectors.
(c) Photographs of two of the settings. Scene design and projections—Patrick Robertson; lighting design—David Hersey. Photos courtesy Noel Staunton, Technical Director, English National Opera, London Coliseum.

In its simplest form, projection requires a light source, the object or slide, and a projection surface. Although it is possible to project an image onto almost any type of surface, a projection *screen* is commonly used. The projector may be placed in front (downstage) of an opaque screen for a front-projection, or at the rear (upstage) of a translucent screen for a rear-projection. In front-projection, it is normally desirable to hide the source from view of the audience. In a rear-projection arrangement, the problem of hiding the source is solved. However, clear space backstage must be maintained between the projector and screen.

**Paint vs. Light** It is important to realize that a projection is *light* and not *paint*, and that there is a world of difference between the two media. Both paint and light, as individual vehicles of expression, have advantages and disadvantages. Each is unique. Do not consider one a substitute for the other.

Color in light is more brilliant than in paint and has a limited value scale by comparison. Therefore, the use of color in projection is more dramatic and eye-catching. If projections are used as backgrounds in substitution of painted scenery, the actor may have to fight for visual attention. Projections, no matter how subtle, convey a heightened sense of theatricality. The most successful use of projection is not as a substitute for realistic background, but as a medium of its own.

The inexperienced designer may be tempted to consider projection as a means of saving either time or money. This reasoning is totally fallacious.

**Figure 19—4**
**Projection Screen Arrangements**

(1) Single-screen rear projection.
(2) Double-screen rear projection.
(3) Front projection screens right and left with rear projection center.
(4) Multiscreen arrangement.
(5) Three-dimensional surface made up of flat planes designed for a single projection.
(6) A projection surface made up of spheres.
(7) Sculptural surfaced planned for many angles of projection.
(8) Slanted surfaces. The downstage screen is scrim, providing the possibility of front, rear, and see-through projections.

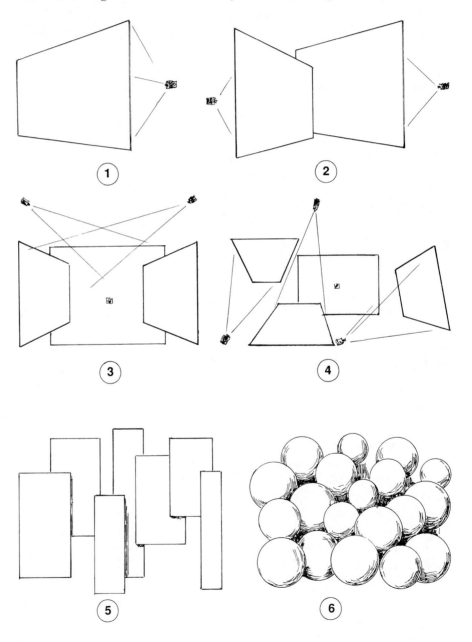

Good projections require a great deal of effort and often more lead time than standard theatrical scenery. Projections must never be considered a last-minute production detail. In addition, projection equipment is very expensive to buy and often difficult to rent.

## THE PROJECTION SURFACE

Aside from increased efficiency of projection equipment, innovative use of the screen or projection surface is perhaps the greatest contribution to the imaginative use of light as scenery. Projected scenery has graduated in a very short time from a large single-screen background to multiscreen compositions in an infinite variety of sizes, shapes, and three-dimensional forms. Figure 19–4 illustrates some screen arrangements and projector positions. They range from a single rear-projection screen to three-dimensional front-projection surfaces.

As soon as the use of projections has been confirmed as the desired technique for a given production, the designers turn to consideration of surfaces. Any material capable of reflecting light may be used as a front-projection surface. Of course, some materials reflect more light than others. And, recalling Chapter 18's discussion of types of reflection, one surface may reflect light differently from another. Brightness and proper dispersion of the projected image is of primary concern to the designer.

**Rear-Projection**     Single-screen rear-projection has been used as background for dramatic productions for some time. The original location of projector and screen was governed by the need to have an operator.

A rear-projection screen must be translucent enough to diffuse the bright spot of the projector's source, yet transparent enough to transmit the image. Very few materials are capable of doing so. The stage-left and stage-right shadow projections in Color Plate 15–4 are rear-projections on common plastic drop-cloth material. The sources show through the plastic and are distracting. To solve this problem, professional rear-screen material must be used.

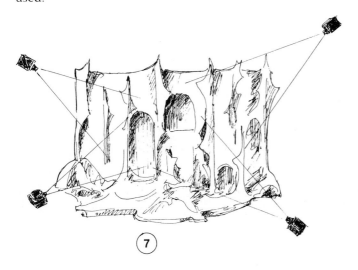

7

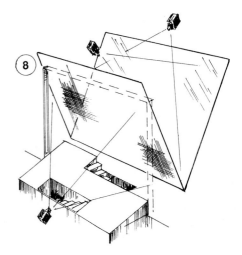

8

A professionally made rear-projection screen is constructed with the greatest density in the center to offset the hot spot of the projector's source. It is seamless and polarized to allow for equal distribution of light. Due to the high density of a rear-projection screen, a great deal of light is lost by absorption and reflection. Consequently, rear-projection requires a brighter source to equal a similar projection from the front.

An advantage of rear-projection is that the projectors can be placed in-line with the screen and are hidden from audience sight. Look ahead momentarily to Figure 19–6, for instance, and note the high angle of the front projector as opposed to the straight-on throw of the rear projector.

Projectors can be equipped with lenses of various focal lengths. However, even the widest of lenses can only achieve a 1:1 ratio of image size to throw distance. In other words, for a 10-foot image, a rear projector must have a least 10 feet of depth upstage of the screen. Some theatres have been designed with extra depth or a special rear-projection booth. But many stages in the United States are simply too shallow to accommodate rear-projection on any large scale.

Before making a final decision on using rear-screen projection for a production, the designers must be sure that screen purchase or rental cost has been considered. Be aware that projecting onto surfaces other than good rear-screen material will produce an inferior image. Rear-screen material is available in many sizes and colors from several theatrical suppliers, including Rosco and Gerriets International.

**Front-Projection**     The greatest advantage of front-projection is that the image can be projected onto a variety of surfaces. It allows for much greater creativity in the design of the screen. Front-projection surfaces may be three-dimensional or they may be broken up to allow for action behind or through the screens. Multiscreen techniques such as those illustrated in Figure 19–5 are best accomplished using front-projection.

A simple technique of slide production for screens of complex shape has been developed by Svoboda. Once the screen and projector are in position, it is simply a matter of placing a piece of unexposed photographic film in the projector where the slide would normally go. Shining a light on the screen exposes the film, producing an exact image of the screen shape and size for the slide.

Front-projection does have the disadvantage of having to throw from a more extreme angle or a greater distance than does rear-projection (Figure

**Figure 19–5**
Multiscreen Technique

The use of many screens is well illustrated by the work of its orginator, Josef Svoboda. While this production of *The Journey* repeats the rectangular screen, the technique can involve screens of various shapes and sizes, each with its individual slide projector. Photos reprinted from *The Sceneography of Josef Svoboda* by permission of Wesleyan University Press. Copyright 1971 by Jarka Burian.

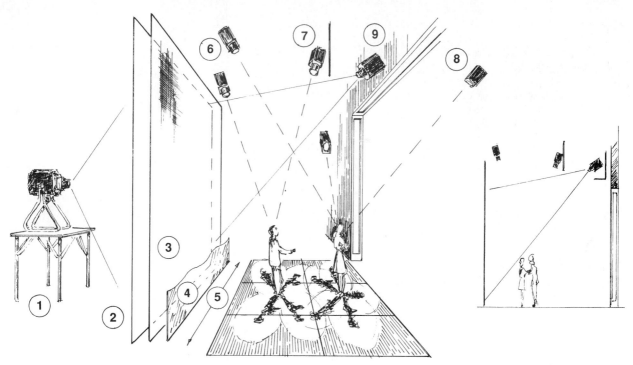

## Figure 19–6
### Projections and the Actor

The effective use of large-scale projections as a background requires special lighting techniques.
(1) Rear-projector.
(2) Rear-projection screen.
(3) Black scrim hung in front of the screen to absorb reflected light from the front.
(4) Ground row.
(5) "Neutral zone."
(6) Back light on actors.
(7) High-angled upstage area lights to keep light and shadows off the screen.
(8) Downstage area lights do not have to be at as steep an angle.
(9) Center of the first electric or bridge position for front projection. The drawing on the right illustrates a front-projection setup. The lighting of the actor remains the same. The black scrim is removed to allow projections from the front. The angle of projection is planned to miss actors at the edge of the neutral zone.

19–6). A high projection angle causes an image to distort because the top of the screen is so much closer to the projector than the bottom. These problems are not insurmountable, but do require slides that have counterdistortion built in. With modern high-intensity lamps, light loss associated with long projection throws is less of a problem than in the past.

Not all distortions need to be corrected. There are times when the distortions of an angled projection are accepted as part of the design, especially if the image is abstract or nonobjective in style.

### LIGHTING THE ACTOR

Lighting of the actor in relation to a projected background requires special attention. Light from acting area instruments hitting the screen causes an image to wash out. Care must be taken to choose lighting angles that will not hit the screen or cause light to bounce off the floor onto the screen. Side-light is particularly useful here. Additionally, back-light is important for separating the actor from the projected background. Ellipsoidal reflector spotlights are the best instrument choice because they produce the least amount of light flair. Top hats are recommended for all instruments in the vicinity of the screen (Figure 19–6).

In addition to the control of distribution, bounce light can be minimized in other ways. The reflectivity of the floor can be deadened with a cover of black or dark gray felt or carpeting. Even common ground cloth material helps to reduce the floor reflection. In the case of *rear-screen* projection, reflected light can be kept off the screen by hanging a seamless black scrim

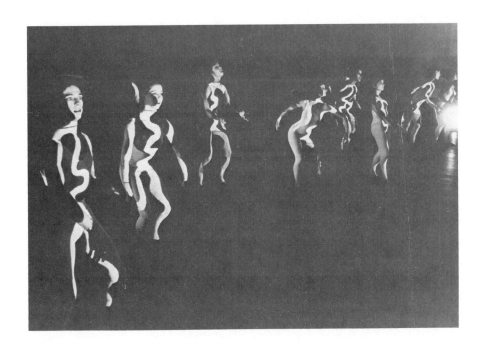

**Figure 19–7**
Projections on the Performer

The abstract form of modern dance adapts easily to the use of projections on the actor or performer, thereby heightening theatricality and visual impact. Shown is *Scenario*, a production of the Nikolais Dance Theatre. Photo by Oleaga.

about a foot downstage of the screen. It serves to absorb the reflected light but does not affect the quality of the image.

The problem of reflected light can also be helped by the design and position of the screen or the image on the screen. A projected image is less likely to suffer from bounce light if it begins 3 or 4 feet above the stage floor. In addition, it is best if a so-called "neutral zone" of approximately 4 feet is maintained between the screen and acting areas. This practice makes it easier to light the actor properly while at the same time preserving the projected image.

**Projection on the Actor**     In the 1950s and 1960s, modern dance and performance art discovered that projections could use the actor as a projection surface. The pioneer in this field has been Alwin T. Nikolais and his dance company. Their performances are a stimulating experience in the theatrical form of sight and sound. Nikolais's imaginative use of light, projections, and performers epitomizes the use of light as scenery (Figure 19–7).

## PROJECTION TECHNIQUES AND EQUIPMENT

Projections can be achieved by a variety of methods. Large-scale shadow projection is possible by using a simple arrangement of slide and light source. A common ellipsoidal reflector spotlight makes an excellent pattern projector. For scenic projections, a lens projector is the most commonly used device. Lens projectors for both moving and still projection come in various sizes and types. The requirements of a specific task dictate which projector is best suited for the job.

## LENS PROJECTORS

A lens projector uses two sets of lenses, each having its own separate function. As illustrated in Figure 19–8, the *condensing lens system* concentrates the light from the source onto the slide. The image of the illuminated slide is then transmitted through another set of lenses called the *objective lens system.* A reflector is most often used to increase the light output of the lamp.

Normally the body of a projector includes the reflector and lamp, condensing lens(es), slide holder, and a fan for cooling. In order to provide a choice of image sizes, the objective lens assembly is housed in a separate *lens tube.* This tube fits into the front of the projector body like the lens barrel of an ellipsoidal reflector spotlight.

**Choice of Lenses**     Projector lenses are available in different focal lengths with the shorter focal lengths providing the widest spread and largest images. The size of a projected image is determined by three things: slide size, focal length of the lens, and throw distance from projector to screen. A designer normally knows the desired image size first. The throw distance is found next by determining where in the theatre the projector can best be located. Finally, the proper lens is selected by using the formulas presented in the box at right.

**Choice of Projectors**     The choice of scenic projectors is quite small and limited further by application. The size of the slide a projector uses varies from the convenient 35mm (1.346 by 0.902 inches) to the large continental size of 9 by 9 inches. However, any given projector will accept only one size. Slide size is an important factor in image brightness. There are several considerations in determining which projector is most appropriate:

1. The longer the throw or the larger the image, the brighter the light source should be.
2. Large slides produce a brighter and clearer image than small slides.
3. The larger the slide format, the more expensive and bulky the equipment.

**Figure 19–8**
The Lens Projector

Shown is a drawing of the optical train of a typical lens projector.

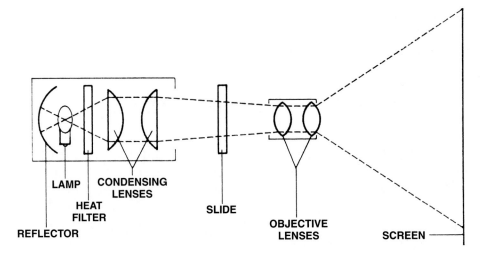

LAMP  CONDENSING LENSES

HEAT FILTER

SLIDE

REFLECTOR

OBJECTIVE LENSES

SCREEN

## THE MATHEMATICS OF LENS PROJECTION

To eliminate trial-and-error methods of selecting lenses and placing projectors, use the following simple formulas:

$$
\begin{aligned}
F &= \text{Focal length of lens} \\
D &= \text{Projection throw distance} \\
S &= \text{Slide size} \\
I &= \text{Image size}
\end{aligned}
$$

$$F = \frac{D \times S}{I}$$

$$D = \frac{F \times I}{S}$$

$$I = \frac{D \times S}{F}$$

Note that all the above measurements must be expressed in the same units, normally inches. If the slide is not square and its horizontal dimension is used, the horizontal dimension of the image will be obtained; if the vertical measurement of the image is needed, the vertical measurement of the slide must be used.

The small 35mm slide is by far the easiest to produce and project, but its image size and intensity have limits. If large and bright images are required, the designer must select from larger format projectors.

### 35MM PROJECTORS

Most people in this country are familiar with Kodak 35mm slide projectors (Figure 19–9a). They have long been the best choice of standard 35mm projectors for a variety of reasons: Light output is superior to other projectors; operation is simple and reliable; and a variety of good-quality lenses are available. Kodak currently manufactures two projector models: the familiar Carousel projector and the more recent Ektagraphic line. Today's Carousel model is intended for home use, while the Ektapro is designed for professional projection applications. The standard lamp for Ektagraphic projectors is an FHS (300-watt, 82-volt, MR-13) with a rated life of 70 hours. An acceptable and brighter substitute is an EXR, which has a rated life of 35 hours.

Kodak sells 25-foot extension cables for the projector's remote controller, allowing control over projectors hung over-stage or placed in the auditorium. However, only three or four extension cables can be used together. Kodak projectors operate on a gravity-feed principle for changing slides. For this

### Figure 19–9
#### 35mm Slide Projector and Lenses

(a) Shown is the Kodak Ektagraphic IIA 35mm slide projector. Photo courtesy Eastman Kodak Company.
(b) Two Kodak projectors with Buhl SF-7 zoom lenses mounted in a stacking dissolve rack.
(c) The Buhl "Keystopper" anti-keystoning lens. Photos courtesy Buhl Optical Company.

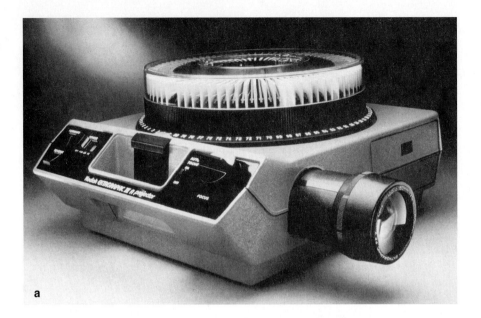

reason, the projectors cannot be tilted too extremely in any direction without danger of slides jamming. Do not attempt to use slide trays that accept more than eighty slides—they will jam.

While Kodak sells a large range of its own lenses, Buhl Optical Company manufactures an even larger range of superior lenses (Figures 19–9b and c). Focal lengths of Buhl lenses made to fit the Kodak projector begin at a very wide angle 1 inch and go to a narrow 11 inches. These lenses are available in varying speeds, with the faster lenses being best for scenic projection.

For greater intensity, Strong International (the maker of follow spots) manufactures a high-intensity xenon-arc lamphouse that works with a Kodak Ektagraphic III projector. It is available with a 500-watt arc lamp delivering 4,000 lumens or a 750-watt lamp providing an intensity of 6,000 lumens. An "eclipser" fade module allows for cross-fading between two or more machines.

**35mm Slide Production**     Anyone with access to a 35mm camera can produce slides that project very well in a Kodak Ektagraphic projector. If

## USING THE KODAK CAROUSEL

Keep in mind the following valuable bits of information about the Kodak Carousel slide projector:

1. The standard lamp recommended by Kodak is the ELH (300-watt, 30-hour life). An acceptable substitute is the ENG (300-watt, 4-hour life). While the life of the ENG is only a fraction of that of the ELH, its light output is greatly increased. It is the ENG that enables the Carousel to be a viable scenic projection unit.

2. The Carousel as wired cannot be dimmed because of its fan and slide-changer motor, although Kodak manufactures a dissolve unit that will cross-fade two projectors. However, it is possible to add an external dimmer in-line with the projector's lamp without any sort of rewiring. A two-pin male plug (Radio Shack Cat. No. 274-342) fits into a pair of holes in the rear of the projector and interrupts power to the lamp. Power need only be directed through any remote dimmer of 300-watt or greater capacity. *Caution:* Power is supplied from the projector, through the dimmer, to the lamp—one may not connect the projector to a conventional stage circuit and dimmer without causing a short circuit.

copying other photographs or designs, a copy stand is a must. Using plastic or glass slide mounts is preferable to the older cardboard mounts because the cardboard tends to warp over time and with heat.

When doing slides for a complex production with a large number of projections, experience has proven that it is best to shoot many more slides than necessary. When making final selections, the director and designers can pick and choose among many possibilities. This practice ultimately saves time and money.

### LARGE-FORMAT SLIDE PROJECTORS

Three companies manufacture large-format slide projectors commonly used in the United States: Ryudensha Company of Japan, Ludwig Pani of Austria, and Reiche and Vogel of Germany. Some of these machines are pictured in Figure 19–10. These projectors are very specialized pieces of equipment, with the most high-powered models costing more than $30,000.

Ryudensha Company's Scene Machine is distributed in the United States by The Great American Market. It uses a 4-by-5-inch glass slide and is available in three models: the 600-watt Mini Scene Machine, the 1,000- or 2,000-watt Scene Machine, and the 2,500-watt HMI Scene Machine. Lenses come in a range of focal lengths between 4 inches (23cm, 50-degree beam spread) and 16 inches (59cm, 12-degree beam spread). A manual as well as a remote-control slide changer with a capacity of five slides can be purchased. Optional effect equipment includes a film loop machine, an effect disc machine, a prism machine, a flicker machine, and a kaleido machine. The Scene Machine has proven to be a good, reliable projector.

**Figure 19–10**
Large Format Slide Projectors

(a) This is the Pani BP4 Scenic Projector. It burns a 4,000-watt HMI lamp and takes a slide size of 18cm × 18cm.
(b) Shown is the Pani BP6 Gold Scenic Projector. It has a bright 6,000-watt HMI lamp with the same slide size as the BP4. Photos courtesy Production Arts Lighting, Inc.
(c) The EQS-20 Scene Machine burns a 2,000-watt incandescent lamp and has a slide size of 4 × 5 inches.
(d) The EMF-25 Scene Machine has a 2,500-watt HMI lamp for greater intensity. Photos courtesy The Great American Market.

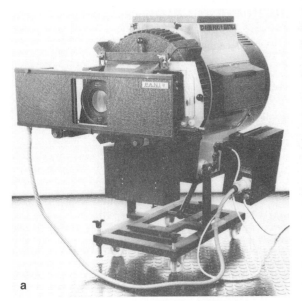

a

b

c

d

Pani projectors are distributed in this country by Production Arts Lighting. Three incandescent-lamp projectors are available: the 2,000-watt BP2 (approx. 52,000 lumens), the 2,500-watt BP 2500 Halogen, and the 5,000-watt BP5 (approx. 130,000 lumens). Arc-lamp projectors are available in three sizes also: the 1,200-watt BP1,2/HMI (approx. 110,000 lumens), the 4,000-watt BP4/HMI (approx. 410,000 lumens), and the high-power 6,000-watt BP6 Gold (approx. 850,000 lumens). All take slides that are 18cm by 18cm (roughly 7 by 7 inches). Remote-control slide changers holding fifteen slides, film loop machines, effects attachments, and a lightning generator are optional equipment. Lenses for all but the BP6 Gold are available with focal lengths from 60cm (8-degree beam spread) to 13.5cm (60-degree beam spread). Two zoom lenses are also available. The BP6 Gold offers eleven lenses having beam spreads from 8 degrees to a wide 71 degrees.

The German Reiche and Vogel projector was for a long time the only very-high-powered scene projector available in this country. The 2,000- and 5,000-watt projectors take a 13cm by 13cm slide, while a larger unit accepts an 18cm by 18cm slide. The usual lenses and optional equipment are available.

**Large-Format Slide Production**    Slides for large-format projectors are much more expensive than the 35mm size, the glass alone being several times the cost of a 35mm slide. If transparencies are used, they are normally sandwiched between two pieces of glass held together in a metal frame. Common sizes are 4 by 5 inches, 5 by 5 inches, and 7 by 7 inches. Photographic production houses can make either black-and-white or color transparencies from any original material in any size desired. Such slides are expensive and take time to produce—two factors that must always be allowed for. Of course, it is possible to transfer design work directly onto the clear glass slides of large-format slide projectors. Rosco manufactures a transparent dye called Colorine designed to be used on glass.

## OTHER PROJECTORS

Many theatrical effects can be created using the foregoing lens projectors and available accessories. There are, however, a number of more specialized types of projectors whose effects range from shadow projection to the projection of ultraviolet light.

**Shadow Projection**    A basic instrument for straight-line shadow projection, which has seen theatrical use for many years, is the *Linnebach projector* (Figure 19–11). Named after its inventor, Adolphe Linnebach, this projector is simply a large metal housing containing a lamp. Along the edge of the open side of the housing is a slot to hold the slide.

Being such a simple device, the Linnebach projector can be homemade. The most important part of the projector is the lamp, whose socket should be mounted in such a manner as to allow adjustment towards and away from the slide. The lamp itself must be high-intensity with the filament remaining

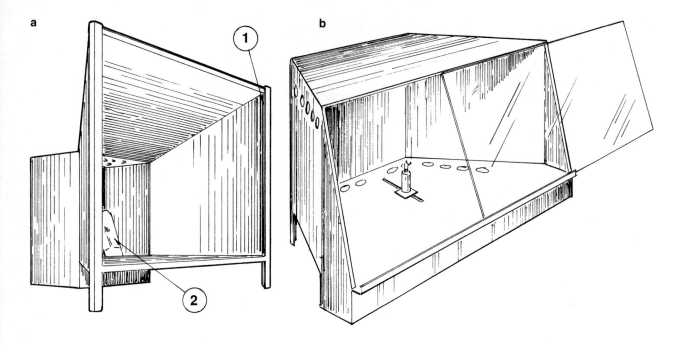

### Figure 19–11
The Linnebach Projector

(a) This simple instrument's key components are:
(1) Slide holder.
(2) Concentrated-filament lamp.
(b) A low-voltage, high-intensity Linnebach. A small, specially built shadow projector using a small source for a sharp projection.

as small as possible. This indicates a low-voltage source such as General Electric's 24-volt FCS quartz lamp. The smaller the filament, the clearer the image.

**The Overhead Projector** The most unusual instrument in the lens projector category is the overhead projector (Figure 19–12). Its large slide deck (about 12 by 12 inches) is a translucent, horizontal surface with the light source underneath. After passing through a vertically mounted objective lens system, the slide image is redirected by a mirror onto the projection surface.

The large area of the slide deck permits hand-painted slides. The photographic process can be omitted, saving time and money. In addition, the horizontal position of the slide deck provides the opportunity of adding movement to the image. Animation is possible using such techniques as moving transparent film across the slide deck, agitating a shallow transparent dish of colored dyes in oil or water, or blowing smoke across the deck.

The overhead projector is not as efficient as a regular lens projector, but because of its wide-angle objective lens system it can be located close to a screen. It is best for rear-projection because an operator is required. Theatrical use is limited due to the low intensity of its light.

**The Opaque Projector** As its name implies, the slide of an opaque projector does not have to be transparent. The material to be projected is reflected by mirrors into the objective-lens system and projected onto a screen. Due to low intensity of the image, the opaque projector is impractical for stage use. However, it is an invaluable tool for the cartooning and painting of stage scenery. A rendering of the painted scenery can be projected onto a drop and readily copied.

**Video Projection**    The television or video projector is a complex and highly specialized piece of equipment that is capable of projecting a video or live televised image. Large-scale video projection equipment has been available for a number of years, but it remains extremely expensive. The problem is simply one of achieving enough image intensity for stage production. The system shown in Figure 19–13 doubles the light output of a single projector to produce 1,500 lumens (a typical 750-watt spotlight lamp delivers 15,000 lumens).

**Effect Projection**    Effect projection can be achieved by using one of a variety of effects projectors or by attaching an effects module to the front of an ellipsoidal reflector spotlight.

Rosco and GAM manufacture animation motor units that can achieve variable speeds and be remotely controlled (Figure 19–14). Animation discs with various patterns create a good sense of movement and can be used in conjunction with gobo projection.

Recently developed automated fixtures, such as Clay Paky's Super Scan Zoom and Cyberlight from High End Systems and Lightwave Research, fall under the category of effect projectors (Figure 19–15). These are both moving mirror units with remote control over an amazing variety of effects and light qualities. Twelve control channels are needed to control the various

**Figure 19–12**
The Overhead Projector

Shown below left is Buhl's Series 202 overhead art projector. It has a high-intensity 1,000-watt lamp for throws of up to forty feet. Photo courtesy Buhl Optical Company.

**Figure 19–13**
Video Projection

Shown below right is the Provision 1500 dual video projection system. The two projectors working together deliver a brightness level of 1,500 lumens. Photo courtesy Spectrel International.

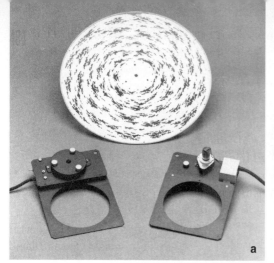

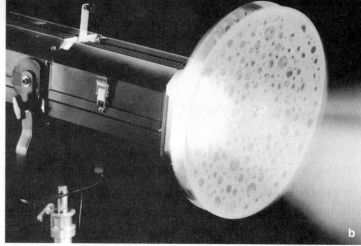

**Figure 19–14**
**Effect Wheels**

(a) Rosco's Animation Effect System offers fixed or variable-speed motor units with several animation discs to choose from. It can be mounted in the color frame of any standard 6-inch instrument. Photo courtesy Rosco.
(b) The Gam Spin/FX has a variable speed double-disc drive using two discs. Photo courtesy The Great American Market.

**Figure 19–15**
**Automated Fixture Effects Projection**

(a) The Cyberlight from High End Systems is an automated fixture effects projector. It has a dual, rotating gobo system; a fixed dichroic color wheel as well as a color mixing system; variable frost and diffusion; and a multi-image prism. It uses a 1,200-watt MSR arc lamp with a color temperature of 5600 degrees. Photo courtesy High End Systems, Inc.
(b) The Super Scan Zoom from Clay Paky offers similar features. It has two rotatable prisms and burns a 1,200-watt HMI arc lamp. Photo courtesy Clay Paky.

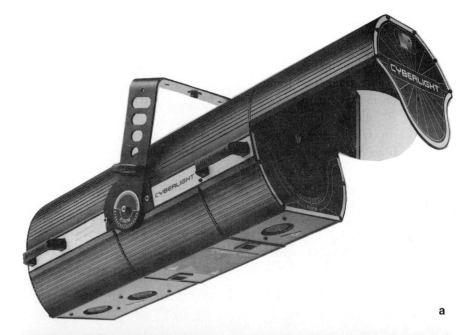

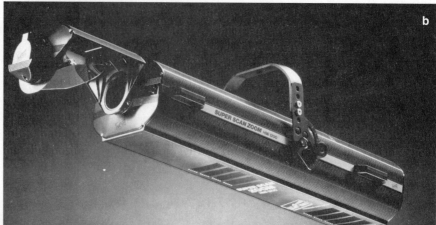

functions of the Super Scan Zoom; the Cyberlight requires twenty-one channels. Both instruments are big and heavy; the Super Scan Zoom is nearly five feet long and weighs in at a hefty 100 pounds. It has a 1,200-watt arc lamp, and the zoom feature provides beam spreads from 8 to 16 degrees. Due to internal color mixing, an infinite variety of color is available. It can project beams of light consisting of four colors, two concentric colors, or a rainbow effect. It provides sixteen gobo pattern combinations and includes variable-speed pattern rotation. It has two variable-speed rotating prisms that greatly add to the repertoire of effects.

**Gobo Projection**     A gobo is a sheet of highly heat-resistant material (usually stainless steel) from which some shape, pattern, or design has been cut (Figure 19–16). When placed at the gate of an ellipsoidal reflector spotlight, the pattern is projected by the lenses onto any appropriate surface.

Gobo projection is an important theatrical design tool. Gobos may be projected as sharp-edged, distinct patterns or may be thrown out of focus to create texture. Many textural qualities can be achieved with the large variety of templates available. Furthermore, gobos can be rotated at variable speeds to create moving texture. Rosco manufacturers a gobo rotator and GAM offers the TwinSpin, which rotates two patterns in opposition to each other (Figure 19–17). Both fit into the drop-in iris slot of a 6-inch ellipsoidal reflector spotlight.

Commercial equipment houses sell gobos in a variety of designs; some are realistic, but most are abstract patterns. Catalogs are available from Rosco and GAM. Custom gobos can be made from any design at a reasonable cost. Long-lasting glass gobos can also be manufactured, but are quite expensive.

a

b

**Figure 19–16**
Gobo Projection

(a) Shown are several of the many gobo patterns available from GAM. Photo courtesy The Great American Market. (b) This is a photograph of Rosco's "Realistic Leaves" gobo template and the image it projects. Photo courtesy Rosco Laboratories, Inc.

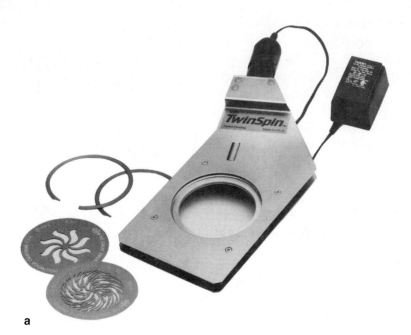

a

b

**Figure 19–17**
Gobo Rotators

(a) Shown is the GAM TwinSpin, a variable-speed pattern rotator. The patterns rotate in opposition to each other. It fits into the drop-in iris slot of a 6-inch ellipsoidal. Photo courtesy The Great American Market.
(b) Rosco's gobo rotator takes a single gobo and is available with fixed- or variable-speed motors. Photo courtesy Rosco Laboratories, Inc.

Patterns can be home-designed and cut from heavy aluminum foil or the bottom of a cheap tin pie plate. An especially useful effect is clouds cut from foil, which can be wrinkled slightly to give out-of-focus soft edges. Unfortunately, gobos made from such materials do not last long under the high temperatures created at the gate of an ellipsoidal.

**Laser Projection**     The term *laser* is an acronym of *light amplification by stimulated emission of radiation.* Laser light is unique because it consists of a single, in-phase wavelength of light. In the relatively few years since their development, lasers have found hundreds of uses, ranging from surgical tools to scanning bar codes at the supermarket. Lasers in the theatre have been used primarily for effects, one the most popular being Tinker Bell in *Peter Pan.* Low-power lasers are harmless but their light output is normally insufficient for stage use. Class II lasers (power up to 1 milliwatt) are usually bright enough, but can cause eye damage if improperly used. Higher-power Class III lasers can be extremely dangerous and their use is carefully regulated. Three-dimensional projections in space, called *holograms,* can be achieved by laser projection. Lasers and their related control equipment are expensive to purchase or rent.

**Ultraviolet Projection**     Ultraviolet light is not visible to the human eye, but it causes certain materials to glow brightly or "fluoresce." Startling and exotic stage effects can be created with the use of ultraviolet light and fluorescent materials. For many years, the best source of ultraviolet light was the carbon arc follow spot equipped with a U-V filter. Today, companies such as Los Angeles's Wildfire manufacture long-throw ultraviolet lighting fixtures as well as fluorescent paints and materials (Figure 19–18).

## PRACTICALS

Practicals refer to onstage, working light sources such as lanterns, lamps, fireplaces, or candles. The design of practicals is the responsibility of the scenic designer and the property department. The wiring and maintenance of such units is the responsibility of the electrics department. Their use is sure to be a concern of the lighting designer. Playwrights or scene designers specify the use of practicals for any of several reasons, including these:

1. The particular light given off by a practical enhances the desired mood of a scene.
2. The use of a practical indicates time of day, season, or time period.
3. Practicals help reinforce the reality of a scene or location.

### FIRE EFFECTS

Often prohibited by fire codes, open fires on the stage are rarely convincing and are difficult to control. However, all too often the demands of a script force the designer to put a fire in full view of the audience.

**Hearth Fires**    If no flames are required from a hearth fire, a glow from lamps buried among burnt logs and scraps of color media will do nicely. If flames must be shown, several options are available. An old stage method that works well from a distance is to shine light on thin streamers of chiffon or China silk as they are blown upward by a small fan. A light smoke effect aids in the illusion. A slowly rotating drum covered with crumpled foil and

**Figure 19—18**
Ultra-Violet Projection

(a) Shown is the WF 400 Flood, a 400-watt blacklight special effects projector.
(b) The WF 250 Effects Lighting Fixture. Photos courtesy Wildfire, Inc.

lit with low-wattage MR-16 or R-type lamps can be convincing. The drum, light sources, and motor can be partially concealed by logs.

Electronic options include flicker generators or a random chase effect programmed into the control system. Flicker generators are available from a number of companies and can produce a fairly realistic effect.

**Torches and Lanterns**    Torches are particularly difficult to simulate. If actual flame is possible, a can of Sterno mounted in the top of the torch works well. *Liquid fuel must never be used.*

Lanterns actually burning oil must never be used on the stage. To begin with, their use is strictly against all fire rules and insurance regulations. An extreme hazard is presented by their use; in the case of an accident, the stage becomes flooded with blazing oil. Fortunately, oil lanterns conventionally have glass chimneys that can be realistically smoke-stained to hide a small lightbulb. If the lantern needs to be carried about, a flashlight battery can be hidden in the base of the lantern (Figure 19–19).

Small lamps can be colored by using Colorine, a commerical transparent dye manufactured by Rosco. Always test the color first. Amber works well, and good results can also be achieved by mixing various colors.

**Candles**    Unlike oil lanterns, candles, which usually extinguish themselves when dropped, are permissible on many stages if properly handled. In some locations they must be encased in transparent mica shields. Candles that self-extinguish when tipped are available commercially. Local fire authorities should be consulted if there is any doubt concerning the legality of using candles onstage. In no case should candles be placed near draperies or other easily flammable materials.

Even if the use of candles is allowed, they probably should be avoided. Their bright light, and particularly their flickering in any air current, can be most distracting for the audience. Very effective simulation can be accom-

**Figure 19–19**
Practicals

An actor uses a practical oil-type lantern that is illuminated by a battery and a small flashlight lamp.

plished with a small battery and lamp or pencil flashlight hidden in a white paper tube. In addition, Rosco and others make quite convincing flicker candles. Complete candles are available, or just the flame module can be purchased for custom work.

## LIGHTING FIXTURES

Chandeliers, wall sconces, table lamps, and similar household lighting fixtures generally offer no problems except for the wattage of the lamps actually used in them. Such fixtures should never be depended on to produce all the light that seems to emanate from them. For proper actor visibility, additional illumination must be provided by stage lighting instruments. This is particularly true when the fixtures have bulbs visible to the audience. If at all bright, they create a most annoying, even blinding, glare. Bare bulbs must always be of extremely low wattage and even then may have to be dimmed. Little usable light will emanate from such fixtures, so the additional stage instruments become doubly important.

If lamp bulbs are shielded by shades, the glare is hidden and extra-large-wattage lamps may be used to give a more realistic effect. Such shades must be quite opaque, or they can be lined with brown paper. An additional baffle over the bulb may be necessary to prevent an unsightly hot spot on the walls and ceilings of a box set.

One rule to remember is that practical lamps should be controlled at the dimmer board. Never allow an actor to switch on a major motivating practical and expect the light board operator to be able to realistically support it. It simply does not work. Work with actors to cover the action of switching practicals on and off, teaching them to hold the moment until the stage lighting responds.

## SPECIAL EFFECTS

Uses of light that are not directly involved in lighting the actor or illuminating the scene are grouped in the category of *special effects*. Examples include explosions, fires, ghosts, and strobe light. Working out special effects is almost always enjoyable but can take a great deal of time. They should never be left to the end as an afterthought.

## MOON AND STARS

Creating a believable moon and stars is not as easy as it might seem. If the background is a cloth drop or cyclorama, a good moon can be made by cutting the desired shape—fully round or crescent—into a large sheet of thin material such as cardboard or plywood. This is then placed against the back of the drop and a spotlight is focused on the cutout from the rear. For front-projection, a gobo or effects machine can be used. A good full moon can be created by using a Fresnel to form the outer edge in conjunction with an iris ellipsoidal forming an inner disk.

Stars can be quite effective, but are tricky to handle. Even tiny "Italian" lights appear as great blobs of light against a dark sky. It is possible, however, to tape the bulb so that only the very tip of the envelope is exposed. If a dark blue or black scrim is hung a few feet downstage of the sky-drop, it will help cut down excessive brightness and help to hide the wiring to the star bulbs.

Another method of creating a good star field is to punch small holes in a black drop and shine light on a white bounce drop located upstage. If a shimmer curtain is placed between the star field and the bounce drop, a wonderful twinkling effect can be achieved.

**Fiber Optics**   By far the best stars are created by using fiber optics. If a light source is located at one end of a tiny thread of glass, it will be conveyed the length of the thread and be emitted with little loss of intensity. Bundles of these threads can be sewn onto a drop with their ends arranged to create a wonderful star field. The drawback to fiber optics is their expense.

## LIGHTNING

Lightning in various forms is called for by many scripts. It can be produced by several methods depending on the desired effect. A convincing display of forks of light springing from the sky is most difficult. However, distant effects can be achieved by either gobo or slide projection. Fortunately, it is usually sufficient to present only the great bursts of high illumination that are the result of a lightning bolt. Such flashes of light can be achieved by arc strikers, strobes, flashbulbs, or photoflood lamps.

Use of an arc striker is an old, but quite effective, theatrical method of producing lightning effects. The rapid striking and breaking contact of an arc source similar to an arc welder gives off a bright burst of light. There is some noise generated, and the light from an arc strike is bright enough to blind. Make sure that the arc source itself is shielded from onlookers.

Today's strobe lights can be very bright and remotely controlled. Many companies—including Diversitronics, AV-PRO, and Lightwave Research—manufacture high-intensity strobe units, most with xenon arc sources (Figure 19–20).

Large photoflash bulbs, although fairly expensive, create a wonderfully bright burst of light. The larger lamps can be mounted in homemade housings to eliminate unwanted spill and hung over-stage. Smaller lamps can easily be placed about the stage and hidden by properties or scenery.

A final method is to switch rapidly on and off a number of intense sources. Momentary contact switches or a control board's "bump buttons" work well for the switching. To be effective, lamps need to have small filaments that respond quickly. This indicates low-voltage sources. However, 120-volt photoflood lamps such as the medium screw base R-32 can be quite effective. Since the color temperature of lightning is very high, it is best to choose lamps with color temperatures over 5,000 degrees Kelvin.

### EXPLOSIONS AND FLASHES

To produce explosive flashes from offstage, the same general techniques can be applied as were suggested for lightning. Sound can be added as appropriate. But, if the script calls for these effects to take place onstage, in view of the audience, a *flash pot* is necessary.

A flash pot is a device that ignites a highly explosive powder called *flash powder*. Available from special effects supply houses, flash powder was once used as a light source for still photography. Figure 19–21 shows one of several flash pot systems available from reputable manufacturers such as Luna Tech, JEM Pyrotechnics, and SFX Design. Use of homemade flash pots is illegal and extremely dangerous.

### SMOKE, FOG, AND HAZE

Dry ice and smoke machines have been used in the theatre for many years to create effects intended to enhance the mood of a scene. The recent popularity of using smoke and haze in the air to accentuate light beams has led to the development of newer and safer methods of production.

**Figure 19–20**
**Strobe Light**

(a) Shown is the DK-56Q-DMX Strobe Cannon from Diversitronics. It allows for variable rate and intensity.
(b) The 1500-DMX Xenon Strobe light distributes a great deal of intensity over a large area. Photos courtesy Diversitronics, Inc.

## Figure 19–21
### Flash Pot System

Shown are photographs of the Pyropak concussion mortar and a two-channel, six-circuit controller. While the concussion mortar is designed for maximum report volume, Luna Tech manufactures several devices for various effects. Photos courtesy Luna Tech, Inc.

**Dry Ice Fog**     As the name implies, dry ice acts more like fog than smoke, in that it tends to cling to the floor and creep along at low levels. Machines to produce dry ice fog are easily and cheaply built or can be purchased from various theatrical suppliers (Figure 19–22). Solid carbon dioxide (dry ice) changes from its solid state to a vapor without becoming a liquid. The rapidity of the change is increased if the dry ice is exposed to hot water.

A 55-gallon drum, an electric immersion heater like those used in home hot-water heaters, and a wire basket to suspend the dry ice are all that is needed to make a dry ice fog machine. When the water is hot, dry ice is dropped in, producing a good deal of fog. This fog can be directed over a short distance by using flexible dryer hose connected to a vent in the lid of the 55-gallon drum.

Such fog gives a splendid effect, although it dissipates rather rapidly. When the dry ice is exposed to the water, it does make a loud bubbling noise. Avoid dry ice burns by wearing gloves when handling.

### Safety Practice

Flash pots are extremely dangerous. Serious injury can result if they are misused. Use only the safe, commercially available flash pot systems—and always follow the directions carefully. Never fire a flash pot close to flammable materials or to people.

Some chemicals and materials that in the past were commonly used in the theatre have been found to be unhealthy. Asbestos is one of these, and another is ammonium chloride (sal ammoniac), used to produce smoke onstage. The use of any substance except pure ammonium chloride is harmful to lungs and should be discontinued. In addition, even pure ammonium chloride must never be heated in contact with metal.

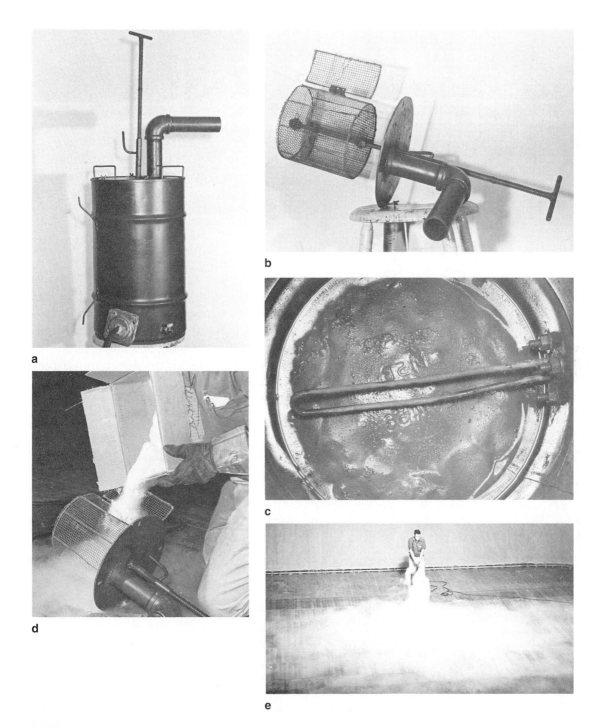

**Figure 19—22**
Dry Ice Fog Machine

(a) Assembled fog machine.
(b) Top removed showing dry ice basket on end of the plunger.
(c) View into the tank revealing electric heating element to heat water.
(d) Loading basket with crushed dry ice. Note that gloves are being used.
(e) The plunging of the ice into hot water produces a blanket of fog. Photos courtesy Richard Thompson.

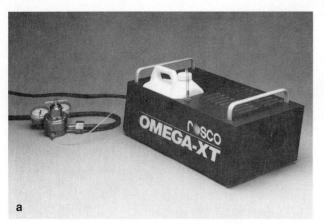

**Figure 19–23**
Smoke/Fog Machines

(a) This is Rosco's Omega-XT Fog Machine. It can produce a variety of fog effects, has a remote control with a timing mechanism, and uses Rosco fog fluid. Photo courtesy Rosco Laboratories, Inc.
(b) Shown are the ZR20 Mk 2 Fog Generator, the J1 Mk2 Smoke Machine, and the JEM Fogger Mk 3; all from JEM. Photos courtesy JEM Smoke Machine Co. Ltd.

**Smoke/Fog Machines** Several manufacturers make very fine portable machines that produce smoke by heating up a special liquid called *fog juice*. The mist tends to rise, but can be kept to the ground similar to dry ice fog by using an attachment that cools the smoke. Plastic hose hidden about the stage is a good way to make the smoke appear wherever wanted. Smoke/fog machines are available in several models varying in the density or quantity of smoke delivered over a period of time. All have the capacity for remote control and some are quieter than others (Figure 19–23).

**Haze Machines** The difference between a smoke machine and a haze machine is that the latter uses either liquid nitrogen or cracked oil to create a long-lasting haze in the air. Haze is not as dense as smoke and does not dissipate as quickly. Hazers are favored for concerts, which are often performed outside under poorly controlled conditions. Hazers are manufactured in a variety of types and are more expensive than either dry ice or smoke machines.

**Controlling Smoke** Anyone using smoke of any nature on the stage is frequently faced with the problem of preventing it from flowing or blowing to where it is not wanted. Heavy fog that tends to hug the stage floor may easily spill over the apron into the auditorium—a touch that is seldom appreciated by the audience (not to mention an orchestra).

The lighter-than-air smoke that rises is subject to the slightest breeze or draft. A ventilator at the top of the stage house may draw it swiftly upward or a cross-draft may set up unwanted eddies and swirls. An exhaust fan that evacuates stale air from the auditorium can bring the smoke billowing into the house.

Each theatre and auditorium will affect smoke and fog in a different manner. The only way to discover how best to use these effects in a given space is to experiment in that facility under conditions that are as close to performance as possible.

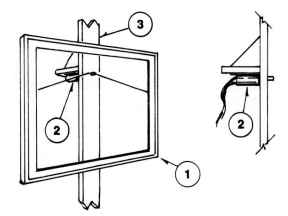

**Figure 19—24**
Electrically Triggered Effects

(1) Picture frame in place.
(2) Solenoid coil mounted on rear of picture batten.
(3) Picture batten. In its off position the spring-loaded pin is extended through the batten to hold the picture frame in place. When current is sent into the coil the pin withdraws and the picture falls.

## ELECTRICALLY TRIGGERED EFFECTS

Designers and technicians are constantly searching for new methods of creating stage illusions. Breakaway properties, pictures falling off the wall, or any number of magical occurrences can be achieved with the help of a device called an *electrical solenoid*.

The magnetic power of the solenoid coil can be used to withdraw the support of a picture on the wall or as a trigger for any other breakaway (Figure 19–24). When a current is passed through the coil of the solenoid it becomes an electromagnet that draws the spring-loaded center pin into the coil. Upon breaking the circuit, the pin is released with considerable force. Either action can be used to trigger a breakaway.

# STAGE LIGHTING PRACTICE: THE LIGHT PLOT AND PRODUCTION

## 20

We now come to a discussion of the lighting designer's basic communication tool: the light plot. The purpose of a light plot is to convey to the production electrician exactly how and where each lighting fixture is to be hung. The plot normally specifies color, circuiting, control, and related information concerning each individual instrument. A great deal of time, preparation, and thought goes into this plot. It represents the lighting designer's "working drawings." Creating a light plot is exacting work, for there is little time in the theatre to remedy any serious mistakes.

### DESIGN DECISIONS

The lighting designer must make many decisions concerning type and position of instruments, color filtering, and dimmer readings. Before going into the specifics of plotting the lights, however, it would be prudent to review the following all-important design considerations: instrumentation, angle and direction, color, and control (Figure 20–1).

### CHOICE OF INSTRUMENT

As previously noted, a particular stage lighting instrument is chosen because it comes closest to satisfying the three requirements of intensity, coverage, and quality of light (Figure 20–2).

**Ellipsoidal Reflector Spotlights**    Adjustable beam spread and shaping, high intensity, and variable quality of light make this instrument the most valuable to the lighting designer. While an ERS is the logical choice for front-of-house applications, this versatile unit also serves well backstage and should be considered along with the Fresnel and PAR fixture.

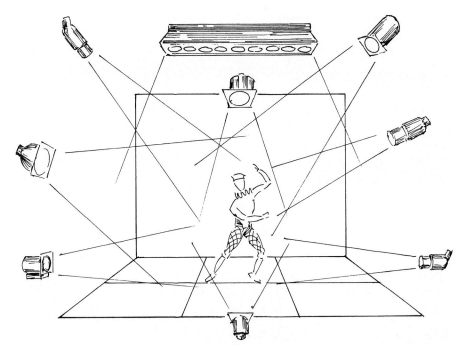

**Figure 20—1**
**Design Decisions**

*Choice of Instrument*—Does it provide the proper quality of light, control possibilities, and beam size/intensity?
*Choice of angle and direction*—Does is create the desired mood and visibility?
*Choice of Control*—Is it used on its own or can it work with others?
*Choice of Color*—Does it provide the proper mood, work with the costumes and scenery, and offer the necessary contrast?

**Fresnels**    These instruments deliver a soft light whose beams blend very easily and therefore are ideal for short throws and upstage areas of a box set. Due to their variable beam spread capability, Fresnels can be used over a wide range of throw distances. The 6-inch Fresnel, lamped from 500 to 1,000 watts, is effective at distances upward of 20 feet. The 8-inch, with lamps up to 2,000 watts, can be useful up to 40 feet. Attached barn doors allow for reasonably good beam shaping. The soft light of a candle, the quality of dusk or an overcast sky, or the scattered, almost shadowless illumination from fluorescent tubes can be reproduced with a Fresnel.

**PAR Fixtures and Beam Projectors**    The light from these instruments cannot be shaped, but their near-parallel rays come closest to those of the sun. This quality can serve as a motivational source, while Fresnel and ERS light act as fill or bounce. The PAR fixture has a lens that breaks up the light, softening the edge of its oval beam. Yet it still delivers a sharp and intense light, harsh in quality. PAR fixtures make good back-lights and deliver a nice quality of light for dance.

**Automated Fixtures**    These remotely controlled instruments produce an intense light that outshines the brightest ERS and PAR fixtures. While their theatrical application is just beginning to be realized, it is obvious that they are here to stay. They make superb specials or can act as intense and flexible side-lighting instruments. Built-in gobo patterns and color versatility can instantaneously act to change the texture and mood of a scene. Their flexibility alone makes them a light source worth considering.

### Figure 20–2
Choice of Instrument

(a) Ellipsoidal Reflector Spotlight
(b) Fresnel
(c) PAR Fixture
(d) Beam Projector

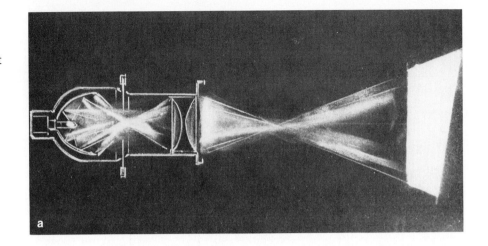

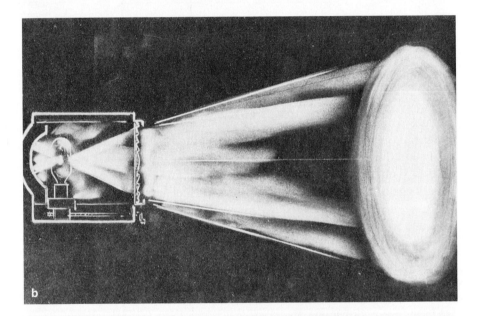

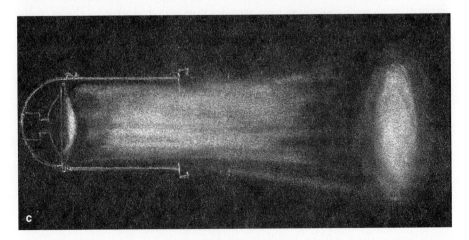

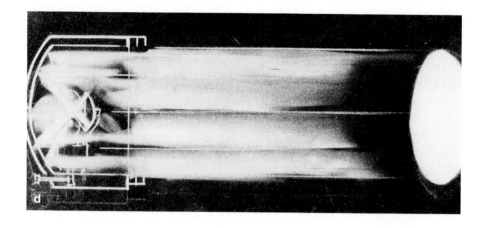

## CHOICE OF ANGLE AND DIRECTION

Angle and direction, along with color, are probably the two most difficult choices for the beginning designer to make.

**Front-Light**     The purpose of two front-lights at various angles to each other, rather than a single unit straightaway, is to add dimension to the actor's body and face. As the angle of front-light is lowered, it tends to flatten features. As the angle is raised, features become sharper, with deeper and deeper shadows. Remember that front-light provides visibility more than any other direction of light.

**Side-Light**     Whether it is a bit frontal or straight out of the wings, side-light offers an exciting direction for both variety and revelation of form. The low-angled side-light commonly used in dance lighting evenly lights the entire height of the body. This angle can be a problem when used in dramatic productions because its light often over-illuminates the scenery. A slightly higher angled side (from 30 to 60 degrees) is often used for theatrical productions. The designer can begin to use richer and more expressive colors in side-light in order to establish a motivational source or simply to set the mood of a scene.

**Back-Light**     Primarily used to create three-dimensionality, back-light offers the additional benefit of separating the actor from the background. Colored light from the back is extremely useful in toning the stage floor, and the choice of color can be more aggressive. Back-light textured by means of gobos can be of great help in establishing mood. Compared to frontal distribution, rear gobos are not as noticeable on the actors; yet, they texture the stage floor well, creating a broken light through which the actors move. Back-light angles should be kept between 45 and 60 degrees.

## CHOICE OF COLOR

Confidence in color selection requires experience—experience in traditional theatrical usage, experience in how colors mix with each other, and experience in how particular colors behave onstage. Lighting laboratories and color mix-boxes help, but a lighting designer ultimately must experiment with the real thing. A masterful use of color is the goal of every lighting designer. Achieving that goal takes time.

Careful consideration must first be given to scenic and costume colors. Unless intended, colored light must not significantly alter the true colors of an actor's skin, clothing, or environment.

Developing a visual memory is important to the successful use of color. A lighting designer's most important color resource is a strong visual memory. People remember feelings or color impressions more readily than actual colors.

Try to analyze and choose color by feeling as well as seeing. For instance, consider: How does sunlight feel? And then try to translate the feeling into color. Don't worry so much about what you think sunlight *should* look like. People associate feelings with certain colors. In creating mood, the lighting designer uses color to tap into those feelings.

Another important consideration is the varying colors of an incandescent lamp under different dimmer settings. Throw distance also tends to affect the intensity or saturation of a color; lighting colors appear less saturated over longer throw distances.

## CHOICE OF CONTROL

At the mention of "control" one normally thinks of dimmer levels—however, control also includes the manner in which instruments and dimmers are assigned to channels. If made arbitrarily, such assignments can complicate the process of cue writing and level setting. The designer must be able to anticipate necessary control assignments based on viewing rehearsals, discussions with the director, and anticipated lighting movement needs.

Setting dimmer levels for the first time is a difficult and time-consuming experience, but be assured that it gets easier. There are two ways of working: writing levels "blind," or writing levels live in the theatre. Learning to set levels blind is a valuable process that could someday mean the difference between an adequate and a good lighting design.

When writing blind, cues and dimmer levels are determined several days before you actually see them onstage. You must take time to think through each preset or stage picture: Which sets of instruments should be reading highest and which control areas should take focus? Levels are recorded on a preset sheet (Figure 20–3), using one sheet for each cue. The completed sheets are then given to your board operator and entered into the memory of the control system. (Electronic Theatre Controls [ETC] has developed a software program called ETCEDIT, which allows a designer to write and edit a show on an IBM PC or compatible computer. The program only works with control consoles manufactured by ETC.) The process of writing blind

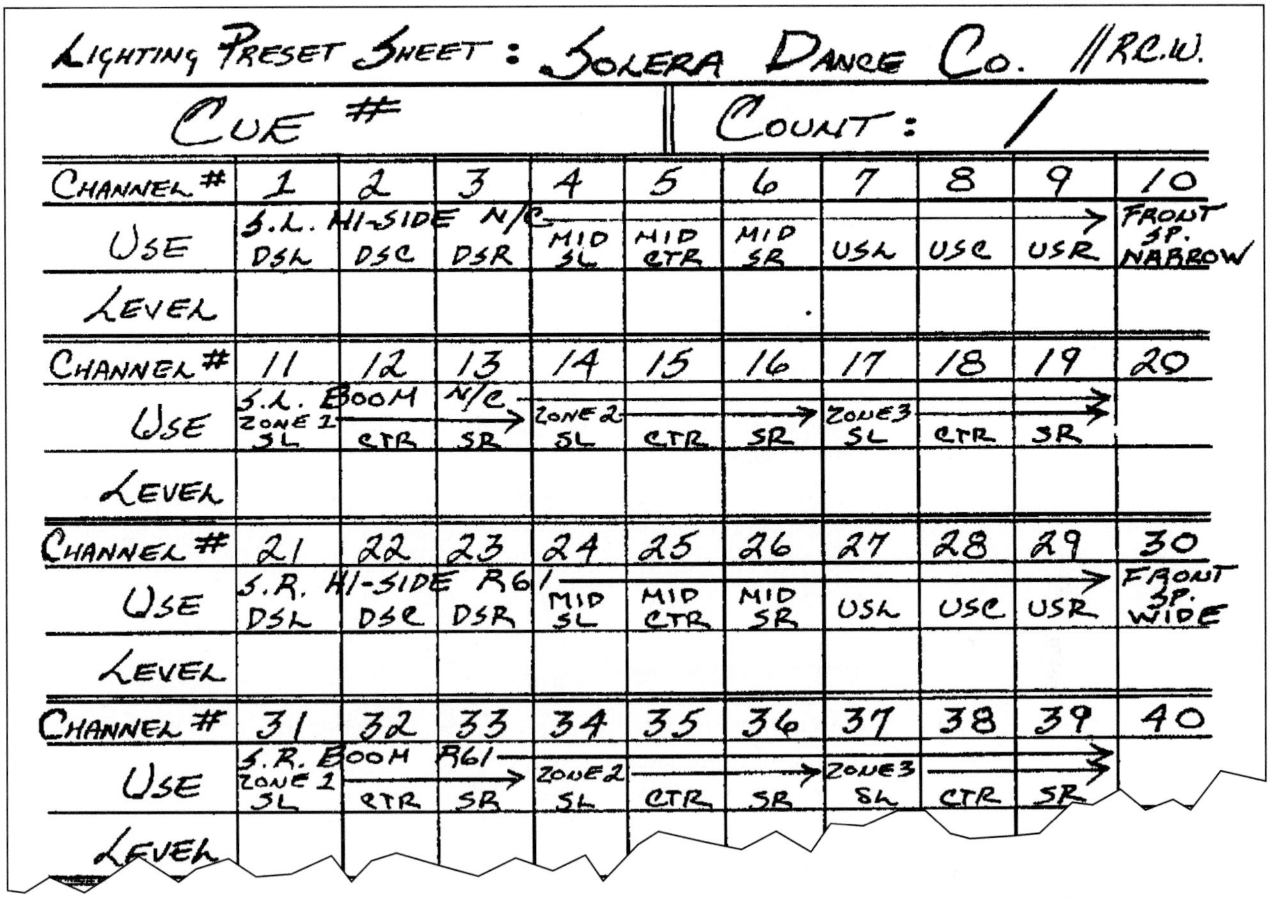

## Lighting Preset Sheet : Solera Dance Co. //R.C.W.

| CUE # | | | | | | COUNT : | | | 1 |
|---|---|---|---|---|---|---|---|---|---|

| CHANNEL # | 1 | 2 | 3 | 4 | 5 | 6 | 7 | 8 | 9 | 10 |
|---|---|---|---|---|---|---|---|---|---|---|
| USE | S.L. HI-SIDE N/C DSL | DSC | DSR | MID SL | MID CTR | MID SR | USL | USC | USR → | FRONT SP. NARROW |
| LEVEL | | | | | | | | | | |
| CHANNEL # | 11 | 12 | 13 | 14 | 15 | 16 | 17 | 18 | 19 | 20 |
| USE | S.L. BOOM N/C ZONE 1 SL | CTR | SR → | ZONE 2 SL | CTR | SR → | ZONE 3 SL | CTR | SR → | |
| LEVEL | | | | | | | | | | |
| CHANNEL # | 21 | 22 | 23 | 24 | 25 | 26 | 27 | 28 | 29 | 30 |
| USE | S.R. HI-SIDE R61 DSL | DSC | DSR | MID SL | MID CTR | MID SR | USL | USC | USR → | FRONT SP. WIDE |
| LEVEL | | | | | | | | | | |
| CHANNEL # | 31 | 32 | 33 | 34 | 35 | 36 | 37 | 38 | 39 | 40 |
| USE | S.R. BOOM R61 ZONE 1 SL | CTR | SR → | ZONE 2 SL | CTR | SR → | ZONE 3 SL | CTR | SR → | |
| LEVEL | | | | | | | | | | |

takes time to learn, but it can result in a better looking product and can cut hours off a lighting rehearsal.

In general, it is best to write and design for the highest dimmer levels to be between 80 and 90 percent. Then, if more light is required, you have room to maneuver. When setting levels, remember that light from two identical sources will be perceived as contrasting when their intensities differ by approximately 15 percent. Depending on the curve of your dimmers, a reading of 20 percent will barely warm the filament, and a reading of 30 percent just begins to produce visible light. Keep in mind the saturation of color filters, for the more saturated filters cut down light transmission significantly.

**Figure 20–3**
**Preset Sheet**

A preset sheet used for recording dimmer levels "blind." It can also function as a designer's cheat sheet.

## THE COLLABORATIVE PROCESS

An attempt has been made throughout this book to emphasize the great importance of collaboration. The lighting designer must be an excellent collaborator because lighting, in the end, unites all of the visual production elements. The significance of superior collaboration skills is heightened by the fact that visual and verbal presentation of lighting ideas is limited by the nature of the medium.

## PRODUCTION COLLABORATION

The very first contact between a director and the designers sets the stage for the collaborative process that follows. The success or failure of this all-important exchange of ideas is determined first and foremost by *attitude*. If the atmosphere surrounding a production team's collaboration is one of acceptance and openness, the process has a good chance of being a positive experience. If such an environment exists and the members of the team become excited by the prospect of shared creation, the experience can be positively exhilarating.

While no formula for success exists, extensive preparation in the form of research coupled with a positive attitude goes a long way. Lighting *storyboards* and *scores* are excellent teaching tools and can be valuable as communication devices.

## THE STORYBOARD

A lighting storyboard consists of a series of sketches illustrating important aspects of a production's intended lighting. A complete storyboard consists of as many sketches as there are major lighting changes in the production. The drawings are often black-and-white value sketches (sometimes referred to as "thumbnail" sketches) and concentrate on the lighting mood or atmosphere of a given scene. Figure 20–4 shows a pair of storyboard-type sketches for a production of *Tosca*. Obviously, a lighting designer's storyboard presentation would take place well after production concept meetings, for a completed scenic design is necessary. On the other hand, the lighting score is a tool that can be useful in early design meetings.

## THE LIGHTING SCORE

Being a "chart" of the lighting, the score is less intimidating than a storyboard for those designers who do not render and draw well. At the same time, the score is capable of presenting more information than a storyboard. As can be seen by the example in Figure 20–5, the top of the score consists of a timeline breakdown of the script. Various concerns and factors affecting the lighting are listed in the left column. The timeline can be constructed in a variety of ways, with the play's acts or scenes making up the most convenient divisions. French scenes can be used for productions requiring a greater number of lighting looks.

The list of design considerations in the left column also varies from production to production, but almost always includes the categories of mood, focus, motivational source, and time of day. Rising and falling action, sense of conflict, brightness level, contrast, color, temperature, and atmospheric conditions are other possibilities. It is recommended that the lighting designer keep the score pictorial (as opposed to verbal), using graphs and color

*Tosca* ACT I S. GRATCH

**Figure 20—4**
**Storyboard Sketches**

Shown are two examples of storyboard sketches from the opera *Tosca* by designer Susan Gratch. Often done as value sketches, they show preliminary lighting ideas.

*Tosca* ACT II S. GRATCH

whenever possible and pictographs instead of words. In this way, the director, as well as the rest of the production team, can "see" the lighting images well before the actual plot is considered.

## THE LIGHT PLOT

The light plot and its accompanying paperwork (the section and hookup or instrument schedule) forms the link between the designer's ideas and the reality of theatrical production. The importance of this piece of paper cannot

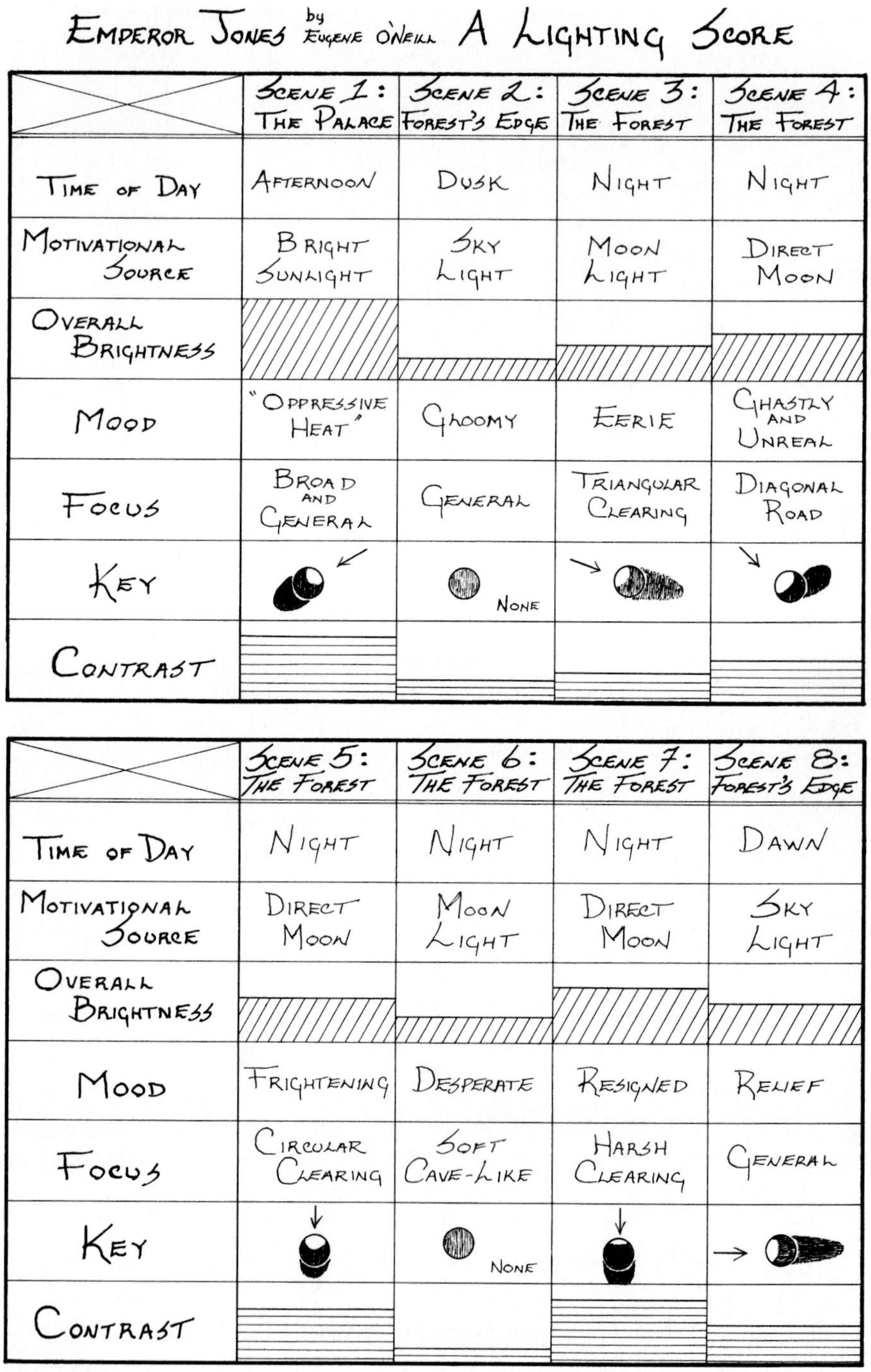

**EMPEROR JONES** by Eugene O'Neill **A LIGHTING SCORE**

| | SCENE 1: THE PALACE | SCENE 2: FOREST'S EDGE | SCENE 3: THE FOREST | SCENE 4: THE FOREST |
|---|---|---|---|---|
| TIME OF DAY | AFTERNOON | DUSK | NIGHT | NIGHT |
| MOTIVATIONAL SOURCE | BRIGHT SUNLIGHT | SKY LIGHT | MOON LIGHT | DIRECT MOON |
| OVERALL BRIGHTNESS | | | | |
| MOOD | "OPPRESSIVE HEAT" | GLOOMY | EERIE | GHASTLY AND UNREAL |
| FOCUS | BROAD AND GENERAL | GENERAL | TRIANGULAR CLEARING | DIAGONAL ROAD |
| KEY | | NONE | | |
| CONTRAST | | | | |

| | SCENE 5: THE FOREST | SCENE 6: THE FOREST | SCENE 7: THE FOREST | SCENE 8: FOREST'S EDGE |
|---|---|---|---|---|
| TIME OF DAY | NIGHT | NIGHT | NIGHT | DAWN |
| MOTIVATIONAL SOURCE | DIRECT MOON | MOON LIGHT | DIRECT MOON | SKY LIGHT |
| OVERALL BRIGHTNESS | | | | |
| MOOD | FRIGHTENING | DESPERATE | RESIGNED | RELIEF |
| FOCUS | CIRCULAR CLEARING | SOFT CAVE-LIKE | HARSH CLEARING | GENERAL |
| KEY | | NONE | | |
| CONTRAST | | | | |

**Figure 20–5**
**Lighting Score**

Shown is an example of a lighting score for a production of *Emperor Jones* by Eugene O'Neill. The lighting score is a means of recording the major lighting looks of a production.

be overstated. It must be 100-percent accurate and complete, so that the "put-in" (hang, circuit, and focus) can proceed in an orderly and rapid fashion. During the process of executing a plot, the designer discovers and remedies many artistic as well as technical problems. Careful and accurate plotting allows this to be accomplished well before the designer sets foot in the theatre.

The following sections cover the process of developing a light plot and executing the design; Chapter 23 delves further into design considerations. A light plot and section for the musical review *Beehive* will be used for illustration purposes (Figure 20–6). The theatre is intimate, with a thrust stage and steep audience rake. Hanging positions over the thrust and audience are created by pipes on 6-foot centers.

## DRAFTING THE PLOT

Whether using a CADD program or drafting by hand, the lighting designer must learn mechanical drawing in order to read and understand scenic draftings as well as execute a lighting plot and section. (If review of the tools and techniques of drafting for the stage is necessary, the reader is referred to Chapter 5.)

The light plot is drawn to $\frac{1}{2}$-inch scale in a manner that allows reproduction through a process known as *blueprinting*. The advantages of *blue-line* reproduction (a variation of blueprinting) are cost and convenience. The disadvantage is that color cannot be reproduced; it would be handy to be able to color-code rather than use some of the current drafting conventions.

The first step in drafting a light plot is to secure a copy of the plan and section of the theatre. Information from these drawings is transferred onto the drafting plates that will soon become light plot and section. Next, details from the scenery ground plan and section are added to the two drawings. Finally, instruments are plotted, color is chosen, and control decisions are made.

---

### LIGHT PLOT ELEMENTS

Working on the premise that some standardization is desirable for any communicative tool, the light plot should include the following elements:

1. A plan of the theatre drawn to scale (preferably $\frac{1}{2}$-inch—*never* $\frac{1}{8}$-inch) showing and labeling all lighting positions
2. A plan of the stage setting drawn to scale in lightweight lines
3. The lighting areas indicated by Roman numerals in heavyweight lines—beginning downstage-left, working stage-right and then upstage
4. Exact instrument placement, type and size, color, and number
5. Title block in the lower right-hand corner; instrument key; instrument annotation key; and color key (if needed)

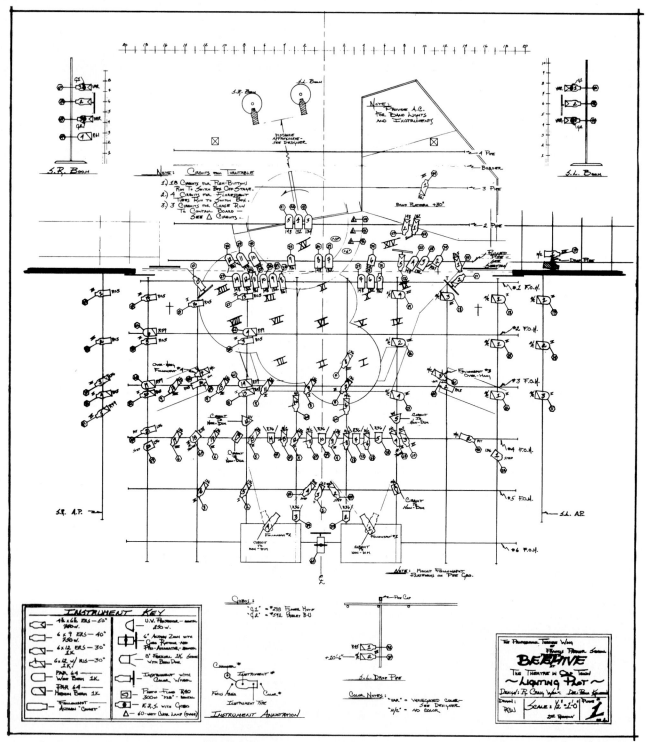

**Figure 20—6**
Light Plot

The ½-inch-scale light plot for a production of *Beehive*, a lively and satiric review of the 1950s' and 1960s' most popular music. The stage thrusts out into a steeply raked and intimate auditorium. See Figure 20–14 for the sectional view.

**Theatre Plan and Section**     A blue-line plan and centerline section, hopefully in $\frac{1}{2}$-inch scale, will be available from the technical director, electrician, or production manager of the theatre. These prints should include all the information needed to draw the theatre plan onto the soon-to-be light plot. However, a theatre plan and section may not show circuits and/or all of the possible light-hanging positions. If this is the case, ask the appropriate producing agent to provide a circuit chart and/or a light-hanging plan. The house will also provide the designer with an up-to-date instrument inventory as well as control specifications. A visit to inspect the theatre is highly recommended.

All rigging for the production should be transferred to the light plot and section. This includes masking, flying scenery and drops, and electric pipes. Critical audience sight points, indicated by a cross, must be included on the lighting plan and section. If drafting by hand, a lighting hanging position is indicated by a single solid line of very light weight (it will later be darkened and made bolder). Each position must be clearly labeled. To save space, it is permissible to show distance to front-of-house positions in a smaller scale, but this deviation should be clearly noted.

Some designers prefer to include a plasterline scale and sometimes an upstage-to-downstage scale in order to facilitate hanging and placement of instruments. The scale for the *Beehive* plot in Figure 20–6 was placed upstage to avoid congestion.

It is advisable to draft the basic lighting plan and section (without instruments) as early as possible in the design process—at least several weeks before the plot deadline. This will allow time to digest the theatre and scenic information as well as save valuable drafting time later.

**Scenery Plan and Section**     The scenic designer should deliver to the lighting designer a copy of the scenery ground plan and section as soon as it is complete. Scenery information transferred to the light plot and section need not be as complete or detailed as on the scenic ground plan. It should only include elements important to the lighting, such as walls, doors, major levels, large pieces of furniture, and so forth. The scenic elements included in the *Beehive* plot are a turntable and wall unit upstage-right, an orchestra platform upstage-left, and the thrust. All this is drafted in lightweight lines so that lighting instruments can be plotted directly over scenery lines.

Plasterline and centerline should be included. If the production requires several sets, the lighting designer may use transparent overlays of each set.

**Instrument Annotation**     One of the several available lighting instrument templates should be used to trace outlines of the various instruments (Figure 20–7). Templates can be ordered in either $\frac{1}{4}$- or $\frac{1}{2}$-inch scale as well as in plan or sectional view. These outlines must be bold enough to stand out from all the other information on the plot. While the lighting instrument should intersect the lighting pipe, the pipe itself should not be drawn through the instrument.

In most situations, instruments are numbered by position, beginning house-right and working house-left. Numbering by position means that all

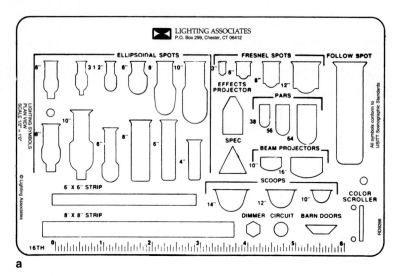

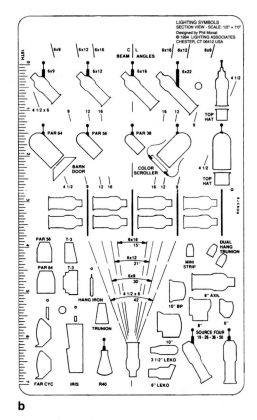

**Figure 20–7**
Lighting Templates

(a) A $\frac{1}{2}$-inch-scale plan view template.
(b) A $\frac{1}{2}$-inch-scale section view template.
Templates courtesy Lighting Associates.

instruments located in each lighting position are numbered consecutively beginning with 1 (Figure 20–6). Some situations, however, may make numbering by position rather confusing (for example, a flexible theatre with a full, overhead lighting grid). In such cases, *all* instruments should be numbered consecutively.

The instrument annotation illustrated in Figure 20–8 is recommended. The instrument number is centered in the rear body of the instrument; the instrument type is indicated by a symbol and located at the barrel position (Figure 20–9); focus area (if used) goes behind the instrument; and the color number is located in front of the lens. In addition, the dimmer or channel number is placed within a hexagon and the circuit number is circled. Both hexagon and circle connect to the rear of the instrument as shown. If the designer does not assign circuits, the circle may be eliminated as in the *Beehive* plot.

**Figure 20–8**
Instrument Annotation

Some designers prefer to place the focus area in front of the instrument, along with the color number.

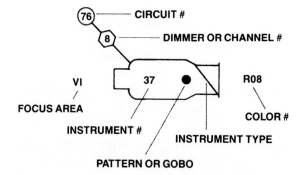

**Instrument and Color Keys**   The instrument key indicates exactly which symbol the designer is using for a specific instrument. This key, which should include wattage as well as beam spread of the instrument, is normally located in the lower left corner of the plate.

The color key explains what numbering and lettering system the designer is using for each brand and type of color medium. For example:

"R" series = Roscolux

800 series = Roscolene

"L" series = Lee Filters

"G" series = GAM Color

**Booms**   A brief discussion about drafting floor stands or booms is necessary at this point. A boom normally consists of a heavy metal base into which is screwed a length of 1¼- or 1½-inch black pipe. Any length of pipe may be used, but booms of any great height must be safely tied off from above. A lighting instrument is then hung off the boom by using a cross-pipe or "side-arm" (Figure 20–10).

A boom can be represented on the light plot in one of two ways:

1.  The boom base is drawn as a circle and located in its proper position on the plan. The pipe is drawn at scaled length and at an angle of 45 to 60 degrees directly out of its base. The various instruments are then shown in relationship to their boom pipe (Figure 20–11a). This is similar to an isometric view.

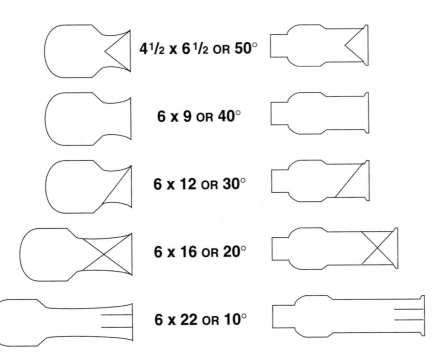

4½ x 6½ OR 50°

6 x 9 OR 40°

6 x 12 OR 30°

6 x 16 OR 20°

6 x 22 OR 10°

**Figure 20–9**
Instrument Types

Use these symbols in the instrument's barrel to indicate beam angle.

**Figure 20–10**
Boom with a Side-Arm

The use of a side-arm allows for easier focus of the instrument.

2. The boom base and pipe are drawn as circles and located in their proper position on the plan. A cross-hatched lighting instrument is drawn in proper relationship to the boom pipe indicating that another view of the instrument appears elsewhere in the plot. An elevation of the boom is then drawn on the side or bottom of the drafting plate and labeled by position name. Instrument specifications are indicated on the elevation (Figure 20–11b; also see Figure 20–6). If a production has a large number of booms, a separate boom plate may be drawn. (*See* Figure 20–13c).

In both methods of plotting boom positions, instrument height(s) must be indicated as in Figures 20–6 and 20–11.

Similar drafting conventions should be used for ladder, box boom, and cove positions where a number of instruments are stacked above each other. Note the drafting for the stage-left drop pipe in the *Beehive* plot.

**Lighting Areas**    As discussed earlier in Chapter 16, lighting areas are determined by the lighting designer, based on several factors: shape and size of the setting, degree of control desired, blocking of the actors, and equipment available. The diameter of the beam of light thrown by a lighting instrument is a function of throw distance and that instrument's beam spread. The beginning designer is wise to make up beam-and-field spread templates for each of the instruments in common use. Such a template, drawn to scale on drafting or tracing paper, can be used as an overlay on a sectional view of the theatre and will quickly show approximate area coverage (Figure 20–12).

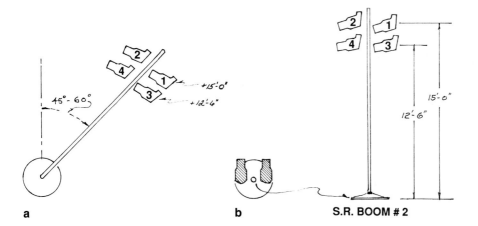

**Figure 20–11**
Representing a Boom
on the Light Plot

(a) The isometric method shows the boom base in its actual position on stage.
(b) The plan and elevation method is often desirable when space on the plan is limited.

S.R. BOOM # 2

a

b

The heavy-weight Roman numerals used as area indicators on the light plot should mark the center of the focus area (Figure 20–6). Roman numerals or letters of the alphabet are suggested in order to keep area numbers distinct from all other numbering on the plot. Circles indicating beam or field spread should *not* be included.

**CADD Light Plots**     Computer-aided design and drafting programs enable a designer to create lighting plots using computer graphics. A new generation of lighting designers is drawing with a mouse rather than a drafting pencil. Architectural firms and much of the entertainment industry are demanding that perspective employees be CADD-literate.

While a number of software programs exist, the two most popular seem to be AutoCad and Generic CAD. Learning to use a CADD program takes time and the software is expensive, but the skill is important for survival in today's highly diverse lighting design field. With access to proper software and equipment, such as a plotter (a mechanical drawing machine capable of drafting a light plot from computer information), the designer need only input the desired lighting instrument information and the system will generate a plot (Figure 20–13) as well as the required paperwork.

**Figure 20–12**
Beam Spread Templates

(a) "Chart-a-Beam" plastic templates available from GAM give spreads for 3½, 4½, and 6-inch ellipsoidals, 6- and 8-inch Fresnels, and PAR-64s. Photo courtesy of The Great American Market.
(b) The lighting designer can make templates using a protractor and drafting paper.

**6 x 12 E.R.S.**
BEAM SPREAD: 16°
FIELD SPREAD: 28°

b

a

**Figure 20–13**
**CADD Plot**

Shown are three pages of a CADD (Computer Assisted Design and Drafting) light plot for a production of *As You Like It* designed by Scott O'Donnell. (a) Over-stage plot.

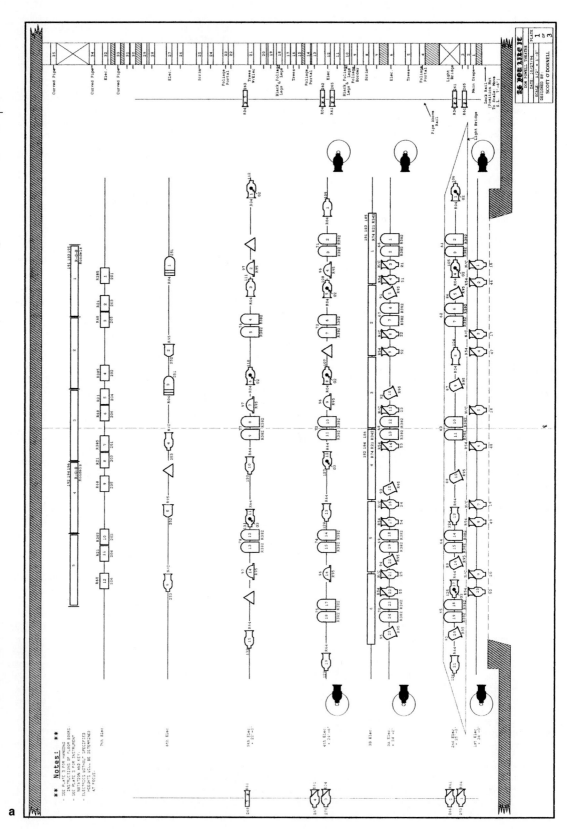

(b) Front-of-house plot.

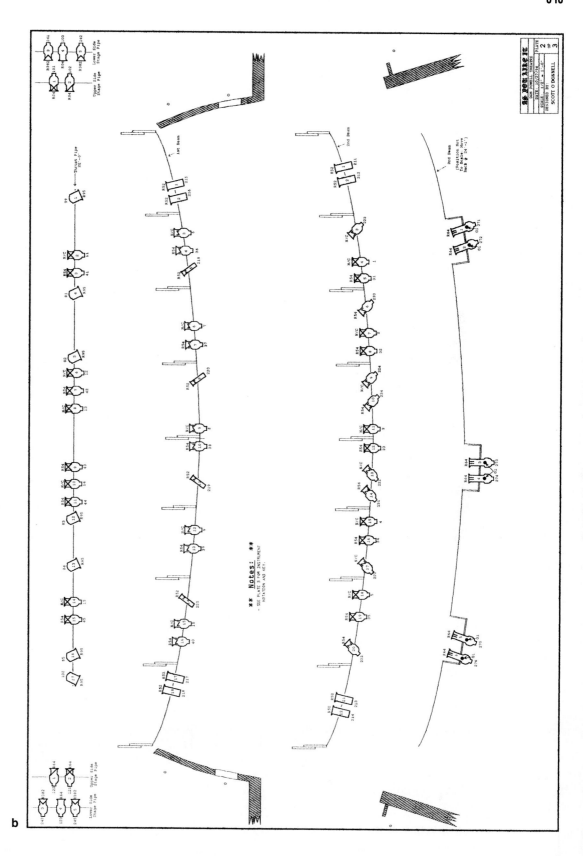

b

(c) Boom plot
and keys.

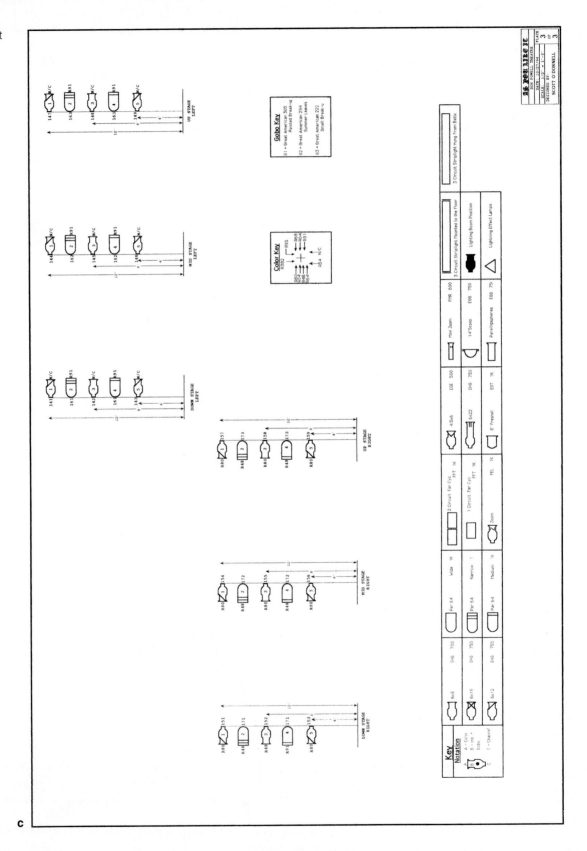

## THE LIGHTING SECTION

A centerline section is an important tool for the lighting designer. The drafting of the section must be completed before lighting instruments are placed on the plot. A section view helps the designer visualize the height and placement of scenery and lighting instruments, thereby improving the accuracy of the light plot. The designer consults the section for vertical sightlines, throw distances, acting levels above or below stage height, and accuracy of lighting angles. Electric trims (height of electric pipes off the stage floor) are determined by using the section (Figure 20–14).

The sectional view is actually a side view with the picture plane being on the centerline. It is as if a large cut was taken through the theatre and auditorium along the centerline and we are looking into the cut surface. If the stage house is drawn on the left-hand side of the drafting plate, we are looking stage-left. If the stage house is on the right-hand side of the drafting plate, we are looking stage-right. Normally only one sectional view is necessary.

It should be understood that the section is primarily a lighting designer's tool. If electric trims are indicated on the plan, the production electrician need never see the section.

As noted earlier, the scene designer provides the lighting designer with a centerline sectional view of the stage that includes horizontal masking at trim height, critical audience sight points, as well as scenery placement. Occasionally various supplementary sectional views are necessary; they can easily and quickly be drafted by the lighting designer.

## THE HOOKUP AND INSTRUMENT SCHEDULE

In most cases, the only paperwork item submitted with the light plot is either a hookup or an instrument schedule. Both pieces of paperwork list anything anyone would ever want to know about each instrument used in the plot. The difference between the two is the order in which they do so.

**The Hookup**     There are two types of hookups: One is arranged by dimmer number and intended for installations that still use a patch panel (left column in the accompanying box); the other is arranged by channel number and used with dimmer-per-circuit systems (right column). Note that items 5 through 9 in both columns contain common information.

As is obvious from Tharon Musser's hookup for *Teddy & Alice* shown in Figure 20–15, all of the information in the accompanying box is not always

**Figure 20–14**
**Lighting Section**

The $\frac{1}{2}$-inch-scale center line section for the *Beehive* light plot shown in Figure 20–6.

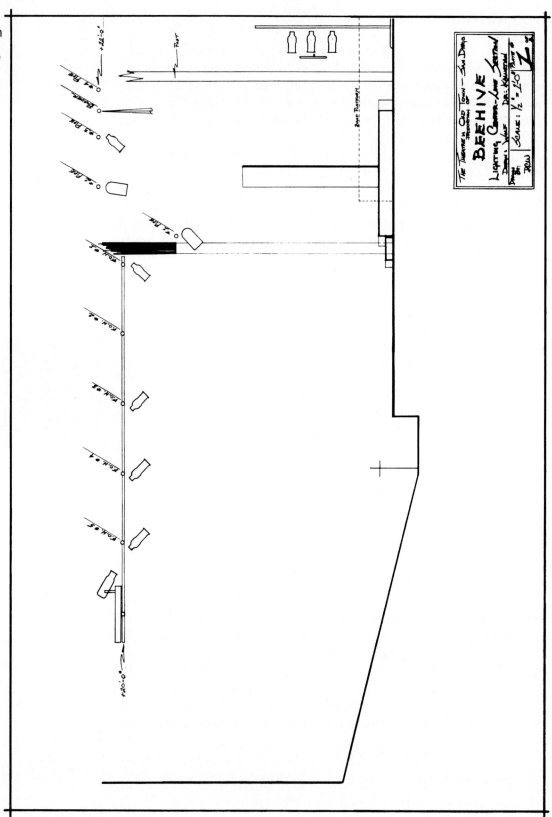

## HOOKUPS

### PATCH PANEL HOOKUP

1. Dimmer number
2. Position name
3. Instrument number
4. Circuit number
5. Instrument wattage
6. Instrument type
7. Color
8. Purpose/focus
9. Remarks

### DIMMER-PER-CIRCUIT HOOKUP

1. Channel number
2. Dimmer/circuit number
3. Position name
4. Instrument number
5. Instrument wattage
6. Instrument type
7. Color
8. Purpose/focus
9. Remarks

necessary. Hookups were originally intended as patching paperwork supplementary to the instrument schedule. With more information included on light plots themselves, a hookup can replace an instrument schedule.

**The Instrument Schedule**   This piece of paperwork lists all instruments by location and instrument number. Its primary use is to provide instrument

**Figure 20—15**
The Hook-up

Shown is one page from the hook-up for the musical *Teddy & Alice*, designed by Tharon Musser.

TEDDY & ALICE — 87 — PAGE 8 OF 9

HOOKUP PALETTE · 152 · 4K. DIMMERS

| CHN | DIM | POSITION & UNIT NUMBER | TYPE | FOCUS | COLOR |
|---|---|---|---|---|---|
| 114 | 132 | NO. 6 ELEC. 3-20 | 6"×16" 750W. L. | BED X·U.C. | 02 |
| 115 | 133 | NEAR COVE · 16 | 6"×16" 1K L.I. | EAGLE | 02 |
| 103 | 134 | NO. 1 GROUND ROW · E | 8'· 12 LT 500W. T-3 | U.S. DROPS | 79 |
| 104 | 135 | NO. 1 GROUND ROW · E | " | " | 67 |
| 105 | 136 | NO. 1 GROUND ROW · E | " | " | 58A |
| 116 | 137 | NO. 1 ELEC. 13 | 6"×16" 750W L.I | · PARTY · ALICE LEE | 65 |
| 117 | 138 | NO. 5 ELEC 12 | 6"×12" 750W. L.I | · WOODS · ALICE LEE | 65 |
| 118 | 139 | SCRIM · STARDROP | #7153-A515 5volt·115amp.CL | STARS · A · | |
| 119 | 140 | SCRIM · STARDROP | " | STARS · B · | |

information that does not appear on the light plot. Information is listed in the following order:

1. Location and instrument number
2. Instrument type
3. Wattage/lamp designation
4. Color number
5. Use/focus area
6. Circuit
7. Dimmer/channel
8. Remarks

## LIGHTING PAPERWORK

Proper planning and the resulting paperwork are critical to a successful design. The best lighting designers are individuals who are creative as well as methodical—character traits not often found together. A variety of types of paperwork have been developed by designers in order to simplify the put-in and the execution of the design. Lighting paperwork and related items include cue sheets and preset sheets, color cut lists, designer "cheat sheets," batten tapes, hanging cardboards, focus charts, and shop orders. Much of this paperwork can be generated by lighting software programs.

**Paperwork Software**    A number of individuals and companies have developed software programs that are intended to ease the lighting designer's paperwork load. Depending on the circumstances of a production, such programs can save the designer or assistant designer a great deal of time. Some initial time and effort is required to enter the lighting data into the computer. However, once the information has been entered, changes and/or additions to keep the paperwork up-to-date are extremely fast and simple. This is a particular advantage to productions that will tour or be revived. If the plot has been drafted with CADD, a supplementary software program can produce paperwork without additional data entry. A hookup produced by Lightwright, Rosco's microcomputer program, is shown in Figure 20–16.

**Cue Sheets and Preset Sheets**    Cue sheets and preset sheets are primarily used with non-computer-based control systems. However, it was suggested earlier in this chapter that a form of the preset sheet is valuable for writing cues blind for any type of control system.

*Cue sheets* are simply a list of a production's lighting cues in numerical order. If using a preset system, information about each cue may include preset number, fade time, and description. If using a computer-based system, information includes fade time, link, delay, profile, and possibly a description. A printer can produce hard copy of cue sheets from any computer-based control console.

*Preset sheets* are used to record dimmer levels for each lighting cue in a production. All dimmers are listed by number and there is space for level information to be penciled in by the operator. A slow process at best, preset sheets must be carefully updated as changes are made by the designer.

```
=======================          =================
TOMMY - BROADWAY - CUT           CHANNEL HOOKUP                    Page   2
=======================          =================                05-28-94
=========================================================================================
  Chn   Dim   Position        Unit   Type            Watts   Purpose        Color
=========================================================================================
( 10 )  512   FOH HIGH         22    6x16 w/TH       1kw     Frts DR        L203+R119
              TRUSS
        512   FOH HIGH         23    6x16 w/TH       1kw     Frts DR        L203+R119
              TRUSS
 - - - - - - - - - - - - - - - - - - - - - - - - - - - - - - - - - - - - - - - - - - - -
( 13 )  297   1 ELECTRIC       13    6x12 w/TH       1kw     Frts UC        L203+R119
        297   1 ELECTRIC       14    6x12 w/TH       1kw     Frts UC        L203+R119
 - - - - - - - - - - - - - - - - - - - - - - - - - - - - - - - - - - - - - - - - - - - -
( 21 )   42   3 BOX BOOM L      9    6x16 w/TH       1kw     Box L Ap L     L202
         42   3 BOX BOOM L     11    6x16 w/TH       1kw     Box L Ap L     L202
 - - - - - - - - - - - - - - - - - - - - - - - - - - - - - - - - - - - - - - - - - - - -
( 22 )   40   3 BOX BOOM L      5    6x16 w/TH       1kw     Box L Ap Ctr   L202
         40   3 BOX BOOM L      7    6x16 w/TH       1kw     Box L Ap Ctr   L202
 - - - - - - - - - - - - - - - - - - - - - - - - - - - - - - - - - - - - - - - - - - - -
( 23 )   38   3 BOX BOOM L      1    6x22 w/TH       1kw     Box L Ap R     L202
         38   3 BOX BOOM L      3    6x22 w/TH       1kw     Box L Ap R     L202
 - - - - - - - - - - - - - - - - - - - - - - - - - - - - - - - - - - - - - - - - - - - -
( 24 )   25   2 BOX BOOM L     10    6x16 w/TH       1kw     Box L DL       L202
         25   2 BOX BOOM L     12    6x16 w/TH       1kw     Box L DL       L202
 - - - - - - - - - - - - - - - - - - - - - - - - - - - - - - - - - - - - - - - - - - - -
( 25 )   23   2 BOX BOOM L      6    6x16 w/TH       1kw     Box L DC       L202
         23   2 BOX BOOM L      8    6x16 w/TH       1kw     Box L DC       L202
 - - - - - - - - - - - - - - - - - - - - - - - - - - - - - - - - - - - - - - - - - - - -
              2 BOX BOOM L      1    6x16 w/TH       1kw     Box L DR       L202
              BOX BO          6x16 w/TH       1kw     Box L DR       L202
```

**Figure 20—16**
**Computer-Generated Hook-up**

Shown is a page of the channel hook-up for the Broadway production of *Tommy* designed by Chris Parry. It was generated by a "Lightwright" software program.

**Color Cut Lists**    Once the plot is complete, a production's color filters must be cut to the correct size and in the correct quantity. A color cut list is organized by color manufacturer and then by color number, and specifies size and quantity. This list may need to be completed quite early in order to allow time for purchasing. Paperwork software programs can generate a cut list including required sheet quantity. If a software program is not being used, it is easiest to generate a color cut list from a hookup or an instrument schedule rather than the plot. If an inexperienced person is cutting color, be sure he or she realizes that a 6-inch color frame doesn't mean a 6-inch cut of color.

**Cheat Sheets**    "Cheat sheet" and "magic sheet" are names given to paperwork that aids a designer in setting and adjusting lighting levels. With the impressive increase in numbers of dimmers, cheat sheets grew out of the need to help a designer remember what is assigned to each control channel or group of channels. While each designer likes to customize his or her own sheets and nearly as many styles exist as do designers, Figure 20—17 illustrates several of the more common types.

Popular forms of cheat sheets list groups of channels by either function or color. Some can be quite elaborate and pictorial. The prime objective in designing a cheat sheet is to keep it clear and brief.

**Batten Tapes**    To expedite hanging and circuiting the electric pipes, a designer may wish to prepare batten tapes for each hanging position. These consist of rolled strips of paper or cloth that have been premarked with centerline and specific instrument information. The tapes are simply attached to the batten, and electricians follow the instructions on the tape. Information may include instrument number, circuit number, instrument type, color, and

## Figure 20-17
### The Magic Sheet

Shown are three examples of magic sheets, sometimes called designer's "cheat" sheets.
(a) A cheat sheet listing by function for *Brigadoon*, designed by Tom Ruzika.
(b) The more pictorial magic sheet used by designer Tom Schraeder.
(c) The magic sheet used by designer Chris Parry for his production of *Tommy*.

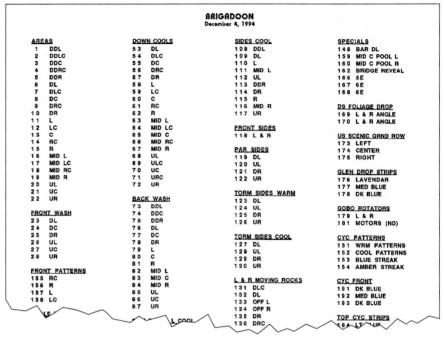

**BRIGADOON**
December 4, 1994

| AREAS | | DOWN COOLS | | SIDES COOL | | SPECIALS | |
|---|---|---|---|---|---|---|---|
| 1 | DDL | 53 | DL | 108 | DDL | 148 | BAR DL |
| 2 | DDLC | 54 | DLC | 109 | DL | 159 | MID C POOL L |
| 3 | DDC | 55 | DC | 110 | L | 160 | MID C POOL R |
| 4 | DDRC | 56 | DRC | 111 | MID L | 162 | BRIDGE REVEAL |
| 5 | DDR | 57 | DR | 112 | UL | 166 | 5E |
| 6 | DL | 58 | L | 113 | DDR | 167 | 6E |
| 7 | DLC | 59 | LC | 114 | DR | 168 | 6E |
| 8 | DC | 60 | C | 115 | R | | |
| 9 | DRC | 61 | RC | 116 | MID R | **DS FOLIAGE DROP** | |
| 10 | DR | 62 | R | 117 | UR | 169 | L & R ANGLE |
| 11 | L | 63 | MID L | | | 170 | L & R ANGLE |
| 12 | LC | 64 | MID LC | **FRONT SIDES** | | | |
| 13 | C | 65 | MID C | 118 | L & R | **US SCENIC GRND ROW** | |
| 14 | RC | 66 | MID RC | | | 173 | LEFT |
| 15 | R | 67 | MID R | **PAR SIDES** | | 174 | CENTER |
| 16 | MID L | 68 | UL | 119 | DL | 175 | RIGHT |
| 17 | MID LC | 69 | ULC | 120 | UL | | |
| 18 | MID RC | 70 | UC | 121 | DR | **GLEN DROP STRIPS** | |
| 19 | MID R | 71 | URC | 122 | UR | 176 | LAVENDAR |
| 20 | UL | 72 | UR | | | 177 | MED BLUE |
| 21 | UC | | | **TORM SIDES WARM** | | 178 | DK BLUE |
| 22 | UR | **BACK WASH** | | 123 | DL | | |
| | | 73 | DDL | 124 | UL | **GOBO ROTATORS** | |
| **FRONT WASH** | | 74 | DDC | 125 | DR | 179 | L & R |
| 23 | DL | 75 | DDR | 126 | UR | 181 | MOTORS (ND) |
| 24 | DC | 76 | DL | | | | |
| 25 | DR | 77 | DC | **TORM SIDES COOL** | | **CYC PATTERNS** | |
| 26 | UL | 78 | DR | 127 | DL | 151 | WRM PATTERNS |
| 27 | UC | 79 | L | 128 | UL | 152 | COOL PATTERNS |
| 28 | UR | 80 | C | 129 | DR | 153 | BLUE STREAK |
| | | 81 | R | 130 | UR | 154 | AMBER STREAK |
| **FRONT PATTERNS** | | 82 | MID L | | | | |
| 155 | RC | 83 | MID C | **L & R MOVING ROCKS** | | **CYC FRONT** | |
| 156 | R | 84 | MID R | 131 | DLC | 191 | DK BLUE |
| 157 | L | 85 | UL | 132 | DL | 192 | MED BLUE |
| 158 | LC | 86 | ULC | 133 | OFF L | 193 | DK BLUE |
| | | 87 | UR | 134 | OFF R | | |
| | | | | 135 | DR | **TOP CYC STRIPS** | |
| | | | | 136 | DRC | 184 LT UR | |

**a**

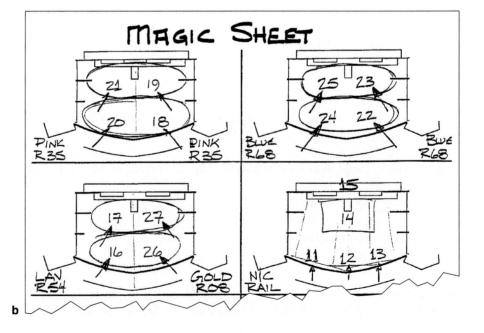

**MAGIC SHEET**

PINK R35    21   19 / 20   18    PINK R35

BLUE R68    25   23 / 24   22    BLUE R68

LAV R54    17   27 / 16   26    GOLD R08

N/C RAIL    15   14    11   12   13

**b**

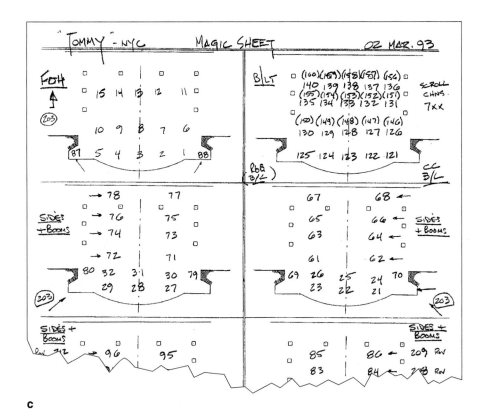

c

even focus. Tapes eliminate any measuring and chalking of the battens and, in combination with hanging cardboards, could eliminate the necessity of an electrician ever having to consult the master light plot. They are particularly valuable for touring productions or when working with inexperienced electricians.

**Hanging Cardboards**     Hanging cardboards are pieces of stiff paper or cardboard onto which a single location and its respective instrumentation have been transferred from the master plot. They can be prepared by an assistant designer or master electrician as soon as the plot is complete. Normally, a copy of the plot is cut up into positions and glued to a cardboard backing. A cardboard is given to an electrician during the put-in, allowing him or her the freedom of hanging and circuiting the position without having to refer to the complete plot. Hanging cardboards may contain more detailed information than the plot and, like batten tapes, are especially useful for touring situations where they can be reused a number of times.

**Focus Charts and Shop Orders**     Two paperwork items that are of primary importance in the commercial theatre are tour focus charts and equipment shop orders. Like cheat sheets, *focus charts* come in many styles and forms, but their function is the same. They provide a concise method of recording light focus. A *shop order* is essentially a contract for the rental of lighting equipment and related hardware between an equipment rental house and a producer represented by the lighting designer. Both of these items are discussed further in Chapter 24.

## REALIZING THE PLOT

The final step in lighting a production is, of course, realizing the plot. This process may be as short as two or three days or as long as two weeks or more and is always the most challenging time for the lighting designer. Let it be said once again that any preparation completed before move-in will pay off tenfold while in the theatre.

### FINAL PREPARATIONS

After completing the plot and before moving into the theatre, the designer must be sure that all supplies are on hand, paperwork is ready, and cues are written.

**Cues**     Writing lighting cues is one of the most simple tasks for the lighting designer, although at first this might not seem to be the case. If a designer attends several rehearsals and concentrates on things other than blocking, the *rhythm* of the production will dictate where most of the cues belong. It is a good idea to note cue placement in the script during one of the final run-throughs before move-in. Cues can then be numbered and presets written. Cues should be numbered sequentially, with inserted cues having a decimal point (for example, Light Cue 12.1).

The cues and their placement must be given to the stage manager, who will "call" the show. This cue-writing session should take place at a sufficiently early date before the technical or first lighting rehearsal and ideally should include both the stage manager and the board operator. The designer should set aside enough time for an uninterrupted discussion of the cues with both people so that they understand *why* a cue happens, and should make sure that both know counts or cue times.

The stage manager must understand that some cue placements will change during the rehearsal process. It is important that each and every cue is assigned a precise moment when it is called. That way, it will be a simple task to change the call of a cue a bit earlier or later.

Cues should be called as follows:

"Warning Light Cue 12" (approximately 30 seconds before "GO")
"Ready Light Cue 12" (approximately 10 seconds before "GO")
"Light Cue 12 . . . GO"

Note that the only time "Light Cue" is not prefaced by another word is on the "GO" call.

**The Production Electrician and Crew**    The lighting put-in must be carefully scheduled well in advance with the technical director in order to coordinate lighting and scenery. A definite crew schedule should be published at least a week before the actual put-in of equipment. This is to ensure adequate participation by crew members and minimize any space conflicts. Equipment must be ready and waiting to be hung. There are certain tasks that are best accomplished by a large crew and others that are more suited to one or two people. Preparing equipment (lamps, lens adjustment, color, gobos, cable, and so on) is best accomplished by the production electrician and perhaps one assistant. The actual hang requires a larger group of four to eight individuals. The production electrician must have all equipment needed for the hang in good ready condition before the larger crew is called. This simple policy allows the production electrician a fighting chance of doing a good job as crew head.

## THE HANG

Just as the goal of the preparation period should be to make the hang go smoothly, the goal of the hanging session should be to make the focus uneventful.

The lighting designer or assistant must be present during the put-in, if for no other reason than to be available for questions. While the responsibility for the put-in lies with the production electrician, the designer can do a great deal of good by being attentive and setting a positive tone. It is important that the entire crew realize that the aim of their work should be toward a good and smooth focus session. If an electrician always keeps the focus in mind, quality of work is usually excellent. The designer should not take a major role in physically hanging the show. This is the crew's job and a designer's energy is best spent elsewhere.

**The Hanging Crew**    It is most efficient for the production electrician to split the crew into groups of two or three people with a group leader reporting back. In this way, one group can begin working on the booms (which always take a good deal of time), another on the first electric pipe, while a third team starts hanging front-of-house. The production electrician coordinates all, checking from time to time on a crew's progress and seeing that everything is being done properly. A given hanging position should be completely hung before cabling is begun. C-clamps should all face the same way (bolts either upstage or downstage) so that the focusing electrician knows where they are. If the designer indicates focus on the light plot, instruments should be roughly aimed in that general direction—this also saves valuable focus time. Instrument adjustments for pan and tilt should be snug, but not so tight that a wrench is required before setting focus.

**Circuits and Cabling**    Depending on the circuit layout of the house, cabling may be the most time-consuming part of the hang. It is often better for the designer not to specify circuits on the light plot, thereby allowing the electricians freedom to cable to best locations. If this is the case, a single person (assistant designer) should be assigned the task of recording circuits onto the hookup or instrument schedule. The only disadvantage of this system is that the patching cannot be completed until circuiting is done and recorded.

Begin circuiting as soon as each position is hung, with one or at most two electricians assigned to the task. It is best to allow one electrician to cable a hanging position alone, due to the complexity of the work. Cable should be attached to the pipe with tie-line (cotton sash cord works well) using bow ties. Adequate slack must be left in the instrument leads, never cabling so taut as to prohibit free instrument focus. If a connection is loose, it should be taped or repaired at the time rather than later during focus. A quality electrician constantly anticipates the needs of the upcoming focus.

## THE FOCUS

Lighting focus takes concentration. If at all possible, electricians should have the stage to themselves during focus hours. Be prepared for the focus: Be on time, be alert, and be efficient. Normally a designer focuses in order, from one instrument to the next in a position. In this case, it is a good idea to have the assistant designer call dimmer or channel numbers to the board operator. This practice cuts down on distractions and saves a good deal of time.

Never begin the focus before an accurate checkout has been completed. Interrupting focus for a lamp or a patch mistake or a bad circuit is a serious waste of time and, more importantly, concentration. Front-of-house is often focused first. Learn to focus two electricians at once. Learn to focus with your back to the light, looking at your shadow. Learn to focus fast. And do not forget to give your crew periodic breaks.

**The Focus Crew**     A focus crew normally consists of the designer, an assistant, the production electrician, two focusing electricians, a board operator, and one or two additional electricians. The production electrician has

**SAFETY PRACTICE**

### Safety Practice

When working overhead, remember to carry a minimum of tools and always tie off your wrench. Take special precautions to avoid falling gel frames, pens and pencils, and gobo holders.

If working with an inexperienced crew, be sure that adequate supervision is provided—even if it seems to be taking too much time.

Remember that proper crew breaks promote safety.

done a full checkout and completed all necessary repairs well before the focus crew arrives. With communications set up, general focus philosophy discussed, and coffee drunk, the focus begins.

A good focus team in action is wonderful and awe-inspiring to watch. Talk is kept to a bare minimum as the electricians keep ahead of the designer, anticipating his or her next move. The team works like a well-oiled piece of machinery. Soon a pace is established and the job is done before anyone realizes that they are hungry or tired.

On the other hand, an unprepared and/or unskilled focus team is dreadful to observe and even more painful to be part of. Headsets do not work, lamps are burned out, one instrument is discovered without a lamp in it at all, shutters stick, cables short out, barrels do not move, and three instruments are hung upside down. By lunchtime, 18 instruments have been focused with 108 left to do, and everyone is tired and feeling mean.

The reality of the situation is that the good team is prepared and their equipment is well maintained, while the poor team is sorry.

## LIGHTING AND TECHNICAL REHEARSALS

The first time a director sees the results of the lighting designer's work is probably at the technical or lighting rehearsal. This should *not*, however, be the first time the lighting designer sees his or her work. The ideal situation is to look at presets during the final run-through before the technical rehearsal. The designer should explain to the cast and director that he or she will be adjusting a few lighting levels and will most probably not be in sequence with the action onstage. (Simply remember to leave them enough light for rehearsal, never blacking out the stage.) This gives the designer a good chance to see the lighting on actors without the added pressure of a technical rehearsal.

The technical and dress period is most crucial to the lighting designer, for this is when the majority of design decisions are made. This is the time when the lighting designer is working the hardest and under the most pressure. Accordingly, the designer *must* be fresh and alert—one cannot see or think for very long with only a few hours of sleep.

**Lighting Rehearsals**    Some directors prefer to sit with the lighting designer and stage manager and move slowly through a production's lighting cues. This practice is usually called a *lighting rehearsal*, and can take several different forms. Some directors like to take the time to build cues during these sessions. Others may want to see presets already written. The precise way of working matters little; what is important is that there are no surprises. Everyone concerned should know how the session will work and what the goals are.

Not all productions need lighting rehearsals. In fact, for many years, it was understood that technical rehearsals were the place to first see the lighting. However, with increased complexity, a special lighting rehearsal is often desirable.

**Technical Rehearsals**    Infamous for being long and laborious affairs, technical rehearsals are disliked by technicians as well as by actors. If proper and thorough preparation has been done and if someone keeps things moving, these rehearsals can be relatively painless. Good judgment must be used in determining when to stop and fix something and when to keep moving on. Tactless people must be banned from technical rehearsals.

It is a good idea for the stage manager to call this rehearsal from the house rather than an isolated booth somewhere. He or she will be in better contact with the director, the designers, the technical staff, and the actors. Always make sure that headsets have been carefully checked out well before the technical rehearsal begins. Nothing is more frustrating (and, unfortunately, more common) than communications problems during a technical rehearsal.

The purpose of a technical rehearsal is to solve technical problems—*not* constantly to adjust light levels, and *certainly not* to write lighting presets. If presets are not complete before the technical rehearsal, the rehearsal should go on without lights. Likewise, this is not the time for a director to adjust blocking, a temptation that sometimes is difficult to resist. If the director gives full attention to the process at hand, results will be better and a conclusion reached sooner.

Always begin a technical rehearsal on time. Pace yourself during the technical rehearsal. Never schedule an open-ended time period; always have a stopping time. Remember to take periodic breaks, and remember that positive reinforcement is a good thing. Remain objective, observe time deadlines, and—above all—be sure that your operators and stage manager understand and record changes as they are made.

## DRESS REHEARSALS

A production normally has two or three dress rehearsals, with the first one primarily devoted to costumes. Lighting level changes must be made during the dress rehearsal process, but the performance may not be stopped except for an exceptionally serious problem. Second and third dresses must never be stopped. The fewer changes made during dress rehearsals, the better the stage manager and operators will learn the show.

The assistant designer should take notes so that the designer can keep his or her eyes on the stage. A designer's remote monitor will enable the assistant to know what cue the designer is in. If a remote doesn't exist, the assistant should follow a script with the cues written in it. Remember that the director's attention is divided among a great number of equally important things during this stage of a production. Never leave after a dress rehearsal without first talking to the director, the stage manager, and the operators.

## PREVIEWS

Previews refer to performances with an audience that take place after the dress rehearsal process but before official opening. The purpose is usually to expose the actors to audience reaction before the production is reviewed. The number of previews can vary from one or two to several weeks' worth; and the role of the lighting designer on these occasions is often dependent upon need. If the production's lighting is complete, there is no reason for the designer to attend all previews. However, if changes continue to be made during the preview process, the designer must be in attendance.

# STAGE LIGHTING AND ELECTRICITY

## 21

A knowledge of electricity may seem nothing more than a bother to the lighting designer-*artist;* but such information is essential for the lighting designer-*practitioner.* At the very least, electricity and basic electronics must be understood well enough to allow for informed choices concerning use and safety. Unfortunately, many individuals believe that electricity is solely the concern of an electrician. This thinking results in a curious mystique that surrounds electrical practice and theory. The fact of the matter is that electrical theory and basic electrical practice are simple and accessible.

### ATOMIC THEORY

According to presently accepted theories, all matter consists of *molecules,* which are made up of *atoms.* Each atom is composed of a positively charged center called the *nucleus.* Around the nucleus are distributed a number of negatively charged bodies called *electrons.* The nucleus of an atom consists of *protons* and *neutrons.* Neutrons have no electrical charge, but each proton has a positive charge that is equal to the negative charge of an electron.

Every normal atom has as many electrons surrounding the nucleus as it has protons within, thus having an equal quantity of positive and negative charges. Hydrogen has one proton in its nucleus and one electron outside it. Helium has two protons and two electrons. Lithium has three of each, carbon has six, copper has twenty-nine, and so on up to uranium, which has ninety-two protons and ninety-two electrons. The electrons are in constant motion, revolving around the nucleus in orbits much the same as the planets revolve around the sun. Figure 21–1 shows a few examples.

In the atom of lithium, the lightest of all metals, the three protons are balanced by two electrons in the inner orbit plus one in the outer orbit. Carbon also has two electrons in the inner orbit and four in the outer orbit, balancing its six protons. Copper requires four orbits to contain its twenty-nine electrons. The various orbits are not all in the same flat plane, but rather they are at angles to each other, somewhat like a number of rubber bands stretched haphazardly about a baseball.

The importance of all this is that the single electron in the fourth and outer orbit of copper can be easily dislodged; only a small force or *voltage* is necessary. An electron removed from its atom is called a *free electron* and forms the basis of the flow of electrical current. All metals are good conductors because they have electrons that are easily dislodged.

## SOURCES OF ELECTRIC CURRENT

Just as water will not flow out of one end of a pipe unless there is water being poured into the other end, free electrons will not move through a conductor unless there is a supply of free electrons being introduced into it. Such a supply of electrons is known as voltage or as an *electromotive force* (EMF). It can be established in a number of ways—with sources including batteries; the action of friction, sunlight, heat, compression, or other phenomena on certain substances; and generators.

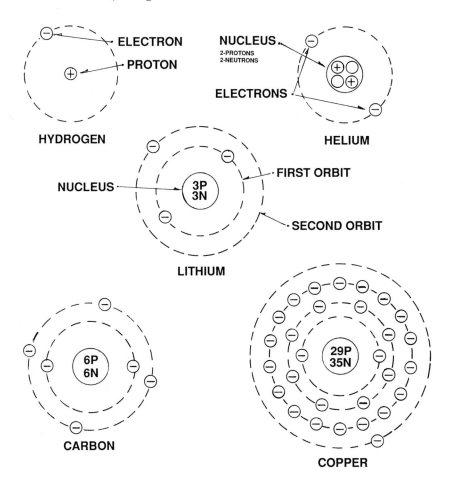

**Figure 21–1**
Schematic Diagram of the Structure of Certain Atoms

Note the single electron in the outer orbit of the copper atom.

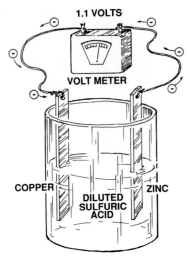

**1.1 VOLTS**

**VOLT METER**

**COPPER**  **ZINC**

**DILUTED SULFURIC ACID**

**Figure 21—2**
A Simple Copper-Zinc-Acid Battery

## BATTERIES

A common device for supplying an EMF is a battery. Figure 21–2 illustrates how a battery works. A strip of copper and a strip of zinc are placed in a glass container filled with a dilute solution of sulfuric acid. A meter connected between the two strips shows a small electric current passing from one to the other. This is caused by the acid attacking the zinc, which dissolves into the solution, releasing two electrons from each of its atoms. These free electrons are left on the zinc strip, and because the acid will not permit them to return to their atoms, they flow through the wire to the copper strip. This is an example of *direct current* (DC).

## OTHER SOURCES

An EMF may be built up in a number of ways other than by a battery. *Electrostatics* produces electricity by rubbing two dissimilar substances together. *Photoelectricity* is the action of sunlight on certain photosensitive materials. *Thermoelectricity* is the application of heat to the junction of two dissimilar metals that have been welded together. *Piezoelectricity* is the mechanical compression of certain crystals. New techniques to produce electricity have been developed, but the method most important to the stage electrician is that of *electromagnetism*: the creation of an EMF through a generator powered by water, steam, or atomic reaction.

## GENERATORS

A generator works by moving a conductor within a magnetic field. The conductor may be moved while the field is stationary, or the field may be moved and the conductor remain stationary. The latter is typical in large installations, but it is easier to understand the operation by considering a moving conductor within a stationary magnetic field.

The two diagrams in Figure 21–3 show a highly simplified *alternating current* (AC) generator, usually called an *alternator*. An armature in the shape of a single coil of wire is rotated through a magnetic field created between the two poles of a magnet. This action induces an EMF in the coil, causing free electrons to accumulate at slip ring 5. The electrons flow off the slip ring through the brush and the connecting wire to a voltmeter and then to slip ring 4, where they reenter the coil. In the second diagram the coil has rotated 180 degrees, reversing the position of its sides. Now the electrons accumulate at slip ring 4, pass through the connecting wire and meter, and reenter the coil at slip ring 5. Each complete revolution of the coil is called a *cycle*. For half of each cycle the electrons move in one direction, and for the other half in the opposite direction. Thus the current is said to be alternating.

Figure 21–4 is a sine curve showing the variation of induced EMF for any portion of the complete cycle of the armature through the magnetic field. At the exact instant that the armature is passing the 0-degree point in its rotation, it is moving parallel to the magnetic field, not through it, and therefore is producing no EMF at all. As it reaches the 30-degree mark, it is

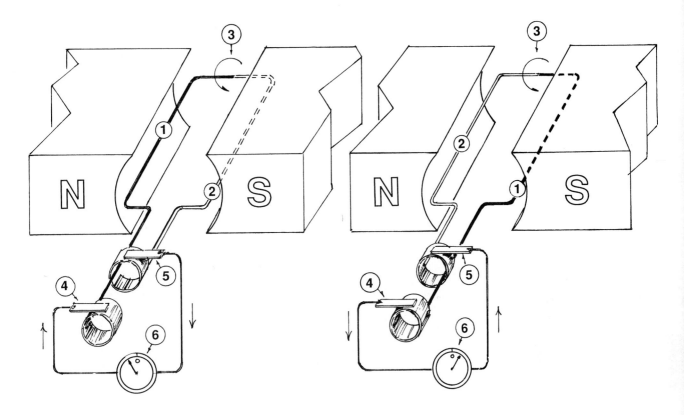

**Figure 21−3**
**Diagram of a Generator (Alternator)**

(1) Side one of the coil.
(2) Side two of the coil.
(3) Direction of rotation of the coil.
(4) Slip ring "A" and brush.
(5) Slip ring "B" and brush.
(6) Volt Meter.

beginning to cut into the magnetic field and generate a small EMF. This is indicated by a line extending from the 30-degree mark to a point slightly later in time. At the 60-degree position an EMF of greater magnitude is produced, and at 90 degrees the maximum EMF is attained. After this the EMF drops back to 0, then it starts to build up in the opposite direction as depicted below the timeline.

For the sake of economy it is practical to build several armatures into a generator. Because they must be at angles to each other, it is obvious that their respective EMFs will not reach any one point at the same instant, but rather they will produce sine curves as indicated in Figure 21−5. Here we see the very common arrangement of three armatures, each producing its own curve out of phase with the others. This is known as *three-phase current* and will be discussed later.

## ELECTRIC UNITS OF MEASUREMENT

A *circuit* is an established path of electrical flow. Four basic measurements can be made in any electric circuit: volts, amperes, ohms, and watts.

### VOLTS

The volt measures the *force* that causes free electrons to flow in a circuit. It is actually a measurement of the difference in electrical potential between two points in a circuit. Another way of putting it is to ask how many more

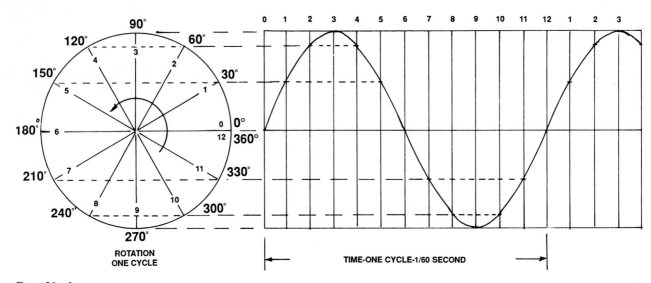

**Figure 21–4**
The Sine Curve Created by
Alternating Current (AC)

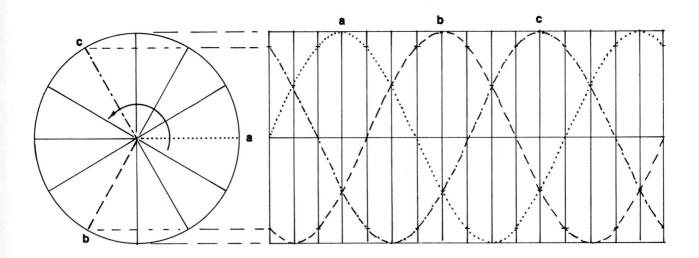

**Figure 21–5**
Three-Phase Sine Curves

Illustrated are the overlapping
sine curves produced by an AC
generator with three armatures
at 120 degrees to one another.

free electrons are there at point A than at point B, to which they will flow if
a path is opened for them. Voltage is also called electromotive force (EMF),
and its symbol is $E$. Standard voltage in the United States is 120 volts.

### AMPERES

The ampere is the *rate of flow* of current through a conductor. It measures how
many electrons pass a given point in 1 second. The mathematical symbol for
the ampere is $I$ (for intensity of current flow). Amperage is used to describe
a circuit's electrical capacity. For instance, most stage circuits carry 20 amps.

## OHMS

Every substance offers some *resistance* to the flow of electrical current. Some, such as copper, offer very little resistance—while others, such as rubber, offer a great deal. In an electrical circuit, larger-diameter wires offer less resistance than smaller ones. The ohm is the measurement of such resistance and its symbol is *R*.

## WATTS

The watt is the *rate of doing work*, whether it is turning an electric motor, heating an electric iron, or causing a lamp to glow. Its symbol is *P*, for power. Wattage can be thought of as "consumption" of electricity, although it must be realized that flowing electrons are never actually consumed.

## THE POWER FORMULA

The power formula is important to know because it expresses the relationship between wattage (P), amperage (I), and voltage (E). It states that the rate of doing work (wattage) is equal to the product of current flow (amperage) and potential (voltage):

$$P = I \cdot E \text{ (called the "pie" formula)}$$

or

$$W = V \cdot A \text{ (using first letters of unit names—called}$$
$$\text{the "West Virginia" formula)}$$

An application of the power formula might be to determine how many 750-watt lamps one could plug into a single 20-amp circuit, as follows:

$$
\begin{array}{l}
W = 750 \text{ per lamp} \\
V = 120 \text{ (U.S. standard)} \\
A = 20 \text{ (given)}
\end{array}
$$

$$X \cdot 750 = 120 \cdot 20$$
$$X = \frac{2,400}{750}$$
$$X = 3.2$$

A 20-amp circuit will carry three 750-watt lamps.

## OHM'S LAW

Ohm's law introduces resistance (R) into a useful formula. It states that amperage (I) equals voltage (E) divided by ohms:

$$I = \frac{E}{R}$$

## ALTERNATING CURRENT

Before development of new techniques, direct current was not an efficient way to transport electricity over long distances. However, it was the only way known in the early days of electricity, and for that reason was installed in the downtown areas of many cities. Today it has almost entirely been replaced by the more versatile alternating current.

### TRANSFORMERS

Alternating current has the distinct advantage of being easily changed from low voltage to high and from high voltage to low by means of transformers. A transformer consists of an iron core, frequently doughnut-shaped, around which are coiled two wires, the primary and the secondary (Figure 21–6). When an alternating current is sent through the primary coil, it sets up a magnetic flux in the iron core, and in turn this flux induces a new current in the secondary coil. It must be understood that there is no electrical connection whatsoever between the two coils. The voltage transformation is solely the result of fluctuating magnetic fields that surround any electrical conductor through which power is flowing.

If the primary has few turns around the core and the secondary has more, the voltage induced in the secondary will be higher than that in the primary. If the primary has more turns than the secondary, then the induced voltage will be lower. These are known as "step-up" and "step-down" transformers, respectively.

### AC SERVICE

Figure 21–6 depicts a portion of a typical arrangement for a modest alternating current service. At the left side of the illustration is seen the AC generator station producing an EMF of 1,200 volts. This is fed to the substation where a transformer boosts it to 6,000 volts. Higher voltages provide less loss in transit (some high-power lines carry as much as 500,000 volts!). As the current nears the neighborhood in which it will be used, it passes through another substation where the EMF is reduced to 600 volts. This is sent out over a local wiring system until it reaches a house, where a small transformer located on a street-side pole finally reduces it to 120 volts.

In this country the most common household service is 120 volts AC at 60 cycles. Many foreign countries use quite different voltages, ranging from 105 to as much as 240 volts, usually at 50 cycles or less.

**Figure 21–6**
Transformers

Schematic drawing of AC transportation from the generating station to the home.

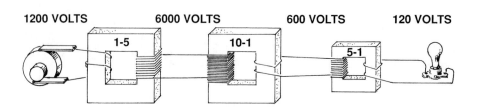

1200 VOLTS   6000 VOLTS   600 VOLTS   120 VOLTS

1-5   10-1   5-1

## TWO-, THREE-, AND FOUR-WIRE SYSTEMS

It is essential for the stage electrician to know which of several possible wiring systems (referred to as "service power") is carrying electricity to the theatre. This is especially true when a touring company moves into an unfamiliar building and must connect its portable control board and other equipment. Figure 21–7 illustrates the three forms of electrical distribution service.

**Two-Wire System**     In a two-wire system, the first line is said to be "hot" and the second "neutral." The potential between the two lines is 120 volts. It should be noted at this point that 120-volt service is often, in fact, closer to 115 volts and may drop to as low as 110 volts. Today's lighting equipment operates well on any of these voltages.

**Three-Wire System**     The second form of service is the three-wire system, in which the two outside (hot) wires usually have a potential of 240 volts between them. However, each hot wire has a potential of only 120 volts between it and the third wire, the common neutral. A familiar domestic application of this service is found in many homes, where the electric lights

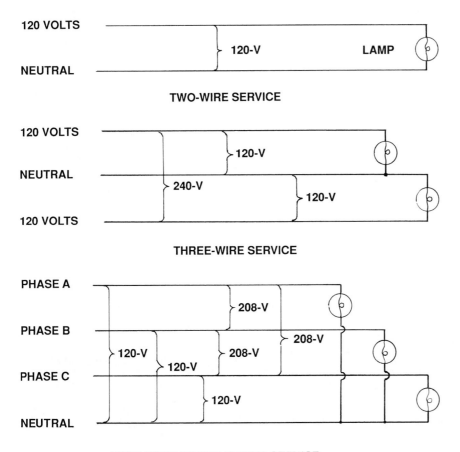

**Figure 21–7**
Electrical Distribution

Illustrated are the three kinds of electrical distribution service. Four-wire, three-phase service is found in most theatres.

are on two or more circuits of 120 volts each, while the electric range and clothes dryer operate on 240 volts.

**Four-Wire System**     The third type of service is popular because of its efficiency in distribution. It is the AC 120–208-volt, four-wire system, also known as the *three-phase system*. The generation of these three phases is illustrated in Figure 21–5. The sine curve of the EMF produced by each phase is at 120 degrees to the others. If the EMF in relation to a common neutral conductor is 120 volts, then any two phases will have a potential of 208 volts (this being the product of 240 volts times the sine value of angle 120 degrees, or .8660). Many motors are built to run on 208 voltage. This type of service is quite commonly found in theatres.

## Safety Practice

Great care must be taken with multiple-wire systems to avoid connecting any apparatus designed for 120 volts across the two hot lines. The 208 or 240 volts will blow lamps at once, ruin other equipment promptly, and provide grave danger of fatal shock. The British, who use 240 volts for all their home lighting, must take precautions that would seem very irksome to us, who are used to our comparatively mild 120-volt service.

### SERIES AND PARALLEL CIRCUITS

Regardless of whether the current reaches the building by two-, three-, or four-wire systems, on the inside it is distributed by two-wire systems like the one diagrammed in Figure 21–7. The various elements that work in these circuits—lamps, switches, dimmers, fuses, and the like—may be connected in either of two ways: series or parallel.

In a series circuit, the flow of current passes through the various elements successively. The top diagram of Figure 21–8 shows that the current must pass through each of the four lamps, one after the other, before returning by the neutral wire. If one of the lamps burns out, the circuit is broken and current can't flow.

The center diagram illustrates the same four lamps connected "in parallel." A portion of the total current can flow simultaneously through each lamp.

**Combination Circuits**     Almost all practical lighting circuits are a combination of series and parallel. The bottom diagram of Figure 21–8 shows a typical example. The switch and fuse are in series with each other and they are also in series with each of the lamps. But the four lamps are in parallel with one another. If the switch is opened or the fuse blown, all the lamps will be extinguished. One of the lamps may be removed, however, and the

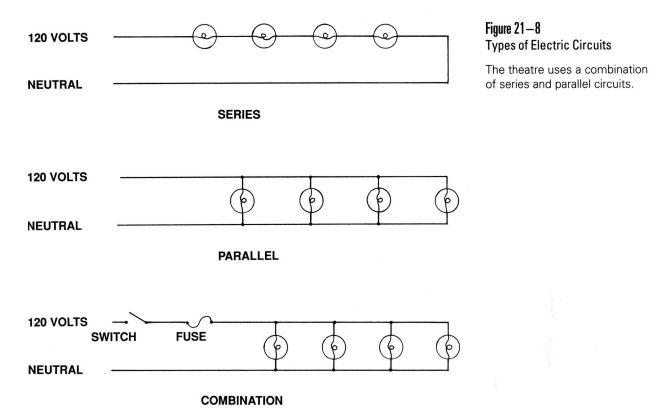

**Figure 21–8**
Types of Electric Circuits

The theatre uses a combination
of series and parallel circuits.

remaining three will not be affected. In other words, the series portion is used to control the circuit as a whole, while the parallel portion is valuable as a distributor of the current.

In stage lighting, switches and fuses are replaced by circuit breakers. These breakers and the dimmers are put in series with the stage lights for the sake of control. The circuit breaker can act as a switch, but its primary function is to protect the entire circuit against a short circuit or an overload that would result in a dangerously high flow of current.

The stage lighting instruments themselves are always in parallel, such as several spotlights ganged on one dimmer or the lamps in one color circuit of a striplight. In each case they are simultaneously under the control of the dimmer and the circuit breaker, but each is independent of the other. If they were connected in series, none would burn at full brightness. And, like strands of old Christmas tree lights, if one lamp fails, no lamps can burn (the broken filament acting like a switch).

**Circuit Capacity**　　An important calculation in parallel circuitry is to quickly ascertain the ampere flow in a circuit. This is usually necessary when several stage instruments are ganged together or several striplights are fed through each other.

Suppose we have four spotlights ganged on one circuit, each one burning a 500-watt lamp. We may invert the power formula ($P = I \cdot E$) to read

$I = \dfrac{P}{E}$, then:

$$I = \dfrac{4 \times 500}{120} = 16.67 \text{ amperes}$$

If our circuit is fused at 20 amperes we are safe. But if we wish to change the lamps to the more powerful 750-watt variety, then:

$$I = \dfrac{4 \times 750}{120} = 25 \text{ amperes}$$

This is too much for our 20-ampere circuit, so we must go back to the 500-watt lamps or put one or two of the spotlights on a different circuit.

## CONDUCTORS AND INSULATORS

As noted earlier, materials that have few electrons in the outer orbit of their atomic structure readily support flow of electricity. Such materials are called *conductors*. Everything offers some resistance to electrical flow, but metals are relatively good conductors, and silver is the best of any substance known.

Due to its cost, the use of silver for extensive wiring is not very practical. Less expensive copper is the best alternative. Its conductivity is almost as good as that of silver, it is relatively inexpensive, and it is easy to work with—to form into wires and other parts. Aluminum is seeing more use for some applications, and brass is valuable for large, permanent parts that need to be especially rugged. Other materials are also used for special purposes, but by and large copper is the conductor of choice for electric wires, switch parts, and the like.

Just as there is no material that is 100-percent conductive, so there is nothing that has 100-percent insulative properties. However, there are many

### Safety Practice

**Short Circuits**

An important rule to remember is that *electricity will always follow the path of least resistance.* Some sort of insulation is necessary to prevent the electrons that are flowing in a conductor from short-circuiting—that is, escaping into other channels. This "short" may result in severe shock to anyone coming in contact with the new and unprotected channel of flow. And, because it may offer little resistance, this new channel may allow a higher current than the legitimate circuit was designed to carry, thereby causing damage to it.

materials that serve well. Glass and ceramics are excellent for small permanent parts such as sockets and switches. Rubber and fiber are used for wires and cables. Many insulating plastics have been developed for assorted uses. The most useful *insulator* of all is dry air. If this were not so, every open socket or wall outlet would drain off current!

Permanent wiring such as stage circuits, which should be laid by a licensed electrician only, have a solid copper core through which the current flows. Temporary wiring cable used on the stage always has a core made up of a number of small strands of wire. This is to provide proper flexibility in handling and laying. Standard stage cable consists of three such cores, each surrounded by a strong rubber insulation. For physical strength, tough fiber cords are laid alongside the strands of wire, and everything is surrounded by either a rubber and/or fiber sheathing.

## GROUNDING

National electrical codes specify that all new electrical installations be *grounded*. Grounding requires that a circuit or cable have three rather than two wires. The third, the ground wire, is designed to offer an emergency path through which the current can flow in case of a short circuit.

The ground wire of a stage lighting instrument is connected to its metal housing. If a short circuit occurs and the housing becomes "hot," the current will flow through the ground wire safely to earth.

## WIRE COLOR CODES

The wires of a stage cable or circuit are always covered with rubber insulation, color-coded as follows:

$$black\ or\ red\ =\ "hot"\ line$$
$$white\ =\ "neutral"\ or\ "common"\ line$$
$$green\ =\ ground$$

## STAGE CABLE

Stage cable comes in different sizes, measured by *gauge*. Gauge relates to the diameter of the wire, with smaller wire having larger gauge numbers, as can be seen in the table below. Each wire size is designed to carry a specific maximum current measured in amps. These limits should never be exceeded. The most useful sizes are as follow:

| Size (gauge number): | 18 | 16 | 14 | 12 | 10 | 8 | 6 |
|---|---|---|---|---|---|---|---|
| Capacity (amperes): | 3 | 6 | 15 | 20 | 25 | 35 | 50 |

The most common (nearly standard) stage circuit has a capacity of 20 amps. Accordingly, the most common cable is No. 12, Type SO (rubber coated). Ordinary lamp cord (or zip cord), which has a 16- or 18-gauge core, may be used on occasion. However, such use must be for very small loads and very short runs.

**Safety Practice**

Care must be taken in wiring plugs onto cable that the ground wire in particular is attached to the proper pin of the connector (see "Stage Connectors" later in this chapter).

Always remember that *"green"* is *"ground."*

**Care and Handling**   When not in use, cable should be neatly coiled in large coils (diameter of approximately 2 feet), tied with tie-line, and hung up for storage. It is a good idea to permanently attach a length of black tie-line next to the female connector on all pieces of cable. Such a line can be used to secure the cable to a batten as well as to tie the coil together when it is stored. Cable length marking codes should be maintained and connectors should be periodically checked for proper strain relief. Cables with damaged or cracked rubber coating should be discarded.

**Cable Accessories**   Cables that allow an electrician to plug multiple lighting instruments into a single circuit are called "two-fers," "Y-connectors," "spiders," or "three-fers." They allow the electrician to plug two or three instruments into one circuit, always remembering that 20 amps is circuit capacity.

*Adaptors* are the other type of cable accessory. Simple adaptors are seldom more than 2 feet long, with a different connector on each end. They allow an electrician to plug something with one type of connector into an outlet having a different type. Applications are numerous, but an example of the use of an adaptor would be plugging a backstage work light equipped with a pin connector into an "Edison" or parallel-blade socket.

## STAGE CONNECTORS

Hanging positions of stage lighting instruments must change from production to production. *Connectors* are electrical plugs that provide this flexibility. They are rated by amperage according to their electrical capacity. Ordinary household plugs with parallel blades, sometimes called "Edison" plugs, are occasionally used in small facilities because they are inexpensive and readily available. However, their use is discouraged because they are easily disconnected in error and are not designed for large amounts of current.

The two connectors most commonly used in the theatre are twist-locks and pin connectors.

## TWIST-LOCK CONNECTORS

Used in many educational and community theatres, the twist-lock connector solves the problem of two connectors pulling apart. It is designed with prongs that allow the male and female caps to be easily and firmly locked together (Figure 21–9a).

Unfortunately, manufacturers have created an amazingly large number of twist-lock blade configurations. The most common stage twist-lock has a capacity of 20 amps and comes in several styles. The most significant difference among these styles is in the third or grounding blade. In two different models, a part of the grounding blade is bent either toward the center of the plug or toward the outside. These two variations are commonly called "pin-in" or "pin-out," respectively, and cannot be used interchangeably.

When wiring a twist-lock, always be sure that the grounding (green) wire is connected to the grounding prong, which is marked "G" or has a green screw head. Twist-lock plugs are available in a wide variety of amperages.

## PIN CONNECTORS

Pin connectors were used as stage connectors long before twist-locks were invented. The standard size has a capacity of 20 amps and consists of a heavy-duty fiber or plastic body with sturdy brass pins and sockets (Figure 21–9b). Most professional theatres use pin connectors because rental house equipment comes standardly equipped with that connector. They have the disadvantage of not always giving a firm electrical connection and are easily pulled apart by mistake unless the two cables or connectors are tied together.

Pin connectors have a split down the center of each brass pin (hence the name "split-pin" connector). When a pin does not make good connection, electrical arcing occurs causing the connector to overheat. To avoid this, the individual pins can be "split" or slightly separated with a small knife blade.

Pin connectors are available for two different types of stage cable: rubber cable (Type SO) and individual fiber-covered leads from lighting instruments. The rubber cable type has a single hole in the back of the connector

**Figure 21–9**
**Stage Connectors**

(a) Female and male three-wire (grounded) twist-lock connectors.
(b) Male and female three-wire pin connectors. Photo courtesy Union Connector Company.

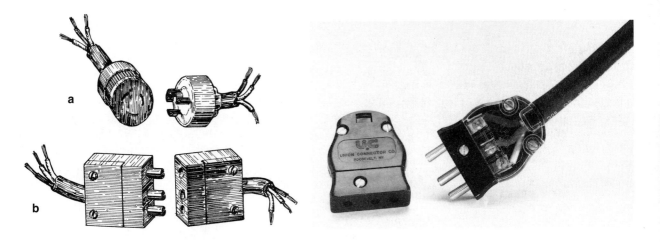

while the other type has three smaller holes. These two connector types may not be used interchangeably.

The grounding pin is always the *center* pin in a pin connector. In addition to the standard 20 amps, pin connectors are available in 60- and 100-amp sizes.

## WIRING CONNECTORS

Proper wiring of stage connectors is important to ensure against short-circuiting or loose connections that can result in arcing within the plug. As pointed out earlier, stage cable consists of three groups of small strands of copper wires, each surrounded by a rubber sheathing. This rubber sheathing must be stripped away by using a cutting tool called a "wire stripper."

The easiest method of wiring a pin connector is to twist the small strands together in order to form a more cohesive single strand. The exposed wire is then wrapped around the connector's screw terminal (Figure 21–10). Be sure to take the following precautions: (1) Expose only as much bare wire as necessary. (2) Always wrap the wire in the direction the screw turns when tightened (clockwise). (3) Be sure that the connector's strain relief is effective. The strain relief mechanism of a stage connector grips the rubber coating of a cable. This ensures that any pulling tension is placed on the cable rather than on the connecting terminals.

A better and safer technique of wiring a connector involves "tinning" the exposed copper wire. The tinning process simply requires soldering all the small copper strands together to form one stiffer strand. This tinned lead can then be connected to the terminal as explained before.

A third technique involves the use of a small connecting device commonly called a "Sta-kon" (Figure 21–11). The Sta-kon is soldered or pinched onto the exposed wire with a crimping tool. The ring is then placed around the screw terminal of the connector. A Sta-kon must be properly sized for the wire and, when in place, the three Sta-kons must not make contact with one another.

Perhaps it is obvious, but a male connector must never be "hot" or "live." For example, leads from a lighting instrument always terminate in a male connector so that it plugs into the "live," shielded female connector.

**Figure 21–10**
Steps in Wiring a Pin Connector

(a) Remove cover plate.
(b) Wrap wire around screw terminal clockwise, making sure the green (ground) wire is attached to the center screw terminal.
(c) Tighten screws and replace cover plate, making sure the strain relief is effective.

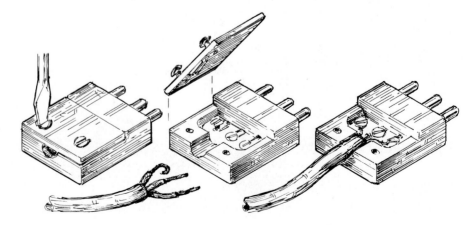

**Figure 21—11**
Solderless Terminals

A special crimping tool is required to securely attach the copper wire to the "Sta-kon" terminal.

## SWITCHES

A switch is a device that is put into a circuit to interrupt and restore the flow of current as desired (to "open" and "close" the circuit). There are many types of mechanical switches, from the familiar domestic wall-type switch to large knife-blade arrangements that handle hundreds of amperes. Like everything else electrical, which type and size to use depends on the duty the switch is expected to perform and the load it is intended to handle.

Most theatre circuits are equipped with a *circuit breaker* that protects the circuit from an overload and also functions as a switch.

A switch commonly found backstage in the theatre is a *disconnect box*. This is a heavy-duty switch housed in a metal box that may also contain fuses (Figure 21–12). The disconnect is permanently mounted in the theatre to receive temporary lighting control equipment, allowing quick and easy access to a power supply. A touring production might carry its own disconnect box, fused to the proper amperage for a traveling control system or other electrical apparatus. In this case, the disconnect is wired to a larger amperage power supply in order to protect the touring equipment from a power overload.

**Figure 21—12**
Disconnect Box

Shown is a 300-amp three-phase disconnect. Power enters at the top and goes through knife switches (shown in off position) and fuses to copper buss bars. Touring "road boards" and auxiliary equipment are connected to the buss bars by means of lugs or bolts.

A *contactor* is an electrically operated device in which a small switch controls a larger, remotely located switch. When operated, the conveniently located smaller switch activates a magnet that opens or closes a switch capable of handling hundreds of amperes. A contactor provides the benefits of high current being kept away from the operator. Additionally, the loud noise created by large magnetic switches is kept away from the audience.

## CIRCUIT PROTECTION

If an electric circuit suffers damage that results in a short circuit, ampere flow increases to a point where *something* must burn out. The same thing happens in the case of an overload (for instance, too many lamps connected to the circuit). By using the power formula, we see that if six 500-watt lamps are connected to a 120-volt circuit, 25 amperes will flow through it. If 14-gauge wire having a capacity of 15 amps is used in the circuit, its limit is greatly exceeded. Again, something must burn out.

### FUSES

To protect against overloads and short circuits, circuit breakers or fuses of suitable capacities are inserted to form the weakest link in the electrical chain.

### Figure 21–13
Fuses and a Circuit Breaker

(a), (b), & (c) Knife-blade cartridge fuses, capacities as indicated.
(d), (e), & (f) Ferrule-tipped cartridge fuses.
(g) A typical circuit breaker.
(h) & (i) Standard plug fuses.
(j) & (k) Type-S fuses (note the difference in threads as shown in the inserts).

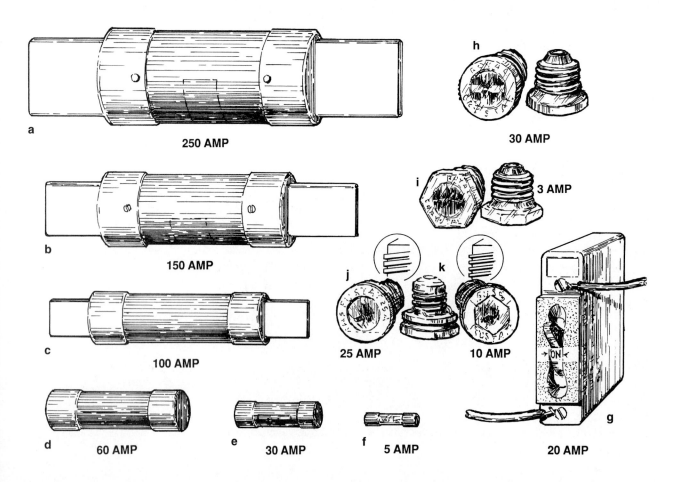

a   250 AMP

b   150 AMP

c   100 AMP

d   60 AMP     e   30 AMP     f   5 AMP

h   30 AMP

i   3 AMP

j   25 AMP     k   10 AMP

g   20 AMP

If the current flow increases to dangerous levels, it is the fuse that gives way, breaking the circuit and preventing more serious damage. The fault is then located and corrected, and a new fuse is inserted with a minimum of trouble. Figure 21–13 shows various forms of fuses in common use at the voltages usually encountered in stage lighting circuitry.

Some older homes still use plug-type fuses that screw into a socket like a lamp. There is a special and very useful variation of this fuse known as nontamperable or "type S." It has different screw threads for various amperages so that no one can change to a higher-capacity fuse.

The other type of fuses are cartridge fuses, available in contact types, sizes, and ratings as listed in the box below.

## CARTRIDGE FUSES

| CONTACTS | LENGTHS | CAPACITIES |
|---|---|---|
| Ferrule | 2 inches | up to 30 amperes |
| | 3 inches | 31 to 60 amperes |
| Knife-blade | $5\frac{7}{8}$ inches | 61 to 100 amperes |
| | $7\frac{1}{8}$ inches | 101 to 200 amperes |
| | $8\frac{5}{8}$ inches | 201 to 400 amperes |
| | $10\frac{3}{8}$ inches | 401 to 600 amperes |

If a fuse continues to blow whenever replaced, it is a sign that there is either an overload or a short circuit. Immediate steps should be taken to eliminate the hazard. Over-fusing or bypassing a fuse is a dangerous and foolish practice that can cause a fire.

### CIRCUIT BREAKERS

Because of their convenience, circuit breakers have replaced fuses in most applications. A circuit breaker is a form of switch that automatically opens when the flow of current becomes higher than it should. A thermal circuit breaker detects excessive current flow through a buildup of heat. Magnetic breakers react to the larger magnetic field created by greater-than-normal amperage. Magnetic breakers can be reset immediately; thermal breakers may need a short period of time to cool before resetting.

## TESTING EQUIPMENT

A stage electrician must have ready access to various testing tools in order to troubleshoot electrical problems that invariably arise precisely when time is most critical. These tools range from the simplest test lights to sophisticated meters.

**Figure 21–14**
Neon Test Light

A handy tool for testing electrical circuits.

A test light such as the one shown in Figure 21–14 lights up if an electrical circuit is "live." Test lights should be inexpensive, easy to carry, and hard to break. The neon tester shown in the figure should prove most satisfactory.

A *continuity tester* contains a battery power supply enabling an electrician to test a circuit to see that it is complete. This type of tester is particularly useful for detecting burned-out lamps where the broken filament has opened the circuit. The Great American Market sells a combination circuit/continuity tester called GAM CHEK (Figure 21–15a). It is made for pin connectors only.

More sophisticated testing equipment in the form of meters can read voltage, amperage, and resistance (ohms) in a circuit. Most meters combine several functions, such as the Simpson V. O. M. (volt-ohm meter) shown in Figure 21–15b. Amprobe manufactures a meter by the same name, which measures volts, ohms, and amperage. Meters are fairly delicate and are also fairly expensive.

**Figure 21–15**
Test Equipment

(a) The GAM CHEK is an electrical tester that can check continuity, power, and polarity. Photo courtesy The Great American Market.
(b) A volt-ohm meter with digital read-out. Photo courtesy Simpson Electric Company.

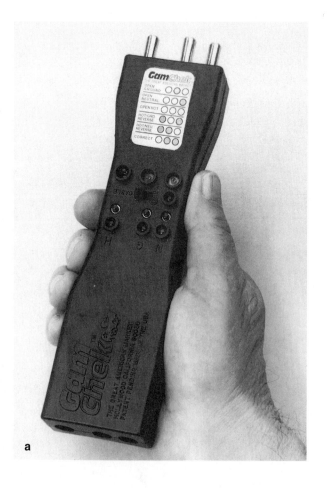

a

b

## Safety Practice

Electrical safety, like most everything else, is a matter of common sense. If you don't know what you're doing, don't do it! Attention to the following points will be helpful:

1. Always remember that electrical current will follow the path of least resistance and that your body could be that path.
2. Insulation is a good thing. Tools should be insulated with plastic or rubber handles. Soles of shoes should provide good insulation.
3. Electrical fires are most commonly caused by heat buildup caused by arcing or a short circuit.
4. Know the locations of electrical (red) fire extinguishers.
5. Fuses and circuit breakers protect equipment and ensure circuit safety. Never attempt to bypass them.
6. Never use a metal ladder for electrical work unless it is insulated with rubber footpads on all legs. Wooden ladders are always safest.
7. Be particularly wary of damp or wet conditions. Water is a fairly good electrical conductor.
8. Strain relief in electrical connectors is important.
9. Green is ground.
10. Voltage kills.

# LIGHT SOURCES 22

Today's lighting designer is fortunate to have the choice of a wide variety of light sources. All theatrical light sources are in the form of *lamps*. A lamp is composed of the *light source* (the filament in an incandescent lamp), a glass envelope or *bulb*, and a *base*.

During the second half of the twentieth century great advances were made in lamp design and manufacturing. Development of the tungsten-halogen lamp in the 1950s brought about a revolution in lighting instrument design. In 1954 the first practical arc lamp, filled with xenon gas, was introduced by a firm called Osram. In 1971 a xenon arc lamp was put to use in a theatrical follow spot, the Xenon Super Trouper. This lamp was destined to be the forerunner of today's great variety of arc lamp sources. Compact-filament low-voltage lamps, combined with new reflectors, have created a source of parallel rays of light unheard of two decades ago. Incandescent light sources rated at 600 watts recently developed for new ellipsoidal reflector spotlights are brighter than standard 1,000-watt lamps.

More than ever before, theatrical lighting designers must be aware of the great potential provided by the various light sources at their command. The theatre uses three basic types of lamps:

1. *Incandescent*—Light is given off by a glowing metal filament.
2. *Arc*—An electrical arc gives off intense illumination.
3. *Gaseous discharge*—Light production depends on the reaction of gases to an electric arc.

## INCANDESCENT LAMPS

The most common source of light used on the stage today is the incandescent filament lamp: a glass bulb containing a tungsten filament that emits light

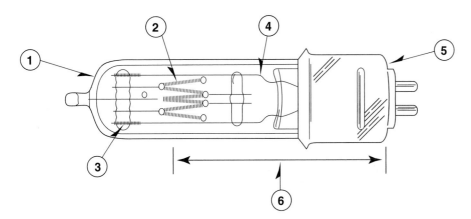

**Figure 22–1**
Parts of a Tungsten-Halogen
Incandescent Lamp

(1) Quartz-glass bulb filled with
halogen gas.
(2) Biplane filament.
(3) Filament supports.
(4) Lead-in wire.
(5) Medium 2-pin base.
(6) L.C.L. (light center length).

when an electrical current is passed through it. The three important parts of
an incandescent lamp, as illustrated in Figure 22–1 and to be discussed in
detail later in this chapter, are these:

The *bulb*—the glass envelope that encloses the inert gas or vacuum
The *base*—which holds the lamp in proper position and provides electrical
contact
The *filament*—which passes the current, yet offers enough resistance to cause the
transformation of electrical energy into light energy

The glass bulb or envelope contains either an inert gas or a vacuum to
prevent the metal filament from oxidizing. Tungsten, the same wire used in
toasters and toaster ovens, is relatively resistant to electrical flow. As a result,
it heats up and glows when a current is passed through it.

There are two basic categories of incandescent lamps: the *standard incandescent lamp* and the *tungsten-halogen lamp.* Thomas Edison developed the standard incandescent lamp in 1879, and it really has not changed much over
the years. The tungsten-halogen lamp is an incandescent light source with a
special quartz glass envelope containing a halogen gas. At the outset, it was
a popular theatrical lamp because of its small size and increased efficiency.

## TUNGSTEN-HALOGEN LAMPS

The development of the tungsten-halogen lamp (sometimes called the *quartz
lamp*) led to significant changes in the lighting industry. The most important
of these was the creation of smaller and more powerful lighting instruments
designed specifically for these lamps. This new line of instruments set the
lighting designer free from the restrictions of relatively archaic equipment.
Not only were the T-H (tungsten-halogen) lamps much more compact than
standard incandescent lamps, but they also were able to maintain initial intensity throughout their life span.

The secret of this significant innovation is the halogen-family gas (usually
iodine) introduced into the bulb. As a tungsten filament burns, particles evap-

These photographs from a Sylvania catalog show the darkening of a standard incandescent
bulb. Photos courtesy Osram
Sylvania Inc.

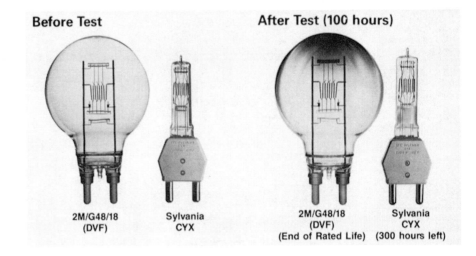

orate from the filament and deposit themselves on the cooler glass envelope.
The result of this process is a gradual darkening of the bulb and a decrease
in light output (Figure 22–2). However, in T-H lamps the halogen gas col-
lects the tungsten particles and redeposits them at the hottest point within
the bulb, the filament. (The lamp ultimately fails only because the halogen
gas does not redeposit the particles evenly.) The desired reaction between
the tungsten particles and halogen gas requires considerably more heat than
that created within a standard incandescent lamp. To provide proper temperatures, the T-H glass envelope is made smaller and constructed out of
strong quartz glass (thus the name "quartz lamp").

### LAMP FILAMENTS

All stage lighting instruments use reflectors in order to increase the efficiency
of their light source. The smaller the light source, the more efficiently a
reflector carries out its job of gathering and precisely redirecting the light
rays. The ideal lamp filament would be what is referred to as a "point source."
We have a long way to go toward achieving such a source, but attempts have
been made to make tungsten filaments as compact as possible. The tungsten
wire is often coiled (designated "C") in order to maintain as small a size as
possible. In the case of some tungsten-halogen lamp filaments, the wire is
double-coiled (designated "CC") and called a coiled coil.

**Filament Forms**    There exist many different filament configurations. The
barrel and corona filaments (Figures 22–3a and 22–3b) are used for floodlights
and household lamps because they distribute their light equally in all directions. The monoplane and biplane filaments (Figures 22–3c and 22–3d), used
in spotlights, emit most of their light in two opposite directions—from the
front and rear of the filament. This permits a larger portion of the light to
be gathered and redirected by a reflector or a lens. The coiled coil, a common
tungsten-halogen lamp filament, tends to be a bit longer and narrower than
other filaments (Figure 22–3e).

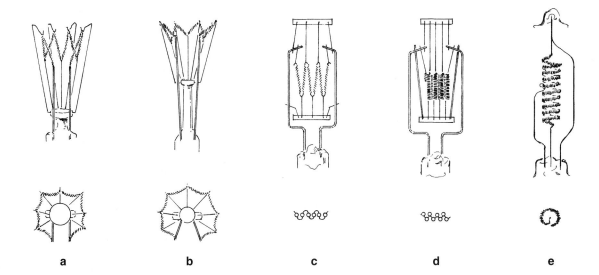

No matter what form a filament takes, the tungsten metal becomes supple when it heats up. In this state, any excessive jarring of the filament can cause it to break. Spotlight filaments such as the biplane and the coiled coil are particularly susceptible to this sort of breakage. Lighting instruments should be handled carefully when their lamps are burning.

**Light-Center Length**    The LCL (light-center length) of a lamp is the distance from the center of the filament to some predetermined place in the base. With a screw-base lamp, the measurement is to the contact button at the bottom of the base. With a prefocus base, it is to the fins; with the 2-pin, it is to the base of the pins (Figure 22–1). It is particularly important to be aware of the LCL when a lamp is used in conjunction with a reflector or a lens. The center of the filament must exactly align with the focal points of such optical devices.

## LAMP BULBS

The bulbs (or envelopes) of standard incandescent lamps are made of ordinary glass, while the bulbs of tungsten-halogen lamps are made of the more heat- and pressure-resistant quartz glass. As a result, the normal glass envelope of the standard incandescent lamp needs to be larger than the T-H bulb in order to dissipate the heat given off by the filament.

**Quartz Envelopes**    A disadvantage of the T-H lamp is that the quartz glass envelope cannot be touched by fingers. No matter how clean your hands happen to be, oil from the skin is deposited on the glass and will react with the quartz when it is heated. The result of this reaction not only weakens the envelope (possibly causing an explosion), but also produces a frosted effect on the glass.

**Bulb Shapes**    Bulbs come in a variety of shapes, each designated by a letter or letters (Figure 22–4). The A (arbitrary) and PS (pear-shape with

**Figure 22–3**
Filament Types

The upper row shows a side view and the bottom row an end view of:
(a) The barrel.
(b) The corona.
(c) The monoplane.
(d) The biplane.
(e) The coiled coil.

**Figure 22—4**
Typical Bulb Shapes

(A) Arbitrary designation.
(S) Straight side.
(PS) Pear shape.
(T) Tubular.
(PAR) Parabolic aluminized reflector.
(G) Globular.
(R) Reflector.
(C) Cone shape.

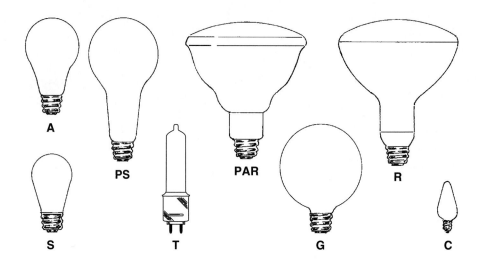

straight sides) are common forms of household lamps. Lamps used in stage lighting instruments were once globe-shaped (G) to allow even dissipation of heat. Today's tungsten-halogen lamps are nearly all tubular (T) in shape, allowing the filament to be brought closer to a reflector. There are a number of other shapes, some of which are purely decorative. The familiar R-type and PAR lamps will be discussed separately later in this chapter.

**Bulb Size**     The size of a bulb is designated by a numbering system which may seem unnecessarily complex, but which is at least standardized. The diameter of the bulb at its largest point is expressed in eighths of an inch. For example, the common T-6 quartz lamp has a tubular envelope and is six-eighths (or three-quarters) of an inch in diameter.

**Bulb Finishes and Color**     Lamps used on the stage usually are made of clear glass, which is essential for any source used in an instrument with a reflector or lens. Common A and PS lamps are most readily available with an inner finish called "frosted." A frosted finish diffuses the light, thereby reducing glare. These lamps can be ordered in the clear-glass style, and often are used that way in signs and for scenery effects.

There are many kinds of finishes available, some purely decorative and others for special applications. Low-wattage PAR lamps can be bought with colored lenses, and small G and A lamps have colored bulbs. These lamps can be put to good use for decorative purposes.

### LAMP BASES AND SOCKETS

A lamp base provides three important functions:

1. It precisely holds the lamp in a predetermined position, critical to the proper operation of a reflector.
2. It conducts electrical current from the socket to the filament.
3. It allows for quick and easy lamp replacement.

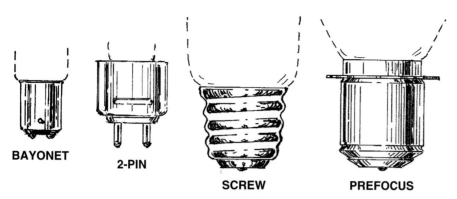

**BAYONET**

**2-PIN**

**SCREW**

**PREFOCUS**

**Figure 22–5**
Common Base Types

In addition to those shown, the bi-post base is used for high wattage lamps. It looks like a large 2-pin base.

Base and socket assemblies are similar to connectors in an electrical circuit. They exist for convenience in changing the lamp. The electrical contact part of the base is made of brass or aluminum. In the medium-sized screw base of a common household lamp, the button at the bottom conducts the electricity to the filament. The return path of electricity is through the aluminum screw-base rim.

**Base Sizes and Shapes**     Normally the size of a base varies with the wattage of a lamp. Large bases are called "mogul," middle-sized bases are called "medium," and small bases are called "miniature."

There is a huge variety of types of bases, but the most common theatrical bases are the screw base, the prefocus base, and the 2-pin base (Figure 22–5). Screw bases work well for low- to medium-wattage lamps whose filaments do not need to be precisely aligned. Prefocus and 2-pin bases are used on medium- to high-wattage lamps that need proper alignment. A base called the bi-post, which looks like a large 2-pin, is used for very high-wattage lamps.

Most tungsten-halogen stage lamps use either a prefocus, 2-pin, or double-ended base (Figure 22–6). The prefocus base slips into its socket and requires slight pressure downward and a turn before the lamp "clicks" into alignment. The 2-pin lamp slides straight into its socket and is held in place by a pressure plate. Excessive handling or jarring may cause this lamp to dislodge from its base, and therefore care must be taken with instruments requiring this lamp. The double-ended lamp is held in place by two metal contacts, mounted so that they protrude through the reflector of an instrument. Depending on the design of the lighting instrument, these lamps can be difficult to get properly seated. Care must be taken not to damage either the contacts or the seal of the lamp base.

## R-TYPE AND PAR LAMPS

The R-type (reflector-type) and PAR (parabolic aluminized reflector) lamps are discussed separately here because each is essentially a self-contained lighting instrument. Both the PAR and R-type lamps have a mirrored-glass

**Figure 22–6**
Common Theatre Lamps

Shown are three common
tungsten-halogen lamp and
base types.

500W TO
1000W

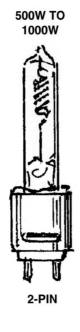

2-PIN

1500W TO
2000W

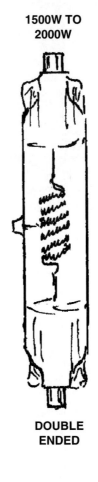

DOUBLE
ENDED

750W TO
1000W

MEDIUM
PREFOCUS

parabolic-shaped reflector that sends light to the lens in parallel rays. Low-wattage versions have standard incandescent filaments, while the brighter and larger sizes have a small quartz lamp placed at the focal point of the reflector. Both PAR and R-type lamps are extremely efficient and have found many uses in the theatre.

**R-Type Lamps**      All R-type lamps consist of a single-piece glass bulb that is inside-frosted to varying degrees, depending on the desired beam spread. Their field of light is generally smooth and even, with a soft beam edge. Being light and fairly fragile, they are intended for indoor use.

The following range of R-type lamps is available:

30-watt R-20 ($\frac{20}{8}$ or $2\frac{1}{2}$-inch diameter); spot (38°); medium screw base
50-watt R-20; spot (38°); medium screw base
75-watt R-30; flood (130°) and spot (50°); medium screw base
100-watt R-40; flood (120°) and spot (36°); medium screw base
150-watt R-40; flood (110°) and spot (37°); medium screw base

300-watt R-40; flood (120°) and spot (40°); medium screw base

500-watt R-40; flood (115°); mogul screw base

750-watt R-52; medium flood (70°); mogul screw base

1,000-watt R-60; medium flood (80°); mogul screw base

The smaller R-20 variety can be tucked away in tight places for special effects or to solve a particular lighting problem. The R-40 flood and spot lamps have long been used in striplights for cyclorama and backdrop lighting. In this application, the floods are used for lighting close and the spots for longer throws. The higher-wattage flood lamps are seldom used in the theatre because PARs are brighter and more able to throw long distances.

**PAR Lamps** The parabolic aluminized reflector lamp is made out of heavy, heat-resistant glass and can be used outdoors. It has a molded-glass lens, which determines beam spread and, to some degree, shape (Figure 22–7). The range of available PAR lamps is as follows:

35-watt PAR-20; flood (40°), narrow flood (30°), and narrow spot (8°); medium screw base

50-watt PAR-30; flood (42°), narrow flood (32°), and narrow spot (12°); medium screw base

75-watt PAR-30; flood (42°), narrow flood (32°), and narrow spot (12°); medium screw base

100-watt PAR-38; flood (30°) and spot (15°); medium screw base

150-watt PAR-38; very wide flood (55°), flood (30°), and spot (10°); medium screw base

200-watt PAR-46; very wide flood (63° × 65°), medium flood (11° × 26°), and narrow spot (9° × 13°); medium side-prong base

300-watt PAR-56; wide flood (19° × 42°), medium flood (11° × 23°), and narrow spot (8° × 10°); mogul end-prong base

500-watt PAR-64; wide flood (19° × 58°), medium flood (9° × 24°), and narrow spot (7° × 10°); extended mogul end-prong base

1,000-watt PAR-64; wide flood (24° × 48°), medium flood (12° × 28°), narrow spot (7° × 14°), and very narrow spot (6° × 12°); extended mogul end-prong base

Note that beam shape becomes oval beginning with the 200-watt PAR-46. Comparison of the beam spread of PAR lamps with that of comparable R-type lamps indicates that the PAR lamp is intended for longer throws.

Automobile headlights have used PAR lamps for years, but it took rock concert lighting to introduce these powerful lamps to the theatre. Quartz PAR-64 lamps are mounted in a very simple housing (aptly named a PAR can) and have the ability to throw a highly concentrated beam of light over a considerable distance. The light has a very distinctive quality because of its nearly parallel rays and its sheer intensity. The beam is oval due to the filament shape. It has a very soft and fuzzy edge, making it possible to blend one beam with another.

**Figure 22–7**
**PAR-64 Lamp**

A drawing of a PAR-64 showing its extended mogul end-prong base and a photograph of a FFS (wide PAR).

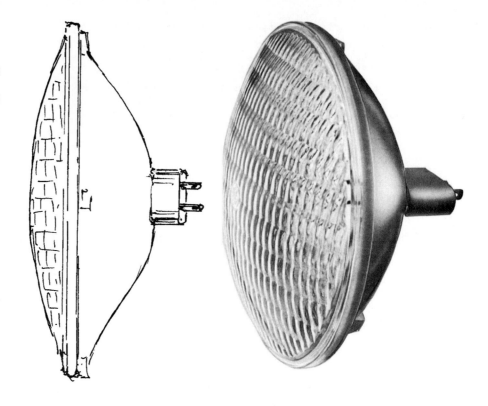

Par-38 and -56 lamps are used in striplights to throw an intense wash of light on a drop or act as color-toning border lights. As with R-type lamps, one can alter the beam spread of a PAR fixture by changing the lamp.

### LOW-VOLTAGE LAMPS

Low-voltage light sources are lamps designed to operate with less than 120 applied volts. Sealed-beam automobile headlights operate to full potential on only 12 volts. Aircraft lamps, useful in the theatre for special purposes, operate on 24 volts. The advantage of low-voltage lamps for theatre applications is in the intensity and quality of the light they emit. The lower the voltage applied to a lamp filament, the smaller the filament can be. Therefore, low-voltage sources have filaments that really do begin to approach the much-desired point source of light. The more closely a point source is approximated, the better the light can be controlled through use of reflectors and lenses.

**Power Sources**    Low-voltage lamps such as aircraft landing lamps (ACLs) deliver a highly coherent light that is intense and harsh in quality. To use such lamps on the stage, however, a low-voltage power source is necessary. A variable-voltage transformer is a good equipment investment for a theatre, but it is fairly expensive. One alternative that will work in certain situations is a continuous-duty automobile battery charger. This is actually a step-down transformer from 120 to 12 volts. A second alternative is an auto-transformer dimmer, which functions by reducing the voltage to a lamp (not true of SCR and other electronic dimmers). By measuring the output of an auto-transformer dimmer with a voltmeter, it can be set to provide any voltage up to 120.

**MR-11 and MR-16 Lamps**     The MR-16 (miniature reflector, 2-inch diameter) lamp was originally developed as a light source for the Kodak Carousel slide projector (Figure 22–8). It is a 12-volt, T-3 (tubular, $\frac{3}{8}$-inch diameter) tungsten-halogen lamp built into a dichroic reflector. The reflector is designed to allow nonvisible light (ultraviolet and infrared) to pass through, while reflecting only visible rays. This results in the light beam having less heat and less harmful ultraviolet radiation. These little reflector lamps have been put to wide use in display and museum lighting, and are a valuable theatrical light source. They are bright and extremely compact. Twelve-volt MR lamps are available in the following types, all with 2-pin bases:

20-, 35-, and 50-watt MR-11; flood (30°), medium flood (20°), and spot (10°)

20-watt MR-16; flood (36°) and narrow spot (12°)

35-watt MR-16; flood (38°), spot (18°), and narrow spot (8°)

50-watt MR-16; very wide flood (60°), flood (38°), medium flood (30°), narrow flood (24°), and narrow spot (12°)

75-watt MR-16; flood (38°), medium flood (24°), and narrow spot (14°)

It should be noted that 120-volt versions of the MR-16 lamp do exist. They burn very hot and require glass filters. The 12-volt MR-16 is used in a variety of lighting instruments including striplights, but its most interesting application is on its own as a tiny spotlight. Mounted in what appears to be an extremely small PAR fixture, this lamp can be tucked into the tightest of spaces. While it does require low voltage, recent developments have led to transformers that can be dimmed and located remotely. The light is of good quality with a harshness that is typical of low voltage, but unusual from such a small source. The narrow beam spreads allow the light to be projected over considerable distances.

## ARC LIGHT

The first electric light source to be used in the theatre was an arc light in the form of limelight. Blocks of calcium oxide (lime) were used in place of the

**Figure 22–8**
The MR-16 Lamp

(a) Nine MR-16 lamps make up the MicroBrute LV9 fixture. Each of the three vertical rows can be aimed separately. Application is greater for television and film, but such a unit can be of value for special theatre needs. Photo courtesy The Great American Market.
(b) The MR-16 lamp with its miniature 2-pin base and dichroic reflector. Photo courtesy General Electric Company.

a

b

more recent carbon rods in spotlights, each requiring an operator. In fact, there are reports that the quality of limelight was so flattering that patrons bemoaned the installation of more modern incandescent light sources in many theatres.

Arc light is impressive because of its brilliance. A streak of lightning during a thunderstorm is an example of arc light on a grand scale. An electric arc light source is composed of two electrodes separated from each other in order to create a gap across which the current must jump.

## CARBON ARC

Carbon arc became popular as a theatrical source because of its great intensity and high color temperature. Broadway musical productions required a follow spot that could throw a high-intensity light over a long distance. The carbon arc follow spot, first marketed in 1948 by Strong International, was the solution.

Two copper-coated carbon rods, about the size of pencils, were mounted within a housing along with a reflector and lenses. Electricity was conducted to the tips of the rods via the copper coating. The rods were brought together to begin the flow of electricity and then backed off to create a gap. Air, being a good resistor, caused the arc to glow brightly.

Today, a xenon arc lamp takes the place of the carbon rod in Strong's line of Trouper and Super Trouper follow spots.

## ARC LAMPS

Two tungsten electrodes in a strong glass enclosure of gas under high pressure produce an intense light source when the current arcs between the electrodes. Because the arc is shielded from the oxygen in the air, the tungsten electrodes do not burn up as do the carbons in a carbon arc follow spot.

**The Xenon Lamp**     Developed in 1954 by Osram Corporation, the XBO xenon short-arc was the first arc lamp light source. Filled with high-pressure xenon gas, this lamp burns with a brilliant, cool light. It maintains a color temperature of approximately 6,000 degrees Kelvin.

A 75-watt xenon lamp is roughly as bright as a 1,000-watt tungsten-halogen lamp, and the xenon lamp's life is twice as long! Because of its efficiency and long life, it became the standard lamp for follow spots and motion picture projectors.

A drawback of xenon arc lamps is the very high pressure built up within the bulb. Explosion-proof lamp housings are required for xenon sources. Like carbon arc, the xenon arc can only operate with a DC (direct current) power supply. Therefore, a transformer that meets the needs of the individual lamp is necessary equipment. No arc source can be electrically dimmed. Therefore, mechanical dimmers are provided as a part of the stage instruments that use arc sources.

**Metal Halide Arc Lamps**     Several years ago GTE Sylvania and Osram Corporation joined forces to become Osram Sylvania. They have had much to do with the development of the newest arc sources: the HMI and HTI metal halide arc lamps (Figure 22–9). Their bulb is quartz glass filled with metal halides. They have a very short arc, which works extremely well with the optics of projectors and stage lighting equipment. The internal pressure within the bulb is lower than xenon, eliminating the need for expensive explosion-proof housings.

HMI lamps have color temperatures ranging between 5,600 and 6,000 degrees Kelvin. The 575-watt HMI lamp used by Clay Paky's Golden Scan automated fixture burns at 5,600 degrees Kelvin and operates at 95 volts. Its intensity is equivalent to a 2,000-watt incandescent lamp, with its 750-hour average life being twice that of the incandescent lamp. The 1,200-watt HMI used by Clay Paky's Superscan is as bright as a 5,000-watt incandescent lamp with twice the life.

HMI sources are also available in the form of PAR lamps. They offer a choice of four lenses: narrow spot (7° × 8°), medium flood (9° × 21°), wide flood (26° × 56°), and super wide flood (47° × 47°). They are very bright and have high color temperatures and long lives.

The 400-watt HTI lamp used by the Vari∗Lite VL4 wash luminaire requires 55 volts and burns at 4,800 degrees Kelvin. It is as bright as a 1,000-watt incandescent lamp and has a similar life expectancy. Osram Sylvania also offers a 250- and a 400-watt HTI lamp with a dichroic reflector.

**Figure 22–9**
**Arc Sources**

Shown are three metal halide arc lamps from Osram Sylvania.
(a) 4,000-watt HMI
(b) 600-watt HTI
(c) 150-watt HTI
Photos courtesy Osram Sylvania Inc.

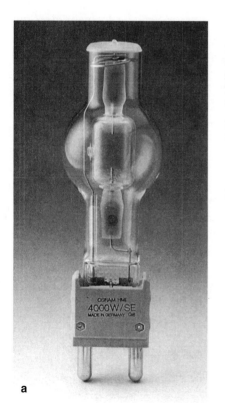

a

b

c

## GASEOUS DISCHARGE LAMPS

The most familiar form of a gaseous discharge lamp is the fluorescent tube, which never achieved its promise of becoming a major light source in the theatre. Current passing through a pressurized mercury vapor causes a gaseous discharge, predominantly in the ultraviolet zone. This energy is absorbed by the phosphorous coating on the inside walls of the tube and is emitted as light.

Because the fluorescent tube is a line of light and not a point source, its uses in the theatre are limited to producing a wash of light on a cyclorama or backdrop. The shape of the lamp makes it difficult to achieve smooth color blending. Dimming is possible with special equipment. Fluorescent hoods can be installed with black light fluorescent tubes to flood the stage with ultraviolet light for black light effects.

## LAMP LIFE

The rated average life for the common household lamp is at least 750 burning hours, but for stage lamps it is as low as 200 hours. Rated average life is determined by the manufacturer, who burns a number of lamps under normal conditions until either (1) they burn out completely, or (2) their light output drops to 80 percent of what it was originally.

Rated average life is presumed to apply under usual operating conditions. But a lamp's life may be shortened in a number of ways. A filament gives out more quickly if burned while enclosed in an excessively hot place such as one from which its own heat cannot escape (lighting instruments are specifically ventilated for this purpose). Rough handling may break some interior part, even though the outer appearance has not changed. And, in the case of some lamps, burning in the wrong position results in early failure. Proper burning position, if important, is always marked on the end of the bulb.

### LAMP VOLTAGE

If a lamp designed to be used on 120-volt service is fed with only 110 volts, it will last almost four times as long as it would on 120 volts. However, there will be only about 74 percent as much light. On the other hand, if this same lamp is fed 130 volts, there will be 31 percent more light, but the lamp will last only a third as long. Stage lamps often last far longer than rated life because they have been burned at low dimmer readings.

This relationship of voltage, intensity, and life must be kept in mind, especially in conjunction with "long-burning" lamps. A 75-watt "long-life" household lamp may burn twice as long, but it burns less brightly.

### WATTAGE AND LUMEN OUTPUT

The general public has been taught by lamp manufacturers to equate the wattage of a lamp with its brightness. If our 75-watt reading lamp is too dim,

| Watts | Volts | Bulb Shape | Order Code | LIF Code | Description | Case Quantity | Approx. Initial Lumens | Color Temp. K | Filament Design | MOL in. (mm) | LCL in. (mm) | Rated Average Life Hours | Fig. No. |
|---|---|---|---|---|---|---|---|---|---|---|---|---|---|
| **Clear, for VBU Operation** | | | | | | | | | | | | | |
| 500 | 120 | T12 | 21799 | | DEB-500T12/8 | 12 | 9000 | 2850 | C-13D | 6 1/8 (155.6) | 3 1/2 (88.9) | 800 | 2 |
| 500 | 120 | T12 | 21795 | | DNS-500T12/9 (29) | 12 | 11000 | 2950 | C-13D | 6 1/8 (155.6) | 3 1/2 (88.9) | 200 | 2 |
| 500 | 120 | T12 | 39134 | | EGC-Q500/5CL/P | 12 | 12700 | 3150 | CC-8 | 6 (152) | 3 1/2 (88.9) | 500 | 1 |
| 500 | 120 | T4 | 39135 | | EGE-Q500CL/P (25) | 12 | 10450 | 2950 | CC-8 | 6 (152) | 3 1/2 (88.9) | 2000 | 1 |
| 750 | 120 | T12 | 22100 | | DNT-750T12/9 | 12 | 17000 | 3000 | C-13D | 6 1/8 (155.6) | 3 1/2 (88.9) | 200 | 2 |
| 750 | 120 | T6 | 39136 | | EGF-Q750/4CL/P | 12 | 20400 | 3200 | CC-8 | 6 (152) | 3 1/2 (88.9) | 500 | 1 |
| 750 | 120 | T6 | 39137 | | EGG-Q750CL/P | 12 | 15750 | 2900 | CC-8 | 6 (152) | 3 1/2 (88.9) | 2000 | 1 |
| 1000 | 120 | T6 | 38853 | | EGJ-Q1000/4CL/P | 12 | 27500 | 3200 | CC-8 | 6 (152) | 3 1/2 (88.9) | 500 | 1 |
| 1000 | 120 | T6 | 39138 | | EGM-Q1000CL/P | 12 | 21500 | 3000 | CC-8 | 6 (152) | 3 1/2 (88.9) | 2000 | 1 |
| 1000 | 220 | T11 | 30531 | T15 | FKE | 12 | 23000 | 3050 | C-13 | 6 5/16 (160) | 3 1/2 (88.9) | 750 | 2 |
| 1000 | 240 | | 30532 | | | 12 | 23000 | 3050 | C-13 | 6 5/16 (160) | 3 1/2 (88.9) | 750 | |
| 1000 | 220 | T6 | 30533 | | EWE | 12 | 26500 | 3200 | CC-8 | 6 (152) | 3 1/2 (88.9) | 250 | 1 |
| 1000 | 240 | | 30534 | | | 12 | 26500 | 3200 | CC-8 | 6 (152) | 3 1/2 (88.9) | 250 | 1 |

we simply replace it with a 100-watt lamp. But, as we learned in the previous chapter, wattage is the rate of doing work. It is not necessarily an accurate measure of lamp intensity. Lamp manufacturers use a measure of intensity called the *lumen* to measure the light output of a lamp. Figure 22–10 shows how two lamps with identical physical specifications can be very different in brightness (compare EGJ and EGM). Note that as lumen output is increased, lamp life is significantly decreased.

**Figure 22–10**

Comparison of Wattage, Color Temperature, Life, and Lumen Output

Compare the 1,000-watt EGJ and EGM lamps. Table courtesy General Electric Company.

## COLOR TEMPERATURE

As previously discussed in Chapter 15, most people consider the color of light emitted from an ordinary lamp to be white. However, so-called "white" light is relative and the actual color of light given off by sources can vary greatly. The method we have to identify the color makeup of any light source is called *color temperature*, and it is measured in degrees Kelvin (°K).

In an effort to standardize light source color notation, a light-emitting device called a "blackbody" was developed. When heated, it emits light consisting of various color wavelengths. The blackbody responds to heat in much the same way that a tungsten filament does. It begins to glow a very warm red-yellow, moves toward "white" as more heat is applied, and finally appears to approach blue when a great deal of heat is applied. The color wavelengths of light emitted by the blackbody are identified by a sophisticated meter called a "spectrophotometer." Any color of light can thus be equated with the temperature of heat applied to the blackbody, resulting in a meaningful Kelvin figure.

This is fairly important for a lighting designer to understand because theatre sources vary in color from standard incandescence, which is around 3,000° K, to much cooler arc lamps, which can be as high as 6,000° K. Obviously, the same filter placed in front of two such different sources will project very different colors. For all practical purposes, no one will notice a source color difference of less than 200° K, but any more of a difference will be noticeable. The color temperature of stage lamps is often printed on their containers and is always noted in catalogues. A general rule to go by is the higher the color temperature, the cooler the light. Always remember that dimming a source decreases its color temperature significantly.

## THE ANSI LAMP CODE

The American National Standards Institute (ANSI) has established a system for identifying lamps using a three-letter code called the "ANSI code." If one lamp differs in any way from another, it is assigned a separate ANSI code (Figure 22–10). Although the three-letter codes are totally nondescriptive by themselves, they have greatly simplified the process of specifying lamps. One may order a lamp by simply providing the supplier with its ANSI code.

## COMMON STAGE INSTRUMENT LAMPS

A lighting instrument is often designed with a certain lamp or lamps in mind. The instrument's ventilation, base type and size, and reflector specifications may all be determined by the choice of lamp. All stage lighting manufacturers provide specific lamp recommendations for their instruments, usually allowing a choice of several different lamps depending on the user's preference. The table below is a sampling from the catalogues of several instrument manufacturers.

### RECOMMENDED LAMPS

| | Watts | ANSI Code | Color Temp. | Lumens | Life (hours) |
|---|---|---|---|---|---|
| 6″ Ellipsoidals | | | | | |
| | 500 | EGE | 3,000° K | 10,450 | 2,000 |
| | 750 | EGG | 3,000° K | 15,750 | 2,000 |
| | 750 | EHF | 3,200° K | 20,400 | 300 |
| | 750 | EHG | 3,000° K | 15,400 | 2,000 |
| | 1,000 | EGJ | 3,200° K | 27,500 | 400 |
| | 1,000 | FEL | 3,200° K | 27,500 | 300 |
| 6″ Fresnels | | | | | |
| | 500 | BTL | 3,050° K | 11,000 | 750 |
| | 750 | BTN | 3,050° K | 17,000 | 500 |
| | 1,000 | BTR | 3,200° K | 27,500 | 200 |

Note that several lamps of the same wattage are listed, but their color temperature, lamp life and lumen output differ.

The stage electrician should be familiar with all possible variations in lamp manufacture and have access to up-to-date lamp catalogues. Not only

**Safety Practice**

A good electrician follows several simple rules when working with the various light sources found in the theatre:
1.  Always unplug a lighting instrument before replacing
    a bad lamp.
2.  Lamps are expensive, so be sure to treat them with care.
3.  Keep fingers off quartz bulbs.
4.  The envelope of a burning lamp gets too hot to handle even with the
    best of gloves.

are these catalogues useful when ordering spare lamps, but they also offer
quick access to special-application lamps such as flashbulbs, low-voltage
lamps, arc lamps, and photofloods. The two major manufacturers in the
United States are willing to supply you with their current catalogues. Write
either to their regional sales offices or to the following addresses:

Osram Sylvania
100 Endicott Street
Danvers, MA 01923

General Electric Company
Lighting Business Group
Nela Park
Cleveland, OH 44112

# STAGE LIGHTING PRACTICE: DESIGN

## 23

This chapter presents lighting layouts for different types of production in a variety of spaces. We will examine simplified designs for a realistic interior "box set" in the proscenium theatre; an "in-the-round" production in an arena theatre; and a drama designed for the thrust stage.

The following examples have been simplified for clarity and ease of presentation. Each lighting layout is deliberately designed to show the minimum number of instruments necessary to achieve acceptable design and visibility. Additional commentary on the individual layouts offers suggestions for embellishing the basic designs, assuming more equipment is available.

## DESIGN PRACTICE: THE PROSCENIUM THEATRE

When a proscenium theatre is used in the traditional manner, the main action of the play takes place upstage of the proscenium line. In this case, front-light for the downstage acting areas comes from a lighting position typically located in the ceiling of the auditorium. Front-light for upstage areas comes from the first electric pipe.

Let us assume that the theatre we are using is of medium size. The stage has a 30-foot-wide and 18-foot-high proscenium opening. There is ample provision for hanging scenery and lighting instruments above the stage. About 20 feet out from the proscenium line is a ceiling beam-port for mounting front spotlights.

### A REALISTIC INTERIOR

Realistic interiors often call for some variation of the conventional box setting, either with or without a ceiling piece. As one might expect, the existence of a ceiling has a great effect on lighting possibilities. The primary

**Figure 23–1**
Realistic Interior: Sketch

action takes place within the walls of this set, while the backgrounds seen through windows and doors are of less importance. The lighting is often motivated by apparent sources such as sunlight through the windows, light from sconces, or firelight. In practically all cases it is realistically plausible.

Figure 23–1 is a sketch of such a setting. In the upstage-left wall, a door leads into the kitchen. Upstage-center, a flight of stairs comes down into the living room, and just to the right an exterior door leads out to the porch. In the stage-right wall is a four-window alcove that looks out onto the porch.

Two lighting scenarios are involved. Act I takes place in the afternoon of a somewhat overcast day, and Act II is later that evening.

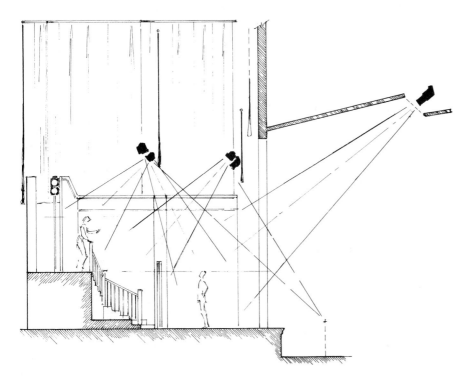

**Figure 23–2**
Realistic Interior: Center Line Section

Note how the height and placement of the over-stage masking borders is determined by using the audience sight point.

**Figure 23–3**
Realistic Interior Schedule and Plot

(a) Instrument schedule.
(b) Lighting layout. Instruments have been numbered sequentially for ease of identification.

**Sectional View**    Figure 23–2 is a centerline section of the stage and auditorium, showing lighting positions and angles. Especially useful is the elevation of the upstage landing and steps leading to it. The beam spreads shown from several of the instruments indicate the amount of coverage in a given area. The centerline of the beam is used to determine vertical angle. The sight point (indicated by a cross symbol) located in the auditorium represents the first row of audience seating. Lines from this point past the masking borders show whether or not lighting instruments are hidden from audience view.

| INSTRUMENT NO. AND LOCATION | TYPE | USE | LAMP | COLOR | CHANNEL | REMARKS |
|---|---|---|---|---|---|---|
| 1 - CEILING SLOT | 6 x 16 ERS | AREA 2 | 1K | R02 | 2 | |
| 2 - " " | 6 x 16 " | AREA 1 | 1K | R02 | 1 | |
| 3 - " " | 6 x 16 " | AREA 3 | 1K | R02 | 3 | |
| 4 - " " | 6 x 16 " | AREA 4 | 1K | R02 | 4 | |
| 5 - " " | 6 x 16 " | SPECIAL | 1K | R02 | 9 | SOFA |
| 6 - " " | 6 x 16 " | AREA 1 | 1K | R60 | 11 | |
| 7 - " " | 6 x 16 " | SPECIAL | 1K | R60 | 19 | SOFA |
| 8 - " " | 6 x 16 " | AREA 2 | 1K | R60 | 12 | |
| 9 - " " | 6 x 16 " | AREA 4 | 1K | R60 | 14 | |
| 10 - " " | 6 x 16 " | AREA 3 | 1K | R60 | 13 | |
| 11 - 1ST ELECTRIC | 6 x 12 " | AREA 9 | 750 | R02 | 27 | |
| 12 - " " | 6" FRESNEL | AREA 5 | 750 | R02 | 5 | CIRCUIT w/ #13 |
| 13 - " " | 6" " | AREA 6 | 750 | R02 | 5 | CIRCUIT w/ #12 |
| 14 - " " | 6 x 9 ERS | SPECIAL | 750 | R02 | 26 | STAIR + LANDING |
| 15 - " " | 6" FRESNEL | AREA 9 | 750 | R02 | 8 | |
| 16 - " " | 6" " | AREA 7 | 750 | R02 | 6 | |
| 17 - " " | 6" " | AREA 5 | 750 | R60 | 15 | |
| 18 - " " | 6 x 9 ERS | SPECIAL | 750 | R02 | 26 | UPPER LANDING |
| 19 - " " | 6" FRESNEL | " | 750 | R02 | 28 | WINDOW SEAT |
| 20 - " " | 3½" ERS | " | 400 | R60 | 37 | FRAME ON TROPHY |
| 21 - " " | 6" FRESNEL | AREA 6 | 750 | R60 | 15 | |
| 22 - " " | 6 x 12 ERS | SPECIAL | 750 | R02 | 35 | FRAME TO ARCH- AREA 9 |
| 23 - " " | 6" FRESNEL | " | 750 | R02 | 28 | WINDOW SEAT |
| 24 - " " | 6" " | AREA 7 | 750 | R60 | 16 | |
| 25 - " " | 6" " | AREA 9 | 750 | R60 | 18 | |
| 26 - 2ND ELECTRIC | 8" FRESNEL | AREA 1 | 1K | R09 | 21 | BARNDOOR OFF SCENERY |
| 27 - " " | 6" " | STAIRS | 750 | R02 | 10 | " " " " |
| 28 - " " | 8" " | AREA 2 | 1K | R09 | 22 | |
| 29 - " " | 8" " | AREA 1 | 1K | N/C | 31 | |
| 30 - " " | 6" " | AREA 8 | 750 | R02 | 7 | |
| 31 - " " | 8" " | AREA 3 | 1K | R09 | 23 | |
| 32 - " " | 6" " | STAIRS | 750 | R60 | 20 | |
| 33 - " " | 6" " | AREA 8 | 750 | R60 | 17 | |
| 34 - " " | 8" " | AREA 2 | 1K | N/C | 32 | |
| 35 - " " | 8" " | AREA 4 | 1K | R09 | 24 | |
| 36 - " " | 3½" ERS | SPECIAL | 400 | N/C | 37 | FRAME ON TROPHY |
| 37 - " " | 8" FRESNEL | AREA 3 | 1K | N/C | 33 | |
| 38 - " " | 8" " | AREA 4 | 1K | N/C | 34 | |
| 39 - BOOM #1 | 6" " | KITCHEN | 750 | N/C | 36 | |
| 40 - BOOM #2 | 6" " | HALL | 750 | R02 | 25 | CIRCUIT w/ #41 |
| 41 - BOOM #2 | 6" " | LANDING | 750 | R02 | 25 | CIRCUIT w/ #40 |
| 42 - SPOTLINE PIPE #2 | 8" " | STREET LIGHTS | 1K | R62 | 41 | CIRCUIT w/ #43 |
| 43 - " " #2 | 8" " | " " | 1K | R62 | 41 | CIRCUIT w/ #42 |
| 44 - " " #2 | 8" " | " " | 1K | R62 | 41 | |
| 45 - " " #1 | PORCH LIGHT | PRACTICAL | 100 | N/C | 42 | |
| 46 - " " #1 | " | " | 100 | N/C | 42 | FIXTURE IN VIEW |
| 47 - " " #1 | 14" ERF | WINDOW WASH | 750 | R02 | 29 | |
| 48 - HALL | 9" ERF | WALL WASH | 500 | R02 | 30 | |
| 49 - " | CEILING FIXTURE | PRACTICAL | 3 @ 40w | N/C | 38 | |
| 50 - SR WALL | WALL SCONCE | " | 2 @ 40w | N/C | 39 | |
| 51 - STAIRS | " " | " | 2 @ 40w | N/C | 40 | |

a

**Instrument Schedule and Layout**     Figure 23–3a is the instrument schedule for the layout in Figure 23–3b. For ease and clarity of presentation, the instruments are numbered consecutively throughout rather than consecutively by position. The two cross symbols on the plan indicate critical side sight points from the extreme seats house-left and house-right in the front row. These sight points are used to determine what the audience can see through door openings and windows and beyond side masking. Refer to the instrument schedule for details such as instrument type, focus area, color and

**b**

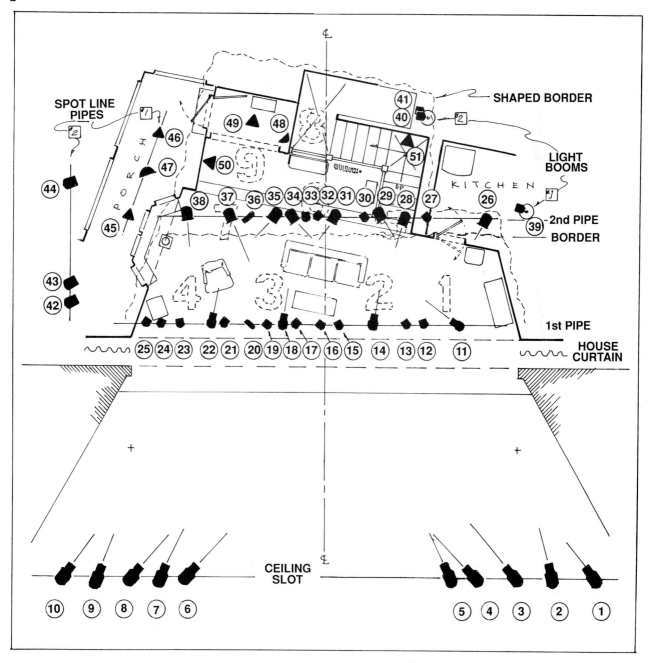

channel assignment. Take the time to refer back and forth between the reading and the plot.

### THE LIGHT PLOT

The lights in this plot must accommodate both scenes of the play. It is expected that the primary light source for the afternoon of Act I is daylight coming through the stage-right windows. The source of illumination in the evening of Act II is interior lighting, including the practical sconces located on the set.

The designer has chosen to use two lights from the front, colored in R02 (bastard amber) and R60 (no-color blue). There are also two lights from the back colored in R09 (pale amber gold) and no-color. The color key in Figure 23−4 indicates position of these instruments.

Act I has the stage-right R60 front-light and no-color back-light reading 70 to 80 percent on their dimmers. The stage-left R02 front-light and R09 back-light read 90 to 100 percent. This provides the look of natural interior day light and offers enough color and intensity contrast to maintain interest. Act II has the R60 front-light reading at 60 to 70 percent and the no color back-light is not reading at all. The R02 front-light reads 50 to 60 percent, and the R09 back-light reads 70 to 80 percent. The warmer color produced by lower dimmer readings from the stage-left instruments should simulate interior incandescent lighting. For color contrast, the blue front remains at a medium-high reading. Taking the no-color back-light out completely should create a sense of darkness and shadow from one direction, a good feeling for evening.

**Downstage Areas**     In dividing the stage into lighting areas, we find that four across the front will be fine as long as a center stage sofa special covers the overlap of areas 2 and 3. To cover these four areas we mount 1,000-watt 6-by-16 or 20-degree ellipsoidals in the ceiling position. A look at the section shows that the angle from the beam-port to the downstage areas is roughly 45 degrees. This represents a good angle for visibility. The ellipsoidal reflector spotlight is an ideal front-of-house instrument due to its beam control

**Figure 23−4**
Realistic Interior: Color Key

Shown is the color key for the light plot in Figure 23−3.

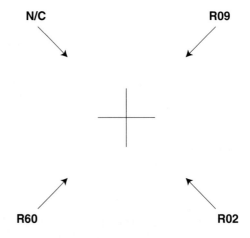

capabilities. For a shorter throw than the one in our sample theatre, or for larger lighting areas, the 30-degree 6-by-12 ERS would be a good choice.

An important skill for a lighting designer to learn is the ability to examine a light plot to determine where scenery, masking, or the architecture of the theatre might interfere with the path of light. In choosing mounting positions for the beam-port instruments, we have attempted to maintain the desired 45-degree horizontal angle. But note that we must mount instrument #2 somewhat in from the end of the ceiling beam-port in order to reach the extreme downstage-left corner of area 1 without being cut off by the proscenium arch. In addition, the color blend hitting the stage-left wall from the blue R60 in instrument #6 and the warm R02 in instrument #2 will be better with #2 moved a bit towards center. In like manner, instrument #9 must move somewhat nearer the center.

Therefore, we have sacrificed to some extent the ideal angle, but it is a necessary compromise. The remaining area instruments can be placed just about where we prefer them. All instruments are carefully shuttered so as not to spill distracting light on the face of the stage apron and, in the case of #2 and #9, on the proscenium arch.

**Back-Light**     Each of the four downstage areas is lit with two additional 8-inch Fresnel back-lights. A Fresnel is ideal for good blending from area to area, and the high-wattage 8-inch instrument is able to punch through the area lights without any trouble. Barn doors cut the light beam from spilling too far downstage and, in the case of instrument #26, off the top of the scenery wall. The upstage areas would be back-lit with another bank of Fresnels from a third electric pipe; but, for the sake of simplicity, we have chosen to exclude these instruments.

The back-light helps to separate the actors from their backgrounds and gives them a pleasing, sculptural look. In addition, its R09 color from stage-left reinforces the feeling of daylight in Act I and, when lowered on the dimmers, provides a nice glow of incandescent light in the night scene of Act II.

**Upstage Areas**     To cover the upstage areas (areas 5, 6, 7, and 9) we use 6-inch Fresnels mounted on the first electric pipe. Fresnels are picked for this location because the soft edge of their beams makes blending between the areas easy. In addition, no sharp and distracting beam patterns will appear on the walls of the set. Instruments #13, #15, and #16 can be focused close to the 45-degree angle for their respective areas; but #12 must move a bit center in order not to hit the wall just stage-right of the kitchen door. Likewise, #17, #21, and #24 are close to the desired angle, but instrument #25 (into area 9) must slide onstage to avoid the stage-right set wall.

The special step area and landing (area 8) are lit with 6-inch Fresnels from the second electric pipe. See the section (Figure 23–2) for an indication of vertical angle.

**Color**     All of the area lights from one direction must be consistent in regard to color. The house-left instruments are colored in R60 because the light outside the window can be considered cool in both acts. The corresponding house-right front-lights are colored in the warmer R02. This color choice is particularly useful because the two colors mix toward white light and will look quite natural on the actors and scenery.

**The Stairway**     Of course, the stairway must not be overlooked. But rather than consider it another area, it is preferable to handle it as a special problem because of its different levels. To light it properly and avoid spilling, we use an ERS in soft focus from the first pipe. Its beam is framed to the stairs themselves and only high enough to cover an actor moving up and down. This is instrument #14 (a 6-by-9 or 40-degree). It will have an R02 filter because warm color seems most appropriate and will blend well with the other colors. When the stairs bend stage-right toward the landing (area 8), a pair of 6-inch Fresnels take over. These instruments (#27 and #32) are used for blending and to avoid harsh shadows on the wall behind the staircase.

**Practicals**     There are five practicals on the set. Instrument #51 is a wall sconce at the first stair landing; #49 is a ceiling light located in the vestibule; #50 is another wall sconce on the upstage-right wall; and #45 and #46 are porch lamps. Note that the triangular "special" symbol is used for these fixtures.

All except the two porch lights should be on their own dimmers, and (as explained in Chapter 19) actual control of the fixtures should be in the hands of the light board operator and stage manager, not the actor. The actors must be instructed to mime switching the practicals on and off while the light board operator does the actual operation.

**Backing and Support Lights**     Backing and support lights are valuable in achieving the illusion required of a box set production. They must be given the same priority as the more traditional visibility lighting.

Beginning in the kitchen, we have hung a 6-inch Fresnel on a boom at a height of 14 feet to simulate a ceiling light. This light, without a color filter, illuminates an actor moving through the kitchen door and shines an interesting light into the living room when the door is open. A second boom holds two 6-inch Fresnels (#40 and #41) at 16 feet off the stage floor and focused down the "hallway" at the top of the stairs. These two instruments, colored in R02, light actors coming into view from behind the wall so that they don't appear to emerge from a black hole.

The upstage-right archway is an important area lit by a special ERS (#22) from the first electric. This instrument is placed in fairly soft focus and shuttered to the arch in order to light an actor entering from the porch door. In addition, the backing wall is washed with a small scoop (#48) colored in the warm R02 to dissipate shadows created by the frontal ERS.

Outside the stage-right window is another larger scoop (#47) that is used as a window-wash during the overcast afternoon scene. More direct sunlight would require different instrumentation in this position, perhaps

PAR fixtures. In the night scene of Act II, instruments #42, #43, and #44 shine in the bay windows imitating streetlights, casting long and eerie shadows into the living room.

**Specials**     These are non-area lighting instruments used for special visibility or effect. As mentioned earlier, the center stage sofa specials (6-by-16 or 20-degree instruments #5 and #7) from the front-of-house ceiling beamport are important not only for accenting action on the sofa, but also because the sofa is located between two lighting areas.

Several Fresnels act as specials into the window seat area from the first electric. These instruments (#19 and #23) fill in where the light for areas 4 and 7 cannot cover adequately.

Instrument #18 is a 6-by-12 ERS focused onto the stair landing for special accent on an actor playing there.

Instrument #20 is framed on a trophy, accentuating its symbolic significance to the play.

**Control**     Even though we attempted to keep the number of instruments to a bare minimum, our schedule still lists a total of fifty-one units. While several instruments (such as the exterior streetlights and the two hall-light Fresnels on boom 2) can be ganged, our layout still requires no fewer than forty-two dimmers. And this figure means that we have to gang areas together.

Two areas that might work together would be 5 and 6. If we place the two R02 Fresnels (#12 and #13) into one dimmer, and the two R60 Fresnels (#17 and #21) into another dimmer, we save two dimmers. Note that like colors always are controlled together. Other ganging choices must be determined by the blocking and desired movement of light.

**Possible Additions**     If more equipment and control were available, we might double-hang the stage-right front-lights. This would allow for more of a distinction between Act I and Act II. A better sense of night could be conveyed if a second set of instruments was colored in more saturated blue or lavender. It would also be possible to vary the angle of the two stage-right sources, thereby accentuating the difference in time of day between the two acts.

**Adding a Ceiling**     If the scene designer adds a ceiling, it would likely eliminate the second electric pipe. However, the first electric pipe must remain, and provisions for it must be made.

All back-light is lost with the second electric pipe. In such a case, the lighting designer must do everything possible to compensate. Extra light flowing into the room from the stage-right windows is a possibility. A set of high side instruments from the first electric pipe is another possibility. In-house cove and box boom positions can be used to provide light that wraps around the performer better than traditional front-light. Some ceilings can have false beam structures built into them, which can accommodate a lighting position.

## DESIGN PRACTICE: ARENA PRODUCTION

The term *arena* is derived from Roman amphitheaters where the audience surrounded the action on all sides and the lighting was nature's. Present-day arena theatres, such as the Arena Stage in Washington, D. C., are fine examples of modern technology working in combination with one of the oldest and most intimate of staging configurations: theatre-in-the-round (Figure 23–5).

### SPECIAL CONSIDERATIONS

Due to audience sightlines, scenery in the arena must be kept to a minimum so as not to block view. Because the audience surrounds the playing space, lighting must be from all directions. Typically, lighting throw distances are shorter in the arena than in proscenium or thrust theatres and the audience is closer to the actors.

**Functions of Arena Lighting**     Visibility remains, of course, the primary function in arena production lighting. The actors should be effectively, although not identically, lit for all members of the surrounding audience. Lighting must focus the spectators' attention to the acting areas, providing good

**Figure 23–5**
Arena Stage Lighting Positions

(a) A perspective view of an arena stage showing the lighting grid.
(b) A sectional view of the same arena showing the various positions and angles of distribution.
  (1) A masking valance and the nearest frontal position behind it.
  (2) The extreme lighting position on the outer edge of the grid.
  (3) A central position over the acting area.
  (4) Special boom position in the aisle for a very low angle.

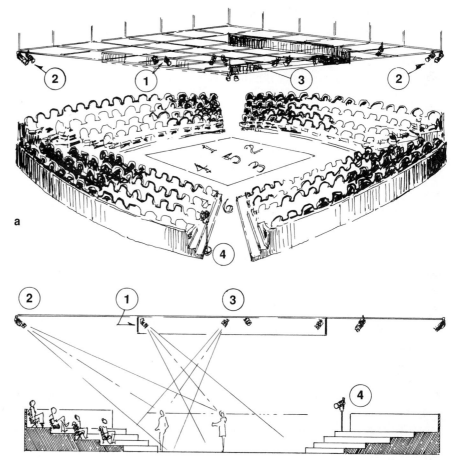

definition and precision of form. Tight and specific area control is often desirable in the arena, adding another requirement, this time of a compositional nature, to the designer's list. Mood must be accomplished by means of intensity and color toning, but both within limited ranges. In addition, the color, texture, and compositional makeup of the stage floor takes on greater visual importance in arena production due to audience viewing angle.

**Accuracy of Focus**     With the audience arranged closely—often too closely—around the playing area, instruments that have hard-to-control beams are of little value. Ellipsoidal reflector spotlights are the best choice. Striplights may be used discreetly and with side maskings to give an overall tonality of rather low intensity. Fresnels must be focused with particular accuracy. In addition, a top hat or barn doors must be added to control the beam spill. PAR fixtures are seldom useful due to their extreme lens flare.

The smaller $3\frac{1}{2}$- or 4-inch ellipsoidals are very useful in an arena space with a low grid. Adjustable field spreads up to 50 degrees are a necessity, making zoom ellipsoidals an ideal choice.

**Arena Lighting Areas**     On the proscenium stage, each area must be covered by a minimum of two spotlights and ideally a third back-light. In an arena, however, where the actor is seen from all sides, more instruments are necessary. There are two popular approaches to the solution. One is that three instruments per area be used, evenly distributed around the area and thus at 120 degrees from one another. The second approach uses four lights on each area, putting them 90 degrees from each other and shooting along the diagonals of the space.

**Color in the Arena**     With either approach, the system of using one warm and one cool color on each area is no longer applicable. In the three-instrument plan, the third instrument is assigned a neutral color, such as light lavender. Opposite a warm filter such as light pink, the lavender appears cool. Opposite a cool filter like a blue tint, the lavender appears warm. Light bastard amber or no color can also be quite effective in this application.

The four-instrument system suggests two color variations. In the first, a warm and a cool are used opposite each other. The other two instruments have a neutral tint. An alternate approach is to use two warms, each opposite the other. The remaining two instruments contain two cools, also opposite each other (Figure 23–6). The latter system often proves most satisfactory.

A word of warning about the saturation of filters used in arena production: Because the directionality of the light on each side of each area is so definite, colors appear very strong on the actors. This is more pronounced than in a proscenium production where there is far more mixing of different beams. Or perhaps this seems true because the audience is so close to the action. In any event, use of the more saturated colors is rarely advisable.

**Unmasked Instruments**     It would be fruitless in a temporary arena setup to attempt to hide the instruments from the audience. They can, of course, all have top hats and be hung and maintained in a neat manner, with wiring

**Figure 23—6**
Arena Color Key

Shown is a possible color key for the arena using four lights per area and a warm/cool approach.

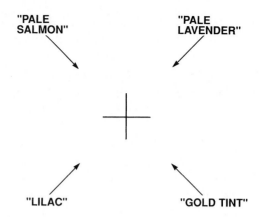

carefully tied off. But a frank acceptance of the fact that the instruments are there for all to view is better than a lot of makeshift, dust-catching, and fire-prone draperies.

However, if a space has been specifically designed for arena production, a false ceiling can be provided with openings through which the beams of light may be focused. Instruments can be safely hung off catwalks well above the ceiling and out of sight. Catwalks must be arranged so that an electrician can reach all instruments for ease of maintenance, focusing, and color changes.

Another solution is the tension wire grid (look ahead to Figure 23–12). Such a grid is suspended over the entire room, allowing great flexibility of instrument placement as well as safe and simple hanging and focus. While the initial expense of such a system is greater than that of others, safety and lower long-term labor costs more than compensate.

**Lighting the Audience**     A difficult problem in any form of arena production is keeping beams of light out of the eyes of spectators seated close to the stage. As long as directors block their actors at the very edge of the arena stage, a compromise is necessary between a well-lighted actor and a half-blinded spectator. Unfortunately, the problem isn't limited to light in the eyes of the audience. Arena audience members look across the stage at other audience members. If the people opposite are lit to any degree, they distract focus from the actors.

To solve the problem, the angle of the instrument or instruments spilling into the audience can be raised, but this compromise only helps to an extent. If the first row of the audience can be raised higher than the stage level, or be set back from it, or both, the problem can be greatly eased. In any event, this is one of the greatest challenges confronting the lighting designer in arena production.

**DESIGNING THE LIGHTING**

The lighting designer need not attempt to create the same lighting picture for everyone in the arena audience. Experience has shown that such an approach is quite restrictive and leads to fairly bland lighting. Nonetheless, the

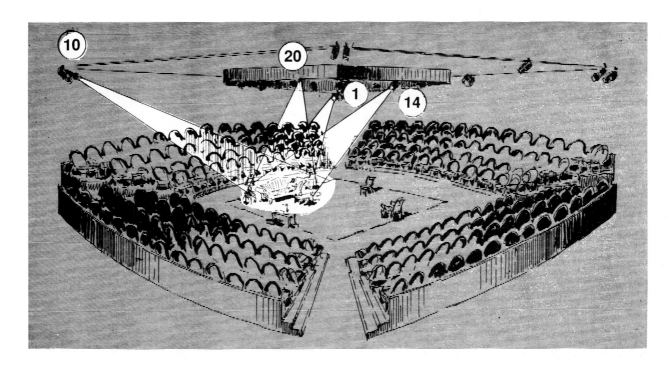

**Figure 23—7**
Lighting an Arena Area

This drawing illustrates area #1 being lit from four angles. The numbers refer to instrument numbers found on the light plot in Figure 23–8.

designer should always be concerned about the quality of lighting from all viewing angles in an arena theatre.

Figure 23–7 illustrates a sample arena layout with properties in place on the stage floor. There are two boxes in which lighting instruments may be hung overhead. The plot and an instrument schedule for a suitable lighting design are shown in Figure 23–8. Refer to these illustrations as you read what follows.

**The Light Plot** The designer has divided the stage into five areas numbered clockwise 1 through 4 with area 5 in the center. Dashed lines on the layout mark the approximate limits of these areas, although it is understood that actually they will overlap one another with their lights blending smoothly.

The area allocation indicated in Figure 23–8 represents an absolute minimum. If the actors play any corners of the stage, they will be poorly lit. Nine areas, three across and three deep, would provide better coverage. It would also nearly double the number of instruments required.

The instruments have been numbered systematically, from the top, clockwise around the stage, in the outer box first and then the inner. From each corner of the outer box, a pair of 6-inch 30-degree ellipsoidal reflector spotlights is focused on the two closest areas. From the inner box, two 40-degree Mini-ellipses are focused on each of the same areas. Looking at area 1 as an example, note that the vertical angle of the Mini-ellipse spotlight is higher than that of the 6-inch ERS. This is done to avoid distracting spill into the audience. The higher angle also means a shorter throw, so a 40-degree rather than a 30-degree instrument is chosen. The ERS is used here because the

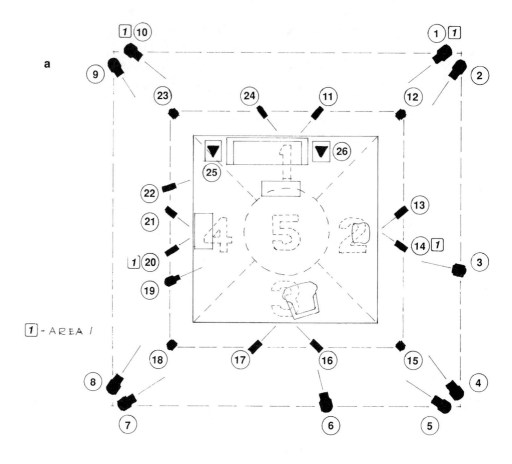

**Figure 23–8**
Arena Schedule and Plot

(a) Instrument schedule with instruments lighting area #1 indicated.
(b) Layout of the lighting instruments. Note the various lighting angles to area #1. In the arena, lighting instruments are often numbered sequentially.

| No. | INSTRUMENT | PURPOSE | LAMP | COLOR | REMARKS |
|---|---|---|---|---|---|
| • 1 | 30° 6" E.R.S. | AREA 1 | 750 W. | G325 | |
| 2 | 30° 6" E.R.S. | AREA 2 | 750 W. | G325 | |
| 3 | 8" FRESNEL | MOONLIGHT SPECIAL | 1000 W. | G815 | FOCUS CENTER |
| 4 | 30° 6" E.R.S. | AREA 2 | 750 W. | G790 | |
| 5 | 30° 6" E.R.S. | AREA 3 | 750 W. | G790 | |
| 6 | 30° 6" E.R.S. | COUCH SPECIAL | 750 W. | G105 | FRAME TO COUCH |
| 7 | 30° 6" E.R.S. | AREA 3 | 750 W. | G364 | |
| 8 | 30° 6" E.R.S. | AREA 4 | 750 W. | G364 | |
| 9 | 30° 6" E.R.S. | AREA 4 | 750 W. | G940 | |
| • 10 | 30° 6" E.R.S. | AREA 1 | 750 W. | G940 | |
| 11 | 40° MINI-ELLIPSE | AREA 4 | 500 W. | G325 | TOP SHUTTER |
| 12 | 6" FRESNEL | AREA 5 | 500 W. | G325 | TOP HAT |
| 13 | 40° MINI-ELLIPSE | AREA 3 | 500 W. | G325 | TOP SHUTTER |
| • 14 | 40° MINI-ELLIPSE | AREA 1 | 500 W. | G790 | TOP SHUTTER |
| 15 | 6" FRESNEL | AREA 5 | 500 W. | G790 | TOP HAT |
| 16 | 40° MINI-ELLIPSE | AREA 4 | 500 W. | G790 | TOP SHUTTER |
| 17 | 40° MINI-ELLIPSE | AREA 2 | 500 W. | G364 | TOP SHUTTER |
| 18 | 6" FRESNEL | AREA 5 | 500 W. | G364 | TOP HAT |
| 19 | 50° 6" E.R.S | CENTER ACCENT | 750 W. | CLEAR | FOCUS CENTER |
| • 20 | 40° MINI-ELLIPSE | AREA 1 | 500 W. | G364 | TOP SHUTTER |
| 21 | 40° MINI-ELLIPSE | AREA 3 | 500 W. | G940 | TOP SHUTTER |
| 22 | 40° MINI-ELLIPSE | COUCH SPECIAL #2 | 500 W. | G360 | SHUTTER TO COUCH |
| 23 | 6" FRESNEL | AREA 5 | 500 W. | G940 | TOP HAT |
| 24 | 40° MINI-ELLIPSE | AREA 2 | 500 W. | G940 | TOP SHUTTER |
| 25 | FIXTURE | TABLE LAMP #1 | 40 W. | - | GANG WITH #26 |
| 26 | FIXTURE | TABLE LAMP #2 | 40 W. | - | GANG WITH #25 |

upper portion of its beam can be shuttered to prevent light from glaring into the eyes of the spectators.

Area 5, in the center, is lit from the four corners of the inner box by 6-inch Fresnels. Here the problem of spill light annoying the audience is less extreme than in the outer areas. Nonetheless, top hats are used on the instruments. The typical soft-edged Fresnel beam pattern is useful to blend this center light with the illumination on the adjacent areas.

**Color**    The color system, using GAM filters, is that of opposite warms and cools. The warm light, working diagonally out of the upper right corner of the layout, is from a GAM No. 325 (bastard amber) filter. The identical color might have been employed also from the lower left, but the designer preferred to use a slightly different tint, GAM No. 364 (pale honey). In like manner, the cools are not identical. From the lower right is a GAM No. 790 (electric blue), while opposite it is a GAM No. 940 (light purple). The light purple is not an especially cool color, but it has been chosen here because the nature of the drama warrants it. If it was a starker and more dramatic piece, we might have selected a combination of G790 and G830 (north sky blue) for the cools. The versatile G940 might have been one of the warms, with perhaps no color at all in the opposite instruments.

**Specials**    A few specials have been provided. On the right side of the plot is an 8-inch Fresnel with a G815 (Moody blue) filter to give the effect of moonlight for a brief scene. Instrument #6 is focused carefully on the couch and colored in a romantic G105 (antique rose) for a scene played there. Toward the upper left corner is another couch special, colored in G360 (amber blush), for a different scene. Also on the left, a wide-beamed ellipsoidal reflector spotlight without color (instrument #19) serves as an accent on the central area for a special moment there. The two table lamps at either end of the couch are practical fixtures, meaning that they will be lit at some point in the production.

**Control**    Twenty-four dimmers would be necessary for this simple arena layout, assuming that we can repatch one of the specials. Arena and thrust lighting almost always require tighter and more individual control than proscenium production.

## DESIGN PRACTICE: THRUST STAGE PRODUCTION

While normally larger in scale, thrust production has many of the same characteristics as the arena. It is an intimate form, with the audience viewing the action from three sides. The stage floor almost always takes on a special importance due to steep audience rake. As in the arena, the performer must be lit from all sides. Lighting angles that may cause spill into the audience must be avoided.

## THE THEATRE

Figure 23–9 is a perspective drawing of a thrust theatre showing lighting positions and other features of such an auditorium. Thrust theatres often have ramps that lead up to the front of the stage from beneath the audience. These are called *vomitory* entrances and exits. Placing a lighting boom in these ramps with an instrument shooting onto the stage creates an interesting and dramatic angle of light.

Lighting position #4 in Figure 23–9, the tormentor boom, might very well be a permanent lighting ladder such as the one shown upstage of it.

Note that an actor playing downstage is seen from all sides by the audience, which wraps well around the thrust. As in the arena, side-light for some audience members is front-light for others.

Many thrust theatres have a balcony, the front rail of which provides a valuable lighting position.

Any theatre designed with a thrust stage must include provision for ample mounting positions for the lighting instruments. The simplest manner of doing this is a grid of pipes or other mounting structures over the entire stage and auditorium. It should extend in all directions at least as far from the edge of the stage as the height of the grid above the stage floor. There should be adequate circuits provided on this grid, more than enough to accommodate all anticipated instruments.

Boxes or valances to hide the instruments can be provided. However, these devices are not completely effective. The necessity to hang lights in any location on the grid makes them difficult to mask. Today's audience has come to accept exposed lighting instruments, particularly in arena and thrust theatres. Instruments neatly cabled are seldom a distraction.

### Figure 23–9
### Thrust Stage Lighting Positions

A perspective view of a thrust stage showing its various lighting positions. The stage division into areas varies with each production.
(1) Outer valance position.
(2) Second valance and over-stage grid.
(3) Wing ladder for side lighting.
(4) Tormentor boom.
(5) Vomitory rail.
(6) Gutter.
If a balcony exists, there will also be a balcony rail position.

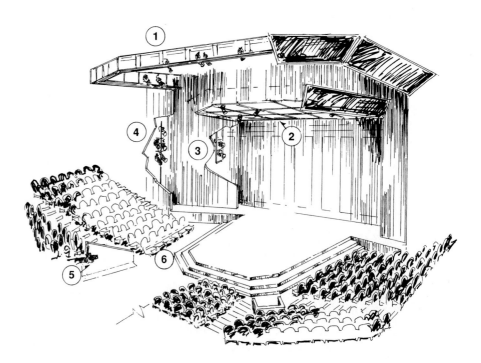

The spectators in the side seats particularly will find that the lenses of instruments focused in their general direction are in full view. But as long as top hats are used, this should not be too much of an annoyance. Care must be taken to mask or frame off the upper part of the beams from such instruments to be sure they do not glare directly into the eyes of those seated facing them. Fresnels, if used, should be provided with barn doors. Once again, a tension wire grid rather than awkward pipe grids is a good choice.

## DESIGN CONSIDERATIONS

The arrangement of set pieces and properties often dictates how a thrust stage is best divided into lighting areas. Each area requires several instruments focused on it from different directions because actors are seen from at least three sides at the same time. Top- or back-lighting is essential to set off the actor from the background. Care must be taken to avoid, as much as possible, light spilling into the audience. Blending and toning are best accomplished by the use of soft-beamed spotlights throwing color washes over large portions of the stage. The stage floor becomes a major scenic element in most thrust houses because of the steep audience rake. As in the arena, lighting color, texture, and composition are readily apparent on the floor.

**Distribution**     There are many possible variations for instrument placement in the thrust theatre. Varying the angle of instruments into an area provides good visual variety. However, a low angle is possible only from the front due to spill into the audience. Therefore, a designer will often treat an area with a low-angle front-light as well as use color washes from the front. Five to seven instruments per area is not unusual in thrust lighting. The absolute minimum is three, allowing for little or no variety.

**Color**     As with arena staging, strong colors are not desirable on the thrust stage—although a designer can be somewhat bolder due to the one closed side. Using very light tints, approaching no color, has been a popular color system for the thrust. This look is generally sharp and dramatic in nature. Another system calls for instruments from the front to have very pale tints, with those on the side taking on stronger shades of the same basic colors. Color systems for the arena are also adaptable to the thrust. Color toning the floor is best done from back- or top-light and can add a great deal of variety to the stage picture.

## DESIGNING THE LIGHTING

Figure 23–10 shows a sketch of a typical thrust stage with one area lit. Also shown are the plot and instrument schedule for a thrust production. Refer to these illustrations as you read the following pages.

**Area 1**     Because area 1 is so far upstage, it is lit somewhat from the front, proscenium-style, by two 6-by-12 or 30-degree ellipsoidals (#32 and #36) mounted in the inner box. Two 6-by-16 or 20-degree ellipsoidals (#1 and

**Figure 23–10**
Thrust Stage Lighting

(a) Illustration of the lighting for area #4 from five angles and directions.
(b) The lighting layout with area #4 instruments indicated.
(c) The instrument schedule.

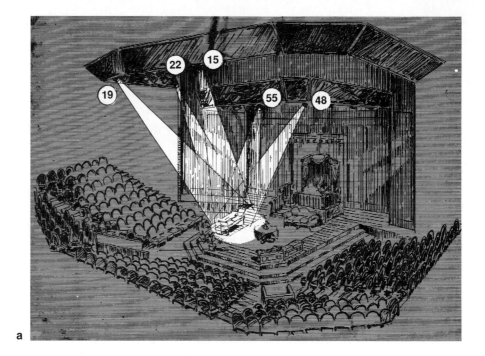

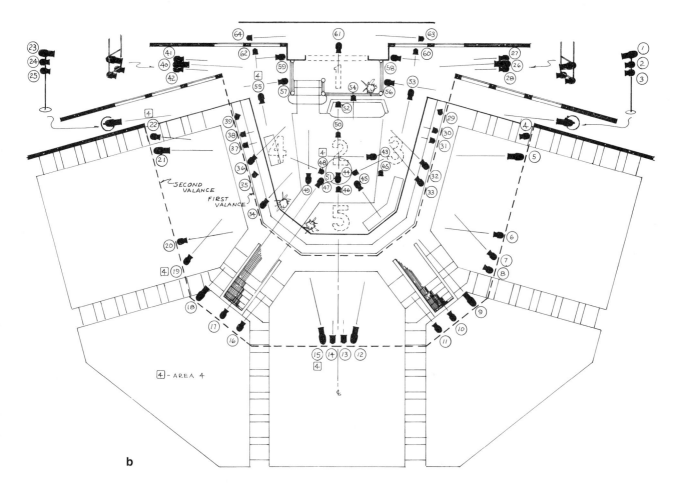

| No. | INSTRUMENT | LOCATION | PURPOSE | LAMP | COLOR | REMARKS |
|---|---|---|---|---|---|---|
| 1 | 6X16 E.R.S. | LEFT BOOM | AREA 1 | 1000 W. | L144 | L. BOOM TOP |
| 2 | 6X12 E.R.S | LEFT BOOM | WASH WARM | 750 W. | L134 | L. BOOM MIDDLE - SOFT EDGE |
| 3 | 6X12 E.R.S | LEFT BOOM | WASH COOL | 750 W. | L119 | L. BOOM BOTTOM - SOFT EDGE |
| 4 | 6X12 E.R.S | 2ND VALANCE-L | AREA 3 | 1000 W. | L141 | |
| 5 | 6X16 E.R.S | 2ND VALANCE-L | AREA 2 | 1000 W. | L141 | |
| 6 | 6X12 E.R.S | 2ND VALANCE-L | AREA 5 | 750 W. | L141 | |
| 7 | 6X12 E.R.S | 2ND VALANCE-L | AREA 3 | 750 W. | L144 | |
| 8 | 6X12 E.R.S | 2ND VALANCE-L | WINDOW SEAT | 750 W. | L144 | |
| 9 | 6X16 E.R.S | 2ND VALANCE-L | AREA 2 | 1000 W. | L117 | |
| 10 | 6X12 E.R.S | 2ND VALANCE-L | LEFT TUNNEL | 750 W. | L142 | FRAME TO TUNNEL |
| 11 | 6X12 E.R.S | 2ND VALANCE-L | AREA 5 | 750 W. | L117 | |
| 12 | 6X16 E.R.S | 2ND VALANCE-C | AREA 3 | 1000 W. | L117 | FRAME OFF AUDIENCE |
| 13 | 8" FRESNEL | 2ND VALANCE-C | WASH COOL | 1000 W. | L119 | BARN DOOR-OFF AUDIENCE |
| 14 | 8" FRESNEL | 2ND VALANCE-C | WASH WARM | 1000 W. | L134 | BARN DOOR-OFF AUDIENCE |
| • 15 | 6X16 E.R.S | 2ND VALANCE-C | AREA 4 | 1000 W. | L152 | FRAME OFF AUDIENCE |
| 16 | 6X12 E.R.S | 2ND VALANCE-R | AREA 5 | 750 W. | L152 | |
| 17 | 6X12 E.R.S | 2ND VALANCE-R | RIGHT TUNNEL | 750 W. | L142 | FRAME TO TUNNEL |
| 18 | 6X16 E.R.S | 2ND VALANCE-R | AREA 2 | 1000 W. | L152 | |
| • 19 | 6X16 E.R.S. | 2ND VALANCE-R | AREA 4 | 750 W. | L151 | |
| 20 | 6X16 E.R.S. | 2ND VALANCE-R | AREA 5 | 750 W. | L153(2) | |
| 21 | 6X16 E.R.S. | 2ND VALANCE-R | AREA 2 | 1000 W. | L153(2) | |
| • 22 | 6X16 E.R.S. | 2ND VALANCE-R | AREA 4 | 750 W. | L153(2) | |
| 23 | 6X16 E.R.S | RIGHT BOOM | AREA 1 | 1000 W. | L151 | R. BOOM- TOP |
| 24 | 6X12 E.R.S | RIGHT BOOM | WASH WARM | 750 W. | L134 | R. BOOM MIDDLE - SOFT EDGE |
| 25 | 6X12 E.R.S | RIGHT BOOM | WASH COOL | 750 W. | L119 | R. BOOM BOTTOM - SOFT EDGE |
| 26 | 6X16 E.R.S | LEFT LADDER | U.R. CORNER | 1000 W. | L141 | L. LADDER TOP - FRAME SIDES |
| 27 | 6X12 E.R.S. | LEFT LADDER | AREA 1 | 750 W. | L141 | L. LADDER BOTTOM - FRAME US |
| 28 | 6X12 E.R.S. | LEFT LADDER | U.L. CORNER | 750 W. | L141 | L. LADDER BOTTOM - FRAME US |
| 29 | 6" FRESNEL | 1ST VALANCE-L | U.L. CORNER | 500 W. | L117 | |
| 30 | 6" FRESNEL | 1ST VALANCE-L | WASH COOL | 500 W. | L119 | BARN DOOR OFF AUDIENCE |
| 31 | 6" FRESNEL | 1ST VALANCE-L | WASH WARM | 500 W. | L134 | BARN DOOR OFF AUDIENCE |
| 32 | 6X12 E.R.S | 1ST VALANCE-L | AREA 1 | 750 W. | L117 | |
| 33 | 6X12 E.R.S | 1ST VALANCE-L | SOFA | 750 W. | L117 | |
| 34 | 6X12 E.R.S | 1ST VALANCE-R | SOFA | 750 W. | L152 | |
| 35 | 6" FRESNEL | 1ST VALANCE-R | BENCH | 500 W. | L152 | |
| 36 | 6X12 E.R.S | 1ST VALANCE-R | AREA 1 | 750 W. | L152 | FRAME BOTTOM |
| 37 | 6" FRESNEL | 1ST VALANCE-R | WASH WARM | 500 W. | L134 | BARN DOOR OFF AUDIENCE |
| 38 | 6" FRESNEL | 1ST VALANCE-R | WASH COOL | 500 W. | L119 | BARN DOOR OFF AUDIENCE |
| 39 | 6" FRESNEL | 1ST VALANCE-R | U.R. CORNER | 500 W. | L152 | |
| 40 | 6X16 E.R.S. | RIGHT LADDER | U.L. CORNER | 1000 W. | L153(2) | R. LADDER TOP - FRAME SIDE |
| 41 | 6X16 E.R.S. | RIGHT LADDER | AREA 1 | 750 W. | L153(2) | R. LADDER BOTTOM - FRAME US |
| 42 | 6X16 E.R.S. | RIGHT LADDER | U.R. CORNER | 750 W. | L153(2) | R. LADDER BOTTOM - FRAME US |
| 43 | 6X16 E.R.S. | GRID OVER STAGE | BENCH | 750 W. | L117 | SOFT EDGE FRAME OFF AUDIENCE |
| 44 | 6" FRESNEL | GRID OVER STAGE | AREA 3 | 500 W. | CLEAR | BARN DOOR OFF AUDIENCE |
| 45 | 6X12 E.R.S | GRID OVER STAGE | LEFT TUNNEL | 750 W. | L103 | FRAME TO TUNNEL |
| 46 | 6" FRESNEL | GRID OVER STAGE | AREA 5 | 500 W. | CLEAR | BARN DOOR OFF AUDIENCE |
| 47 | 6X12 E.R.S | GRID OVER STAGE | RIGHT TUNNEL | 750 W. | L103 | FRAME TO TUNNEL |
| • 48 | 6" FRESNEL | GRID OVER STAGE | AREA 4 | 500 W. | CLEAR | BARN DOOR OFF AUDIENCE |
| 49 | 6X12 E.R.S | GRID OVER STAGE | STEPS | 750 W. | L152 | SOFT EDGE FRAME TO STEPS |
| 50 | 6" FRESNEL | GRID OVER STAGE | AREA 2 D.S. | 500 W. | CLEAR | |
| 51 | 6X12 E.R.S | GRID OVER STAGE | ARCHWAY | 750 W. | L103 | FRAME TO ARCHWAY |
| 52 | 6" FRESNEL | GRID OVER STAGE | AREA 2 U.S. | 500 W. | CLEAR | |
| 53 | 6X12 E.R.S | GRID OVER STAGE | AREA 3 | 750 W. | CLEAR | FRAME L AND TOP |
| 54 | 6" FRESNEL | GRID OVER STAGE | SOFA | 500 W. | CLEAR | |
| • 55 | 6X12 E.R.S | GRID OVER STAGE | AREA 4 | 750 W. | L117 | FRAME R AND TOP |
| 56 | 6X12 E.R.S | GRID OVER STAGE | LEFT RAMP | 750 W. | L103 | FRAME OFF R. WALL |
| 57 | 6X12 E.R.S | GRID OVER STAGE | RIGHT RAMP | 750 W. | L103 | FRAME OFF L. WALL |
| 58 | 6X12 E.R.S | GRID OVER STAGE | UL ENTRANCE | 750 W. | L103 | FRAME OFF R. WALL |
| 59 | 6X12 E.R.S | GRID OVER STAGE | UR ENTRANCE | 750 W. | L103 | FRAME OFF L. WALL |
| 60 | 6" FRESNEL | GRID OVER STAGE | UL CORNER | 500 W. | CLEAR | |
| 61 | 6X12 E.R.S | GRID OVER STAGE | AREA 1 | 750 W. | CLEAR | SOFT EDGE |
| 62 | 6" FRESNEL | GRID OVER STAGE | UR CORNER | 500 W. | CLEAR | |
| 63 | 6" FRESNEL | GRID OVER STAGE | HALLWAY - L | 500 W. | L104 | |
| 64 | 6" FRESNEL | GRID OVER STAGE | HALLWAY - R | 500 W. | L104 | |
| 65 | 6" FRESNEL | GRID OVER STAGE | WINDOW SEAT | 500 W. | CLEAR | BARN DOOR OFF AUDIENCE |

c

#23) strike the area from the booms placed in the ramp entrances on either side of the stage. Two more 30-degree ellipsoidals (#27 and #41) are on the ladders hung in the upstage entrances. Instrument #61, a 40-degree ellipsoidal because of its short throw, acts as a back-light from above the upstage archway.

The colors, working from front to rear on the left side, are Lee No. 117 (steel blue), L114 (no-color blue), and L141 (bright blue). On the right side they are L152 (pale gold), L151 (gold tint), and double L153 (pale salmon). The back-light is clear. The other areas use these same colors for instruments working from the same angles.

**Area 4**     Figure 23–10a highlights the instruments being used for area 4, typical of the other three areas on stage. Instrument #15, a 20-degree ellipsoidal, strikes the area from the front with Lee No. 152. Instruments #19 and #22 are 30-degree ellipsoidals colored in L151 and L153 doubled. The more saturated double salmon (L153) comes from the far stage-right side. Instruments #48 and #55 are both quite steep to avoid spill into the audience, and the 6-inch Fresnel has barn doors as well. The back-light ellipsoidal (#55) has no color and the stage-left Fresnel is colored in L117 (steel blue).

**Color Wash**     A pair of 8-inch Fresnels light the entire set from the front to give a tonal wash that may be varied by dimming the warm and cool instruments to different readings. Two pairs of 6-inch Fresnels located on either side of the inner box work with the 8-inch Fresnels. For the cool wash an L119 (dark blue) is used, and for the warm wash an L134 (golden amber). The golden amber has a warming effect on the rather cool blue, resulting in lavender tones when mixed properly.

**Specials**     A large number of specials have been hung. The extreme up-left and up-right corners, which might be considered areas in themselves, are each covered by three spots from front and sides, plus a back-light. The vomitory entrances are lit from front and back by house-right instruments #10 and #45 and house-left instruments #17 and #47. The upstage-left and upstage-right entrances are lit by instruments #56 through #59, and two 6-inch Fresnels (#63 and #64) illuminate the far upstage hallway. Instrument #51, a 30-degree ellipsoidal, is framed to the upstage-center archway and colored in the versatile L103. Instrument #49 lights the steps leading to the upstage platform area. The bench, the window seat, and the sofa also have appropriate coverage.

Additional specials would be indicated by blocking and traffic patterns. Actors might, for example, be placed on the steps leading down from the platform toward the audience. If this is the case, suitable lighting would have to be provided. If the steps were used a great deal, up to five additional areas might be necessary.

Ellipsoidal reflector spotlights have been used a great deal in this layout because of the good control we have over their beams. When possible they are made soft-edged by shifting the lenses to throw the gate out of focus. This reduces sharp beam edges that result in abrupt changes of intensity on the stage and the actors. For the same reason, Fresnel spotlights are used when their spill light will not be critical. Barn doors or top hats are suggested for all Fresnels.

## VARIATIONS

Our sample lighting layout is designed for a comedy or a light drama with a simple interior setting. Lighting angles are standard for good visibility and the colors are chosen for their pale tints. The arrangements of color (cool on one side and warm on the other) and angle are derived from proscenium lighting and provide good coverage. However, this two-sided color approach allows for little variety or color interest and may not be desirable for a production with a number of scenes each demanding specific lighting.

With a minimum of five instruments on each acting area and a color arrangement as shown in Figure 23–11, the designer is provided with several more options, as follows:

1. The two warms can act as key-light with the cools filling.
2. The two cools can act as key with the warms filling.
3. Any one instrument (except the back-light neutral) can be lowered in intensity or dropped out completely, causing a color shift as well as a compositional change.

If more than the minimum five instruments per area is possible, even greater variety of color and distribution can be achieved.

**Side Angle**    For more dramatic productions, the vertical angle of the sidelights can be raised, with the following results:

1. Higher angle distribution causes sharper facial and body shadows.
2. Spill into side audience seating is more controllable.
3. Area control is tighter.

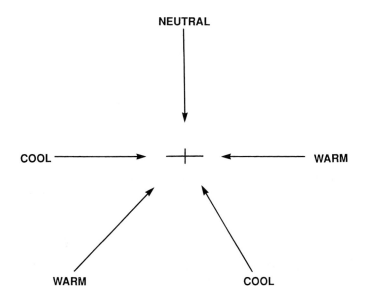

**Figure 23–11**
Thrust Color Key

Shown is a possible color key for lighting a thrust area from five directions.

a

b

**Figure 23–12**
Tension Wire Grid

(a) View from the grid of the Keck Theatre at Occidental College in Los Angeles. The woven cable grid is weight-bearing and offers complete access to overhead lighting positions. This full-ceiling grid was installed by Hoffend & Son.
(b) View from the stage. The Keck is a unique courtyard theatre with a seating capacity of 475.

**Texture**     Texture achieved by patterns or gobos can break up the sometimes flat and dull surface of the thrust stage. High side- or back-light is often a desirable angle for such treatment.

## THE FLEXIBLE STAGE

Another form of performance space that should not go without mention is the popular "black box." This flexible space is primarily intended as an actor's performance space rather than a production facility, but lighting nonetheless is often required. Black box seating can be set up in any number of configurations that will, as a result, define the playing space. Common seating arrangements are as follows:

1. One-sided, or full front (a proscenium-type orientation)
2. Two-sided, or corner staging
3. Three-sided, or thrust staging
4. Four-sided, or arena staging
5. Aisle—with seats on two sides of a central aisle

### LIGHTING THE BLACK BOX

Lighting the flexible space is not very different from lighting one of the several theatre forms previously examined, except that the lighting positions are generally closer to the stage. In order to provide adequate lighting, hanging positions must be kept flexible. A cross-pipe grid over the entire space is a fair solution to the problem of flexibility. Such a grid allows lighting instruments to be hung in any position and focused in any direction.

A better solution is the tension wire grid (Figure 23–12). One-eighth-inch wire rope is woven in all directions, forming a weight-bearing surface upon which an electrician can walk. Pipes supported from the ceiling are arranged to allow complete hanging flexibility with a minimum of time and effort. The lighting instruments shoot through the thin wire mesh as shown in the photograph. This grid is ideal for the flexible space as well as extremely useful in arena or thrust situations.

# 24 LIGHTING FOR THE COMMERCIAL THEATRE AND OTHER FORMS

This chapter gives special attention to lighting for the commercial theatre, which includes Broadway as well as the nation's regional theatres. It also investigates design for forms of performance other than theatre, such as dance and opera. Finally, the chapter touches on the many possibilities for lighting in such diverse areas as theme parks, concerts, architecture, television and film, restaurants, museums, industrials, and displays—all of which may require the expertise of a theatrical lighting designer.

## LIGHTING ON BROADWAY AND THE PRODUCTION OF *THE WHO'S TOMMY*

New York's Broadway has always been, and still remains, the premier theatrical entertainment center of the United States. People come from all over the world to see Broadway productions. It is an extremely commercial theatre with tough competition and great reward for achievement. While many practices are identical to those of any commercial theatre, some are unique to the Broadway stage.

### THE BROADWAY LIGHTING DESIGNER

There are no designers who work exclusively on Broadway. Despite the potential for high pay, there is not enough work to keep more than a handful of designers busy even on a part-time basis. New York–based lighting designers spend much of their time traveling about the country, working at regional and other commercial venues. Most of these individuals spent a number of years working as assistants to more established Broadway designers before they were rewarded their first Broadway show. Many of them designed off- and off-off-Broadway for many years, learning the ropes and meeting directors and producers.

A producer hires the artistic staff for a production, but the director is normally chosen first and often consulted. It is frequently the director (or occasionally the scenic designer) who recommends an individual lighting designer for the show. Accordingly, the experience of having worked with a number of people on a variety of productions is essential to achieving a Broadway show.

**The United Scenic Artists**     Before being eligible to light a show on Broadway, or at a number of the larger commercial theatres across the country, the designer must become a member of the United Scenic Artists Union (USA). This union represents professional scenic artists (painters), scenic designers, costume designers, and lighting designers. It consists of one local union (829) divided into three regions: Eastern, Central, and Western.

To be admitted to this organization, an applicant must first undergo an interview and portfolio review with members of the regional examination committee. On a rare occasion, a designer may be admitted to the union based on portfolio only. Normally, the lighting applicant must pass a rigid examination offered once a year in New York, Chicago, or Los Angeles. Exams vary from region to region, but usually include a take-home portion that is administered approximately one month before the "in-town" exam. The latter usually involves eight hours of drafting and designing at a site selected by the union. A nonrefundable examination fee must be paid in order to attempt the exam. If it is passed, the designer pays an initiation fee (currently $2,500) and becomes a USA member. Dues and assessments are approximately $300 per year.

Membership in the union is often the first major hurdle faced by a young designer looking to work professionally. The interview and portfolio review process is designed to eliminate individuals whom the committee judge to be underqualified for membership. The exam itself is kept difficult to assure that only the most capable designers are allowed entrance to the union.

Regional offices are located at the following addresses:

16 West 61st Street, New York, NY 10023

176 West Adams, Chicago, IL 60603

5410 Wilshire Boulevard, Suite 407, Los Angeles, CA 90036

Write your regional business agent for exam dates and information.

When working under a United Scenic Artists contract, a designer must receive a minimum fee. Established designers may ask for and often get a great deal more than this minimum. It is not uncommon for a well-known designer to receive, in addition to a straight fee, a royalty based on a percentage of the gross receipts.

## EQUIPMENT IN THE BROADWAY THEATRE

Unlike anywhere else in the country, the commercial theatres commonly referred to as "Broadway houses" have no lighting equipment of their own.

All is rented. There may be a dimmer for the house lights and possible wiring in conduit from backstage to front-of-house positions. A high-amperage company switch providing power for dimmers will be found close to the stage area. Everything else must come in with the show. This includes instruments and their accessories, all control equipment and cable, dimmers and plugging boxes, cable sufficient to connect all instruments to the dimmers, booms for offstage instruments, work lights, and all special rigging supplies.

**Equipment Rental and Shop Orders**     Because all expenses related to the production must be approved by the producer or business manager, the lighting designer must work within the figures that they have in mind. The normal rental contract calls for a payment of 10 percent of the value of the equipment for the first three weeks of the rental (e. g., an ellipsoidal reflector spotlight that costs $400 rents for $40 for the first three weeks). A lower percentage is charged for the next three weeks, and rental is further reduced for the remainder of the run of the production. Most producers make a practice of asking for competitive bids from the few companies that are engaged in the rental of lighting equipment for the stage. Others have a favorite rental house and always work with this same company. A producer may depend on the lighting designer to recommend a firm. The major New York–area rental and supply houses are Bash, Four Star, Production Arts, and Vanco.

Even if competitive bids are not required by the producer, the rental house must provide a cost estimate based on an equipment list called the *shop order*. This paperwork is generated by one of the various software programs as soon as the light plot is completed. It lists each and every piece of rental equipment in specific detail. It also specifies all necessary "perishables" (materials that will be used up and, therefore, must be purchased by the production), such as tape and tie-line.

After a bid is approved, the shop requires at least a week to gather and prepare the equipment necessary for a Broadway show. If it is a large show with specialized equipment such as automated fixtures or projectors, much more lead time is needed. For this reason, the Broadway lighting designer must complete the plot several weeks earlier than is required of a designer working primarily with in-house equipment.

***Tommy* Shop Order**     Figure 24–1 shows part of the equipment list for the national tour of the Broadway production of *The Who's Tommy*, designed by Chris Parry. The production opened at the La Jolla Playhouse and the lighting was redesigned for Broadway and again for touring. Note that the order includes everything needed, from lighting instruments to radio control batteries.

## HIRING ELECTRICIANS

Even more significant than equipment rental costs are the wages paid to the electricians who set up and run the show. In New York and many commercial

## Figure 24–1

*Tommy* Shop Order

Shown is the shop order for the tour of the musical *The Who's Tommy,* designed by Chris Parry.

FINAL ELECTRICAL EQUIPMENT LIST
"THE WHO'S TOMMY - GOIN' MOBILE"
May 26, 1994

| | |
|---|---|
| Load In Dallas: | September 27, 1993 |
| Manager: | George MacPherson<br>The Pinball Touring Company<br>ATP / Dodger<br>1501 Broadway<br>Suite 2015<br>New York, NY 10036<br>(212) 391-8160<br>(212) 944-7616 FAX |
| Designer: | Chris Parry<br>(619) 942-2697<br>(619) 942-2697 FAX |
| Associate: | David Grill<br>(201) 825-0391<br>(201) 825-2643 FAX |
| Production Electrician: | Mark Davidson<br>(201) 440-9224 Shop |
| Shop: | Steve Terry<br>Wayne Lawrence<br>Production Arts Lighting<br>35 Oxford Drive<br>Moonachie, NJ 07074<br>(201) 440-9224<br>(201) 440-2612 FAX |

GOIN' MOBILE
FINAL - Electrical Equipment List

### EQUIPMENT TOTALS

| | |
|---|---|
| 15 | 4½x6½ 1k |
| 6 | 4½x6½ Dataflash w/DMX 512 Prom |
| 18 | 6x9 1k |
| 35 | 6x12 1k |
| 44 | 6x16 1k |
| 17 | Source 4 426 575w |
| 45 | Source 4 419 575w |
| 1 | Source 4 410 575w |
| 2 | 30°-60° Baby Zoom 750w |
| 6 | PAR 16 EZK 150w |
| 5 | PAR 16 EYC 75w Short Nose |
| 6 | PAR 16 EYF 75w w/Transformer |
| 56 | PAR 46 NSP 200w |
| 26 | PAR 46 NSP 200w Custom Housing to fit into Deck |
| 2 | PAR 64 MFL 1k |
| 38 | PAR 64 NSP 1k |
| 8 | PAR 64 NSP 1k Short Nose |
| 22 | 6" Fresnel 1k |
| 26 | 7" Arri Fresnel 2k |
| 12 | 2Lt Broad Cyc 1500w w/Hangers |
| 10 | 2 Lt Ianiro Orion 1k |
| 5 | 6' 9Lt PAR 56 12v 240w VNSP Motorized Lite Curtains |
| 3 | Wildfire 400w Flood UV |
| 7 | Mini 10 500w |
| 6 | Stik Up 100w |
| 2 | Pani HMV 1202 1200w Followspot |
| 16 | Vari*Lite VL-2C |
| 5 | Vari*Lite VL-4 w/Tophats |
| 4 | Vari*Lite VL-5 w/Stipple Lens |
| 48 | Data Flash w/DMX 512 Prom, Reflector, & Yoke |
| 3 | Super Nova Strobe |
| 3 | F100 Fogger w/Remote Trigger |
| 1 | Rosco Pencil Fogger |
| 2 | Fogmaster 3000 |
| 1 | Theatre Magic Haze Master w/25' Output Hoses |
| 4 | Bowens Fan - Variable Speed w/Yokes |
| 8 | Color Ram w/Source 4 Plate |
| 18 | Color Ram w/PAR 64 Plate |
| 26 | Color Ram w/7" Arri Fresnel Plate |
| 1 | Wybron Scroller w/Source 4 410 Plate |
| 12 | Wybron Scroller w/PAR 64 Plate |
| 1 | Howard Eaton 4 RPM Flicker Wheels w/Diffusion Glass |
| 2 | 12" Mirror Ball w/Variable Speed Motor |
| 6 | Twin Spin |
| 2 | Blue Police Beacons |

Page 2

GOIN' MOBILE
FINAL - Electrical Equipment List

| | |
|---|---|
| 7 | Source 4 Iris' |
| 16 | 6" Tophat |
| 22 | Source 4 Tophat |
| 10 | 6" Halfhat |
| 8 | 10" Tophat |
| 8 | 10" Barndoor |
| 400 | Safety Cables |
| 20 | Template Holders |
| | |
| 1 | Custom Addressable DMX Triggered Contact Closure w/Amiga Interface Cables and Connectors |
| 1 | Set Midi Cables (Amiga to Artisan) |
| 4 | LMI L86 96x2.4k DMX 512 Dimmer Rack |
| 3 | Opto Splitter |
| 1 | DAC |
| 3 | DMX - Data Flash Protocall Converter |
| 8 | 12 Unit Color Ram Control Box |
| 1 | 50 Channel Radio Control Transmitter |
| 2 | 12 Channel Radio Control Receiver |
| 6 | 10 amp 12v Radio Control Dimmer |
| 6 | Radio Control Battery |
| 6 | Radio Control Battery Charger |
| | |
| 2 | Obsession 600 |
| 2 | Obsession LD Monitors |
| 1 | Obsession RFU |
| 1 | Obsession Printer (As fast as possible) |
| 1 | UPS |
| | |
| 3 | A-B Switch Boxes (Cue / Work Lights) |
| | |
| 4 | 5' Unistrut Bar |
| 3 | 7' Unistrut Bar |
| 18 | 10' Unistrut Bar |
| 6 | Unistrut Cart |
| | |
| 2 | 36' Genie Personal Lift |
| | |
| 14 | Custom Quick Mount VL-2C Brackets |
| 1 | Custom Quick Mount VL-4 Brackets |
| 4 | Custom Quick Mount VL-5 Brackets |
| | |
| 3 | Vari*Lite Bumpers |

Page 3

---

GOIN' MOBILE
FINAL - Electrical Equipment List

### IMPORTANT NOTES

- All units to be axial with quartz lamp, clamp, template slot and black color frame unless otherwise stated;

- All units to have clear lenses - NO green or tinted lenses accepted;

- All PAR Cans must have interior protective screening;

- Any substitutions or revisions must be fully disclosed at the time of the bid, these substitutions or revisions are not accepted without permission of the Designer;

- Bidder assumes responsibility for any additional materials that are required on site due to rental shop oversight or error;

- Allow for color scroller color and color scroller loading labor;

- Multi, cable, jumper, control cable, video cable specifics by Electrician;

- Allow for Spare Units, Lamps, Dimmer Cards, Control Cards, Fuses, Control Cables, Scrollers, etc.

theatres elsewhere, these people must be members of the International Alliance of Theatrical Stage Employees union (IATSE), commonly called the IA. Member electricians are paid a substantial hourly wage and prudent use of their time is imperative. Stringent regulations concerning working hours and conditions, which may vary from one local union to another, must be understood and adhered to by the designer.

Every large city across the country has its own IA local. The *business agent* is the union's representative to the public. It is this individual who negotiates labor needs with a producer and subsequently fills the crew call. Often one member of the crew is designated "union representative." This person is responsible for seeing that the rules and regulations of the union are followed and any violations are reported to the business agent.

The electrician who works most closely with the designer is the *production electrician*. This person may or may not be a union member and is hired by the show's producer. It is this electrician who works with the rental house and acts as a liaison between the producers and the IA union. Obviously, the choice of who will serve as production electrician is an important one to the lighting designer.

### PLANNING THE LIGHTING

The biggest difference between designing for Broadway and elsewhere is *time*. Exciting, dramatic lighting designs such as that by David Segal for *Damn Yankees* (Color Plate 24–1a) require extensive preparation and a lot of work—yet time available for the design period and production in the Broadway theatre is so compressed that only the best can survive. The rehearsal period is usually short and the plot must be completed well in advance in order for the shop to have time to prepare the equipment. The familiar adage that "time is money" has never been more appropriate than when a designer is in the theatre with an IA crew. This is where superb preparation and an excellent production electrician really pay off.

***Tommy* Plot**     Figure 24–2 shows the light plot and projector frame plot for the national tour of *The Who's Tommy*. Figure 24–3 is a partial channel hookup for this plot.

The "B Version Towers" referred to on the projector frame plot are designed for a reduced version of the plot. The "stadium light boxes" show well in the production photograph of Color Plate 24–1b.

As can be seen, the light plot calls for seven over-stage electric pipes, extensive side-light, and very little front-of-house lighting. Trims are high at approximately 30 feet, creating a square rather than rectangular stage picture, as can be seen in Color Plates 24–2a and 24–2b. Vari*Lites are used over-stage and color scrollers are used both over-stage and in side-light positions. The video truss noted on the plot can be seen at the bottom of the photograph in Color Plate 24–2.

Reference is made to black "Zetex" in the notes on the plot. Zetex is a heat-resistant material that is hung between lighting instruments and masking borders to keep the velour borders from burning. In this case, the first electric pipe is close enough to the upstage masking border to require the use of Zetex.

## THE PRODUCTION PERIOD

It should be expected that focus conditions will not be ideal. At best, a sound check will be going on simultaneously. At worst, carpenters will still be rigging scenery under a blaze of work light. The job must be done quickly in order to avoid overtime wages for the electricians on the work call. It must also be done absolutely correctly. A subsequent labor call in order to adjust focus means a ladder crew of four people, each hired for the union minimum of four hours.

According to union regulations, under no circumstances whatsoever may the lighting designer or an assistant handle any lighting equipment. One of the union electricians must be requested to do so. This applies to even such innocent actions as handing a wrench to its owner or steadying a ladder on which an electrician is working.

## MOVING THE SHOW

The Broadway designer, more than any other, finds it necessary to design a production for more than one space. Perhaps, like *The Who's Tommy*, the production premieres at one of the nation's regional theatres with the intent of then going to Broadway. Nearly all successful Broadway shows tour at some point after they have opened in New York. The lighting designer needs to be proficient at designing for more than a single theatre.

There are two types of Broadway tours. One is called a "national" tour, which plays for many weeks in a single large city. The second, the "bus-and-truck" tour, jumps from city to city, often playing a week but sometimes playing only one-night stands in each location.

A national tour settles into a major city. The actors get apartments, the IA crew is contracted for a long run, and the put-in period is at least several days. A light plot is usually designed for this specific theatre. The lighting designer is normally in attendance during the technical and dress rehearsals, setting the look of the production before it begins its run.

The light plot for a bus-and-truck tour must be designed to accommodate a number of types and sizes of theatres. Such a production inevitably carries less equipment than was on the Broadway plot. Due to time constraints, various techniques have been developed to make setting up and focusing as

## Figure 24–2
*Tommy* Light Plot and Projector Frame Plot

This is the plot for the national tour of the musical *The Who's Tommy*, designed by Chris Parry.

24–2a

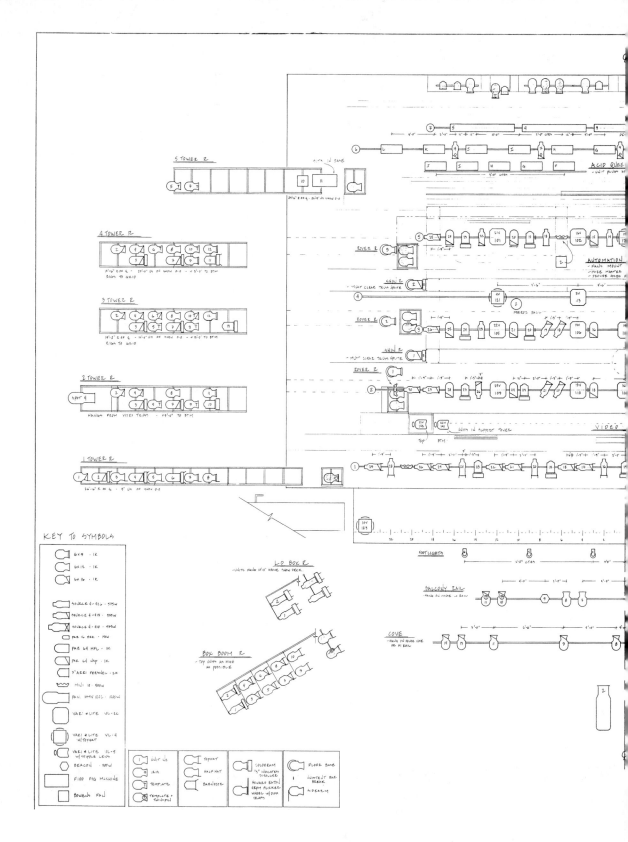

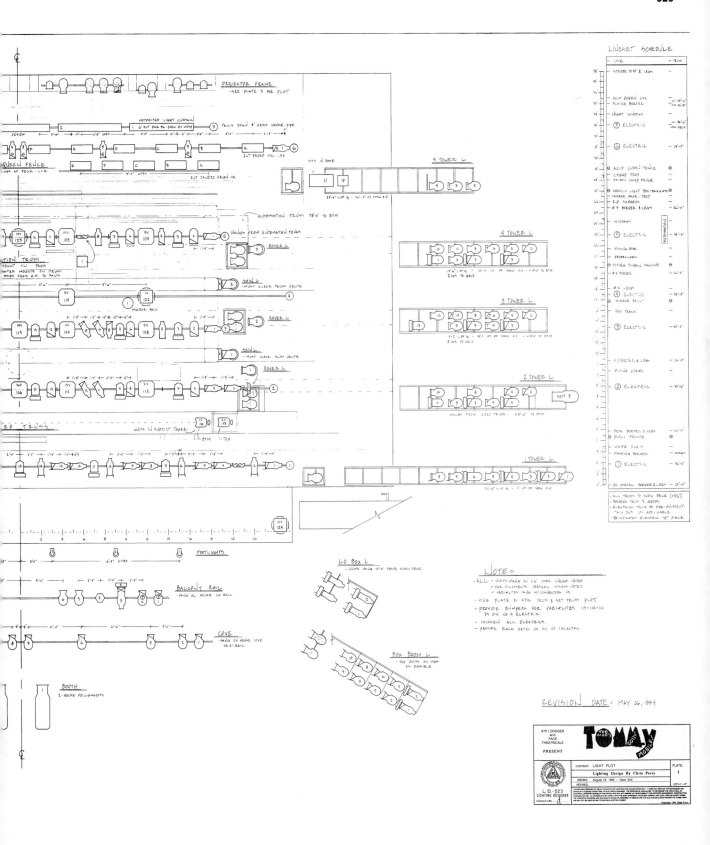

**24–2b**

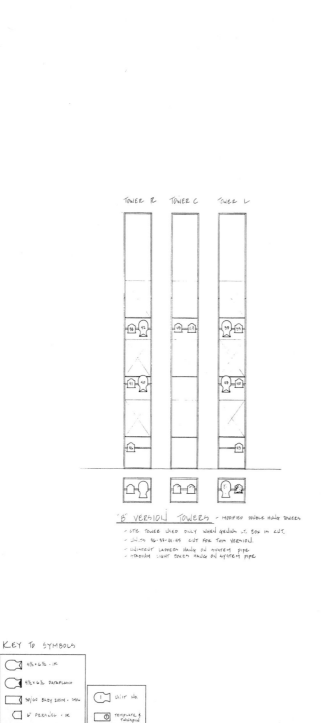

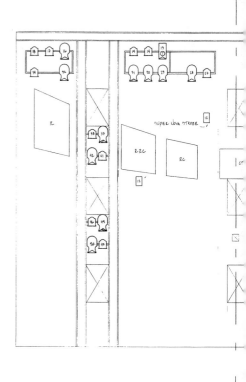

TOWER R    TOWER C    TOWER L

"B" VERSION TOWERS - MODIFIED DOUBLE HUNG TOWERS

- CTR TOWER USED ONLY WHEN GENIUM LT. BOX IS CUT.
- UNITS 36-37-44-45 CUT FOR THIS VERSION.
- UNISTRUT LADDERS HANG ON SYSTEM PIPE
- STADIUM LIGHT BOXES HANG ON SYSTEM PIPE

KEY TO SYMBOLS

| | |
|---|---|
| 4½ × 6½ · 1K | |
| 4½ × 6½ DATAFLASH | |
| 30/60 BABY ZOOM · 250w | |
| 6" FRESNEL · 1K | |

Unit No.

TEMPLATE &
TWINSPIN

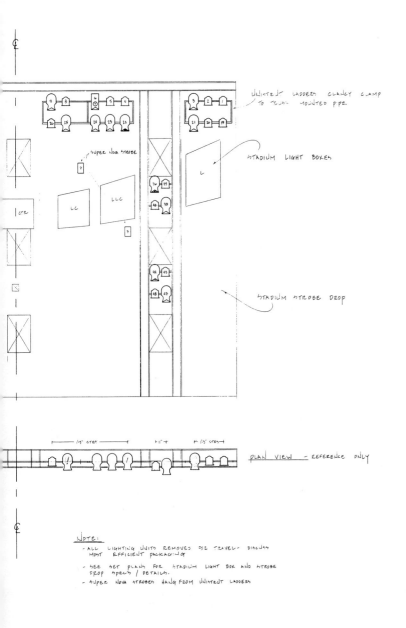

UNISTRUT LADDERS CLANCY CLAMP
TO ECHH MOUNTED PIPE

STADIUM LIGHT BOXES

SUPER NOVA STROBE

STADIUM STROBE DROP

PLAN VIEW - REFERENCE ONLY

NOTE:
- ALL LIGHTING UNITS REMOVES %2 TRAVEL- DISCUSS
  MOST EFFICIENT PACKAGING
- SEE SET PLANS FOR STADIUM LIGHT BOX AND STROBE
  DROP SPECS / DETAILS.
- SUPER NOVA STROBES HANG FROM UNISTRUT LADDERS

REVISION DATE: FEB. 21, 1994

ATP / DODGER and PACE THEATRICALS PRESENT

CONTENT: PROJECTOR FRAME PLOT — PLATE: 3
Lighting Design By Chris Parry
DRAWN: August 23, 1993 – Dave Grill — 1/2"=1'-0"
REVISED:

L.D. - 523
LIGHTING DESIGNER
SIGNATURE

Figure 24—3
*Tommy* Channel Hook-Up

```
=====================                    ================
TOMMY - PINBALL "A"                      CHANNEL HOOKUP                        Page   1
=====================                    ================                      05-26-94
Designer: Chris Parry                                         Producer: ATP / Dodger / Pace
Associate: David Grill                                  Head Electrician: Steve Cooksey
PINBALL - FINAL CUT VERSION
===========================================================================================
Note:  Asterisks indicate Replug Channels
-------------------------------------------------------------------------------------------
  Chn   Dim   Position       Unit   Cir#   Type              Watts   Purpose       Color
=====  ===  ==========       ====   ====   ====              =====   =======       =====
(  3 )  84   COVE              7      6    6x16               1kw    Conductor      N/C
-------------------------------------------------------------------------------------------
(  6 )  81   COVE              4      3    6x16               1kw    Frts CL        L203+R119
-------------------------------------------------------------------------------------------
(  7 )  83   COVE              6      5    6x16               1kw    Frts CLC       L203+R119
-------------------------------------------------------------------------------------------
(  8 )  85   COVE              8      7    6x16               1kw    Frts CC        L203+R119
-------------------------------------------------------------------------------------------
(  9 )  86   COVE              9      8    6x16               1kw    Frts CRC       L203+R119
-------------------------------------------------------------------------------------------
( 10 )  88   COVE             11     10    6x16               1kw    Frts CR        L203+R119
-------------------------------------------------------------------------------------------
( 17 )  60   BOX BOOM L        1      1    S4-419 w/CRam      575w   Wash L C/C     IR H.S.+
                                           w/10" TH                                CRam
        60   BOX BOOM L        2      1    S4-419 w/CRam      575w   Wash L C/C     IR H.S.+
                                           w/10" TH                                CRam
-------------------------------------------------------------------------------------------
( 18 )  66   BOX BOOM R        1      7    S4-419 w/CRam      575w   Wash R C/C     IR H.S.+
                                           w/10" TH                                CRam
        66   BOX BOOM R        2      7    S4-419 w/CRam      575w   Wash R C/C     IR H.S.+
                                           w/10" TH                                CRam
-------------------------------------------------------------------------------------------
( 19 )  65   LO BOX L          1      6    S4-426 w/CRam      575w   Lo C/C L       IR H.S.+
                                           w/10" TH                                m
        65   LO BOX L          2      6    S4-426 w/CRam      5      Lo C/C
                                           w/1
```

easy as possible. Instrumentation might not only be reduced in number, but simplified in type. Lengths of pipe or track might be carried on the truck with instruments already attached. Focus charts such as the one for the Broadway production of *Teddy and Alice*, designed by Tharon Musser (Figure 24—4), as well as other time-saving devices, have been invented by those designers and electricians who frequent the road.

**Focus Charts**     A focus chart is a piece of lighting paperwork intended to record exact focus information for each lighting instrument in use by the touring production. It indicates exact focus location, usually using a grid method of notation. It also specifies shutter cuts and beam edge focus. Figure 24—4c is a sample page from the focus chart for the tour of *The Who's Tommy*. This chart was generated by a Lightwright paperwork program.

**The Road Electrician**     If the designer is fortunate, an experienced head electrician will be assigned to the bus-and-truck production. This *road electrician* travels with the production and, along with the production stage manager, is responsible for making sure that the lighting is faithfully reproduced. Early consultation between the designer and the road electrician concerning equipment and methods of working can lead to a much better production.

It is the designer's obligation to periodically drop in and check on a production during its run. If the lighting has slipped a bit from what was originally set, adjustments must be made.

## DESIGNING FOR THE REGIONAL THEATRE

The middle years of the twentieth century will be remembered for the rebirth throughout the country of professional theatre, too long confined to New York and a few other large centers. Now it is a rare city that does not have at least one repertory or stock theatre, run by professional producers and directors and employing professional actors and designers.

a

FOCUS CHART FOR: _TEDDY AND ALICE_   DATE ___ *87'*

### KEY TO ABBREVIATIONS

O.O.H. = Out of House

O.O.P. = Off of Proscenium

Off Prosc. = . "

H.H. = Head High (To Fingers with Hand Held Above Head)

S.E. = Stage Edge

A.A. = As Above (Same cuts as previous lamp)

⊿ = Angle Shutter

L = Stage Left

R = Stage Right

@ = At

F or FLD = Flood Focus for Fresnels

SP = Spot Focus for Fresnels

¼ SP = Lamp is ¼ way from Full Spot in a Fresnel

H = Hard Edge or Sharp in terms of focus of Lekos

S = Soft Edge or "Fuzzy"   " "   " "   "

M = Medium Edge

₵ = Center Line

*O.F = OFF FOOTS*

**Figure 24—4**
Focus Charts

(a) Key to the focus chart for *Teddy & Alice*, designed by Tharon Musser.
(b) Focus chart for *Teddy & Alice*.
(c) Focus chart for *Tommy*. It was generated with a Lightwright program.

b

## FOCUS CHART FOR: **TEDDY & ALICE**
## POSITION: · UPPER BOX BOOM RIGHT.

| CH / UN | PLUGGED W/ | FOCUS | | | F | TYPE | COLOR |
|---|---|---|---|---|---|---|---|
| 11 / 1 | 0 -2- -U.B.L. 7-8 | D.L. SL OFF PORTAL SR — | • +4 C 12L US H.H. DS O.F | S | 6"x16" 1K LEKO | 02 |
| 11 / 2 | 0 -1- U.B.L 7-8 | D.L SL Δ.A. SR | • +4 C 12L US H.H. DS O.F | S | " | 35Δ |
| 12 / 3 | 0 -4- U.B.L. 3-4 | D.L O/C SL OFF PORTOL SR — | • +4 C 4L US H.H. DS O.F. | S | " | 02 |
| 12 / 4 | 0 -3- U.B.L 3-4 | D.L O/C SL Δ.Δ. SR | • +4 C 4L US H.H. DS O.F. | S | " | 35A |
| 13 / 5 | -6- U.B.L 5-6 | D.R O/L SL OFF COLUMN. SR — | • +4 C 4R US H.H. DS O.F | S | " | 02 |
| 13 / 6 | 0 -5- U.B.L 5-6 | D.R O/L SL Δ.Δ. SR — | • +4 C 4R US H.H. DS O.F | S | " | 35A |
| 14 / 7 | 0 -8- U.B.L 1-2 | D.R. SL — SR O.O.P. | • +4 C 12R US H.H. DS O.F. | S | " | 02 |
| 14 / 8 | 0 -7- U.B.L 1-2 | D.R. SL — SR O.O.P. | • +4 C 12R US H.H. DS O.F. | S | " | 35A |
| 78 / 9 | 10-11-12 | (T) HOUSE FRONT SL O.O.P. SR — | • LEFT US OFF HEADER DS OFF FOOT | m S | " T & S | 64A #210 BRANCHES |
| 78 / 10 | 9-11-12 | (T) HOUSE FRONT SL — SR — | • SL OF ¢ US CLIPS HEADER DS O.F. | m S | " T & S | " |
| 7 / 11 | 9-10-12 | (T) HOUSE FRONT SL O.O.P SR — | • LEFT US OFF HEADER DS O.F | m S | " T & S | 02 #294 LEAVES |
| 79 / 12 | 9-10-11 | (T) HOUSE FRONT SL — SR — | • SL OF ¢ US CLIPS HEADER SLIGHTLY DS O.F. | m S | " T & S | " |

POSITION & NO. __UPPER BOX BOOM RIGHT__
PAGE NO. _1_ OF _42_

```
c ====================              ============
  TOMMY - PINBALL "A"               FOCUS CHARTS                    Page   1
  ====================              ============                    05-26-94
  Designer: Chris Parry                            Producer: ATP / Dodger / Pace
  Associate: David Grill                   Head Electrician: Steve Cooksey
  PINBALL - FINAL CUT VERSION
  ================================================================================
  Note:  Asterisks indicate Replug Channels
  ================================================================================
  ====
  COVE
  ====
  Unit  Purpose              Type              Watts    Color          Dim    Chn
  ================================================================================
    1   Door Frts            6x16              1kw      L201           79   (314 )
                    @
        ----------   ----------
        US             SR                      Sf . + . Hd
        DS             SL                      Sp . + . Fl
        TP             BT                      Axis:
  --------------------------------------------------------------------------------
    2   Door Frts            6x16              1kw      L201           79   (314 )
                    @
        ----------   ----------
        US             SR                      Sf . + . Hd
        DS             SL                      Sp . + . Fl
        TP             BT                      Axis:
  --------------------------------------------------------------------------------
    4   Frts CL              6x16              1kw      L203+R119      81   (  6 )
                    @
        ----------   ----------
        US             SR                      Sf . + . Hd
        DS             SL                      Sp . + . Fl
        TP             BT                      Axis:
  --------------------------------------------------------------------------------
    6   Frts CLC             6x16              1kw      L203+R119      83   (  7 )
                    @
        ----------   ----------
        US             SR                      Sf . + . Hd
        DS             SL                      Sp . + . Fl
        TP             BT                      Axis:
  --------------------------------------------------------------------------------
    7   Conductor            6x16              1kw      N/C            84   (  3 )
                    @
        ----------   ----------
        US             SR                      Sf . + . Hd
        DS             SL                      Sp . + . Fl
        TP             BT                      Axis:
  --------------------------------------------------------------------------------
(continued on next page)
```

## WORKING IN REGIONAL THEATRE

Nearly all regional theatres (called LORT houses, after the type of union contract issued the actors) run apprentice programs—which seldom pay much but which offer exceptional experience and valuable professional contacts. Theatre Communications Group (TCG) publishes a complete list of theatres and programs; it is available by writing to TCG at 355 Lexington Avenue, New York, NY 10017-0217.

An enormous amount of exciting production is going on in regional theatre, using both national and local designers (Figure 24–5). More and more college students and graduates are working in these theatres on a full- or part-time basis. Opportunities abound for learning and making valuable contacts. The chances of assisting a designer or working on the staff are good for the talented and devoted theatre student. The first thing to do is send a resume to either the production manager or artistic director of the theatre. Then telephone and request an interview—it is that simple. Do not be discouraged if you are turned down and seemingly ignored. These individuals are extremely busy, but you will get results if you are willing to be persistent. The following section provides an overview of lighting practices in this segment of the commercial theatre.

## REGIONAL THEATRE PRODUCTION

Many of the professional practices that apply to lighting design on Broadway are also standard for the country's regional theatres. However, accepted practice in the regional theatres varies a great deal from theatre to theatre. Production schemes, ranging from repertory to stock, influence how a lighting designer approaches his or her work. Local IA union rules and regulations differ from city to city. Each theatre has its own in-house equipment, which may be radically different from one to the next. Technical production practices and staffing are unique to each situation.

**Regional Theatre Staff**     Most regional theatres are nonprofit organizations run by a *board of directors*. This is a group of community leaders who have an interest in the arts, but may know little or nothing about the actual operation of a theatre. The theatre's *business manager* and *artistic director* are hired by, and directly responsible to, this board of directors. Each theatre has a permanent staff, the makeup of which depends on the unique needs of the individual theatre. There will most likely be a *production manager* and department heads, including either an *electrics department head* or *house electrician*. This person's duties include maintenance of house equipment and working with each of the production's lighting designers. In addition, this individual has a strong voice in determining put-in and running crew size as well as local interpretation of union rules and regulations.

**Regional Theatre Designers**     A few regional theatres have staff designers, but most hire designers on a show-by-show basis. The way a lighting designer is hired is similar to Broadway practice, with the theatre's artistic director acting like the New York producer. Some regional theatres hire only designers who are United Scenic Artist members, while others pay no attention to union membership. Most theatres have a list of favorite designers, although a production's director can have great influence over this decision.

**Figure 24—5**
**Regional Theatre Production**

A production of Shakespeare's *Twelfth Night* directed by Des McAnuff for the La Jolla Playhouse. Lighting design—Chris Parry, scenery design—Neil Patel, and costume design—Susan Hilferty.

**Designing for Repertory**     Repertory theatres have a unique scheme of production in which different shows are presented each day of the week. Traditional repertory production generally requires daily changeovers from show to show. It may involve as few as two or as many as eight individual productions. The lighting designer must develop a repertory plot that serves as a basis for all shows, adding special instrumentation for each individual production. Repatching and sometimes color changes may take place during changeovers, but extensive refocusing should be avoided in repertory situations. Repertory design requires much more equipment than is normal for a single production, and the demands of an individual show must often be compromised for the sake of the entire production scheme. Remotely controlled color changers are an excellent equipment investment for the repertory theatre. Even more valuable are modern automated fixtures that allow the designer tremendous flexibility in repertory production.

Summer repertory—of Shakespeare or other classics, historical reenactments, and popular fare, especially musicals—has become a tradition in the United States. The repertory experience is an extremely valuable one in the developmental process of any lighting designer.

**Designing for Stock**     The vast majority of regional theatres produce their shows in a stock arrangement, running each production continuously for a period of two to six weeks. (Summer stock productions may run only one week.) Such a scheme requires rapid changeovers from show to show and normally a new lighting design for each production. The stock designer must be able to work quickly and efficiently, remaining one step ahead of the production schedule at all times.

Those theatres that run shows for more than three weeks most often job-in their lighting designers for each production. Those operations with shorter runs may very well employ a resident designer. Either way, the lighting designer is always under a great deal of time pressure. Like repertory production, stock experience is invaluable for the beginning lighting designer.

**What to Expect**     Some regional theatres have a stagehand contract with the local IA union and just as many others have no union labor affiliation. In essence, the regional designer should expect to find a new situation and new challenges in each place he or she designs.

Most cities have their own IA local. Rules and regulations vary radically from local to local as does the quality of work. This fact is of particular concern to the regional designer, for the quality of any local membership can only be known through previous experience or by word-of-mouth. It is wise to carefully evaluate the potential workforce in addition to local rule idiosyncrasies well before a production is mounted.

Stage lighting rental houses have grown in number along with the spread of regional theatres across the country. Some of these local businesses are surprisingly efficient and well stocked. Others are woefully ill equipped and lacking in knowledgeable personnel. The designer must anticipate the possibility of having to go to New York or some other major center for equipment needs, a situation that will surely affect budget and time considerations.

More important than commercial usage is the quite different matter of professional standards. No one should consider for a moment going into any level of commercial theatre unless he or she plans to devote total energy and ability to the routines and the problems that present themselves. It is no place for the casual enthusiast or the dilettante, nor for the easily discouraged, the supersensitive, or the noncooperative.

## LIGHTING DANCE

Dance is most often performed on a proscenium stage with a formal leg-and-border arrangement. At first glance it would seem that dance requires the same sort of light as do other forms of production. But there is one most important difference. When we attend a play we are vitally interested in the faces of the actors to convey character, thoughts, and emotion. This is not true in dance, particularly ballet, in which the position and movement of the dancer's body tell all. A knowledgeable lover of concert dance will scarcely notice a dancer's face and will surely not concentrate on it. The primary concern is movement, revealed and emphasized by light.

### DESIGN CONSIDERATIONS

One method of emphasizing movement is to place the principal axis of light in line with the axis of movement. Thus, a ballerina spinning in a pirouette would have the light hitting straight down on her or straight up from below.

The latter, which has been used for trick effects in modern dance, would probably not be appropriate for classical ballet. Although light from directly overhead tends to make the human body appear shortened, it is still a good way to accent the rapid turning of the dance.

Of course it would be impractical, if not inappropriate, to attempt to cover every single movement of a dance. Fortunately, choreographers often establish several basic movement patterns and repeat them throughout the dance. These patterns echo or reinforce the theme of the dance piece, creating compositions that can be effectively reinforced by the lighting. Provisions can be made for some of the most significant movement and for more general lighting that will best suit the work. The lighting designer must attend as many rehearsals as possible and take careful notes before developing the light plot. Most dances fall into certain basic patterns of movement, which can be covered successfully by one or more of the areas suggested in Figure 24–6.

**Side-Light**    When lighting a theatrical production, it is most likely for the designer to begin with front visibility light and then move on to consideration of side- and back-light angles. In lighting most dance however, the designer begins with the side-lights. Side-lighting is the primary source of figure-modeling light. While a typical theatrical lighting plot for the proscenium theatre has at least half of its equipment located front-of-house, dance plots often have three-quarters of their instruments backstage. This fact should be of interest to the lighting design student in terms of stage circuits as well as design technique. Extra cabling may be required because the theatre does not have the necessary number of circuits backstage for an average dance plot.

### LOCATION OF INSTRUMENTS

Following are the more usual mounting positions for dance lighting instruments (almost invariably ellipsoidal reflector spotlights):

**Low Front**    For a low front position, the lights may be mounted on a low balcony rail. Although light from this angle tends to wash out body form, a little may be desirable for the sake of visibility and/or color washing.

**Medium Front**    Medium front-lights would be mounted on a second balcony rail or in a beam position. Again, this does little for the body and casts shadows of ballet costumes on dancers' legs. This angle corresponds with the 45-degree visibility light common to theatrical presentation and, if necessary, can be used as such.

**High Front**    Roughly at a 60-degree angle, high front is much more useful for theatrical presentation than for dance. This angle casts serious costume shadows on the legs of an otherwise beautiful ballerina. It is, however, a dramatic angle that can be used to emphasize such a mood.

### Figure 24–6
### Dance Patterns

These patterns coincide with the principal movements of the dancers on the stage.
(a) Cross-stage "zones." Dancers enter from and exit into the wings, working in zones that parallel the apron.
(b) Up-and-down stage. Dancers move toward the apron and away again. In ballet, the chorus frequently poses along the sides while the principals take center stage.
(c) The diagonals. An important pattern in modern dance, dancers enter from upstage wings and exit downstage on the opposite side, or vice versa.
(d) Center stage. An obvious location for important dancing.
(e) Special spots. These may be any place on stage (a few possibilities are indicated) in which a tight movement by principal dancers is performed.

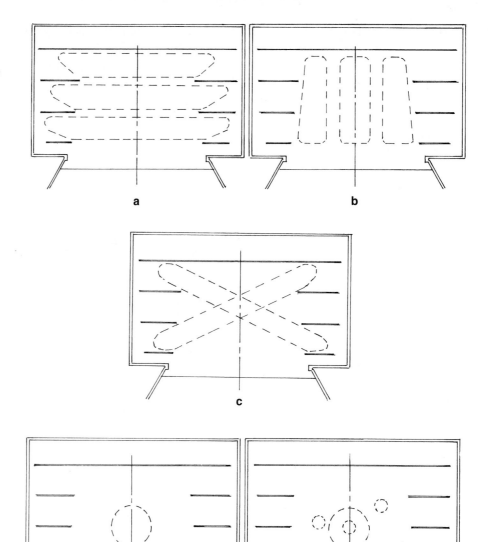

**Low Side**     For the low side position, lights are mounted very low on booms in the wings. Although an unnatural angle, it is flattering to dancers because it tends to lift the body. Low side-lighting instruments are called "shin kickers" or "shin busters" for obvious reasons. They are normally clear or colored with very light tints. Their light can be shuttered off the floor surface in order to eliminate visible scallops from the beams. Gobo patterns placed in low side instruments enhance the sense of movement and add texture and mood to a scene. Instruments can be focused so that patterns are visible only on the dancers and not on the floor.

**Medium Side**     For the medium side position, lights are mounted about 8 or 10 feet above the floor in the wings. This may be regarded as *the* basic dance lighting angle. It throws a wash across the stage with little significant shadowing. It may be desirable to mount an additional spotlight a few feet higher to carry across to the far side of the stage. A third instrument can be mounted a few feet lower to light the close side of the stage. In this case both long- and short-throw ellipsoidals are focused so that the centerlines of their beams are parallel (see Figure 24–7 for details). Gobo patterns placed in medium side instruments shine upon both the dancers and the floor.

**High Side**     Light in the high side position comes from 15 to 20 feet high in the wings or from the ends of electric battens (such units are called "pipe ends"). If too high an angle is chosen, the light will tend to push the dancers down and make them appear squat. However, a 60-degree high side can be very effective for a dramatic moment and is particularly useful in modern dance. Gobo patterns from high side instruments read most strongly on the floor.

**Straight Back**     In the straight back position, light comes from above but also from behind the dancer. This is a very valuable position, for it highlights the body in space, separating it from the background. And it does not cause one dancer to throw a shadow on the next one.

**Diagonal Back**     Like the straight back position, light comes from above and behind the dancer, but from an angle to the side as well. Frequently this is more desirable than straight back because a more visible surface area of the dancer's body is illuminated.

**Down-Light**     In the down-light position, lights are mounted directly overhead, an effect that tends to push the body down. They are useful only for specialized moments.

**Follow Spots**     Light from a follow spot can come from various locations in the auditorium or from some onstage position. This must be kept unobtrusive and should be operated by an individual capable of making it so. Of course, in musical comedy, dance, and some classical ballet, blatant use of follow spots is accepted as traditional.

**Dancers' Spotting Light**     Dancers maintain balance by finding their "center." The lighting designer can help them by placing a "spotting light" or "centering light" in the auditorium. This should be a small $7\frac{1}{2}$- or 15-watt red lamp located at head height, dead center at the rear of the auditorium or on a balcony rail.

## BOOMS

Low and medium side-lighting require floor stands or booms as hanging positions. A dance concert or ballet almost always calls for booms in each wing on both sides of the stage. This can total twelve booms for a large production. It is traditional to hang lighting instruments to the side of booms

**Figure 24—7**
Dance Boom Layout

Instruments are hung on-stage from the boom to take up as little wing space as possible. This illustration shows instrument #1 lighting far stage-left in the second zone while instrument #2 lights mid-stage and #3 close. Instrument #4 is a low angle ''shin.''

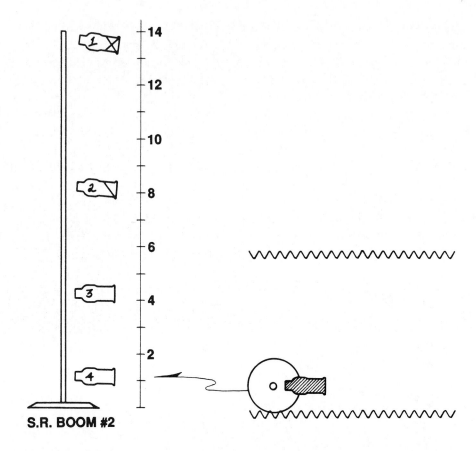

**S.R. BOOM #2**

in the theatre, but for dance they should be mounted straight out from the boom pipes. In this way, the boom will take up as little wing space as possible, allowing more freedom for dancer entrances and exits (often leaps into the wings). Figure 24–7 illustrates a typical dance boom layout.

Booms must be clean and safe, each with a safety tie from the top of the pipe to the grid. Cable to booms is neatest if run up the boom and onto an electric pipe for circuiting. However, many times floor pockets must be used. If this is the case, run the cable straight offstage from the boom and then turn upstage or downstage to floor pocket locations. Cover the cable with carpeting and tape it securely to the floor.

Be aware that inexperienced dancers may try to use light booms as balance bars when warming up. Discourage this practice without being rude.

### COLOR CONSIDERATIONS

For most classic ballet, strong colors are not desirable, but a basic tint certainly is. Pale lavender is frequently used, but tradition may prescribe some other tint. Whatever color is selected becomes the neutral for the particular ballet. The other shades work in relation to it, and when blended together on the stage, approximate the neutral. Thus if lavender is the neutral, a light rose next to it appears quite warm and light blue appears cool. The rose and blue mix together to lavender.

**COLOR PLATE 24–1a**
**THE BROADWAY CAST OF *DAMN YANKEES***
Scenery design—Douglas W. Schmidt, costume design—David C. Woolard, and lighting design—David F. Segal.

**COLOR PLATE 24–1b**
**THE BROADWAY PRODUCTION OF *THE WHO'S TOMMY***
Michael Cerveris as Tommy. The light plot and projector frame plot for the Broadway tour of *Tommy* can be found in Figure 24–2.

Directed by Des McAnuff, scenery design—John Arnone, costume design—David C. Woolard, lighting design—Chris Parry, projections—Wendall Harrington. Photo by Marcus Bryan-Brown.

a

b

a

b

**COLOR PLATE 24–4**
**OPERA: *RAPE OF LUCRETIA***

(a) Act I, scene 1, outside the Roman camp.
(b) Act II, scene 2, Lucretia's garden.
Light plot, section and hook-up are shown in Figures 24–9 through 24–11. Produced by the Cincinnati Conservatory of Music, director—John Eaton, scenery design—Paul Shortt, and lighting design—Cindy Limauro. Photos courtesy Sandy Underwood.

Color Plate 24–3a is a photograph from the classical ballet *La Sylphide*. Principal front-light colors are lilac (R55) and pale amber gold (R09). The cool-looking back-light is no-color blue (R60).

A valuable effect can be achieved by using advancing and receding colors to add apparent depth to the stage. The use of slightly cooler tints on the upstage dancers makes them appear farther away than they would otherwise seem. Likewise, warmer shades on the downstage dancers seem to bring them even further forward. Care must be taken in using this technique, however. The tints must not be so far apart that the dancers visibly change color as they move through the zones.

As illustrated in Color Plate 24–3b, modern dance requires color usage that is appropriately modern. Use of more saturated colors, especially in side-light, is a common technique for expressing mood. No-color light or cool tints are often chosen to express the sometimes dramatic nature of the dance. Remote control color changers mounted on the booms can provide needed variety for a performance comprising several dance pieces.

## CUES

Cue placement for a dramatic piece is often dictated by the rhythm of the work. This is even more true of dance. Movement nearly always corresponds to the music, and cues should do the same. The cues for a ballet should be called by the stage manager from the score. The lighting designer should become very familiar with the music before beginning the design. Cues for modern dance or pieces without scores may need to be called from the action. This requires that the lighting designer and stage manager become very familiar with the movement. Attending preproduction rehearsals is imperative.

## A DANCE PLOT

Figure 24–8 is a $\frac{1}{2}$-inch over-stage light plot for a modern dance concert consisting of three separate pieces. Each of the three pieces is quite modern, with the second piece, "Souvenir," being the most traditional (music from Tchaikovsky's *Souvenir de Florence*).

**Physical Space**     In the case of this performance, the Old Globe Theatre, which often plays in thrust configuration, was used in its proscenium form. Downstage and upstage edges of the dance floor are indicated on the plan. Note that the masking legs step in a bit as they go upstage. This technique accommodates the audience sightlines, which are fairly wide and typical of thrust theatres. The rake of the audience is steep, allowing a good view of the stage from every seat. Most of the audience sees quite a bit of floor surface.

**Distribution**     Front-of-house instruments are not indicated on this plot. However, only eleven instruments were used from the auditorium. They included five 6-by-16s colored in R54 and used as a downstage visibility wash. The other seven instruments were specials for the various dances.

### Figure 24—8
Modern Dance Plot

A $\frac{1}{2}$-inch scale over-stage light plot for a modern dance concert consisting of three separate pieces. It was produced at the Old Globe Theatre and lit by Brenda Berry and Craig Wolf.

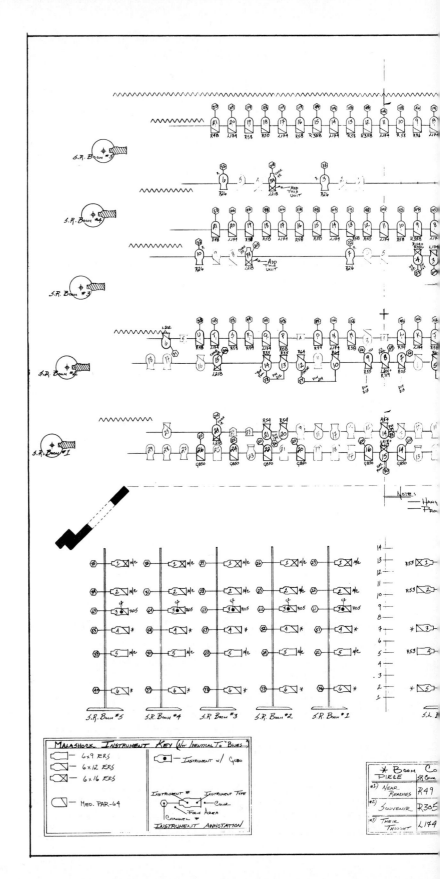

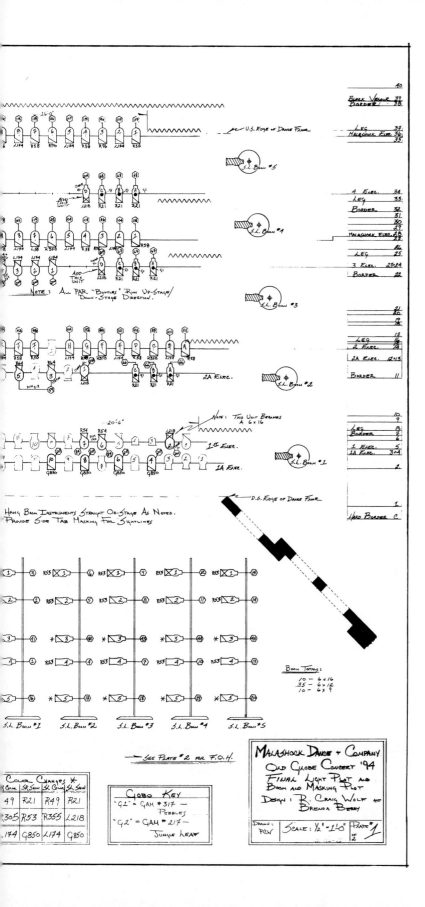

Boom Totals:
10 — 6×16
35 — 6×12
10 — 6×9

S.L. Boom #1  S.L. Boom #2  S.L. Boom #3  S.L. Boom #4  S.L. Boom #5

— SEE PLATE #2 FOR F.O.H.

| COLOR CHANGES ★ | | | |
|---|---|---|---|
| COLOR | SR SHIN | SL DOWN | SL SHIN |
| 49 | R21 | R49 | R21 |
| 305 | R53 | R355 | L218 |
| 174 | G850 | L174 | G850 |

GOBO KEY
"G1" = GAM #317 — PEBBLES
"G2" = GAM #217 — JUNGLE LEAF

MALASHOCK DANCE + COMPANY
OLD GLOBE CONCERT '94
FINAL LIGHT PLOT AND
BOOM AND MASKING PLOT
DESIGN: R. CRAIG WOLF AND
BRENDA BERRY

| DRAWN: RCW | SCALE: ½" = 1'-0" | PLATE 1 of 2 |

The over-stage hang was slightly limited by instrumentation previously hung for a dramatic production ("Blues in the Night"), which was to follow the dance concert. The lightweight instruments with no color or channel notation were hung for "Blues . . ." and not used in the dance concert. Three sets of PAR-64 back-lights were designed, principally one for each dance piece. They were hung seven across the stage with their oval beams running up- and downstage. Three electrics were necessary to cover the depth of the stage. An upstage R54 front wash of 6-by-12s was located on the first electric. The various other over-stage instruments were designed as specials for each piece.

The booms held five instruments each on the stage-left side and six instruments stage-right. The additional stage-right instruments contained a leaf pattern, which provided a swirly breakup for "Souvenir." The top boom instrument (6 × 16) threw far across the stage and was focused a bit high to eliminate too much intensity buildup in the center of the stage. It received top and upstage shutter cuts off the black masking legs. The mid boom instrument (6 × 12) was focused center stage with slight shutter cuts both up- and downstage. The close instrument (6 × 9) was focused to hit about ten feet out from the wings and also received shutter cuts on up- and down-stage edges. The 6-by-12 shins were tilted up just slightly and received top and side shutter cuts. Finally, the color change instruments (6 × 12) were focused straight cross the stage with minor shutter cuts.

**Color**    One bank of back-lights was colored in L174, a medium steel blue. The second was R58, deep lavender. The third consisted of a mixture of color zones in order to create a mottled look on the stage floor for "Souvenir." They too were fairly saturated colors.

A light tint (R53) of lavender was used in the stage-left side-light while no-color was used stage-right. This technique offers a built-in warm and cool side, however slight. The color change instruments generally took more saturated colors that blended with the light tints of the other side-lights. The "Boom Color Changes" key indicates the exact colors used for this performance.

An interesting color and pattern effect was created for "The Near Reaches" by the pipe-end gobo instruments on 2A, 3, and 4 electrics. Their golden amber rays were focused across the stage from a diagonal back direction. The saturated color effectively cut through the other stage lighting to create an appropriately abstract effect.

**Control**    For this dance concert, 220 control channels were used, providing independent control over nearly all instruments. The control system was a Light Palette 90. Note the channel layout for the booms, making it easier to remember individual zones and functions.

## AN OPERA PLOT

Lighting for the opera calls for a heightened theatricality, often combining the techniques of theatre and dance. Traditional operatic scenery suggests reality, but does so on a grand scale. Modern opera design often uses exaggerated techniques that suggest reality in a distorted manner, reminiscent of expressionism. Lighting may follow suit with saturated colors to produce a heightened sense of reality. Exaggerated angles and harsh colors may be used to produce stark images. Follow spots are frequently called for in traditional opera production.

### RAPE OF LUCRETIA

Figure 24–9 is a light plot designed by Cindy Limauro for the Cincinnati Conservatory of Music's production of *Rape of Lucretia.* Scenery was designed by Paul Shortt. Figure 24–10 is the scene designer's cross section, and Figure 24–11 is a part of the designer's hookup. Color Plates 24–4a and 24–4b are production photographs.

Each of the two acts of this opera has two scenes. Act I, Scene 1 takes place at night in a military camp outside of Rome (Color Plate 24–4a). The second scene is an evening interior—inside Lucretia's home. Act II, Scene 1 is the rape scene; and Act II, Scene 2 is an exterior garden (Color Plate 24–4b).

The theatre is a small extended apron with a rather steep audience rake seating approximately 800 people. The control system is a Colortran Prestige 2000.

**Scene 1**    A stormy evening is chosen for this scene, with the atmosphere intended to have an aggressive and dirty feel. The flown tent piece, which can just be seen at the top of the production photograph in Color Plate 24–4a, was lit with down-light from bridge 2 (instruments #22 and #23). A practical brazier is located downstage-left and supported by ambers (R16) from the stage-left torm positions. The front-light for the scene comes from the first beam and is colored in a combination R60/R55 from house-left and R70 from house-right. A high side R76 completes the picture. As the scene progresses, several lights located in the orchestra pit are brought up to accentuate the eerie and uneasy feeling desired by the designer.

**Scene 2**    For this candlelit scene inside Lucretia's house, the designer wanted a softer, yet menacing look. Front-of-house instruments in the second beam replaced those of the first beam, providing a less harsh angle and color of light. While still used, the R76 high side-light was lowered in intensity.

**Scene 3**    The scene in which the rape of Lucretia takes place begins with a very soft and gentle look created by light lavenders isolating the bed and its immediate surroundings. During the rape this shifts to "jagged" lighting angles and colors that emphasize the brutality of the act.

**Scene 4**    The final scene, in which Lucretia dies, takes place in her garden, beautifully textured with break-up leaf gobos colored in R88 (Color Plate 24–4b). The lighting is gentle, with front sources from the second beam colored in R02.

**Figure 24–9**
An Opera Plot

A light plot for *Rape of Lucretia*, produced by the Cincinnati Conservatory of Music, directed by John Eaton with lighting designed by Cindy Limauro. See Color Plate 24–4.

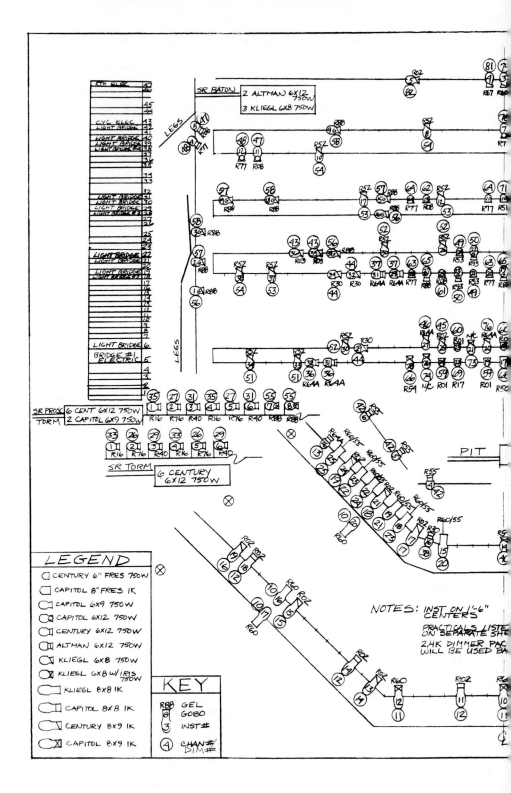

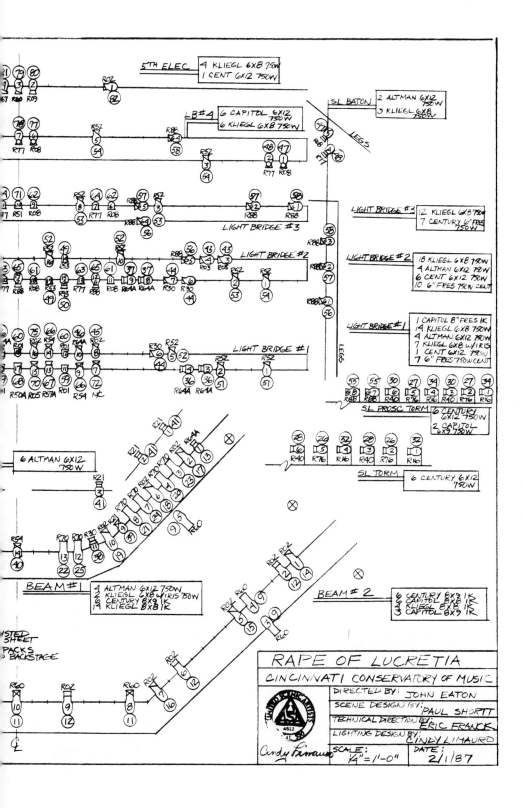

RAPE OF LUCRETIA

CINCINNATI CONSERVATORY OF MUSIC

DIRECTED BY: JOHN EATON
SCENE DESIGN BY: PAUL SHORTT
TECHNICAL DIRECTION BY: ERIC FRANCK
LIGHTING DESIGN BY: CINDY LIMAURO

SCALE: 1/4" = 1'-0"
DATE: 2/1/87

**Figure 24–10**
Section

The center line section for *Rape of Lucretia*, drawn by scenic designer Paul Shortt.

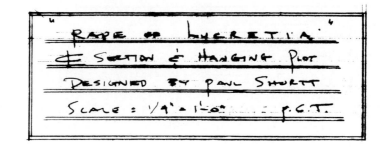

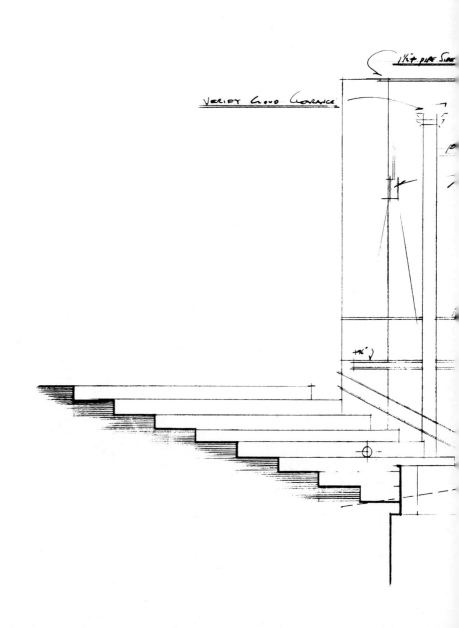

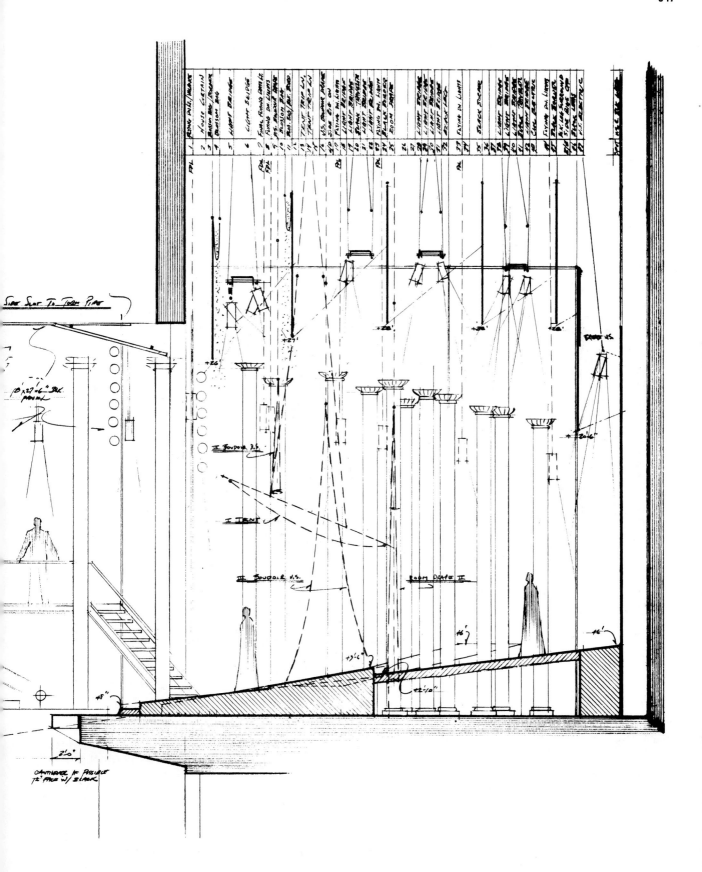

**Figure 24–11**
Hook-Up

A page from the hook-up for *Rape of Lucretia*.

| Channel | Position & Unit # | Type | Focus | Color | Circuit | Dimmer |
|---|---|---|---|---|---|---|
| 1 | SL PLAT CAN DNLTS 1-2-3 | PAR 64 NSP 1K | DOWN LIGHT | R60 | | |
| 2 | SR PLAT CAN DNLTS 1-2-3 | PAR 64 NSP 1K | DOWN LIGHT | R60 | | |
| 3 | RAKE CAN DNLT 2 | PAR 64 NSP 1K | MALE CHORUS DOWNLIGHT | R60 | | |
| 4 | RAKE CAN DNLT 3 | PAR 64 NSP 1K | DOWN LIGHT | R60 | | |
| 5 | RAKE CAN DNLTS 4-5-6 | PAR 64 NSP 1K | DOWN LIGHT | R60 | | |
| 6 | SL RAMP CANS 1-2 SR RAMP CANS 1-2 | PAR 64 NSP 1K | DOWN LIGHT | R60 | | |
| 7 | CENTER RAMP CANS 1-2 | PAR 64 NSP 1K | DOWN LIGHT | R60 | | |
| 8 | RAKE CAN DNLT 1 | PAR 64 NSP 1K | FEMALE CHORUS DOWNLIGHT | R60 | | |
| 9 | #1 BEAM 5 #2 BEAM 3-4 | KLIEGL 8X8 1K | SL PLAT NARRATOR | R60 | | |
| 10 | #1 BEAM 20 #2 BEAM 16-17 | KLIEGL 8X8 1K | SR PLAT NARRATOR | R60 | | |
| 11 | #2 BEAM 8-10-12 | CAPITOL 8X9 1K | DS DECK WASH | R60 | | |
| 12 | #2 BEAM 2-6-9 11-14-18 | CAPITOL 8X8 1K | DS DECK WASH | R02 | | |
| 13 | #1 BEAM 1-26 | ALTMAN 6X12 750W | RAKE HPE | R64A | | |
| 14 | #2 BEAM 1-13 | CENTURY 8X9 1K | RAKE DL | R02 | | |
| 15 | #2 BEAM 5-15 | CENTURY 8X9 1K | RAKE DC | R02 | | |
| 16 | #2 BEAM 7-19 | CENTURY 8X9 1K | RAKE DR | R02 | | |
| 17 | #1 BEAM 2-17 | CENTURY 8X9 1K | RAKE UL | R02 | | |
| 18 | #1 BEAM 6-21 | CENTURY 8X9 1K | RAKE UC | R02 | | |
| 19 | #1 BEAM 10-24 | CENTURY 8X9 1K | RAKE UR | R02 | | |

## WORKING AS A LIGHTING DESIGNER

The theatre has always been the primary training ground for lighting designers. It remains so today, despite the diverse fields in which theatre-trained lighting designers work. Not only does the theatre teach the art of designing with light, it also teaches the art of collaboration. A background in theatrical lighting prepares the designer to work in architecture, for theme parks, in film and television lighting, as well as concerts and a variety of other public events.

### GETTING WORK

It is the rare individual who graduates from a theatre training program and immediately gets work as a designer. The old axiom that people have to "pay their dues" is still true; it's simply another way of saying that experience working in the field is a significant part of becoming a designer. It doesn't matter what the field is.

Whether the work is theatrical, architectural, industrial, or theme parks, an aspiring lighting designer probably must live in or around a fairly large city. Some cities are known for certain types of work. Obvious examples are Los Angeles for film and New York for theatre. It is simply a matter of first determining what field you wish to pursue and then going where major employers in that field are located.

**Architecture**     Architectural firms make a practice of hiring young people as apprentices. Individuals with theatre backgrounds are especially welcome because they have been trained to think both creatively and practically. In addition, working with other people is a skill of the theatrical lighting designer. Chicago, Los Angeles, San Francisco, and New York are hubs of architectural activity. Most large cities have several firms, each of which has a lighting department or an individual who works primarily with lighting. In many cases he or she will have been trained in the theatre. The ability to draft and use a CAD program is of great advantage in landing a job in the architectural world.

The Illuminating Engineering Society (IES) is a national organization primarily made up of architectural lighting engineers and designers. The principal function of this organization is to service its membership by providing an outlet for discussion and the dissemination of up-to-date information on architectural lighting. The IES is also concerned with providing better training in the field of architectural lighting. Local chapters offer beginning and advanced classes that can be of great benefit in gaining industry-specific information.

**Television and Film**     As in architecture, many lighting directors for television and film were trained in the theatre. Television and film lighting is a highly competitive field. However, it is possible to gain entry into the industry by beginning as an apprentice or assistant. Los Angeles and New York are the major film and television centers, although most other large cities offer ample television opportunities. Some universities offer a theatre major with a film or television minor (San Diego State is an example). Most colleges and universities offer some film and television course work.

The National Association of Broadcasters (NAB) holds an annual convention that attracts television workers from across the country. It is a good place to meet people and learn more about the field—and perhaps find a job.

**Industrials and Trade Shows**     Lighting for industrials and trade shows can be a lucrative business. It is primarily done by firms that have gained a reputation over the years for this type of design work. These firms are contracted by industry giants like General Motors or IBM to design and execute the lighting for their product shows. The scope of this design work varies

**Figure 24–12**
**Industrial and Trade Show Design**

Shown is the lighting for one of the automobile manufacturers at the North American International Auto Show at Cobo Hall in Detroit. Lighting system design by Ann M. Archbold of The Secor Group.

from relatively direct and simple illumination to extremely complex and spectacular productions (Figure 24–12). Industrial lighting firms are always looking for people with lighting design talent to apprentice and learn more about the business. They are generally located in larger cities and can be identified simply by looking in the telephone book. Call and ask for the name of the individual to whom you may send a resume.

**Theme Parks**     The rise in popularity of theme parks has made this another lucrative field for lighting designers. Theme parks may be owned and run by large corporations such as Disney or Universal. In this case, one should apply to the human resources department for a position. If at all possible, find out exactly who does the hiring and contact that person directly. Assuming there is work, lighting designers trained in the theatre are welcomed at these large entertainment conglomerates. At other times, small firms consisting of one or two designers are contracted to do the lighting for a certain theme park. When the work comes along, these firms need help to get the job done. Sending a resume and requesting an interview could lead to a good job and provide exceptional experience. Remember that volume of work for the smaller firms varies a great deal. Don't give up if nothing is available immediately. Be persistent without being a nuisance.

Lighting Dimensions International (LDI) holds a national conference each November, which is attended by many lighting designers in diverse fields. Such conferences are a valuable way to meet people and learn more about the various aspects of lighting design. The Themed Entertainment Association publishes a directory of firms working in the industry.

**Concerts**     Concert lighting grew out of the need for special illumination of touring rock concerts. In the beginning, a band member was in charge of the lighting—often nothing more than a few spotlights providing a wash of color on the stage. However, things changed quickly as bands realized the strong dramatic effect color and light had on their audiences. It soon became a necessity to have special lighting and effects. New methods of touring lights were developed and the PAR-64 fixture became an industry standard. More recently, concert lighting has provided the theatre with a whole new generation of automated fixtures (Figure 24–13).

A concert lighting designer often tours with the band, running the lighting console for each performance. Being a part of a concert tour is an extremely valuable experience for any young lighting designer. Such tours hire electricians and it is certainly possible to assist the designer. Jim Moody, who was trained as a theatrical designer, has written an informative book on concert lighting that should be read by anyone interested in the field. It is listed in the bibliography at the back of this book.

**Figure 24–13**
**Concert Design**

Shown is one section of a concert truss containing both fixed instruments and automated fixtures.

**The Theatre**     Working your way up to designing in the theatre is a slow and sometimes frustrating process. Normally, producers will not hire a designer until his or her work has been seen. The paradox is this: How can someone see your work if you can't get hired? You must be prepared to design for little or no money at first. This also means that you will need another job. In fact, most theatrical lighting designers work in other fields. Your first choice for non-design work should be doing something else in the theatre. Stagehands and electricians are always needed and some get paid good wages. Assisting more experienced designers is of great advantage. Such work allows you to stay close to the theatre and meet people who may offer you work in the future. Build up a resume and distribute it frequently.

USITT (United States Institute for Theatre Technology) is the American association of design and production professionals in the performing arts. It sponsors an annual conference usually held in March or April, which is invaluable for meeting other designers, keeping up with state-of-the-art techniques and equipment, and learning more about the art of design through the numerous workshops offered. USITT also provides a job placement service at its national conference. Membership is inexpensive for students and reasonable for others. For information, contact USITT at 10 West 19th Street, New York, NY 10011-4206.

*ArtSEARCH* is a national publication listing available positions primarily in the theatre arts. You may subscribe to this TCG (Theatre Communications Group) service by writing to the following address: *ArtSEARCH*, 355 Lexington Avenue, New York, NY 10017-0217.

The theatre is a wonderful place to work because theatre people enjoy what they are doing. It doesn't take too long to discover whether or not you are cut out for a career in the theatre. But remember—if you think you are, be persistent. Good luck!

# GLOSSARY

**Arc Light**  A spotlight that has for its source an electric current arcing between two electrodes.

**Amperage**  The rate of flow of an electric current through a conductor. The capacity of an electrical conductor.

**Angstrom**  A unit of length used to specify wavelengths of light.

**ANSI**  American National Standards Institute. The ANSI Code is a three-letter code used to identify lamps.

**Asbestos**  Although asbestos is no longer used in the theatre, the term is sometimes used when referring to the Safety Curtain (see Safety Curtain).

**Avista**  Change of scene or movement of scenery in full view of the audience.

**Back Cloth**  English theatre expression for back drop.

**Backstage**  Much the same as *off-stage* but used generally in reference to stage workers and stage machinery rather than to actors.

**Bag Line**  Pick-up or bull line on a sandbag to lift the weight of the bag while trimming or clewing a line-set.

**Barn Doors**  A device consisting of two or four hinged metal flaps which is placed in front of a spotlight to reduce the beam spread in one or more directions.

**Batten**  (1) Pipe batten. Horizontal pipe hung from a line-set of a flying system. (2) Wooden batten. Top and bottom of roll drop.

**Beam Port**  A front-of-house lighting position located in the ceiling of the theatre.

**Blackout**  The instantaneous killing of all stage lights.

**Bleeding**  Brightly colored undercoat of paint showing a second coat.

**Bloom**  Specular reflection from mirror or highly polished surface.

**Boards**  Slang for stage.

**Book**  Set a two-fold of scenery in an open-book position.

**Boom** or **Boomerang**  A vertical pipe for mounting spotlights.

**Bounce**  Reflected diffuse light off the floor or walls.

**Box Booms**  Lighting booms located in front-of-house box-seat positions.

**Break**  To fold or unfold scenery.

**Breakaway**  Scenery or properties rigged to break on cue.

**Breast Line**  Fixed line to wall or gridiron that drags or breasts a piece of hanging scenery into an eccentric position. Also called a *drag line.*

**Bridle**  Means of dividing the load of each liftline by spreading the pick-up points along the batten.

**Bull Line**  Heavy four-stranded hemp rope used on a winch to lift uncounterweighted scenery.

**Bumper**  (1) Low platform downstage of portal against which castered wagons bump. (2) Metal hoop fastened to a batten carrying lighting instruments to protect them from flying scenery and the scenery from hot instruments.

**Bump-up**  Sudden movement of lights to a higher intensity.

**Channel**  A lighting control path. *Channel* replaces the term *dimmer* in modern usage.

**Circuit**  Established paths of electricity.

**Clewing**  Several lines are held together by knots or clew for handling as a single line.

**Company Switch**  A distribution panel with hook-up terminals to supply the power for a traveling company's switchboard. Usually three-wire 220 volts, 600 amps on a side.

**Cross Fade**  To fade from one lighting set-up to another without going through a dimout.

**Cue**  A visual or audible signal from the stage manager to execute a predetermined movement of lights or scenery.

**Cyc**  Short for cyclorama.

**Cyc Knuckle**  Hardware for attaching side arms of a cyc batten to a regular pipe batten.

**Dark House**  No performance or inactive theatre.

**Dead Hung**  A unit of scenery hung directly from the gridiron and not a part of the flying system.

**Deck**  Stage floor.

**Diffusion**  A plastic medium placed in the color holder of a spotlight to break up the light in a variety of ways.

**Dim**  Change the intensity of a light, either brighter or less bright.

**Dimmer**  Apparatus for altering the flow of electric current to cause a light to be more or less bright.

**Dimmer-per-Circuit**  A system in which an individual dimmer is permanently assigned to each stage circuit.

**Disappearance Trap** Special counterweighted elevator trap used as a quick exit or disappearance by an actor.

**Disconnect** *see* Company switch.

**Dolly** A type of wagon.

**Donkey** Electric winch.

**Douser** Mechanical means of putting out a light.

**Downstage** The area nearest the footlights and curtain.

**Draw Line** Operating line of a traveler curtain rigging.

**Dutchman** (1) Condensing lens in a lens projector. (2) Scab or mending cleat. (3) Cloth strip covering a hinged joint.

**Edge-up** Framed scenery maneuver; raise a flat upright on its edge.

**EMF** Electromotive force or voltage.

**End for End** Reverse the position of an object.

**ERF** Short for ellipsoidal reflector floodlights.

**ERS** Short for ellipsoidal reflector spotlights.

**Feel-up** Take slack out of lift lines prior to setting the trim.

**FEV** Short for French Enamel Varnish.

**Fill Light** Wash or soft light that fills in the light on the face from the direction opposite the key light.

**Flag** Small piece of cloth inserted into the lay of the purchase line as a trim mark.

**Flat** In the commercial theatre, the stiffening of two or more hinged wings into a flat plane or wall.

**Flipper** Jog hinged to a single wing.

**Floatdown** Kitelike action when a flat is allowed to fall or float to the floor.

**Flood** Widespread focus on a spotlight. Also, short for floodlight.

**Floodlight** A lighting instrument that produces a broad spread of light. Often misapplied to other lighting apparatus.

**Focus** (1) The direction in which a lighting instrument is aimed.

(2) Adjustment of the size or shape of a light beam.

**FOH** Front-of-house. Anything located on the audience side of the proscenium arch.

**Follow Cue** A cue timed to follow an original cue so quickly it does not warrant a separate cue called by the stage manager.

**Follow Spot** A high-intensity, long throw spotlight requiring an operator in order to follow action on stage.

**Footcandle** The measurement of illumination; the amount of light from one candle that will fall on a surface one foot from the candle.

**Fresnel** (correctly pronounced Fre' nel) A lens recognized by its concentric rings. The spotlight designed to use this lens.

**Front Lighting** Illumination on the stage from instruments placed in the auditorium.

**Frost** *see* Diffusion.

**Funnel** Also known as a top hat. A short metal cylinder placed in front of a spotlight to reduce flare.

**Gobo** A metal cutout used with a spotlight to obtain a patterned beam.

**Grand Drape** Decorative first border in old proscenium-type theatres.

**Greek-it** Fake lettering that has no meaning; doubletalk.

**Grip** Stagehand.

**Gripping** Running scenery on the floor by stagehands or grips.

**Ground Row** Horizontal profile unit of scenery to mask the bottom of a drop or cyclorama.

**Halation** Undesirable diffraction of light from a spotlight. A halo of light around the beam.

**Head Block** Multigrooved pulley or multipulley sheave in a lineset.

**Head Spot** Very narrow beam from a spotlight focused on an actor's head. Also called *pin spot*.

**Hook-up** A lighting schedule which lists instruments by dimmer or channel number.

**House Curtain** Main curtain of a proscenium theatre designed to tie in with the house decorations. Also called act curtain.

**IA** Short for IATSE—International Alliance of Theatrical Stage Employees. The stagehands' union.

**In-one** Foremost downstage acting position, traditionally in front of oleo.

**Interconnect** A flexible system allowing the electrical connection of any stage circuit with any dimmer. Also called patch panel.

**Iris** Mechanical means of closing the aperture of a spotlight.

**Jack** Framed brace to hold scenery upright.

**Jackknife** Pivoting wagon movement like the action of blades in a jackknife.

**Jog** Narrow-width wing.

**Juice** Commercial slang for electricity.

**Jumper** Cable connecting two or more lighting instruments.

**Key Light** Accent or highlight on actor's face, usually from the direction of the motivating light for the scene.

**Keystoning** Distortion of a projected image when the projector is oblique to the screen.

**Klieglight** A type of spotlight sold by Kliegl Bros. *Klieg* is often used as a synonym for any bright light.

**Knife** Steel guide for a tracked wagon.

**Ladder** Hanging ladderlike frame for mounting spotlights.

**Lamp** (1) Correctly, the name of what is often called a light bulb. (2) In the commercial theatre the term for any lighting instrument, particularly a spotlight.

**Lead** Cable from power supply.

**Left Stage** To the actor's left as he or she faces the audience.

**Lekolite** A type of spotlight sold by Strand Lighting. *Leko* is often used as a generic term for any ellipsoidal reflector spotlight.

**Light Leak** Unwanted spill from an instrument or through scenery.

**Line Set** A group of from three to

five lines using the same head block to lift a pipe batten or unit of scenery.

**Lip** A beveled three-ply strip attached so as to overhang the edge of a framed unit of scenery and thereby conceal the open crack of a joint with an adjacent unit.

**Load** Lamp or instrument.

**Load In** When a show's scenery moves into the theatre. The reverse is *Load Out.*

**Loft Block** Individual pulley on the gridiron of a line set.

**Lumen** Intensity measurement of a source of light.

**Make-up** Put together a setting.

**Mask** Conceal from the audience, usually by scenic pieces or neutral hangings, any portion of the backstage area or equipment.

**Mat** Shutter or matting material over the face of a spotlight to change the shape of the beam.

**Muling Block** Pulley to change the horizontal direction of a moving line.

**Offstage** Out of sight of the audience. Away from the center of the stage.

**Ohm** An electrical measurement of resistance in a circuit.

**Ohm's Law** A statement of the relationship of current, electric potential, and resistance in a circuit. It may be expressed by the equation: $I = \dfrac{E}{R}$.

**Oleo** Traditionally the in-one backdrop. A decoratively painted addrop from vaudeville.

**Olivette** Old stand floodlight.

**On and Off** Referring to scenery sitting parallel to the footlights.

**Onstage** In sight of the audience. Toward the center of the stage.

**P and OP** Promp and Opposite Promp. An English and old American method indicating the left and right side of the stage. *Promp* was the side of the prompter or stage manager.

**PAR** Short for parabolic aluminized reflector lamp.

**PAR Head** Slang for PAR 64 lighting instrument.

**Patch Panel** *see* Interconnect.

**P-C** Plano convex lens or lighting instrument.

**Peek** Expose the backstage or see past masking.

**Picture** The general composition of the setting as seen from the average sightline seat.

**Pigtail** Short length of lead cable.

**Pin Spot** *see* Head spot.

**Plot** Short for lighting plot.

**Practical** Descriptive of something that can be used by the actor, like a window sash that can actually be raised or a light that can be switched on and off.

**Pre-set** (1) A pre-arranged lighting set-up held in readiness for later use. (2) Prepositioned scenery that will be revealed later in the scene.

**Prop** Short for *property.* Also refers to anything not real or practical.

**Purchase Line** Flyman's operating line in a counterweight system.

**Quartz-iodine** Early name for what is now known as the tungsten-halogen lamp.

**Raked** Scenery or stage floor angled to the footlights.

**Return** Element of scenery that returns the downstage edge of the setting offstage to the right or left.

**Right Stage** To the actor's right as he or she faces the audience.

**Roundel** A glass color filter for lighting instruments.

**RPF** Short for Rigid Plastic Foam. Styrofoam.

**RUF** Short for Rigid (Poly) Urethane Foam.

**Safety Curtain** Fire-retardant curtain or framed member located directly upstage of the proscenium opening to protect the audience from fire on the stage.

**Sandbag** Counterweight for pin-and-rail flying system.

**Scenography** (In European theatre, *scenographie*) Literally, the graphics of scenery, drawing, and painting. In modern usage, combining the design of scenery, lighting, and costumes into a single visual concept.

**Scoop** Slang for ellipsoidal reflector floodlight.

**Sharp Focus** Sharp-edged focus of a spotlight.

**Shoe** (1) Special construction on the end of the toggle rail, the internal framing member of a flat. (2) Framed platform to encase the legs of furniture for protection on tour.

**Shop Order** A lighting rental equipment list for the purpose of bids.

**Short** Slang for short circuit, the term for the escape of electricity from its prescribed path.

**Show Portal** Framed teaser and tormentor designed especially for the show.

**Shutter** A beam-framing device located at the aperture of an ellipsoidal reflector spotlight.

**Sightline** Line of sight from an audience seat to a point on stage. In perspective, line of sight to a point on object from observation point.

**Slash** A diagonal beam of side lighting on a stage drapery or window curtain creating an arbitrary pattern of light.

**Snatch Block** Pulley block with removable side to permit its insertion into rigging or tackle system without having to rethread all the line.

**Snatching** To hook and unhook a flown piece of scenery during the shift.

**Spike** Mark on floor to locate the working position of scenery or properties.

**Spot Focus** Narrow beam focus.

**Spot Line** A fixed line spotted on the gridiron directly over its working position.

**Spotlight** A lighting instrument with a lens that throws an intense light on a defined area. The term is often misapplied to other lighting instruments.

**Spot Sheave** The special placement of a loft sheave on the gridiron for an additional or single running line.

**Stab** Low trim or tie-off on the bottom rail of the pin-and-rail flying system.

**Stage Left and Stage Right** *see* Left stage and Right stage.

**Stage Peg and Plug** Bolt-threaded peg which fits into an inside threaded plug.

**Stage Screw** Screw-threaded peg.

**Strike** Take down a setting. Remove properties or lights.

**Sunday** Knot used to clew or hold several lines together.

**Surround** or **Shroud** Carry-off platforms that surround a turntable.

**Switchboard** Fixed or movable panel with switches, dimmers, and so forth, used to control the stage lights.

**Tails** Lines dropped from a batten to hang scenery several feet below the batten.

**Teaser** Top or horizontal member of the adjustable frame downstage of the setting.

**Top Hat** *see* Funnel.

**Tormentor** Side or vertical members of the adjustable frame downstage of the setting.

**Traps** System of openings through the stage floor.

**Trick Line** Small line used to trigger a breakaway or trick device.

**Trim** Mark designating the height of a line set. **High Trim** Height of a flow piece when in *out* position. **Low Trim** Height of flown piece when in an *in* (or working) position.

**Tripping** Raising a piece of soft scenery from the bottom as well as from the top.

**Tungsten-Halogen** An improved form of the incandescent filament lamp which contains a small quantity of halogen gas in the bulb.

**Up and Down** Reference to scenery sitting perpendicular to the footlights.

**Upstage** On the stage but away from the audience.

**USA** United Scenic Artists. Theatrical union for scenic artists; scenery, costume, and lighting designers; and allied crafts.

**Voltage** The pressure behind electrical flow.

**Wagon** A platform on casters.

**Wattage** An electrical term for the rate of doing work.

**Wash** Low angle front-of-house lighting sources which illuminate in a general manner.

**Wild** Hinged portion of a setting that is free to move.

**Wing** In the commercial theatre the term *single wing* refers to the basic unit of framed scenery, commonly called a *flat* in the noncommercial theatre.

**Wings** Area offstage right and left, stemming from the era of wings and backdrops.

**X-Rays** Old expression designating the first row of border lights.

**Zone** A single stage-left to stage-right lighting area; most often used in dance lighting.

# ADDITIONAL READING

## SCENE DESIGN

The following books are recommended as additional reading to increase the reader's understanding of the philosophy and historical background of scene design as part of the art of theatre.

## THE DESIGN CONCEPT

Appia, Adolphe. *"Adolphe Appia: A Gospel for Modern Stage." Theatre Arts Monthly*, August 1932.
Entire issue devoted to Appia's influence on present-day scene and lighting design.

Brockett, Oscar G. *The Threatre: An Introduction*, 7th ed. Boston: Allyn & Bacon, 1994.

Burian, Jarka. *Secrets of Theatrical Space*. New York: Applause Theatre Pub., 1995.

Burian, Jarka. *The Scenography of Josef Svoboda*. Middletown, Conn.: Wesleyan University Press, 1971.

Gorelik, Mordeca. *New Theatres for Old*. New York: Samuel French. 1975.

Izenour, George. *Roofed Theatres of Classical Antiquity*. New Haven, Conn.: Yale University Press, 1995.

Izenour, George. *Theatre Design*. New York: McGraw-Hill, 1979.

Jones, Robert E. *The Dramatic Imagination*. New York: Theatre Arts, 1941.

Kernodle, George R. *From Art to Theatre*. Chicago: University of Chicago Press, 1988.

Oenslager, Donald M. *The Theatre of Donald Oenslager*. Middletown, Conn.: Wesleyan University Press, 1978.

Pendleton, Ralph. *Theatre of Robert Edmund Jones*. Middletown, Conn.: Wesleyan University Press, 1977.

Welker, David. *Theatrical Set Design*. Boston: Allyn & Bacon, 1979.

## DESIGN APPLICATION

The following are recommended to broaden knowledge of the practicable application of design principles to modern theatre practices and related theatrical forms.

Aronson, Arnold. *American Set Design*. New York: Theatre Comm., 1985.

Dean, Alexander, and Carra, Lawrence. *Fundamentals of Play Directing*, 3rd ed. New York: Holt, Rinehart and Winston, 1989.

Hainaux, René (editor). *Stage Design Throughout the World Since 1970*. New York: Theatre Arts, 1975.

Nagler, Alois. *Source Book in Theatre History*. New York: Dover, 1952.
Good source book still in print.

Payne, Darwin R. *Materials and Crafts of the Scenographic Model*. Carbondale, Ill.: Southern Illinois University Press, 1987.

Payne, Darwin R. *The Scenographic Imagination*. Carbondale, Ill.: Southern Illinois University Press, 1986.

Vollach and Walther. *Essays and Designs* (illustrated). Black Swan, Conn.: Performing Arts Service, 1997.

## DRAWING AND PAINTING

The following books are recommended to the student scene designer to help develop his skill as a visual artist and draftsman.

Albers, Josef. *The Interaction of Color*. New Haven, Conn.: Yale University Press, 1975.
Still a classic study of color.

Birren, Faber. *A Grammar of Color, based on Munsell*. New York: Van Nostrand Reinhold, 1984.

Chevreul, M. E. *The Principles of Harmony and Contrast of Colors*. New York: Van Nostrand Reinhold, 1981.

*Color Harmony Manual, Ostwald Theory of Color*. Chicago: Container Corporation of America, 1948.
Limited ed., expertly presented.

Itten, Johannes. *The Art of Color*. New York: Van Nostrand Reinhold, 1973.

Jones, Tom Douglas. *The Art of Light and Color*. New York: Van Nostrand Reinhold, 1972.

Parker, W. Oren. *Sceno-Graphic Techniques*. Carbondale, Ill.: Southern Illinois University Press, 1987.

## FURNITURE AND DECORATIONS

The following are recommended as general reference material for designing furniture and decorating interiors.

Flanigan, Michael. *American Furniture from Kaufman Collection*. Washington: National Gallery of Art, 1987.

Gottshall, Franklin H., *How to Make Colonial Furniture*. New York: Macmillan, 1980.

Grant, Ian (editor). *Great Interiors*. London: Hamlyn, 1971.

Hayward, Helena (editor). *World Furniture*. London: Hamlyn, 1971.

Jones, Bernard E. *The Complete Woodworker*. Berkeley, Calif.: Ten Speed Press, 1980.

Meyer, Franz S. *Handbook of Ornament*. New York: Dover, 1957.

Praz, Mario. *An Illustrated History of Interior Decoration*. New York: Thamas Hudson, 1984.

Richter, G. M. *The Furniture of the Greek Etruscan and Roman*. Ithaca, N.Y.: Cornell University Press, 1984.

Strange, T. Arthur. *A Guide to Collectors: English Furniture and Decoration*. London: McCorquodale, 1903.
In the rare book class, but still an excellent compilation and analysis of seventeenth- and eighteenth-century English and French furniture, interior styles.

Strange, T. Arthur. *Historical Guide to French Interiors*. London: McCorquodale, 1903.

Wilson, Jose, and Leaman, Arthur. *Decorating Defined*. New York: Simon and Schuster, 1970.
A dictionary of decoration and design.

## TECHNICAL PRODUCTION

The following books are recommended as additional reading to give the reader a greater insight into scenery construction techniques and general shop practices.

### SCENERY CONSTRUCTION

Arnold, Richard L., *Scene Technology*, 3rd ed. Englewood Cliffs, N.J.: Prentice Hall, 1993.

Bowman, Ned. *Handbook of Technical Practice for the Performing Arts*. Norwalk, Conn.: Scenographic Media, 1975.

Bryson, Nicholas L. *Thermoplastic Scenery for the Theatre*. New York: Drama Book Publishers, 1970.

Burris-Meyer, Harold, and Cole, Edward C. *Scenery for the Theatre*, rev. ed. Boston: Little, Brown, 1972.

*The Complete Woodworker*. New York: David McKay Co., n.d.

Daniels, George. *How to Use Hand and Power Tools*. New York: Van Nostrand Reinhold, 1978.

Dykes Lumber Company, *Moulding Catalog*, No. 49. Dykes Lumber Co., 137 West 24th Street, New York, N.Y., 10011, n.d.

Feirer, John, and Hutchings, Gilbert. *Carpentry and Building Construction*. New York: Scribner, 1981.

Finelli, Patrick M. (editor). *Directory of Software for Technical Theatre*. United States Institute of Theatre Technology, 1988.

Krenov, James. *Worker in Wood*. New York: Van Nostrand Reinhold, 1981.

Ramsey, Charles G. and Sleeper, Harold R. *Architectural Graphic Standards*, 7th ed. New York: Wiley, 1981.

Salaman, R. A. *Carpentry Tools*. New York: Scribner, 1976.

Taylor, Douglas C. *Metalworking for the Designer and Technician*. New York: Drama Book Publishers, 1974.

## THE HANDLING OF SCENERY

The following provide a more specialized knowledge of the various methods of moving scenery, backstage organization, and rigging techniques.

Gillette, A. S. *Stage Scenery*. New York: Harper & Row, 3rd ed. 1980.

Glerum, Jay O. *Stage Rigging Handbook*. Carbondale, Ill.: Southern Illinois University Press, 1987.

*How to Put Rope to Work*. Plymouth Cordage Company, North Plymouth, Mass.

Irving, J., and Searl, C., *Knots, Ties and Splices*. New York: Routledge & Kegan Paul, 1978.

## PAINTING AND PROPERTIES

The following are recommended to expand skill in scene-painting techniques and the building of properties.

Kenton, Warren. *Stage Properties and How to Make Them*. New York: Drama Books, 1978.

Motley. *Theatre Props*. New York: Drama Books, 1976.

Pecktal, Lynn. *Designing and Painting for the Theatre*. New York: Holt, Rinehart and Winston, 1975.

Pinnell, Willard. *Theatrical Scene Painting*. Carbondale, Ill.: Southern Illinois University Press, 1985.

Polunin, Vladimir. *The Continental Method of Scene Painting*. Princeton, N.J.: Princeton Book, 1980.

Veaner, Daniel. *Scene Painting, Tools and Techniques*. Englewood Cliffs, N.J.: Prentice Hall, 1984.

## GENERAL

The following books are recommended as supplementary reading in the generalized area of scene design, technical production, and stage lighting.

American Theatre Planning Board, *A Theatre Check List*. Middletown, Conn.: Wesleyan University Press, 1983.
Guide to planning and construction of proscenium and open stage.

Bellman, Willard F. *Scene Design, Stage Lighting, Sound, Costume and Makeup*. New York: Harper & Row, 1983.

Rossol, Monona, *Stage Fright*. New York: Center for Occupational Hazards, 1986.
Health and safety in the theatre, a very practical guide.

Selden, Samuel, and Rezzuto, Tom. *Essentials of Stage Scenery*. New York: Appleton-Century-Crofts, 1972.

*Theatre Design and Technology*. The official journal of the U.S. Institute of Theatre Technology, 330 West 42nd St., New York, N.Y. 10036.

# THEATRE SOUND

While there are very few books written specifically on theatre sound, the following is a list of those which cover related topics. Under the supplementary heading will be found periodicals and other materials of value to the audio designer and technician.

## GENERAL

Ballou, Glen, (editor). *Handbook for Sound Engineers.* Indianapolis: Howard W. Sams, 1987.
> The most comprehensive of audio reference books.

Bracewell, John. *Sound Design in the Theatre.* Englewood Cliffs, N.J.: Prentice Hall, 1992.
> The best recent text on sound design and technology.

Burris-Meyer, Harold; Mallory, Vincent; Goodfriend, Lewis S. *Sound in the Theatre,* rev. ed. New York: Theatre Arts Books, 1979.
> Fairly outdated, but useful for theatre acoustics.

Collison, David. *Stage Sound,* 2nd ed. London: Cassell, 1982.
> Good reading, but slightly outdated and relates almost exclusively to British practice.

Davis, Don and Carolyn. *Sound System Engineering,* 2nd ed. Indianapolis: Howard W. Sams, 1987.
> Formulas needed to build a sound system.

Davis, Gary, and Jones, Ralph. *The Sound Reinforcement Handbook.* Milwaukee: Hal Leonard, 1987.
> A Yamaha publication with a great deal of valuable information covering practical material not found in other books.

Eargle, John. *The Microphone Handbook.* Plainview, N.Y.: Elar, 1982.
> Good information on stereo microphone techniques.

Huber, David Miles. *Microphone Manual.* Indianapolis: Howard W. Sams, 1988.
> An up-to-date volume covering all types of microphones.

Kaye, Deena, and Lebrecht, James. *Sound and Music for the Theatre.* New York: Back Stage Books, 1992.
> A recent book covering sound design.

Pohlmann, Ken C. *Principles of Digital Audio,* 2nd ed. Indianapolis: Howard W. Sams, 1989.

Sadie, Stanley (editor). *Norton/Grove Concise Encyclopedia of Music.* London: Macmillan, 1988.
> A reference book on classical music.

Sinclair, Ian R. (editor). *Audio Electronic Reference Book.* Oxford: Blackwell Scientific, 1989.
> The inner workings of various audio components.

Thom, Randy. *Audio Craft,* 2nd ed. Washington: National Federation of Community Broadcasters, 1989.
> An excellent introductory book, however it is designed primarily for radio production.

Waaser, Carol M. *Sound and Music for the Theatre.* New York: Richards Rosen, 1976.
> Probably the best of sound *design* books, but badly outdated.

Woram, John M. *The Recording Studio Handbook.* Plainview, N.Y.: Elar, 1981.

## SUPPLEMENTARY

*Audio.*
> A monthly magazine aimed at the consumer, with good articles on audio applications.

Audio Engineering Society (AES).
> This organization publishes tapes and reprints of papers delivered at their annual conventions in addition to their journal listed below.

*db magazine.*
> A bi-monthly publication containing articles primarily of interest to musicians and small recording studios.

*EQ magazine.*
> Published monthly, aimed at project recording and sound equipment.

*Journal of the Audio Engineering Society.*
> Published 10 times a year by the AES, often containing highly technical information and papers on new developments.

*Mix.*
> Published monthly, this magazine is intended primarily for audio professionals.

*Recording Engineer/Producer.*
> A magazine aimed at those working in the recording industry. It is published monthly.

*Schwann.*
> A quarterly guide to all currently available CDs, LPs, and cassettes.

# STAGE LIGHTING

The following books are recommended as supplementary reading in the areas of lighting design and technology. They would form an invaluable nucleus for the private library of anyone genuinely interested in the field.
> The general list contains books of broad approach to the whole stage-lighting field, and offers material of value in several facets of theatre lighting. The supplementary titles contain matter related to specific aspects, and also include a few periodicals that frequently carry articles of interest to the lighting designer for the stage.

## GENERAL

Bellman, Willard F. *Lighting the Stage: Art and Practice,* 2nd ed. New York: Crowell, 1974.

Bentham, Frederick. *The Art of Stage Lighting,* 2nd ed. New York: Theatre Arts Books, 1976.
> Covers the field well, but for the American reader the British terminology is sometimes confusing.

Burian, Jarka. *The Scenography of Josef Svoboda.* Middletown, Conn.: Wesleyan University Press, 1971.

Cunningham, Glen. *Stage Lighting Revealed.* Cincinnati: Betterway Books, 1993.

An inexpensive, basic book on lighting design and production.

Gillette, J. Michael. *Designing with Light,* 2nd ed. Mountain View, Calif.: Mayfield, 1989.

Hays, David. *Light on the Subject.* New York: Limelight Editions, 1989.
A wonderful book on the basics of lighting design.

McCandless, Stanley. *A Method of Lighting the Stage,* 4th ed. New York: Theatre Arts Books, 1958.
This little book has had more influence on lighting design in the United States than any other.

Moody, James L. *Concert Lighting.* Boston: Focal Press, 1989.
The first book published concerned with the field of concert lighting.

Palmer, Richard H. *The Lighting Art: The Aesthetics of Stage Lighting Design,* 2nd ed. Englewood Cliffs, N.J.: Prentice Hall, 1994.
An interesting book on the aesthetics of stage lighting design.

Pilbrow, Richard. *Stage Lighting,* rev. ed. New York: Drama Book Publishers, 1979.
A delightful book covering the theories of this English designer.

Rosenthal, Jean, and Wertenbaker, Lael. *The Magic of Light.* Boston: Little, Brown, 1972.

Watson, Lee. *Handbook of Lighting Design.* New York: McGraw-Hill, 1990.
Part One of this new volume covers lighting design of all the specialty areas, while Part Two concerns itself with employment and working in the profession.

## SUPPLEMENTARY

Bureau of Naval Personnel. *Basic Electricity.* New York: Dover Publications, 1962.
A clear and simple presentation of the fundamentals of electricity.

Colortran, Inc.: Burbank, Calif. Equipment Catalogues.

Electronic Theatre Controls: Middleton, Wisc. Equipment Catalogues.

General Electric Company. Cleveland. *Fundamentals of Light and Lighting.* 1956.
Excellent material on color, sources, and behavior of light.

General Electric Company. Cleveland, Ohio. *#9200 Lamp Catalog.*

Illuminating Engineering Society, New York: *IES Lighting Handbook.*
Pertinent information on color, instruments, equipment, and use.

Jones, Robert Edmond. *The Dramatic Imagination.* New York: Theatre Arts Books, 1941.
Just for the inspiration.

Kook, Edward F. *Images in Light for the Living Theatre.* New York: Privately printed, 1963.
An interesting survey on the use of projections in the theatre.

McCandless, Stanley. *A Syllabus of Stage Lighting,* 11th ed. New York: Drama Book Publishers, n.d.
A historical reference book and dictionary of stage-lighting terms.

Osram Sylvania, Inc. Danvers, Mass. *Osram Sylvania Product Catalog.*

Penzel, Frederick. *Theatre Lighting Before Electricity.* Middletown, Conn.: Wesleyan University Press, 1978.

Strand Lighting, Rancho Dominguez, Calif. Equipment Catalogues.

Warfel, William. *The New Handbook of Stage Lighting Graphics.* New York: Drama Book Publishers, 1990.
A very helpful publication addressing lighting graphic standards and paper work. A must for the student lighting designer.

Warfel, William B., and Klappert, Walter A. *Color Science for Lighting the Stage.* New Haven, Conn.: Yale University Press, 1981.
Color filter analysis.

*TCI* magazine.
A magazine covering the business of entertainment technology and design.

*Lighting Dimensions.*
A magazine for lighting designers and technicians published by the same company as *TCI* magazine.

*Theatre Design and Technology.*
A publication of the United States Institute of Theatre Technology.

# INDEX